GROWTH AND DEVELOPMENT OF CHILDREN: A BIO-CULTURAL PERSPECTIVE

GROWTH AND DEVELOPMENT OF CHILDREN: A BIO-CULTURAL PERSPECTIVE

Edited by
MADHU BALA SHARMA

SERIALS PUBLICATIONS
NEW DELHI (INDIA)

First Published - 2009

ISBN: 978-81-8387-248-5

Published by

SERIALS PUBLICATIONS
4830/24, Prahlad Street, Ansari Road
Darya Ganj, New Delhi-110002 (India)
Phone : 23245225 Fax : 91-11-23272135
E-mail: serials@satyam.net.in

CONTENTS

FOREWORD

Physical growth and development of children, though genetically determined, are considerably influenced by social, economic and physical environment. Growth pattern of a growing child reflects the nutritional state of the child. Indeed a child's growth rate is the single best indicator not only of his/her state of health and nutrition but also indicates his/her psychological situation. It is increasingly realized now that physical growth and development of children form important themes of Biological Anthropological Research as it provides vital information about the health profile of a particular population. Thus, a well-designed growth study is a powerful tool with which the health and nutritional status of a particular population and that of a nation can be assessed.

In the developing country like India, under-grown children and unhealthy adults are a national liability and pose a larger threat to its economy and human resource. Indian Council of Medical Research launched a countrywide survey of physical growth of infants and children belonging to different socio-economic background in different parts of the country, in the year 1956-57. As a result, for the first time, the Growth Standards for Indian children were evolved in accordance with age, sex and socio-economic status. However, these standards are quite old now and as the socio-economic scenario of the country has changed substantially, it needs review. In order to overcome these shortcomings it was decided to launch the present comprehensive growth study to encompass both cultural and physical factors of the populations that may influence the growth pattern of the children.

The present volume is the outcome of research undertaken at national level by the Anthropological Survey of India, under its Ninth Five Year Plan Project "Growth and Development of Children: Bio-cultural Perspectives". Various methodologies were employed as both physical anthropologists and cultural anthropologists participated in it. This massive project focused on children, aged between 6 years to 10 years. In first phase of the project, ten reports, highlighting population data not only from different ecological regions of the country but also from different socio-economic categories were prepared. These are included here. In the last chapter Dr. Madhu Bala Sharma, Deputy Director and Project

Coordinator has evaluated comprehensively the growth-pattern and nutritional statuses of children belonging to different ethnic groups, placed in varied ecological zones and representing diverse socio-economic conditions, with special reference to NCHS standards for European Children and ICMR standards for Indian children. The present study also highlights that malnutrition is no longer linked to inadequate food or health problem but it is closely related to the ignorance about the nutritious value of food items and flawed food habits, which are often standardized by religion and caste considerations, over time. In order to overcome the problem of malnutrition and retarded growth, the precise data presented in this volume will help provide input to the policy makers who ultimately prepare the national plans.

V. R. Rao
Director-in-Charge

INTRODUCTION

MADHU BALA SHARMA

The growth is defined as a process by which an individual attains maximum size until certain age in his genetic constitution in a given environment. It is characterized according to Garn (1952), by changes in magnitude, increments in the size of the organs, increase in the thickness of tissues or changes in the individuals as a whole. Related to the term growth, another term development, refers to the functional maturation and progressive changes occurring during the life history of some tissue differentiation; as well as changes in complexity and proportion. Normal growth and development of every living organism is a function of both genetic and environmental factors.

Many studies indicate that the pattern of physical growth and development; though genetically determined, is strongly influenced by socio-economic and nutritional status. Growth and development of children not only concern with physical growth but also mental and social development and personality of the child. It is well established that psychological factors like love, tender care and proper parent-child relationship influence the social, emotional and physical development of the child. Many studies also indicate that physical environment such as sunshine, good housing, lighting, ventilation, sanitation and economic factors indicating standard of living connected with nutrition and the life style of the people influence the growth and development. There are other factors which control growth and development such as birth order of the child, birth spacing, birth weight, in single and multiple pregnancy, education of parents, occupation of parents, nature of family, family size and food habits etc.

It is well established that nutrition influences growth and development of the children before and after birth in addition to above-mentioned factors. In order to estimate the nutritional status of any population, it is very essential to study their nutritional pattern in relation to socio-cultural and inorganic environments (Margaret Mead, 1964). In a multi-ethnic and geographically vast country like India, food and food habits vary from region to region and season to season and are guided by religious and caste considerations more than socio-economic factors so that people suffer from hunger and malnutrition due to ignorance, superstition and nature of food fed rather than non-availability of adequate food. Besides, the social and demographic factors that influence the occurrence of malnutrition in children include family income, family size, parental education, parenting style (affection, attention) and other measures such as presence of intellectual stimulation and factors of environment.

In India, two per cent of the pre-school children suffer from severe form of protein-energy malnutrition (PEM); 4.6 per cent suffer from different grades of Vitamin A deficiency. Likewise; 40 to 60 per cent are found to be anemic. About 35 to 40 per cent of the total deaths occur among children below five years of age. It is one of the most vulnerable periods mainly due to easy susceptibility to malnutrition and infection. It has also been observed that stunted growth of Indian children is mainly due to poor nutrition. To overcome this problem, the Government of India has launched a number of large-scale nutritional projects for feeding children such as Applied Nutritional Programme, the School lunch programme, the Special Nutrition Programme and Integrated Child Development Scheme (ICDS). These programmes are mainly meant for undernourished children in age range of new born to six year and school going children up to primary level and for expectant and nourishing mothers belonging to under privileged and weaker sections including the tribal communities of the country. They provide not only supplementary food but also services like health care, immunization, nutrition, education etc.

The study of growth and development of human physique, especially of infants and children, is considered to be an important area of research as it provides determinants of nation's health. A child's growth rate reflects, better than any other single index, his state of health and nutrition and also indicates his psychological situation. Thus, a well-designed growth study is a powerful tool with which the health and nutritional status of the population can be monitored.

Historically, earlier interest in human growth and development was confined to technologically advanced countries especially Great Britain and U.S.A. In developing countries, however, it did not receive much attention it deserve because of the low priority attached to it. It was soon realized that for any country, undernourished children and unhealthy adults are national liability and posed greater threat to its economy and well being. Hence the middle of this century witnessed a boon of scientific researches in this field. In India credit goes largely besides few sporadic studies, to the Indian Council of Medical Research and the National Institute of Nutrition for initiating systematic countrywide surveys on physical growth and the nutritional status of infants and children from different parts of the country and from different socio-economic and religious backgrounds in the year 1956-57. This gigantic task was finally accomplished by an active co-operation of clinicians and anthropologists from various medical institutes and Universities lasting over a decade. As a result, for the first time, Growth Standards for Indian children were evolved according to age, sex, socio-economic status, religion and state wise.

The growth standard for Indian children evolved by ICMR are now more than forty five years old and the socio-economic scenario of the country have changed significantly. There is an urgent need to find out the change in the ICMR growth standards. Besides, the ICMR study overlooked the fact whether the group studied is an ethnic/endogamous entity. The population in India is an amalgamation of varied ethnic groups with different socio-economic level in different ecological background. It has been emphasized that individual growth standards for each endogamous populations are required because of the genetic determination of growth pattern (Tanner, etal 1965) and their modification by particular environment and nutritional habits of such populations (Roberts, 1960; Prader et al 1963; Parsons, 1965; Tanner, 1966; Garn and Rohamann, 1966; Heirnaux, 1968). It was also felt necessary that future studies should be conducted in close coordination by inducting scientists from Physical Anthropology and Cultural Anthropology field so as to have the synthetic view of the problem. So, during the ninth plan, interdisciplinary scientific investigation, on the growth and development of Indian children, was launched under the ambit of the project *"Growth and Development of Indian Children: Biocultural Perspectives" by Anthropological Survey of India* by inducting scientists from both disciplines Physical Anthropology and Cultural Anthropology. Dr. (Mrs.) M.B. Sharma, Superintending Anthropologist (Physical) and Dr D.B. Mondal, Superintending Anthropologist (Cultural) were given the responsibility by the Director, Anthropological Survey of India, Kolkata to co-ordinate and execute the above mentioned Project. The research designs on Biological aspect of growth and development of children and its statistical analysis on biological and biocultural parameters was designed by Dr. (Mrs.) Madhu Bala Sharma, SA (P), whereas the research design on Cultural aspects of growth was prepared by Dr. D.B. Mondal, SA (C).

The main objectives of the study are:

1. To study the pattern of growth and development of children belonging to some selected communities in terms of fourteen anthropometric variables such as weight, stature, sitting height, Bi-acromial breadth, Bi-iliac breadth, Head Circumference, Chest Circumference, Mid-upper arm circumference, Calf girth, Total arm length, Fore-arm length and Skin fold at triceps, biceps and sub-scapular. Data on Head circumference, Chest circumference, Calf girth, Total length, Fore-arm length is not presented which will be published later on.

2. To evaluate the extent of malnutrition among these children through the use of nutritional anthropometry.
3. To figure out the frequency of various common nutritional deficiency signs.
4. To evaluate the growth pattern among the children in terms of their socio-economic background such as per capita income, occupation of parents, parent's education, family type, family size and parity of child studied.
5. To evaluate the hygienic environment in the study area and its impact on the reoccurrence of infectious disease.

The study was implemented through multi-disciplinary approach inducting scientists from Physical Anthropology and Cultural Anthropology discipline. The study was conducted on minimum 400 unrelated school going children aged between 6 years to 10 years from each selected endogamous community. The communities were selected for investigation according to their numerical strength from different ecological zones and preferably those who were not studied earlier with regard to growth of children. In large-scale anthropometric survey it was difficult to follow strictly random statistical sampling method for collecting data, so no strict sampling design was followed. But care was taken to measure minimum 35 unrelated children of each sex in each age group. Those children who had been bed ridden for more than 15 days during six months preceding the time of investigation, those who suffered from any ailment in the preceding one month, those with physical deformity or clinical evidence of endocrine disfunctioning and those with any chronic disease were excluded from the study. In order to assess the growth of children fourteen anthropometric measurements were taken as per schedule II (Annexure I) and the cross sectional data thus collected were subjected to statistical analysis as per Annexure III. Each child was examined for presence of clinical signs which are related to inadequate nutrition and which can be seen or felt in superficial epithelial tissues such as skin, the eyes, the hair and the buccal mucosa such as Angular stomatitis, Dry/Scaly skin, Discoloured hair, Flag/Coarse hair, Spongy bleeding gums, Pale conjunctiva of lower eyelid. The detail regarding identification of these clinical signs are given in Annexure III.

The data on the second component of the project i.e., cultural aspects including information on the education level of both parents, weaning practice, demographic parameter, total family income, occupation and type of food eaten by the populations under investigation were collected as per Schedule No. 1 (Annexure IV) by paying visit to the home of each child measured. In order to understand the living condition and socio-economic background, information on hygienic conditions, food habit, sanitation, potable water, education status etc. was collected as per schedule No. III (Annexure V).

Under the ambit of the project *"Growth and Development of Children: Bio-cultural Perspective"* eleven communities namely *Ahir* of Haryana, *Yadav* of Uttar Pradesh, *Ghase Mali* of Maharashtra, *Mala* of Andhra Pradesh, *Poundrakshtriya* of West Bengal, *Bauri* of West Bengal, *Oroan* of West Bengal, *Kaibarta* of Assam, *Lushai* of Mizoram *Nicobarese* of Car Nicobar Island and *Dangi* of Rajasthan were studied during 1999-2000 to study the variation in growth pattern in different geo-climatic and socio-cultural perspective. A Workshop on this project was conducted by the Coordinators Dr. (Mrs.) M.B. Sharma and Dr. D.B. Mondal in October 2000, as per the guideline of the project where these reports were thoroughly discussed. During the workshop, it was also decided to prepare brief and concise reports for early publication of results. It was also felt necessary that the reports should be edited thoroughly before publication. I, Dr. (Mrs.) M.B. Sharma was given the responsibility by Dr. R.K. Bhattacharya, Director, Anthropological Survey of India to edit the volume, being one of the Coordinators of the project, and the researchers were accordingly instructed to send a brief report on the communities studied for editing of the reports. I accepted the responsibility bestowed on me to bring out the volume in present shape.

The present volume has been divided into 11 chapters. Paper on growth and development of *Bauris* children, aged between 6 and 10 years, could not be included due to non-availability of brief report in time. But the data has been utilized while evaluating growth among the 11 populations studied under the ambit of ninth plan project 'Growth and Development of Children : Biocultural Perspective'. Report on Bauris children will be published seperately.

The Chapter-I discuss the growth pattern of *Yadav* children studied in the *Urban* area of Varanasi city of District Varanasi, Uttar Pradesh on 401 unrelated school going children, aged between 6 and 10 years. The children studied belong mainly to middle-income group. The growth and dental pattern exhibits that the rate of growth is high and also earlier in girls in comparison to that of boys. The girls have pre-adolescent growth spurt between age 9 years and 10 years. The growth trend in Yadav children is in close agreement with several studies on human populations (Eveleth and Tanner, 1976). However, the boys exhibit higher mean values for all the characters than girls except at age 10 years and sexual dimorphism is not well marked. The Yadav children are marginally malnourished as assessed by different anthropometric measurements. The majority of children have good or satisfactory health status.

Chapter-II is on a cross-sectional study on growth and development of 420 *Ahir* children (209 boys and 211 girls) studied in village Simha,

Khampura/Khampra, Khaspur and Deroli in Narnaul tehsil and Mahendergarh district of Haryana. They are mainly agriculturist and a few of them are in government and private services. The area under study is semi-arid. A steady growth was observed in both the sexes with advancement of age except for Skinfold measurement. It is very interesting to note in this study the girls of 6 years age exhibits higher mean values for all the anthropometric measurements as well as have more number of permanent teeth as compared to boys of same age group. But for rest of the age groups boys show more number of permanent teeth as well as higher mean values for all the anthropometric measurements. Pre-adolescent growth spurt is observed between age 8 and 9 years among the girls. Clinical signs as well as nutritional status derived based on anthropometric measurements reveal that the Ahir children in general are healthy.

Chapter-III deals with the growth and development of *Oroan* children aged from 6 years to 10 years of North 24 Paraganas district of West Bengal. The Oroan is a scheduled tribe and majority of them are concentrated in Chotanagpur plateau of Bihar and its adjoining areas in West Bengal, Orissa and Madhya Pradesh. The growth patterns indicate that the sexual dimorphism is not well marked in respect to linear anthropometric measurements. In the initial stages i.e. at 6 and 9 years the boys have slightly higher mean values than the girls at a given age categorie, but in girls, between age 8 years to 10 years the growth accelerated and at 10 years superceded the mean values of all anthropometric measurements, except that of Skinfold measurements. The eruption of more number of teeth in girls in comparison to boys of corresponding age indicates that girls mature earlier than the boys. The growth trend in Oroan children is in close agreement with several studies on human populations (Eveleth and Tanner, 1976). The height and weight deficit classification of Oroan children reveal that majority of the children are normal and very few of them are mild malnourished. The study reveal that there is no clear cut impact of various socio-cultural factors such as parity of child, per capita income, literacy level of parents on growth of Oroan children. This may be due to small sample size, which may not be statistically viable to derive any conclusion.

Chapter-IV is on growth and development of *Poundrakshtriya* or Pods children studied in Canning Block in South 24 Paraganas of West Bengal. Poundrakshtriya is the well-known scheduled caste of West Bengal and most of them are landless and work as labourers. They belong to poor income group.

Only 23.65 per cent of them are educated beyond primary level, over all picture of education is not encouraging. Majority of them are living in poor and unhygienic environment. Only few children are immunized against DTP, Polio, BCH and Measles because of lack of awareness, reluctance and fear. The growth and development of children has been assessed metrically under above-mentioned background. It is found that linear measurements increase with the advancement of age from 6 to 10 years age group in both boys and girls. The mean value of triceps, biceps and sub scapular is higher in girls than boys. The bisexual dimorphism with respect to Skinfold at triceps, biceps and sub scapular region are well marked. The boys experience highest absolute gain with respect to weight, stature, sitting height, bi-acromial diameter, bi-illiocristal diameter, upper arm circumference between the age 9 and 10 years whereas among the girls this gain is observed between the age 6 and 7 years and again between the age 10 years and 11 years thus resulting in higher mean values for all the measurements in girls at 11 years age than the boys of corresponding age. The girls experience pre-adolescence spurt between 10 and 11 years which is approximately one year late in comparison to universal pattern of growth among the girls.

Chapter-V is on growth and development of *Kaibarta* children of Assam aged between 6 years and 10 years. The Kaibarta are one of the sixteen-schedule caste populations of Assam as per constitution (1950). The gradual increase in mean values of weight and all linear measurements through 6 to 10 years indicate a regular and gradual growth among the Kaibarta children. It was observed from the absolute growth rate among all body dimensions, the stature increases at a faster rate as compared to other body dimensions. Sitting height and weight increases at a rather slower rate than stature. The rate of growth of biacromial is relatively slower than the sitting height and height whereas, bi-iliocristal diameter is marked by the slowest rate of growth than all other body dimensions. Distance curve for girls show higher average value than the boys at the age of 10 years for body dimensions like weight, height, sitting height, bi-acromial and bi-iliac diameter which start increasing at higher rate from 7 years onwards. In case of skin fold measurements, higher curve showed by the girls reflect greater fat deposition in them through age 6 to 10 years, except triceps at 7 years, than their male counterpart at corresponding ages. The study indicates that in the initial age i.e., 6 years, the mean values for all the linear measurements are higher in boys as compared to girls but at subsequent groups i.e., from 7 years to 10 years, the rate of growth is more in girls. It may be due to pre-adolescent spurt, as the girls mature earlier than the boys. This is also supported by the dentition pattern in boys and girls at different ages. Sex differences were noticed at the age of 6 years with respect to weight, height, sitting height and bicep skin fold and at the age of 10 years in case of height, bi-acromial and bi-iliac diameter and skin fold at sub scapular and bicep level.

Nutritional status of children based on Height deficit and Weight deficit classification reveal that majority of children are malnourished. The malnutrition among the Kaibarta children could be due to their poor socio-economic condition, low level of education, unawareness of nutritional science and medium sized family.

Chapter-VI deals with the growth and development of *Lushai* children of Mizoram situated in the North Eastern part of India. Mizoram is a land of deep valleys and hills and is inhabited by multi-ethnic groups having a mongoloid strain. In the present study 407 children (215 boys and 192 girls) from age group 6 to 10 years of Lushai tribe in rural areas in Aizwal district in Mizoram have been studied. The growth trend in Lushai children with respect to all linear measurements is in close agreement with several studies on human populations. From the velocity curves of linear measurements it was seen that between the age of 6 and 10 years minimum change in dimension is noticed at bi-iliocristal diameter of all the body dimensions. Bi-acromial dimensions grow more than bi-iliocristal dimensions. Sitting height and weight grows more than bi-acromial and bi-iliocristal diameter. The rate of growth of sub-scapular skin fold is relatively more than that of triceps and bicep skin fold. When the distance curve of either sex was compared, it was seen that boys have greater measurements than those of girls from 6 to 8 years, and as the age advances this difference decreases and at the age of 10 years the girls supersede the boys with respect to all linear measurements. This indicates that the preadolescent growth spurt appears at an early age among the girls than the boys. Nutritional assessment based on height, weight and upper arm circumference by age revealed that majority of children are marginally malnourished. The girls enjoy better nutritional status as compared to boys. The socio-cultural factors such as family size, family type and literacy level of parents appear to affect the growth of children to some extent.

Chapter-VII deals with growth and development among the *Nicobarese* children of Car Nicobar Island in the background of their socio-cultural and physical environment. The Nicobarese are Mongoloid people speaking an Austro-Asiatic language. The mean average values of all the linear anthropometric measurements in boys at age 6 years and 7 years is greater than those of girls of corresponding age, but from age 8 years onwards the girls mean values as compared to boys increases at a greater rate and by 10 years of age, its values supersede the mean values of all the measurements than those of boys. This indicates that the girls experience pre-adolescent spurt earlier than that of boys. Nutritional status of children based height-deficit and weight-deficit classification reveal that majority of children are classified under normal category; whereas, a few of them come under mild malnourished category. It is interesting to note that frequency of children in normal category decreases as age increases in both the sexes.

Chapter-VIII is on growth and development of 427 *Ghase Mali* children (195 boys and 232 girls) aged between 6 years and 10 years in Nagpur belonging to lower socio-economic status in Nagpur district, Maharashtra.

The mean values of the selected measurements gradually increase with the advancement of age. The differential growth rate is evident from the velocity curve among boys and girls through time in various body dimensions. Bisexual dimorphism is not well marked among Mali children. The biological age or maturity rate based on eruption of number of permanent teeth indicates that the girls mature earlier than the boys of corresponding age. Nutritional status, based on weight for age, and mid upper arm circumference for age deficit classification indicate that the children are suffering with moderate malnourished to malnourished categories. Whereas, nutritional status based on height for age, classified majority of children in normal categories. The children belonging to higher income and educated parents have better health and growth than those belonging to lower income parents. The girls enjoy better nutritional status as compared to boys. Socio-cultural factors such as family size, family type and literacy level of parents affect the growth of children to some extent.

Chapter-IX reveals the growth and development of *Mala* children studied in the rural areas of East Godavari district of Andhra Pradesh. The Mala is the second largest scheduled caste group of the State and are concentrated in the coastal districts of Godavari. The Malas are economically poor. Most of them are agricultural labourers and a few are in government and private sectors. The study was carried out on 453 school-going children (214 boys and 239 girls) aged between 6 years and 10 years. The growth trend in Mala children is in close agreement with several studies in human populations (Eveleth and Tanner, 1976). The growth of children show regular increase in all the anthropometric traits with advancing age, except for some deceleration in between 7 and 8 years, as is found in other human populations and presents the universal pattern of growth among the children (Johnston, *et al* 1975), except for the skin fold measurements. The height and weight deficit classification of Mala children reveal that only a few children are observed to be normal, while a majority of them are found to be malnourished and fall much below the NCHS standards of height and weight for respective ages. The malnutrition among Mala children could be due to their poor economic condition and unawareness of nutritional science. Mala children are also prone to various diseases due to lack of proper health and Medi-care facilities in the areas of their habitation, which ultimately leads to poor or stunted growth.

Chapter-X discusses the growth pattern of *Dangi* children of Udaipur district of Rajasthan, residing in rural areas. The Dangi are Yaduvanshi who have originally migrated from Mathura via Gujarat and settled in Mewar region of Rajasthan. They exhibit gradual increase in the mean values for different measurements with the advancement of age. The boys experience between 6 years and 7 years whereas the girls experience between 6 years and 7 years and 8 years and 9 years. The Dangi children show higher growth rate with respect to stature, weight and sitting height than the Indian (pooled) children (ICMR) but slower than children belonging to socio-economic class-I category (ICMR) and US children (NCHS). It was observed that socio-economic factors such as family size, family type, literacy level of parents, per capita income and parity of child do affect the growth of the children to some extent. Because of nutritional anthropometry it was observed that more than 95% children are in normal state of health, which indicates that they take a balanced diet.

Chapter-XI deals with the evaluation of growth of children belonging to 11 populations studied under the ambit of ninth plan project with reference to NCHS and ICMR standards for European and Indian children respectively. The children belonging to socio-economic class-I category (ICMR), Yadav of U.P, Ahir, Oroan show statures matching to those of US children. But the difference increases due to slower growth rate in some Indian groups with the advancement of age; whereas, the Oroan and Ahir children come closer to the height of US children because of accelerated growth rate with the advancing age. This indicates that the Oroan, Ahir and Yadav children have the genetic potential for growth similar to that of US children but due to low standard of living and nutrition they fail to achieve the maximum genetic potential. The Kaibarta, Dangi, Mali, Lushai, Poundrakshtriya and Mala have shorter height than the children belonging to socio-economic class-I category (ICMR 1972) but taller than Indian (pooled) children (ICMR 1972). Among the Indian children the trunk height, as compared to stature is much shorter than the US children. This indicates that the rate of growth of trunk in Indian children is slower, whereas the growth rate of lower extremity is greater than that of US children. Weight at successive ages is much less than that of US children while the stature is comparatively closer to US children–indicative of leanness. The leanness among the Indian children indicates that they are comparatively malnourished. The malnutrition among the Indian children is due to ignorance about nutritional science and nature of food, which is principally guided by their religious and caste considerations, rather than non-availability of adequate quality food. In the present study, the majority of children studied for growth and development belongs; to lower to middle socio-economic strata and more likely are victims of malnutrition and infectious disease alliance. The children who are the victims of such alliance exhibits retarded growth and development and poor health in comparison with the expected growth and development at their age as per NCHS standards.

Madhu Bala Sharma

LIST OF CONTRIBUTORS

Barua S., Anthropologist (P), Anthropological Survey of India, 27, Jawaharlal Nehru Road, Kolkata-700 016.

Bhattacharyya Sarmistha, Research Associate(P), Anthropological Survey of India, Eastern Regional Centre, 2, Rippon Street, Kolkata-700 016.

Chatterjee Mitali, Research Associate(P), Anthropological Survey of India, 27, Jawaharlal Nehru Road, Kolkata-700 016.

Das Bandana, Research Associate (P), Anthropological Survey of India, North East Regional Centre, Mawblei, Madanriting, Block-B, Shillong-793 024.

Dasgupta S., Research Associate(C), Anthropological Survey of India, Central Regional Centre, CGO Complex, Seminary Hills, Nagpur-440 006.

Debi Bharati, Asst. Anthropologist(C), Anthropological Survey of India, 27, Jawaharlal Nehru Road, Kolkata-700 016.

Dinda A., Research Associate (C), Anthropological Survey of India, Central Regional Centre, CGO Complex, Seminary Hills, Nagpur-440 006.

Joardar B.N., Anthropologist (C), Anthropological Survey of India, North West Regional Centre, 192/1, Kaulagarh Road, Dehradun-248 195.

Mallik Gautam, Research Associate (C), Anthropological Survey of India, 27, Jawaharlal Nehru Road, Kolkata-700 016.

Mandal D.B., Suptdg. Anthropologist (C) & Co-ordinator, Growth and Development of Children: Bio-Cultural Perspective, Anthropological Survey of India, Eastern Regional Centre, 2, Rippon Street, Kolkata-700 016.

Mukherjee P. Aditi, Research Associate (P), Anthropological Survey of India, Central Regional Centre, CGO Complex, Seminary Hills, Nagpur- 440 006.

Mukherjee S.K., Research Associate (C), Anthropological Survey of India, North East Regional Centre, Mawblei, Madanriting, Block-B, Shillong-793 024.

Nanda Mandira, Research Associate (P), Anthropological Survey of India, Western Regional Centre, 16, Madhuban, Udaipur-313 001.

Rao J.S. Jaya Sankar, Research Associate (P), Anthropological Survey of India, Southern Regional Centre, Manab Bhavan, 93/12 and 94/12 Bogadi, Mysore-570 006.

Ramana G.V., Research Associate(C), Anthropological Survey of India, Southern Regional Centre, Manab Bhavan, 93/12 and 94/12 Bogadi, Mysore-570 006.

Ravi Kattoju, Anthropologist (C), Anthropological Survey of India, Andhra Pradesh Field Station, C/O Dept. of Anthropology, Andhra University, Waltair-530003.

Sahani Ramesh, Asst. Anthropologist (P), Anthropological Survey of India, North East Regional Centre, Mawblei, Madanriting, Block-B, Shillong-793 024.

Saheb Yaseen, S., Anthropologist (P), Anthropological Survey of India, Southern Regional Centre, Manab Bhavan, 93/12 and 94/12 Bogadi, Mysore-570 006.

Sharma Madhu Bala, Deputy Director (P) and Co-ordinator, Growth and Development of Children: Bio-Cultural Perspective, Anthropological Survey of India, North West Regional Centre, 192/1, Kaulagarh Road, Dehradun-248 195.

Urade B.P., Anthropologist (P), Anthropological Survey of India, Eastern Regional Centre, 2, Rippon Street, Kolkata-700 016.

1

GROWTH AND DEVELOPMENT OF YADAV CHILDREN (AGED 6 TO 10 YEARS) OF VARANASI DISTRICT, UTTAR PRADESH: A BIO-CULTURAL PERSPECTIVE

MADHU BALA SHARMA & B. JOARDAR

"The term growth and development refers to the process by which the fertilized ovum eventually attains adult status. Growth principally implies changes in size of the body as a whole or of its separate parts; development embraces other aspects of differentiation of form, but principally involves changes in the function, including those largely shaped by interaction with the structural, emotional or social environment".(Vaughan, and Litt. 1952).

Many studies indicate that the pattern of growth in Man though genetically defined, is strongly influenced by nutritional status in addition to various environmental conditions. It is well established that psychological factors like love, tender care and proper parent child relationships influence the social, emotional and physical development of child. Many studies also indicate that physical environment (such as sun-light, good housing, ventilation, sanitation), economic factors (indicating standard of living, nutritional status and life style of people which in turn determined by education level of parents, their occupation, family size, familty type) and food habits which are culturally defined influence the growth and development of children. Besides, there are other factors, which have bearing on biology of growth and development such as birth order of child, birth spacing, birth weight in single and multiple pregnancy etc. Thus a child's growth rate reflects, better than any other simple index, his state of health and nutrition. "A well designed growth study is a powerful tool to monitor the health of the population or it pinpoints subgroups of a population whose share in economic and social benefits is less than it might be. During a country's development, it was observed that infant mortality rate goes down, so the importance of monitoring growth rate increases" (Eveleth and Tanner, 1976).

Physical growth and development though an integral part of human biology has received serious attention at the hands of researchers in physical anthropology all over the world. It is through their combined effort that a wealth of information on the subject is now available on a global basis and new information is being added. Initially, the study of growth and development was confined to technologically advanced countries especially Great Britain and the U.S.A.. In developing countries however, it did not receive the attention it deserved because of low priority attached to it. But it was soon realized that for any nation undergrown children and unhealthy adults were national liability and posed a great threat to its economy and well being. (Eveleth and Tanner, 1976). Hence the middle of this century witnessed a boon of scientific researches in this field. In India credit goes largely to the Indian Council of Medical Research and the National Institute of Nutrition for initiating systematic countrywide surveys on physical growth and the nutritional status of infants and children from different parts of the country and from different socio-economic status, religion and region, besides a few sporadic studies (Singh, 1968; Singh,1969; Sharma,1963, 1970; Singh, 1970; Malik and Singh,1978; Kaul, 1971; Reddy, 1989; Bhowmick, 1993, Nath, *et.al.* 1991; Rao *et. al.* 1997). The growth standard for Indian children evolved by ICMR are now more than forty-three years old and the socio-economic scenario of the country have changed significantly and there is urgent need to find out whether there is any change in the ICMR growth standard. Besides, the ICMR study does not take into consideration whether the group studied is an ethnic/endogamous group. The population in India is an amalgamation of various ethnic groups with different socio-economic level in different ecological background. It has been emphasized that individual growth standards for each endogamous populations are required because of the genetic determination of growth pattern (Tanner, *et. al.*, 1965) and their modification by particular environment and nutritional habits of such populations (Roberts, 1960; Prader et.al. 1963; Parsons, 1965; Tanner, 1966; Garn and Rohamann, 1966; Heirnaux, 1968; Birkbeek, K. 1973). In an effort to add further information an attempt has been made to evaluate the physical growth and development of Yadav children aged between 6 years to 10 years of Eastern Uttar Pradesh in Varanasi district in the backdrop of their socio-cultural and physical environment.

Area of Study: Varanasi is one of the eastern most districts of Uttar Pradesh and lies between the parallels of 24^0 232 and 25^0 352 north latitude and 82^0 112 and 83^0 342 east longitude (Gazetteers of India, U.P., Varanasi; 1965:1). It is one of the most ancient cities of the world. In the *Atharva Veda* we find the reference of Kashi. In the *Ramayana*, the *Mahabharata* and the *Satapathas Brahmana* Kashi is mentioned as a powerful country (Pandey: 1979 : 29-31). Varanasi is famous for its traditional scholarship and its sacred traditions "centering the cult of Vishwanath" and "the cult of the Ganges (Vidhyarthi *et al:* 1979 : 14-15).

The People: The Yadavs in general believe that they are the descendents of the Lord Krishna and they had Brij as their original home. They are mainly distributed in Bihar, Haryana, Madhya Pradesh and Uttar Pradesh especially in Western, Central and Eastern U.P. Singh (*n.d*) has rightly observed that it is difficult to propose that they migrated to these vast areas in recent times and they had Brij as their original home. In Uttar Pradesh some of them use Chowdhury and Singh as surnames. In Varanasi district they consider the Brahmins and Rajputs as their superior and all other communities lower than themselves. But other communities consider them to be in the middle rung of the regional caste heirarchy (Singh). In Uttar Pradesh and Bihar they have becomed a dominant political force. Even ordinary person of the community claims his proximity to regional and even national leaders. The Yadavs or Ahirs or Gwalbands are agriculturists; though their traditional occupation is that of grazer, milkman and cattle breeder (Gazeteers of India, U.P. Varanasi; 1965: 86-9).

Material and Methods: The present study was carried out in the urban area in Varanasi city of District Varanasi in Uttar Pradesh from November 1999 to January 2000 on 401 unrelated school going children of Yadav community aged between 6 years to 10 years. The data were collected from eighteen schools scattered over Varanasi city. The children were selected by purposive random sampling techniques and care was taken to measure minimum 35 children of each sex in each age group. It has been recognised that assessment of correct age is a pivotal factor in any growth study. The date of birth of children were noted from enrolement registers of the school and then corroborated them with the information supplied by their parents and teachers. Anthropometric measurements such as weight, stature, sitting height, bi-acromial breadth, bi-iliac breadth, mid-arm-circumference and skinfold at tricep, biceps and subscapular point were taken on each selected child following the technique of Martin and Saller (1957) and Singh and Bhasin (1968). Each child was also examined for the presence of clinical signs which are related to inadequate nutrition and observations were made according to Jelliffe (1966) and Latham (1979). The data on pattern of tooth eruption were also collected in order to establish the chronological age and physical maturation. In order to collect the data on cultural aspects including information on education background of both the parents, the weaning practice, demographic factors, family size, family type, parity of the child, total family income, occupation and pattern of food intake, household survey was conducted for all 401 children measured. In order to understand the living condition and socio economic background 100 household out of 401 sample was randomly selected. Information pertaining to housing pattern, number of rooms, ventilation, availability of sunlight, cleanliness of house, source of potable water, personal cleanliness, availability of health facilities, health care system, practice of breast feeding, taboos regarding food items, supplementary food facilities, food habits, basic amenities available in the households as well as developmental programmes in that area etc., was collected as per schedule.

The anthropometric data were statistically analyzed to inerprete the growth pattern according to the age and sex of the children. Cross tabulation of the mean values and Standard deviation of five selected anthropometric measurements have been done for parity, family size, family type and literacy level of parents of the wards. Cross tabulation for per capita income could not be done because the informants were reluctant to divulge the information about their total income inspite of lots of persuation by the investigators.

RESULTS AND DISCUSSIONS

Socio-cultural Factors

Information regarding civic amenities prevalent in the studied area reveals that the lanes and bylanes are mostly dirty. Stray dogs, oxes, cows and sometimes even pigs roam about freely on the lanes and bylanes. This is specially true in the areas like Dasaswamedh, Mansarovar Jangambari, Agastkundah, Harishchandra Ghat, Bengali tola, Rampura, Sonia, Aurangabad, Railway Colony, Mishir Pokhra, Chittupur etc. The houses within the areas are not organised in planned way and hence they are crowded. Most of the houses are not well ventilated and sunlight hardly finds way inside except Pandeypura and Ravindrapuri, the housing condition of which is much better. In the above mentioned areas the houses are well-ventilated and not over crowded.

From the household survey the information on, family size, family type, marital status, occupational pattern, income, literacy etc. are obtained. The analysis of data reveals that most of the children (91%) in our sample live in nuclear family (Table 1). Majority of children (73%) live in medium sized family (Table 2). Literacy level of the parents is not satisfactory. More than 50 per cent (51.76%) of mothers are non-literate while about 14.57 per cent of fathers are non-literate (Table 3). Eight per cent of fathers and 1.76%of mothers are graduate. The father/guardian of the wards are generally day labourer, cook in caterer's establishment or sweet shop, rickshaw puller, tea stall owner, peddlers, automobile mechanic and such other meneal jobs. A few are engaged in white collar jobs like police constable, bank employee, teacher or lawyer.

Table 1
Type of Family in Which Yadav Boys and Girls Live

	Number of families			
Type of family	*Boys*	*Girls*	*Total*	*Per cent*
Nuclear	184	181	365	91.02
Joint	17	19	36	8.98
Total	201	200	401	100

Table 2
Size of the Family in Which Yadav Boys and Girls Live

	Number of families		*Total*	
Size of family	*Boys*	*Girls*	*Boys+Girls*	*Per cent*
Small (< 3)	3	4	7	1.7
Medium size (4-6)	154	139	293	73.07
Large size (7-9)	41	50	91	22.69
Extra large (10 & above)	3	7	10	2.49

Table 3
Level of Literacy of the Parents of Yadav Children

	Father		*Mother*	
Level of literacy	*No.*	*%*	*No.*	*%*
Illiterate	58	14.57	206	51.76
Primary	50	12.56	33	8.29
Middle	131	32.91	96	24.12
Secondary	60	15.08	38	9.55
Senior Secondary	58	14.57	17	4.27
Graduate	32	8.04	7	1.76
Post Graduation	1	0.25	0	0
Professional degree & others	8	2.01	1	0.25
Total	398	100	398	100

The living condition in which the children live is depicted in Table 4. 99 per cent of these wards live in pucca house. Majority of these children live in one (55%) or two room (23%). Condition of ventilation is alarming. Only in six per cent case it is well ventilated. In 62 per cent houses sunlight is not available. In 75 per cent household there is no separate kitchen so cooking is done in living room which might have adverse effect on the health of the ward. Cleanliness in majority of the houses (63%) is satisfactory. 98 per cent of these houses have flush laterines. 84 per cent of these houses use tap water while 14 per cent use hand pump and three per cent have well. Personal cleanliness in 13 per cent houses is very good, while in 52 per cent houses it is satisfactory and in 35 per cent case it is good. In majority of these households (84%) utensils are cleaned and stored properly. Majority of them avail allopathic medicare; whereas, seven per ent of them avail homeopathy medicare alongwith allopathic treatment. Almost all the children were immunized for BCG, polio, diptheria, tetanus, measles and tuberculosis under various immunization programmes launched by Government in this area. But not a single ward was immunized for Hepatitis B.

Table 4
Living Conditions Among the Yadav of Eastern Uttar Pradesh (Survey Based on 100 Households)

Living Conditions	*No. of Households %*
No. of thatched houses	1
No. of masonary built houses	99
No. of bunglows	0
No. of household having own house	1
No. of households staying rented house	
Average No. of rooms	
1 room	55
2 room	23
3 room	10
4 room	8
5 room	1
6 & above	3
No. of houses having good ventilation	6
No. of houses having satisfactory ventilation	39
No. of houses having poor ventilation	55
No. of houses having sun light	38
No. of houses having no sunlight	62
Cleanliness of the houses-Good	8
Satisfactory	63
Poor	29
No. of houses having-	
Flush latrines	98
Pit type latrine	2
No. of houses who go field for toilet	-
No. of households avail protected water supply	84
No. of households avail unprocessed water supply	16
No. of households availing pipe water	84
Wells	2
Hand Pumps	14
No. of household availing stream water	0
No. of households having washing and bathing facilities near their dwellings	100
No. of households having washing and bathing facilities far away from their houses	0
Personal cleanliness-	
Very Good	13
Good	35
Satisfactory	52
Poor	0
Utensils cleaned properly	84
Utensils not cleaned properly	16
Utensils stored properly	84
Utensils not stored properly	16

Traditionally the Yadavs are vegetarian but the younger generation now-a-days has started taking non-vegetarian food outside. In our sample 62 per cent is non-vegetarian and out of which only three per cent are regular non-vegetarian. Their staple food consists of wheat and rice. They occasionally take *bajra* during winter season. They take pulses such as *moong* and *arhar*. Majority of them relish *arhar* dal and rice. They take milk and milk products. 58 per cent children are given milk regularly. 37 per cent takes milk occasionally and five per cent do not take milk at all. Consumption of leafy vegetable and fruits is less even though they can afford it. On the other hand they consume *pakora, samosa, kachouri* and other deep fried food in significant quantity. It is reported that, breast feeding is initiated immediately after birth in order to stimulate the physiologic process of lactation and establish the milk supply, to provide colostrum with its immunological benefits. They start weaning after six months of child birth in order to fulfil the demand of growing child. The breast feeding continue as long as the mother bears milk or it is terminated because the mother has become pregnant again or has decided that the child has reached the proper size or stage of development.

Though some of the Yadav of Varanasi is educated but they do not have the knowledge regarding either essential nutrients, their nutritive value and their specific functions or the fact that their need and quantity vary with individual's metabolic requirement arising out of age, sex, physical activity, pregnancy, lactation and physical growth and development. So it is concluded that under nutrition among the Yadav children may be more due to the result of ignorance of nutrition or health requirements rather than affordability.

DATA ON GROWTH

The cross sectional data on growth of the Yadav boys and girls in the age range 6-10 years for all growth characteristics are tabulated (Table 5) in terms of mean for specific age-group and sex, their standard errors, standard deviations, co-efficient of variation, average rate of increment per year and per cent growth per annum. The distance curve and velocity curve for these characteristics are shown in Fig. 1-18.

The value of co-efficient of correlation between selected body measurements to observe the degree of correlation or concommitant variation between two variables are shown for boys and girls by age. The mean value and standard deviation are tabulated for five selected measurements as mentioned above with respect to parity, family size, family type and literacy level of parents of the wards.

WEIGHT

The weight is the largest composite body measurement which sums up the growth and increment of all the the organs and bodily parts and is probably the best indicator of health and nutrition.

Table 5
Anthropometric Variables of Yadav Children by Age and Sex

		Boys					Girls				
Measurements	*Age*	*6yrs.*	*7yrs.*	*8yrs.*	*9yrs.*	*10yrs.*	*6yrs.*	*7yrs.*	*8yrs.*	*9yrs.*	*10yrs.*
1. *Weight*											
N		41	39	43	35	42	35	36	41	47	41
Mean		19.28	19.95	22.72	26.06	26.88	17.8	19.69	21.81	23.07	27.2
S.E.		0.49	0.41	0.54	0.68	0.51	1.5	0.36	0.31	0.47	0.63
S.D.		3.107	2.557	3.526	4.025	3.311	2.951	2.172	3.208	3.247	4.017
C.V.		16.12	12.82	15.52	15.45	12.32	16.58	11.03	14.71	14.07	14.77
Absolute Growth			0.67	2.77	3.34	0.82		1.89	2.12	1.26	4.13
% Growth			0.48	13.88	14.7	3.15		10.69	10.77	5.78	17.9
2. *Height*											
Mean		117.9	119.6	125.9	132.3	134.2	111.6	120.6	123.4	127.4	134.81
S.E.		0.92	0.77	1.2	0.98	0.84	1.22	0.84	0.93	1.12	1.2
S.D.		5.75	4.732	3.259	5.742	5.398	7.143	4.978	5.783	7.612	7.567
C.V.		4.94	4.01	4.93	4.4	4.07	6.49	4.19	4.74	6.04	5.68
Absolute Growth		1.7	6.28	6.38	1.94		9.01	2.83	3.97	7.41	
% Growth			1.44	5.25	5.07	1.46		8.07	2.35	3.22	5.82
3. *Sitting Height*											
Mean		63.48	64.23	66.87	69.75	70.39	61.08	64.28	65.93	67.36	70.44
S.E.		0.3	0.37	0.5	0.43	0.41	0.62	0.54	0.45	0.51	0.54
S.D.		3.139	2.258	3.259	2.53	2.599	3.62	3.215	2.786	3.485	3.423
C.V.		5.01	3.58	4.93	3.68	3.74	6.01	5.07	4.28	5.23	4.93
Absolute Growth		0	0.8	2.64	2.88	0.64		3.2	1.65	1.43	3.08
% Growth			1.3	4.1	4.3	0.9		5.2	2.6	2.2	4.6

Contd...

Measurements Age	Boys					Girls				
	6yrs.	7yrs.	8yrs.	9yrs.	10yrs.	6yrs.	7yrs.	8yrs.	9yrs.	10yrs.
4. Bi-acromial Breadth										
Mean	25.87	26.2	27.42	28.76	29.02	24.47	26.23	26.89	27.24	29.54
S.E.	0.23	0.23	0.26	0.25	0.22	0.29	0.19	0.24	0.26	0.24
S.D.	1.45	1.44	1.689	1.486	1.41	1.699	1.126	1.495	1.781	1.485
C.V.	5.68	5.57	6.23	5.24	4.92	7.04	4.35	5.63	6.61	5.1
Absolute Growth		0.33	1.22	1.34	0.26		1.76	0.66	0.35	2.3
% Growth		1.3	4.7	4.9	0.9		7.2	2.5	1.3	8.4
5. Bi-illiac Breadth										
Mean	18.24	18.54	19.32	20.33	20.88	17.66	18.99	19.58	19.97	21.3
S.E.	0.19	0.15	0.2	0.22	0.25	0.2	0.31	0.29	0.18	0.26
S.D.	1.213	0.899	1.269	1.263	1.573	1.141	1.813	1.824	1.207	1.615
C.V.	6.73	4.91	6.65	1.573	7.62	6.55	9.68	9.43	6.11	7.67
Absolute Growth		0.3	0.78	1.01	0.55		1.33	0.59	0.39	1.33
% Growth		1.64	4.21	5.23	2.71		7.53	3.11	1.99	6.66
6. Mid-Upper arm Circumference										
Mean	14.98	15.08	15.38	16.87	16.97	14.85	15.21	16.1	16.2	17.34
S.E.	0.18	0.19	0.19	0.36	0.22	0.2	0.15	1.22	0.19	0.23
S.D.	1.138	1.192	1.208	2.077	1.417	1.145	0.873	1.368	1.263	1.431
C.V.	7.69	7.9	7.79	12.49	8.45	7.82	5.82	8.6	7.88	8.35
Absolute Growth		0.1	0.27	1.52	0.1		0.36	0.89	0.1	1.14
% Growth		0.67	1.79	9.9	0.59		2.42	5.85	0.62	7.04

Contd...

		Boys					Girls				
Measurements	*Age*	*6yrs.*	*7yrs.*	*8yrs.*	*9yrs.*	*10yrs.*	*6yrs.*	*7yrs.*	*8yrs.*	*9yrs.*	*10yrs.*
7. Skinfold at Tricep											
Mean		6.3	6.32	6.77	6.74	7.08	7.62	7.16	8.3	7.63	8.08
S.E.		0.21	0.29	0.2	0.43	0.43	0.22	0.29	0.32	0.32	0.34
S.D.		1.3	1.689	1.319	2.518	2.765	1.316	1.722	2.022	2.199	2.177
C.V.		20.91	27.09	20.42	40.11	39.53	17.52	24.39	24.67	29.13	27.38
Absolute Growth			0.02	0.45	-0.03	0.34		-0.46	1.14	-0.67	0.45
% Growth			0.32	7.12	0.44	5.05		6.04	15.92	8.07	5.89
8. Bicep											
Mean		3.83	3.92	4.03	3.91	4.03	4.46	4.32	4.74	4.41	4.39
S.E.		0.14	0.17	0.11	0.23	0.23	0.13	0.21	0.2	0.16	0.18
S.D.		0.853	1.073	0.713	1.342	1.45	0.784	1.214	1.276	1.067	1.37
C.V.		22.57	27.11	18.7	34.81	36.39	17.84	29.18	27.26	24.45	26.22
Absolute Growth			0.11	0.09	-0.16	0.12		-0.24	0.52	-0.35	0.02
% Growth			2.85	2.18	2.86	3.15		5.38	12.32	6.96	0.45
9. Subscapular											
Mean		5.54	5.19	6.17	6.06	6.15	6.5	6.24	7.05	7.18	7.99
S.E.		0.19	0.18	0.19	0.4	0.29	0.21	0.31	0.34	0.36	0.48
S.D.		1.2	1.126	1.252	2.319	1.849	1.264	1.828	2.111	2.418	2.721
C.V.		21.94	22.01	21.65	38.84	30.44	19.74	29.71	30.32	34.04	34.39
Absolute Growth			-0.35	0.98	-0.11	0.09		-0.26	0.81	0.13	0.81
% Growth			6.32	18.88	1.78	1.49		4	12.98	1.84	11.42

The yearly increment of mean weight increases for both boys and girls during 6-10 years of age (Table 5; Fig. 1). For boys the mean weight increases from 19.28 kg. at the age 6 years to 26.88 kg. at age 10 years . For the girls the increase is from a mean weight of 17.8 kg. at the age 6 to 27.20 kg. at the age 10 years. It is observed that the rate of growth is slightly higher among the boys in comparison to girls up to 9 years of age. Then by the end of 10 years rapid growth of the Yadav girls takes place, so that girls are havier than the boys in this period of life. Between the age 6 and 9 years Yadav boys are havier than the girls of corresponding age. Increments of mean weight from year to year are unequal, and so the curve of mean weight by sex and age is not quite linear (Fig. 2). The increase of weight from 6 to 10 years in case of boys is 7.60 kg.; whereas, in the case of girls it is 9.40 kg. The t-values for sexual dimorphism, however show a significant difference for age 6 and 9 years at 5% level.

In the present study, it is observed that there is no direct influence on body weight of children of family size, type and literacy level of the parents (Table 14). The erroneous results may be due to very small sample size. It is the presumption that birth weight of the child is influenced by parity of the child. It is observed that the child of second parity is heavier than the child of first parity in both boys and girls. The regression equation for boys and girls $y = 2.12x + 6.02$ ($r = 0.895$) and $y = 2.218x + 4.17$ ($r = 0.981$) respectively have been calculated and presented in Fig. 19.

HEIGHT/STATURE

Height is one of the largest composite measurement and has a very wide range of variation at any age level. Between the ages of 6 yrs. to 10 yrs there is approximately a linear increase in mean height for both boys and girls (Fig. 3). Upto 9 years of age, boys are taller than girls of corresponding age group. But at 10 years the girls are slightly taller than the boys. The t-values indicate that at age 6,8 and 9 years the difference for height of girls and boys is significant at 5% level.

Increment of mean height from year to year are unequal so the curve of mean height by sex and age is not quite linear (Fig. 4). Among the girls highest absolute growth in height is observed from 6 to 7 years followed by 9 to 10 years whereas among the boys rate of growth is high in 7 to 9 years. There is a tendency towards flattening of boy's slope between 9 and 10 years; whereas, in case of girls at no age the girl's slope diminishes. The mean height for boys and girls at 6 years was 117.91 cms. and 111.60 cms. respectively and at 10 years boys have the mean height of 134.21 cms which is 0.61 cms less than the height of girls of corresponding age. The total increase in height from 6 to 10 years is 16.30 cms (13.82%) for boys and 23.21 cms (20.80%) for girls. The boys attained maximum increment or spurt of 5.25 % at 7 and 8 years; whereas, the girls attained maximum increment or spurt of 8.07% at 6 and 7 years followed by second spurt of 5.82% at 9 and 10 years.

No specific trend has been observed with respect to literacy level of parents on height among the boys whereas the girls of 6 and 7 years age of both literate parents are taller than that of the girls of non-literate parents (Table 15). The boys of all ages living in nuclear family are taller than those living in joint families except the girls in age group 6 years and 8 years. Because of small sample size no specific trend is observed with respect to family size in both boys and girls. The boys and girls of second parity are taller than the children of first parity except the girls aged 9 years. This may be due to some variation in sampling. The regression equation for boys and girls $Y = 4.526\ X + 89.77$ ($r = 0.98$) and $Y = 5.322\ X + 80.99$ ($r = 0.98$) respectively have been calculated and represented in Figure 20.

SITTING HEIGHT

The sitting height is an aggregate of trunk height, height of head and neck and as such rate of growth of sitting height vertex is directly dependent upon its three components.

Mean value of sitting height showed a continuous increase at different ages irrespective of sex (Fig. 5). The boys attained maximum gain of 2.88 cms with the rate of increment of 4.30 per cent at age 8 and 9 years and between 7 and 8 years the rate of increment is 4.1 per cent. The girls attained the maximum gain of 3.20 cms with the rate of increment of 5.20 per cent at the age 6 and 7 years. The rate of increment slowed down gradually upto 9 years of age. From 9 years onward the rate of increment sharply accelerated and the girls attained a gain of 3.8 cms i.e 4.6 per cent at the age between 9 and 10 years. The total increase from 6 to 10 years is 6.91 cms for boys and 9.36 cms for girls indicating that the rate of growth of sitting height is faster among the girls than that in the boys (Fig. 6). The 't' value for sexual dimorphism, however, shows significant difference for 6 years and 9 years at 5% level.

Mean sitting height of children vis-a-vis their parents education level, family size, family type and parity of wards is shown in Table 16. It was observed that the children of literate father and non-literate mother shows the higher mean values of sitting height than those of children of non-literate father and literate mothers except in children of age group 9 and 10 years but the difference is not statistically significant. These erroneous results may be due to inadequate sample size in each category sex and age wise.

In general boys and girls living in nuclear families have higher sitting height than that of those living in joint families except the girls of 9 and 10 yaears. The boys of second parity shows higher value of sitting height in comparison to boys of first parity. Among the girls the sitting height increases upto fourth parity in all the age groups with few exception which may be due to small sample size.

The regression equation for sitting height on age for boys and girls y = 1.934x + 51.472 (r = 0.978) and y = 1.98x + 49.978 (r = 0.898) respectively have been recorded and plotted (Fig. 21).

BI-ACROMIAL DIAMETER

The boys and girls showed gradual increase of the mean values with the advancing age (Table 5 Fig. 7). Absolute gain of 1.76 cms was recorded among the girls with the increment rate 7.2 per cent at 6 and 7 years and gain of 2.3 cms was observed with increment rate 8.4 per cent at 9 and 10 years. Gain of 1.22 cms and 1.34 cms were observed among the boys with increment rate 4.7 per cent and 4.9 per cent at the age 7 and 8 and 8 and 9 years respectively. The velocity curves for boys and girls (Fig. 8) indicate that the growth spurt of lesser intensity among the girls is between age 6 and 7 years, whereas, in boys it is spread over the span of 7 to 9 years. The girl attained second growth spurt of greater intensity between the age 9 and 10 years whereas in case of boys it is being delayed. From this it was concluded that the girls attained growth spurt earlier than the boys as observed with respect to other parameters. The distance curve for boys showed higher values up to 9 years of age but at 10 years the values for girls supersede the values of that of boys. The regression equation of bi-acromical breadth on age of boys and girls y = 0.886x+20.366,(r = 0.976) and y = 1.115x + 17.954 (r = 0.962) respectively and plotted in Fig. 22. The 't' values shows significant difference at 5 % level between boy's and girl's bi-acromial breadth at age 6 years and 9 years.

Mean value of biacromial diameter of boys and girls according to the parent's literacy level, family size, family type and parity of child is shown in Table 17. The percentage of couples where both parents are literate, and father illiterate and mother literate is very small so it may not be statistically viable to draw any conclusion. It is interesting to note that the boys and girls of literate father and non-literate mother depicts the higher mean value of biacromial breadth than those of literate father and literate mother. This difference is well marked in case of boys.

It is observed that mean value of biacromial breadth decreases as the family size increases but the decrease is not statistically significant. The boys and girls living in a nuclear family showed the higher mean value than those living in joint family except the girls of age 9 and 10 years. The girls aged 9 and 10 years living in joint families showed better growth than those living in nuclear families.

BI-ILIAC BREADTH

With the advancement of age from 6 years the mean value of bi-iliac breadth increases among both boys and girls (Table 5, Fig. 9). Increments of mean bi-iliac breadth are unequal. In the inital age i.e. 6 years bi-iliac breadth of boys is greater than girls but later on among the girls rate of growth from 6 years to 7 years is 7.53 per cent; whereas, among the boys it is only 1.64 per cent. This leads to greater value of bi-iliac breadth among the girls from the age of 7 years onward (Fig. 9). The boys experience a gain of 2.64 cms whereas the girls gain 3.64 cms through age 6 years to 10 years. From velocity curve (Fig.10) it is seen that the rate of growth is high between age 7 and 9 years among the boys which later on drops down to 2.71 per cent. Whereas, the girls experience high rate of growth of bi-iliac breadth i.e. 7.53 per cent from 6 to 7 years and 19.30 per cent from 9 to 10 years. The regression equation of bi-iliac breadth on age for boys and girls $y = 0.707x + 13.806$ and $y = 0.826x + 12.848$ respectively have been calculated and plotted (Fig. 23). Significant sexual dimorphism is observed beween boys and girls at the age 6 yrs. with respect to bi-iliac breadth at 5% level.

The mean values of bi-iliac breadth of children according to the literacy level of their parents, family type, family size and parity of wards is shown in Table 18 . It is observed that the children of literate father and non-literate mother have better growth of bi-iliac breadth in comparison to those of both literate parents. In other two categories of parents the sample size is not statistically valid to draw any conclusion. No clear cut trend is observed with respect to the family size. The children living in nuclear family shows higher mean value of bi-iliac breadth than those living in joint families except the girls of age 9 and 10 years.

It is observed the child of second parity is having greater mean value of bi-iliac breadth incomparison to child of first parity. For rest of parity the trend is not clear. This may be due to small sample size in each category.

MID-UPPER ARM CIRCUMFERENCE

The mean values of upper arm circumference showed a continuous increase at different ages among both the sexes (Table 5, Fig. 11). In case of boys the maximum gain of 1.52 cms was observed between 8 and 9 years whereas in case of girls the maximum gain of 1.14 cms was recorded between 9 and 10 years followed by 0.89 cms between 7 and 8 years (Fig. 12). The greater rate of increment in case of boys was found 9.90 per cent at 9 years and among the girls 7.04 per cent at 10 years.

TRICEP SKINFOLD

The skinfold thickness is an indication of how much energy reserve are available for the body. The changes in the thickness of subcutaneous fat is associated with the energy storage and expenditure during the process of growth.

It is observed from Table 5 (Fig.13) that the skinfold thickness at triceps increases gradually upto 8 years of age in boys and girls but between the age 8 and 9 years the negative growth was observed both in boys and girls (Fig 14). Thereafter, the average triceps skinfold measurement increases. The value of skinfold at tricep in girls is higher than that of boys at all the ages. The 't'- values for sexual dimorphism show significant difference for 6, 7 and 8 years at 5 per cent level. The value of co-efficient of variation and range in each age group in both boys and girls is large indicating variations in tricep skinfold were of high magnitude. The skinfold at tricep is not highly correlated with skinfold at bicep and subscapular region.

BICEP SKIN FOLD

This skinfold was measured over the bicep muscle on the anterior side of the left arm, half way between the acromion and elbow. It was observed that the thickness of bicep skinfold increases in boys through age 6 to 10 yrs except at age 9 yrs; whereas, in girls reverse trend was observed except at age 8 yrs (Table 5). Off all ages the mean value of bicep skinfold in girls is greater in comparison to boys of corresponding age (Fig. 15) but the t-values for bisexual dimorphism show that difference is significant at 5% level in age 6 yrs and 8 yrs.

From the velocity curve (Fig. 16) the negative growth was observed at the age between 8 to 9 yrs among the children of both the sexes. The similar trend was observed in case of tricep skinfold. Among the girls the positive growth rate i.e. 12.32 per cent was observed from the age 7 and 8 years preceded and followed by negative growth at the 6 to 7 and 8 to 10 yrs respectively . Whereas, in boys highest rate of growth i.e. 3.15 per cent was observed from the age 9 to 10 yrs. The value of co-efficient of variation and range in each age group in both boys and girls shows that the variation in bicep skinfold is of high magnitude.

SUB SCAPULAR SKIN FOLD

The mean value and other statistical constants for subscapular skinfold are shown in Table 5. Mean value of subscapular skinfold in girls of all ages from 6 to 10 yrs is significantly greater than that of boys of corresponding age. The subscapular skinfold thickness increases with the advancing age except at 7 yrs among the girls. But among the boys the value of subscapular skinfold keeps on fluctuating with advancing age i.e. skin fold thickness shows negative growth between age 6 to 7 yrs and 8 to 9 yrs. (Fig. 17).

The velocity curve (Fig. 18) shows that the boys experience rapid growth i.e. 18.54 per cent of growth during the period between 7 to 8 yrs whereas between the age 6 to 7 and 8 to 9 the boys experience negative growth at slow rate i.e. 6.32 per cent and 1.49 per cent respectively. The high value of co-efficient of variation in each age group in both boys and girls indicate that the variation in subscapular skinfold is high.

Table 6
Test Significance 't' Test Values to Depict Bisexual Difference in Yadav Children

Character	*6 yrs boy vs 6 yrs girl*	*7 yrs boy vs 7 yrs girl*	*8 yrs boy vs 8 yrs girl*	*9 yrs boy vs 9 yrs girl*	*10 yrs boy vs 10 yrs girl*
Weight	2.1268**	0.4757	1.2382	3.6069**	0.3955
Stature	4.1935**	0.8811	2.3863**	3.3023**	0.4150
Sitting Height	3.0610**	0.0773	1.4231	3.5978**	0.0748
Biacromial breadth	3.8280**	0.1009	1.5246	4.2064**	1.6352
Biiliac breadth	2.1454**	1.3444	0.7550	1.3010	1.1999
Tricepskinfold	4.3830**	2.1301**	4.0862**	1.6699	1.8330
Bicep skinfold	3.3528**	1.4353	3.1496**	1.8175	1.1532
Sub scapularskinfold	3.3779**	2.9659**	2.3098**	2.1240**	3.5949**
Mid-upperarmcircumference	0.4947	0.5417	2.6586**	1.6899	1.1834

**Significant at 5% level.

CO-RELATION CO-EFFICIENT BETWEEN SOME SELECTED MEASUREMENTS

Co-relation co-efficient between some selected measurements is shown in Table 7 for the ages 6 to 10 yrs. sexwise. A significantly simplified picture of the degree of relationship of various physical characters may be obtained by averaging the correlation co-efficients representing various age levels in both boys and girls separately. The results depicted in Table 7 show relatively moderate to high positive correlation of stature with weight and stature with sitting height. The biacromial breadth is moderately correlated with bi-iliac breadth except among the girls aged 7 yrs. this correlation is very poor. Mid upper arm girth have relatively moderate to high positive correlation with tricep skinfold and calf girth in both boys and girls. The skinfold thicknesses at tricep and subscapular region have moderate to high positive correlation in both boys and girls (r = 0.44-0.92).

To expose and evaluate relationships, correlation must be thought of, not as something that measure casual relationship, but only as measure of co-variation (Kaul, 1991). The significant correlation between the two variables do not prove actual association between participating variables. Correlation co-efficients, in the opinion of Chaurasia (1978) are of little importance in cross-sectional growth analysis because of the fact that they explain only association and not the variation.

From this it is concluded that though the different part of the body grow differentially but they grow proportionately and simultaneously.

DENTAL MATURITY

The data on *dental maturity* has been collected, because the children under study are yet to attained the pubertal maturity. Dental maturity can be ascertained by counting the number and type of teeth erupted and relating this to standard figures Dental maturity is less influenced by the postnatal environment than in case of sexual maturation because the teeth are laid

Table 7

Co-efficient of Correlation (r) Between Selected Physical Variables According to Age in Yadav Boys and Girls

	Values of co-efficient of Correlation (r)											
	Boys (Age in Years)						*Girls (Age in Years)*					
Variables	*6*	*7*	*8*	*9*	*10*	*Total*	*6*	*7*	*8*	*9*	*10*	*Total*
Stature/Weight	0.79*	0.84**	0.69*	0.71*	0.71*	0.748*	0.65**	0.74*	0.74*	0.60*	0.65*	0.67*
Stature/Sitting ht.	0.88**	0.74*	0.92**	0.84**	0.83**	0.842*	0.89**	0.22*	0.87**	0.69*	0.75*	0.78*
Bi-acromial breadth/Bi-iliac breadth	0.55*	0.68*	0.73*	0.56*	0.70*	0.644*	0.72*	0.20*	0.52*	0.79*	0.71*	0.58*
Mid-upper arm girth/Tricep skinfold	0.61*	0.75*	0.83**	0.50*	0.75*	0.688*	0.62*	0.60*	0.66*	0.57*	0.66*	0.62*
Tricep skinfold/Subscapular skin fold	0.74*	0.63*	0.92**	0.92**	0.69*	0.780*	0.44*	0.70*	0.72*	0.80*	0.83*	0.69*

** High correlation
* Moderate correlation
Low correlation

down early in growth and require little interaction with environment later. The deciduous teeth erupted from about 6 months to 2 years can be used as measure of physiological maturity during this period. The permanent teeth dentition provide a measure from about 6 yrs to 13 yrs. (Eveleth and Tanner, 1976).

The sample size, mean and standard deviations of number of permanent teeth errupted on maxilla and mandible and in total on both the jaws are presented in Table 8 by age and sex of children. It has been observed in both boys and girls that the eruption of permanent teeth on mandible are earlier than on maxilla.

At any given year of age girls have more permanent teeth than that of the boys except in 6 years age group (Table 8). At age 10 years, the girls (19.48 ± 6.81) have more permanent teeth than that of boys(17.61 ± 2.294) and the difference is statistically significant. The biological age and maturity rate based on eruption of permanent teeth indicates that the girls mature earlier than the boys of corresponding age.

NUTRITIONAL STATUS, ASSESSMENT BASED ON ANTHROPOMETRIC MEASUREMENTS

Incidence of Malnutrition on the Basis of Weight Deficit

(Vishveshwar Rao's classification): Use of weight in the assessment of nutritional status of an individual give the current status of the subject. It gives a picture of the not-so-long-off changes in nutritional supplies.

The children studied are grouped in to five categories of malnutrition based on Vishveshwar Rao's classification using NCHS standards (Table 9) out of 201 boys , 90 (44.78%) fall in the Grade I and 72 (35.82%) in Grade II of malnutrition. Only 21 (10.45%) boys are classified to have normal nutrition whereas 8.46% fall under Grade IV category of malnutrition. In case of girls, 84 (42.0%) falls in the Grade I and 73 (36.50%) in Grade II of Vishveshwar Rao's classification. Only small number i.e. 11 (5.50%) girls had normal nutritional status and 6 (3.00%) of grade IV malnutrition.

It is thus evident that only about 7.88 % of the children studied aged 6 to10 yrs. are normal on the basis of Vishweshwar's classification (weight deficit). The sex distribution of normal children is, however, in favour of boys (Boys = 10.45%; Girls = 5.50%).

Incidence of Malnutrition on the Basis of Height Deficit

Height deficit gives a picture of the post nutritional status as per Vishweshwar Rao's classification using NCHS standards. It is a reflection of the availability of nutrients to the body over a period of time. If the supplies have been inadequate the individual will be stunted, that is, will have less height than expected for age.

Table 8

Erupation of Permanent Teeth on Maxilla and Mandible among the Yadav Children Aged 6-10 Years Sexwise

	Male							Female						
		Maxilla		Mandible		Total			Maxilla		Mandible		Total	
Age Group (in yrs.)	N	Mean	S.D.	Mean	S.D.	Mean	S.D.	N	Mean	S.D.	Mean	S.D.	Mean	S.D.
6	39	5.44	1.481	6.77	1.527	12.21	2.821	32	5.16	2.195	6.03	2.215	11.19	3.972
7	39	6.28	1.694	8.00	1.340	14.28	2.552	36	6.72	1.387	7.86	1.367	14.58	2.253
8	43	7.58	1.418	8.05	1.698	15.63	3.686	40	7.38	1.812	8.20	2.954	15.80	2.967
9	35	7.86	1.222	8.86	1.570	16.71	2.421	46	8.28	1.637	9.17	1.650	17.46	2.716
10	41	8.15	1.424	9.46	1.171	17.61	2.294	40	9.35	2.286	10.13	1.691	19.48	3.681

Table 9
Distribution of Yadav Children in Various Grades of Malnutrition (by Weight Deficit)

Categories of Malnutrition		BOYS (Age in years)						GIRLS (Age in years)						
		6	7	8	9	10	Total Boys	6	7	8	9	10	Total Girls	Total B + G
Normal	N	6	3	4	5	3	21	3	1	3	2	2	11	32
	%	14.6	7.69	9	14.29	7.14	10.45	7.69	2.78	7.5	4.26	4.88	5.5	7.88
Grd. I	N	19	16	18	17	20	90	15.00	21	17	16	15	84	174
	%	46.3	41.03	40.91	48.57	47.6	44.78	42.86	58.33	40	34	36.6	42	43.39
Grd. II	N	14	16	17	12	13	72	45.0	11	14	16	17	73	145
	%	34.2	41.03	38.64	34.29	39	35.82	42.86	30.56	35	34	41.5	36.5	36.16
Grd. III	N	2	3	5	1	6	17	0	3	7	11	5	26	43
	%	4.88	7.69	11.36	2.86	14.3	8.46	0	8.33	17.5	23	12.2	13	10.72
Grd. IV	N	0	1	0	0	0	1	2	0	0	2	2	6	7
	%	0	2.56	0	0	0	0.50	5.71	0	0	5.71	4.88	3	1.75

The distribution of various grades of malnutrition according to age on the basis of height deficits is shown in Table 10. Out of the total 201 boys, 50 (24.88%) were found to be of normal height, 137 (68.16%) found to be of mild retarded height for age and only 14 (6.97%) of boys were having poor stunted height for age indicating they have been poorly nourished for longer period of life. Out of 200 girls, 34 (17.00%) fall under the normal category,138 (69.0%) under mild retardation i.e. marginally malnourished and 28 (14.0%) under poor height reflecting severe malnutrition over a long period of time. Only 20.95% of the children irrespective of their sex,showed normal height for age. The study showed the girls were poorly nourished in comparison to boys over all ages.

Incidence of Malnutrition in Various Grades of Malnutrition Based on Mid upper Arm Circumference Deficit for Age

The distribution of various grades of malnutrition according to age on the basis of mid-upper arm circumference deficit is shown in Table 11. Out of the total 201 boys, 145 (72.14%) were found to be normal or well nourished, 39 (19.40%) were moderately nourished and only 1 (0.50%) boy was reported to be severely malnourished. It was reported out of 200 girls, 122 (61.0%) are classified in Normal, 52(26.0%) in moderately malnourished and only 4 (2.00%) in severely malnourished categories. On the whole out of 401 children, 267 (66.58%) are normal, 91 (22.69%) are moderate nourished and only 5 (1.25%) are severely malnourished. The study reflects comparatively more girls are malnourished than boys.

CLINICAL ASSESSMENT OF NUTRITION STATUS

This method is only useful in detecting the advanced stage of nutrition deficiency and it is based on the examination of epithecal tissues especially the skin, eyes,and mouth. The observation of various signs believed to indicate deficiency of certain vitamins or nutrients (Jelliffe, 1966; Latham, 1979).

Before observing the nutritional deficiency signs the general health of children by eye estimation only was observed (Table 12). It was recorded that 68.66% of boys are having good health, 24.88% satisfactory and little over 6% possess poor health. Among the girls 69% are having good and very good health, 25% satisfactory good health and only 6% poor health.

In the present study nine nutritional deficiency signs such as pigmentation of skin, angular stomatitis, dry scaly skin, flag/coarse hair, spongy bloody gums, yellow teeth, pale conjectiva and yellow colour in the base of nails were observed and are shown in Table 13. It was observed that not a single child exhibits yellow teeth, pale conjunctiva, yellow colour in the base of the nail, flag/coarse hair and pigmentation of skin. The clinical signs observed among the children (Table 13) are discussed below.

Table 10
Distribution of Yadav Children in Various Categories of Malnutrition (by Height Deficit)

	Sex	*BOYS (Age in years)*						*GIRLS (Age in years)*						
Categories of Malnutrition	*Age*	*6*	*7*	*8*	*9*	*10*	*Total Boys*	*6*	*7*	*8*	*9*	*10*	*Total Girls*	*Total B + G*
Normal	N	18	7	12	8	5	50	5	10	7	6	6	34	84
	%	43.9	17.95	27.27	22.9	11.91	24.88	14.29	27.8	17.5	12.8	14.6	17	20.95
Mild retardation	N	23	30	24	26	34	137	21	25	29	31	32	138	275
	%	56.1	76.92	54.55	74.3	80.95	68.16	60	69.44	70	66	78.1	69	68.58
Poor	N	0	2	8	1	3	14	9	1	5	10	3	28	42
	%	0	5.13	18.18	2.86	7.14	6.97	25.71	2.78	12.5	21.3	7.32	14	10.47
Grand Total							201						200	

Table 11

Distribution of Yadav Boys and Girls in various Categories of Malnutrition According to Mid-upper Arm Circumference

	Sex	*BOYS*						*GIRLS*						
Categories of Malnutrition	*Age in yrs.*	*6*	*7*	*8*	*9*	*10*	*Tota Boys*	*6*	*7*	*8*	*9*	*10*	*Total Girls*	*Total Boys+Girls*
Severe Malnutrition	N	0	0	0	0	1	1	1	0	0	3	0	4	5
	%	0	0	0	0	2.38	0.5	2.86	0	0	6.38	0	2	1.25
Moderate malnutrition	N	3	7	3	2	1	16	5	3	6	4	4	22	38
	%	7.32	17.95	6.82	5.71	2.38	7.96	14.29	8.33	12.5	8.51	9.76	11	9.48
Mild Malnutrition	N	5	6	10	8	10	39	10	12	9	14	7	52	71
	%	12.2	15.38	22.73	22.9	23.81	19.4	28.57	33.3	22.5	29.8	17.1	26	22.69
Normal	N	33	26	31	25	30	145	19	21	26	26	30	122	267
	%	80.49	66.67	70.45	71.4	71.43	72.14	54.29	58.3	65	55.3	73.2	61	66.58

Table 12
Distribution of Yadav Boys and Girls According to Health Status Predicted by Eye Estimation

	Sex	*BOYS*						*GIRLS*						
Categories of Malnutrition	*Age in yrs.*	*6*	*7*	*8*	*9*	*10*	*Tota Boys*	*6*	*7*	*8*	*9*	*10*	*Total Girls*	*Total Boys+Girls*
Good	N	26	28	32	23	29	138	19	27	28	28	36	138	276
	%	63.41	71.79	72.73	65.71	69.05	68.66	54.29	75	68.29	59.57	87.8	69	68.83
Satisfactory	N	9	9	11	8	13	50	14	7	10	15	4	50	100
	%	21.95	23.08	25	22.86	30.95	24.88	40	19.44	24.39	31.91	9.76	25	24.94
Poor	N	6	2	1	4	0	13	2	2	3	4	1	12	25
	%	14.63	5.13	2.27	11.43	0	6.47	5.71	5.55	7.32	8.51	2.44	6	6.23

Table 13
Incidence of Nutritional Deficiency Signs (Age Combined) Among Yadav Boys and Girls

	BOYS		*GIRLS*		*BOYS + GIRLS*	
Clinical Signs	*N*	%	*N*	%	*N*	%
Dry skin	20	9.95	16	8.00	36	8.98
Angular Stomatitis	10	4.98	9	4.50	19	4.72
Spongy bleeding gums	2	1	0	0.00	2	0.5
Discolour hair	0	-0	1	0.50	1	0.25

Dry and Scaly Skin

This is a very common type of clinical sign caused by the deficiency of Vitamin-A. It was observed that 20 (9.95%) boys were having dry skin; whereas, 16 (8.0%) girls exhibits dry skin. On an average 8.98% of children studied are having vitamin-A deficiency.

Angular Stomatitis

Angular stomatitis is caused due to vitamin B-complex deficiency. It was observed that the incidence of this vitamin deficiency is quite low as compared to vitamin A. It was observed that only 10 boys (4.98%) and 9 Girls (4.50%) are suffering with angular stomatitis. On an average 4.72% of children studied are suffering with vitamin B-complex deficiency.

Spongy Gums

This is caused due to the deficiency of vitamin C. Children at age 7 years (1.33%) and 9 years (1.22%) were reported to have spongy gums. Only 0.5% of the children studied were having vitamin C deficiency.

Discolour Hair

Only one girl child aged 10 years exhibits discoloured hair out of 401 children of both sexes examined.

Discussion

Health is a composite and cumulative effect of number of factors, hygienic living conditions, improved purchasing capacity and above all, education and immunity against the diseases. The relationship between literacy, awareness, accessibility of health services, inadequate utilization of health facilities with the use of immunization process is well documented by Gopalan, S. (1995). Nutrition is perhaps the foremost of all the basic factors for a healthy life and for building up resistance against environmental stresses. Margaret Mead (1964,1977) emphasized the need for a holistic approach to study the nutritional pattern. She stressed that an understanding of the nutritional pattern of the people requires a careful analysis of their social, cultural, biological and inorganic environments".

Table 14
Mean and Standard Deviation for Weight of Yadav Children Aged from 6 Through 10 Years by Literacy Level of Both the Parents, Parity of Children, Family Size and Family Type

	Boys															Girls														
	6			7			8			9			10			6			7			8			9			10		
Literacy level	N	*Mean*	S.D.	N	*Mean*	S.D.	N	*Mean*	S.D.	N	*Mean*	S.D.	N	*Mean*	S.D.	N	*Mean*	S.D.	N	*Mean*	S.D.	N	*Mean*	S.D.	N	*Mean*	S.D.	N	*Mean*	S.D.
Father & Mother both literate	13	18.27	3.509	21	19.93	2.619	15	22.37	3.642	12	25.50	4.421	17	26.74	3.623	16	16.91	2.764	14	20.21	2.016	20	21.78	3.58	25	23.34	2.918	16	26.69	4.179
Mother literate Father illiterate	4	20.13	4.11	2	18.75	0.754	1	19.50	0	5	28.20	5.507	3	28.83	2.255	0	0.00	0	1	18.50	0	3	21.67	3.79	2	23.25	5.303	1	27.00	0
Mother illiterate Father literate	20	19.73	2.765	15	20.10	2.772	27	23.06	3.496	11	26.04	3.053	20	26.78	3.206	16	19.00	2.536	15	20.00	2.345	15	20.03	5.57	16	22.56	3.829	17	27.71	4.456
Mother illiterate Father illiterate	3	19.50	2.5	1	20.50	0.00				7	25.50	3.926	2	26.25	4.596	3	16.17	4.537	6	17.75	1.508	2	23.75	3.89	4	23.38	2.955	7	27.14	2.673
Family size																														
Small family (<3)	0	0.00	0	0	0.00	0	0	0.00	0	0	0.00	0	0	0.00	0.00	0	0.00	0	0	0.00	0	0	0.00	0	3	22.75	0.354	1	19.00	0
Medium family (4-6)	29	19.64	2.793	29	20.19	2.494	33	22.89	3.642	29	26.17	4.349	35	26.97	3.581	28	18.23	2.888	26	19.40	2.218	29	22.02	3.32	29	23.16	3.418	27	26.83	3.308
Medium large family (7-9)	9	18.50	4.146	10	19.25	2.741	9	21.61	2.902	6	25.20	1.949	7	26.43	1.185	7	16.07	2.729	9	20.72	1.856	8	21.69	3.04	14	22.14	2.453	13	28.58	4.703
Large family (10>)	2	17.25	1.768	0	0.00	0	1	27.00	0	0	0.00	0	0	0.00	0	0	0.00	0	1	18.00	0	3	20.17	3.01	1	26.50	0	0	0.00	0
Family type																														
Nuclear	32	19.52	2.737	36	20.06	2.624	39	22.81	3.316	32	26.19	4.173	41	26.88	3.352	32	17.98	2.903	30	19.53	2.189	37	21.95	3.22	44	22.93	3.288	39	27.17	4.002
Joint	8	18.31	40.91	3	18.67	1.041	4	21.88	5.808	3	24.67	1.528	1	27.00	0	3	15.83	3.329	6	20.50	2.075	3	20.17	3.01	3	25.17	1.756	2	27.75	6.01
Parity																														
1	11	19	3.302	12	19.08	3.363	13	22.65	4.284	12	25.42	3.547	14	27.29	4.2	10	17.50	3.358	12	17.50	3.358	14	20.82	2.81	10	23.55	3.052	9	25.61	4.878
2	12	20.08	4.033	8	22.00	2.549	11	23.91	3.714	11	26.18	5.396	8	26.19	4.139	9	18.28	3.289	10	19.40	2.525	8	22.31	4.07	15	22.83	3.569	12	27.71	3.922
3	7	19.86	1.887	9	19.89	2.043	9	20.00	1.118	6	28.58	3.262	8	28.00	4.237	11	17.82	2.714	9	20.17	1.887	11	22.50	3.55	10	23.00	2.625	8	26.06	2.597
4	7	17.64	2.428	4	21.00	2.972	2	22.50	1.411	2	23.25	0.354	9	25.33	4.198	2	18.01	2.828	4	19.63	2.359	4	22.50	3.11	4	23.88	3.376	4	31.13	4.956
5 & above	3	19.50	0.817	6	18.33	1.772	8	24.25	2.586	4	25.25	1.25	1	28.50	0	3	17.17	2.718	1	22.00	0	3	23.33	3.4	8	22.63	3.879	8	27.38	2.891

Table 15
Mean and Standard Deviation for Height of Yadav Children Aged from 6 Through 10 Years by Literacy Level of Both Parents, Parity of Children, Family Size and Family Type

	Boys															Girls														
	Age Group															Age Group														
	6			7			8			9			10			6			7			8			9			10		
Literacy level	N	Mean	S.D.	N	Mean	S.D.	N	Mean	S.D.	N	Mean	S.D.	N	Mean	S.D.	N	Mean	S.D.	N	Mean	S.D.	N	Mean	S.D.	N	Mean	S.D.	N	Mean	S.D.
Father & Mother both literate	13	115	5.16	21	119	5.14	15	125	9.1	12	131	4.02	17	134	4.87	16	109	6.43	14	122	5.57	20	123	5.6	25	127	4.95	16	134	9
Mother literate Father illiterate	4	119	7.31	2	116	0.14	1	115	0	5	135	6.48	3	141	6.01	0	0	0	1	111	0	3	119	3.3	2	128	6.44	1	133	0
Mother illiterate Father literate	20	120	5.73	15	121	4.28	27	127	7.09	11	133	5.37	20	134	5.51	16	115	6.48	15	121	4.29	15	125	6.2	16	127	10.6	17	134	6.05
Mother illiterate Father illiterate	3	118	3.12	1	121	0	0	0	0	7	131	8.64	2	132	5.73	3	108	10.5	6	117	2.8	2	125	10	4	132	9.98	7	137	9.12
Family size																														
Small family(<3)	0	0	0	0	0	0	0	0	0	0	0	0	0	0	0	0	0	0	0	0	0	0	0	0	3	136	2.23	1	118	0
Medium family (4-6)	29	119	5.61	29	120	4.97	33	126	7.69	29	133	6.08	35	134	5.87	28	112	7.28	26	19.4	2.22	29	124	5.9	29	128	7.19	27	135	7.48
Medium large family (7-9)	9	115	5.2	10	119	4.48	9	120	8.78	6	130	4.32	7	135	2.91	7	108	6.56	9	20.7	1.86	8	123	6.2	14	125	7.23	13	136	6.96
Large family (10>)	2	111	4.6	0	0	0	1	134	0	0	0	0	0	0	0	0	0	0	1	18	0	3	119	4.2	1	144	0	0	0	0
Family type																														
Nuclear	32	119	5.73	36	120	4.94	39	126	7.66	32	133	5.92	41	134	5.53	32	112	7.11	30	120	4.68	37	124	5.9	44	127	7.68	39	135	7.71
Joint	8	115	5.48	3	119	2.78	4	122	10.2	3	128	3.05	1	134	0	3	111	9.13	6	125	5.12	3	119	4.2	3	134	5	2	140	5.66
Parity																														
1	11	119	6.6	12	117	5.23	13	125	7.86	12	131	6.04	14	134	5.87	10	111	7.39	12	120	5.58	14	122	5.2	10	128	9.29	9	131	8.85
2	12	119	6.76	8	122	5.23	11	129	8.55	11	131	4.93	8	132	6.22	9	110	7.69	10	119	5.15	8	122	4.4	15	128	6.13	12	136	6.67
3	7	118	2.71	9	1'20	4.22	9	121	5.41	6	138	5.69	8	138	5.02	11	114	7.22	9	124	3.71	11	125	6.9	10	128	6.47	8	137	10.50
4	7	114	4.8	4	121	4.22	2	129	10.5	2	129	5.02	9	132	3.57	2	115	2.97	4	118	2.99	4	127	8.9	4	122	7.09	4	136	5.38
5 & above	3	119	5.02	6	119	3.06	8	129	6.36	4	134	5.64	1	138	0	3	109	7.38	1	126	0	3	121	0.5	8	128	9.66	8	134	4.46

Table 16

Mean and Standard Deviation for Sitting Height of Yadav Children Aged from 6 Through 10 Years by Literacy Level of Both Parents, Parity of Children, Family Size and Family Type

	Boys															Girls														
	6			7			8			9			10			6			7			8			9			10		
Literacy level	N	*Mean*	S.D.	N	*Mean*	S.D.	N	*Mean*	S.D.	N	*Mean*	S.D.	N	*Mean*	S.D.	N	*Mean*	S.D.	N	*Mean*	S.D.	N	*Mean*	S.D.	N	*Mean*	S.D.	N	*Mean*	S.D.
Literacy level	6 N	Mean	S.D.	7 N	Mean	S.D.	8 N	Mean	S.D.	9 N	Mean	S.D.	10 N	Mean	S.D.	6 N	Mean	S.D.	7 N	Mean	S.D.	8 N	Mean	S.D.	9 N	Mean	S.D.	10 N	Mean	S.D.
Father & Mother both literate	13	62.9	3.26	21	64.2	2.48	15	66.6	3.5	12	69.4	2.3	17	70.5	2.25	16	59.7	3.54	14	65	4.25	20	66.1	3	25	67	2.94	16	70.5	3.86
Mother literate Father non-literate	4	62.9	5.03	2	63.6	1.77	1	61.9	0	5	70.8	1.32	3	74.7	0.5	0	0	0	1	62.7	0	3	64.6	2.31	2	66	2.3	1	70.5	0
Mother non-literate Father literate	20	63.8	2.89	15	64.4	2.25	27	67.2	3.1	11	69.7	2.3	20	69.8	2.67	16	62.7	3.2	15	64.6	2.31	15	66	2.80	16	67.4	3.63	17	70	3.11
Mother and Father both non-literate	3	63.7	3.44	1	63.4	0	0	0	0	7	69.7	4.04	2	69.9	1.77	3	60.1	4.65	6	62.5	2.21	2	66.2	2.35	4	69.7	4.04	7	69.9	1.77
Family size																														
Small family (<3)	0	0	0	0	0	0	0	0	0	0	0	0	0	0	0	0	0	0	0	0	0	0	0	0	3	67.2	3.54	1	64.1	0
Medium family (4-6)	29	64.1	3.04	29	64.4	2.37	33	67	3.2	29	69.7	2.75	35	70.3	2.8	28	67.8	3.45	26	64.7	2.76	29	66.1	2.86	29	67.5	3	27	70.5	5.53
Medium large (7-9) family	9	61.9	3.05	10	63.7	2.07	9	66.2	4	6	70	1.52	7	71	1.52	7	58.3	3.47	9	64.3	3.32	8	65.7	0.02	14	66	3.21	13	70.7	3.13
Large family (10>)	2	60.1	1.84	0	0	0	1	69.8	0	0	0	0	0	0	0	0	0	0	1	54.8	0	3	65.3	2.77	1	77.3	0	0	0	0
Family type																														
Nuclear	32	63.7	3.16	36	64.2	2.32	39	67	3.1	32	64.8	2.68	41	70.4	2.66	32	61.3	3.52	30	64.3	2.68	37	66	2.86	44	67.2	3.61	39	70.4	3.54
Joint	8	62.2	3.11	3	64.7	2.76	4	65.5	5.1	3	69.6	0.78	1	70.3	0	3	59.2	5.63	6	64.2	5.72	3	65.3	2.77	3	69.1	0.82	2	72.3	0.35
Parity																														
1	11	63.7	3.8	12	63	2.29	13	66.6	3.9	12	69	2.92	14	70.4	2.4	10	61	4.43	12	63.6	4.04	14	62.5	2.54	10	67.1	3.22	9	70.1	5.53
2	12	64.5	3.06	8	66.4	1.9	11	67.6	3.2	11	69.3	1.81	8	69.1	3.04	9	59.9	3.17	10	63.6	2.95	8	65.2	2.21	15	67.4	3.19	12	71.1	2.94
3	7	62.7	2.5	9	64.7	2.11	9	64.9	2.1	6	72.1	2.51	8	72	2.78	11	62.2	3.28	9	66.1	2.27	11	66.8	3.26	10	67.4	2.89	8	70.00	2.98
4	7	61.8	2.63	4	64.2	2.72	2	67.9	3.4	2	68.7	2.33	9	69.6	2.27	2	62.7	3.33	4	64	3.61	4	68.4	3.12	4	67.7	3.08	4	71.9	3.15
5 & above	3	63.8	3.28	6	63.2	1.26	8	68.2	2.9	4	70.4	1.94	1	70.2	0	3	59.7	3.75	1	66.4	0	3	63.5	0.77	8	87.6	5.37	8	69.2	1.47

Table 17

Mean and Standard Deviation for Biacromial Breadth of Yadav Children Aged from 6 Through 10 Years by Literacy Level of the Parents, Family Size, Family Type and Parity of Children

Boys

	6			7			8			9			10		
Literacy level	N	Mean	S.D.	N	Mean	S.D.	N	Mean	S.D.	N	Mean	S.D.	N	Mean	S.D.
Father and Mother both literate	13	24.99	1.49	21	25.9	1.772	15	27.1	1.866	12	28.6	1.639	17	28.78	1.268
Mother literate Father non-literate	4	26.48	1.52	2	25.3	0.071	1	25.5	0	5	29.2	2.026	3	29.9	0.781
Mother non-literate Father literate	20	26.21	1.34	15	26.4	1.204	27	27.7	1.607	11	28.8	1.104	20	29.05	1.5
Mother and Father both non-literate	3	26.57	0.86	1	25.6	0	0	0	0	7	28.7	1.709	2	29.45	3.182
Family size															
Small family (3)	3	28.2	2.623	1	26.7	0									
Medium family (4-6)	29	26.18	1.51	29	26.1	1.525	33	27.4	1.729	29	28.9	1.515	35	29	1.517
Medium Large family (6-9)	9	25.1	1.1	10	26	1.565	9	27.5	1.834	6	28.8	1.531	7	29.09	0.958
Large family (10 & above)	2	24.85	0.5	0	0	0	1	29.6	0	0	0	0	0	0	0
Family type															
Nuclear family	32	26.12	1.45	36	26.1	1.569	39	27.5	1.707	32	28.8	1.483	41	29.01	1.444
Joint family	8	24.82	1.13	3	25.8	0.625	4	27.8	1.855	3	27.9	1.804	1	29.4	0
Parity															
1	11	25.99	1.42	12	25.3	1.599	13	27.4	1.994	12	28.8	1.672	14	28.88	1.258
2	12	25.85	2.07	8	26.9	1.565	11	27.9	1.752	11	28.6	1.828	8	28.44	1.602
3	7	26.31	0.67	9	26.2	1.417	9	26.5	1.063	6	29.5	1.088	8	29.63	1.082
4	7	25.37	1.32	4	26.6	1.156	2	28.2	0.919	2	28.1	0.989	9	29.02	1.879
5 & above	3	25.6	0.28	6	25.8	1.178	8	27.7	1.668	4	28.4	0.46	[illegible]	30.2	0

Girls

	6			7			8			9			10		
Literacy level	N	Mean	S.D.	N	Mean	S.D.	N	Mean	S.D.	N	Mean	S.D.	N	Mean	S.D.
Father and Mother both literate	16	24.1	1.413	14	26.39	1.016	20	26.87	1.762	25	26.98	1.736	16	29.36	1.876
Mother literate Father non-literate	0	0	0	1	25.3	0	3	26.4	0.721	2	27.25	2.616	1	30.1	0
Mother non-literate Father literate	16	24.99	1.699	15	26.21	1.147	15	26.89	1.354	16	27.19	1.679	17	29.72	1.4
Mother and Father both non-literate	3	23.63	3.102	6	26.03	1.571	2	27.8	1.131	4	29.08	2.035	7	29.07	0.842
Family size															
Small family (3)															
Medium family (4-6)	28	24.65	1.731	26	26.08	1.156	29	27.01	1.594	29	27.2	1.48	27	29.56	1.498
Medium Large family (6-9)	7	23.74	1.612	9	26.79	0.953	8	27.01	1.191	14	26.81	1.972	13	29.7	1.411
Large family (10 & above)	0	0	0	1	25	0	3	25.37	0.643	1	31.5	0	0	0	0
Family type															
Nuclear family	32	24.58	1.711	30	26.21	1.145	37	27.01	1.501	44	27.16	1.819	39	29.52	2.127
Joint family	3	23.27	1.665	6	26.28	1.232	3	25.37	0.643	3	28.43	1.059	2	29.8	0.621
Parity															
1	10	24.8	1.652	12	26.11	1.214	14	26.45	1.612	10	27.3	1.328	9	29.04	1.771
2	9	24.43	1.979	10	26.4	1.276	8	27.44	2.025	15	27.05	1.627	12	29.87	1.491
3	11	24.51	1.842	9	26.2	1.115	11	26.89	1.11	10	27.53	1.238	8	29.18	1.566
4	2	24.55	1.202	4	26.25	1.193	4	27.03	1.717	4	25.68	2.986	4	30.73	1.873
5 & above	3	24.3	1.791	1	26	0	3	27.26	0.189	8	27.93	2.252	8	29.36	0.6081

Table 18
Mean and Standard Deviation for Bi-illiac Diameter of Yadav Children Aged from 6 Through 10 Years by Literacy Levelof Both Parents, Parity of Children, Family Size And Family Type

	Boys															Girls														
	6			7			8			9			10			6			7			8			9			10		
Literacy level	N	Mean	S.D.	N	Mean	S.D.	N	Mean	S.D.	N	Mean	S.D.	N	Mean	S.D.	N	Mean	S.D.	N	Mean	S.D.	N	Mean	S.D.	N	Mean	S.D.	N	Mean	S.D.
Father & Mother both literate	13	17.85	1.124	21	18.54	1.085	15	19.15	1.326	12	20.19	1.151	17	20.57	0.962	16	17.33	1.267	14	18.72	0.503	20	19.70	2.347	25	19.97	1.154	16	21.48	2.023
Mother literate Father illiterate	4	19.10	0.898	2	18.00	0.707	1	17.20	0	1	20.36	0	3	21.37	1.518	0	0	0	1	17.80	0	3	18.90	0.608	2	20.05	2.051	1	20.20	0
Mother illiterate Father literate	20	18.30	1.326	15	18.60	0.693	27	19.49	1.225	11	20.47	1.062	20	21.07	2.031	16	17.99	0.982	15	19.41	2.755	15	19.45	1.331	16	19.79	1.326	17	21.15	1.466
Mother illiterate Father illiterate	3	18.43	1.159	1	18.20	0	0	0.00	0	7	20.31	1.588	2	20.85	1.768 F	3	17.63	1.305	6	18.28	0.621	2	20.25	0.354	4	20.70	1.029	7	21.43	1.215
Family size																														
Small family(<3) 0																										3	19.232.757		1	19.70
Medium family (4-6)	29	18.30	1.287	29	18.51	0.969	33	19.36	1.405	29	20.47	1.319	35	20.82	1.726	28	17.71	1.220	26	18.59	0.642	29	19.52	1.239	29	20.04	1.237	27	21.10	1.395
Medium large family (7-9)	9	18.21	1.073	10	18.62	0.755	9	19.10	0.822	6	19.62	0.833	7	21.13	0.496	7	17.44	1.009	9	19.04	0.669	8	19.28	1.089	14	19.72	1.044	13	21.85	2.012
Large family (10>)	2	17.50	1.414	0	0	0	1	19.80	0	0	0	0	0	0	0	0	0	0	1	19.00	0	3	18.23	0.907	1	21.70	0	0	0	0
Family type																														
Nuclear	32	18.43	1.065	36	18.56	0.935	39	19.32	1.291	32	20.38	1.307	41	20.90	1.606	32	17.68	1.121	30	18.96	2.013	37	19.68	1.868	44	19.96	1.233	39	21.27	1.640
Joint	8	17.51	1.619	3	18.30	0.625	4	19.25	1.406	3	19.80	0.985	1	20.00	0	3	17.47	1.793	6	19.17	0.320	3	18.23	0.907	3	20.17	1.201	2	21.85	2.051
Parity																														
1	11	17.78	1.622	12	18.23	0.747	13	18.88	1.379	12	20.42	1.158	14	21.20	2.426	10	17.62	1.173	12	18.64	0.623	14	19.09	0.983	10	19.89	1.314	9	20.79	1.704
2	12	18.44	1.30	8	19.29	0.813	11	20.10	1.369	11	19.86	1.249	8	21.25	3.169	9	17.16	1.349	10	19.89	3.342	8	19.70	1.234	15	20.16	1.300	12	21.38	1.391
3	7	18.89	0.511	9	18.14	0.826	9	18.68	1.057	6	21.40	1.543	8	20.70	1.112	11	18.07	0.934	9	18.59	0.468	11	18.96	1.335	10	19.84	0.883	8	21.41	2.251
4	7	17.76	0.812	4	18.83	0.750	2	19.50	1.839	2	20.45	0.071	9	20.72	0.814	2	17.40	1.131	4	18.75	0.412	4	19.95	1.103	4	20.00	0.735	4	21.23	1.742
5 & above	3	18.77	0.309	6	18.55	0.647	8	19.63	0.458	4	20.20	1.263	1	21.50	0	3	17.93	0.822	1	18.80	0	3	20.60	1.019	8	20.41	1.571	8	21.25	1.339

In the present study emphasis have been given to collect information on the nutritional pattern followed by Yadav community of Varanasi. It has been observed that the food habits of these people are guided by religious and caste considerations rather than socio-economic factors. It is observed that people suffer from hunger and malnutrition due to ignorance, superstition and their food habits rather than non availability of adequate food.

It has been reported that the hygienic conditions around their houses were very poor. They keep their utensil and kitchen clean and they have access to processed pipe water even then there were great chances to be infected from their surroundings. Though no specific information was sought from the mothers on this score, but indirect evidence indicates that diarrhoea, the most frequent form of gastro-intestinal infection, is quite high among the children under 5 years. It was reported that the under nourished children are more prone to frequent infections (Gorden *et. al.* 1968; Mata *et. al.*,1971; Mortorell *et. al.*, 1975; Jenkins 1981and Sharma, 1982).

The children who were victims of this alliance i.e malnutrition and infection especially diarrhoea exhibit retarded growth and development (Mortorell *et. al.* 1975; Sharma, 1982, Kaul, & Nyamongo, 1990, Black, *et. al.* 1984). The comparative slow rate of growth and development of Yadav in comparison to NCHS standards for corresponding age may be attributed to malnutrition and infection alliance which is common in this population.

The variation in body dimensions and proportions at any stage of growth and development would occus as a result of differential growth rates and sex differences. There exist relationship between variability and rates of growth (Boas 1932; Schulz, 1926 etc.) The variability in body dimensions as judged from co-efficient variation and range of maximum and minimum, reveals higher values during periods of faster growth and lower values during period of slower growth.

In the present study it is observed that all the measurements have gradual increase in mean values with advancing age with a fluctuating discrepancies of a minor nature because the data is cross sectional. This is shown by the regression lines drawn for some important selected measurements i.e. weight (Fig. 19), Stature (Fig. 20), Sitting height (Fig. 21), bi-acromial breadth (Fig. 22), bi-iliac breadth (Fig. 23) against age. The value of r in the regression equations for all the five characters for girls are high as compared to that for boys. This indicates that the rate of growth is high or earlier, in girls incomparison to that in boys. However, the boys exhibits higher mean value for all the characters than girls this is due to higher mean value at the initial stage i.e. at 6 yrs of age.

Similarly, sex differences in the rates of growth of various body dimensions became evident if one examines the graphic representations

Table 19
Comparative Data on Yadav Children; Weight

	6		*7*		*8*		*9*		*10*		
Group	*Mean*	*S.D.*	*Mean*	*S.D.*	*Mean*	*S.D.*	*Mean*	*S.D.*	*Mean*	*S.D.*	*Authors*
Boys											
United States	22.0	3.37	24.7	3.97	27.8	4.86	31.2	6.79	33.7	6.48	NCHS, 1960
India (Socio-economic Class I)	18.7	2.87	21.0	2.87	22.0	3.46	24.7	4.24	25.9	4.77	ICMR, 1972
India (Pooled)	16.3	2.68	18.0	3.03	19.7	3.37	21.5	4.47	23.5	5.26	ICMR, 1972
Uttar Pradesh	16.3	2.39	18.1	2.88	19.6	3.08	21.8	5.76	23.8	7.19	ICMR, 1972
Yadav, Haryana	17	2.68	20.95	3.29	23.21	4.07	24.58	4.09	27.10	4.881	Ravi and Rao, 2000 (unpublished)
Yadav, Andhra Pradesh	15.38	0.85	17.18	1.17	19.41	1.25	21.53	1.61	24	1.62	Rao and Busi (1991)
Yadav, Uttar Pradesh	19.28	0.49	19.95	0.41	22.72	0.54	26.06	0.68	26.88	0.51	Present study
Girls											
United States	21.6	3.68	24.2	4.16	27.5	5.36	31.4	6.8	35.2	8.18	NCHS, 1960
India (Socio-economic Class I)	18.1	2.88	19.7	3.84	21.6	4.32	23.6	4.66	26.7	5.00	ICMR, 1972
India (Pooled)	16.0	2.63	17.6	2.92	19.4	3.25	21.3	3.77	23.6	5.74	ICMR, 1972
Uttar Pradesh	16.2	2.64	17.7	2.89	19.6	2.68	21.6	3.15	23.8	3.84	ICMR, 1972
Yadav, Haryana	16.98	2.3	19.01	2.829	19.6	2.39	22.61	3.58	24.67	3.524	Ravi and Rao 2000 (unpublished)
Yadav, Uttar Pradesh	17.8	1.5	19.69	0.36	21.81	0.31	23.07	0.47	27.2	0.63	Present study

Table 20
Comparative Data on Yadav Children : Stature

	6		7		8		9		10		
Group	*Mean*	*S.D.*	*Mean*	*S.D.*	*Mean*	*S.D.*	*Mean*	*S.D.*	*Mean*	*S.D.*	*Authors*
Boys											
United States	118.6	5.17	124.5	5.52	130	5.67	135.5	6.72	140.2	6.81	NCHS, 1960
India (Socio-economic Class I)	118.8	5.83	119.7	5.29	123.9	6.15	128.4	8.37	135.4	9.78	ICMR, 1972
India (Pooled)	108.5	7.15	113.9	5.2	119.3	7.34	123.7	9.28	128.4	9.99	ICMR, 1972
Uttar Pradesh	108.1	7.16	112.9	11.54	118.4	7.55	122.8	11.95	127.8	14.13	ICMR, 1972
Yadav, Haryana	111.604	7.932	123.232	6.843	128.712	7.836	132.465	6.864	137.869	7.966	Ravi & Rao 2000 (Unpublished)
Yadav, Andhra Pradesh	105.86	3.29	112.30	3.34	118.25	3.25	123.01	3.56	128.99	2.99	Rao and Busi (1991)
Yadav, Uttar Pradesh	117.91	0.92	119.61	0.77	125.89	1.2	132.27	0.98	134.21	0.84	Present study
Girls											
United States	117.8	5.52	123.5	5.87	129.4	6.26	135.5	7	140.9	7.37	NCHS, 1960
India (Socio-economic Class I)	112.6	6.56	116.3	7.15	122.8	6.76	127.1	7.28	132.5	7.81	ICMR, 1972
India (Pooled)	107.4	8.65	112.8	8.49	118.2	7.71	122.9	7.35	128.4	8.02	ICMR, 1972
Uttar Pradesh	106.7	10.87	111.8	11.29	117.3	8.49	122.2	8.04	127.9	7.98	ICMR, 1972
Yadav, Haryana	113.36	6.756	120.25	7.65	122.419	6.01	129.812	6.854	134.07	7.25	Ravi & Rao, 2000 (Unpublished)
Yadav, Uttar Pradesh	111.6	1.22	120.6	0.84	123.43	0.93	127.4	1.12	134.81	1.2	Present study

indicating rates of growth in boys and girls. In the present study, pre-adolescence puberty is seen to set in among the girls between 9 and 10 years of age; whereas, among the boys it is yet to set in. Consequently, spurt in the growth of various dimensions takes place earlier in girls. This results in the differences between two sexes are phase difference and vary in magnitude.

Cross tabulation of the mean values and standard deviation of five selected measurements i.e. weight, stature, sitting height, bi-acromial breadth and bi-iliac breadth have been done for literacy level of both parents, family size, family type and parity. The analysis indicates that above mentioned factors are related to growth and physique of the children. Absence of consistent differences in physical characterstics may be due to very small sample size which is not statistically viable to derive at any conclusion.

COMPARISON WITH SELECTED POPULATIONS

Since majority of growth studies are restricted to few bodily dimensions such as height and weight, the comparison of the present data also has been limited to these composite measurements. Thus the mean body weight and mean height of Yadav boys and girls are compared with other selected groups studied (Table 19 and 20).

It was observed that the Indian children (ICMR, 1972) were shorter and lighter than their counterparts in the United States (NCHS, 1977). The body weight and height of Yadav children of Uttar Pradesh (present study) and Yadav of Haryana (Ravi & Rao, Unpublished) are closer to that of Indian children belonging to socio-economic class I (ICMR, 1972. Fig. 24, 27). The lowest body weight were observed among Indian children (Pooled) ICMR and children of Uttar Pradesh (ICMR) of both the sexes. The Yadav boys of Andhra Pradesh (Rao and Busi, 1991) occupy the lowest position with respect to weight and height (Fig. 24, 26) at the initial stage i.e. at 6 yrs but supercede the mean values of weight for Indian (Pooled), ICMR, 1972 at age 8 yrs.

It was apparent from the graph (Fig. 26, 27) that the pattern of growth among the children of United States were similar to that of Yadav children of Haryana (Ravi and Rao, n.d.) from age 7 yrs onward. At age 6 years the height of children of United States is almost similar to the height of Indian boys belonging to Socio-economic class I (ICMR) as the age advances the difference between the heights of two groups increases. This is due to the higher rate of growth among the children of the United States than that of Indian children (Socio-economic class I category). The Yadav boys of Uttar Pradesh(present study) were closer to the boys of United States in height at age 6 and 7 yrs but between the age 7 to 8 yrs rate of growth slowed down drastically in Yadav boys of U.P. which accounts for their shorter stature. From above it is concluded that the Indian children have the genetic potential for growth more or less similar to children of United States. The better growth potential among the children of United States than that of India are due to the better environmental factors such as living conditions, health and hygiene, nutrition, immunization etc. enjoyed by the children of United States.

From Fig. 24-27, it is apparent that the United States children occupy the highest position with respect to height and weight of comparable populations. Whereas, the Yadav of Uttar Pradesh (present study) and Yadav of Haryana (Ravi and Rao) and Indian children belonging to higher socio-economic group occupy the middle position with slight variation which were attributed to differential rate of growth. The children of Uttar Pradesh State (ICMR, 1972) and Indian children from different economic strata (pooled) ICMR, 1972, were at the lowest level with respect to height and weight.

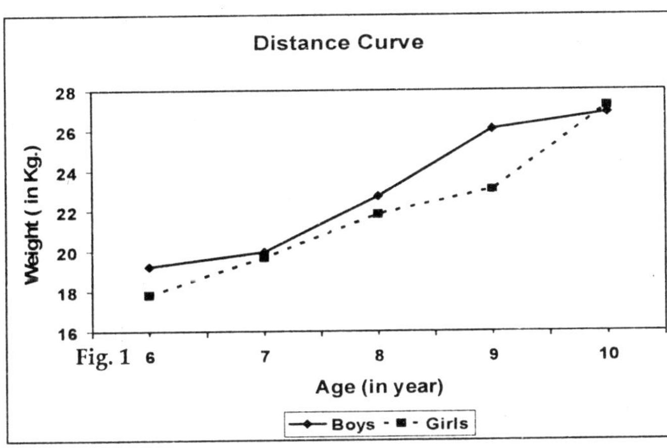

Fig. 1

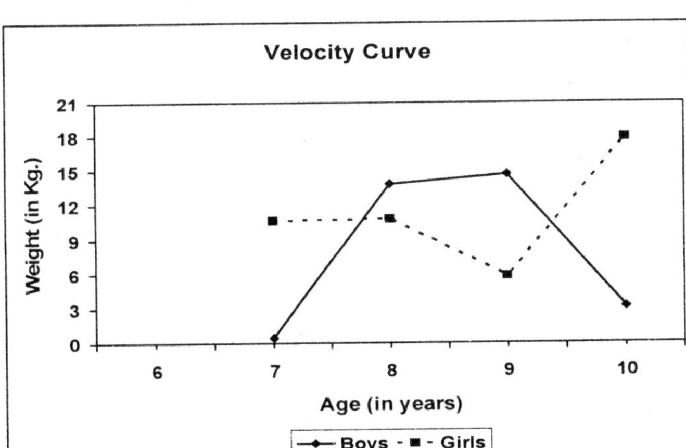

Fig. 2

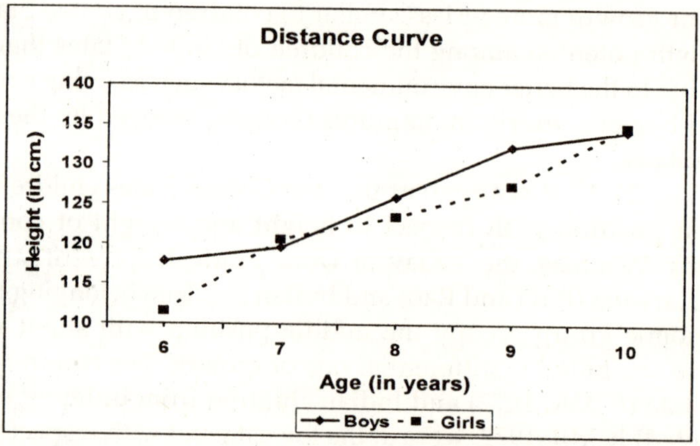

Fig. 3

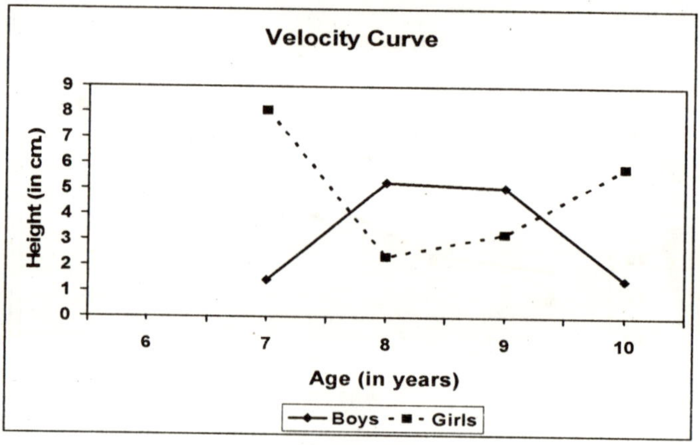

Fig. 4

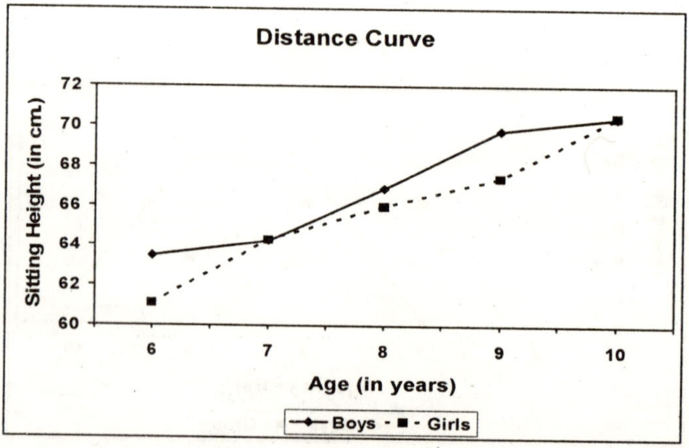

Fig. 5

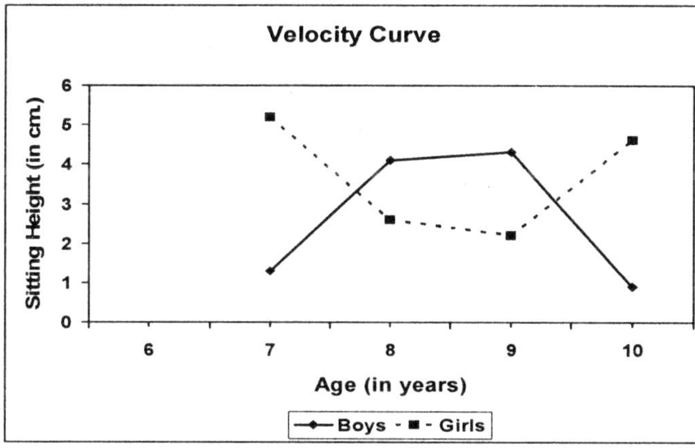

Fig. 6

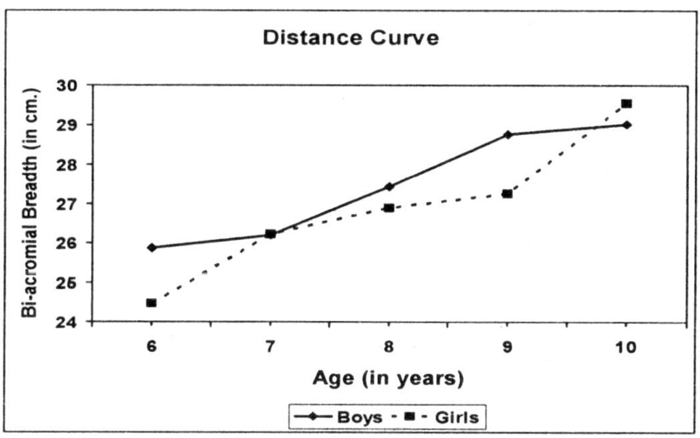

Fig. 7

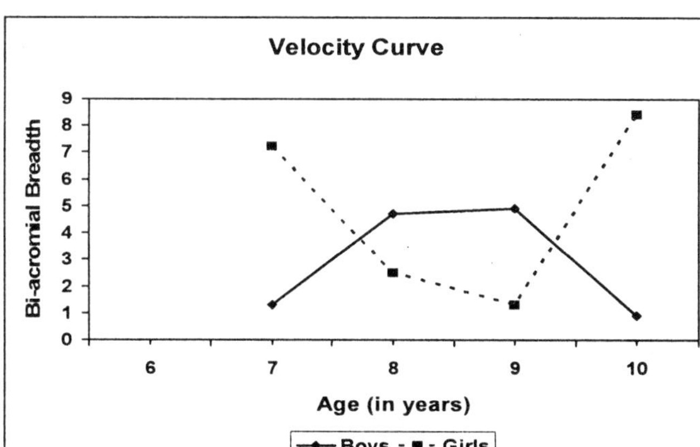

Fig. 8

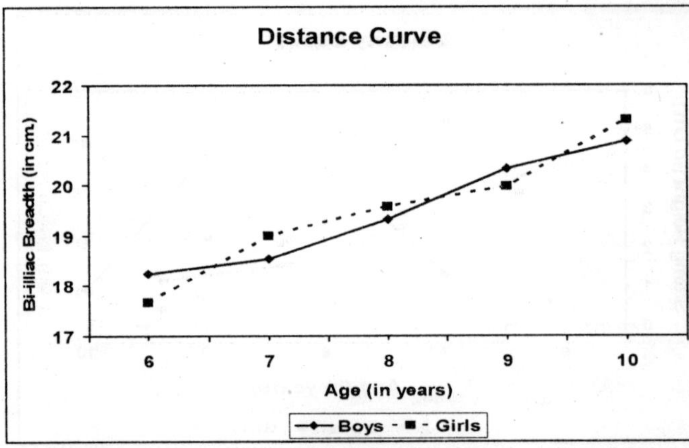

Fig. 9

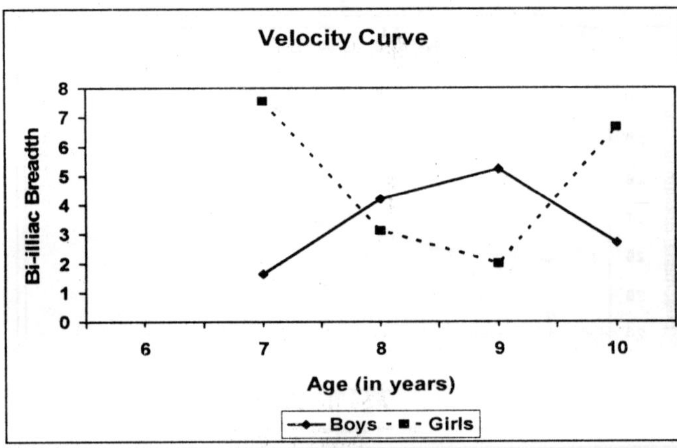

Fig. 10

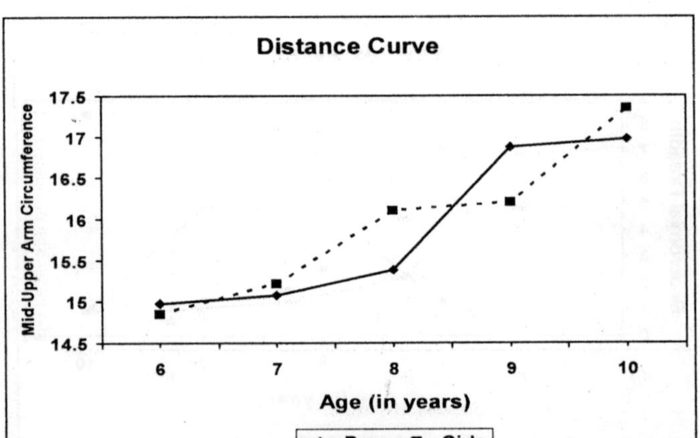

Fig. 11

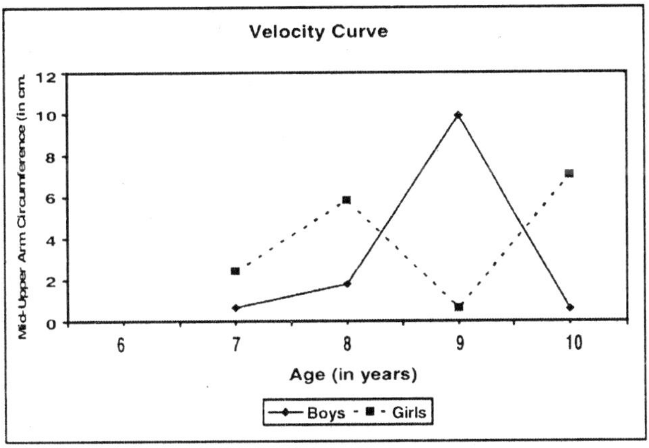

Fig. 12

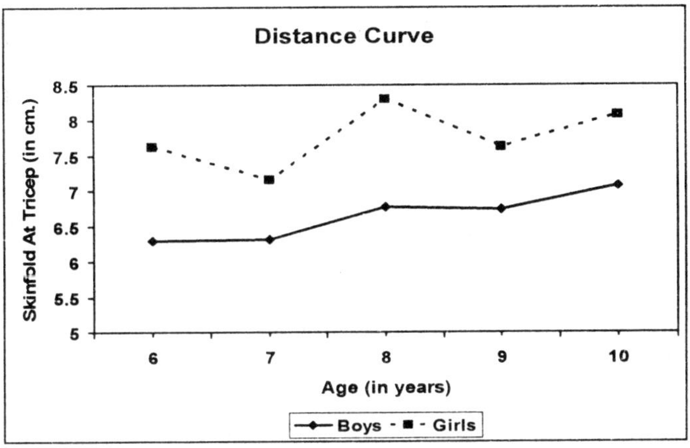

Fig. 13

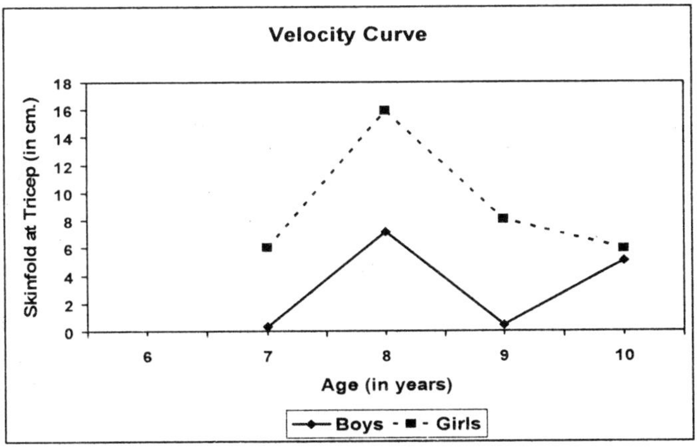

Fig. 14

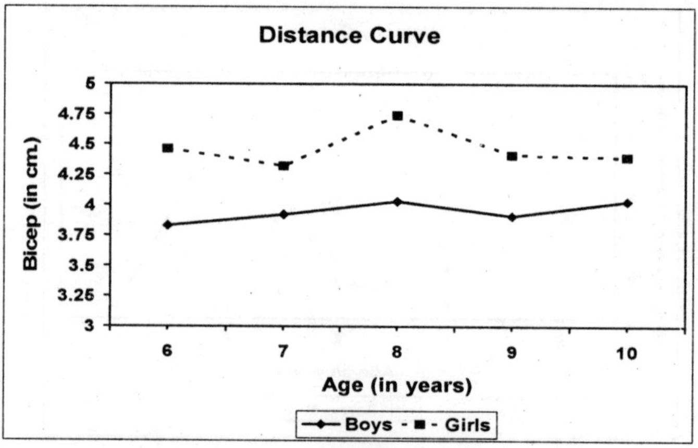

Fig. 15

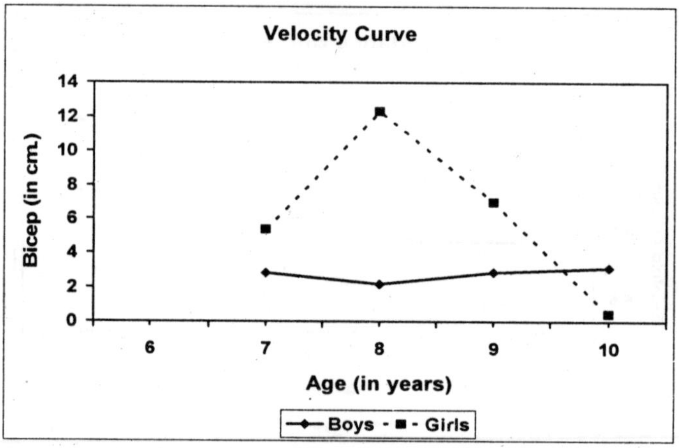

Fig. 16

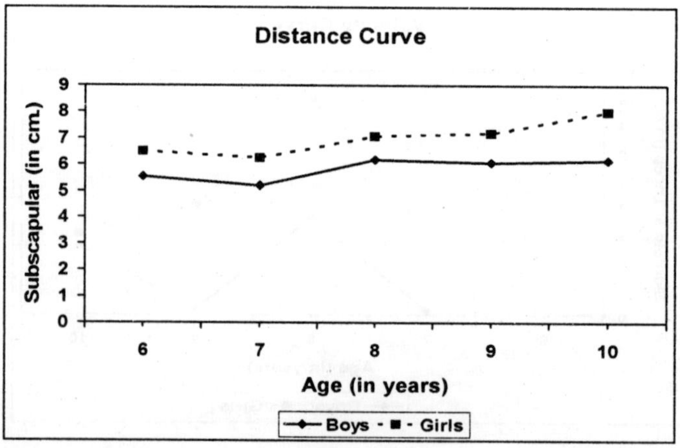

Fig. 17

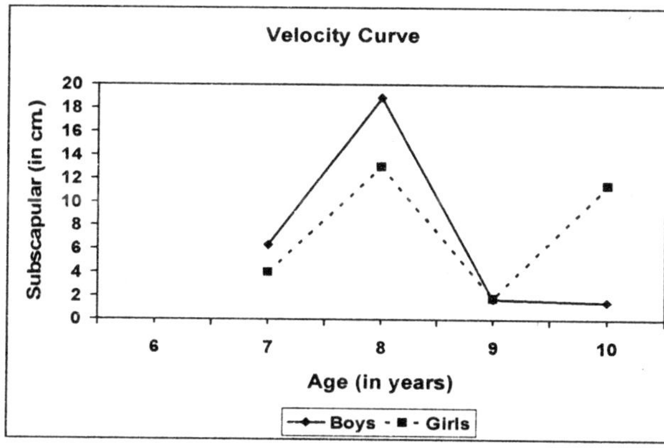

Fig. 18

REGRESSION LINES FOR YADAV BOYS AND GIRLS

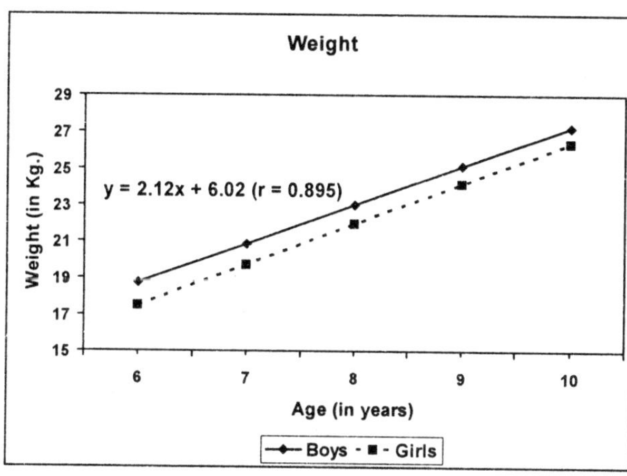

Fig. 19

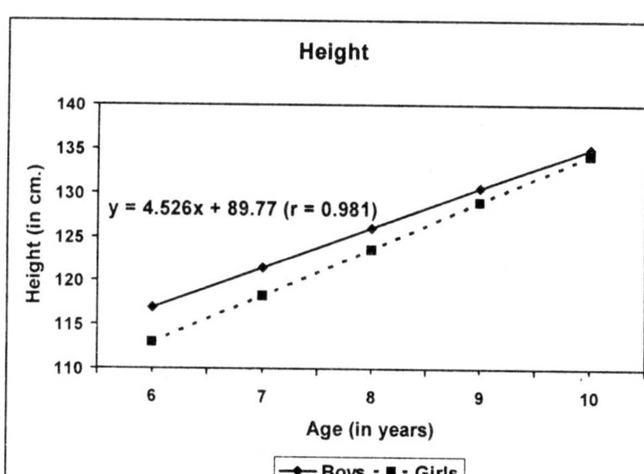

Fig. 20

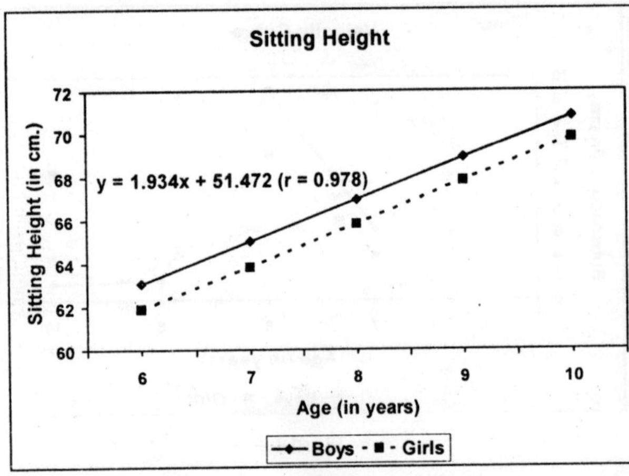

Fig. 21

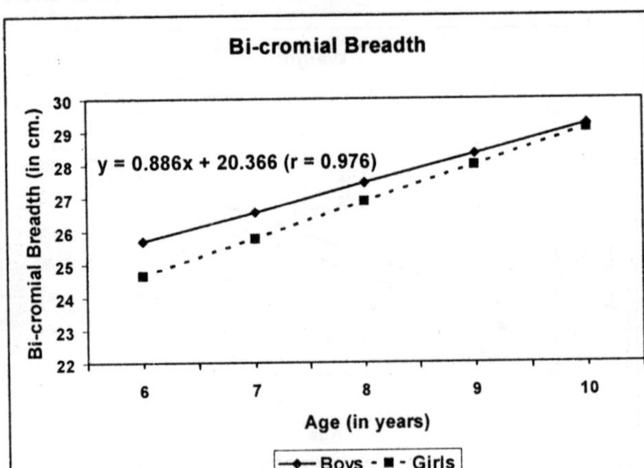

Fig. 22

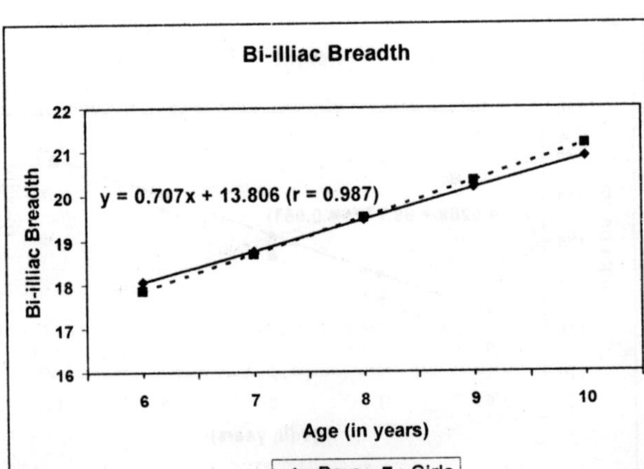

Fig. 23

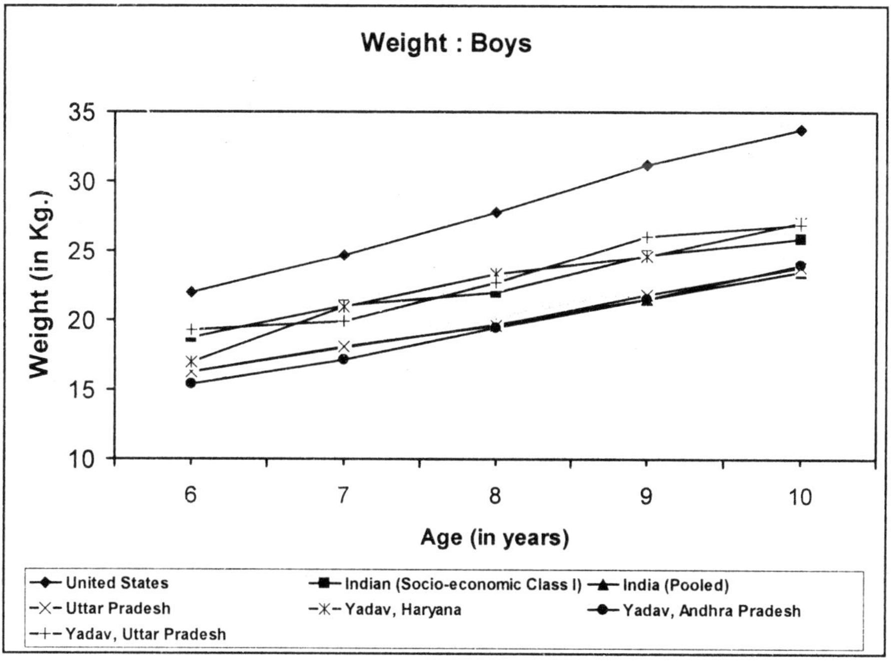
Weight : Boys
35
30
25
20
15
10
Weight (in Kg.)
6
7
8
9
10
Age (in years)
United States
Indian (Socio-economic Class I)
India (Pooled)
Uttar Pradesh
Yadav, Haryana
Yadav, Andhra Pradesh
Yadav, Uttar Pradesh

Fig. 24

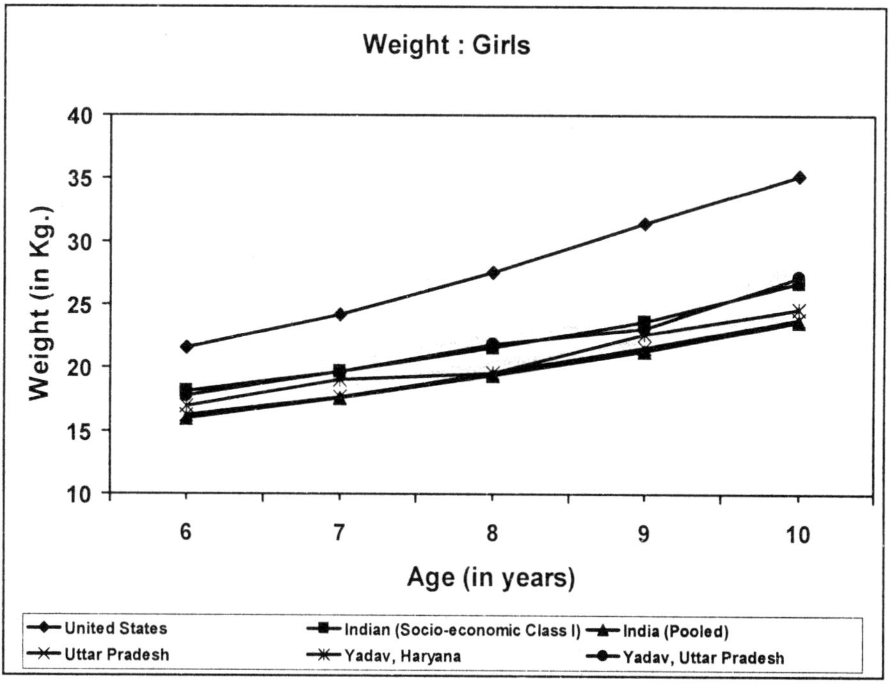
Weight : Girls
40
35
30
25
20
15
10
Weight (in Kg.)
6
7
8
9
10
Age (in years)
United States
Indian (Socio-economic Class I)
India (Pooled)
Uttar Pradesh
Yadav, Haryana
Yadav, Uttar Pradesh

Fig. 25

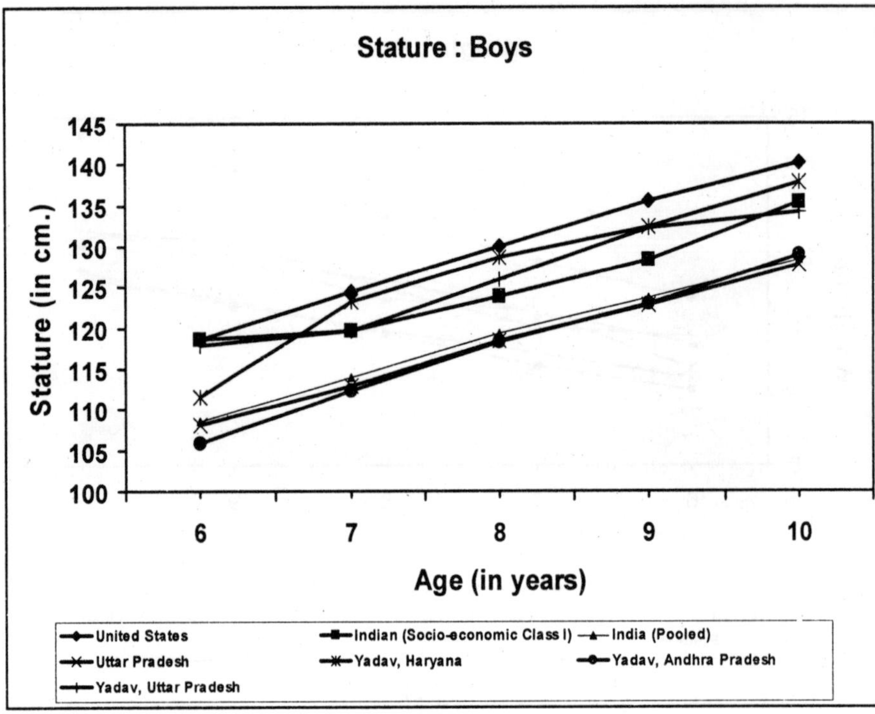
Stature : Boys
145
140
135
130
125
120
115
110
105
100
Stature (in cm.)
6
7
8
9
10
Age (in years)
United States
Indian (Socio-economic Class I)
India (Pooled)
Uttar Pradesh
Yadav, Haryana
Yadav, Andhra Pradesh
Yadav, Uttar Pradesh

Fig. 26

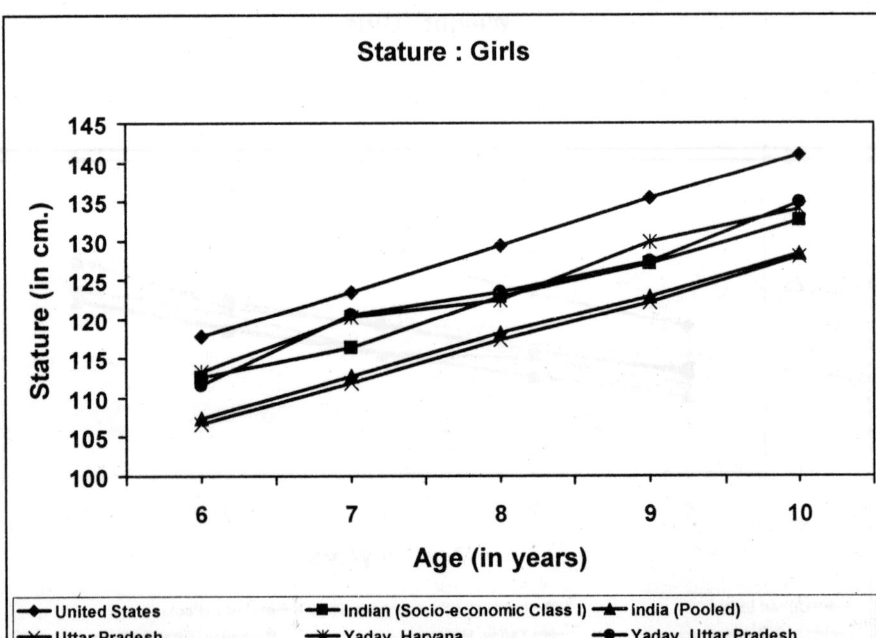
Stature : Girls
145
140
135
130
125
120
115
110
105
100
Stature (in cm.)
6
7
8
9
10
Age (in years)
United States
Indian (Socio-economic Class I)
india (Pooled)
Uttar Pradesh
Yadav, Haryana
Yadav, Uttar Pradesh

Fig. 27

References

Bhowmick, D. C. (1993), A Cross Sectional Growth Study of the School Children of Medinipur, *Anthropological Survey of India*, Calcutta.

Black R. E., K. H. Brown, and S. Becker (1984), Effects of Diarrhoea Associated with Specific Enteropathogens on the Growth of Children in Rural Bangladesh, Pediatrics, 73 (6): 799–805.

Boas, F. (1932), Studies in Growth, In *Human Biology*, 4: 307-50.

Chaurasia, A. R. (1978), Correlates of Age with Height and Weight of Children, In *Indian Journal of Pediatrics*, 45: 48-51.

Eveleth, P. B. and J. M. Tanner (1976), International Biological Programme World Wide Variation in Human Growth. Cambridge University Press, Cambridge, London, New York-Melbourne, Page 1.

Garn, S. M. and C. G. Rohman (1966), Interaction of Nutrition and Genetics in the Timing of Growth and Development, In *The Paediatric Clinics of North America*, 13: 353-361.

Gomez, F., R. R. Galvan, S. Frenk, J. C. Munoz, R. Chavez and J. Vazquez (1956), Mortality in Second and Third Degree Malnutrition, In *Journal of Tropical Paediatrics*, 2: 77-83.

Gopalan, Sarla (1995), Towards Better Nutrition for Women and Children Problem and Programmes. Lecture Delivered at Second Annual Foundation day of the Nutrition Foundation of India, November 29, 1995.

Gorden, J. E., W. Ascoli, , I. J. Mala, , M. A. Guzman, and N. S. Scrimsshaw (1968), Nutrition and Infection Field Study in Guatemalan Villages, 1959-1964. VI: Acute Diarrhoeal Disease and Nutritional Disorder in General Disease Incidence, In *Archives of Environmental Health*, 16:424.

Government of India (1965), *Gazetteers of India, Uttar Pradesh, Varanasi*, Government of India Press, Allahabad.

Hiernaux J. (1968), Bodily Shape Differentiation of Ethnic Groups and of the Sexes Through Growth, In *Human Biology*, 40: 44-62.

ICMR (Indian Council of Medical Research) 1972. Growth and Physical Development of Indian Infants and Children, In *Technical Report No. 18*, New Delhi.

Jelliffe, D. B. (1966), The Assessment of the Nutritional Status of the Community. *WHO Monograph Series No. 53*, Geneva: WHO.

Jenkins C. L. (1981), Patterns of Growth and Malnutrition among Pre School Children in Belize, In *American Journal of Physical Anthropology*, 56: 169-178.

Kaul, S. (1971), Physical Growth and Development (Human)–A Study Based on Kashmiri Pandit Boys of School Going Age in Srinagar, Kashmir Ph.D. Thesis, Punjab University, Chandigarh, (unpublished).

Kaul, S. (1991), Co-relation in Human Growth Analysis, In *Indian Journal of Physical Anthropology & Human Genetics*, Vol. 17(2 & 3): 105-112.

Kaul, S. S. and I. K. Nyamongo, (1990), Ecology, Growth and Nutritional Status, Ashish Publishing House, New Delhi.

Latham, M. (1979), Human Nutrition in Tropical Africa Second Edition, Rome.

Malik, S. L. and I. P. Singh (1978), Growth Trends among Male Bodhs of Ladakh– A High Altitude Population, In *American Journal of Physical Anthropology*, 48: 171–176.

Martin, R. & K. Saller (1957), *Lehrbuch der Anthropologic. Suttgart.*

Mata, L. J. J. Urrutia and A. Lechtig (1971), Infection and Nutrition of Children of a Low Socio-economic Rural Community, *American Journal of Clinical Nutrition*, 24: 249–259.

Mead, M. (1964), Food Habits Research: Problmes of the 1960's. Nat Acad. Sci. Nat. Res. Coun. Washington.

Mead M. (1997), Contemporary Implications of the State of Art. In L. Greene (Ed.) Malnutrition, Behaviour and Social Organisation. Acad. Press, New York.

Morterell, R., C. Yarbrough, A. Lechtig, J. P. Habicht and R.E. Klein (1975), Diarrhoeal Diseases and Growth Retardation in Pre. School Guatemalan Children, In *American Journal of Physical Anthropology*, 43: 341–346.

Nath, Surinder, Varsha Sachdeva and Meena Chauhan (1991), Progression of Maturation Sequence in Stature and Linear Measures of the Extremities and Sex Differences among Lodhas of West Bengal, In *Indian Journal of Physical Anthropology and Human Genetics*, 17 (2.3), 205–218.

NCHS (National Centre for Health Statistics) 1977 NCHS Growth Curves for Children, Birth to 18 Years, United States. Vital and Health statistics, Series 11, No. 165, 1977.

Pandey, R. (1979), Kashi Through the Ages. Sandeep Prakashan, Delhi.

Parsons, P. A. (1965), Growth in a Sample of Australian Aborigins from one to Twenty-three Months of Age, In *Growth* 29: 207-211.

Prader, A., J. M. Tanner & G. A. Von Harnack (1963), Catch up Growth following Illness or Starvation. An Example of Developmental Canalization in Man. In *Journal of Pediatrics*, 62: 646-659.

Rao., B. Dharma and B. R. Busi, *et. al.* (1991), Physical Growth and Regression Characteristics among Yadav Boys of Visakhapatnam District, Andhra Pradesh, India, In *Indian Journal of Physical Anthropology and Human Genetics*, 17 (2 & 3): 223-232.

Rao, B. S. , D. S. S. Girija Vani and B. R. Busi (1997), A Study of Growth in Physical and Physiological Variables among Mala Boys of Visakhapatnam District, Andhra Pradesh, In *Journal of Human Ecology*, 8: 361–367.

Rao, Visweswara (1980), Efficiency of Anthropometric Indices for the Diagonosis of Malnutrition, In *Courier*, 30: 113-121.

Ravi, K. and J. S. Rao (2000), Growth and Development of Children: Bio-cultural Perspectives-A Study of the AHIRS (Yaduvanshi) of Haryana (Unpublished).

Reddy, K. N. (1989), Growth and Physical Changes during Adolescence among Bhil Boys of Rajasthan, *Anthropological Survey of India*, Calcutta.

Roberts, D. F. (1960), Effects of Race and Climate on Growth of African Children, In *Human Growth*, Ed. J.M. Tanner, p. 59-72. London-Pergamon.

Sharma, J. C. (1963), Age Changes in Bodily Proportions of Maharashtrians. Ph.D. Thesis, Punjab University, Chandigarh, (unpublished).

Sharma, J. C. (1970), Physical Growth and Development of the Maharashtrians. Ethnographic and Folk Culture Society, U.P. Lucknow, India.

Sharma, J. C. (1982), Physical Growth and Development and Protein-calorie-malnutrition in Tribal Children of Central India, In *Bulletin Socio Bionaturalist*. Bhopal.

Schultz, A. H. (1926), Foetal Growth of Man and other Primates, *Quat. Rev. Biol.* 1:465.

Singh, Bageshwar n.d. The Yadavas, In the People of India: Uttar Pradesh Volume (Unpublished); Anthropological Survey of India, Govt. of India.

Singh, I. P. & M. K. Bhasin (1968), Anthropometry. Kamala-Raj Publication, Delhi.

Singh, Lakhbir (1969), Biological Survey of Punjabi males with Special Reference to Age Changes. Ph.D. Thesis, Punjab University, Chandigarh, (unpublished).

Singh, Lakhbir (1970), Physical Growth of Lahaulis from Birth to Maturity. Ph.D. Thesis, Punjab University, Chandigarh (unpublished).

Singh, Raghubir (1968), Somatometric Study of the Punjabi Hindu Khatri (male) with Special Emphasis on Growth (cross-sectional) and Relationship between Arm Girth and Body Weight Measurements. Ph.D. Thesis, Delhi University, (unpublished) Delhi.

Tanner, J. M.; R.H. Whitehouse and M. Takaishi (1965), Standards from Birth to Maturity for Height, Weight, Height Velocity and Weight Velocity: British Children. Archives of Disease in Childhood, 41:454-464.

Vaughan, V. C. and I. F. Litt (1952), Growth and Development in Nelson's Text Book of Pediatrics Thirteen edition ed. By Behram, Vaughen and Sounders.

Vidyarthi, L. P., Makhan Jha and B. N. Saraswati (1979), The Sacred Complex of Kashi: A Microcosm Civilisation, Concept Publishing Company, Delhi.

2

GROWTH AND DEVELOPMENT OF CHILDREN: BIO-CULTURAL PERSPECTIVES– A STUDY ON THE AHIRS (YEDUVANSHI) OF HARYANA

Kattoju Ravi & Jadhav S. Jaya Sankar Rao

This study is a part of the national project "Growth and Development of Children: Bio-cultural Perspective" launched by Anthropological Survey of India during the Ninth Five Year Plan. The present paper is on growing Ahirs (Yeduvanshi) children (6 years to 10 years of age) of Mahendragarh district, Haryana.

The Ahir claim to be the descendants of Lord Krishna of Mathura. The Ahir are an agricultural community who are mainly concentrated in the districts of Mahendragarh, Rewari and Gurgaon of Haryana. The community is broadly divided into three divisions (*vansh* or *khamp*) namely Goalvanshi, Yeduvanshi and Nandvanshi, which are endogamous in nature. Each *vansh* or *khamp* is further divided into a number of *got* which are exogamous in nature. The Ahirs of the villages under the study i.e., Seehma, Khampura/Khampra, Khaspur and Deroli Ahir belong to the Yeduvanshi division. The Yeduvanshi of this area form a territorial group of 26 villages locally called *chabbis kheda.* The villages under the study as mentioned above come under this territorial group. Reportedly, there are about 64 *got* under the Yeduvanshi division. They are saap, Munad, Jagam, Khosya, Panihar, Lamba, Kansalya, Simalval, Bickwalia, Kathas, Jundack, Khola, Seegadiya to mention a few. Among the Ahirs (Yeduvanshi) of Mahendragarh district, the marriageable age for boys is between 18 and 22 years and for girls it is between thirteen and eighteen years.

The four villages under the study namely Seehma, Khampura/ Khampra, Khaspur and Deroli Ahir come under Ateli Development Block, Narnul tahsil and Mahendragarh district. The district comes under semi-arid/semi-desert area, and it is almost a flat surface. The climate is very hot during summers and cold during winters.

The staple food of the Ahirs (Yeduvanshi) is unleavened bread (*roti*) made of wheat and *bajra*. They consume pulses like red gram (*chana*), green gram (*moong*), *arhar* and black gram dal (*urad dal*). Some of the malefolk consume alcoholic drinks purchased from the market. Smocking of huble buble (*hooka*) is the general practice of the men. By and large the Ahir (Yeduvanshi) are vegetarian. Only some members of the working class take non-vegetarian food occasionally. Among the younger generation consumption of eggs is common; this they consider as a vegetarian food item since it is un-fertilised. They consume milk and milk products such as *lassi* and curds (*dahi*). Children are given milk and milk products as daily diet. They also consume clarified butter *desi ghee* or *makhan* along with bread (*roti*) of wheat or *bajra*. The people take adequate staple food, which is balanced with consumption of pulses, vegetables, milk and milk products (curds, *lassi*, *desi-ghee* and *butter/makhan*). They consider *lassi* as a preventive of bacterial disorder. They commonly believe that on consumption of lassi, the infection if any will be drained out through urination. The infants are given breast feeding as long as mother can provide the same.

MATERIAL & METHODS

The data for the present study was collected during November 1998 to January, 1999. The present study consists of 420 unrelated school going children (boys 209; girls 211). The study was carried out in the rural areas of Ateli block, Narnul tahsil, Mahendragarh district of Haryana. The data was collected from four villages viz. Seehma, Khampura/Kahmpra, Khaspur and Deroli Ahir. The data was collected from five different age group, ranging from 6 years to 10 years. Atleast forty children were studied under each age group of both the sexes separately. Anthropometric measurements such as Weight, Stature, Sitting height, Biacromial diameter, Bi-iliocristal diameter, Mid upper arm circumference, Triceps skin fold, Sub-scapular skin fold and Biceps skinfold. Parity of the child, dental pattern and clinical signs were recorded. The exact date of birth of the subjects were recorded from the school register and also cross checked through the subject's parents. The children taken for the study are mostly from the rural areas and all the subjects are from the same social status with economic stratification. The techniques employed in measuring boys and girls are of Martin and Saller (1959). Observation of deficiency signs was taken according to Jelliffe (1966) and Latham (1979).

RESULTS

The literacy among the 420 households of the Ahir (Yeduvanshi) community is above the national average literacy. Of the total population of 2752 individuals, as many as 1912 individuals (69.48 per cent) are literate. Among the males 1103 (82.22 per cent) and among the female 809 persons (58.04 per cent) are literate. (Table 1). Only five males and two females are reported to be semi-literates.

Table 1
Literacy Rate among the Ahirs of the Four Villages under Study in Mahendragarh District, Haryana

Literacy	*Male*	*%*	*Female*	*%*	*Total*	*%*
Literate						
Primary	405	29.82	458	32.86	863	31.36
Upper Primary	272	20.03	224	16.07	496	18.02
Secondary	287	21.13	87	6.24	374	13.59
Higher Secondary	91	6.70	23	1.65	114	4.14
Graduation	38	2.80	14	1.00	52	1.90
Post Graduation	10	0.74	3	0.22	13	0.47
	1103	82.22	809	58.04	1912	69.48
Semi-literate	5	0.37	2	0.14	7	0.25
illiterate	250	18.41	583	41.82	833	30.27
Total	1358		1394		2752	

The analysis on family types reveal that out of 420 families, majority of them are of nuclear type 190 (45.24 per cent), while as many as 122 families (29.05 per cent) are of vertically extended type. Reportedly, a good number of families 94 (22.38 per cent) are of mixed extended type. Only nine families (2.14 per cent) are of horizontally extended type while the remaining five (1.19 per cent) are either incomplete or broken families.

The major primary occupations among the Ahir (Yeduvanshi) shows that majority of them are engaged in agriculture, followed by service. They are mostly recruited in armed services like Central Reserve Police Force, Indo-Tibetan Border Police, Border Security Force, Army , Navy etc. Only few members are engaged in other pursuits such as masonry, watch repairing, camel cart driving etc. Their secondary occupations are agricultural labour, dairying, farming, and petty business.

Their housing pattern reveal that their houses are spacious having on an average four rooms for every house with large windows for sufficient sunlight and ventilation. The civic amenities in the villages under the study are not satisfactory. The roads are not properly laid and the villages lack adequate drainage system and soak pits. Hence, the water that is utilized for bathing and washing of clothes is driven on to the roads, making them unworthy for vehicular traffic with many pot holes. These pot holes form a breeding place for mosquitoes and flies resulting in the spread of Malaria, Typhoid and other water born diseases.

Most of the houses are devoid of latrines (61.67%). Only 48 houses possess flush latrines (38.33%). Even if the houses have septic latrines, some members go out to defecate–a process of continuity and change. As majority of the houses have milch cattle (buffaloes or cows) or drought cattle like camels, a separate place is provided for them. The sand/soil where the cattle are tied is changed frequently to keep the surroundings dry and also to keep the cattle warm during winter season. In all the four villages under the study tube wells have been introduced for every locality (*mohalla*) with over head tanks by the village panchayats. However, the surroundings of the tube wells are not clean.

The analysis on the living conditions (Table 2) of the Ahir (Yeduvanshi) in the four villages under the study show that out of 120 households surveyed as many as 81 households (68.33 per cent) live in masonry built houses and about 38 households (31.67 per cent) live in both thatched and masonry built houses. Only two households are exclusively living in thatched houses and one household in a bungalow). Almost all the

Table 2
Living Conditions Among the Ahirs of Four Villages of Mahendragarh District, Haryana

Living Conditions	*No. of Households*	%
No. of thatched houses	38	31.67
No. of masonry built houses	118	98.33
No. of bungalows	1	0.83
No. of households having owned house	119	99.17
No. of households staying in rented house	1	0.83
Average No. of Rooms.	3.84 (4 rooms)	-
No. of houses having good ventilation	10	8.33
No. of houses having satisfactory ventilation	109	90.83
No. of houses having poor ventilation	1	0.83
No. of houses having sunlight	120	100
No. of houses having no sunlight	-	-
Cleanliness of the houses-good	7	5.83
Cleanliness of the houses-satisfactory	109	90.83
Cleanliness of the houses- poor	4	3.33
No. of houses having flush latrines	46	38.33
No. of houses having pit type latrine		
No. of houses who go to field for toilet	82	68.33
No. of households avail protected water supply	-	-
No. of households avail unprocessed water supply	120	100
No. of households availing pipe water	-	-
No. of households availing stream water	-	-
No. of households having washing and bathing facilitis-nearby their dwellings	106	83.33
No. of households having washing and bathing facilities far away from their houses	14	11.67
Personal cleanliness-Good	14	11.67
Personal cleanliness- Satisfactory	104	86.67
Personal Cleanliness- Poor	2	1.67
Utensils cleaned properly	120	100
Utensils not cleaned properly	-	-
Utensils store properly	120	100
Utensils not stored properly	-	-

households–119 constituting 99.17 per cent have their own house and only one household reported to have been living in a rented house. Regarding ventilation and availability of sunlight, it is reported by 10 households (8.33 per cent) that they have good ventilation, while the rest 109 households i.e. 90.83 per cent have satisfactory ventilation. Only one household has poor ventilation. All the 120 households, (100.00 per cent) reportedly get enough sunlight. As far as cleanliness is concerned only seven houses constituting 5.38 per cent show good cleanliness. Majority of the houses–109 (70.83 per cent) show satisfactory cleanliness and in only four houses (3.33 per cent) cleanliness is poor. All the 120 households avail unprocessed/unprotected water from the tube wells. The water is being lifted either by electric pumpsets or hand pumps. They also draw water from open wells manually.

The analysis on health and hygiene among the Ahir (Yeduvanshi) in the four villages under the study (Table 3) reveal that all the 120 households avail health facilities allopathic system of medicine. Among them about nine households (7.50 per cent) also avail indigenous system of medicine and about seven households (5.83 per cent) avail ayurvedic system of medicine. As many as 113 households (94.27 per cent) reported to have been availing immunization programmes while the remaining seven households (5.8 per cent) have not availed the same either due to negligence or due to lack of awareness. Under the immunization programmes a large number of households–107 (89.2 per cent) have availed Polio drops for their children. During our field work too, pulse polio programme was in operation and the health department in the villages could reach a target of 90 per cent. As many as 114 (95 per cent) households availed D.P.T. vaccine facilities. A large number of households–109 (90.8 per cent) availed Measles vaccine as well as Tetanus vaccine. Only 55 households (45.83 per cent) reported to have availed supplementary food facility to their children through government agency i.e., Anganwadi institutes.

Developmental Programmes for the Children

Most of the children are covered under various immunization schemes such as D.P.T., B.C.G., Measles and Polio/Pulse Polio. Parental care is being extended to the expectant mother and child, and anti natal care to the new borns and the mothers through Primary Health Centres and Anganwadis.

Mid Day Meal Scheme was initiated on 15th November, 1995 for Primary School children in the State of Haryana. Under this scheme rice and wheat are distributed to all the Primary School children irrespective of caste and creed. This scheme was initiated to encourage primary education for all children in the state. The ration of 1.5 Kg. of rice and 1.5 Kg. of wheat per child per month is being issued to the children on the last working day of the month on assessing the percentages of attendance.

Table 3
Details of Health and Hygiene Among the Ahirs of Four Villages, Mahendragarh Distrit, Haryana

Health and Hygiene	*No of households*	*%*
No of households in which member/members suffer from diseases	1	0.83
No of households availing health facilities	120	100.00
No of households not availing health facilities		
No of households availing Allopathic medicines	120	100.00
No of households availing Ayurvedic medicines	7	5.83
No of households availing indiginous medicines	9	7.50
No of households availing Homeopathic medicines		
No of households availed immunization programme	113	94.20
No of households who have not availed immunization programme	7	5.83
No of households who availed polio drops	107	89.20
No of households who availed DPT vaccine	114	95.00
No of households who have availed Measles vaccine	109	90.83
No of households who availed Tetanus vaccine	109	90.83
No of households who practise breast feeding	120	100.00
No of households who do not practise breast feeding		
No of households where breast feeding is regular	120	100.00
No of Households where breast feeding is irregular	-	-
No of Households who observe taboos in taking food	120	100.00
No of Households who do not observe any taboos in taking food	-	-
No of Households availing supplementary foods	55	45.83
No of Households not availing supplementary foods	65	54.17
No of Households availing supplementary foods through government	55	45.83
No of Households availing supplementary foods trough NGOs	-	-
No of Households having separate kitchen	71	59.17
No of Households having no separate kitchen	49	40.83
No of Households using wood as fuel for cooking	120	100.00
No of Households using smoke stove for cooking	-	-
No of Households using coal as fuel for cooking	-	-
No of Households using kerosene as fuel for cooking	73	60.83
No of Households using cowdung cakes as fuel for cooking	120	100.00
No of Households using L.P.Gas as fuel for cooking	10	8.33

The cross-sectional growth data on Ahir (Yeduvanshi) boys and girls in the age range six to ten years of Mahendragarh district, Haryana are statistically analysed. It is known fact that during preadolescence and adolescence period linear growth will be more than the transverse growth hence much attention was focused on the linear measurements. The following measurements along with weight and skin fold measurements were shown in Table 4 and discussed below:

Weight

Age changes in weight gives a general idea of the gross body growth. A change in body weight may be the result of changes in health of an individual, changes in dietary supplies or even changes in one's physical activity (Kaul and Nyamongo, 1990).

A steady increase in weight is observed in both boys and girls from 6 to 10 years. It is seen from the Table 4 that boys were heavier than the girls. The mean weight of boys at six years is 17 Kg. and at ten years it is 27.1 Kg., whereas, in the case of girls the mean weight at six year is 17 Kg. and at ten years it is 24.7 Kg. The total increase in weight from six to ten years in the case of boys is 10.09 Kg. while girls have shown an increase of 7.69 Kg. only.

The coefficient of variation in boys is high at eight years and ten years. Whereas, in the case of girls the c.v. value is high at nine years, seven years and at ten years.

The distance curve (Fig. 1) shows a steady increase in weight from six to eight years in boys then it showed a slight decrease in the age group 8-9 years then it shown a steady increase from nine years onwards. While in girls there is a steady increase upto seven years then between 7 to 8 years a dip, is observed and again from eight years it has shown an increase in weight as the age advances.

As we discussed in the above about the net gain of weight in each age it is substantiated with the velocity curve which shows the similar type of curves, it is shown in Fig.2.

Stature

Stature is also represented as total body length or height. The mean height of boys and girls increased steadily from the age 6 years to 10 years. It is observed that boys are taller than the girls except in the age group six years. The mean height of the boys at six years is 112.0 cm. while the mean height of the girls at six years is 113 cm. The mean height of boys at ten year is 138 cm. and for girls at ten years it is 134 cm. The increase in height from six years to ten years for boys is 26.26 cm and for girls it is 20.70 cm. Among boys if we see the net growth at each age, at the age six to seven years 11.63 cm. followed by 5.48 cm. at 7 to 8 years, 3.75 cm; at 8 to 9 years and at 9 to 10 years the increment in growth is just 2.40 cm. Whereas, girls show a high of 7.4 cm at 8 to 9 years followed by 6.89 cm at 6 to 7 years, 4.25 cm. growth at 9 to 10 years and a very less amount of growth at 8 to 9 years 2.16 cm.

The co-efficient of variation among boys is high at 8 and 6 years while girls shown a high of c.v. value at 7 years.

The distance curve (Fig. 3) showed a steady increase from six to ten years both in boys and girls, but at the starting age i.e., at six years girls are taller than the boys. The velocity curve (Fig. 4) shown the rate of growth is high at 6 to 7 years in boys while in girls it is in 8 to 9 years.

Table 4
Mean, Standard Error, Standard Deviation and Co-efficient of Variation of Eight Body Measurements of the Ahir (Yaduvanshi) Boys and Girls of Haryana

Sex		*Boys*	*Girls*	*Boys*	*Girls*	*Boys*	*Girls*	*Boys*	*Girls*	*Boys*	*Girls*
age	*(yrs)*	*6*	*6*	*7*	*7*	*8*	*8*	*9*	*9*	*10*	*10*
Sample	*(N)*	43	45	40	42	40	42	44	41	42	41
Weight	Mean	17.00	17.00	21.00	19.00	23.12	19.60	24.60	22.60	27.10	24.70
	S.E.	0.40	0.30	0.50	0.43	0.64	0.36	0.61	0.55	0.75	0.55
	S.D.	2.67	2.30	3.30	2.82	4.06	2.39	4.09	3.57	4.88	3.52
	C.V.	15.70	14.00	16.00	14.90	17.52	12.20	16.60	15.80	18.00	14.30
	Abs.			3.95	2.04	2.26	0.58	1.36	3.01	2.52	2.07
	% growth			23.23	12.02	10.78	3.05	5.85	15.36	10.25	9.15
Stature	Mean	112.00	113.00	123.00	120.00	128.70	122.00	132.00	130.00	138.00	134.00
	S.E.	1.20	1.00	1.10	1.18	1.23	0.92	1.03	1.07	1.22	1.13
	S.D.	7.93	6.80	6.80	7.64	7.83	6.00	6.86	6.85	7.96	7.25
	C.V.	7.11	6.00	5.60	6.36	6.08	4.91	5.18	5.28	5.78	5.42
	Abs.			11.63	6.89	5.48	2.16	3.75	7.4	5.4	4.25
	% growth			10.42	6.07	4.44	1.79	2.91	6.04	4.07	3.274
Sit.hight	Mean	59.40	60.00	65.00	62.90	66.93	63.80	68.00	66.70	70.10	68.60
	S.E.	0.61	0.50	0.60	0.57	0.64	0.55	0.53	0.47	0.64	0.59
	S.D.	4.02	3.30	3.60	3.69	4.08	3.50	3.52	3.05	4.14	3.80
	C.V.	6.78	5.90	5.60	5.87	6.10	5.49	5.18	4.58	5.86	5.54
	Abs.			5.34	2.71	2.22	0.92	1.07	2.92	2.61	1.86
	% growth			8.99	4.5	3.43	1.46	1.59	4.57	3.83	2.78
Biacr.dia	Mean	24.50	25.00	27.00	25.90	28.05	26.40	28.60	27.60	29.60	28.80
	S.E.	0.27	0.20	0.30	0.21	0.28	0.20	0.24	0.25	0.29	0.26
	S.D.	1.77	1.50	1.80	1.38	1.78	1.30	1.60	1.66	1.94	1.70
	C.V.	7.21	6.30	6.80	5.33	6.35	4.95	5.63	6.01	6.57	5.93
	Abs.			2.25	1.33	1.27	0.5	0.51	1.26	0.99	1.15
	% growth			9.17	5.41	4.74	1.93	1.81	4.77	3.46	4.16

Contd...

Sex		Boys	Girls	Boys	Girls	Boys	Girls	Boys	Girls	Boys	Girls
age	*(yrs)*	*6*	*6*	*7*	*7*	*8*	*8*	*9*	*9*	*10*	*10*
Sample	*(N)*	*43*	*45*	*40*	*42*	*40*	*42*	*44*	*41*	*42*	*41*
Bi-ilo.dia	Mean	17.70	18.00	20.00	18.70	20.17	19.00	20.80	20.20	21.40	20.80
	S.E.	0.21	0.20	0.20	0.23	0.23	0.16	0.22	0.21	0.20	0.24
	S.D.	1.39	1.10	1.20	1.50	1.49	1.09	1.46	1.39	1.31	1.55
	C.V.	7.89	5.90	6.00	8.04	7.43	5.79	7.09	6.88	6.11	7.44
	Abs.			1.79	0.77	0.67	0.23	0.6	1.27	0.67	0.56
	% growth			10.1	4.28	3.43	1.22	2.97	6.69	3.22	2.76
Triceps	Mean	6.05	6.60	5.70	6.66	6.27	6.00	5.93	6.37	5.89	6.66
	S.E.	0.24	0.20	0.20	0.20	0.31	0.15	0.26	0.16	0.22	0.20
	S.D.	1.57	1.20	1.40	1.32	1.98	0.98	1.77	1.04	1.47	1.33
	C.V.	26.10	18.00	24.00	19.90	31.67	16.40	29.90	19.90	25.10	16.50
	Abs.			-0.321	0.104	0.54	-0.664	-0.334	0.368	-0.041	0.293
	% growth			-5.304	1.584	9.424	-9.96	-5.326	6.131	-0.69	4.599
Biceps	Mean	3.78	3.50	3.10	3.57	3.27	3.18	3.34	3.15	2.95	3.31
	S.E.	0.15	0.10	0.10	0.14	0.16	0.09	0.17	0.11	0.10	0.10
	S.D.	1.00	0.80	0.70	0.91	1.04	0.59	1.17	0.73	0.70	0.67
	C.V.	26.50	23.00	22.00	25.50	31.88	18.70	33.00	20.50	23.80	23.50
	Abs.			-0.656	0.096	0.15	-0.386	0.065	-0.029	-0.383	0.156
	% growth			-17.34	2.762	4.8	-10.809	1.984	-0.91	-11.467	4.942
Subscapular	Mean	5.33	5.50	5.40	5.73	5.60	5.28	5.22	5.75	5.72	5.49
	S.E.	0.16	0.10	0.10	0.17	0.18	0.08	0.17	0.15	0.16	0.13
	S.D.	1.07	0.80	0.80	1.10	1.15	0.57	1.17	0.99	1.05	0.85
	C.V.	20.10	14.00	16.00	19.30	20.59	10.80	22.40	15.50	18.40	17.20
	Abs.			0.02	0.249	0.255	-0.453	-0.383	1.089	0.504	-0.254
	% growth			0.375	4.54	4.766	-7.901	-6.833	20.628	9.651	-4.416

Sitting Height

It gives a measure of the total development of the upper body when the subject is seated erect and head placed in the F.H. plane. The mean value of boys and girls increased with the change in age. The mean value at six years and ten years in boys is 59.4 cm and 70.1 cm respectively. In the case of girls the mean at six years is 60 cm and at 10 years it is 68.6 cm. The sitting height also shown similar type of growth as we have seen in stature i.e., at the six year age girls were taller than boys but in the rest of the ages, boys were taller than girls. The increase in sitting height from six years to ten years for boys is 11.24 cm and for girls of similar years it is 8.39 cm. In boys it is observed that during the six to seven years a maximum growth of 5.34 cm while in girls of same age it is just 2.70 cm. Minimum growth among boys is seen in eight to nine years i.e., 1.07 cm while in girls a maximum growth is observed (2.92). Boys shown 2.61 cm of growth at 9 to 10 years and 2.22 cm of growth at 7 to 8 years. Girls shown 1.86 cm at 9 to 10 years while very poor growth is observed at 7 to 8 years (0.92 cm).

The co-efficient of variation is high among boys at 6 years and 8 years. Basing on the mean values the distance curve for boys and girls has been drawn (Fig. 5). It is noticeable that the age distance curve of girls is high in the initial age i.e., six years and thereafter, the curve for boys overcome that of girls. The velocity curve for boys and girls are shown in Fig. 6. It is observed that the absolute growth at the 7 to 8 years in girls is minimal and in boys it is at 8 to 9 years.

Bi-acromial Diameter

A steady increase in the average values is observed both in boys and girls as the age advances i.e., from 6 years to 10 years. The mean value for boys at 6 years and 10 years is 24.5 cm and 29.6 cm respectively whereas in the case of girls the mean value at six years is 25 cm and at ten years it is 28.8 cm. On an average the growth of bi-acromial diameter in boys for a period of five years is 5.02 cm and in girls for the same period it is 4.24 cm. This shows that during five year period boys showed higher growth than girls. The year wise growth shows that a maximum of growth is seen at 6 to 7 years in boys (2.25 cm) while in girls it is 1.33 cm for the same age group. Similarly, minimum growth among boys is seen at 8 to 9 years (0.51 cm) and among girls it is at 7 to 8 years (0.50 cm). The coefficient of variation is high at six years among boys while in girls it is high at six years and nine years.

Taking the mean values into consideration, the distance curve for boys and girls have been plotted in the graph shown in Fig. 7. It is interesting to note from the graph that at the age group nine years girl showed a sudden spurt, which is proceeding ahead to boys. Velocity curves were also drawn basing on the absolute growth (Fig. 8).

Bi-iliocristal Diameter

An increase in the average values for both boys and girls from 6 years to 10 years is observed.

The mean value for boys at six years is 17.7 cm and for ten years it is 21.4 cm. while for girls the mean value at 6 years is 18 cm and for 10 years it is 20.8 cm. The absolute growth in 5 years is noted by subtsracting the ten years mean value to six years mean value. The increase from 6 to 10 years in boys is 3.73 cm and girls it is 2.83 cm only. The coefficient of variation is high for six years, eight years and nine years among boys while it is high at seven years and ten years for girls. The year wise increase in growth is maximum at six to seven years 1.79 cm for boys and for girls it is at eight to nine years 1.27 cm. Minimum increase of growth among boys is seen in eight to nine years 0.60 cm and in girls it is in seven to eight years 0.20 cm.

Distance curve for boys and girls are drawn in the graph (Fig. 9) basing on the average values. It is observed from the graph that at nine years girls started showing transverse growth spurt. Velocity curves (Fig. 10) were also drawn basing on the absolute growth per annum.

Triceps Skinfold

Skinfold measurements give an indication of how much energy reserves are available for the body. These reserves are in the form of fat and are available mainly at the subcutaneous layers of the body, where besides acting as energy reserves for the body, they act as insulators for the body against cold and provide the body its characteristic contours.

It is quite interesting to observe that a decreasing tendency in the triceps skinfold is observed upto nine years in girls and in boys right through 6 years to 10 years. The mean value goes on decreasing as the age advances except at eight years in boys. The mean tricep skinfold for boys at 6 years is 6.05 cm and at 10 year it is 5.89 cm. Among girls the mean tricep skinfld at 6 years is 6.6 mm and at 10 years it is 6.66 mm. The maximum loss in triceps skinfold is at 6 to 7 years and 8 to 9 years (0.34) for boys and for girls it is at 7 to 8 years (0.66 mm).

Distance curves were drawn (Fig. 11) basing on the average values. Among the boys the graph shows a downward trend upto 7 years and then it showed an increment in 8 years from there it again decreased upto 10 years while in girls the curve increased upto 7 years and in 8th year it decreased and again it increased in 9 year and 10 year.

Velocity curve (Fig. 12) showed negative growth at seven year, nine year and ten year among boys while among girls it showed negative growth only at eight years.

Sub Scapular Skinfold

The mean and standard deviation for both boys and girls are shown in Table 4. The mean value for sub-scapular skinfold among boys increased from 6 years to 10 years except in the age group of nine years. The mean at 6 years is 5.33 mm and the mean at 10 years is 5.72 mm. In girls the mean has intermittently increased from six years to seven years then it decreased in eight years and again it increased in nine years then it again decreased in ten years. Among girls the mean value at 6 years is 5.5 mm and the mean value at 10 years is 5.49 mm. The c.v. values are very high for all the age groups among both the sexes.

Distance curves were drawn basing on the average values and are shown in the Fig. 15. The velocity curves (Fig. 16) shown a negative value among boys at the 9 years age group. The rest of the ages shown positive growth similarly, among girls negative growth is observed at 8 years age group only.

Biceps Skinfold

A decreasing tendency is observed in both boys and girls. In girls it is observed upto nine years. Whereas, in boys it is upto 10 years. The mean of biceps skinfold among boys at 6 years is 3.78 mm and at 10 years it is 2.95 mm and among girls at 6 years 3.5 mm and at 10 years 3.31 mm. The mean value among boys decreased from 6 to 7 years and then increased upto nine years and again in the 10th year it decreased while among girls the mean value increased upto seven years then it decreased upto nine years and again it increased in the tenth year. This is also shown in the distance curve (Fig. 17). The c.v. values are very high among both the sexes for all the age groups.

The velocity curve (Fig.18) for biceps skinfold shows negative growth among boys at seven and tenth age group, whereas, among girls it is in eighth and ninth age group.

The value of co-relation (r) is shown in Table 5 for both boys and girls. It is observed from the table that the co-relation co-efficient between the height and weight; stature and sitting height, biacromial breadth and bi-iliac breadth are significant for all the ages among both the sexes but, for chest circumference and head circumference the co-relation co-efficient is insignificant for all the age groups among the boys and girls. It is observed from the table that the co-relation co-efficient is significant for triceps and subscapular skinfold among boys and girls for all the age groups except, for the age group seven years and ten years among boys and among girls it is insignificant at eight years. When it is seen bisexually girls show higher "r" value for height vs. weight at six years but for rest of the ages boys show higher 'r' value. The 'r' value for biacromial diameter vs. bi-iliocristal diameter is high among girls than to boys except in sixth and eighth age group. The value of "r" for head circumference vs. chest circumference is high among boys than to girls except ninth age group. The height vs. sitting height's value is high among boys for all the age groups except tenth age group wherein, girls show higher "r" value.

Table 5
Corelation Co-efficient of Related Measurements Among the Ahir (Yeduvanshi) of Haryana

Age	*Traits*	*Boys*	*Girls*
6 Years	HTvs WT	0.834908	0.911964
	HTvsSH	0.896533	0.872797
	BID vs BiiLD	0.83704	0.608299
	HCD vs CHC	0.456441	0.335526
	TSF vs SSF	0.626564	0.633966
7 Years	HTvs WT	0.900617	0.857476
	HTvsSH	0.878396	0.814363
	BID vs BiiLD	0.696482	0.807741
	HCD vs CHC	0.466784	0.342435
	TSF vs SSF	0.437486	0.581556
8 Years	HTvs WT	0.886501	0.811563
	HTvsSH	0.912226	0.611585
	BID vs BiiLD	0.818763	0.602678
	HCD vs CHC	0.41478	0.319121
	TSF vs SSF	0.819127	0.25222
9 Years	HTvs WT	0.845812	0.788478
	HTvsSH	0.872426	0.839242
	BID vs BiiLD	0.695249	0.761737
	HCD vs CHC	0.349729	0.424457
	TSF vs SSF	0.785325	0.564234
10 Years	HTvs WT	0.899419	0.785344
	HTvsSH	0.854012	0.893842
	BID vs BiiLD	0.689879	0.728139
	HCD vs CHC	0.33057	0.309048
	TSF vs SSF	0.327435	0.53821

HT = Height; WT = Weight; SH = Sitting height;
BID = Biacromial diameter; BILLD = Bi-iliocristal diameter;
HCD = Head circumference;
CHC = Chest circumference; TSF = Skinofold at triceps;
SSF = Skinfold at subscapular

Assessment of Nutritional Status Based on Anthropometric Indices

The current and past nutritional status of an individual can be assessed based upon some anthropometric indices. An attempt has been made to find out the nutritional status with the following indices:

1. weight for age or weight deficit classification
2. height for age or height deficit classification
3. Mid upper arm circumference classification

Weight for Age or Weight Deficit Classification

Observing weight of an individual we can assess the nutritional status. It also provides the exact picture of the not-so-long off changes in nutritional supplement.

The modified Gomez classification proposed by Vishveshwar Rao (1979) has been applied to the present study and the frequencies along with the percentages are shown in the Table 6. The table reveals that, among boys in the age group of eight years 17.50% of children fall in the normal category. 45 per cent of boys of 7 years fall under grade-I malnutrition, 40.90% boys of ninth year age group fall under grade-II malnutrition. Under grade–III and grade IV 25.58% and 4.65% of sixth age group are malnourished respectively. Similarly 19.51 per cent girls of ten years fall under normal category. 42.85% girls of seven years come under grade–I malnutrition, 48.78% of girls of nine years represent grade II malnutrition. Whereas, eight year girls show 38.09% gap of grade III malnutrition under grade IV 9.75% of 9 year and 10 year girls are malnourished.

The overall picture (i.e., both boys and girls) shows that 37.38% are in grade-II malnutrition and 31.66% are in grade I malnutrition. 18.57% and 3.57% are in grade III and grade IV malnutrition respectively. It is observed that only 8.80% of children are normal. When we consider both the sexes individually boys are relatively less malnourished than girls. 35.40% of boys are in grade I malnutrition, whereas, girls are only 27.96%, 34.92% of boys are in grade II malnutrition when compared to girls 39.81%. In grade III and grade IV malnutrition boys are 14.83% and 1.43% respectively, while girls are 22.27% and 5.68% respectively. 6.66% of boys are normal while girls are only 2.14%.

Height for Age or Height Deficit Classification

Generally, it is understood that, through the height of an individual the past or very-long-off nutritional status can be assessed. Studying apart from socio-ecological condition, family background etc. to over come the past nutritional status under the present study height for age or height deficit classification has been analysed for both boys and girls and its frequencies along with the percentages are shown in the Table 7.

Around 60.71% of the total observed individuals of both boys and girls show mild retardation, 28.09% are normal and 11.19% of children are in poor condition. By observing both the sexes separately 33.01% of boys are normal in comparison to girls 23.22%, 63.50% of girls fall under mild retardation in comparison to boys 57.89% and only 9.09% of boys are poor to 13.27% of girls. It is interesting to observe that in 6 years boys 30.23% are in poor state and at the age of seven years no individual falls under poor category. Among girls at the age of 10 years 21.95% are in poor state.

Mid upper Arm Circumference Classification

The extent of malnutrition is also observed through the thickness of mid upper arm circumference (MUAC). It has been calculated among the present study and its frequency along with their percentages are shown in Table 8. 48.33% of observed children (both sexes combined) are normal, 29.28% show mild malnutrition, and 16.19% are under moderate

Table 6
Weight for Age or Weight Deficit Classification of Ahir Children

	Boys (age in years)						Girls (age in years)						
categories	*6*	*7*	*8*	*9*	*10*	*total*	*6*	*7*	*8*	*9*	*10*	*total*	*total Boys + Girls*
Grd iv M.N.	2			1		3		2	2	4	4	12	15
	[4.65]			[2.27]		[1.43]		[4.76]	[4.76]	[9.75]	[9.75]	[5.68]	[3.57]
Grd iii M.N.	11	1	4	6	9	31	7	8	16	5	11	47	78
	[25.58]	[2.50]	[10.00]	[13.63]	[21.42]	[14.83]	[15.55]	[19.04]	[38.09]	[12.19]	[26.82]	[22.27]	[18.57]
Grd ii M.N.	14	16	13	18	12	73	19	11	16	20	18	84	157
	[32.55]	[40.00]	[32.50]	[40.90]	[28.57]	[34.92]	[42.22]	[26.19]	[38.09]	[48.78]	[43.90]	[39.81]	[37.38]
Grd i M.N.	13	18	16	13	14	74	16	18	8	9	8	59	133
	[30.23]	[45.00]	[40.00]	[29.54]	[33.33]	[35.40]	[35.55]	[42.85]	[19.04]	[21.95]	[19.51]	[27.96]	[31.66]
Normal	3	5	7	6	7	28	3	3		3		9	37
	[6.97]	[12.50]	[17.50]	[13.63]	[16.66]	[6.66]	[6.66]	[7.14]		[7.31]		[2.14]	[8.80]
Total	43	40	40	44	42	209	45	42	42	41	41	211	420

* M.N.= Malnutrition
Grd. = Grade

Table 7
Height for Age or Height Deficit Classification of Ahir Children

	Boys (age in years)						Girls (age in years)						
categories	*6*	*7*	*8*	*9*	*10*	*total*	*6*	*7*	*8*	*9*	*10*	*total*	*total Boys + Girls*
Poor	13		2	2	2	19	5	5	6	3	9	28	47
	[30.23]		[5.00]	[4.54]	[4.76]	[9.09]	[11.11]	[11.90]	[14.28]	[7.31]	[21.95]	[13.27]	[11.19]
Mild retardation	21	23	23	30	24	121	26	20	32	30	26	134	255
	[48.83]	[57.50]	[57.50]	[68.18]	[57.14]	[57.89]	[57.77]	[47.61]	[76.19]	[73.17]	[63.41]	[63.50]	[60.71]
Normal	9	17	15	12	16	69	14	17	4	8	6	49	118
	[20.93]	[42.50]	[37.50]	[27.27]	[38.09]	[33.01]	[31.11]	[40.47]	[9.52]	[19.51]	[14.63]	[23.22]	[28.09]
Total	43	40	40	44	42	209	45	42	42	41	41	211	420

[Values in parentheses are percentages]

Table 8
Mid Upper Arm Circumference Classification of Ahir Children

categories	*Boys (age in years)*						*Girls (age in years)*						*total Boys + Girls*
	6	*7*	*8*	*9*	*10*	*total*	*6*	*7*	*8*	*9*	*10*	*total*	
Severe MN	5 [11.62]			2 [4.54]		7 [3.34]		2 [4.76]	1 [2.38]	4 [9.75]	1 [2.43]	8 [3.79]	15 [3.57]
Moderate MN	6 [13.95]	2 [5.00]	3 [7.50]	9 [20.45]	9 [21.42]	29 [13.87]	8 [17.77]	7 [16.66]	9 [21.42]	7 [17.07]	8 [19.51]	39 [18.48]	68 [16.19]
Mild MN	10 [23.25]	15 [37.50]	10 [25.00]	9 [20.45]	11 [26.19]	55 [26.31]	10 [22.22]	17 [40.47]	16 [38.09]	7 [17.07]	18 [43.90]	68 [32.22]	123 [29.28]
Normal	21 [48.83]	22 [55.00]	24 [60.00]	23 [52.27]	19 [45.23]	109 [52.15]	26 [57.77]	16 [38.09]	16 [38.09]	22 [53.65]	14 [34.14]	94 [44.54]	203 [48.33]
>Normal	1 [2.32]	1 [2.50]	3 [7.50]	1 [2.27]	3 [7.14]	9 [4.30]	1 [2.22].			1 [2.43]		2 [0.94]	11 [2.61]
Total	43	40	40	44	42	209	45	42	42	41	41	211	420

malnutrition. Only 2.61% of children are above normal. 52.15% of boys are normal to 44.54% of girls. 26.31% of boys are normal to 44.54% of girls. 26.31% of boys are mild malnourished to 32.22% of girls. 13.87% of boys are moderately malnourished in comparison to 18.48% of girls. 3.79% of girls are severely malnourished to 3.34% of boys. Only 0.94% of girls are above normal in comparison to boys 4.30%.

Dental Pattern

The development of teeth is much more important for the facial growth because discrepancies in relation to maxillary and mandibular basal arches will result in the severe type of malocclusion.

Mean and standard deviation (S.D.) of the number of permanent erupted teeth in both the jaws combined by age and sex, are presented in Table 9. Boys show more number of permanent teeth than girls at every given year of age, except in 6 years. At 10 years boys show higher number of permanent teeth than girls. Boys shown more than 19 permanent teeth at ten years (by visual observation) i.e., 2 pairs of incisors at maxilla and mandible, one pair of first molar at both the upper and lower jaw. One pair of premolars at both the jaws and the remaining 3-4 teeth is either canine or the 2nd molar in both the jaws. In girls at ten years they show more than 17 permanent teeth i.e. 2 pairs of incisors at maxilla and mandible, one pair of first molar at both upper and lower jaw, one pair of premolars at both the jaws and the remaining 1-2 teeth is either canine or the 2nd molar.

Table 9
Mean and Standard Deviation of Erupted Permanent Teeth Among the Ahir Children

Sex		*Boys*			*Girls*	
			Parameter			
Age in years	*No*	*Mean*	*SD*	*No*	*Mean*	*SD*
6+	44	3.82	4.02	45	5.80	4.04
7+	40	10.40	4.44	42	10.12	3.76
8+	40	13.40	4.43	42	10.17	3.24
9+	44	15.91	5.05	41	14.51	5.05
10+	42	19.17	6.16	41	17.09	5.97

Clinical Signs

The observation of people according to clinical specifications forms an important practical method for the assessment of the state of nutrition of the community. The observations are made on examination of various signs believed to indicate deficiency of certain vitamins or nutrients. This examination is relatively easy.

Nine types of nutritive deficiency signs are observed for both boys and girls and are shown in Table 10 and Table 11 respectively. Before

Table 10
Clinical Signs and Nutritional Deficiency Signs Among Boys

	Age Groups in Years											
	6		*7*		*8*		*9*		*10*		*Total*	
Clinical Signs	*No*	*%*	*No*	*%*	*No*	*%*	*No*	*%*	*No*	*%*	*No*	*%*
General Health												
Very good												
Good	8	18.60	7	17.50	10	25.00	16	36.36	15	35.72	56	26.79
Satisfactory	23	53.48	30	75.00	27	67.50	22	50.00	24	57.14	126	60.28
Week	12	27.90	3	7.50	3	7.50	6	13.64	3	7.14	27	12.91
Nutrition deficiency signs												
Pigmentation of skin												
Present	21	48.83	15	37.50	18	45.00	19	43.18	16	38.09	89	42.58
Absent	22	51.16	25	62.50	22	55.00	25	56.82	26	61.91	120	57.41
Angular Stomatitis												
Present	9	20.93	4	10.00	5	12.50	11	25.00	4	9.53	33	15.78
Absent	34	79.06	36	90.00	35	87.50	33	75.00	38	90.47	176	84.21
Dry scaly skin												
Present	20	46.51	17	42.50	12	30.00	19	43.18	15	35.72	83	39.71
Absent	23	53.48	23	57.50	28	70.00	25	56.82	27	64.28	126	60.28
Discoloured hair												
Present	8	18.60	7	17.50	6	15.00	8	18.18	7	16.67	36	17.22
Absent	35	81.39	33	82.50	34	85.00	36	81.82	35	83.33	173	82.77
Flag/coarse hair												
Present	14	32.55	5	12.50	6	15.00	5	11.36	10	23.80	40	19.13
Absent	29	67.44	35	87.50	34	85.00	39	88.64	32	76.20	169	80.86

Contd...

	Age Groups in Years											
	6		7		8		9		10		Total	
Clinical Signs	*No*	*%*	*No*	*%*	*No*	*%*	*No*	*%*	*No*	*%*	*No*	*%*
Spongy bleeding gums												
Present	1	2.32	0	0.00	0	0.00	0	0.00	0	0.00	1	0.47
Absent	42	97.67	40	100.00	40	100.00	44	100.00	42	100.00	208	99.52
Yellowish teeth												
Present	8	18.60	17	42.50	18	45.00	25	56.82	26	61.91	94	44.97
Absent	35	81.39	23	57.50	22	55.00	19	43.18	16	38.09	115	55.02
Pale conjactiva												
Present	9	20.93	1	2.50	2	5.00	4	9.09	1	2.38	17	8.13
Absent	34	79.06	39	97.50	38	95.00	40	90.91	41	97.62	192	91.86
Yellow colour at nails' base												
Present	2	4.65		0.00	1	2.50	0	0.00	0	0.00	3	1.43
Absent	41	95.34	40	100.00	39	97.50	44	100.00	42	100.00	206	98.56

Table 11
Clinical Signs And Nutritional Deficiency Signs Among Girls

	Age Groups in Years											
	6		*7*		*8*		*9*		*10*		*Total*	
Clinical Signs	*No*	*%*	*No*	*%*	*No*	*%*	*No*	*%*	*No*	*%*	*No*	*%*
General helth												
Very good												
Good	5	11.11	11	26.19	5	11.90	5	12.20	7	17.08	33	15.63
Satisfactory	30	66.67	25	59.52	34	80.96	30	73.14	26	63.41	145	68.72
Weak	10	22.22	6	14.28	3	7.14	6	14.63	8	19.51	33	15.63
Nutrition deficiency signs												
Pigmentation of skin												
Present	21	46.67	14	33.33	10	23.80	11	26.82	14	34.14	70	33.17
Absent	24	53.33	28	66.67	32	76.20	30	73.18	27	65.86	141	66.82
Angular Stomatitis												
Present	4	8.89	5	11.90	5	11.90	4	9.76	5	12.20	23	10.90
Absent	41	91.11	37	88.10	37	88.09	37	90.24	36	87.80	188	89.09
Dry scaly skin												
Present	21	46.67	17	40.48	13	30.96	9	21.96	5	12.20	65	30.80
Absent	24	53.33	25	59.52	29	69.04	32	78.04	36	87.80	146	69.19
Discoloured hair												
Present	13	28.89	25	59.52	18	42.86	30	73.18	30	73.18	116	54.97
Absent	32	71.11	17	40.48	24	57.14	11	26.82	11	26.82	95	45.02
Flag/coarse hair												
Present	15	33.33	11	26.19	7	16.67	9	21.96	9	21.96	51	24.17
Absent	30	66.67	31	73.81	35	83.33	32	78.04	32	78.04	160	75.82

Contd...

	Age Groups in Years											
	6		*7*		*8*		*9*		*10*		*Total*	
Clinical Signs	*No*	*%*	*No*	*%*	*No*	*%*	*No*	*%*	*No*	*%*	*No*	*%*
Spongy bleeding gums												
Present	0	0	0	0	1	2.39	0	0	0	0	1	0.47
Absent	45	10	42	100	41	97.61	41	100	41	100	210	99.52
Yellow teeth												
Present	6	13.33	10	23.80	10	23.80	23	56.10	19	46.34	68	32.22
Absent	39	86.67	32	76.20	32	76.20	18	43.90	22	53.66	143	67.66
Pale conjactiva												
Present	5	11.11	5	11.90	4	9.52	2	4.88	3	7.31	19	9.00
Absent	40	88.89	37	88.10	38	90.48	39	95.12	38	92.69	192	90.99
Yellow colour at nails' base												
Present	4	8.89	3	7.14	3	7.14	1	2.43	4	9.76	15	7.10
Absent	41	91.11	39	92.86	39	92.86	40	97.57	39	90.24	196	92.89

observing the nutrition deficiency signs it is felt utmost essential to assess the general health of children. General health of each child was recorded by using grading techniques in the respective column by simple observation (i.e. either very good, good, satisfactory or weak). Most of the children for all ages seem to be satisfactory. Only in six years age group about 27.90% of boys are weak, where as in nine years 36.36% of boys are in good health condition. Among girls more than 60% show satisfactory health condition. Maximum number of weak girls (22.22%) are found in 6 years and minimum number of weak girls (7.14%) in eight years age group. Maximum number of good health condition among girls is seen in 7 years (26.19%). Pigmentation of skin (niacin deficiency) is high among boys (42.85%) than girls (33.17%). The deficiency of vitamin B-Complex (angular stomatitis) is high among boys (15.78%) than girls (10.90%). The observance of dry scaly skin (Vitamin–A) is found among both boys (39.71%) and girls (30.80%). As most of the children show this deficiency it is felt that it may be because of dry weather as the data was collected during dry winter season with all that the region is semi arid. About 54.97% girls showed discoloured hair and 24.17% of flag/ coarse hair. Very little per cent of spongy bleeding gum is seen but yellowish teeth is very high both among boys and girls (44.97% and 32.22% respectively). A negligible per cent of pale conjunctive and yellow colour at the base of the nail is observed in both sexes.

Impact of Various Socio-cultural Factors Over Growth

Mean and standard deviation (S.D.) were calculated for weight, height, sitting height, biacromial diameter and bi-iliocristal diameter based on the literacy level of both the parents, birth order (parity) of the child, family size, family type and per capita income. The various socio-cultural factors are considered in order to know its impact on the growth of the children. The results of weight, height, sitting height, biacromial diameter and bi-iliocristal diameter according to the various socio-cultural factors are shown in the Table 12 to 16.

Mean and standard deviation (S.D.) were calculated basing on the literacy level of the parents. It is observed from the tables that only a sizeable number of samples are available in the first and third group whereas, in the second and fourth group it is very difficult to arrive at a conclusion, as not more than two/three children are available in each age group. For all the five measurements undoubtedly, both boys and girls showed better growth in the first group i.e. father and mother both literate group exceptionally in certain age groups i.e. sixth, ninth and tenth among boys and among girls seventh and eighth age groups wherein, a higher growth is seen in third group i.e. mother non-literate , father literate. Since more number of mothers are non-literate a good number of sample is observed in third group.

Table 12

Mean and Standard Deviation for Weight of Children Aged from 6 to 10 Years by Literacy Level of Both the Parents, Parity of Child, Family Size, Family Type and Per Capita Income of the Ahir (Yeduvanshi) of Haryana

	Boys															*Girls*														
	6			*7*			*8*			*9*			*10*			*6*			*7*			*8*			*9*			*10*		
	N	*Mean*	*S.D.*	*N*	*Mean*	*S.D.*	*N*	*Mean*	*S.D.*	*N*	*Mean*	*S.D.*	*N*	*Mean*	*S.D.*	*N*	*Mean*	*S.D.*	*N*	*Mean*	*S.D.*	*N*	*Mean*	*S.D.*	*N*	*Mean*	*S.D.*	*N*	*Mean*	*S.D.*
Literacy level																														
Father and Mother both literate	14	16.79	2.73	12	21.17	3.15	16	24.03	5.07	11	23.59	3.15	9	26.94	5.21	16	17.31	2.4	12	18.83	2.71	17	19.41	2.69	7	23.21	4.11	12	24.71	2.41
Mother lit., father non-lit.	1	19.00	0	0	0	0	0	0	0	0	0	0	1	36.00	0	0	0	0	0	0	0	0	0	0	0	0	0	1	33.00	0
Mother non-lit., father lit	28	17.03	2.71	25	20.96	3.54	21	22.65	3.33	29	25.03	4.44	31	26.95	4.69	27	16.59	2.14	27	18.94	2.67	24	19.56	2.11	30	22.13	3.42	26	24.15	3.53
Mother & Father non-lit	0	0	0	2	19.00	1.41	1	22.50	0	3	23.33	3.01	1	23.00	0.00	2	19.50	2.82	3	21.16	4.90	1	23.50	0	4	25.12	3.47	1	31.00	0
Family Size																														
Small family(<3)	8	18.06	1.99	10	21.80	4.00	9	24.16	3.71	10	25.05	5.50	11	28.22	5.48	7	16.85	1.52	6	19.16	2.62	2	20.25	3.25	3	21.16	2.32	5	22.90	3.72
Medium family (4-6)	19	16.92	3.03	19	21.28	3.26	19	22.89	3.92	26	25.01	3.33	19	28.28	4.64	17	16.73	1.88	14	19.39	3.31	23	19.39	2.13	19	22.21	3.66	27	24.75	3.62
Medium large family (7-8)	10	17.60	2.14	6	20.33	1.81	6	22.25	2.41	5	21.60	2.81	7	23.21	2.50	10	18.55	2.07	14	18.5	2.54	9	18.50	1.58	12	23.50	4.18	4	26.12	1.84
Large family (09)	6	14.83	1.14	5	18.70	0.74	6	23.75	5.40	3	24.16	3.47	4	25.12	2.72	11	16	2.62	8	19.12	2.13	8	21.25	2.56	7	22.78	1.27	5	24.80	2.63
Family type																														
Nuclear	18	17.47	2.70	17	20.85	3.35	24	22.81	3.55	19	24.05	4.14	16	28.43	5.55	16	17.06	2.09	17	19.00	2.51	19	19.18	2.06	20	21.77	3.90	25	24.24	3.70
Joint	25	16.66	2.54	23	21.02	3.16	16	23.81	4.55	25	24.98	3.92	25	26.24	4.17	29	16.93	3.36	25	19.02	2.97	23	19.93	2.53	21	23.40	2.93	16	25.34	2.98
Birth order																														
Birth order 1	16	16.71	2.35	13	21.96	4.51	9	21.50	3.75	10	24.10	3.65	8	26.75	3.71	16	17.68	1.82	11	18.18	2.22	14	19.57	1.90	12	22.00	2.32	10	23.75	2.55
Birth order 2	9	17.94	2.27	8	20.62	2.02	8	25.18	3.97	10	25.25	4.46	16	26.21	3.92	7	16.57	1.87	12	19.45	2.52	6	17.41	0.78	10	22.8	3.73	10	23.60	2.75
Birth order 3	6	17.41	3.28	10	21.05	2.56	5	22.10	3.23	12	24.70	4.69	5	33.70	6.15	7	17.78	2.47	7	19.57	3.86	10	19.30	2.45	4	25.37	4.99	11	25.09	4.21
Birth order 4<	12	16.45	2.68	9	19.00	0.74	18	23.50	3.90	12	24.29	3.08	12	25.75	3.84	15	16.03	2.36	12	19.00	2.58	12	20.95	2.39	15	22.23	3.36	10	26.2	3.39
Per capita Income																														
Group-1(0-400)	22	16.27	2.40	17	20.44	2.64	22	22.16	3.7	24	23.58	4.31	20	26.43	4.64	23	17.02	1.96	19	19.24	2.70	20	19.95	2.29	12	22.21	2.34	23	25.11	3.97
Group -11(401<)	21	17.76	2.80	22	21.30	3.79	18	24.5	4.23	19	26.03	3.45	21	28.05	5.31	22	16.93	2.66	22	18.85	3.02	22	19.27	2.49	29	22.78	4.00	17	24.15	2.95

Table 13
Mean and Standard Deviation for Stature of Children Aged from 6 to 10 Years by Literacy Level of Both the Parents, Parity of Child, Family Size, Family Type and Per Capita Income of the Ahir (Yeduvanshi) of Haryana

	Boys															Girls														
	6			7			8			9			10			6			7			8			9			10		
	N	Mean	S.D.	N	Mean	S.D.	N	Mean	S.D.	N	Mean	S.D.	N	Mean	S.D.	N	Mean	S.D.	N	Mean	S.D.	N	Mean	S.D.	N	Mean	S.D.	N	Mean	S.D.
Literacy level																														
Father and Mother both literate	14	108.45	7.26	12	123.85	8.24	16	129.00	9.14	11	130.63	5.75	9	137.51	8.89	16	114.92	6.55	12	120.22	6.86	17	121.65	6.86	7	130.58	8.45	12	135.75	7.33
Mother lit., father non-lit.	1	114.70	0	0	0	0	0	0	0	0	0	0	1	144.50	0	0	0	0	0	0	0	0	0	0	0	0	0	1	151.90	
Mother non-lit., father lit	28	113.07	8.04	25	123.12	6.27	21	128.20	7.27	29	133.48	7.52	31	138.01	7.84	27	111.99	6.42	27	120.00	5.46	24	122.73	5.46	30	128.93	6.12	26	132.78	6.15
Mother & Father non-lit	0	0	0	2	119.9	10.2	1	133.20		3	129.93	3.21	1	132.80		2	119.55	11.1	3	122.63	4.90	1	127.8		4	135.05		1	142.20	
Family Size																														
Small family (<3)	8	116.48	7.46	10	124.92	8.09	9	130.55	6.97	10	134.62	8.60	11	139.00	7.73	7	111.57	4.98	6	119.35	10.70	2	124.4	10.70	3	128.26	5.68	5	129.04	6.68
Medium family (4-6)	19	111.25	7.17	19	124.58	6.63	19	127.53	7.90	26	132.83	5.54	19	139.97	7.70	17	113.12	6.22	14	120.58	5.75	23	121.96	5.75	19	129.33	7.66	27	134.64	6.88
Medium large family (7-8)	10	112.99	7.59	6	120.40	2.99	6	127.78	7.16	5	129.26	7.34	7	132.17	6.49	10	117.79	6.02	14	119.90	4.28	9	120.16	4.28	12	130.10	6.87	4	134.80	5.58
Large family (09)	6	103.88	3.43	5	118.10	2.76	6	130.61	7.92	3	127.43	3.69	4	134.82	6.24	11	110.85	6.90	8	120.95	4.71	8	125.75	4.71	7	131.28	3.16	5	135.54	8.20
Family type																														
Nuclear	18	112.71	8.80	17	123.15	7.06	24	127.72	7.16	19	132.60	7.05	16	140.26	8.73	16	113.88	6.38	17	120.20	5.66	19	121.61	5.66	20	129.06	7.67	25	133.16	6.57
Joint	25	110.80	6.95	23	123.28	6.51	16	130.19	8.30	25	132.36	6.57	25	136.35	7.02	29	113.07	6.82	25	120.28	6.07	23	123.08	6.07	21	130.52	5.68	16	135.52	7.82
Birth order																														
Birth order 1	16	113.52	6.98	13	124.00	8.32	9	124.37	7.47	10	132.03	5.12	8	137.07	7.24	16	115.13	5.74	11	117.29	6.38	14	121.91	6.38	12	127.24	6.29	10	133.61	5.28
Birth order 2	9	113.90	5.86	8	123.97	5.23	8	132.46	7.33	10	134.96	8.80	16	136.91	6.12	7	111.50	5.13	12	122.78	2.16	6	118.36	2.16	10	131.13	5.49	10	132.69	6.65
Birth order 3	6	111.03	9.31	10	124.76	6.88	5	127.24	8.07	12	131.63	7.16	5	146.28	10.72	7	115.44	8.21	7	120.14	6.73	10	121.8	6.73	4	136.75	7.43	11	133.48	8.56
Birth order 4<	12	107.60	7.80	9	119.76	3.12	18	129.62	6.78	12	131.58	4.90	12	136.20	7.07	15	111.37	6.63	12	120.50	4.12	12	125.55	4.12	15	129.14	6.24	10	136.62	7.03
Per capita Income																														
Group-1(0-400)	22	110.20	8.17	17	122.39	6.32	22	126.12	7.36	24	131.05	7.29	20	137.65	7.59	23	113.43	6.17	19	120.70	5.91	20	123.27	5.91	12	130.28	5.34	23	134.30	7.35
Group -11(401<)	21	113.07	7.59	22	123.81	7.44	18	131.88	7.39	19	134.35	6.16	21	138.44	8.50	22	113.07	7.78	22	119.91	6.13	22	121.65	6.13	29	129.62	7.47	17	134.21	7.26

Table 14
Mean and Standard Deviation for Sitting Height of Children Aged from 6 to 10 Years by Literacy Level of Both the Parents, Parity of Child, Family Size, Family Type and Per Capita Income of the Ahir (Yeduvanshi) of Haryana

	Boys															Girls														
	6			7			8			9			10			6			7			8			9			10		
	N	Mean	S.D.	N	Mean	S.D.	N	Mean	S.D.	N	Mean	S.D.	N	Mean	S.D.	N	Mean	S.D.	N	Mean	S.D.	N	Mean	S.D.	N	Mean	S.D.	N	Mean	S.D.
Literacy Level																														
Father and Mother both literate	14	57.97	3.67	12	65.41	3.91	16	67.50	4.48	11	69.27	2.86	9	69.49	6.36	16	61.28	3.44	12	63.12	3.95	17	63.83	4.08	7	67.96	3.04	12	68.85	3.27
Mother lit., fathernon-lit.	1	63.80		0	0	0	0	0	0	0	0	0	1	73.50		0	0	0	0	0	0	0	0	0	0	0	0	1	77.40	
Mother non-lit., father lit	28	60.15	4.20	25	64.34	3.59	21	66.45	4.00	29	68.48	3.84	31	70.87	3.41	27	59.26	2.94	27	62.73	3.19	24	63.72	3.18	30	66.21	2.79	26	68.05	3.81
Mother & Father non-lit.				2	63.50	2.68	1	67.00		3	66.46	2.48	1	65.90		2	64.05	2.19	3	63.53	7.73	1	65.90		4	68.47	4.51	1	71.60	
Family Size																														
Small family (<3)	8	62.08	3.39	10	66.11	3.75	9	68.08	3.29	10	68.57	4.43	11	71.30	3.53	7	59.38	2.44	6	63.40	3.06	2	65.60	4.6	3	64.83	2.29	5	65.82	3.14
Medium family (4-6)	19	58.90	4.23	19	64.53	3.93	19	66.48	3.77	26	68.19	3.02	19	71.80	3.63	17	60.90	3.59	14	62.96	4.33	23	63.74	2.65	19	67.06	3.46	27	68.70	3.87
Medium large family (7-8)	10	59.52	3.76	6	64.81	1.79	6	66.26	5.44	5	67.28	3.60	7	68.02	3.61	10	61.90	2.97	14	62.55	3.41	9	62.38	3.49	12	66.73	2.92	4	69.75	1.64
Large family (09)	6	57.00	1.27	5	62.46	1.19	6	67.30	3.75	3	65.66	2.04	4	67.82	5.33	11	58.79	3.73	8	63.00	3.05	8	65.17	4.32	7	66.71	1.49	5	69.84	3.48
Family type																														
Nuclear	18	59.95	4.96	17	64.84	3.85	24	66.53	3.61	19	67.66	3.31	16	71.78	4.07	16	60.55	3.05	17	62.72	3.70	19	63.24	2.35	20	66.77	3.50	25	68.02	3.84
Joint	25	58.96	3.02	23	64.61	3.32	16	67.53	4.52	25	68.25	3.59	25	69.9	4.01	29	60.27	3.78	25	63.00	3.61	23	64.28	4.10	21	66.71	2.48	16	69.46	3.42
Birth order																														
Birth order 1	16	59.64	3.98	13	65.55	4.87	9	65.52	3.07	10	67.87	3.19	8	69.87	4.25	16	61.25	3.72	11	62.19	3.46	14	63.87	2.86	12	66.18	2.45	10	68.36	2.63
Birth order 2	9	60.26	3.51	8	64.73	2.55	8	69.12	3.95	10	68.63	4.08	16	70.35	3.21	7	59.37	2.80	12	63.76	3.86	6	63.23	1.49	10	66.35	2.83	10	67.50	2.94
Birth order 3	6	59.66	4.35	10	65.15	2.90	5	65.14	4.01	12	67.83	3.77	5	74.92	4.07	7	61.34	3.04	7	62.57	3.53	10	63.02	4.29	4	70.10	3.56	11	68.46	5.09
Birth order 4<	12	58.20	3.84	9	62.98	1.62	18	67.16	3.99	12	67.75	2.73	12	69.72	4.10	15	59.44	3.51	12	62.85	3.48	12	64.69	3.79	15	66.56	2.83	10	70.05	3.20
Per capita Income																														
Group-1(0-400)	22	59.05	4.17	17	63.91	3.06	22	65.79	4.13	24	67.71	3.75	20	70.23	4.38	23	60.20	3.12	19	62.62	3.62	20	63.83	3.65	12	66.38	2.78	23	68.6	4.23
Group-11(401<)	21	60.06	3.94	22	65.19	3.97	18	68.33	3.66	19	68.75	3.26	21	71.19	3.98	22	60.18	3.55	22	63.08	3.91	22	63.80	3.45	29	66.88	3.20	17	68.64	3.38

Table 15

Mean and Standard Deviation for Bi-iliocristal Diameter of Children Aged from 6 to 10 Years by Literacy Level of Both the Parents, Parity of Child, Family Size, Family Type and Per Capita Income of the Ahir (Yeduvanshi) of Haryana

	Boys															Girls														
	6			7			8			9			10			6			7			8			9			10		
	N	*Mean*	*S.D.*	*N*	*Mean*	*S.D.*	*N*	*Mean*	*S.D.*	*N*	*Mean*	*S.D.*	*N*	*Mean*	*S.D.*	*N*	*Mean*	*S.D.*	*N*	*Mean*	*S.D.*	*N*	*Mean*	*S.D.*	*N*	*Mean*	*S.D.*	*N*	*Mean*	*S.D.*
Literacy Level																														
Father and Mother both literate	14	17.63	1.08	12	19.86	1.2	16	20.11	1.5	11	20.69	1.47	9	21.03	1.20	16	17.81	0.92	12	18.56	1.52	17	18.87	1.33	7	20.65	1.86	12	21.09	17.10
Mother lit.,	1	18.4	0	0	0	0	0	0	0	0	0	1		23.30	0	0	0	0	0	0	0	0	0	0	0	0	0	1	23.20	0
Mother non-lit., father lit,	28	17.68	1.59	25	19.35	1.18	21	20.21	1.59	29	20.79	1.54	31	21.50	1.30	27	17.93	1.07	27	18.71	1.47	24	19.02	0.95	30	19.97	1.17	26	20.51	1.40
Mother & Father non-lit.	0	0	0	2	19.00	3.41	1	20.50	0	3	20.53	1.27	1	21.70	0	2	19.40	1.27	3	20.20	0.14	1	19.20	0	4	21.52	1.53	1	23.10	0
Family Size																														
Small family (<3)	8	18.27	1.11	10	19.64	1.37	9	20.84	1.23	10	20.97	1.41	11	21.55	1.28	7	17.50	1.08	6	19.23	1.30	2	19.55	1.25	3	20.03	0.95	5	19.66	1.28
Medium family (4-6)	19	17.83	1.43	19	19.47	1.10	19	19.82	1.40	26	20.96	1.30	19	21.70	1.19	17	18.00	0.96	14	18.87	1.89	23	18.85	1.11	19	20.18	1.45	27	20.85	1.46
Medium large family (7-8)	10	17.8	1.29	6	19.66	1.07	6	19.75	1.41	5	20.00	1.55	7	20.25	1.07	10	18.33	1.23	14	18.52	1.11	9	18.67	0.73	12	20.36	1.55	4	21.32	1.05
Large family (09)	6	16.45	0.8	5	19.12	0.89	6	20.66	1.62	3	19.96	1.90	4	21.92	1.09	11	17.85	0.78	8	18.47	1.24	8	19.45	1.08	7	20.22	0.87	5	21.10	1.82
Family type																														
Nuclear	18	17.88	1.44	17	19.50	1.11	24	20.03	1.41	19	20.63	1.27	16	21.76	1.26	16	18.03	0.91	17	18.81	1.46	19	18.71	0.99	20	20.16	1.60	25	20.64	1.51
Joint	25	17.59	1.32	23	19.50	1.19	16	20.36	1.55	25	20.90	1.57	25	21.23	1.29	29	17.92	1.10	25	18.67	1.50	23	19.16	1.11	21	20.30	1.10	16	21.00	1.52
Birth order																														
Birth order 1	16	17.84	1.13	13	19.86	1.53	9	19.80	1.31	10	21.17	1.38	8	21.17	1.06	16	18.25	1.12	11	18.30	1.31	14	18.79	1.12	12	19.66	0.59	10	20.45	1.29
Birth order 2	9	18.25	1.00	8	19.18	0.88	8	20.91	1.67	10	20.59	1.24	16	21.23	0.98	7	17.28	0.73	12	19.21	1.52	6	17.93	0.47	10	20.90	1.09	10	20.48	1.40
Birth order 3	6	17.56	1.84	10	19.52	0.96	5	19.02	1.21	12	20.90	1.71	5	22.66	1.80	7	18.01	1.34	7	18.92	1.74	10	19.41	1.00	4	21.35	1.65	11	20.93	1.50
Birth order 4<	12	17.21	1.47	9	19.23	0.72	18	20.34	1.27	12	20.51	1.32	12	21.39	1.32	15	17.93	0.72	12	18.51	1.27	12	19.30	0.91	15	19.95	1.55	10	21.27	1.71
Per capita Income																														
Group-1 (0-400)	22	17.42	1.22	17	19.19	1.05	22	19.76	1.37	24	20.24	1.79	20	21.53	1.41	23	18.16	0.86	19	18.53	1.57	20	19.14	1.04	12	20.23	1.09	23	20.81	1.60
Group-11(401<)	21	18.02	1.53	22	19.72	1.27	18	20.67	1.53	19	21.43	1.34	21	21.40	1.27	22	17.76	1.21	22	18.90	1.50	22	18.85	1.18	29	20.24	1.57	17	20.82	1.56

Table 16

Mean and Standard Deviation for Biacromial Diameter of Children Aged from 6 to 10 Years by Literacy Level of Both the Parents, Parity of Child, Family Size, Family Type and Per Capita Income of the Ahir (Yeduvanshi) of Haryana

	Boys															Girls														
	6			7			8			9			10			6			7			8			9			10		
	N	Mean	S.D.	N	Mean	S.D.	N	Mean	S.D.	N	Mean	S.D.	N	Mean	S.D.	N	Mean	S.D.	N	Mean	S.D.	N	Mean	S.D.	N	Mean	S.D.	N	Mean	S.D.
Literacy Level																														
Father and Mother both literate	14	24.03	1.60	12	26.91	2.31	16	28.08	1.95	11	28.00	1.33	9	29.26	1.87	16	25.05	1.39	12	25.48	1.29	17	26.16	1.43	7	26.67	2.75	12	28.84	1.12
Mother lit., father non-lit.	1	24.10	0	0	0	0	0	0	0	0	0	0	1	31.00		0	0	0	0	0	0	0	0	0	0	0	0	1	32.90	0
Mother non-lit., father lit	28	24.81	1.85	25	26.70	1.64	21	28.07	1.78	29	28.75	1.70	31	32.18	9.86	27	24.10	1.44	27	25.97	1.37	24	26.47	1.19	30	27.40	1.35	26	28.56	1.73
Mother & Father non-lit	0	0	0	2	26.05	1.20	1	27.80		328.10	1.25		129.20			2	26.60	1.69	3	26.8	1.75	1	28.20	0	4	29.07	1.84	1	31.60	0
Family Size																														
Small family(<3)	8	25.65	1.80	10	27.17	2.05	9	28.41	1.69	10	28.58	1.77	11	30.07	2.21	7	24.17	0.80	6	25.95	1.35	2	26.70	1.10	3	27.30	1.02	5	27.74	1.47
Medium family (4-6)	19	24.41	1.59	19	27.33	1.63	19	27.99	1.68	26	28.90	1.48	19	29.84	1.9	17	24.51	1.50	14	26.05	1.37	23	26.50	1.12	19	27.55	1.65	27	28.87	1.78
Medium large family (7-8)	10	24.91	1.42	6	26.01	0.84	6	27.58	1.63	5	27.30	1.20	7	28.47	1.28	10	25.42	1.31	14	25.80	1.46	9	25.47	1.35	12	27.80	2.00	4	29.05	0.92
Large family (09)	6	22.85	1.17	5	24.80	0.64	6	28.2	2.07	3	27.76	0.96	4	28.67	1.05	11	24.05	1.71	8	25.67	1.08	8	26.98	1.19	7	27.74	0.91	5	29.20	1.42
Family type																														
Nuclear	18	24.94	1.92	17	27.09	1.85	24	28.06	1.67	19	28.42	1.83	16	30.17	2.42	16	24.51	1.25	17	25.91	1.18	19	26.44	0.99	20	27.41	1.83	25	28.59	1.79
Joint	25	24.24	1.54	23	26.54	1.72	16	28.05	1.88	25	28.68	1.55	25	29.16	1.42	29	24.57	1.64	25	25.86	1.47	23	26.33	1.49	21	27.86	1.40	16	29.11	1.44
Birth order																														
Birth order 1	16	24.66	1.72	13	27.03	2.08	9	27.55	2.10	10	28.26	1.30	8	29.42	1.26	16	25.06	1.25	11	25.55	0.98	14	26.58	0.83	12	27.58	0.98	10	28.92	1.04
Birth order 2	9	25.18	1.10	8	26.73	1.61	8	28.53	1.82	10	29.05	1.77	16	29.32	1.71	7	24.57	1.19	12	26.00	1.36	6	24.90	1.23	10	27.77	1.50	10	27.88	1.24
Birth order 3	6	24.75	2.04	10	27.62	1.41	5	28.12	1.44	12	28.74	1.76	5	32.16	2.08	7	24.41	1.75	7	26.37	1.64	10	26.19	1.36	4	29.10	2.23	11	28.73	2.2
Birth order 4<	12	23.77	1.75	9	25.51	1.04	18	28.07	1.54	12	28.25	1.31	12	28.87	1.64	15	24.06	1.61	12	25.77	1.37	12	27.05	1.03	15	27.22	1.72	10	29.65	1.45
Per capita Income																														
Group-1 (0-400)	22	24.12	1.82	17	26.38	2.21	22	27.44	1.59	24	28.06	1.61	20	29.37	1.86	23	24.50	1.42	19	25.82	1.34	20	26.30	1.24	12	27.48	0.90	23	28.87	2.03
Group-11 (401<)	21	24.97	1.65	22	26.81	1.98	18	28.81	1.76	19	29.06	1.56	21	29.86	2.00	22	24.50	1.70	22	25.96	1.47	22	26.46	1.39	29	27.71	1.90	17	28.77	1.23

Mean and standard deviation (S.D.) were calculated for the above said five measurements according to the family size of the household units and the value of different measurements were shown in table number 12-16. The mean value for weight, height, sitting height, biacromial and bi-iliocristal diameters show that it is high in small family both among boys and girls, it is high in medium family except for bi-iliocristal diameter. The higher mean value for bi-iliocristal diameter is seen in small family. It is evident from the table that among boys and girls the acceleration of growth neither slowed nor increased drastically, anyhow a slight swing in growth is observed from medium large family to small family when compared to large family which clearly indicates that smaller the family size better the availability of food and better in the growth progress.

The type of family is also studied and it has been categorized into two types i.e. nuclear and joint, basing on these division mean and standard deviation (S.D.) were calculated for weight, height, sitting height, biacromial diameter and bi-iliocristal diameter and is shown in table number 12 to 16. It is observed from the table that among boys the six year children and ten year children of nuclear family type show higher growth whereas the rest of age groups i.e. seven, eight and nine show high rate growth under joint family type. Similarly among girls under nuclear family type the six year age group children showed better growth while, the rest age group show high rate of growth in the other type of family i.e. joint family.

As we have calculated mean and standard deviation (S.D.) for the above said five measurements, here also the same parameters were calculated for mean and standard deviation according to the birth order (parity) of the subject. It is interesting to note from the Tables 12 to 16 the mean values for different measurements is not decreasing from birth order one to birth order four and above among both boys and girls. An increased growth is observed in birth order two group and birth order three group for all ages among both the sexes when compared to birth order one and birth order four and above. Since the sample size is also unevenly distributed among different categories there is every possibility of variation in the mean values.

The mean and standard deviation were analysed basing on the per capita income of the family and it is divided into two groups. In the first group if the per capita income is less than 400 it is categorized as group I and if the per capita income is 401 and above it is classified under group II. Undoubtedly among boys the mean value is high in group II for all the five measurements. Among girls the mean value is high in group I for six, seven and eight years, the rest nine and ten years show higher growth in the other group i.e. group II.

Finally in a nut shell to say the impact of socio-cultural factors like per capita income, literacy level of parents, family size, family type and birth order of the child, have not revealed a clear cut picture over weight, stature, sitting height, biacromial diameter, bi-iliac diameter. It is also not out of context to mention that the sample size when distributed into subgroups it is not evenly distributed as a result a haphazard picture is observed which turns down to our hypothesis. Thus it is very difficult to conclude whether the socio-cultural factors definitely have impact over growth or not.

Discussion

The shapes of the distance curve for weight, height, sitting height, biacromial diameter and bi-iliocristal diameter are strikingly similar between boys and girls. They almost start at the same point with a spindle shape divergence between 7 to 9 years before they settle for a parallel trend widely separated each other. In all the curves slowing down of the velocity at the age of 8 years for girls and for boys it is at 9 years. Consequently the velocity curves of all the above characters among boys show a strikingly similar pattern i.e., an inverted right tick mark (gradually lowering of velocity upto 9 years before increasing at 10 years) while girls show an inverted "s" shape with a spurt in the velocity between 8 and 9 years and a dip before and after these two ages in the rate of growth. The pattern observed for longitudinal and breadth measurement are not reflected in the skinfold measurement. It is well known fact that the deposition of fat are result of the state of health or nutritional intake and largely free from age depended growth factor.

Similarly if we observe the co-efficient of variation the dip in the value of co-efficient of variation is prominent at the age of 8 years among girls for all the linear measurements and for skinfold measurements and among boys it is seen at the nine year age group for some measurement.

Classification of different nutritional status categories agewise with reference to the standard values (NCHS and ICMR) for various indications of nutritional influences exhibit no uniform and parallel comparable proportions of in dial categories while around 50% of the individual in different age group classes are observed to be normal or above for mid upper arm circumference. The classification based on height for age index exhibits more number of normal children in comparison to the children classified based on weight for age. The classification based on weight for age and height for age exhibit greater proportion of normal children the height for age than the later Index. A general pattern that can be observed is that at 6 years age level the proportions of various indical classes in all the three categories (boys and girls) show more or less equal proportions and as the age progresses the girls show a declining proportion with reference to their male counterpart towards the near normal categories.

From the results obtained, it is evident that as far as their weight stature, sitting height, bi-iliocristal diameter the Ahir (Yeduvanshi) children showed higher growth than the standard values given on Hindus by the ICMR, 1984. The values were also high for stature and sitting height when compared to kisi boys and girls of Keroka urban council of Kenya (Samvit S. Kaul and Issac, K. Nyamongo, 1990).

Comparison of Present Study with Some Selective Population

The Ahir (Yeduvanshi) of the present study has been compared with some of the selective population for weight and height. Boys were compared with five other populations namely Punjabi (Sidhy L.S. 1969); Gaddi Rajput (Singh, S.P., 1980), Kinnaura (Malhotra, R, 1975); Rajput Kullu (Singai *et al*, 1987) and Bonda tribe (Dharma Rao, B, *et al*, 2000). While, girls were compared with two population only they are Gaddi Rajput (Singh, S.P. 1980) and Rajput Kullu (Singal, *et al*, 1987). The Table 17 shows that the mean weight of the present study as well as some of the selective population of both boys and girls. Fig. 17 and 19 also represents the distance curve for weight of Ahir (Yeduvanshi) boys and girls with and some other populations. It is observed from the table and graph that the Bonda tribal boys showed better weight than the Ahir (Yeduvanshi) boys. While Punjabi boys, Kinnaura boys, Rajput Kullu boys showed higher weight than Ahir (Yeduvanshi) boys at 6 years, for the rest of the years i.e., 7 years, 8 years and 10 years. Ahir (Yeduvanshi) boys showed better weight than the above said three population. Gaddi Rajput children are less in weight of all the compared population.

Table 17
Comparison of Mean Weight of the Present Study With Some of the Selective Population

Sex	*Age (Year)*	*Punjabi*	*Gaddi Cajput*	*Kinnaura*	*Rajput Kullu*	*Bonda tribe*	*Present study*
Boys							
	6	17.26	16.39	18.06	17.75	19.83	17.00
	7	20.18	17.61	19.50	20.00	23.35	20.95
	8	21.88	18.62	20.62	21.50	25.02	23.12
	9	24.33	21.28	23.10	19.25	27.33	24.57
	10	25.30	22.10	24.12	21.60	28.54	27.09
Girls							
	6	0.00	15.95	0.00	17.40	0.00	16.97
	7	0.00	17.09	0.00	17.00	0.00	19.01
	8	0.00	18.01	0.00	19.30	0.00	19.59
	9	0.00	19.83	0.00	22.60	0.00	22.60
	10	0.00	21.60	0.00	22.80	0.00	24.67

Among girls Ahir (Yeduvanshi) children showed better weight than Rajput Kullu and Gaddi Rajput girls except at the age six years, Rajput Kullu girls showed a slightly higher weight and at nine years the mean weight of Ahir (Yeduvanshi) girls and Rajput Kullu girls are one and the same.

Similarly Table 18 shows the mean height of the Ahir (Yeduvanshi) and some of the selective population of both the sexes. It is also shown in fig. 18 and 20. It is observed from the table and graph that the Bonda tribal boys showed higher growth than Ahir (Yeduvanshi) boys upto the age of nine years while in the tenth year Ahir (Yeduvanshi) boys supercede the Bonda tribal boys. The rest population namely the boys of Punjabi, Gaddi Rajput, Kinnaura, Rajput Kullu shown lesser growth than Ahir (Yeduvanshi) boys. Rajput Kullu boys showed different growth from 7 years to nine years. Very poor growth is observed among Gaddi Rajput boys. This evidences that the high altitude people are shorter. Just like weight here also girls showed a similar type of trend. Ahir (Yeduvanshi) girls are far ahead to Rajput Kullu girls and Gaddi Rajput girls.

Table 18
Comparison of Mean Height of the Present Study with Some of the Selective Population

Sex	*Age (Year)*	*Punjabi*	*Gaddi Rajput*	*Kinnaura*	*Rajput Kullu*	*Bonda Tribe*	*Present study*
Boys	6	108.50	104.30	107.70	108.60	119.45	112.60
	7	116.30	110.87	112.10	108.60	126.35	123.23
	8	121.60	114.90	115.50	125.20	129.90	128.71
	9	126.70	120.48	121.50	118.50	134.69	132.46
	10	130.60	123.69	124.20	124.90	137.13	137.86
Girls	6	0.00	103.69	0.00	106.00	0.00	113.36
	7	0.00	108.13	0.00	112.60	0.00	120.25
	8	0.00	112.12	0.00	119.40	0.00	122.41
	9	0.00	117.29	0.00	125.00	0.00	129.81
	10	0.00	122.53	0.00	124.00	0.00	134.06

(a) Sidhu, L. S. (1969), (b) Singh, S. P.(1980), (c) Malhotra, R. (1975), (d) Singh *et. al.*, (1980) (e) Dharma Rao, B. *et. al.*, (2000), (f) Present study Ahir (Yeduvanshi).

Acknowledgements

The authors are very much indebted to Dr. R. K. Bhattacharya, Former Director, Anthropological Survey of India for giving us an opportunity to work under this project. We are also grateful to Dr. Swaran Singh, Deputy Director and Head of Office, North West Regional Centre, Anthropological Survey of India, Dehradun for providing the necessary facilities and gave encouragement for both of us during our field work and while drafting the report. We are also grateful to Dr. V R Rao and Shri S S Sastry for giving us inspiration while drafting this report. We are also grateful to Dr. (Mrs.) Madhubala Sharma and Dr. D. B. Mondal, Project Co-coordinators of this project for giving us guidance from time to time during our field work and while drafting this report.

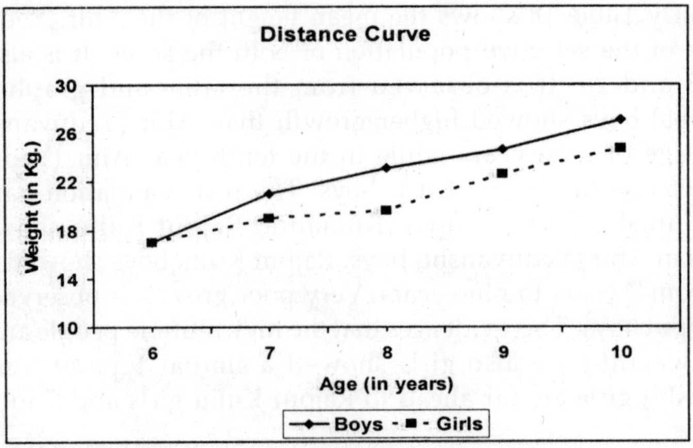

Fig. 1

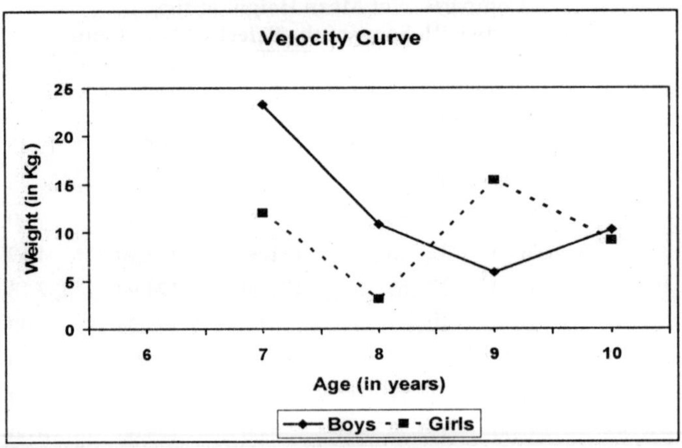

Fig. 2

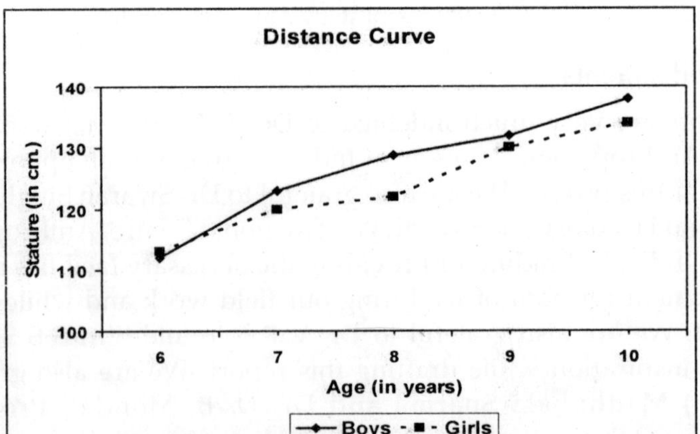

Fig. 3

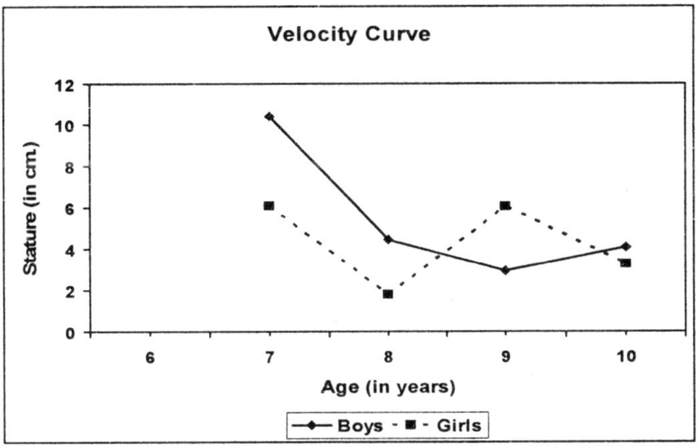

Fig. 4

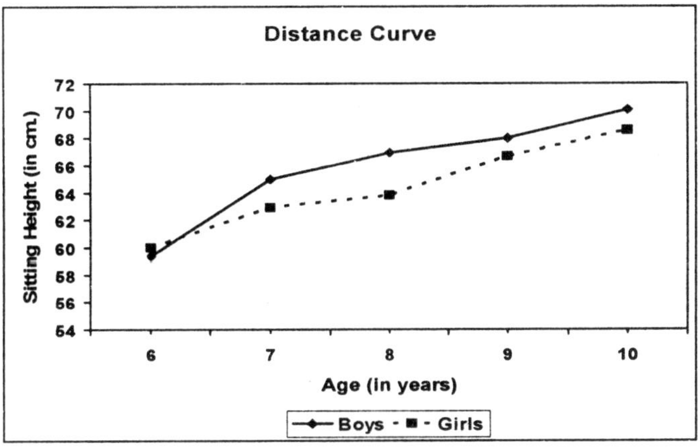

Fig. 5

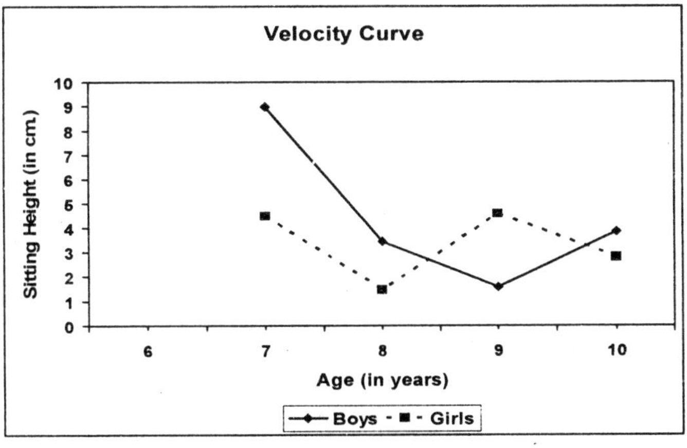

Fig. 6

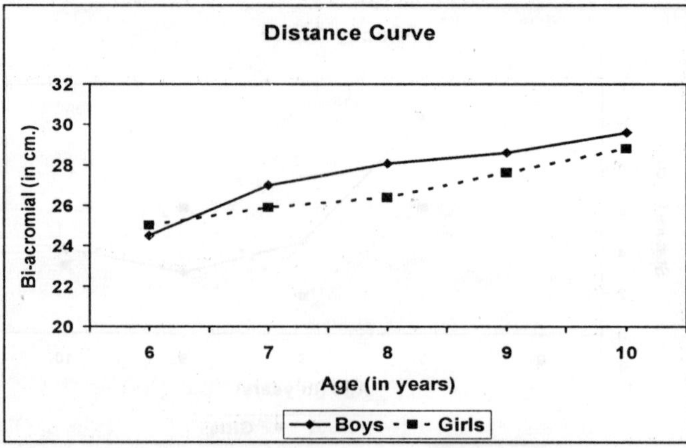

Fig. 7

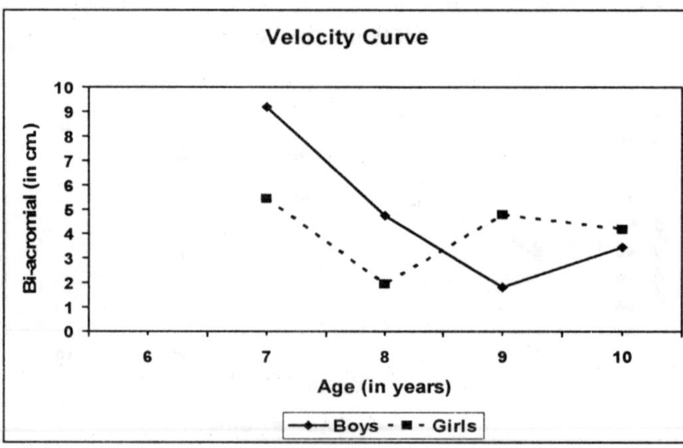

Fig. 8

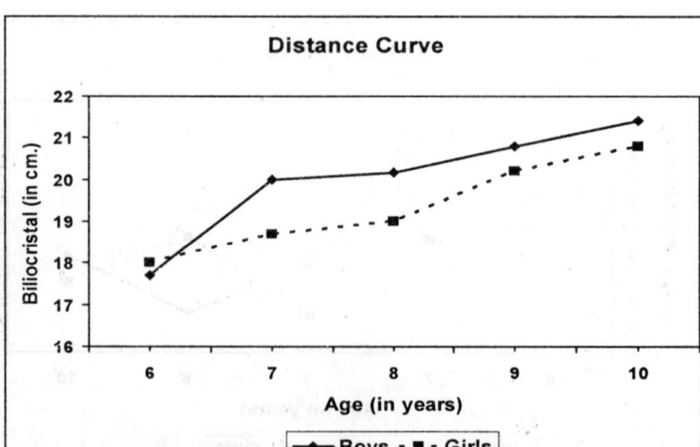

Fig. 9

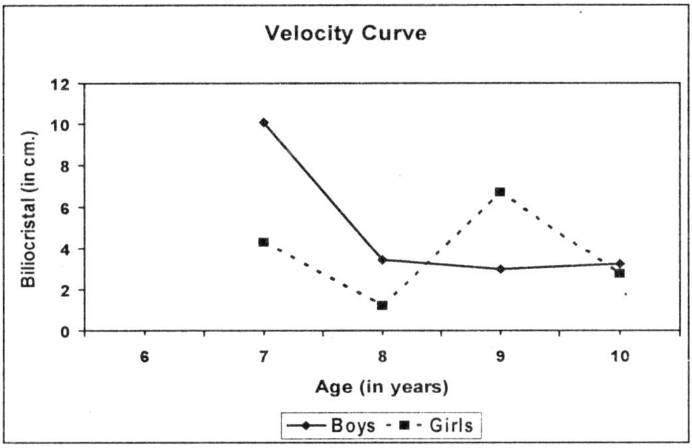

Fig. 10

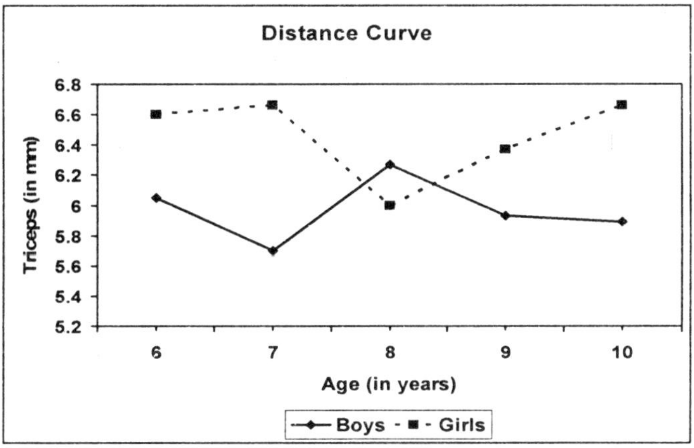

Fig. 11

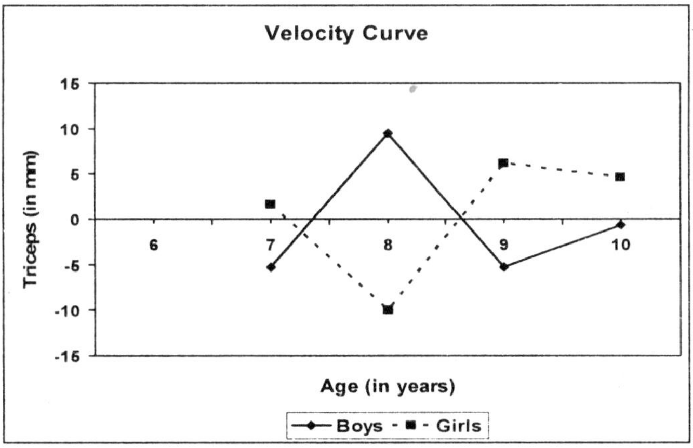

Fig. 12

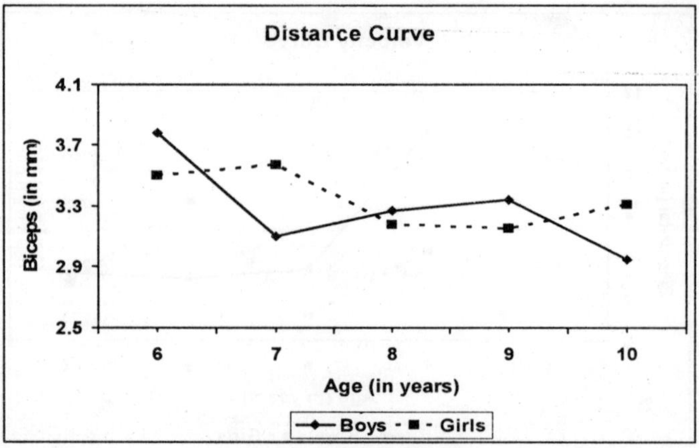

Fig. 13

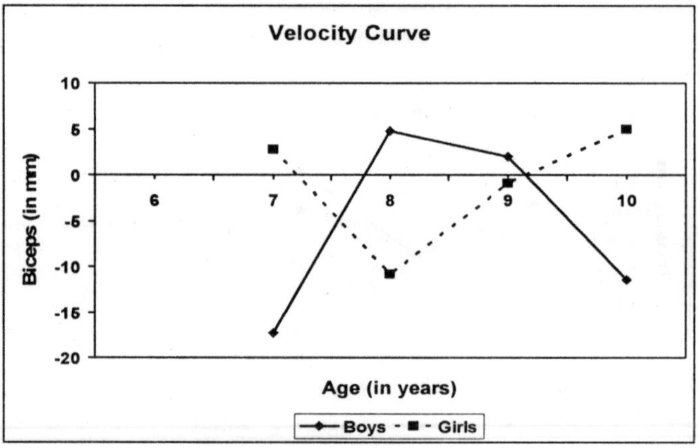

Fig. 14

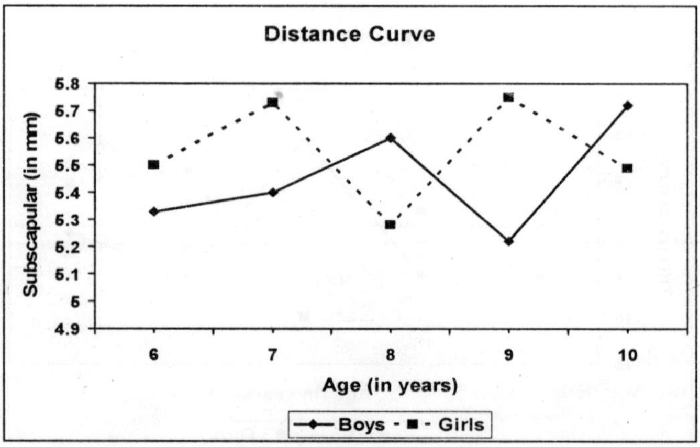

Fig. 15

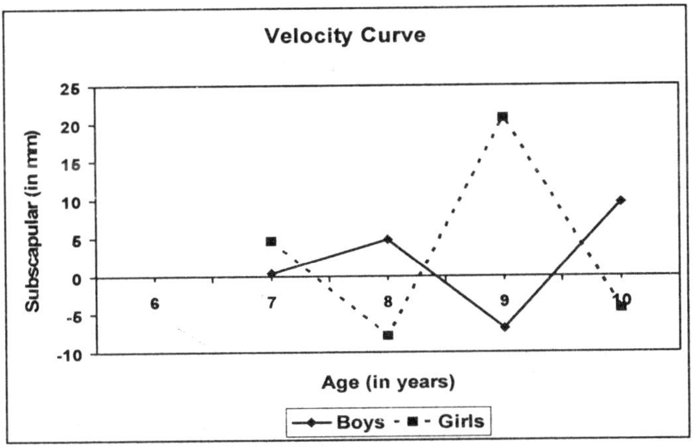

Fig. 16

References

Dharma Rao, B., V.L.N. Rao and B.R. Busi (2000), Growth Progression in Physical and Physiological Variables among Bondo Tribal Boys in Orissa, *Man in India*, 80 (182) pp. 157-67

I.C.M.R. (1984), *Technical Report Series No. 18:* Growth and Physical Development of Indian Infants and Children ICMR, New Delhi.

Jelliffe, D. B. (1966) The Assessment of the Nutritional Status of the Community *W.H.O. Monograph Series, No. 53,* Geneva: WHO.

Latham, M. (1979) Human Nutrition in Tropical Africa 2nd Edition, Rome: F.A.O.

Malhotra, R. (1975), A Study of Physical Growth and Developmental Status of High Altitude Population in the Himalayas (A Cross-sectional Study of Kinnaura Male Rajputs) Ph.D. Thesis (Unpublished), Punjab University, Chandigarh.

Martin, R. and K. Saller (1959), Lehrbuchh der Anthropologic Stuttgart.

Samvit, S. Kaul and Issac, K. Nyamongo (1990), Ecology, Growth and Nutritional Status, New Delhi. Ashish Publishing House, 8/81, Punjabi Bagh.

Sidhu, L. S. (1969), Biological Survey of the Punjabi Males with Special Reference to Age Changes, Ph.D. Thesis. Punjab University, Chandigarh.

Singal, P., D.P. Bhatnagar and Meera Bawa (1987), Physical Growth and Somatotypes in Rajput Children of Kullu Valley (ms).

Singh, S.P. (1980), Physical Growth of Gaddi Rajputs of Dhauladhar Range of the Himalayas, Z. *North. Anthrop.*, 71 : pp. 65-81

Vinod Kaul (1979), Age Changes in Dental Arches: A Study of Growth of Dental Arches in the Jats of Haryana. Ph.D. Thesis. Punjab University, Chandigarh (Unpublished).

3

GROWTH OF THE ORAON CHILDREN (AGED 6 YEARS TO 10 YEARS) OF SUNDARBAN, WEST BENGAL: A BIO-CULTURAL PERSPECTIVE

S. BARUA, MITALI CHATTERJEE & GAUTAM MALLIK

This report is a part of the national project, "Growth and Development of Children: Bio-Cultural Perspective" launched by the Anthropological Survey of India during the 9th Five Year Plan. The present report is on the growth of Oraon children aged from 6 years to 10 years of Sandeshkhali (I) Block of North 24 Parganas district of West Bengal. In fact, Sandeshkhali (I) Block of North 24 Parganas district belongs to the greater Sundarban area of the undivided Bengal, though geo-morphological and geo-vegetative features of the Sandeshkhali Block are quite different from the typical Sundarban belt of Southern Bengal.

The Oraon is a Scheduled Tribe, majority of whom concentrated in Chotanagpur plateau of Bihar and its adjoining area in West Bengal, Orissa and Madhya Pradesh. It is believed that the Oraon migrated to Chotanagpur plateau and its adjoining area from South India in the remote historical past (S.C. Roy, 1915: 1984). From Chotanagpur area many small groups of Oraon were transplanted to various parts of West Bengal and North East India, Assam in particular, during the British rule in India. Besides, some other small groups of Oraon also migrated voluntarily to the adjoining area of West Bengal. The Oraons belong to the Proto-North Dravidian linguistic group speaking 'Kurukh' language (Subramanium, 1971).

According to 1981 census the total population of Oraon of the undivided 24 Parganas districts were 38.307, majority of whom were distributed in the Sandeshkhali Police Station area. The Oraons of Sandeshkhali Police Station and Sandeshkhali (I) Block form the population of the present study. The area from were the Oraons had been included in the present study is encircled by the tributaries of Ichamati river: Betni on the north and Baunia on the South. Kalinagar trading centre is hardly half kilometre from the main Nazat trading centre around which the Oraons under study are concentrated. However, Nazat trading centre is separated from the Kalinagar trading centre by the tributary river Betni.

The Oraons of this belt were traditionally agriculturists, practicing wet paddy cultivation like those of the neighbouring Bengali Muslims and caste Hindu Bengalees of South Bengal. Of late, Bengali Muslims and caste Hindu Bengalees of the area started brackish water fishery as their main avocation because of their lucrative nature discarding their traditional caste or community occupations. In brackish water fishery, saline water from the tributaries of Ichamati river, Betni and Baunia, are drained into agricultural lands or paddy lands until the lands become flooded with brackish water. In the process, the vast area of agricultural lands in the Sandeshkhali (I) Block remain flooded with brackish water throughout the year. These flooded lands are used for tiger prawn culture and brackish water fisheries. Tiger prawns being produced in huge quantities in these flooded lands are often sold to the multinational companies for export to the foreign countries.

Due to the increase in salanity of the agricultural lands owned by the tribals, the tribals were compelled to lease their lands to the fisheries owners and to take up other occupations. A very few of them practice their own fisheries in their agricultural lands. It has also been reported that 91 Oraon families out of 318 Oraon families being surveyed are landless; out of these 91 families, nine families owned *barga* land (share cropping land) ranging from a few katha to eight bighas. Of these bargadars only three *bargadar* families had to lease their barga lands for fisheries, since the lands became unfit for agriculture. Hence the parents of the Oraon children had given up their traditional occupations and had taken up other avocations, fisheries in particular or occupations centering around fish trade as porters in the fish trading centre. It has been reported that only 3.75% of the males are involved in agriculture and none of the female are engaged in agricultural works. Besides, there are a very few rickshaw pullers and service holders.

Rice is the staple food of the Oraons of this region and it is generally taken along with pulses or vegetables or both. They are non-vegetarian and consume meat and fishes as and when available or when they can afford to by them. However, fishes are, in most of the time, available to them. The adult male Oraons consume high quantity of rice beer and distilled liquor. The field rats which form one of the delicacy of their food items have now become scarce due to the great decrease in cultivable lands and change in soil condition due to brackish water fisheries. Now a days plentiful of brackish water and estuarine fishes are available to them.

Bhattacharya *et. al.* (1994) suggested that the diet of these Oraons is deficient mainly in calories, calcium, vitamin A and vitamin B_2. Hence the Oraons are in a state of adverse nutritional situation which is further aggravated by high intestinal parasitic load among them.

They construct mud houses with thatched roofs but due to salinity of the soils these huts hardly last more than a year. However, a very few rich families have well built concrete buildings. Government had provided some families (about 5%) with masonry (bricks) houses with tile roofs but due to soil conditions these houses hardly last beyond five years. Their houses are neat, clean, spacious and well ventilated .

A total of 318 Oraon families were surveyed for the present study. The average number of individuals per family is 5.68. The distribution by the size of the family is given in Table 1. The table suggests that only 22.33% of the families are large and very large (7 to more than 10 members in the family).

Table 1
Family Size of the Oraon

Family Size (No. of individuals in a family)	*Total No. of families*	
	No.	*%*
-3	15	4.71
6-9	232	72.96
7-9	65	20.45
10+	6	1.88
Total	318	100

Average No. of individuals per family or per household = 5.68

The literacy rate seems of be high (58.40%) as compared to that of the other rural and tribal populations. This higher value of the literacy rate is because of the fact that persons who are able to read and write are considered to be literate. Of late, school going children had increased in this area because of the fact that free rations (mid-day meals in the form of uncooked rice and pulses) are given to the school going children. However, these free rations are shared by all the family members of the children so the school going children may not get the requisite food items. The literacy rate among the Oraons has been given in Table 2. The table suggests that more females are non literate (58.87%) than the males (41.60%). It should be mentioned in this connection that 16 females (including one female beyond class 10) were reported to have reached class 10 and beyond. Not even single female has reached the college level.

It had been reported in the present study that 91.20% of the total families avail of allopathic system of medicine; only 8.80% of the families avail of homeopathic system of medicine along with the traditional system, this may be due to the economic reasons. However, Government's immunization programme had reached them with success. All the Oraons had availed of this Government's immunization programme. All the Oraon children that have been included in this study have availed of various vaccines included in the Government immunization programme (such as BCG, measles, DPT and polio vaccine/drops). It should be mentioned that many of the government developmental programmes such as the Jawahar Rojgar Yojna, Employment Assurance Scheme and National Rural Employment Programme and Training of Rural Youth for self employment could not be implemented successfully because of lack of infrastructural facilities. However under certain governmental scheme, a few of the Oraons (a few fathers of the studied children) were provided with rackshaws for their livelihood. Public health engineering department of the state government had provided drinking water to the Oraons of the area and as such two to three villages or three to four hamlets are provided with a main drinking water source. Despite the regular supply of drinking water to the Oraons, they use pond water for bathing and washing of household utensils. This pond water is often contaminated with intestinal parasites. From the previous study of Bhattacharya (1994) it has been observed that this population has high intestinal parasitic load. A good number of them have scabies. Majority of the Oraon families use straw (paddy straw) supplemented by wood as fuel for cooking their food.

Table 2
Literacy Rate Among the Oraons

	Male		*Female*		*Total*	
	N	*%*	*N*	*%*	*N*	*%*
Non Literate	379	41.6	498	58.87	877	49.91
Literate	532	58.4	348	41.13	883	50.09
Primary	342	37.43	259	30.61	600	34.15
Upper Primary	137	15.04	73	8.63	210	11.95
Secondary	41	4.5	15	1.77	56	3.19
Higher Secondary	9	0.99	1	0.12	10	0.57
Graduate	3	0.33	-	-	3	0.17
Post Graduate	-	-	-	-	-	-
Polytechnic	1	0.11	-	-	1	0.06
Total	911	-	846	-	1757	-

Material and Methods

Certain anthropometric traits (stature, body weight, sitting height, biacrominal breadth or diameter, bi-iliocristal breadth or diameter, skin fold thicknesses at triceps, subscapular and biceps region) were taken from Oraon school children from 6 years to 10 years of age, from 9 Primary, one Junior Basic and one High Schools near Nazat main trading centre. A total of 213 males and 206 females are included in the study.

The sample children were the residents of the villages of the Bayarmari, Nazadt and Daakshin Akhraatala Mouzas of Sandeshkhali (I) Block.

Houses (households) of the children were thoroughly interviewed for taking information on their socio-cultural life and economic persuits.

The correlation coefficients (*r*) between certain anthropometric measurements, and also between each of the anthropometric measurements and age were estimated for both the sexes following standard method. The test of linearity of relationship between the anthropometric traits, and also between each of anthropometric traits and the age of the individual was performed based on the testing of linearity of regression and on the non significance of the correlation ratio. The comparison between various *r* values was made following Fisher's Z-transformation method (Fisher, 1954). Distance (growth) curve for various anthropometric traits was constructed from the mean values at different ages. The growth velocity curve was constructed from the differences of the two mean values at the successive ages. In fact, growth velocity is the annual increase in the mean values of the anthropometric traits. Besides, other statistical constants were estimated using standard statistical procedure. Available computer software were used for obtaining various results and curves.

Results and Discussions

The ethno history of the population under study has been described at length in the preceding section. The probable socio-cultural determinants and the ecological condition that may have some bearing on the growth and development of the Oraon children have already been described at length as above.

Anthropometric Traits and Growth Process

Present study indicates that the children in each age categories from 6 years to 10 years do not show significant differences between the sexes in respect of linear anthropometric measurements. However, in respect of height, weight and sitting height the males of 6 years and 7 years have slightly higher values than the females counterpart of that age categories ('t' test of significance shows $P \geq 0.05$). Regarding these traits, children from 8 years to 10 years do now show sex differences (Table 3). Further in respect of skin fold thickness at tricepts, subscapular and biceps, females in each age categories have slightly higher values than their males counterpart as the 't' values are either significant or almost significant at 5% level of probability. This is because of the fact that the females have more subcutaneous fat than their male counterpart. This has also been reported by Tanner (1962) among the British population.

The studies of correlations, i.e., relationship between anthropometric characters among the adult human individuals were undertaken by Pearson (1898,1933) and Pearson and Lee (1903), who reported that

Table 3

Mean (± S.E.) of the Anthropometric Measurements of Oraon Children by Age and Sex

Sex/Age	Total No. Surveyed	Height (cm.)	Weight (Kg.)	Sitting Height (cm)	Bi-acron Diameter (cm)	Bi-iliocrist diameter (cm)	Skinfold thickness at Triceps (mm)	Subscapular (mm)	Biceps (mm)
Male									
6 Yrs	42	112.75	17.88	59.26	23.89	17.21	5.14	4.8	4.45
		(-0.82)	(-0.34)	(-0.46)	(-0.24)	(-0.81)	(-0.17)	(-0.16)	(-0.17)
7 Yrs.	53	122.25	21.43	63.25	25.8	18.28	4.83	4.81	4.41
		(-0.68)	(-0.34)	(-0.46)	(-0.18)	(-0.16)	(-0.16)	(-0.15)	(-0.2)
8 Yrs.	54	128.25	23.58	65.79	26.93	18.84	4.94	4.82	4.32
		(-0.62)	(-0.3)	(-0.41)	(-0.19)	(-0.14)	(-0.26)	(-0.14)	(-0.16)
9 Yrs.	32	134.36	26.86	68.59	27.98	20.14	5.39	5.42	4.4
		(-0.8)	(-0.41)	(-0.26)	(-0.19)	(-0.12)	(-0.26)	(-0.19)	(-0.22)
10 Yrs.	32	140.12	30.2	71.65	29.33	20.85	4.95	4.93	4.09
		(-1.45)	(-0.95)	(-0.95)	(-0.36)	(-0.28)	(-0.19)	(-0.2)	(-0.21)
Female									
6 Yrs.	34	110.11	16.56	57.34	23.13	16.71	5.86	5.09	4.98
		(-0.75)	(-0.37)	(-0.5)	(-0.23)	(-0.21)	(-0.22)	(-0.21)	(-0.19)
7 Yrs.	50	120.58	20.37	61.69	25.3	18.25	5.83	5.3	4.99
		(-0.6)	(-0.3)	(-0.5)	(-0.34)	(-0.15)	(-0.2)	(-0.18)	(-0.19)
8 Yrs.	52	128.2	23.3	65.59	26.77	19.11	5.59	5.11	4.58
		(-0.62)	(-0.41)	(-0.53)	(-0.25)	(-0.18)	(-0.17)	(-0.16)	(-0.16)
9 Yrs.	30	134.95	26.77	68.49	28.07	19.93	5.94	5.8	5.25
		(-0.73)	(-0.49)	(-0.57)	(-0.22)	(-0.22)	(-0.22)	(-0.27)	(-0.25)
10 Yrs.	40	140.23	31.31	71.69	29.39	21.1	6.67	6.97	5.06
		(-0.95)	(-0.8)	(-0.61)	(-0.31)	(-0.22)	(-0.26)	(-0.67)	(-0.26)

Figures in parenthesis are S.E. (Standard Error)
Bi-acrom. Diameter = biacromial diameter; Bi-illocrist diameter = bi-illiocristal diameter, diameter and breadth convey the same meaning here.

relationship seemed to exist among certain anthropometric characters. In India such studies among the adult human individuals were carried out by Mahalanobis (1940), Mahalanobis and Bose (1941), and Mahalanobis *et. al* (1949) who also found some significant correlations among certain anthropometric characters. They found the values of correlation coefficient (r) to range between + 0.0438 (nasal breadth and nasal length) and + 0.6862 (nasal index and upper facial height) in the U.P. anthropometric survey data. Genoves (1967) found significant correlations between the measurements of various long bones and stature among the Meso-Americans. However the nature and degree of relationships among certain somatometric traits other than head and face measurements depend on the body physique (somatotype) and the climatic condition (Roberts, 1978). In the present report it has been attempted to find out the correlations between height and weight, height and sitting height, biacromial breadth and bi-iliocristal breadth, and between skin fold thickness at triceps and skin fold thickness at subscapular region. The correlation coefficient (*r*) values between the aforesaid mentioned anthropometric characters have been shown in Table 4. The table suggests that among the Oraon growing children there exists strong and positive correlations between the aforesaid mentioned anthropometric traits, and the value of '*r*' ranges from + 0.62 (between skin fold thickness at triceps and skin fold thickness at subscapuler) among the females to + 0.98 (between height and weight) among the males. Further the values of the coefficient of correlations (*r*) are much higher in the males than in the females. In both males and females weight, height, biacromial breadth and skin fold thickness at triceps respectively are linearly related to height, sitting height, bi-iliocristal breadth and skin fold thickness at subscapular region as mentioned in the table. However in the females the skin fold thickness at triceps is not linearly correlated with skin fold thickness at subscapular area though the relationship is statistically significant at 5% level of probability. Existence of significant relationship between all these anthropometric traits in these growing children can be suggested to be due to the fact that all these anthropometric traits are equally involved in the growth process.

Table 4

Correlations Between Some Anthropometric Traits in the Oraon Children

Pair	*Value of r* *Male*	*Value of r* *Female*
Weight and Stature	+0.98*+	+0.91*+
Height (stature) and Sitting Height	+0.97*+	+0.86*+
Biacromial diameter and Bi-iliocristal diameter	+0.97*+	+0.79*+
Triceps skinfold thickness and subscapular skinfold thickness	+0.89*+	+0.62*+

* Significant at 5% level of probability

* Relationship between traits is linear.

Mean values of weight, height (stature), sitting height, bi-acromial diameter, bi-iliocristal diameter, and of skin fold thicknesses at triceps, sub scapular and biceps are given in Table 3. The table shows that with the increase of age in both the sexes, there are increases in the mean values of weight, height, sitting height, biacromial diameter and bi-iliocristal diameter. However in case of mean values of skin fold thickness of triceps, biceps and subscapular region there seem to be no increase or decrease with age. However only in the females, the mean value of skin fold thickness at triceps and subscapular region seem to increase gradually from 9 years onward.

The present study indicates that among the Oraon males (aged 6 years to 10 years), the weight and standing height (stature) of the individuals are positively, linearly and highly correlated with their age (r = + 0.78). However in the Oraon females, the weight, standing height (stature) and sitting height are linearly and highly correlated with the age (r = + 0.79). Though the other anthropometric traits (sitting height, biacromial diameter and bi-iliocristal diameter in males and biacromial diameter and bi-iliocristal diameter in females) are significantly correlated with the age of the individuals, are not linearly related with the age. Non linear relationship between age and sitting height; between age and biacromial diameter; and between age and bi-iliocristal diameter can be suggested to be due to the variation among individuals in growth pattern in respect of these characters. The correlation coefficient values between age and various anthropometric traits. In fact, among the females skin fold thickness at the subscapular region is to some extent influenced by the growth processes as the correlation coefficient value is highly significant at 5% level of probability (r = +0.39).

Distance curves of growth in stature (height), weight, sitting height, biacromial diameter and bi-iliocristal diameter of the average Oraon children aged 6 to 10 years by sex are given in Figure 1. It is apparent from that the distance curves of growth in stature, sitting height and biacromial breadth are similar and overlap each other from 8 years onward, however before 8 years the males have slightly higher mean value than those of their female counterpart. Whereas in respect of weight and bi-iliocristal breadth there are slight differences between the distance curves of the males and the females.

Growth velocity measured in terms of annual increment in the mean values (i.e. gain in the mean values per year) for height, weight, sitting height, bi-acromial diameter and bi-iliocristal breadth have also been noted among the Oraon children from 6 years to 10 years. Velocity curves (or velocity growth curves) thus obtained for these anthropometric traits have been given in Figures 2. From the velocity growth curves, it is apparent that there are no much differences in respect of rate of gain per year in height, sitting height and biacromial diameter. However there is sudden spurt (abrupt increase) in the rate of gain (per year) in weight and bi-iliocristal diameter in the female children from 9 years onward. This can be explained from the point of view that such an increase in female children is to make way for the adolescent growth processes. In females adolescent growth starts earlier than the males.

The subcutaneous fat layer measured in term of skin fold thickness has also curve of its own and somewhat complicated one. The distance and velocity curves of skin fold thickness taken at the triceps, subscapular and biceps region have been shown in Figures 1 and 4. As mentioned earlier, in the females skin fold thicknesses at triceps and subscapular region is involved in the growth process as skinfold thickness at triceps and subscapular region is significantly correlated with the age. In females growth velocity curve in respect of skinfold thickness at triceps and subscapular area shows an abrupt spurt in the rate of gain per year from 8 years onward perhaps to make way for the adolescent growth processes. Since in the males skinfold thicknesses are not involved in the growth process as skin fold thicknesses are not correlated with the age of the individual. It would be meaningless to interpret the distance growth curve and velocity curves for skin fold thicknesses in the Oraon males.

Dental Pattern

Eruptions of deciduous dentition and permanent dentition take place in all normal human individuals from some months after birth to maturity (and in many cases even after maturity) along with growth and development process. By 30 months (from birth) all the deciduous teeth appear in the human individuals. Thus all the children above 30 months will show a complete set of deciduous teeth, thereafter(after sometime) the deciduous teeth start shedding off just at the time of formation of permanent teeth. By six years (6 years) onward some permanent teeth become visible. Eruption of a permanent tooth, begins just after the completion of enamel formation which remains embedded in the mandibular or the maxillary gum just two to three years before the tooth become visible by the naked eye. Hence the best way to study the eruptions of permanent teeth(or tooth) in the growing children from three years onward is by X-ray radiography. However, this has not been done in the present study. The eruption of permanent teeth is to a greater extent is genetically controlled and less effected by environment. In the present study, permanent first molars had been reported among 56.40% of the Oraon children of 6 years of age and among cent per cent of the children in each of the other age categories; central incisors had been noticed among 41.25% of the children of 6 years, among 89.50% of the children of 7 years and among cent per cent children of each of the other age categories; lateral lower incisors were seen among 43.50% of children of 7 years, among 89.50% of the children of 8 years, and cent per cent children of each of the other age categories; lateral upper incisors had been reported among 11.00% of the children of seven years, among 38.00% children of 8 years, among 96.50% children of 9 years and cent per cent children in 10 years age categories; first premolars had been reported among 63.00% of the children of 10 years; lower canines had been reported among 43.26% children of 10 years age group. Dental caries either in a tooth or some teeth had been reported among 68.50% of the Oraon children understudy.

Table 5
Correlations Between Age and Various Anthropometric Measurements in the Oraon Children

Age	*Value of r* *Male*	*Value of r* *Female*
Weight	+0.79*+	+0.84*+
Stature (Standing height)	+0.85*+	+0.90*+
Sitting height	+0.74*+	+0.80*+
Biacromial diameter	+0.75*	+0.73*
Bi-iliocristal diameter	+0.72*	+0.75*
Skinfold thickness at triceps	-0.02 NS	+0.18*
Skinfold thickness at Subscapular	+0.11 NS	+0.39*
Skinfold thickness at Biceps	-0.07 NS	+0.04 NS

NS = r-value not significant at 5% level of P.
* = r-value significant at 5% level of P.
+ = Relationship is linear.

Nutritional Anthropometry and General Health Condition

Anthropometric traits like stature and weight have been used in assessing the nutritional status of the children (Bolzan *et. al,* 1999; Frisancho, 1990, Naidu and Rao, 1994; Jelliffe, 1966). In the present study, Gomez classification as proposed by Vishveshwar Rao (1980) using NCHS standards for age and sex was followed. The classification taken into consideration that the person who is undernourished will have a weight deficit. Using the Vishveshwar Rao's classification using the reference standards for age and sex it has been reported that about 26% of the Oraon children (both male and female separately) come under malnourished group; of which about 78% (in both the sex) of the children are of mild type (Grade I). About 74% of the Oraon children are found to be normal without malnutrition. The nutritional status of Oraon children basing on Vishveshwar Rao's (1980) classification is given in the Table 6. Further using the data on height, Vishveshwar Rao's classification basing on NCHS standards for age and sex was done on the Oraon children and has been shown in the Table 7. The classification indicates the children who are below the height expected for their age have retarded growth. The Table 7 suggests that about 6% of the Oraon children have mild retarded growth in height whereas majority of the Oraon children(about 94%) have normal growth in height.

Table 6
Nutritional Status of the Oraon Children Based on Vishveshwar Rao's (1980) Classification Using NCHS Standard for Age and Sex in Respect of Weight

Sex	Total No. Surveyed	Normal	Malnutrition			
			Grade-I	Grade-II	Grade-III	Grade-IV
Male	213	157	43	13		
	%	73.71	20.19	6.1		
Female	206	152	43	11		
	%	73.79	20.87	5.34		
Total	419	309	86	24		
	%	73.75	20.52	5.73		

Table 7
Assessment of Normal Growth in Height (Stature) of the Oraon Children Based on Nutritional Vishveshwar Rao's (1980) Clasification Using NCHS Standard for Age and Sex in Respect of Height (Stature)

Sex	Total Number	Normal	Mild Retardation	Poor
Male	213	199	14	
%		93.43	6.57	
Female	206	193	13	
%		93.69	6.31	
Total	419	392	27	
%		93.56	6.44	

Body mass index or BMI = weight in kg./height^2 in metres) is often used as proxy measure for body fatness because it is correlated with body mass and percentage of body fat in general population. Hence, body mass index (BMI) has been used as a measure of nutritional status in certain populations. The mean body mass index(BMI) in the Oraon children by age and sex are as follows: *MALE* ; 14.00 (6 years), 14.27(7 years), 14.30 (8 years), 14.84 (9 years), 15.24(10 years); *FEMALE*: 13.63 (6 years), 13.99 (7 years), 14.14. (8 years), 14.677 (9 years), 15.85 (10 years). Thus, body mass index (BMI) in the Oraon of each age and sex categories is much lower than those in the Argentinian children for that age and sex categories studied by Bolzan *et al* (1999). However, from this we cannot claim that nutritional status of the Oraon children are much lower than those of the Argentinian children because of the fact that the BMI of the adult as well as of the growing children is to a significant extent is genetically controlled (Moll *et. al,* 1991 ; Price *et. al* 1990; Stunkard *et. al,* 1990; Katzmarzyk *et. al,* 1999). Katzmarzyk *et. al* (1999) suggested that there are strong influences of ethnicity, genetic and geoclimatic factors in determining the BMI of growing children in a population. Further, BMI is significantly correlated with the age of individuals (r = + 0.54 for male and r = + 0.48 for female) in this population.

Thus, it can be seen that using nutritional Vishveshwar Rao's (1980) classification basing on NCHS standards for age and sex, Oraon children of Nazat area (Sundarban area) are much better off than the other tribal children and other non tribal children from other rural area of India as the frequency of Malnourished (including retarded in respect of growth in height) children is much lower. Bhattacharya *et. al* (1994) reported that Oraons of the Nazat (present study area) are in a state of adverse nutritional situation. Bhattacharya *et. al* (1994) report on inadequacy of food and nutrients intake was based on some anthropometric characters(with Indices) like body-weight, weight-height index and the skin fold thicknesses of the adult Oraons individuals, and on the quantitative analysis of nutritive values of the consumed food items. Despite this state of adverse nutritional situation in the adult individuals, the growing Oraon children in the present study do not show or show lesser degree of malnutrition; as in the Oraon children of 6 years to 10 years the body weight is strongly and linearly correlated with the age so also the BMI is significantly correlated with the age in addition to Vishveshwar Rao's method of classification on their nutritional status. This is because the present Oraon children are better fed than their adult counterpart studied 10 years ago. Bhattacharya *et. al* (1994) conducted their studies 10 years ago. Now due to rampant brackish water fisheries, a large quantity of protein diet in the form of fishes are easily available to them. Further free cereals like rice and pulses are given to them by the government through school authorities.

Angular stomatitis had been reported among 2.5% of the Oraon male children and among 1.75% among Oraon female children. Night blindness was reported among 1.8% of the female children and about 0.57% among the male children. About 0.57% of the male children had yellowish teeth and none of the female children showed yellowish teeth.

Is there any Effect on Parity, Family Income and Literacy of the Mothers on the Anthropometric Traits of the Growing Oraon Children

Mean values of the anthropometric traits by parity of the Oraon male children of different age groups as well as of the Oraon female children of different age groups are given in Table 8 and 9. However, statistical tests performed according to the standard method suggest that there is no significant differences between the children of different parities at different age groups (except among the children of six years males in some cases) in respect of mean values of weight, stature, sitting height, biacromial diameter and bi-iliocristal diameter. Such a non-significance effect of parity or birth order on the mean anthropometric values of the Oraon children can be attributed to the inadequate or small sample size.

Anthropometric dimensions of the growing Oraon children by their mothers' literacy status have been given in Tables 10 and 11. The tables

Table 8

Mean Values and S.D. of Some Anthropometric Traits by Parity of the Oraon Male Children of Different Age Groups

Age/ Parity	No.	Weight (kg)		Height (in cm)		Sitting Height (in cm)		Biacromial diameter (in cm)		Bi-illiocristal diameter (in cm)	
		Mean	S.D.	Mean	S.D.	Mean	S.D.	Mean	S.D.	Mean	S.D.
6 Years											
1st Parity	13	17.5	2.08	111.7	5.29	58.66	2.11	23.23	1.12	16.74	1.02
2nd Parity	16	18.19	1.94	113.28	4.02	59.67	2.05	23.73	1.31	17.16	1.23
3rd Parity	7	17.57	2.83	113.57	5.96	60.17	3.72	24.4	1.47	17.36	1.04
4th & more	6	18.25	2.16	112.65	6.96	58.42	5.42	25.12	1.96	18.2	0.32
7 Years											
1st Parity	14	19.55	2.42	117.59	4.71	60.91	3.25	24.87	1.29	17.75	1.01
2nd Parity	13	22.65	1.8	125.24	2.31	64.64	3.64	26.3	0.94	18.55	1.09
3rd Parity	13	22.61	2	123.55	4.14	64.27	2.00	26.39	1.02	18.87	1.46
4th & more	13	21.04	2.24	122.99	4.18	63.28	2.69	25.69	1.45	18.01	0.75
8 Years											
1st Parity	14	23.00	2.49	127.76	5.9	64.56	4.05	26.43	1.71	18.88	1.42
2nd Parity	15	23.33	1.73	128.19	3.2	65.77	2.26	27.00	1.21	18.87	0.88
3rd Parity	11	24.23	1.56	129.35	3.2	66.62	1.67	27.24	1.08	18.9	0.67
4th & more	14	23.93	2.59	128.69	4.94	66.37	3.06	27.1	1.31	18.73	0.8
9 Years											
1st Parity	11	27.82	1.54	135.87	3.02	68.88	3.85	28.26	1.32	20.41	0.65
2nd Parity	14	26.36	2.45	133.95	4.16	68.58	1.93	27.63	0.64	19.99	0.77
3rd Parity	4	25.87	1.43	134.08	4.46	68.07	2.63	28.27	1.05	19.97	0.36
4th & more	3	27.00	3.56	131.13	7.53	68.13	2.98	28.2	1.31	20.03	0.46
10 Years											
1st Parity	14	29.29	4.76	139.29	8.2	71.16	6.13	28.55	1.69	20.5	1.69
2nd Parity	7	32.86	4.25	143.34	5.7	72.47	4.29	30.04	1.89	21.37	1.11
3rd Parity	3	32.00	6.38	142.07	12.62	72.17	5.58	29.6	3.27	21.17	0.39
4th & more	8	28.81	5.35	138.03	6.82	71.56	4.63	28.9	1.48	20.54	1.08

Table 9

Mean Values of Some Anthropometric Traits by Parity of the Oraon Female Children of Different Age Groups

Age/ Parity	No.	Weight (kg)		Height (in cm)		Sitting Height (in cm)		Biacromial diameter (in cm)		Bi-illiocristal diameter (in cm)	
		Mean	S.D.	Mean	S.D.	Mean	S.D.	Mean	S.D.	Mean	S.D.
6 Years											
1st Parity	7	17.43	2.48	111.89	3.09	58.34	2.28	22.87	1.3	16.9	0.6
2nd Parity	11	16.53	2.02	109.51	4.93	58.18	2.68	23.00	1.41	16.79	1.72
3rd Parity	3	14.83	0.24	106.83	4.00	56.5	0.85	23.17	2.13	16.57	1.03
4th & more	13	16.54	1.98	110.41	3.98	56.28	3.28	23.53	0.87	16.58	1.02
7 Years											
1st Parity	12	20.08	2.19	120.04	3.67	61.4	4.22	25.06	1.54	17.8	0.98
2nd Parity	11	20.23	2.66	119.56	5.37	59.75	3.6	24.3	2.25	18.04	0.93
3rd Parity	13	20.00	1.62	121.59	4.00	62.2	2.93	24.54	4.57	18.39	0.84
4th & more	14	21.07	1.67	121.19	3.75	62.98	2.51	25.9	1.08	18.52	1.05
8 Years											
1st Parity	13	22.12	2.4	126.49	3.11	65.66	2.62	26.31	1.61	18.85	1.36
2nd Parity	13	23.31	3.47	128.27	5.58	65.62	4.73	27.12	1.74	19.71	1.28
3rd Parity	15	23.23	3.09	128.2	4.85	64.29	4.48	26.55	1.39	18.8	1.18
4th & more	11	24.77	1.81	130.14	2.44	67.24	1.64	27.56	1.4	19.14	1.02
9 Years											
1st Parity	9	25.83	2.3	135.13	3.55	67.78	2.93	28.58	1.35	19.69	1.27
2nd Parity	6	27.08	2.98	134.02	5.22	68.68	4.43	27.32	1.21	20.02	1.01
3rd Parity	10	26.8	2.4	134.74	3.15	67.98	2.26	28.04	1.06	19.71	1.21
4th & more	5	28.00	3.03	135.94	4.41	68.54	2.74	28.14	1.16	20.74	0.71
10 Years											
1st Parity	7	29.21	5.29	137.73	4.05	70.9	2.09	28.00	1.87	20.00	0.88
2nd Parity	11	31.82	5.77	141.28	5.86	71.77	3.37	29.73	1.98	21.31	1.63
3rd Parity	8	31.44	5.42	139.84	7.9	71.92	5.17	29.21	1.77	21.54	1.39
4th & more	14	31.89	3.59	140.86	5.34	71.87	3.9	29.93	1.77	21.24	1.16

Table 10
Anthropometric Diamensions of the Male Oraon Children by Age and by Mother's Literacy Status

Age of the children and literacy status of the mother		*Weight (kg)*		*Height (in cm)*		*Sitting Height (in cm)*		*Biacromial diameter (in cm)*		*Bi-illiocristal diameter (in cm)*	
	No.	*Mean*	*S.D.*	*Mean*	*S.D.*	*Mean*	*S.D.*	*Mean*	*S.D.*	*Mean*	*S.D.*
6 Years											
Mother Literate	9	16.61	1.59	110.5	4.81	58.89	2.83	23.00	0.87	16.82	1.08
Mother Illiterate	31	18.24	2.3	113.5	5.42	59.31	3.31	24.1	1.63	17.22	1.1
7 Years											
Mother Literate	10	20.00	2.59	118.6	4.72	61.33	3.61	24.6	1.08	17.76	1.08
Mother Illiterate	41	21.68	2.33	122.9	4.45	63.59	3.03	26.1	1.25	18.4	1.2
8 Years											
Mother Literate	8	23.19	1.3	127.1	3.08	65.41	1.79	26.6	1.53	18.56	1.27
Mother Illiterate	46	23.65	2.33	128.5	4.72	65.86	3.21	27.00	1.36	18.89	0.94
9 Years											
Mother Literate	6	26.08	2.52	132.1	3.42	68.02	1.72	27.6	1.32	20.18	0.68
Mother Illiterate	25	26.96	2.26	134.9	4.66	68.66	3.17	28.1	1.03	20.1	0.7
10 Years											
Mother Literate	6	28.5	2.36	137.8	5.62	70.62	3.15	28.3	1.73	20.72	1.21
Mother Illiterate	26	30.6	5.79	140.7	8.58	71.65	6.00	29.6	2.01	20.88	1.64

Table 11
Anthropometric Dimensions of the Female Oraon Children by Age and by Mothers' Literacy Status

Age of the children and literacy status of the mother		*Weight (kg)*		*Height (in cm)*		*Sitting Height (in cm)*		*Biacromial diameter (in cm)*		*Bi-illiocristal diameter (in cm)*	
	No.	*Mean*	*S.D.*	*Mean*	*S.D.*	*Mean*	*S.D.*	*Mean*	*S.D.*	*Mean*	*S.D.*
6 Years											
Mother Literate	9	17.61	1.96	110.7	4.71	58.23	1.98	23.00	0.99	16.6	0.79
Mother Illiterate	24	16.04	2.18	110.0	4.3	57.63	2.43	23.1	1.36	16.71	1.37
7 Years											
Mother Literate	10	20.3	2.44	120.1	4.35	60.49	4.00	24.4	2.4	18.68	1.1
Mother Illiterate	39	20.35	2.00	120.6	4.27	61.77	3.31	25.5	2.36	18.11	0.99
8 Years											
Mother Literate	11	23.36	3.15	128.2	3.79	65.44	4.16	26.4	2.45	19.02	1.72
Mother Illiterate	40	23.26	2.91	128.3	4.6	65.74	3.74	26.9	1.59	19.1	1.12
9 Years											
Mother Literate	4	26.38	4.35	134.6	4.29	67.48	3.28	28.5	0.92	19.78	1.07
Mother Illiterate	26	26.81	2.37	135.0	3.98	68.64	3.11	28.00	1.31	19.96	1.2
10 Years											
Mother Literate	5	33.7	5.8	141.4	5.95	73.26	3.18	29.9	1.96	20.9	1.3
Mother Illiterate	35	30.97	4.83	140.1	6.03	71.46	3.86	29.3	2.09	21.13	1.42

Table 12

Anthropometric Dimensions of the Male Oraon Children by Annual Per Capita Income of the Families to which the Children Belong

Age group and Annual per capita income in the family		*Weight (kg)*		*Height (in cm)*		*Sitting Height (in cm)*		*Biacromial diameter (in cm)*		*Bi-illiocristal diameter (in cm)*	
	No.	*Mean*	*S.D.*	*Mean*	*S.D.*	*Mean*	*S.D.*	*Mean*	*S.D.*	*Mean*	*S.D.*
6 Years											
Less than Rs. 4000/-	34	17.78	2.31	112.8	5.53	58.99	3.38	23.81	1.66	17.16	1.2
Rs. 4001/- to Rs. 8000/-	8	18.25	1.71	112.55	4.24	60.4	1.31	24.2	0.71	17.46	0.82
More than Rs. 8000/-											
7 Years											
Less than Rs. 4000/-	29	21.87	2.37	123.45	4.66	63.83	2.92	26.03	1.3	18.52	1.27
Rs. 4001/- to Rs. 8000/-	19	20.55	2.64	120.24	5.24	62.09	3.88	25.47	1.44	17.92	1.04
More than Rs. 8000/-	5	22.2	1.6	122.88	1.17	64.3	1.17	25.7	0.88	18.26	0.89
8 Years											
Less than Rs. 4000/-	42	23.55	2.31	128.3	4.45	65.78	3.18	26.85	1.36	18.84	0.94
Rs. 4001/- to Rs.8000/-	10	23.85	1.96	128.52	5.1	65.9	2.74	27.36	1.43	18.72	0.98
More than Rs. 8000/-	2	22.75	0.25	126.00	1.9	65.45	0.25	26.85	1.55	19.55	1.75
9 Years											
Less than Rs. 4000/-	23	26.98	2.41	134.1	4.68	68.49	3.34	27.98	1.21	20.1	0.65
Rs. 4001/- to Rs. 8000/-	9	26.56	2.1	135.02	3.97	68.82	1.3	27.99	0.66	20.23	0.82
More than Rs. 8000/-											
10 Years											
Less than Rs. 4000/-	20	29.88	5.74	140.94	8.78	71.79	5.84	29.68	2.11	20.8	1.51
Rs. 4001/- to Rs. 8000/-	10	29.00	3.92	137.07	5.92	70.45	3.21	28.49	1.64	20.98	1.76
More than Rs. 8000/-	2	35.00	7.00	147.25	4.85	76.25	6.65	30.35	1.55	20.75	1.15

Table 13

Anthropometric Dimensions of the Female Oraon Children by Annual Per Capita Income of the Families to which the Children Belong

Age group and Annual per capita income in the family		*Weight (kg)*		*Height (in cm)*		*Sitting Height (in cm)*		*Biacromial diameter (in cm)*		*Bi-illiocristal diameter (in cm)*	
	No.	*Mean*	*S.D.*	*Mean*	*S.D.*	*Mean*	*S.D.*	*Mean*	*S.D.*	*Mean*	*S.D.*
6 Years											
Less than Rs. 4000/-	28	16.68	2.17	110.62	4.19	57.66	2.82	23.31	1.31	16.82	1.27
Rs. 4001/- to Rs. 8000/-	3	16.5	2.68	108.53	4.77	56.33	2.34	21.93	0.19	16.07	1.03
More than Rs. 8000/-	3	15.5	0.41	106.23	3.85	57.33	2.85	22.63	0.49	16.3	0.85
7 Years											
Less than Rs. 4000/-	36	20.24	2.16	120.31	4.06	61.55	3.36	25.24	2.66	18.15	0.99
Rs. 4001/- to Rs. 8000/-	11	20.32	1.92	120.96	5.26	61.1	3.92	25.26	1.54	18.39	1.05
More than Rs. 8000/-	3	22.17	0.24	122.33	0.61	65.63	0.42	26.2	0.57	18.93	1.37
8 Years											
Less than Rs. 4000/-	39	23.47	3.17	128.35	4.95	65.55	3.92	26.81	1.64	19.21	1.31
Rs. 4001/- to Rs. 8000/-	8	22.69	2.49	127.7	2.74	65.48	4.51	26.83	2.74	18.71	1.42
More than Rs. 8000/-	5	22.8	0.93	127.84	0.99	66.08	0.91	26.36	0.85	18.96	0.3
9 Years											
Less than Rs. 4000/-	24	26.4	2.59	134.68	4.09	68.52	3.33	28.03	1.4	19.9	1.25
Rs. 4001/- to Rs. 8000/-	5	28.1	2.91	135.4	3.54	68.12	2.51	28.28	0.51	20.4	0.49
More than Rs. 8000/-	1	29.00		138.1		69.6		28.2		18.5	
10 Years											
Less than Rs. 4000/-	25	30.9	5.28	140.69	6.15	71.62	4.1	29.08	2.07	21.18	1.51
Rs. 4001/- to Rs. 8000/-	12	31.79	4.87	139.19	5.87	71.74	3.2	29.94	1.57	21.06	1.23
More than Rs. 8000/-	3	29.83	5.17	140.43	5.12	72.03	3.82	29.77	2.1	20.67	1.16

and the statistical tests suggest that there is no influence of mothers' literacy status on their children's anthropometric dimensions or more specifically on the growth of the children(test of significance of difference of the means suggests $p > 0.05$). This finding can be attributed to inadequate data and small sample size. The anthropometric dimensions of the Oraon children by fathers' educational level has not been shown in this report because of the fact that child care i.e. nurturing of children(including school going children) is the duty of the mothers and womenfolks in this community, and the fathers or the menfolks spent less time (or no time at all) in child care. However the statistical test performed suggest that there are no significance differences between the children of literate fathers and those of illiterate fathers in respect of weight, height, bi-iliocristal diameter and biacromial diameter.

Anthropometric dimensions of the growing Oraon children were compared among themselves according to per capita income age wise and sex wise, i.e., compared among children of the families with per capita income below Rs. 4000/- annually, Rs. 4001/- to Rs. 8000/- annually, and above Rs. 8000/- annually (3 categories of families). Due to inadequate data and small sample sizes, no clear cut influences of family income on the anthropometric dimensions of the children have been reported in this community, as in many cases (i.e. many age groups) there are no significant differences between the economic categories in respect of means of the anthropometric traits (see Tables 12 and 13).

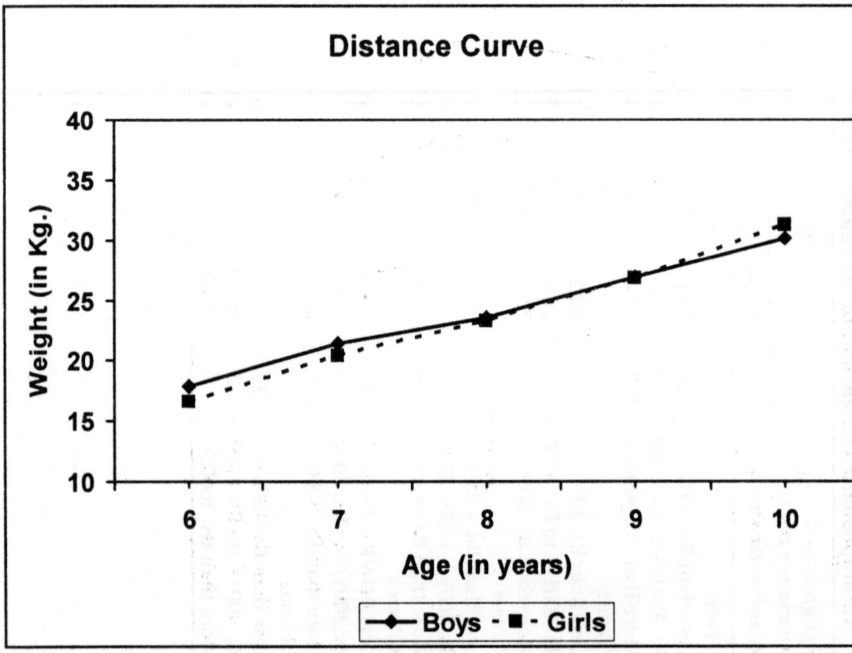

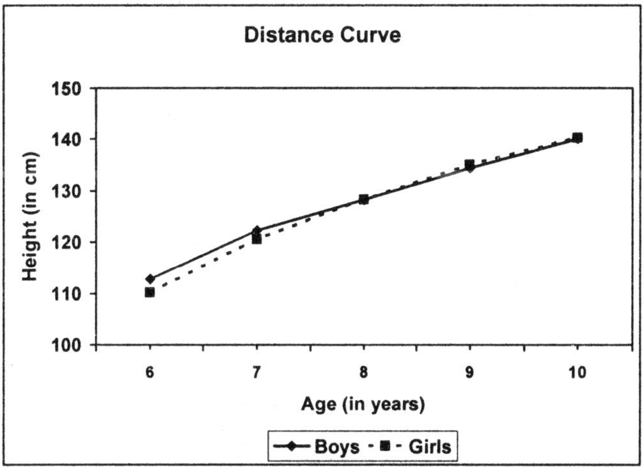
Distance Curve
Height (in cm)
150
140
130
120
110
100
6
7
8
9
10
Age (in years)
Boys
Girls

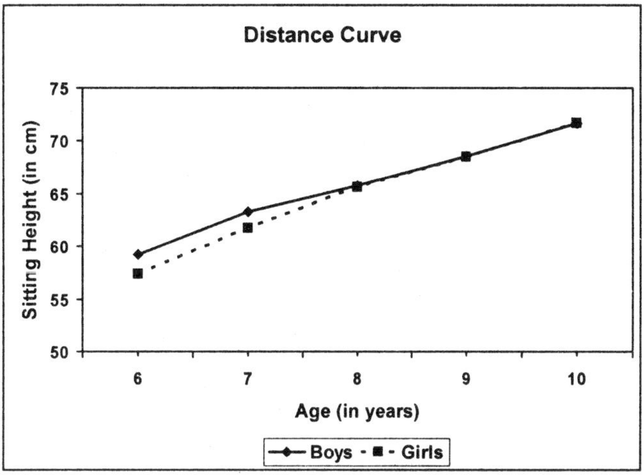
Distance Curve
Sitting Height (in cm)
75
70
65
60
55
50
6
7
8
9
10
Age (in years)
Boys
Girls

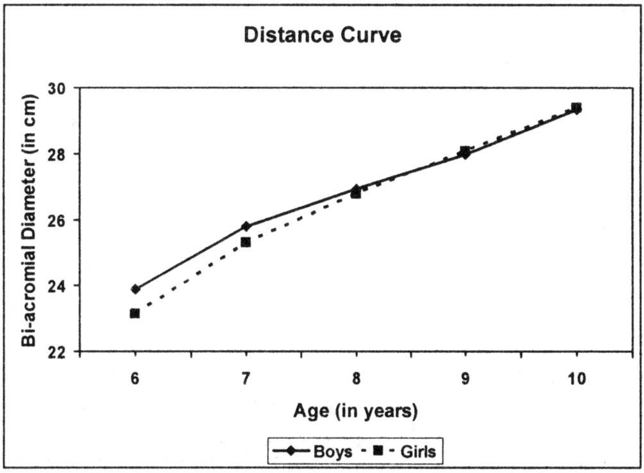
Distance Curve
Bi-acromial Diameter (in cm)
30
28
26
24
22
6
7
8
9
10
Age (in years)
Boys
Girls

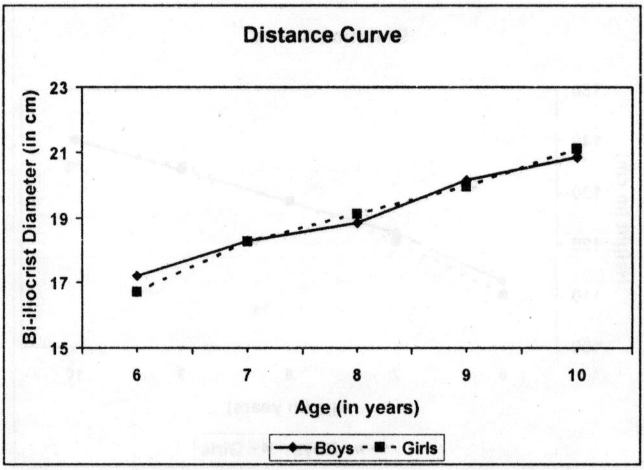
Distance Curve
Bi-iliocrist Diameter (in cm)
23
21
19
17
15
6
7
8
9
10
Age (in years)
Boys
Girls

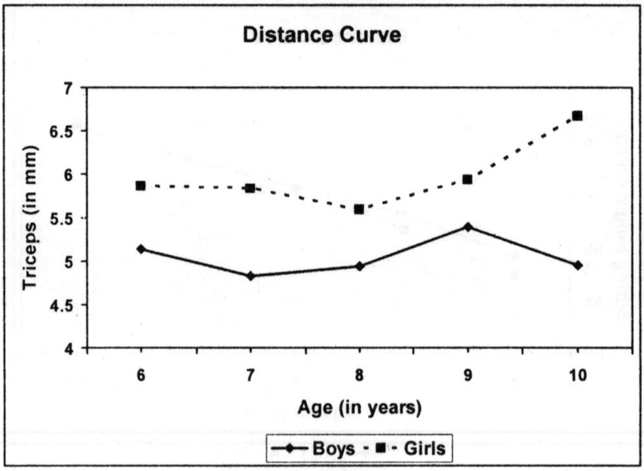
Distance Curve
Triceps (in mm)
7
6.5
6
5.5
5
4.5
4
6
7
8
9
10
Age (in years)
Boys
Girls

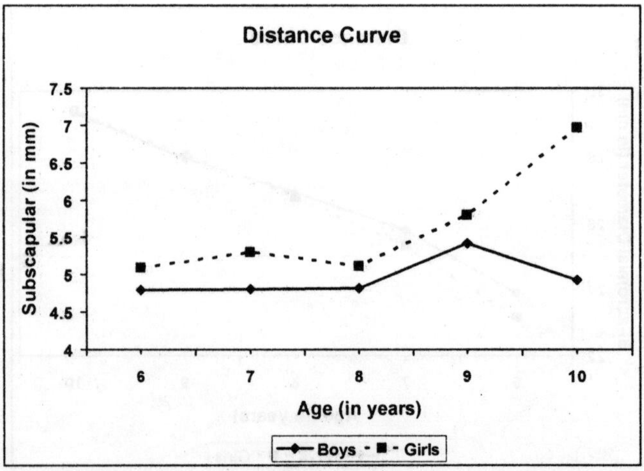
Distance Curve
Subscapular (in mm)
7.5
7
6.5
6
5.5
5
4.5
4
6
7
8
9
10
Age (in years)
Boys
Girls

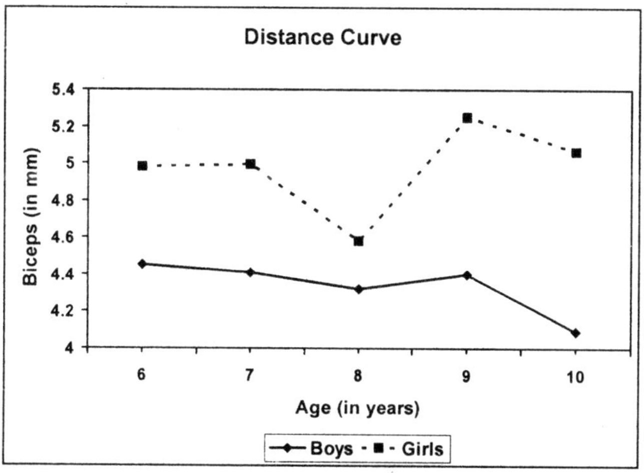

Figure 1: Distance Curve (growth curve) for the anthropometric traits

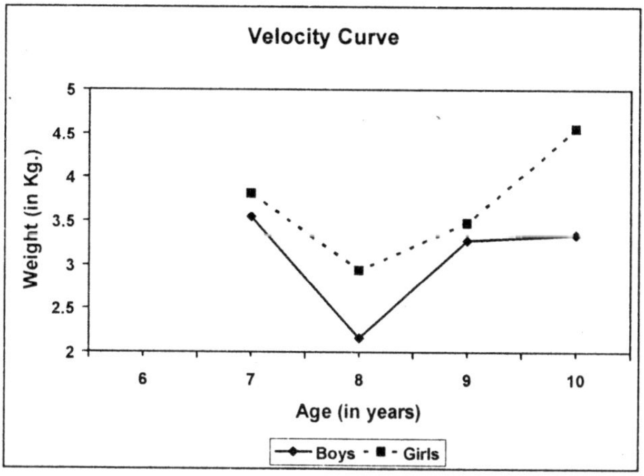

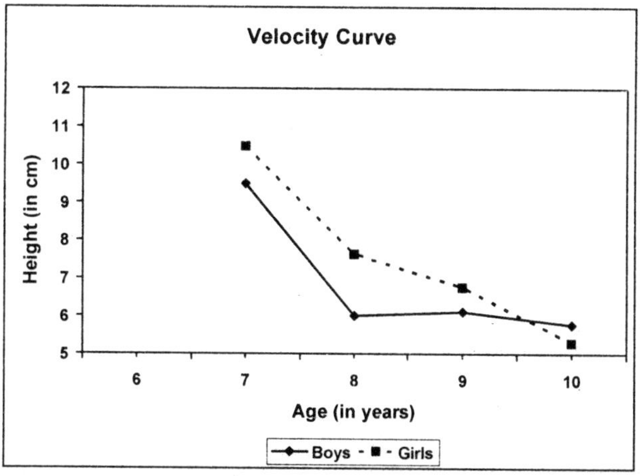

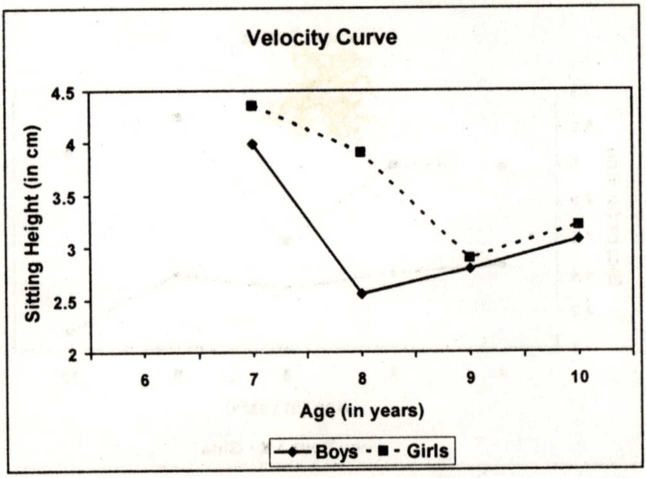
Velocity Curve
Sitting Height (in cm)
4.5
4
3.5
3
2.5
2
6
7
8
9
10
Age (in years)
Boys
Girls

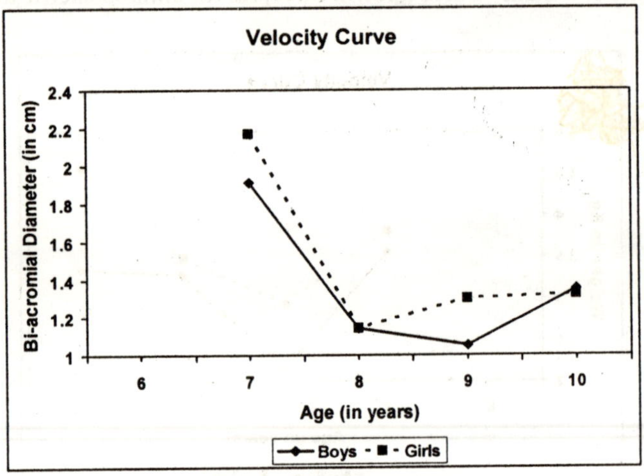
Velocity Curve
Bi-acromial Diameter (in cm)
2.4
2.2
2
1.8
1.6
1.4
1.2
1
6
7
8
9
10
Age (in years)
Boys
Girls

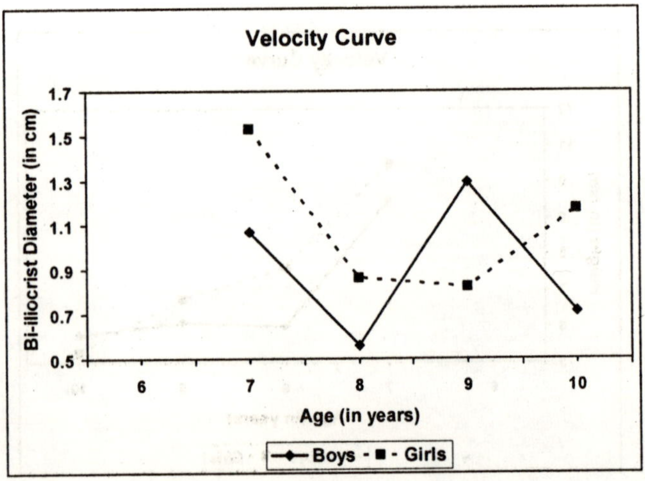
Velocity Curve
Bi-iliocrist Diameter (in cm)
1.7
1.5
1.3
1.1
0.9
0.7
0.5
6
7
8
9
10
Age (in years)
Boys
Girls

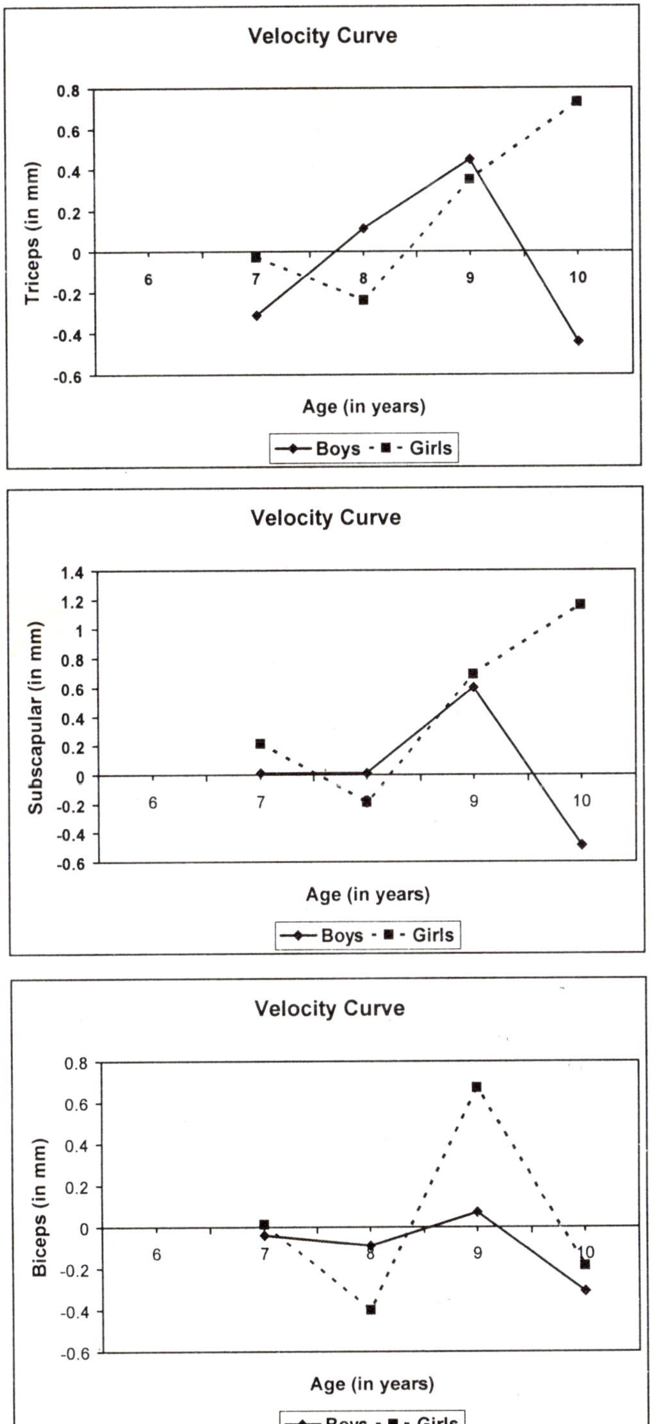

Figure 2: Velocity Curve for Weight, Stature and Sitting Height

References

Bhattacharya, K. K., S. Mondal, G. C. Ghosh (1994), Nutritional Status of the Oraon of Sundarban, West Bengal, *J. Anthrop. Surv. India*, 43: 31-66.

Bolzan, A., L. Guimarey, A. R. Erzancho (1999), Study of Growth in Rural School Children from Buenos Aires, Argentina using Upper Arm Muscle Area by Height and Other Anthropometric Dimensions of Body Composition, *Ann. Hum. Biol.*, 26:185-193.

Fisher, R.A. (1954), *Statistical Methods for Research Workers*. London: Oliver Boyd.

Frisancho, A. (1990), *Anthropometric Standards for the Assessment of Growth and Nutritional Status*. Ann. Arobor: The Univ. Michigan Press.

Genoves, S. (1967), Proportionality of the Long Bones and Their Relation to Stature among Meso-American, *Am.J. Phys. Anthrop.*, 26: 67-77.

Jeliffe, D. B. (1966), *The Assessment of the Nutritional Status of a Community*, Geneva: T.R.S. World Health Organisation.

Katzmarzyk, P. T., M. C. Mahaney, U. Blangero, Guck. Jing-Jong and R.M. Malina (1999), Potential Effects of Ethnicity in Genetic and Environmental Source of Variability in Stature, Mass and Body Mass of Children, *Hum. Biol.*, 71-977-987.

Mahalanobis, P.C. (1940), Anthropological observations on Anglo-Indian of Calcutta: Statistical measurements of seven characters. *Rec. Ind. Mus.* 23: 151-187.

Mahalanobis, P. C. and C. Bose (1941), Correlations Between Anthropometric Characters in Some Bengal Castes and Tribes, *Sankhya*, 5: 249-260.

Mahalanobis, P. C., D. N. Majumdar and C. R. Rao (1949), Anthropometric Survey of United Province, *Sankhya*, 9: 89-327.

Moll, P. P., T. L. Burn and R. M. Leauer (1991), The Genetic and Environmental Source of Body Mass Index Variability: The Masculine Ponderosity Family Study, *Am. J. Hum. Genet.*, 49: 1243 –1255.

Naidu, A. and N. Rao (1994), Body Mass Index: A Measure of Nutritional Status in Indian Populations, *European Journal of Clinical Nutrition*, 48: 131-140.

Pearson, K. (1898), Mathematical Contribution to the Theory of Evolution, V. On the Reconstruction of Stature of the Prehistoric Races. Philos. Trans. A. 192:169-244.

Pearson, K. and, A. Lee (1903), Preliminary Note in Interracial Characters and Their Correlation in Man, *Biometrika*, 2: 357-462.

Pearson, K. (1933), On the Relationships of Certain Characters in Man (males). *Ann. Eugen.*, 5:364–412.

Price, A. A., R. Ness, P. Laskerzewski (1990), Common Major Gene Inheritance of Extreme Over Weight, *Hum. Bio.*, 62 : 747–765.

Roy. S. C. (1915) (1984), *The Oraons of Chota Nagpur*, Ranchi: Man in India Office, p. 16.

Rao V. (1979), As Cited from *National Nutrition Monitoring Bureau: Report of the Year 1979*, Hyderabad: NIN, ICMR.

Stunkard, A. J. , J. R. Harris and E. L. Pedersen (1990), The Body Mass Index of Twins who have been Reared Apart, *New Engl. J. Med.*, 322: 1483–1487.

Subramanium, P. S. (1971), *Dravadian Verb. Morphology: A Comparative Study*. Dept. of Linguistics. Publication No. 24. Annamalai University Annamalainlger.

Tanner, J. M. (1962), Growth at Adolescence: With a General Consideration of the Effects of Heredity and Environmental Factors upon Growth and Maturation from Birth to Maturity (2nd edition). Oxford : Blackwell Scientific Publications.

Visweswara Rao, K. (1980), Efficiency of Anthropometric Indices for the Diagnosis of Malnutrition Courrier, 30,113.

4

CROSS SECTIONAL STUDY OF GROWTH AND DEVELOPMENT OF POUNDRAKSHTRIYA CHILDREN OF CANNING SUB-DIVISION, DISTRICT SOUTH 24 PARGANAS, W.B.

BHARATI DEVI & SHARMISTHA BHATTACHARYYA

The present study was undertaken among a scheduled caste of deltaic region of West Bengal, namely the Poundra Kshtriyas of Pods under the ambit of well designed ninth plan project "Growth and Development of Children: Bio-Cultural Perspectives" launched by Anthropological Survey of India. Their largest concentration is in the south 24 Parganas district. In south 24 Parganas again, Canning Block I is inhabited by six scheduled castes namely the Bagdis, Jeles, Kaoras, Namasudras, Rajbhanshis and the Pods. As per the records of the Block Development Office, they together constitute 53.6 per cent of the total population of the area, which is higher than the district figure of 34.4 per cent. Of the six groups just mentioned the proportion of the Poundrakshtriyas or Pods in the Block is 93 per cent. Canning Block-I was selected as the locale of the present study.

There are many views regarding the origin, relationship and distribution of the Pods. Bankim Chandra Chatterjee, the great Bengalee novelist, traced probable relationship of the Pods with the Pundras mentioned in the Mahabharata. He further considered them as one of the chief races distributed between Magadha and the sea. Hunter (1875) opined that the Pods were a low Sudra residents of 24 Parganas. He added that they were said to be the offspring of a Sunri father and a Napit mother. While Risley (1891) mentioned that the people were of uncertain origin but the educated members of the caste claimed a mixed decent from a Kayastha father and a Napit mother. Guha (1935) considered the Radhiya Brahmans, Dakshin Rarhiya Kayasthas and the Pods as representative of three sections of the Bengalee people of the Central Deltaic region. He, on the basis of physical characters noticed the Pods to be different from the Brahmans and Kayasthas of Bengal. Mahalanabis (cited by Roy 1402 BS) measured the genetical distance of the people. Mahendra Nath Karan (1335 BS), an insider of the caste, traced a glorious past of the people. He believed that the people were victimized and degraded wrongfully by the Brahmans. Nihar Ranjan Roy (1402 (BS) considered them as a member of the lower stratum of the Hindu Society. In a recent study Purnendu Ghosh (1406 BS) has opined that the Pods are one of the low caste of the Hindu society.

Whatever may be the conjectures or findings, the present social status of the caste is that of a scheduled one. They bear surnames like Mandal, Naskar, Sardar, Mirdha. Paik, Sanfui, Gayen, Baidya and so on.

The caste is endogamous. There are a number of gotras like Kashyap, Sandilya, Madhukulya etc. They prefer clan endogamy. Marriage is regulated by descent. Marriage within five ascending generations of the father and three ascending generations of the mother is avoided. They observe pollution at birth and death. A son observe 30 days of pollution at the death of either of his parents. But recently there is a trend to reduce the pollution period from 30 to 13 days by wearing a sacred thread that is offered by the priest during the shradh ceremony. The thread thus worn is neither hereditary nor obligatory afterwards.

They profess Hinduism and worship Hindu gods and goddesses like Lakshmi, Narayan, Kali, Shiva, Durga, Saraswati etc. Over and above, their religion shows as adoption of local or regional deities of the Sunderban like Banabibi, Bara Kachari etc. who are worshipped by them. Gods and goddesses like Panchananda and Shasthi are associated with child welfare.

Materials and Methods

Data were collected from Canning Block during November 1998 to February 1999. Altogether 347 children (176 boys and 171 girls) of 6-10 yrs. were measured anthropometrically using scientific instruments.

In all, nine absolute anthropometric measurements had been taken both in boys and girls. A standard anthropometer and a set of sliding and spreading calipers were used. Measurement was taken following Martin (1928). All linear measurements were taken in centimeters. The body weight was recorded in kologram with the help of a portable weighing machine. The circumference measurements were taken with a steel tape. For measuring the subcutaneous fat, Holten skinfold caliper was used. Each jaw of caliper measures 6 mm to the nearest 0.1 mm (Tanner, 1952). Falling of milk teeth and the eruption of various permanent teeth in both upper and lower jaw were noted. Clinical signs and types of nutrition deficiency signs of the Poundrakshtriya children, were also noted as per guideline.

Statistical calculation like mean, standard error (SE), standard deviation (SD), coefficient of variation (CV) along with their standard error were calculated for all measurements. T-test for sexual dimorphism, was also calculated. Graphs on distance and velocity curves and line of regression are drawn for some of the selected characters such as weight, stature, sitting height, bi-acromial breadth, bi-iliac breadth on age.

Besides, attention was paid on the dentition pattern of the children and clinical signs of nutritional deficiency, as well. Data on socio-cultural background with a bearing on the project were also collected. A section of the children were subjected to non-verbal psychological tests in order to assess the mental development of the children. Actual food intake of a section of the population for seven consecutive days was also recorded through programme for an understanding of the nutritional status of the people. Data on cultural perspectives were collected following traditional anthropological methods like structured schedule, case history, participant observation and interview.

Two-way processes were adopted while collecting data. Poundrakshtriya students of required age-range were picked up for measurement and observation at random with the assistance of local teachers from Malerdhar Free Primary School, Dighir Par Purbapara Free Primary School, Korakathi Junior Basic School and Rai Baghini Junior Basic School. Household census data was collected from the respective houses of the measured students.

Utmost care was taken in discerning the age, particularly of the children, as it is one of the vital and decisive factors in determining individual growth and development. Age of child was determined by respective original birth certificate (if available) and by putting the ego in a relative time frame against his/her junior or senior, as the case may be. The information was checked and rechecked from different elderly members of the family or neighbouring one.

Result and Discussion

With this brief note let the demographic situation be discussed in detail. As already stated the data center round 347 children of whom 176 are male and 171 female. Absolute numbers of male children in the ages between 6 to 10 years are 36,36,35,34 and 35 while the number of female children are 34,34,34,35 and 34 respectively.

These children belonged to 321 families scattered over six contiguous villages namely Malerdhar Dighir Par, Kumarshaw, Nikarighata, Korakathi and Hinchekhali within a radius of 10-12 kms from Canning Sadar.

There are 1725 individuals, of whom 847 are male and 874 are female, living in 321 families. Sex ratio of the studied sample is 1035 female per 1000 male.

The literacy rate of the children upto 5 years of age have been excluded from consideration for obvious reasons. Of the rest about 5 per cent are illiterate. Forty two per cent had the scope of primary schooling including the current children of 6-10 years of age group (Table 1). Education beyond primary level is confined among 23.65 per cent of the population of whom only 1.8 per cent has crossed the limit of the school. Only 0.7 per cent individuals are graduates. There is a master degree holder and an allopathic doctor in the population studied. Male female disparity is marked.

Usual age at marriage is 21-25 years for the male and 16-20 years for the female. Monogamy is the norm. Nuclear family is the predominant type of family (73.8%) (Table 2). Most of the families (77.2%) are of medium size (4-6 membered) (Table 3).

The people are mostly landless and they work as labourer. The proportion of agricultural or daily labour is 22.8 per cent and 28.9 per cent respectively. Only 5.2 per cent are engaged in agriculture. The type of occupation followed by the people are skilled labour (10.2%), taxi driver (0.5%), rickshaw van puller (7.6%), fishing (0.3 %), business (18.8% mostly petty), service (4.4%), carpenter (3%) and teacher (0.3%) etc. (Table 4).

30.2 per cent women are engaged as maid servant. The category of skilled labourer (like bidi rolling, ampoule making and batik printing) involves 46.5 per cent women (Table 5). Petty business (17.0%), fishing (0.6%), midwifery (1.3%) and agricultural labourer (2.5%) etc., are some of the salient type of women's economic involvement. Widows and deserted women come forward to earn for the sustenance of their family. And young adolescent and unmarried girls work to procure money for dowry and other related expenses for timely marriage.

Most of the families (69%) are not economically sound. Their annual income ranges between 5000/- to 25,000/- approximately.

Table 6 includes family size, monthly income and per capita income of the Poundrakshtriya family. It is seen from the table that mean number of family members varies between 2.2 to 2.6 whereas mean number of children are 2.9 to 3.3. All children included for the study belongs to family having an average monthly income between Rs. 1590.14 to Rs. 1885.46 and per capita income varies between Rs. 312.33 to 360.90 only.

Poor economic condition has a direct bearing with the standard of living of the people as well as nutrition and development of children. Standard of living as assessed from a number of parameters like landholding, dwelling pattern, food habit, household belonging and so on reveals that the general mass is living a hard pressed life. The children do not get balanced diet. They are not living in a healthier environment. Majority of them live in clustered households erected without any planning for free flow of air and light. There is no arrangement for proper sanitation. Small ponds or puddles are their main source of water and serves all purposes other than drinking. Drinking water is drawn from tube well.

Table 1
Literacy Position of the Poundra Kshatriyas

Age Group in Years	*Illiterate*		*Literate*		*Primary*		*Secondary*		*Madhyamik*		*Higher Secondary*		*Graduate*		*Post Graduate*		*Professional*		*Total*	
	M	*F*	*M*	*F*	*M*	*F*	*M*	*F*	*M*	*F*	*M*	*F*	*M*	*F*	*M*	*F*	*M*	*F*	*M*	*F*
6-Oct	12	35	-	-	207	196	7	4											226	235
Nov-15	6	12	-	2	44	49	52	52											102	115
16-20	7	13	1	5	8	13	29	13	4	1	2	-							51	45
21-25	3	21	3	4	7	12	11	20	1	-	-	1	-	1					25	59
26-30	7	78	11	18	13	24	19	25	1	1	-	-	1	-					52	146
31-35	19	42	22	11	30	3	28	14	-	1	1	-	4	-	1				105	71
36-40	17	25	19	5	25	4	25	5	2	-	-	-	2	-	-		1		91	39
41-45	3	11	12	1	8	1	18	-	-	-			1	-	-				42	13
46-50	3	13	4	1	2	-	9	1	-	-	-	-	1	-	-		-		19	15
51-55	1	12	3	2	1	1	4	1	1	-	-	-	1	-	-		-		11	16
56-60	4	24	3	-	1	-	3	-	-	-	-	-							11	24
61-65	2	7	5	2	5	-	-	-	-	-	-	-	-	-	-		-		12	9
66-70	2	9	3	-	-	-	-	-	-	-	-	-	-	-	-				5	9
71-75	2	2	1	-	1	-	-	-	-	-	-	-	-	-	-		-		4	2
76-80	2	-	-	-	-	-	-	-	-	-	-	-	-	-	-				2	
81-85	1	1	-	-	1	-	-	-	-	-	-	-	-	-	-		-		2	1
86	-	1	-	-	-	-	-	-	-	-	-	-	-	-	-		-			1
	91	306	87	51	353	303	205	135	9	3	3	1	10	1	1		1		760	800

Table 2
Family Size of the Poundra Kshatriya

Members in a family	*Number of family*	*Per cent*
2	1	5
3	15	
4	85	
5	100	77.2
6	63	
7	27	
8	14	15.6
9	9	
10	3	
11	1	2.2
12	2	
13	1	
Total	321	100

Table 3
Family Type of the Poundra Kshatriya

Family Type	*Number of family*	*Percent*
Nuclear	237	73.8
Joint	84	26.1
	321	99.9

Table 4
Primary Occupation of Male Poundrakshatriya

Types of Occupation	*No. of person involved*	*Percentage*
Cultivator	20	5.2
Agricultural Labour	87	22.8
Daily Wage Labour	108	28.3
Skilled Labour (mason, bidi rolling, tubewell repairers, cycle repairers, iron-grill maker, motor mechanic, tractor operator etc.)	39	10.2
Taxi Driver	2	0.5
Rickshaw/Van Puller	29	7.6
Fishing	1	0.3
Carpenter	1	0.3
Medical/Ayurvedic Practitioner	2	0.5
Teacher	3	0.8
Brewary	1	0.3
Service (Police, custom, railway, health department, salesman, hotel boy etc.)	18	4.4
Business (Decorator, tourism, husking mill, shallow pump owner, kerosene oil dealer)	5	1.3
Petty Business (Glass ampule manufacturer, fish seller, extraction and selling of crab's oil, rice processing and selling, vegetable and fruit seller and goldsmith)	67	17.5
Total	383	100

Table 5
Occupation of Female Poundrakshatriya

Types of Occupation	*No. of Person Involved*	*Percentage*
Agricultural Labour	4	2.5
Unskilled Labour (maid servant)	48	30.2
Skilled Labour (bidi rolling, ampule making and batih printing)	74	46.5
Midwifery/Nursing	2	1.3
Fishing	1	0.6
Brewary	1	0.6
Service	2	1.3
Petty Business (Rice processing and selling, tailoring, fruit and vegetable seller, paper packet maker)	27	17
Total	159	100

Table 6
Size, Monthly Income and Percapita Income of the Poundrakshtariya Family

Age	*Mean No. of Family Members*	*Mean No. of Adult*	*Mean No. of Children*	*Mean Monthly Income of the Family in Rs.*	*Per Capita Income in Rs.*
6	5.29	2.23	3.06	1590.14	317.89
7	5.39	2.43	2.96	1827.86	360.9
8	5.87	2.36	3.33	1724.35	312.33
9	5.75	2.65	3.1	1885.46	335.47
10	5.52	2.62	2.9	1758.8	334.86

The percentage of immunization of newborn babies against DTP, Polio, BCG and measles are 53, 49, 7 and 6 per cent respectively. The reasons for not going for immunization are lack of awareness, reluctants and fear.

This is in brief the background information against which growth and development of children has been assessed metrically.

Table 7 shows body measurements of Poundrashtriya children. It is seen that mean weight, stature, sitting height, biacromial diameter, bi-iliocristal diameter, upper arm girth are gradually increasing with the advancement of age from 6 to 10 years in both boys and girls.

Weight

In Poundrakshtriya boys the maximum absolute gain of 3.04 kg. with the rate of increment 14.07 per cent for weight at 9 and 10 years of age group. Whereas in girls the greater absolute gain of 3.24 kg. with high rate of increment 20.69 per cent in 6 and 7 years age group.

From the initial phase of study it is seen that, distance curve for weight (Fig. 1) in Poundrakshtriya boys is slightly higher than girls after 9 years but at 10 years the curve in girls supersedes the boys. The boys are heavier in weight than the girls. It is also observed from the velocity curve for both boys and girls (Fig. 2). Among the boys the rate of growth curve

Table 7
Anthropometric Variables of Poundrakshatriya Children by Age and Sex

	Boys					Girls				
Age in Years	*6*	*7*	*8*	*9*	*10*	*6*	*7*	*8*	*9*	*10*
Weight (in kg)										
N	36	36	35	34	35	34	34	34	34	35
Mean	17.19	18.53	19.69	21.6	24.64	15.66	18.9	19.47	21.68	23.44
S.E. of mean	0.52	0.5	0.44	0.42	0.59	0.32	0.64	0.41	0.68	0.6
S.D.	3.13	3.0	2.59	2.42	3.51	1.85	3.76	2.4	3.97	3.55
C.V.	18.21	16.19	13.15	10.37	14.25	11.81	19.89	12.33	18.31	15.14
Absolute growth		1.34	1.16	1.91	3.04		3.24	0.57	2.21	1.76
% growth		7.79	6.26	9.7	14.07		20.69	3.02	11.35	8.12
Stature (in cm)										
N	36	36	35	34	35	34	34	34	34	35
Mean	109.17	114.87	117.75	124.74	129.26	106.99	115.2	119.16	123.24	129.01
S.E. of mean	1.38	1.17	0.06	0.83	1.07	1.08	1.35	1.08	1.22	0.87
S.D.	8.28	7.01	5.68	4.83	6.33	6.29	7.87	6.32	7.14	5.16
C.V.	7.58	6.1	4.82	3.87	4.9	5.88	6.83	5.3	5.79	3.99
Absolute growth		5.7	2.88	6.99	4.62		8.21	3.96	4.08	5.77
% growth		5.22	2.51	5.94	3.62		7.67	3.96	4.06	5.77
Sitting height (in cm)										
N	36	36	35	34	35	34	34	34	34	35
Mean	58.1	61.11	62.59	65.83	67.69	57.32	61.3	62.76	65.02	67.23
S.E. of mean	0.67	0.6	0.48	0.52	0.47	0.57	0.71	0.49	0.89	0.5
S.D.	4.03	3.58	2.86	3.03	2.84	3.35	4.11	2.86	5.17	2.97
C.V.	6.94	5.86	4.57	4.6	4.19	5.84	6.7	4.56	7.95	4.42
Absolute growth		3.01	1.48	3.24	1.86		3.98	1.46	2.26	2.21
% growth		15.18	2.42	5.18	2.82		6.94	2.38	3.6	3.39
Biacromial breadh (in cm)										

Contd...

	Boys					Girls				
Age in Years	*6*	*7*	*8*	*9*	*10*	*6*	*7*	*8*	*9*	*10*
N	36	36	35	34	35	34	34	34	34	35
Mean	23.15	24.39	24.8	26.09	27.21	22.71	23.83	24.68	25.82	26.87
S.E. of mean	0.27	0.29	0.2	0.24	0.25	0.23	0.3	0.27	0.26	0.29
S.D.	1.64	1.74	1.16	1.38	1.45	1.34	1.74	1.58	1.55	1.7
C.V.	7.08	7.13	4.68	5.29	5.33	6.04	7.3	6.4	6	6.33
Absolute growth		1.29	0.41	1.29	1.12		1.12	0.85	1.14	1.05
% growth		5.36	1.68	5.2	4.29		4.93	3.57	4.62	4.07
Billiocristal breadth (in cm)										
N	36	36	35	34	35	34	34	34	34	35
Mean	17.43	18.08	18.32	19.07	19.99	16.89	18.03	18.59	19.11	19.62
S.E. of mean	0.21	0.22	0.19	0.18	0.22	0.18	0.2	0.24	0.2	0.2
S.D.	1.26	1.34	1.15	1.05	1.33	1.04	1.19	1.42	1.19	1.17
C.V.	7.23	7.41	6.28	5.51	6.65	6.16	6.6	7.64	6.23	5.96
Absolute growth		0.65	0.24	0.75	0.92		1.14	0.56	0.52	0.51
% growth		3.73	1.34	4.08	4.81		6.75	3.12	2.8	2.67
Mid Upperarm Circumference										
N	36	36	35	34	35	34	34	34	34	35
Mean	13.87	14.11	14.49	14.82	15.43	13.57	14.24	14.38	15.25	15.13
S.E. of mean	0.17	0.16	0.2	0.18	0.14	0.14	0.2	0.16	0.24	0.18
S.D.	1.05	0.95	1.2	1.08	0.81	0.8	1.17	0.93	1.37	1.04
C.V.	7.57	6.73	8.28	7.29	5.25	5.89	8.22	6.47	8.98	6.87
Absolute growth		0.24	0.38	0.33	0.61		0.67	0.14	0.87	0.12
% growth		1.78	2.69	2.28	4.12		4.94	0.98	6.05	0.79
Triceps Skin Fold (in mm)										
N	36	36	35	34	35	34	34	34	34	35
Mean	5.88	5.4	5.28	5.13	5.27	6.34	6.15	5.98	6.24	6.14
S.E. of mean	0.19	0.19	0.19	0.14	0.15	0.21	0.24	0.24	0.28	0.22
S.D.	1.15	1.15	1.15	0.84	0.87	1.22	1.39	1.41	1.65	1.28
C.V.	19.58	21.29	21.78	16.37	16.51	19.24	22.6	23.58	26.44	20.85
Absolute growth		-0.48	-0.12	-0.15	0.14		-0.19	-0.17	0.26	-0.1
% growth		-8.16	-2.22	-2.84	2.73		-2.99	-2.76	4.35	-1

Contd...

	Boys					Girls				
Age in Years	*6*	*7*	*8*	*9*	*10*	*6*	*7*	*8*	*9*	*10*
Subscapular Skin Fold										
N	36	36	35	34	35	34	34	34	34	35
Mean	4.26	4.22	4	4.1	4.28	4.72	4.97	4.59	5.31	5.46
S.E. of mean	0.12	0.14	0.13	0.13	0.1	0.15	0.19	0.15	0.22	0.17
S.D.	0.75	0.86	0.67	0.74	0.59	0.88	1.09	0.85	1.3	0.98
C.V.	17.61	20.38	16.75	18.05	13.79	18.64	21.93	18.52	24.48	17.95
Absolute growth		0.4	0.22	0.1	0.18		0.25	0.38	0.72	0.15
% growth		0.94	5.21	2.5	4.39		5.3	7.65	15.69	2.75
Biceps Skin Fold										
N	36	36	35	34	35	34	34	34	34	35
Mean	4.26	3.23	3.13	3.18	3.18	3.6	3.68	3.13	3.67	3.67
S.E. of mean	0.13	0.12	0.11	0.11	0.08	0.11	0.14	0.11	0.17	0.61
S.D.	0.75	0.72	0.66	0.66	0.48	0.64	0.84	0.62	1.02	0.96
C.V.	17.61	22.29	21.09	20.75	15.09	17.78	22.83	19.81	27.79	26.16
Absolute growth		-1.03	-0.1	0.95	0		0.08	-0.55	0.54	0
% growth		-24.18	-3.09	1.6	0		2.22	14.94	17.25	0

decreases after 9 and 10 years but in girls the velocity curve raises gradually upward after 9 and surpasses the boys at 10 years.

The regression equation of weight on age for Poundrakshtriya boys and girls are Y = 4.78+1.96 x, r = 0.98, y = 2.93+2.14x, r = 0.98 respectively (Fig. 19).

Stature

At 8 and 9 years age the Poundrakshtriya boys show the maximum absolute gain in stature of 6.99 cms with rate of growth per annum is 5.94 per cent. Among the girls the greater absolute gain is 8.21 cms with rate of increment 7.67 per cent at the age 6 and 7 years.

From the distance curve (Fig. 3) it is found that both boys and girls show more or less same trend and after 9 years both the curves merge together. The velocity curve for stature (Fig.4) shows the maturity trend fluctuates in both the sexes. In girls stature is slightly higher after 9 years but growth is more or less same after 10 years in both boys and girls.

The line of regression for stature on age in Poundrakshtriya boys and girls are y = 78.64+5.07x, r = 0.99, y = 77.28+5.18x, r = 0.99 respectively (Fig. 20).

Sitting Height

From Table 7 it is seen that the boys attain maximum gain of 3.24 cms with the rate of increment of 5.18 per cent at 8 and 9 years age group. The Poundrakshtriya girls at 6 and 7 years attain the maximum gain of 3.98 cms with the rate of increment 6.94 per cent for sitting height.

The distance curve (Fig. 5) fluctuates much in both the sexes. The curve is higher in boys up to 9 years after that it goes up slightly than girls and then the curve merge together. The velocity curve (Fig. 6) moves up and down in both boys and girls. The curve is higher in boys up to 8 years and after 9 years it goes down gradually. But in girls the curve is more or less steady up to 9 years and it surpasses the boys after 10 years of age group.

The regression equation of sitting height on age for both boys and girls are y = 44.25+2.31x, r = 0.99 and y = 45.22+2.22x, r = 0.99 respectively (Fig. 21).

Biacromial Diameter

The Poundrakshtriya boys and girls attain maximum absolute gain of 1.29 cms and 1.12 cms respectively at 8 and 9 years. Similarly the greater rate of increment in both boys and girls are 5.36 per cent and 4.93 per cent at 6 and 7 years of age. After that the increment slows down and again goes up to 5.20 per cent in boys and 4.62 per cent in girls at 8 and 9 years of age.

The distance curve for biacromial diameter (Fig.7) in Poundrakshtriya boys is higher than girls up to 9 years but after 10 years of age the curves merge with the girls. But in girls, the curve is more or less steady. The velocity curve for biacromial diameter goes up and down in both boys and girls. The velocity curve (Fig. 8) in boys comes down after 9 years; whereas, in girls the curve goes slightly up after 9 years.

The line of regression for biacromial diameter on age for boys and girls are y = 17.23+0.99x, r = 0.99, y = 16.37+1.05x, r = 0.99 respectively (Fig. 22).

Bi-iliac Diameter

The Poundrakshtriya boys attain absolute gain of 0.92 cms with rate of increment 4.81 per cent at 9 and 10 years of age. The Poundrakshtriya girls attain maximum gain of 1.14 cms with rate of increment 6.75 per cent at 6 and 7 years of age.

The distance curve of bi-iliac diameter in boys (Fig.9) show that the curve moves up after 8 years and then it goes down. The distance curve of girls show that after 7 years the curve goes upward and then the curve surpasses the boys at 10 years. From the velocity curve (Fig.10) it is found that the rate of increment in boys gradually increases after 7 to 9 years but after 9 years it declines. In girls the increment is well marked after 10 years.

The regression equation of bi-iliac diameter (Fig. 23) on age for Poundrakshtriya boys and girls are y = 13.60+0.62x, r = 0.99 and y = 12.69 + 0.72x, r = 0.98 respectively.

Mid Upper Arm Girth

The Poundrakshtriya boys attain maximum gain of 0.61 cms with increment rate of 4.12 per cent at the age group of 9 and 10 years. The Poundrakshtriya girls attain gain of 0.87 cms with growth per cent per annum 6.05 at 8 and 9 years age group. The distance curve (Fig. 11) of the Poundrakshtriya boys show that the curve moves up after 9 years and then goes down after 10 years. In girls it is found that the curve moves up and down but it surpasses the boys after 10 years of age group. The velocity curve for upper arm girth (Fig. 12) in boys goes up after 8 years and continue it up to 9 years but at 10 years it goes down whereas in girls the curve move up and down then the curve gradually rises up after 10 years and supersedes the boys.

Skinfold Thickness Triceps

The mean value of triceps skinfold thickness of Poundrakshtriya boys are more or less same in all the age group. It ranges from 5.13 ± 0.14 mm to 5.88 ± 0.19 mm. But the girls show slight increment as age increases. In boys, the maximum gain of 0.14 cms with rate of increment 2.73 per cent at 9 and 10 years. Whereas in the Poundrakshtriya girls maximum gain of 0.26 mm with rate of increment 4.35 per cent at 8 and 9 years age group.

The distance curve for triceps thickness (Fig. 13) is very high in girls specially after 10 years than boys. It shows a clear picture of sexual dimorphism. The velocity curve for triceps (Fig. 14) in Poundrakshtriya boys and girls show up and down. The curve in boys comes down after 10 years but in girls the curve for triceps goes up after 10 years.

Sub-scapular

From Table 7 it is found that the mean value of sub-scapular skin fold thickness is not marked in all ages among the Poundrakshtriya boys. But the Poundrakshtriya girls show a continuous increase at different ages. In boys, absolute gain is greater 0.18 mm with the rate of increment of 4.39 per cent at 9 and 10 years age. In girls, the maximum gain of 0.72 mm with rate of increment 15.69 per cent at 8 and 9 years age group.

From the distance curve for sub-scapular (Fig. 15) skin fold it is seen that in boys after 8 years the curve goes slightly up. The Poundrakshtriya girls show that the curve moves up and down but after 10 years a sharpest increase is noticed. Sexual differences is marked. The velocity curve of boys and girls (Fig. 16) shows that the curve after 8 years goes up again moves back after 10 years in boys whereas in girls the curve moves up and down and then it markedly increases after 10 years of age.

Biceps

The mean value of biceps thickness in the Poundrakshtriya boys are more or less same in all ages. But the girls show slight increase of mean value at different ages. In boys absolute gain is greater 0.95 mm with the rate of increment 1.60 per cent at 8 and 9 years. The Poundrakshtriya girls show maximum gain 0.54 mm with rate of increment of 17.25 per cent at 8 and 9 years age group.

The distance curve for biceps in boys (Fig. 17) shows that the curve is more or less steady up to 10 years and after 10 years it moves back. The curve of biceps in girls shows that it goes up and down and after 10 years of age it sharply increases. Sexual differences is very marked. The velocity curve of biceps (Fig.18) shows that the curve in boys move slightly up at 8 years then it goes back after 10 years. In Poundrakshtriya girls the curve moves very markedly after 10 years of age. The increment of biceps in girls is more pronounced at 8 and 9 years.

Table 8 shows t-test for sexual difference in anthropometric characters of Poundrakshtriya children. Bisexual diamorphism for skin fold at triceps ($t^2 = 7.57$, $p<0.01$), sub-scapular ($t^2=10.14$, $p<0.01$), biceps ($t^2 = 5.32$, $p<0.01$) are very much pronounced.

The co-relation co-efficient between some of measurements of the Poundrakshtriya children are presented in Table 9.

The value of coefficient of co-relation(r) between stature and weight among the boys is high 0.912 in 6 years age group. Whereas, in girls it is high 0.929 in 8 years age group. Co-relation between stature and sitting height is high r= 0.990 in boys of 10 years age. High co-relation between bi-acromial breadth and bi-iliocristal breadth in both boys and girls are 0.961 in 9 years and 0.982 in 6 years respectively. From the table it is seen that all five anthropometric characters are highly co-related.

Table 8
t-Test for Sexual Difference of Anthropometric Characters in Poundrakshtriya Children

	t-test
Weight	0.51
Stature	0.22
Sitting Height	0.23
Bi-Acromial Diameter	1.14
Bi-Iliocristal Diameter	1.86
Fore Arm Length	0.56
Total Arm Length	1.65
Upper Arm Circumference	1.65
Tricept	7.57***
Sub-scapular	10.14***
Biceps	5.32***

d.f. = 413
** = Significant at 0.02% level
*** = Significant at 0.01% level

Dentition

A cross-sectional dental examination was made to study the fallen of milk-teeth and eruption of permanent teeth by age and sex among the rural children of Poundrakshtriya.

Here teeth is classified into four categories such as milk-teeth, fallen teeth, just erupted and permanent teeth. It is seen that persistence of milk teeth is high i.e. 44 per cent (Table 10) and frequency of fallen teeth 18 per cent is noticed in the boys of 6 years age. Just erupted teeth is common 21 per cent and high percentage of permanent incisor teeth (Table 11) it varies from 23 to 64 per cent among the Poundrakshtriya girls. In boys permanent incisor teeth occur 15 to 64 per cent.

Frequency of carries is high 38 per cent among the Poundrakshtriya boys whereas in girls it is 37 per cent.

It is found that incisor and canine erupt earlier in girls. It agrees with the earlier findings. First permanent molar erupt after 7 years of age, high frequency of 35 per cent is noticed among the girls of 8years age group. At 9 years of age cent per cent of first permanent molar is found in both the sexes.

Assessment of Nutritional Status

In weight deficit classification according to Vishveshwar Rao (1979) grade II and III is more or less dominant in boys and girls (Table 12), it occurs between 21 to 53 per cent only

Table 9

Correlation Co-efficient of Some Anthropometric Characters of the Poundrakshtariya Children

	Children									
	6 Years		*7 Years*		*8 Years*		*9 Years*		*10 Years*	
	Boys	*Girls*	*Boys*	*Girls*	*Boys*	*Girls*	*Boys*	*Girls*	*Boys*	*Girls*
Stature & Weight	0.912	0.894	0.865	0.8	0.885	0.92	0.905	0.83	0.885	0.842
Stature and Sitting Height	0.842	0.987	0.989	0.991	0.986	0.992	0.982	0.936	0.99	0.987
Biacromial bred and Bi-iliocristal Bred	0.809	0.982	0.934	0.952	0.955	0.954	0.961	0.948	0.955	0.936
Chest Chir and head Cir.	0.882	0.943	0.93	0.64	0.811	0.956	0.979	0.949	0.925	0.95
Triceps and Subscapular	0.561	0.626	0.719	0.703	0.725	0.682	0.6	0.828	0.618	0.825

Table 10
Occurance of Incisor According to Age and Sex of Poundrakshatriya Children

	Children											
	6 Years		7 Years		8 Years		9 Years		10 Years		11 Years	
Categories	Boys	Girls	Boys	Girls	Boys	Girls	Boys	Girls	Boys	Girls	Boys	Girls
Milk Teeth	16	12	8	5	2	1	1	1	1	1	1	-
%	44.44	35.29	22.22	14.71	5.71	2.94	2.94	2.94	2.78	2.86	2.94	-
Fallen Teeth	9	6	5	4	3	1	2	1	1	1	1	1
%	17.65	11.76	13.89	8.57	8.57	2.94	5.88	2.94	2.78	2.86	2.94	2.94
Just Erupted	6	7	4	5	2	3	1	1	2	1	1	1
%	16.67	20.59	11.11	14.71	5.71	8.82	2.94	2.94	5.56	2.86	2.94	2.94
Parmanent Teeth	5	9	19	20	28	29	30	31	32	32	31	32
%	13.89	26.47	52.78	58.82	80	85.29	88.24	91.18	88.89	91.43	91.18	94.12

Table 11
Occurance of Permanent Teeth According to Age and Sex of Paundrakshatriya Children

	Children											
	6 Years		*7 Years*		*8 Years*		*9 Years*		*10 Years*		*11 Years*	
Categories	*Boys*	*Girls*	*Boys*	*Girls*	*Boys*	*Girls*	*Boys*	*Girls*	*Boys*	*Girls*	*Boys*	*Girls*
Incisor Number	11	16	23	25	28	32	31	32	34	33	32	33
%	15.28	23.53	31.94	36.77	40	47.05	55.59	57.06	64.45	64.21	74.12	79.06
Canine Number					10	11	19	21	25	26	30	31
%					14.29	16.17	27.94	30.88	34.72	37.14	44.11	45.59
I Permanent Molar Number					11	12	34	34	36	35	34	34
%					31.43	35.29	100	100	100	100	100	100
I Pre Molar Number							10	9	12	11	20	22
%							14.7	13.23	16.67	15.71	29.41	32.35
II Permanent Molar Number							4	5	15	14	21	22
%							5.88	7.36	20.05	20	30.51	32.37
II Permanent Pre-molar Number							1	1	4	3	9	10
%							1.47	1.17	5.55	5.72	13.24	14.7

Table 12
Weight for Age or Weight Deficit Classification of Poundrakshatriya Children

	Children											
	6 Years		*7 Years*		*8 Years*		*9 Years*		*10 Years*		*11 Years*	
Categories	*Boys*	*Girls*	*Boys*	*Girls*	*Boys*	*Girls*	*Boys*	*Girls*	*Boys*	*Girls*	*Boys*	*Girls*
Grade IV												
Malnutrition	-	4	-	2	-	2	1	6	3	8	4	7
%	-	11.76	-	5.88	1	5.88	2.94	17.65	8.57	22.86	11.76	20.59
Grade III												
Malnutrition	11	15	11	7	15	12	15	16	12	15	12	12
%	30.56	44.12	30.56	20.59	41.67	35.29	44.12	47.06	34.29	42.86	35.29	35.29
Grade II												
Malnutrition	11	8	13	13	12	18	14	6	11	9	12	7
%	30.56	23.53	36.11	38.24	33.33	52.94	41.18	17.65	31.43	25.71	35.29	20.59
Grade I												
Malnutrition	8	5	6	7	5	1	2	3	5	2	5	6
%	22.22	14.71	16.67	20.59	13.89	2.94	5.88	8.82	14.29	5.71	14.71	17.68
Normal	6	2	6	5	4	1	2	3	4	1	1	2
%	16.67	5.88	16.67	14.71	11.11	2.94	5.88	8.82	11.43	2.86	2.94	5.88
Total	36	34	36	34	36	34	34	34	35	35	34	34

Height deficit classification of the Poundrakshtriya children shows that mild retardation is very predominant in both boys and girls (Table 13), it varies from 38 to 79 per cent.

Mid-upper arm circumference includes four categories such as normal, malnutrition, moderate malnutrition and severe malnutrition. Moderate malnutrition is common in Poundrakshtriya boys and girls (Table 14), it occurs between 21 to 67 per cent.

Observation of Clinical Signs and Nutrition Deficiency Signs

General health of the Poundrakshtriya children has been classified into three categories such as good, satisfactory and weak (Table 15).

It is found that in male high frequency of good health 50 per cent occurs at 6 years age group whereas, in Poundrakshtriya girls good health occurs 47 per cent in 7 years age. In boys satisfactory general health 11 per cent found in the age group of 10 years but in girls it is only 3 per cent in 9 years age group. In boys weak health occurs between 47 to 68 per cent, whereas in girls it varies from 53 to 71 per cent.

Clinical Observations

Pigmentation of skin in Poundrakshtriya boys show 36 per cent in 7 years but in girls it occurs 57 per cent in 10 years age group. Angular stomatitis is very common 59 per cent among the boys of 9 years but in girls it occurs 50 per cent in 6 years age group. Frequecy of dry scaly skin is 83 per cent in the boys of 8 years age group whereas, in girls it occur very high 85 per cent in 9 years age group.

Discolour hair occur 68 per cent in the boys of 9 years whereas in girls 71 per cent is noticed in the age group of 7. Coarse hair is very common 44 per cent among the boys of 10 years but the girls possess only 32 per cent.

Spongy bleeding gum occur 62 per cent among the boys of 9 years but in girls it occur 69 per cent in 10 years age group. In boys 73 per cent yellow teeth in 9 years but in Poundrakshtriya girls it occur 85 per cent in 7 years age group. Pale conjunctiva is 82 per cent among the boys of 9 years; whereas, in girls it is 91 per cent in the same age group. Yellow colour at the base of nail occur 41 per cent in the boys of 9 years but in girls it occur 68 per cent.

Impact of Socio-cultural Factors on Growth of Children

From examination of Tables 16-19 it is found that impact of socio-cultural factors such as literacy level of parents, family size, family type, parity of the children and per capita income on growth pattern of the children are not well marked. This may be due to very small sample size.

Table 13
Height for Age or Height Deficit Clasification of Poundrakshatriya Children

	Children											
	6 Years		7 Years		8 Years		9 Years		10 Years		11 Years	
Categories	*Boys*	*Girls*	*Boys*	*Girls*	*Boys*	*Girls*	*Boys*	*Girls*	*Boys*	*Girls*	*Boys*	*Girls*
Poor	16	7	11	8	16	11	10	18	10	7	10	13
%	44.44	20.59	30.56	23.53	45.71	32.35	29.41	52.94	28.57	20	29.41	38.24
Mild Retardation	17	27	23	21	18	21	23	13	22	27	22	20
%	47.22	79.41	63.89	61.76	51.43	61.76	67.65	38.24	62.86	77.14	64.71	58.82
Normal	3	-	2	5	1	2	1	3	3	1	2	1
%	8.33		5.56	14.71	2.86	5.88	2.94	8.82	8.57	2.86	5.88	2.94
Total	36	34	36	34	35	34	34	34	35	35	34	34

Table 14
Mid-upper Arm Circumference of Poundrakshatriya Children

	Children											
	6 Years		*7 Years*		*8 Years*		*9 Years*		*10 Years*		*11 Years*	
Categories	*Boys*	*Girls*	*Boys*	*Girls*	*Boys*	*Girls*	*Boys*	*Girls*	*Boys*	*Girls*	*Boys*	*Girls*
Severe Malnutrition	10	16	5	15	16	12	15	15	10	17	12	14
%	27.78	47.06	13.89	44.12	45.71	35.29	44.12	44.12	28.57	48.57	35.29	41.18
Moderate Malnutrition	15	14	24	7	9	18	11	13	16	13	13	9
%	41.67	41.18	66.67	20.59	25.71	52.94	32.35	38.23	45.71	37.14	38.23	26.47
Malnutrition	7	2	6	9	6	3	4	3	8	5	5	8
%	19.44	5.88	16.67	26.47	17.14	8.82	11.76	8.82	22.86	14.29	14.71	23.53
Normal	4	2	1	3	4	1	4	3	1	-	4	3
%	11.11	5.88	2.78	8.82	11.43	2.94	11.76	8.82	2.86		11.76	8.82
Total	36	34	36	34	35	34	34	34	35	35	34	34

Table 15
Clinical Signs and Nutrition Deficiency Signs of the Ponurakshatriya Children

	Children											
	6 Years		7 Years		8 Years		9 Years		10 Years		11 Years	
Categories	*Boys*	*Girls*	*Boys*	*Girls*	*Boys*	*Girls*	*Boys*	*Girls*	*Boys*	*Girls*	*Boys*	*Girls*
General Health												
Good	18	10	14	16	17	14	11	9	15	11	16	8
%	50	29.11	38.89	47.06	48.57	41.18	32.35	26.47	41.67	31.43	47.96	23.53
Satisfactory	1	-	2	-	-	-	-	1	4	-	1	2
%	2.78		2.78					2.94	11.11		2.94	5.39
Week	17	24	21	18	18	20	23	24	17	24	17	24
%	47.22	70.59	58.33	52.94	51.43	58.82	67.65	70.59	47.22	68.57	50	70.59
Nutrition Deficiency Signs												
Pigmentation of skin												
Present	7	13	13	7	8	12	12	14	8	20	7	15
%	19.44	38.23	36.11	20.59	22.36	35.29	35.29	41.18	22.22	57.14	20.59	55.88
Absent	29	21	23	27	27	22	22	20	28	15	27	19
%	80.56	61.76	63.89	79.41	77.14	64.71	64.71	58.82	77.78	42.86	79.11	55.88
Angular Stomats												
Present	17	17	20	14	17	11	20	12	15	11	12	18
%	47.22	50	55.56	41.18	48.57	32.35	58.82	35.29	41.67	31.43	35.29	52.94
Absent	19	17	16	20	18	23	14	22	21	24	22	17
%	32.78	50	44.44	58.82	51.43	67.65	41.18	64.71	58.33	68.57	64.71	50
Dry Scaly Skin												
Present	28	25	19	28	29	23	26	29	26	27	24	30
%	77.78	73.53	52.78	82.35	82.86	67.65	76.47	85.29	72.22	77.14	70.59	88.24
Absent	8	9	17	6	6	11	8	5	10	8	10	4
%	22.22	26.47	47.22	17.65	17.14	32.35	23.53	14.71	27.78	22.86	29.41	11.76

Contd...

	Children											
	6 Years		*7 Years*		*8 Years*		*9 Years*		*10 Years*		*11 Years*	
Categories	*Boys*	*Girls*	*Boys*	*Girls*	*Boys*	*Girls*	*Boys*	*Girls*	*Boys*	*Girls*	*Boys*	*Girls*
Discolour Hair												
Present	20	21	18	24	22	16	23	21	24	17	23	21
%	55.56	61.76	50	70.59	62.86	47.06	67.65	61.76	66.67	48.57	67.65	61.76
Absent	16	13	18	10	3	18	11	13	12	18	11	13
%	44.44	38.23	50	29.41	37.14	52.94	32.35	38.24	33.33	51.43	32.35	38.24
Flag/Coarse Hair												
Present	15	9	14	11	12	11	8	11	16	11	13	12
%	41.67	26.47	38.89	32.35	34.29	32.35	23.53	32.35	44.44	31.43	38.24	35.29
Absent	21	25	22	23	23	23	26	23	20	24	21	22
%	58.33	73.53	61.11	67.65	65.71	67.65	76.47	67.65	55.56	68.57	61.76	64.71
Spongy Bleeding												
Present	12	16	16	18	15	15	21	20	19	24	20	20
%	33.33	47.06	44.44	52.94	42.86	44.12	61.76	58.82	52.78	68.57	58.82	58.82
Absent	24	18	20	16	20	19	13	14	17	11	14	14
%	86.67	52.94	55.56	47.06	57.14	55.88	38.24	41.18	47.22	31.43	41.18	41.18
Yellow Teeth												
Present	15	22	17	29	22	28	25	28	23	27	28	22
%	41.67	64.71	47.22	85.29	62.86	82.35	73.53	82.35	63.89	77.14	82.35	64.71
Absent	21	12	19	5	13	6	9	6	13	8	6	12
%	58.33	35.29	52.78	14.71	37.14	17.65	26.47	17.65	36.11	22.86	17.65	35.29
Pale Conjunctive												
Present	29	30	20	30	27	29	28	31	22	30	29	29
%	80.56	88.23	55.56	88.24	77.14	85.29	82.35	91.18	61.11	85.71	85.29	85.29
Absent	7	4	16	4	8	5	6	3	14	5	5	5
%	19.44	11.76	44.44	11.76	22.86	14.71	17.65	8.82	38.89	14.29	14.71	14.71

Contd...

	Children											
	6 Years		7 Years		8 Years		9 Years		10 Years		11 Years	
Categories	*Boys*	*Girls*	*Boys*	*Girls*	*Boys*	*Girls*	*Boys*	*Girls*	*Boys*	*Girls*	*Boys*	*Girls*
Yellow Colour in the base of Nail												
Present	8	17	10	19	14	19	14	23	9	21	9	21
%	22.22	50	27.78	55.88	80	55.08	41.18	67.65	25	60	26.47	61.76
Absent	28	17	26	15	21	15	20	11	27	14	25	13
%	77.78	50	72.22	44.12	60	44.12	58.82	32.35	75	40	73.53	38.24
Other Observations												
Tunsil	2	3	1	2	3	1	2	4	1	2	4	3
%	5.56	8.82	2.77	8.86	8.57	2.94	5.88	11.76	2.77	5.71	11.76	8.33
Pus in Cat	4	5	1	3	4	3	3	2	2	2	2	2
%	11.11	14.71	2.77	8.82	11.43	8.82	8.82	5.08	5.56	5.71	5.88	5.88
Enisrged buily	3	-	1	-	1	-	-	-	-	-	-	-
%	8.82	2.77		2.86								
White Patch	2	4	2	4	2	2	2	3	2	5	2	2
%	5.56	11.76	5.56	11.76	5.71	5.88	5.88	8.82	5.56	14.29	5.88	5.88
Black Patch	1	1	2	1	1	-	2	1	-	1	2	-
%	2.77	2.94	5.56	2.94	2.86		5.88	2.94		2.86	5.88	
Crake Sole	2	2	3	2	3	2	4	2	-	2	1	-
%	5.56	5.88	8.33	5.88	8.57	5.83	11.76	5.88		5.71	2.94	
	4	5	3	4	5	7	3	6	4	3	4	2
	11.11	14.71	8.33	11.76	14.29	20.59	8.82	17.65	11.11	8.57	11.76	5.88

Table 16
Mean and Standard Deviation for Weight of Poundrakshatriya Children Aged from 6 to 10 Years by Literacy Level of Both the Parents, Parity of Children, Family Size and Family Type

	Boys															Girls														
	6			7			8			9			10			6			7			8			9			10		
	N	*Mean*	S.D.	N	*Mean*	S.D.	N	*Mean*	S.D.	N	*Mean*	S.D.	N	*Mean*	S.D.	N	*Mean*	S.D.	N	*Mean*	S.D.	N	*Mean*	S.D.	N	*Mean*	S.D.	N	*Mean*	S.D.
Literacy Level																														
Father & Mother both literate	14	15.8	1.72	14	17.2	2.16	13	20	2.36	9	21.1	2.23	12	24.9	3.52	14	15.7	1.52	14	18.1	2.47	15	19.8	2.67	12	23	2.03	11	23.03	2
Mother lit., Father Non-lit.	4	18	1.84	8	19	2.69	5	18.7	1.08	9	20.7	1.31	5	24.9	3.61	4	14.4	0.82	3	21.2	2.41	2	20.5	2	3	21	2.83	2	21.5	1.5
Mother Non-lit., Father lit.	6	16.3	2.38	5	20.4	3.31	6	19.6	3.34	11	22.5	3.03	10	23.3	3.24	6	13.9	1.13	5	17.7	2.89	6	19.4	1.42	10	20.5	3.94	6	23.6	2
Mother & Father Non-Lit.	12	19	4.01	9	18.6	2.83	9	19.7	2.52	5	22.4	1.85	6	23.8	2.05	10	16.8	1.96	12	19.7	3.94	11	18.7	2.08	11	18.9	1.88	16	23.8	2
Family Size																														
Small family (<3)	2	16.5	1.41	5	15.6	0.86	0	0	0	1	22	0.01	3	25.3	3.56	0	0	0	2	18.5	1.5	0	0	0	1	32.5	0.01	0	0	0
Medium family (4-6)	28	17.3	3.37	26	21.7	3.98	30	19.9	2.71	27	21.2	2.09	28	24.1	3.39	32	15.5	1.91	26	18.8	3.16	25	19.7	2.27	26	21.1	3.36	26	23.8	2.7
Medium large family (7-9)	5	17.6	2.33	5	19.5	2.28	5	18.5	1.09	4	23	3.74	3	23.3	2.49	2	16	0.01	4	19.8	2.14	8	18.9	2.92	7	22.1	3.49	9	21.7	2.2
Large family (10>)	1	15	0.01	0	0	0	0	0	0	2	24	1	1	23	0	0	0	0	2	18.8	0.25	1	20	0.001	0	0	0	0	0	0
Family Type																														
Nuclear	25	17.7	3.46	28	23.4	2.79	26	19.6	2.71	26	21.3	2.08	26	24.8	3.85	26	15.5	1.91	22	19.3	3.02	24	19.6	2.34	28	21.8	3.18	28	24.1	3.6
Joint	11	16	2.09	8	20.1	3.03	9	20	2.15	8	22.6	3.09	9	23.8	2.22	8	15.9	1.4	12	18	2.98	10	19.5	2.59	6	20.9	2.64	7	20.8	1.1
Parity																														
1	5	15.5	2.45	14	18.6	2.97	10	20.1	3.18	11	21	1.64	16	25.3	3.42	14	15.5	1.78	6	19.1	2.39	9	18.8	1.8	10	21.6	2.08	6	24.9	3.2
2	15	16.6	3.95	14	19	2.52	12	19.1	2.31	8	21.2	2.37	6	25.3	3.89	7	16.4	1.57	10	18.3	3.25	13	20	2.08	8	21.4	2.57	11	23	2.8
3	10	17.7	2.21	4	16	0.61	6	20.6	2.59	7	21.2	1.97	9	23.8	1.99	9	15.6	2.05	13	20	2.61	6	18.8	1.63	3	23	2.94	6	23.4	2
4	5	17.1	2.36	3	19	4.97	6	19.7	1.46	5	22.1	1.36	3	25	2.45	1	13	0.001	1	16	0.001	3	20.7	0.87	7	20.8	1.6	6	25	2.5
5 to above	1	15	0.01	1	20	0.12	1	17.2	0.01	3	22.3	2.87	1	20	0	3	15.3	0.47	4	17.1	1.75	1	17	0.001	6	21.1	3.28	6	21.3	1
Per Capita Income																														
Rs.101-200	3	16.3	3.01	5	18.7	2.79	6	19.3	1.46	2	22	1	1	23	0	8	16.1	1.99	7	19.9	2.78	3	19	0.82	8	19.4	2.31	7	22.6	2.5
Rs.201-300	14	16.6	2.02	13	18.4	3.16	18	19.8	2.6	18	22	2.8	13	23.1	2.03	10	15.3	1.63	14	18.4	2.84	18	19.4	2.49	16	21.2	3.32	20	23.8	2
Rs.301-400	16	17.9	3.83	11	19.4	3.21	10	19.9	3.08	13	20.4	1.57	14	26	2.8	12	15.2	1.5	6	19	4.46	7	20.1	2.65	7	23.9	4.08	5	24.8	2.18
Rs.401 and above	3	16.8	1.25	7	17.4	1.66	1	18	0.01	1	24.5	0	7	23.9	2.16	4	16.9	1.88	7	18.6	2.31	6	19.3	2.31	3	22.5	3.44	3	22.3	0.9

Table 17
Mean and Standard Deviation for Stature of Poundrakshatriya Children Aged from 6 to 10 Years by Literacy Level of Both the Parents, Parity of Children, Family Size and Family Type

	Boys															Girls														
	6			7			8			9			10			6			7			8			9			10		
	N	Mean	S.D.	N	Mean	S.D.	N	Mean	S.D.	N	Mean	S.D.	N	Mean	S.D.	N	Mean	S.D.	N	Mean	S.D.	N	Mean	S.D.	N	Mean	S.D.	N	Mean	S.D.
Literacy Level																														
Father & Mother both literate	14	1053.4	62	14	1119	66	13	1183	39	9	1243	47	12	1284	56	14	1068	60	14	1128	51	15	1200	64	12	1239	69	11	1314	26
Mother lit., Father Non-lit.	4	1099.6	49	8	1161	72	5	1182	47	9	1229	37	5	1287	53	4	1077	56	3	1160	54	2	1189	14	3	1272	32	2	1282	34
Mother Non-lit., Father lit.	6	1069.8	82	5	1177	71	8	1172	52	11	1368	54	10	1302	30	6	1032	46	5	1120	47	6	1185	45	10	1251	59	6	1271	47
Mother & Father Non-Lit.	12	1144.8	85	9	1164	59	9	1185	55	5	1276	35	8	1292	27	10	1096	52	12	1176	56	11	1185	61	11	1189	30	16	1288	48
Family Size																														
Small family (<3)	2	1065	53	5	1165	70	0	0	0	1	1245	0	3	1287	40	0	0	0	2	1080	18	0	0	0	1	1430	0	0	0	0
Medium family (4-6)	28	1094.1	90	28	1155	72	30	1222	59	27	1240	49	28	1296	57	32	1073	66	26	1143	63	25	1196	60	26	1224	56	26	1305	46
Medium large family (7-9)	5	1094.5	90	5	1155	52	5	1139	28	4	1290	36	3	1271	64	2	1056	1	4	1199		8	1191	60	7	1233	56	9	1251	47
Large family (10>)	1	1047	0	0	0	0	0	0	0	2	1260	21	1	1280	0	0	0	0	2	1139	14	1	1202	0	0	0	0	0	0	0
Family Type																														
Nuclear	25	1107.2	87	28	1140	21	26	1175	61	26	1245	48	26	1256	53	26	1068	47	22	1151	62	24	1233	62	28	1225	59	28	1297	51
Joint	11	1056.4	59	8	1174	62	9	1171	52	8	1258	49	9	1277	47	8	1083	56	12	1055	72	10	1198	70	6	1228	51	7	1251	44
Parity																														
1	5	1080.8	81	14	1154	68	10	1181	69	11	1232	37	16	1297	57	14	1089	60	6	1124	49	9	1163	44	10	1216	61	6	1287	55
2	15	1091.7	69	14	1149	63	12	1169	47	8	1244	43	6	1306	48	7	1062	65	10	1150	64	13	1209	60	8	1229	47	11	1286	32
3	10	1099.6	60	4	1109	43	6	1171	61	7	1252	47	9	1281	58	9	1056	56	13	1168	70	6	1173	30	3	1	49	5	1308	31
4	5	1102.6	60	3	1143	69	6	1205	34	5	1253	49	3	1278	49	1	990	0	1	1097	0	5	1221	38	7	1218	50	6	1300	37
5 to above	1	1012	0	1	1210	0	1	1121	0	3	1296	32	1	1230	0	3	1090	26	4	1117	44	1	1155	0	6	1234	55	6	1277	39
Per Capita Income																														
Rs.101-200	3	1073	63	5	1152	54	6	1162	56	2	1285	16	1	1280	0	8	1073	54	7	1161	50	3	1195	18	8	1172	33	7	1288	82
Rs.201-300	14	1081.8	73	13	1144	63	18	1169	53	18	1258	43	13	1266	40	10	1064	60	14	1165	55	18	1193	66	16	1235	59	20	1288	54
Rs.301-400	16	1104	84	11	1157	66	10	1203	59	13	1223	32	14	1328	57	12	1065	56	6	1122	66	7	1169	41	7	1294	49	5	1313	42
Rs.401 and above	3	1091	65	7	1113	56	1	1176	0	1	1290	0	7	1276	45	4	1112	41	7	1137	49	6	1170	47	3	1263	49	3	1268	38

Table 18
Mean and Standard Deviation for Siting Height of Poundrakshatriya Children Aged from 6 to 10 Years by Literacy Level of Both the Parents, Parity of Children, Family Size and Family Type

	Boys															Girls														
	6			7			8			9			10			6			7			8			9			10		
	N	Mean	S.D.	N	Mean	S.D.	N	Mean	S.D.	N	Mean	S.D.	N	Mean	S.D.	N	Mean	S.D.	N	Mean	S.D.	N	Mean	S.D.	N	Mean	S.D.	N	Mean	S.D.
Literacy Level																														
Father & Mother both literate	14	567.6	34.94	14	595.9	43.64	13	630.4	28.82	9	643.7	34.88	12	680.4	32.45	14	572.1	31.4	14	614.9	42.28	15	634.8	35.09	12	656.3	34	11	677.2	31.35
Mother lit., Father Non-lit.	4	598	21.05	8	617.3	32.39	5	599	9.17	9	653.7	26.34	5	674	8.88	4	588.8	26.99	3	603.3	41.15	2	634.5	0.5	3	620.7	34.8	2	667.5	5.5
Mother Non-lit., Father lit.	6	576.3	37.08	5	617.6	18.14	8	621	20.64	11	670.3	25.43	10	670.3	20.75	6	553.2	42.26	5	610.8	64.09	6	627.8	26.26	10	669.2	75.56	6	671.5	26.87
Mother & Father Non-Lit.	12	593.3	46.4	6	625.6	20.04	9	638.8	30.77	5	666.8	24.04	8	681.5	35.36	10	580.7	26.14	12	614.2	23.53	11	616.3	16.33	11	630.9	26.12	16	669.9	30.96
Family Size																														
Small family (<3)	2	560.5	24.5	5	584	24.28	0	0	0	1	639	0.001	3	696	23.28	0	0	0	2	600	15	0	0	0	1	644	0.001	0	0	0
Medium family (4-6)	28	584.3	42.8	26	617.2	37.67	30	625.6	30.27	27	653.6	30.46	28	676.3	25.46	32	574.2	33.77	26	612.2	45.59	25	633.2	28.63	26	652.7	58.26	26	673.8	31.3
Medium large family (7-9)	5	573.6	29.99	5	606.6	17.98	5	628	15.48	4	685.5	18.04	3	675.3	44.32	2	557.5	24.5	4	629.3	19.46	8	609.1	21.74	7	642.1	16.65	9	668.2	24.17
Large family (10>)	1	569	0.01	0	0	0	0	0	0	2	677	12	1	640	0.01	0	0	0	2	604	2	1	634	0.01	0	0	0	0	0	0
Family Type																														
Nuclear	25	587.4	42.73	28	607.3	38.93	26	625.7	31.59	26	653.5	31.66	26	682	29.61	26	572.8	33.2	22	615.3	43.11	24	631.1	31.21	28	650.6	34.16	28	670.7	28.17
Joint	11	566.6	29.6	8	624.5	15.71	9	626.7	17.49	8	673.9	18.27	9	662	17.23	8	574.8	34.53	12	608.8	36.93	10	619	18.46	6	648.3	38	7	679	34.48
Parity																														
1	5	566.8	47.54	14	608.6	37.91	10	614.8	29.73	11	652.6	36.74	16	671.4	30.2	14	583.2	29.44	6	607.7	29.99	9	629.7	20.09	10	651.4	34.31	6	671.3	21.11
2	15	583	47.78	14	614	37.26	12	625.5	22.38	8	671.1	20.94	6	679.8	11.87	7	575.3	34.74	10	610.9	40.57	13	633.1	31.64	8	637.5	39.81	11	680.4	32.98
3	10	583.5	26.04	4	608.3	20.69	6	627.7	20.62	7	641.7	16.5	9	673.7	26.63	9	564.7	36.05	13	621.4	40.56	6	614.8	36.49	3	631.7	42.29	6	656.5	24.1
4	5	591	26.48	3	603.3	35.18	6	639.3	37.36	5	676.4	18.14	3	712.7	24.24	1	515	0.01	1	650	0.01	5	631	12.05	7	670.1	85.36	6	675	27.66
5 to above	1	548	0.01	1	640	0.01	1	651	0.01	3	653.7	36.75	1	667	0.01	5	567	10.8	4	590	49.29	1	596	0.01	6	651.3	37.44	6	671.8	31.51
Per Capita Income																														
Rs. 101-200	3	551.7	18.35	5	615	19.67	5	626	33.25	2	678.5	25.5	1	640	0.001	8	570.8	33.61	7	620.9	29.43	3	632.7	36.38	8	646.5	29.75	7	689.7	20.28
Rs. 201-300	14	575.9	31.28	13	598.9	34.83	18	623.4	22.06	18	665	27.13	13	678.9	27.08	10	582.8	23.08	14	617.9	31.63	18	623.1	34.21	16	632.6	37.18	20	668.7	27.23
Rs. 301-400	16	590.4	47.29	11	635.6	27.84	10	632.9	34.7	13	646.2	31.82	14	672.7	31.52	12	563.8	37.49	6	582.5	43	7	637	13.18	7	681.4	80.07	5	667	28.56
Rs. 401 and above	3	584.3	34.87	7	592.3	35.64	1	600	0.01	1	656	0.01	7	686.6	18.48	4	582.8	33.87	7	621.6	52.85	6	627.3	9.21	3	681.7	24.94	9	664.7	35.31

Table 19
Mean and Standard Deviation for Biacromial Diameter of Poundrakshatriya Children Aged from 6 to 20 Years by Literacy Level of Both the Parents, Parity of Children, Family Size and Family Type

	Boys															Girls														
	6			7			8			9			10			6			7			8			9			10		
	N	Mean	S.D.	N	Mean	S.D.	N	Mean	S.D.	N	Mean	S.D.	N	Mean	S.D.	N	Mean	S.D.	N	Mean	S.D.	N	Mean	S.D.	N	Mean	S.D.	N	Mean	S.D.
Literacy Level																														
Father & Mother both literate	14	225.4	10.9	14	241.2	18.8	13	250.7	13.6	9	255.3	6.1	12	273.1	14.9	14	227.1	11.8	14	235.9	13.6	15	253.1	15.7	12	260.9	14.4	11	271.3	23.4
Mother lit., Father Non-lit.	4	223.8	8.6	8	246	14.8	5	244.8	5.4	9	261.9	13.3	5	267.2	4.7	4	229	15	3	239.3	13.9	2	239.5	5.5	3	246.3	13.6	2	254	2
Mother Non-lit., Father lit.	6	234.5	16.4	5	248.4	9.1	8	245.3	11.6	11	261.8	15.8	10	269.9	13.1	6	220	11.3	5	242.2	13.1	6	244.2	19.4	10	263.8	18.9	6	265.5	10.1
Mother & Father Non-Lit.	12	239.7	19.4	9	243.6	19.8	9	248.3	10	5	267.4	16.1	8	276.5	17.2	10	230.4	14.4	12	239.2	22.6	11	241	13.4	11	252.2	6.4	16	269.9	13.3
Family Size																														
Small family (<3)	2	230	0	5	243.4	12.6	0	0	0	1	257	0	3	281.7	11.7	0	0	0	2	231	11	0	0	0	1	255	0	0	0	0
Medium family (4-6)	28	231	18.2	26	244.2	19.4	30	248.3	12.3	27	256.7	10.4	28	270.1	13.7	32	227.3	13.8	26	237.9	19.1	25	247.7	14.5	26	257.1	15.4	26	268	18.8
Medium large family (7-9)	5	236.4	7.3	5	242.8	5	5	246.2	5.2	4	280.3	11.5	3	284.7	15.8	2	223.5	0.5	4	245.8	7.3	8	244.4	20.1	7	262.6	16.1	9	270.7	10.1
Large family (10>)	1	224	0	0	0	0	0	0	0	2	281	11	1	263	0	0	0	0	2	235.5	0.5	1	245	0	0	0	0	0	0	0
Family Type																														
Nuclear	25	233.6	17.6	28	243.6	19.04	26	249.1	12.9	26	256.5	10	26	273.2	16.3	26	225.9	14.5	22	240	19.3	24	249.4	15.8	28	256	14.2	28	267.3	17
Joint	11	226.8	12.2	8	248.4	8.56	9	244.9	5.5	8	275.3	14.7	9	269.1	5.8	8	230.9	8	12	235.3	12.9	10	240.6	14.3	6	268.2	17.4	7	274.1	15.9
Parity																														
1	5	231.8	15.2	14	245.7	19.51	10	250.7	14.6	11	256.9	8.1	16	267.1	13.6	14	229.8	13.1	6	237.7	8	9	247.9	11	10	260.2	16.3	6	262.7	10.9
2	15	230	20.8	14	243.8	16.4	12	247.2	12.7	8	269	13.7	6	272.7	10.9	7	227.7	15.9	10	235.9	16.9	13	248.6	16.3	8	259.8	14.3	11	271.8	17.6
3	10	232.6	12.5	4	238.5	11.41	6	247.8	4.6	7	248.9	4.9	9	274.9	13.4	9	223.4	12.7	13	236.9	21.3	6	236.3	13.8	3	257.7	5.3	6	270.8	9.1
4	5	235.8	6.2	3	239.7	18.57	6	245	8	5	268	15.2	3	291.7	11.3	1	214	0	1	262	0	5	258.8	10.5	7	252.4	15.8	6	274.3	14.8
5 to above	1	220	0	1	253	0.001	1	250	0	3	270.7	15.2	1	266	0	3	227.7	6.6	4	243.8	10.1	1	217	0	6	259.7	16.9	6	261.2	23.5
Per Capita Income																														
Rs. 101-200	3	229.7	5.9	5	249.4	3.01	6	243.7	7.9	2	275	18	1	263	0	8	228.3	11	7	238.3	11.2	3	240.3	16.2	8	258.1	11.4	7	264.4	25.7
Rs. 201-300	14	230.6	15.2	13	235	18.36	18	248.4	11.2	18	262.7	13	13	274.4	12.1	10	219	10.9	14	240.1	22	18	242.9	15.9	16	256.5	16.9	20	270.6	15.6
Rs. 301-400	16	231.9	19.6	11	252.3	17.62	10	249.8	13.9	13	257.2	12.7	14	268.8	16.9	12	230.5	14.6	6	235	16.9	7	258.6	11.3	7	261.6	17.2	5	268	8
Rs. 401 and above	3	235.3	6.9	7	243.1	12.8	1	248	0	1	251	0	7	275.9	12.1	4	234.3	9.8	7	237.4	10.9	6	248	12.4	3	259.2	10.3	3	267	4.9

Comparison with Other Indian Populations

The anthropometric parameters of the Poundrakshtriya children have been compared with "All India" growth pattern of the children in statewise (ICMR, 1972).

The highest weight in both boys and girls are 18.1 Kg. and 17.4 Kg. in 6 years age group, 19.8 Kg. and 19.9 Kg. in 7 years age, 22.1 Kg. and 21.4 Kg. in 8 years age group respectively are found in Orissa and low weight are found in Maharashtra (Poona) such as 15.2 Kg. and 15.1 Kg. in 6 years age group, 16.7 Kg. and 16.3 Kg. in 7 years age, 18.1 Kg. and 18 Kg. in 8 years age group in both boys and girls. In 9 years age group it is seen that highest weight 23.7 Kg. occupied by the boys of Orissa and the girls of Delhi 23.5 Kg. and low weight is noticed in both boys and girls of Kerala 19.8 Kg. In 9 years group weight is high in both boys and girls are 26 Kg. and 26.2 Kg. respectively of Delhi and weight is low 21.5 Kg. and 21.7 Kg. in girls of Maharashtra. The weight of the Poundrakshtriya children occupy the intermediate position.

Tall stature includes 113.1 cms and 113.3 cms in 6 years age group, 117.2 cms and 117.3 cms in 7 years age group, 124.6 cms and 123 cms in 8 years age and 128.3 cms and 126.9 cms in 9 years age group in boys and girls respectively of Orissa. In 10 years age group tall stature are noticed 131.8 cms in boys of Orissa and 132.6 cms in girls of Jammu and Kashmir. Low stature are noticed for both boys and girls 106.1 cms and 105.9 cms in 6 years age, 111.5 cms and 111.1 cms in 7 years, 117.5 cms and 116 cms in 8 years, 122.3 cms and 121.5 cms in 9 years age group respectively of Madras. In 10 years age group low stature 125.4 cms and 125 cms are found in both boys and girls in Kerala. The stature of the Poundrakshtriya children are neither taller, the children of Madras, nor shorter the children of Orrissa.

Sitting height is very high in 6 years age group among the children of Jammu and Kashmir 63.4 cms in boys and 60.8 cms in girls. Sitting height is high in both boys and girls 63.3 cms and 62.5 cms in 7 years age, 65.5 cms and 64.7 cms in 8 years age group and 67.6 cms and 66.6 cms in 9 years age group respectively of Punjab. In 10 years age group high frequency of sitting height 70 cms in boys and 70.8 cms in girls are found in Jammu and Kashmir. Sitting height is low among the children of Kerala, the values varies between 57.8 cms to 65 cms in boys and 57.3 to 64.5 cms in girls. In Poundrakshtriya children sitting height is more closer to the low values of Kerala.

The children of Jammu and Kashmir possess high bi-iliocristal diameter in 6 years to 10 years age group. The value varies between 18.6 cms to 21.2 cms in boys and 18.2 cms to 22.1 cms in girls. Bi-iliocristal diameter is low among the children of Kerala, it varies between 16 cms to 18.3 cms in boys and 15.8 to 18.3 cms in girls. Bi-iliocristal diameter of the Poundrakshtriya children is neither high like the children of Jammu and Kashmir nor low like the children of Kerala.

Summary and Conclusion

From the metric analysis it is found that in Poundrakshtriya children weight, stature, sitting height, biacromial diameter, Bi-iliocristal diameter, head circumference, chest circumference, upper arm girth and calf girth are generally increasing with the advancement of age from 6 to 10 years age group.

The mean values of triceps, biceps and sub-scapular skinfold thickness in Poundrakshtriya girls show slight increment as age increases.

The maximum absolute gain with rate of increment is higher in weight, sitting height, bi-acromial diameter, bi-iliocristal diameter, chest circumference, upper arm girth and calf girth among the boys of 8 and 9 years and the girls of 6 and 7 years age group.

Distance and velocity curves are much pronounced in girls for weight, sitting height, bi-iliocristal diameter, chest circumference, calf girth, triceps, biceps and sub-scapular skin fold specially at 10 years age group.

Line of regression in the Poundrakshtriya boys is higher in weight, stature, biacromial diameter, bi-iliocristal diameter, chest circumference, triceps and biceps.

In skin fold at triceps, sub-scapular and biceps, sexual difference is highly marked in Poundrakshtriya children.

Co-relation is high between stature and weight, stature and sitting height, bi-acromial diameter and bi-iliocristal diameter, chest circumference and head circumference in both the sexes of the Poundrakshstriya children.

Anthropometric characters of the Poundrakshtriya children when compared with All Indian (ICMR-1972) different populations it is seen that weight occupies the intermediate position not higher than Orissa or not lesser than Maharashtrian children. The stature of the Poundrakshtriya children are neither taller than the children of Madras nor shorter than the children of Orissa. Sitting height is more closer to the low value of Kerala. Bi-iliocristal diameter of the Poundrakshtriya is in between high value of the children of Jammu and Kashmir and low value of Kerala. Both head circumference and chest circumference of the Poundrakshtriya children are low when compare with other Indian populations.

Grade II and Grade III malnutrition is very common in both boys and girls of the Poundrakshtriya in weight deficit classification Vishveshwar Rao (1979). In height deficit classification, mild retardation is predominant in both boys and girls (Vishveshwar Rao 1979). Moderate malnutrition is very common among the boys and girls of the Poundrakshtriya in Mid-upper Arm circumference. (ICMR 1972).

The eruption of permanent teeth is slightly delayed in Poundrakshtriya children in comparison to other Bengali population (Banerjee, *et.al.* 1985).

Girls are suffering from very high prevalence of Vitamin A, Vitamin C and Niacin deficiencies, and anemia is common among them. Whereas, the boys suffer from riboflavin, Niacin and Pyridoxine deficiencies.

Impact of socio-cultural factors on growth pattern of Poundrakshtriya children is not marked. Physical development and mental development are inter-related. In order to assess the mental ability of the children about 25 per cent of them were subjected to two simple-type of psychological tests, namely Koh's Block Design Test and Raven's Progressive Matrices Test.

The result of the Block Design Test reveals that 62.3 per cent children belong to below average 10 level category. None could reach the maximum level. Colour matrices test also yielded result in the same direction. Children to the tune of 68.5 per cent belong to the below average IQ level category, Preponderance of the category might be due to factors like malnutrition and lack of awareness due to less exposure to mass media in rural context. Male female disparity is also marked.

Thus all the findings point to the fact of malnutrition and undernourishment of the People. In sum it may be concluded that most of the Poundrakshtriya children of Canning are living in a distressed condition and the impact is clear on their development-both physical and mental. They are placed much below the optimum standard laid down by the ICMR.

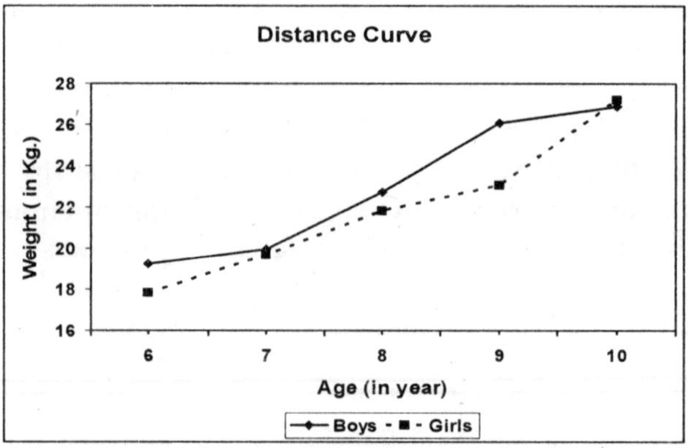

Fig. 1

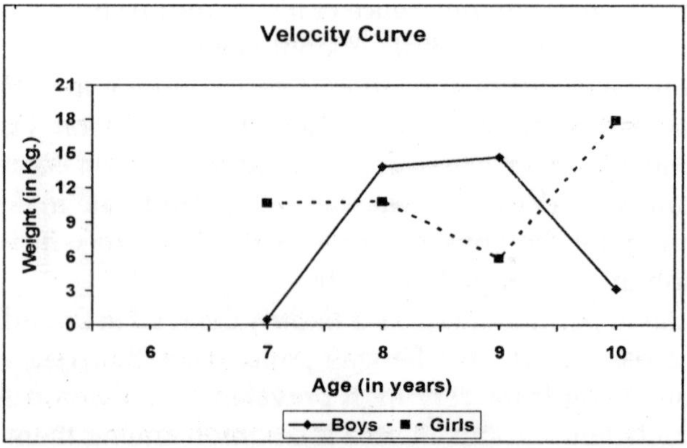

Fig. 2

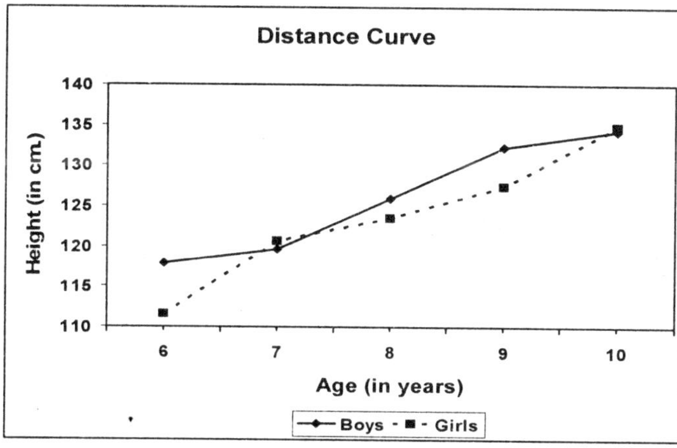

Fig. 3

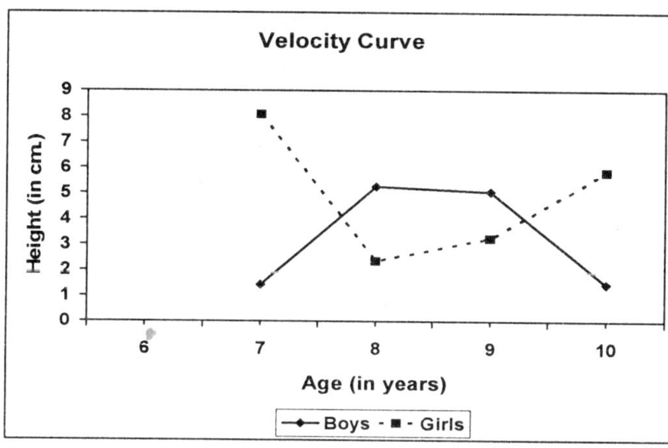

Fig. 4

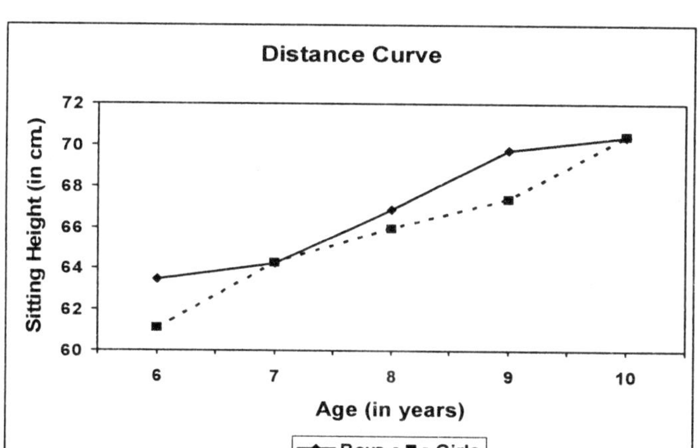

Fig. 5

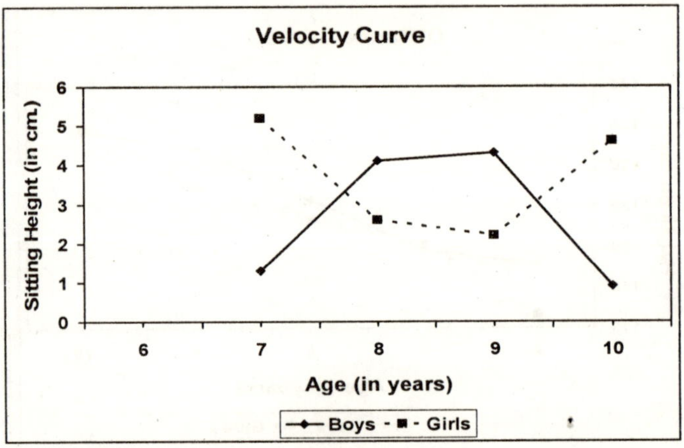

Fig. 6

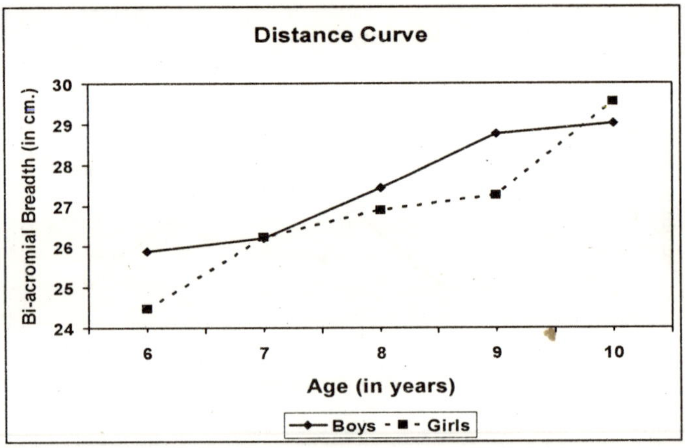

Fig. 7

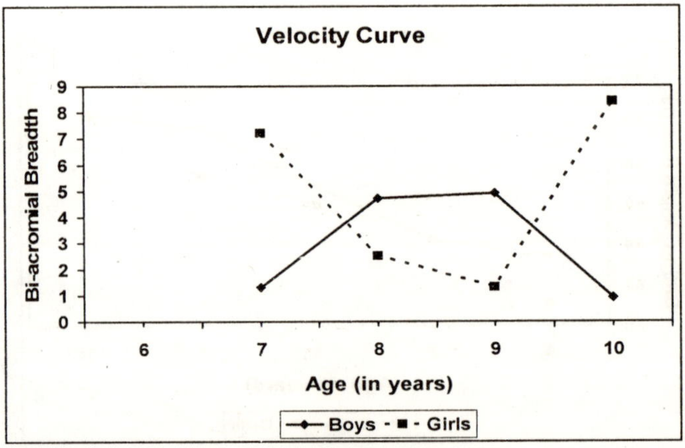

Fig. 8

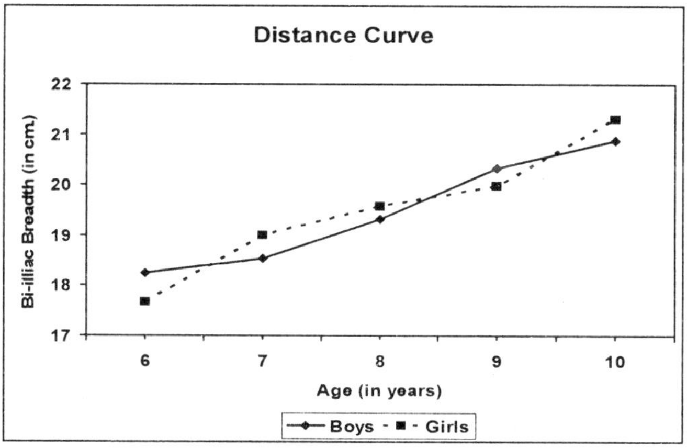

Fig. 9

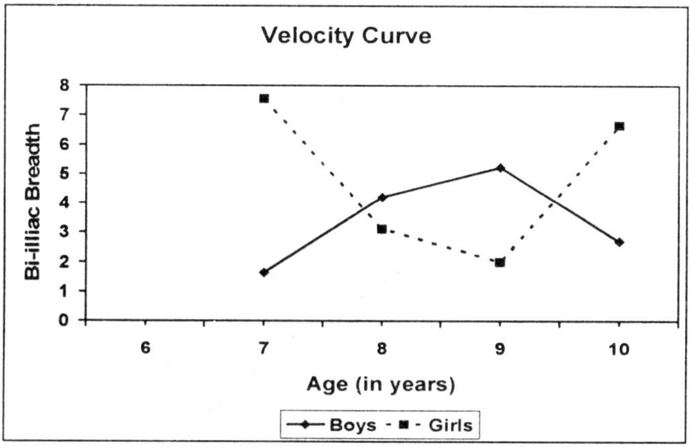

Fig. 10

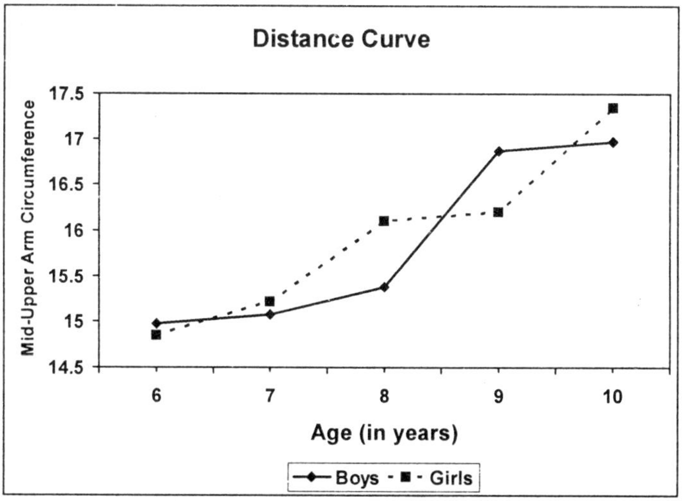

Fig. 11

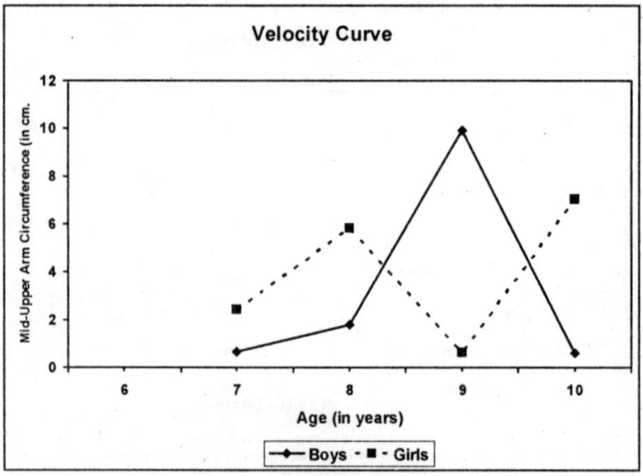

Fig. 12

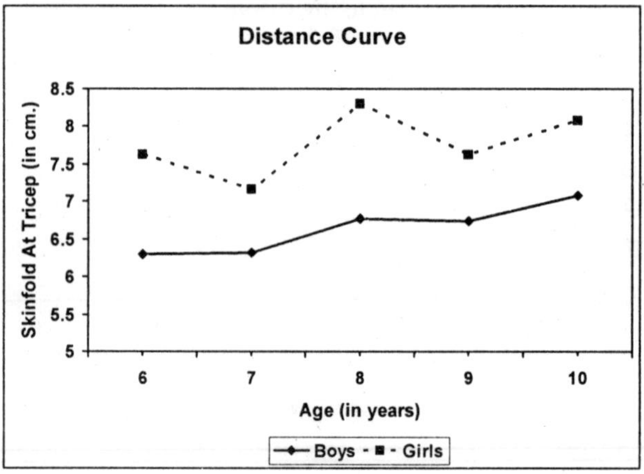

Fig. 13

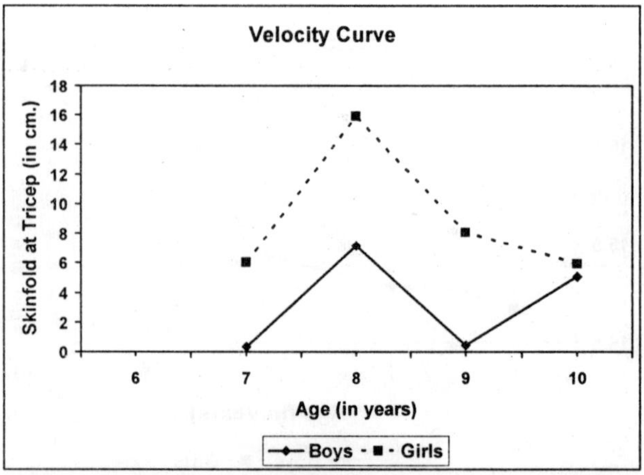

Fig. 14

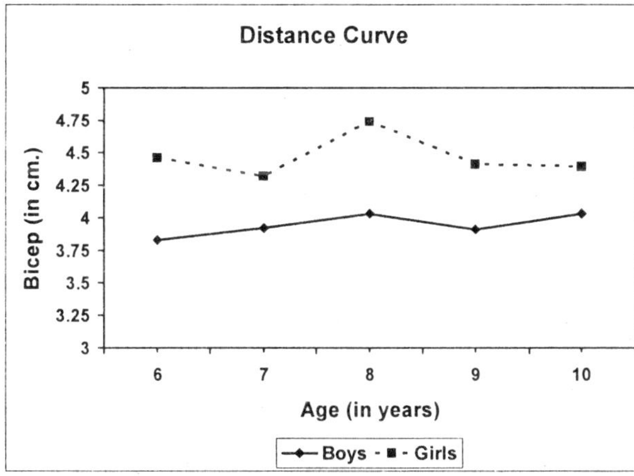

Fig. 15

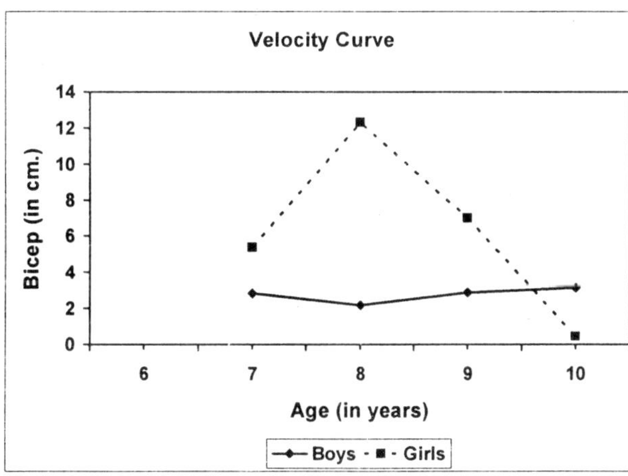

Fig. 16

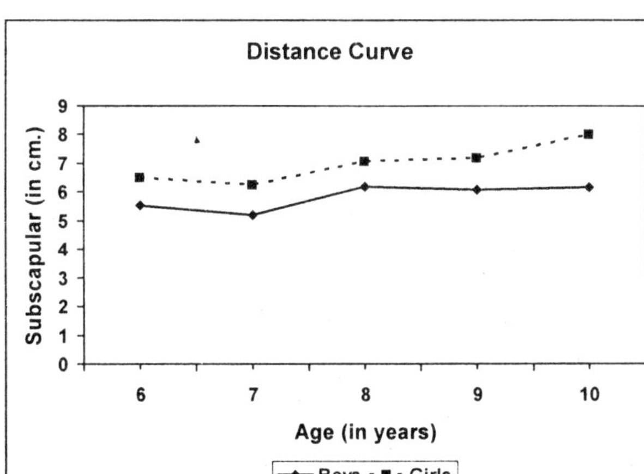

Fig. 17

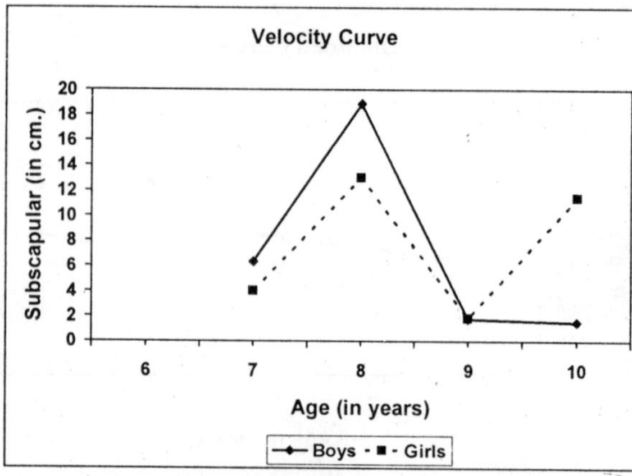

Fig. 18

LINE OF REGRESSION POUNDRA KSHATRIYA

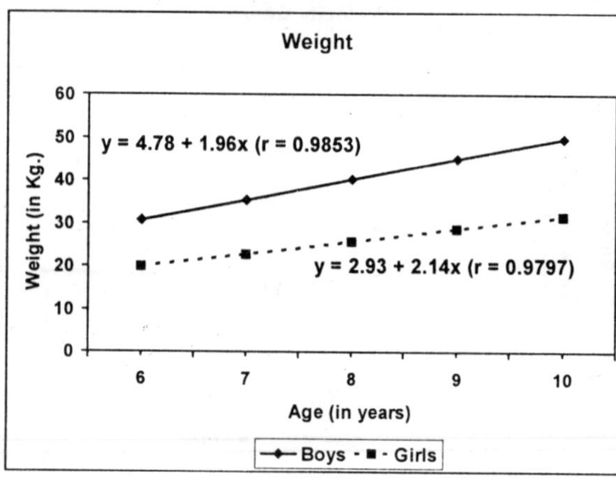

Fig. 19

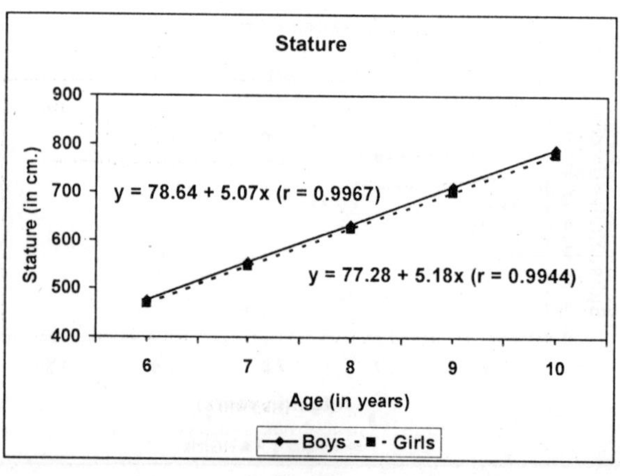

Fig. 20

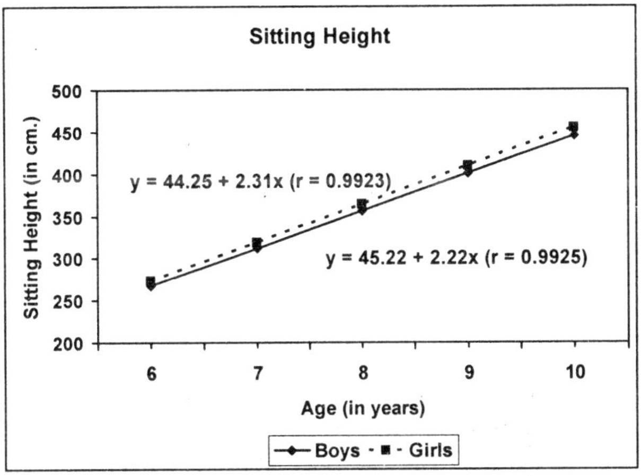

Fig. 21

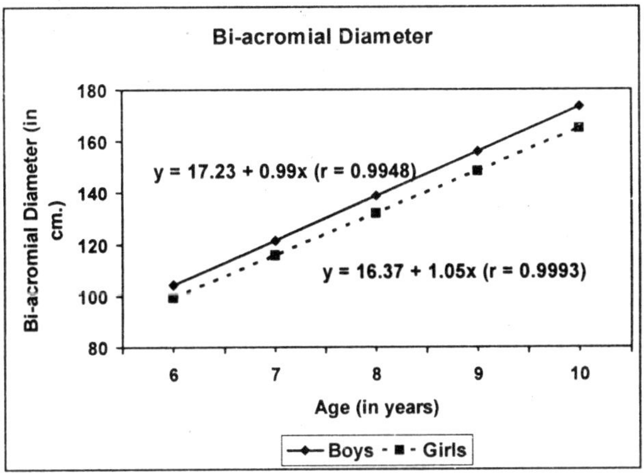

Fig. 22

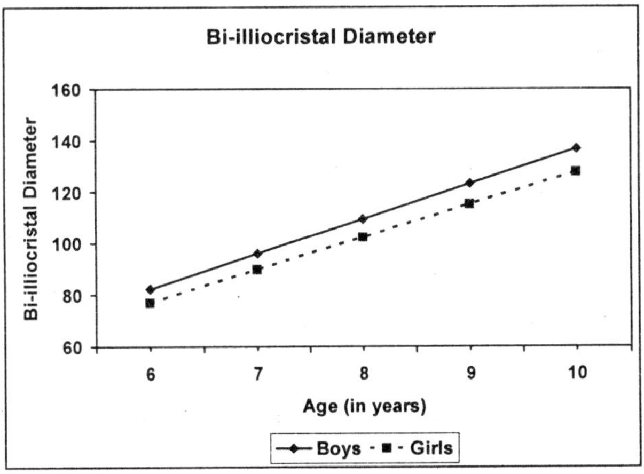

Fig. 23

References

Banerjee, A. R., Papiya Banerjee and Krishna Dutta (1985), Eruption of Permanent Teeth among the Bengalees. In Dental Anthropology Application and method (ed.) Rami Reddy. Inter India Publications, New Delhi.

Chatterjee, B.C. (1872), Cited by Risley, H.H. (1891).

Ghosh, Purnendu (1406), *Dakshin Chabbis Parganar Janagosthi O Adbasider Jiban-Samaskriti.* Paschimbanga: Dakshin Chabbis Parganar Jela Sankhya. Pp 131-148 Govt. of W. Bengal, Deptt. of Information and Culture, Kolkata.

Guha, B. S. (1935), Racial Affinities of the People of India. In *Census of India,* 1931, Vol. I, India.

Hunter, W.W. (1973), A Statistical Account of Bengal Vol. II (Reprint). D.K. Publishing, Delhi.

Indian Council of Medical Research (1972), Growth and Physical Development of Indian Infants & Children, *ICMR Tech. Rep. Series No. 18,* Medical Enclave, New Delhi.

Mahalanabis, P.C. 1402 (BS) Cited in Nihar Ranjan Roy.

Martin, R. (1928), Lehrbuch der Aanthropologie. Jena: Gustar Fischer.

National Nutrition Monitoring Bureau (1979), Report of the year 1979., NiN, ICMR Hyderabad.

Risley, H. H. (1891), The Tribes and Castes of Bengal , Vol. 2, pp 176-177. Calcutta: Bengal Secretarial Press.

Roy Nihar Ranjan 1402 (BS) *Bangalir Itihas (Adi Parba)* Calcutta: Deys Publishing.

Tanner, J. M. (1952), The Assessment of Growth and Development in Children, *Arch. Dis. Child.* 27: 10-33.

Sen, T. (1988), Growth and Development of Bengalee Girls. Anthropological Survey of India, Govt. of India, Calcutta.

World Health Organisation (1986), Use and Interpretation of Anthropometric, Indicators of Nutritional Status. *Report of WHO Working Group, Bulletin of the WHO 64,* No. 6, 929-941.

World Health Organisation (1995), Physical Status. The Use and Interpretation of Anthropometry. *Report of a WHO Expert Committee, Who Technical Report Series* 854.

5

GROWTH AND DEVELOPMENT OF KAIBARTA CHILDREN OF ASSAM: A BIO-CULTURAL PERSPECTIVE

Bandana Das

The growth is an active dynamic evolutionary process by which an individual attain maximum size until certain age in his or her genetic constitution in a given environment. In the study of the mechanism of evolutionary change and the study of individual differences in structure and function: growth and development occupies a central place, which is influenced by mixture of heredity and environmental effect. The genetical control of growth rate is manifested most simply through the inheritance of differential growth pattern of the human body. These differential growth-velocities are responsible for the appearance of characteristic human shape in embryogenesis and for the change of shape from that of the young to the adult development that varies from population to population due to their different genetically constitution and effect of the environment. Tanner (1962) pointed out the period of adolescence is the time of growing up. It lasts almost about eight to ten years and has no sharp beginning or end. It is the period of transition from childhood to adulthood. Evidently, it shows the importance of studying the growth and development of children.

Many studies indicated that the pattern of physical growth and development, though genetically determined, it is strongly influenced by socio-economic and nutritional status. "A child's growth rate reflects, better than any other single index. His state of health and nutrition also indicate his or her psychological situation. Thus, a well-designed growth study is a powerful tool with which the health and nutritional status of the population can be monitored." (Eveleth and Tanner, 1990).

With this view Anthropological Survey of India undertook an inter-disciplinary systematic scientific investigation under the project 'Growth and Development of Children: Bio-cultural perspective'.

The present study was taken up under the above mentioned project as no such systematic study on growth and development along with the bio-cultural perspective to see its impact on growth among the Kaibarta children of Assam has been made so far.

Land and People

The present field of investigation was carried out in district Kamrup of Guwahati, capital of Assam. The Assam state is situated in the extreme north-eastern region of India between 24^0 and 28^0 North latitude and $89^050'$ and 96^0 East longitude. A natural gap between North Guwahati and Guwahati is created by the river Brahmaputra which flows across the entire length of the state from East to West.

The Kaibartas are one of the sixteen Scheduled Caste populations of Assam. Numerically they occupy the second largest position among the sixteen communities constituting 7.4% of total population of Assam. They are found almost in all plains districts of Assam. Their language is Assamese belonged to Indo Aryan language. Their primary occupation is fishing.

Material and Method

The data were collected from the Kaibarta community, residing in Uzanbazar and Kharghuli in Guwahati and Monikarneswar, Rajaduwar, Silsekhow, Dihingsatra and Mazgaw in North Guwahati. Data have been collected from school and by house survey of the respective subjects in the month from February to March'99.

Eight absolute anthropometric measurements were taken on 352 children consisting of 175 boys and 177 girls from the age group of 6 to 10 years of apparently normal and healthy children. Weight, stature/height vertex, sitting height, bi-acromial diameter, bi-iliocristal diameter, triceps, biceps and subscapular were taken into consideration along with mid-upper arm circumference, clinical sign for general health and dental pattern. Information on some socio-cultural factors like occupation, per capita income, literacy level of parents, family type and family size were also considered to see its impact on growth.

Various statistical constants were calculated for all measurements, age and sexwise as per the guideline of the project. The mean, standard deviation, co-efficient of variation with their standard error absolute growth rate, 't' test for inter-group differences and sexual diamorphism were calculated. Distance and velocity curves were also plotted. Regression equation $Y = b x + a$, co-relation co-efficient between height and weight, height and sitting height, bi-acromial and bi-iliocristal breadth, skinfold thickness at triceps and subscapular were calculated. Classification of children according to weight for age, height for age and mid-upper arm circumference were computed to see the nutritional status. Frequency distribution of children with erupted teeth and clinical sign, per capita income, frequency distribution of family size and literacy level of parents were calculated to see the impact on growth and development.

Results and Discussion

Occupation

Though the traditional main occupation of the Kaibartas was fishing or fish trade, the present study showed more inclination towards other occupation. However, most of them were engaged in low paid job like chowkidar, electrician, military, police, ticket collector in inland water transport etc. which was not adequate to run their day to day requirement and meet their daily expenditure. And those who were engaged in business or daily earner were not in service but economically steady. Low economic condition of the Kaibartas have obviously affected the growth and development of children. The mean per-capita income of parents was calculated and tabulated age and sex wise (Table 1). It ranges between Rs. 8,401 to Rs. 11,602. However, majority of the Kaibarta families were found below poverty line as their per capita income was below India's standard per capita income which is Rs. 10,770.

Table 1
Distribution of Mean, S.D. for Per Capita Income of Kaibarta Children

	Per Capita income of Boys		*Per Capita income of Girls*	
Age Group in years	*Mean*	*S.D.*	*Mean*	*S.D*
6	10,063	5577.56	10.044	4329.38
7	8,401	4299.00	8,517	3972.77
8	10,086	6669.42	11,602	6835.63
9	10,915	4627.06	10,207	6349.54
10	10,442	7921.65	10,103	5273.53

Literacy Level of Parents

The literacy level i.e. primary, middle, higher secondary and graduate level in both parents of boys and girls are shown in Table 2. Parents show high frequency up to higher secondary level. Specially most mother's education was limited within middle and higher secondary level

Table 2
Literacy Level of Parents of Kaibarta Children

Father of Boys						
					Literate Father	
Age group of children	*No. of Father*	*Illiterate Father*	*Primary*	*Middle*	*Hgr. Secondary*	*Graduate*
6	35	2	3	4	18	8
7	35	2	4	5	14	10
8	34	1	2	2	16	13
9	34	Nil	2	2	16	14
10	35	2	1	3	18	11
Total	173	7	12	16	82	56
Percentage		4.05	6.94	9.25	47.40	32.37

Mother of Boys						
					Literate Mother	
Age group of children	*No. of Mother*	*Illiterate Mother*	*Primary*	*Middle*	*Hgr. Secondary*	*Graduate*
6	35	4	4	10	15	2
7	35	6	4	9	12	4
8	34	6	3	8	11	6
9	33	6	4	8	9	6
10	35	6	4	9	12	4
Total	172	28	19	44	59	22
Percentage		16.28	11.05	25.58	34.30	12.79

Father of Girls						
					Literate Father	
Age group of children	*No. of Father*	*Illiterate Father*	*Primary*	*Middle*	*Hgr. Secondary*	*Graduate*
6	35	1	2	4	12	16
7	34	1	3	4	16	10
8	35	1	2	3	12	17
9	32	1	3	3	13	12
10	35	1	2	2	14	16
Total	171	5	12	16	67	71
Percentage		2.92	7.02	9.36	39.18	41.52

Contd...

Mother of Girls						
					Literate Mother	
Age group of children	*No. of Mother*	*Illiterate Mother*	*Primary*	*Middle*	*Hgr. Secondary*	*Graduate*
6	36	5	5	8	14	4
7	35	5	4	9	12	5
8	34	3	4	10	10	7
9	35	4	3	8	12	8
10	35	2	5	8	13	8
Total	175	19	21	42	61	32
Percentage		10.86	12.00	24.00	34.86	18.28

comparatively which might have affect the efficiency of knowledge for proper management of health of their children and thus restrain the growth and development of the children.

Family Type

A child being brought up in a nuclear family expect to attain better growth and development compare to a child from a joint family as the child gets better attention nourishment. In the present study all the families were nuclear and no joint families were found. However, the present findings of growth and development among the Kaibarta children indicate less impact of family type on the growth and development of Kaibarta children.

Family Size

Family size is an important factor to assess the nutritional status of a growing child. From the size of the family one can know how much a child partakes of his/her family's total income and thus large family size has an impact on nutritional status of the child. In the present study (Table 3) high frequency was found in the medium size of family that consists of 4 to 6 members and this might have affected their nutritional status with the prevailing lower economic condition among the Kaibarta people and thus might have affected their growth and development of the Kaibarta children to a great extent. (Table 3).

Anthropometric Variables

Weight

Weight is an important measurement, which gives the idea of sum total of growth in all dimensions. Mean values of weight (Table 4) showed gradual increase in weight from 6 years to 10 years in both the sexes i.e. 17.30 kg to 24.44 kg for boys, whereas in case of girls it was 15.75 kg to 26.04 kg. The girls were found to be heavier than their male counterpart at the age of 8 and 10 yrs.

Table 3
Distribution of Family Size of Kaibarta Children

Boys				
Family Size				
Age Group	*Small (1-3)*	*Medium (4-6)*	*Large (7-9)*	*Total*
6	5	28	2	35
7	3	31	1	35
8	4	31	-	35
9	2	32	-	34
10	4	30	2	36
	18	152	5	175
Percentage	10.28%	86.86%	2.86%	
Girls				
Family Size				
6	7	29	-	36
7	6	26	3	35
8	6	29	-	35
9	6	30	-	36
10	1	33	1	35
	26	147	4	177
Percentage	14.69%	83.05	2.26%	

The calculated value of standard deviation and co-efficient of variation showed greater variation in all the age groups.

The frequency of absolute growth (Table 4) was found to be higher at 9 yrs among boys i.e. 2.61 while in case of girls it was recorded at 10 yrs. i.e. 3.33. However the relative rate of growth of boys was found to be higher at 7 yrs i.e. 12.77% whereas in case of girls it was found to be of 18.98% for the same age.

Distance curve of boys for weight (Fig.1) remains at a higher level from 6 to 7 yrs. whereas the girls surpassed that of boys at 8 and 10 yrs. Both the curves crosses at 8 yrs. probably the pre-adolescent spurt starts from the age of 8 yrs.

It was distinct from the velocity curves (Fig 2) that the rate of growth as higher among girls for all the age group than the boys except between 8 and 9 yrs. Between 9 and 10 yrs. growth rate was accelerated in case of girls, while among boys it was deaccelerated.

The regression equation for weight on age (Table 6) for boys and girls $y = 7.66530+1.663886$ ($r = 0.994$) and $y = 0.60\ x+2.7$ ($r = 0.996$) respectively was recorded (Fig. 17).

The 't' test for sexual dimorphism (Table 7) showed significant result at 6 yrs of age at 1% level.

Stature

It is an important composite measurement, which help us to assess the total vertical growth of the children. The mean value of stature (Table 4) show the gradual increase in both the sexes from 6 to 10 yrs. which ranges from 111.51 cm. to 129.77 cm. and 106.86 cm. to 134.59 cm. boys and girls respectively. The increment of stature was prominent in girls after 10 yrs. though it was lower in early ages. Value of S.D. and C.V. denoted distinct variation of stature among the children.

The value of absolute growth (Table 4) which shows rate of growth of stature accelerated at 7 yrs. of age for both the sexes as the higher frequency of absolute growth was found for both the sexes, at that age. While the lower frequency was recorded at 10 yrs. and 8 yrs. among boys and girls respectively.

The frequency of relative rate of growth was found to be higher at 7 yrs. and accelerated intermittently in either sexes. The relative rate of growth deaccelerates from lower age to higher age.

Distance curve of stature (Fig. 3) of boys is higher than the girls from 6 to 8 yrs., whereas, it rises higher among girls than the boys from 9 to 10 yrs. The distance curve of girls is abruptly increased from 9 to 10 yrs. and is at higher level whereas in case of boys it is at lower level than the girls of the same age, which indicates the spurt of growth for the girls at that age.

Velocity curve of stature (Fig. 4) clearly showed rate of increment among girls was higher than the boys for all age group. The rate of growth was found to be increased among the girls beyond 10 yrs. whereas in case of boys it was diminished for the same age. This may be due to girl's earlier attainment of maturity than the boys. The regression equation for stature (Table 6) of boys and girls y=87.25x+4.25 and y=96.67x+3.86 respectively was recorded (Fig. 18). Value of 't' test for sexual dimorphism in stature (Table 7) showed significant result at 6 and 10 yrs. of age at 1% level.

Sitting Height

It is one of the most important measurement of the linear growth, which help to assess the development of trunk. The distribution of mean values of sitting height (Table 4) showed gradual increase from 6 yrs. to 10 yrs. in either sexes. The lesser value of S.D. and C.V. showed less variation or slow rate of growth of sitting height in both the sexes.

Maximum absolute and relative rate of growth in sitting height exhibited by both the sexes between the age group of 6 and 7 yrs. In case of girls growth rate was increased between the age group of 9 and 10 years while in boys it was decreased.

Distance curve of sitting height of boys (Fig. 5) remains higher from 6 to 9 yrs. than the girls while the girls surpassed the boys at 10 yrs. which indicated that development of trunk of girls was more pronounced than the boys at that age.

The velocity curve of sitting height (Fig. 6) showed that the relative rate of growth was higher among girls than their male counterparts. Maximum differences was seen between 6 and 7 yrs. in both the sexes. The pattern of growth rate was more or less similar up to 9 yrs. of age in both the sexes but it deaccelerates among boys beyond it whereas it accelerates in case of girls.

The regression equation (Table-6) of boys and girls y = 51.97 x +1.7 and y = 47.36x+2.33 respectively was recorded (Fig. 19).

The 't' for sexual dimorphism sitting is well marked with respect to height in 6 yrs. only at 1% level.

Bi-acromial Diameter

Mean values of bi-acromial diameter ranges from 23.99 cm. to 27.45 cm and 23.40 cm. to 28.56 cm from 6 to 10 yrs. for Kaibarta boys and girls respectively. However, the mean value increases with the change of age in either sexes, and the sex difference is more marked at the age of 9 yrs. (1.69 cm.)

The rate of absolute growth (Table 4) shows less variation in the growth and development of bi-acromial breadth of both the sexes.

The relative rate of increment seems to be higher in both the sexes at the age of 7 yrs; whereas, the lower increment was recorded at 8 yrs. Between 9 and 10 years of age the girls experienced a sudden increase in biacromial diameter thus supercedes the value of bi-acromial diameter of boys. From the above it can be said that, the boys shoulder was narrower than that of girls as the girls shoulder was broaden with the change of age.

Distance curve of bi-acromial diameter (Fig. 7) of boys shows higher at 6 and 9 yrs. than the girls whereas among the girls it shows higher at 10 yrs. than the boys. Although both the curves were crossed at 8 yrs. the curve was prolonged after 9 yrs. in case of girls whereas in case of boys it was almost similar to that of 9 yrs. which indicate growth of biacromial breadth for boys after the age of 9 yrs was slow whereas for girls at that age it was faster.

Velocity curve of bi-acromial diameter (Fig. 8) of boys showed that the rate of growth accelerated between the age group of 8 and 9 yrs. while in case of girls it was seen between the age of 6 and 7 yrs. At the age of 9 to 10 yrs. rate of growth for boys decelerated while it was accelerated in case of girls.

The regression equation for boys and girls y = 18.67x+0.89 (r = 0.996) and y = 21.10x+0.75 (r = 0.706) respectively was recorded (Fig. 20).

The value of 't' for sexual dimorphism in bi-acromial diameter showed significant result at the age of 10 yrs. at 1% level.

Bi-Iliocristal Diameter

It helps to assess transverse growth of hip. The mean values show gradual increase (Table 4) with the change of age in both the sexes, which was slightly higher in case of girls from 7 yrs. onwards than their male counterparts.

The absolute growth of bi-iliocristal dimension (Table 4) showed higher rate of growth of girls than the boys for all the age groups. Between 9 and 10 yrs. while it was decelerated in case of boys but it was accelerated to its maximum in case of girls.

The relative rate of growth was higher for boys at the age of 9 yrs. while in case of girls it was at the age of 10 yrs.

The distance curve of bi-iliocristal diameter (Fig. 9) for girls showed higher from 7 yrs. onwards with maximum difference at the age of 10 yrs. than the boys, which indicates broader hip of girls compare to boys.

The velocity curve (Fig. 10) of girls showed higher rate of growth than the boys in all the age groups. The rate of increment was found to be much higher among girls than among boys. The spurt accelerates rapidly among the girls whereas it was decelerated among the boys from 9 yrs. to 10 yrs. of age.

The regression equation (Table 6) for boys and girls $y = 13.36x+0.66$ ($r = 0.973$), $y = 22.80x+0.81$ ($r = 0.436$) respectively was recorded (Fig. 21).

For sexual dimorphism 't' value showed highly significant difference at the age of 10 years at 1% level. (Table 7).

Triceps Skin Fold

The amount of accumulation of fat can be assessed by measuring the thickness of skin fold at triceps, biceps and sub scapular. The distribution of mean value (Table 5) showed irregular increment with the change of age in both the sexes. Slightly higher increment was observed at the age of 7 yrs. in both the sexes. However the girls shows higher values than the boys for all age groups except at 7 yrs. where the boys showed higher value.

The maximum rate of absolute growth of both the sexes was noticed between the age 6 and 7 yrs. The negative value of rate of absolute growth of both the sexes was recorded at the age of 8 to 9 yrs., which means there was no growth in those ages. On the other hand the rate of absolute Growth was recorded positive at 10 yrs. with slight change over 9 years of age for boys only.

Distance curve (Fig.11) for girls shows higher level in comparison to boys for all age groups except at 7 yrs. which indicates that fat deposition at triceps is more in case of girls compared to boys throughout their growth period except at the age of 7 yrs.

The velocity curve for both the sexes (Fig.12) showed maximum rate of growth at the age of 7 yrs. followed by 10 yrs. Both the curves showed negative rate of growth between 7 and 9 yrs. which indicates that there was no increment in growth of this dimension in that period. Variation of rate was more in case of boys than the girls.

The 't' value shows no significant result of sexual dimorphism for both the sexes (Table 7) for triceps skinfold thickness in any age group.

Sub Scapular Skin Fold

In case of boys the distribution of mean value (Table 5) was not found uniform.

At the age of 9 yrs. slightly higher value was observed for boys which were followed by 6 and 10 yrs., whereas in case of girls it was found at 10 yrs. followed by 9 and 8 yrs. However, the girls show less variation over the boys for all age groups.

The absolute growth of boys showed higher frequency at the age group of 9 yrs. and for girls it showed higher frequency at 7 yrs. Negative rate of growth among boys was noticed at 7 and 8 yrs where as among girls it was seen at 8 yrs. which indicate that there was no growth. After 9 yrs of age the rate was found to be increased in girls while in case of boys it is decreased.

Distance curve of sub scapular skin fold (Fig.13) showed opposite trend between boys and girls. However, the curve for girls remains at a higher level than that of boys with more difference at 8 yrs followed by 10 yrs, which indicates that the deposition of fat at subscapulr is more in case of girls in comparison to boys throughout their growth periods.

Velocity curve of subscapuar skin fold (Fig.14) for boys showed higher than that of girls at 9 yrs. and 10 yrs whereas girls surpassed the boys at 7 yrs. Growth of boys was decelerated with negative trend from 7 to 8 yrs. while in case of girls it was observed at 8 yrs. after that it showed positive trend and increase rate of growth up to 10 yrs. In case of boys in 10 yrs. of age boys growth was decelerated.

In sexual dimorphism 't' value (Table 7) showed significant differences in 8 and 10 yrs of age at 1% level.

Biceps Skin Fold

The mean values of thickness of skin fold at biceps (Table 5) showed slightly higher value for girls in comparison to boys with the change of age. During the growth period of 6 to 10 yrs. maximum deposit of fat at bicep showed in case of boys at the age of 7 yrs. while in case of girls it was at the age of 6 yrs. and 10 yrs.

The absolute growth showed maximum rate for boys at the age of 7 yrs. and for girls at the age of 9 yrs. The frequency of absolute growth for boys showed negative rate of growth at the age of 8 yrs while the girls showed at 7 and 8 yrs. which means there was no growth for that period.

The relative rate of growth of biceps among boys was found to be higher than the girls at 7 yrs. followed by 9 yrs. The rate of increment was found to be decelerated in either sexes with the change of age as expected.

Table 4
Distribution of Mean, Standard Error, Standard Deviation, Co-efficiant of Variation and Absolute Growth of Five Anthropometric Measurements, Among the Kaibarta Children of Assam

		Boys						Girls				
Age Group	*No.*	*Wt. Kg.*	*Ht. cm.*	*St.H. cm.*	*Bi-acro cm.*	*Bi-illiac cm.*	*No.*	*Wt. Kg.*	*Ht. cm.*	*St. Ht. cm.*	*Bi-acro cm.*	*Bi-iliac cm.*
6 yrs	35						36					
	M	17.30	111.51	61.85	23.99	17.64		15.75	106.86	59.88	23.40	17.02
	S.E.	0.39	0.92	0.42	0.18	0.13		0.29	0.91	0.35	0.25	0.15
	S.D.	2.33	5.46	2.52	1.11	0.79		1.76	5.49	2.15	1.53	0.92
	C.V.	13.46	4.89	4.07	4.62	4.47		11.17	5.13	3.59	6.53	5.40
	Ab. G.	-	-	-	-	-		-	-	-	-	-
	%	-	-	-	-	-		-	-	-	-	-
7 yrs	35						35					
	M	19.51	117.77	64.20	25.05	18.02		18.74	116.80	63.67	25.03	18.09
	S.E.	0.45	1.04	0.51	0.24	0.19		0.70	1.06	0.50	0.21	0.21
	S.D.	2.67	6.20	3.03	1.45	1.13		4.14	6.31	2.96	1.24	1.26
	C.V.	13.68	5.26	4.71	5.78	6.27		22.09	5.40	4.64	4.95	6.96
	Ab. G.	2.21	6.26	2.35	1.06	0.38		2.99	9.94	3.79	1.63	1.07
	%	12.77	5.61	3.79	4.41	2.15		18.98	9.30	6.32	6.96	6.28
8 yrs	35						35					
	M	20.75	121.43	65.61	25.76	18.51		20.96	121.37	65.37	25.84	18.73
	S.E.	0.36	0.98	0.39	0.22	0.19		0.41	0.92	0.45	0.22	0.17
	S.D.	2.15	5.82	2.32	1.31	1.15		2.46	5.44	2.68	1.28	1.03
	C.V.	10.36	4.79	3.53	5.08	6.21		11.73	4.48	4.09	4.95	5.49
	Ab. G.	1.24	3.66	1.41	0.71	0.49		2.22	4.57	1.70	0.81	0.64
	%	6.35	3.11	2.19	2.83	2.71		11.84	3.91	2.67	3.23	3.53

Contd...

	Boys						Girls					
Age Group	*No.*	*Wt. Kg.*	*Ht. cm.*	*St.H. cm.*	*Bi-acro cm.*	*Bi-illiac cm.*	*No.*	*Wt. Kg.*	*Ht. cm.*	*St. Ht. cm.*	*Bi-acro cm.*	*Bi-iliac cm.*
9 yrs	*34*						*36*					
	M	23.36	126.87	67.69	27.09	19.32		22.72	126.79	67.71	26.71	19.61
	S.E.	0.55	1.33	0.63	0.28	0.21		0.52	0.97	0.54	0.24	0.14
	S.D.	3.23	7.76	3.69	1.69	1.27		3.18	5.83	3.26	1.44	0.84
	C.V.	13.82	6.11	5.45	6.23	6.57		13.77	4.59	4.81	5.39	4.28
	Ab. G.	2.61	5.44	2.08	1.33	0.81		1.76	5.42	2.34	0.87	0.88
	%	12.57	4.47	3.17	5.16	4.37		8.39	4.46	3.57	3.36	4.69
10 yrs	*36*						*35*					
	M	24.44	129.77	69.33	27.45	19.41		26.04	134.59	70.25	28.56	21.05
	S.E.	0.64	1.20	0.52	0.25	0.18		0.75	1.31	0.58	0.32	0.25
	S.D.	3.89	7.20	3.54	1.55	1.11		4.49	7.74	3.46	1.94	1.46
	C.V.	15.91	5.54	5.14	5.64	5.71		17.23	5.75	9.92	6.79	6.93
	Ab. G.	1.08	2.90	1.66	0.36	0.16		3.33	7.80	2.54	1.85	1.44
	%	4.62	2.28	2.45	1.31	0.82		14.65	6.15	3.75	6.92	7.34

Table 5
Distribution of Mean, Standard Deviation, Coefficient of Variation and Absolute Growth of Three Skinfold Measurements

		Boys				Girls		
Age Group	*No.*	*Triceps mm*	*Subscapular mm*	*Biceps mm*	*No.*	*Triceps mm*	*Subscapular mm*	*Biceps mm*
6 yrs	35				36			
	Mean	4.75	4.68	3.30		4.81	4.80	4.04
	S.E.	0.16	0.15	0.12		0.16	0.11	0.12
	S.D.	0.98	0.94	0.75		0.97	0.68	0.84
	C.V.	20.63	20.08	17.92		20.16	14.16	18.06
	Ab. G.	-	-	-		-	-	-
	%	-	-	-		-	-	-
7 yrs	35				35			
	Mean	5.03	4.44	3.76		4.96	5.18	3.94
	S.E.	0.17	0.14	0.13		0.18	0.45	0.26
	S.D.	1.03	0.86	0.78		1.07	2.69	0.86
	C.V.	20.47	19.36	27.50		21.57	21.93	40.10
	Ab. G.	0.28	-0.24	0.46		0.15	0.38	-0.10
	%	5.89	-5.12	13.93		3.11	7.91	-2.47
8 yrs	35				35			
	Mean	4.51	4.36	3.48		4.71	5.17	3.82
	S.E.	0.14	0.10	0.11		0.15	0.19	0.15
	S.D.	0.87	0.61	0.66		0.90	1.17	1.02
	C.V.	19.29	13.99	23.18		19.11	22.63	24.60
	Ab. G.	-0.52	-1.08	-0.28		-0.25	-0.01	-0.12
	%	10.33	-1.80	-7.44		-5.04	-0.19	-3.04

Contd...

Age Group	No.	Boys Triceps mm	Boys Subscapular mm	Boys Biceps mm	No.	Girls Triceps mm	Girls Subscapular mm	Girls Biceps mm
9 yrs	34				36			
	Mean	4.22	4.75	3.58		4.60	5.19	3.95
	S.E.	0.17	0.18	0.14		0.19	0.21	0.17
	S.D.	1.02	1.06	0.83		1.18	1.26	0.94
	C.V.	24.17	22.31	18.96		25.59	24.27	25.82
	Ab. G.	-0.29	0.39	0.10		- 0.10	0.02	0.13
	%	-6.43	8.94	3.73		- 2.12	0.38	3.40
10 yrs	36				35			
	Mean	4.38	4.49	3.60		4.64	5.46	4.04
	S.E.	0.17	0.13	0.16		0.12	0.21	0.14
	S.D.	1.04	0.83	0.99		0.73	1.28	1.58
	C.V.	23.74	18.48	20.74		15.73	23.44	21.28
	Ab. G.	0.16	0.16	0.02		0.03	0.27	0.09
	%	3.79	5.47	0.55		0.65	5.20	2.27

Table 6

Distribution of Regression Equation of Some Measurements on Age for Male and Female Measurements

Ses	*Height on age*	*Height on age*	*Sitting height on age*	*Bi-acromial diameter on age*	*Bi-iliocristal diameter on age*
Male	y = 7.66530x + 1.663886 r = 0.994	y = 87.25x +4.25 r = 0.996	y = 51.97x +1.7 r = 0.997	y = 18.67x +0.89 r = 0.996	y = 13.36x +0.66 r = 0.973
Female	y = -0.60x +2.7 r = 0.996	y = 96.67x +3.86 r = 0.705	y = 47.36x +2.33 r = 0.969	y = 21.10x +0.75 r = 0.706	y = 22.80x +-0.81 r = 0.436

The distance curve (Fig. 15) of both the sexes for bicep skin fold run almost parallel with maximum difference at 6 yrs and 10 yrs. However the curve was found to be higher among girls rather than boys throughout their growth period from 6 to 10 yrs.

The velocity curve for bicep skin fold (Fig.16) of boys showed much higher at the age of 7 yrs while that of girls showed negative rate of growth at that age that means there was no gain of growth during that period . Boys showed negative rate at 8 yrs. Maximum rate of growth for girls showed at 9 yrs. and 10 yrs. The maximum difference of velocity curves was found at 10 yrs. in positive growth.

In sexual dimorphism 't' value showed significant difference at 6 and 10 yrs. at 5% level (Table 7).

Table 7
Distribution of Value of 'T' Test for the Measurements for Sexual Diamorphism

	Age Groups				
Measurements	*6 yrs*	*7 yrs*	*8 yrs*	*9 yrs*	*10 yrs*
Weight	3.18**	0.92	0.38	0.84	1.36
Height	3.59**	0.65	0.04	0.05	2.72**
Sitting Height	3.60**	0.74	0.40	0.02	1.11
Bi-acromial	1.91	0.06	0.25	1.03	2.73**
Bi-ilio.	1.26	0.24	0.86	1.15	5.46**
Tricep	0.26	0.28	0.97	1.53	1.25
Subscapular	0.64	1.57	3.78**	1.59	3.94**
Bicep	4.37**	0.62	1.82	1.68	2.07*

Significant at 5% level* at 1% level **

Co-Relation

Co-relation between (Table 8) height and weight, height and sitting height, biacromial and bi-iliocristal diameters and triceps and sub scapular skin fold showed positive in nature and highly significant at 1% level in all the age groups for both the sexes. Skin fold between triceps and sub scapular at 6 yrs of both the sexes and corelation between biacromial and bi-iliac diameter of girls at the age of 8 showed insignificant results. However, the significant result between height and weight, height and sitting height, biacromial and bi-iliocristal diameter and biceps and sub scapular skin fold indicates that they are closely related to each other.

Dental Pattern

Permanent incisor starts to erupt from 6th year to 9th year. Permanent canine starts to erupt from 11th to 12th year and both first and 2nd premolar from 9th to 12th year, permanent first molar from 6th to 7th year of age and second molar from 12th to 14th year of age and thus show the chronological age of the child (Table 9).

Table 8
Values of Correlation, Co-efficient Between Height and Weight; Height and Sitting Height; Bi-acromial and Bi-iliac Breadth; Skinfold at Tricep and Subscapular for Boys and Girls

Age Group	*Height & Weight*	*Height & Sitting Height*	*Bi-acromial & Bi-ilio. Breadth*	*Skinfold at tricep & subscapular*
Boys				
6 yrs	0.7842**	0.875**	0.5817**	0.3044
7 yrs	0.8662**	0.922*	0.7435**	0.5445**
8 yrs	0.8326**	0.82**	0.6372**	0.5369**
9 yrs	0.8853**	0.8752**	0.6556**	0.558**
10 yrs	0.8217**	0.9344**	0.8394**	0.5103**
Girls				
6 yrs	0.8145**	0.8345**	0.7875**	0.1475
7 yrs	0.7557**	0.9198**	0.7053**	0.7645**
8 yrs	0.5663**	0.8361*	0.2449	0.5402**
9 yrs	0.7403**	0.7234**	0.719**	0.4744*
10 yrs	0.7914**	0.8079**	0.4946**	0.4483**

Significant at 5% level * Significant at 1 % level **

The present findings showed slight variation in the eruption of dental pattern (Table 9). The observed frequency of Kaibarta children with permanent incisor indicate that it starts from 6 years of age and continued upto 10 years of age in case of boys whereas in case of girls eruption completed by 8 years of age. In case of permanent canine it starts to erupt at the age of 8 years in both the sexes and continued beyond 10 years. The frequency distribution of children with premolar showed in case of boys it starts to erupt from 9 years of age while in case of girls from 8 years of age and continued beyond 10 years in both the cases.

First molar starts to erupt from 6 years and continued upto 10 years of age in case of boys whereas in case of girls eruption of first molar completed by 8 years of age.

Eruption of second molar showed by the frequency distribution of boys and girls that it starts from 9 years with very low frequency of 2.94 but at the age of 10 years the frequency of girls erupted second molar was higher as compared to boys indicated that girls are slightly ahead than the boys with the erupted permanent teeth.

Clinical Sign

The frequency distribution of clinical sign (Table 10) shows the nutritional deficiency among children. It shows that most of the children suffered from dry scaly skin followed by angular stomatitis which are associated with ribo-flavin and vitamin A deficiency respectively. All the clinical signs are influenced by the deficiency of vitamin B, mineral, protein, fat and carbohydrates. Probably the Kaibarta children are in want of the aforesaid sources of energy to combat various kinds of clinical symptoms.

Table 9
Number and Percentage Distribution of Cases Either Deciduous and with Erupted Permanent Teeth in Kaibarta Boys and Girls According to Age

			Boys				Girls			Boys					Girls				
Age Group	*Jaw*	*No.*	*i*	*c*	*m*	*No.*	*i*	*c*	*m*	*I*	*C*	*P*	*istM*	*2ndM*	*I*	*C*	*P*	*istM*	*2ndM*
6		35				36													
	UP		35	35	35		34	36	36				16		1			16	
			(100.00)	(100.00)	(100.00)		(94.44)	(100.00)	(100.00)	NIL	NIL	NIL	(45.71)	NIL	(2.77)	NIL	NIL	(44.44)	NIL
	LOW		31	35	35		35	36	36	4			18					16	
			(88.57)	(100.00)	(100.00)		(97.22)	(100.00)	(100.00)	(11.41)	NIL	NIL	(51.42)	NIL	NIL	NIL	NIL	(44.44)	NIL
7		35				35													
	UP		13	35	35		21	35	35	22	NIL	NIL	30	NIL	14	NIL	NIL	25	NIL
			(37.14)	(100.00)	(100.00)		(60.00)	(100.00)	(100.00)	62.84)	-	-	(85.71)	-	(40.00)	-	-	(71.42)	-
	LOW		1	35	35		9	35	35	34	NIL	NIL	32	NIL	26	NIL	NIL	26	NIL
			(2.85)	(100.00)	(100.00)		(25.71)	(100.00)	(100.00)	(97.14)	-	-	(91.42)		(74.28)	-	-	(74.28)	-
8		35				35													
	UP		16	33	35		1	22	35	19	2	NIL	34	NIL	34	13	NIL	35	NIL
			(45.71)	(94.28)	(100.00)		(2.85)	(62.85)	(100.00)	(54.27)	(5.71)	-	(97.14)	-	(97.14)	(37.14)	-	(100.00)	-
	LOW		4	33	35		NIL	25	35	31	2	NIL	34	NIL	35	10	NIL	35	NIL
			(11.42)	(94.28)	(100.00)		-	(71.42)	(100.00)	(88.56)	(5.71)	-	(97.14)	-	(100.00)	(28.57)	-	(100.00)	-
9		34				36													
	UP		NIL	16	27		NIL	12	30	34	18	7	33	NIL	36	24	6	34	1
		-	(47.05)	(79.41)		-	(33.33)	(83.33)	(100.00)	(52.94)	(20.59)	(97.05)	-	(100.00)	(66.67)	(16.66)	(94.44)	(2.77)	
	LOW		2	12	27		NIL	10	18	32	22	7	33	1	36	26	18	36	1
			(5.38)	(35.29)	(79.41)		-	(27.77)	(50.00)	(94.11)	(64.70)	(20.59)	(97.05)	(2.94)	(100.00)	(72.22)	(50.00)	(100.00)	(2.77)
		36				35													
	UP		NIL	7	22		NIL	9	12	36	29	14	34	3	35	26	23	35	4
		-	(19.44)	(61.11)		-	(25.71)	(34.28)	(100.00)	(80.55)	(38.89)	(94.44)	(8.33)	(100.00)	(74.28)	(65.71)	(100.00)	(11.42)	
	LOW		1	9	23		NIL	12	12	35	27	13	35	3	35	23	23	35	5
			(2.77)	(25.00)	(63.88)		-	(34.28)	(34.28)	(97.22)	(75.00)	(36.11)	(97.22)	(8.33)	(100.00)	(65.71)	(65.71)	(100.00)	(14.28)

Table 10
Percentage Distribution of Kaibarta Children With Clinical Sign

Age Group in years	*No. of Boys*	*Pigmentation of the skin*	*Angular Stomatities*	*Dry scaly skin*	*Discolour of hair*	*Coarse hair*	*Spongy bleeding gum*	*Yellowish teeth*	*Pale conjunctiva*	*Yellow colour nail*
6	35	-	5.71 (2)	11.42 (4)	2.85 (1)	-	-	8.53 (3)	2.85 (1)	-
7	35	-	2.85 (1)	42.85 (15)	-	-	2.85 (1)	-	-	-
8	35	2.85 (1)	2.85 (1)	20.00 (7)	2.85 (1)	-	2.85 (1)	-	-	-
9	34	2.94 (1)	2.94 (1)	2.94 (1)	-	-	-	2.94 (1)	-	-
10	36	-	2.77 (1)	11.11 (4)	2.77 (1)	-	2.77 (1)	5.55 (2)	2.77 (1)	5.55 (2)
Age Groupin years	*No. of Girls*									
6	36	-	2.77 (1)	8.33 (3)	2.77 (1)	-	-	5.55 (2)	-	-
7	35	-	-	14.28 (5)	2.85 (2)	-	2.85 (1)	8.57 (3)	-	-
8	35	-	2.77 (1)	20.00 (7)	-	2.85 (1)	-	11.42 (4)	2.85 (1)	-
9	36	2.77 (1)	2.77 (1)	5.55 (2)	-	2.85 (1)	-	-	-	2.77 (1)
10	35	-	-	2.85 (1)	-	2.85 (1)	-	-	-	-

Assessment of Nutritional Status based on Anthropometric Indices

In the present study an attempt has been made to find out the nutritional status with the following indices.

1. Weight for age or weight deficit classification
2. Height for age or height deficit classification
3. Mid upper arm circumference classification

Weight for Age or Weight Deficit Classification

Weight for age gives a good indication of size at different stages of life of individual.

The entire data was classified according to weight deficiency based on the different grades of the malnutrition (Table 11) using NCHS (1977) data as standard. It was observed that the frequency of 66.28% of the boy suffered from different kinds of malnutrition; whereas, it was found to be higher in case of girls where the frequency was 76.27%. However, the frequency of malnutrition of boys found to be higher at 8 yrs followed by 9 and 10 yrs., whereas, the girls showed higher frequency at 8 yrs followed by 6, 9 and 10 yrs. respectively. In normal category boys frequency was found to be higher as compare to girls which indicated that the girls suffered from weight deficit compare to boys. This shows the magnitude of malnutrition which might have affected growth and development of Kaibarta children and checked their normal weight due to which majority of children were found to be under weight.

Height for Age or Height Deficit Classification

In the present study more than fifty per cent of children were found in normal category which shows normal growth in height with age. However in both the sexes approximately 31% of children were suffering from mild retardation, which may be due to poor and imbalanced diet that might have caused to stunt the normal growth of growing children (Table 12).

Mid Upper Arm Circumference Classification

Arm circumference helps to evaluate the condition of muscle development and skin fold thickness act as an significant index of body fat and thereby of calorie reservoir. It has been again pointed out that measurement of arm girth at a time do provide an objective basis to learn to what extent an individual had in his or her growth years suffered deficit growth process due to protein-calorie malnutrition. (Jelliffe 1966; Beaton and Bengao 1976). In the present study children were categorized according to the standard of malnutrition for the sexes (Table 13) using ICMR (1972) data on children belonging to Socio-economic class I, as standard.

It was observed that more than fifty per cent children suffered from different categories of malnutrition which provide evidence for poor

Table 11
Weight for Age Classification for Boys and Girls

	Age Group											
	6 Yrs		7 Yrs		8 Yrs		9 Yrs		10 Yrs		Total	
Boys	N	%	N	%	N	%	N	%	N	%	N	%
Grade IVMalnutrition	1	0.57	Nil	-	Nil	-	Nil	-	Nil	-	1	0.57
Grade IIIMalnutrition	Nil	-	1	0.57	Nil	-	5	2.86	4	2.28	10	5.71
Grade IIMalnutrition	6	3.43	5	2.86	11	6.28	11	6.28	15	8.57	48	27.43
Grade I Malnutrition	10	5.71	15	8.57	16	9.14	8	4.57	8	4.57	57	32.57
Normal	18	10.28	14	8.00	8	4.57	10	5.71	9	5.14	59	33.71
Total	35	19.99	35	20.00	35	19.99	34	19.42	36	20.56	175	99.99
Girls												
Grade IVMalnutrition	Nil	-	Nil	-	Nil	-	Nil	-	Nil	-	Nil	-
Grade IIIMalnutrition	3	1.70	1	0.56	1	0.56	5	2.82	6	3.40	16	9.04
Grade IIMalnutrition	12	6.78	16	9.04	7	3.95	12	6.78	8	4.52	55	31.07
Grade I Malnutrition	13	7.34	8	4.52	20	11.30	11	6.21	12	6.78	64	36.16
Normal	8	4.52	10	5.65	7	3.95	8	4.52	9	5.08	42	23.73
Total	36	20.34	35	19.77	35	19.76	36	20.34	35	19.78	177	100.00

Table 12
Height for Age Classification

Boys categories	*6 Yrs*		*7 Yrs*		*8 Yrs*		*9 Yrs*		*10 Yrs*		*Total*	
Boys	*N*	*%*	*N*	*%*	*N*	*%*	*N*	*%*	*N*	*%*	*N*	*%*
Poor	1	0.57	Nil	-	Nil	-	Nil	-	Nil	-	1	0.57
Mild Retardation	7	4.00	7	4.00	9	5.14	13	7.43	14	8.00	50	28.57
Normal	27	15.42	28	16.00	26	14.86	21	12.00	22	12.57	124	70.86
Total	35	20.00	35	20.00	35	20.00	34	19.43	36	20.57	175	100.00
Girls Categories												
Girls												
Poor	Nil	-	Nil	-	Nil	-	Nil	-	Nil	-	Nil	-
Mild Retardation	20	11.30	11	6.21	10	5.67	7	3.95	7	3.95	55	31.07
Normal	16	9.04	24	13.56	25	14.12	29	16.38	28	15.82	122	68.93
Total	36	20.34	35	19.77	35	19.79	36	20.33	35	19.77	177	100.00

Table 13
Distribution of Kaibarta Children According to the Mid-upper Arm Circumference

Boys categories	*6 Yrs*		*7 Yrs*		*8 Yrs*		*9 Yrs*		*10 Yrs*		*Total*	
Boys	*N*	*%*	*N*	*%*	*N*	*%*	*N*	*%*	*N*	*%*	*N*	*%*
Severe Malnutrition (75% Stand.)	Nil	-	Nil	-	Nil	-	1	0.57	2	1.14	3	1.71
Moderate Malnutrition (75.1-80%)	7	4.0	3	1.71	5	2.86	5	2.86	8	4.57	28	16.00
Malnutrition (80.1-85%)	8	4.57	13	7.43	18	10.29	12	6.86	15	8.57	66	37.72
Normal (85.1%)	20	11.43	19	10.86	12	6.86	16	9.14	11	6.28	78	44.57
Total	35	20.00	35	20.00	35	20.01	34	19.43	36	20.56	175	100.00
Girls Categories												
Girls												
Severe Malnutrition (75% Stand.)	2	1.13	4	2.26	1	0.56	4	2.26	1	0.56	12	6.78
Moderate Malnutrition (75.1-80%)	9	5.09	9	5.09	5	2.82	7	3.95	11	6.21	41	23.16
Malnutrition (80.1-85%)	7	3.95	12	6.78	13	7.34	6	3.39	12	6.78	50	28.25
Normal (85.1%)	18	10.17	10	5.65	16	9.04	19	10.73	11	6.21	74	41.81
Total	36	20.34	35	19.77	35	19.77	36	20.34	35	19.77	177	100.00

nutritional status. The boys show highest frequency of malnutrition at the age of 10 yrs. and the girls at 7 yrs. Though in the severe category of malnutrition frequency of both the sexes was found to be lower compared to other categories but the girls show higher frequency than the boys. Thus higher frequency of malnutrition among the girls compared to boys showed the effect of their normal growth and development. Higher frequency of boys under normal category indicated that the boys suffered less from protein calorie malnutrition compared to girls.

Impact of Cultural Factors on Growth of Children

To observe the impact of cultural factors such as per capita income or economic condition, literacy level of parents, family size, family type, birth order of child/parity of the ward more distinctively on the growth and development of children, the children were classified categorically for each bio-cultural factors separately and the statistical constant mean and standard deviation of their anthropometric measurements like height, weight, sitting height, bi-acromial diameter and bi-iliocristal diameter have been calculated accordingly.

In literacy level (Table 14) children were classified into four categories according to their parents literacy level, as both parents literate, both parents non-literate, father literate mother non-literate and mother literate father non-literate. It was noticed that in both parents literate group, at 8 and 9 years of age, the boys were slightly heavier, taller with more sitting height, more bi-acromial breadth and more bi-iliocristal breadth; among the father literate and mother non-literate group, the boys and girls show that the biacromial breadth is more in 6 and 10 years of age.

No significant growth in considered measurements of children was noticed through all the age group equally in any particular family size group (Table 15). Hence the impact of family size on growth and development is abstruse.

In family type as no joint family were found, all the families were nuclear type, the impact of family type on growth and development could not be found out.

The children were classified into five categories according to their parity first, second, third, fourth and fifth (Table 16). It was noticed that the boys of first parity were slightly heavier at 6 and 7 years of age, slightly taller at 7 years, having slightly broad bi-iliocristal breadth at the age of 6 years. The boys of second parity were slightly heavier, taller with broader bi-acromial diameter at 8 years of age. The boys of third parity were slightly heavier and taller with slightly more sitting height and broader bi-acromial breadth at 10 years of age. The boys of fourth parity were slightly heavier, taller with more sitting height with broader bi-acromial breadth at the age of 9 years only. The boys of fifth parity were slightly taller with slightly more sitting height at 6 years of age only.

Table 14
Distribution of Mean and Standard Deviation of a Few Measurements of Kaibarta Children Aged from 6 to 10 Years by Literacy Level of Both Parents

		Boys																		Girls						
		Both parents literate			*Father literate Mother illiterate*			*Mother literate Father literate*			*Both parents illiterate*			*Both parents illiterate*			*Father illiterate Mother illiterate*			*Mother illiterate Father illiterate*			*Both parents illiterate*		
	Age	*N*	*Mean*	*S.D.*	*N*	*Mean*	*S.D.*	*N*	*Mean*	*S.D.*	*N*	*Mean*	*S.D.*	*N*	*Mean*	*S.D.*	*N*	*Mean*	*S.D.*	*N*	*Mean*	*S.D.*	*N*	*Mean*	*S.D*
Weight	6	30	17.13	2.44	3	17.83	0.62	1	20.00	0.00	1	18.00	0.00	30	15.66	1.82	4	16.75	1.08	0	0.00	0.00	1	14.00	0.00
	7	28	19.67	2.85	5	19.70	1.16	0	0.00	0.00	2	16.75	0.25	28	18.51	2.65	5	21.10	8.46	1	16.00	0.00	0	0.00	0.00
	8	27	21.05	2.25	5	19.20	1.32	0	0.00	0.00	1	20.00	0.00	32	21.01	2.51	1	18.50	0.00	0	0.00	0.00	1	21.00	0.0C
	9	27	23.85	2.96	6	21.92	3.67	0	0.00	0.00	0	0.00	0.00	28	22.51	3.37	2	22.75	1.25	0	0.00	0.00	1	23.00	0.00
	10	27	24.70	3.91	5	24.80	4.62	2	23.00	0.45	0	0.00	0.00	33	25.69	3.91	1	40.00	0.00	0	0.00	0.00	1	26.00	0.00
Stature	6	30	111.01	5.46	3	112.26	3.69	1	120.70	0.00	1	115.00	0.00	30	106.65	5.83	4	109.52	1.93	0	0.00	0.00	1	107.00	0.00
	7	28	118.15	6.45	5	118.70	2.94	0	0.00	0.00	2	110.25	2.75	28	117.44	6.22	5	115.36	6.80	1	112.00	0.00	0	0.00	0.00
	8	27	122.00	5.32	5	118.40	2.31	0	0.00	0.00	1	123.50	0.00	32	121.21	5.47	1	118.00	0.00	0	0.00	0.00	1	129.50	0.00
	9	27	127.60	6.73	6	124.36	11.22	0	0.00	0.00	0	0.00	0.00	28	126.78	6.28	2	126.65	2.65	0	0.00	0.00	1	127.50	0.00
	10	27	130.21	6.40	5	132.20	10.50	2	125.00	2.00	0	0.00	0.00	33	134.11	7.55	1	149.00	0.00	0	0.00	0.00	1	136.00	0.00
Sitting height	6	30	61.57	2.50	3	63.30	1.84	1	65.80	0.00	1	62.00	0.00	30	59.64	2.28	4	61.02	1.49	0	0.00	0.00	1	61.50	0.00
	7	28	64.46	3.13	5	64.46	1.13	0	0.00	0.00	2	59.90	1.56	28	61.86	11.14	5	63.64	2.96	1	62.00	0.00	0	0.00	0.00
	8	27	65.72	2.26	5	64.88	2.32	0	0.00	0.00	1	64.00	0.00	32	65.30	2.75	1	65.40	0.00	0	0.00	0.00	1	65.50	0.00
	9	27	67.91	3.80	6	67.01	3.71	0	0.00	0.00	0	0.00	0.00	28	67.60	2.94	2	65.95	2.45	0	0.00	0.00	1	66.20	0.00
	10	27	69.43	3.41	5	70.06	4.97	2	67.60	0.40	0	0.00	0.00	33	69.99	3.35	1	76.80	0.00	0	0.00	0.00	1	72.50	0.00
Bi-acromial diameter	6	30	23.89	1.11	3	24.40	0.56	1	26.00	0.00	1	24.00	0.00	30	23.27	1.51	4	24.37	1.55	0	0.00	0.00	1	22.40	0.00
	7	28	25.16	1.53	5	25.20	0.44	0	0.00	0.00	2	23.15	0.21	28	25.11	1.08	5	25.16	1.79	1	24.00	0.00	0	0.00	0.00
	8	27	25.79	1.17	5	24.64	1.28	0	0.00	0.00	1	27.00	0.00	32	25.88	1.21	1	23.00	0.00	0	0.00	0.00	1	27.50	0.00
	9	27	27.17	1.57	6	26.71	2.53	0	0.00	0.00	0	0.00	0.00	28	26.79	1.50	2	25.75	1.25	0	0.00	0.00	1	27.70	0.00
	10	27	27.48	1.40	5	27.96	2.66	2	26.50	0.00	0	0.00	0.00	30	28.41	1.77	1	33.80	0.00	0	0.00	0.00	1	28.30	0.00
Bi-iliac diameter	6	30	17.63	0.81	3	17.76	0.71	1	18.50	0.00	1	17.00	0.00	30	16.88	0.88	4	18.00	0.79	0	0.00	0.00	1	17.40	0.00
	7	28	17.98	1.17	5	18.10	0.86	0	0.00	0.00	2	16.45	0.45	28	18.21	1.08	5	17.80	2.00	1	17.30	0.00	0	0.00	0.00
	8	27	18.68	1.09	5	17.30	0.87	0	0.00	0.00	1	19.50	0.00	32	18.73	1.01	1	18.30	0.00	0	0.00	0.00	1	19.50	0.00
	9	27	19.47	1.30	6	18.93	1.02	0	0.00	0.00	0	0.00	0.00	28	19.62	0.88	2	19.45	1.05	0	0.00	0.00	1	19.50	0.00
	10	27	19.35	0.96	5	19.94	1.82	2	19.00	0.00	0	0.00	0.00	33	20.95	1.42	1	23.80	0.00	0	0.00	0.00	1	21.50	0.00

Table 15

Mean and Standard Deviation of a Few Measurements of Kaibarta Children Aged 6 to 10 Years by Family Size

		Boys									Girls								
		1 to 3			*4 to 6*			*7 to 9*			*1 to 3*			*4 to 6*			*7 to 9*		
	Age	*N*	*Mean*	*S.D.*	*N*	*Mean*	*S.D.*	*N*	*Mean*	*S.D.*	*N*	*Mean*	*S.D.*	*N*	*Mean*	*S.D.*	*N*	*Mean*	*S.D.*
Weight	6	5	17.40	1.14	28	16.79	2.60	2	17.00	1.41	7	15.85	1.54	29	15.72	1.86	0	0.00	0.00
	7	3	19.00	1.07	31	19.67	2.77	1	16.00	0.00	6	21.66	8.26	26	18.15	2.79	3	18.00	1.00
	8	4	20.75	1.50	31	20.75	2.28	0	0.00	0.00	6	20.08	2.01	29	21.15	2.56	0	0.00	0.00
	9	2	21.75	3.88	32	23.46	3.23	0	0.00	0.00	6	22.83	2.63	30	22.70	3.32	0	0.00	0.00
	10	4	22.25	1.89	30	24.40	3.90	2	29.50	0.70	1	26.00	0.00	33	26.18	4.67	1	24.00	0.00
Stature	6	5	113.18	1.04	28	107.33	6.05	2	115.25	0.35	7	107.30	4.54	29	106.75	5.85	0	0.00	0.00
	7	3	120.13	4.58	31	117.86	6.30	1	108.00	0.00	6	117.56	7.33	26	111.42	6.58	3	118.56	3.50
	8	4	121.55	5.77	31	121.74	5.30	0	0.00	0.00	6	119.38	3.53	29	121.78	5.81	0	0.00	0.00
	9	2	126.45	5.58	32	126.90	7.94	0	0.00	0.00	6	126.95	1.66	30	126.76	6.46	0	0.00	0.00
	10	4	126.12	5.88	30	129.35	6.90	2	141.85	0.91	1	129.00	0.00	33	134.87	8.01	1	13.08	67.20
Sitting height	6	5	61.82	1.14	28	59.74	2.80	2	63.00	1.40	7	60.00	1.89	29	59.79	2.34	0	0.00	0.00
	7	3	64.93	1.36	31	64.29	3.23	1	61.00	0.00	6	64.08	3.18	26	63.60	3.15	3	63.46	1.90
	8	4	65.65	2.69	31	65.61	2.36	0	0.00	0.00	6	64.28	2.78	29	65.59	2.69	0	0.00	0.00
	9	2	66.40	0.84	32	67.75	3.77	0	0.00	0.00	6	67.65	1.41	30	67.72	3.59	0	0.00	0.00
	10	4	69.07	1.57	30	69.08	3.67	2	73.75	0.35	1	68.50	0.00	33	70.40	3.57	1	67.20	0.00
Biacromial diameter	6	5	24.34	0.23	28	23.18	1.23	2	23.50	0.70	7	23.42	1.23	29	23.39	1.64	0	0.00	0.00
	7	3	24.83	0.28	31	25.14	1.52	1	23.00	0.00	6	25.23	1.85	26	26.98	1.18	3	25.06	1.01
	8	4	26.50	1.73	31	25.66	1.28	0	0.00	0.00	6	26.05	0.85	29	25.79	1.39	0	0.00	0.00
	9	2	27.10	1.55	32	27.09	1.72	0	0.00	0.00	6	26.00	0.78	30	26.86	1.53	0	0.00	0.00
	10	4	26.75	1.19	30	27.35	1.40	2	30.50	1.41	1	29.00	0.00	33	28.56	2.03	1	28.00	0.00
Bi-iliac diameter	6	5	18.02	0.43	28	17.00	0.84	2	17.25	0.35	7	16.78	0.39	29	17.08	1.02	0	0.00	0.00
	7	3	17.43	0.60	31	18.13	1.19	1	16.50	0.00	6	18.73	1.62	26	17.97	1.22	3	17.90	0.96
	8	4	18.25	1.04	31	18.54	1.19	0	0.00	0.00	6	18.80	1.24	29	18.72	1.03	0	0.00	0.00
	9	2	18.65	0.21	32	19.30	1.34	0	0.00	0.00	6	19.31	0.45	30	19.68	0.92	0	0.00	0.00
	10	4	19.00	0.41	30	19.30	0.98	2	21.90	0.84	1	21.14	0.00	33	21.08	1.50	1	19.60	0.00

Table 16

Mean and Standard Deviation of a Few Measurements of Kaibarta Children Aged 6 to 10 Years by Parity

		Boys															Girls														
		1			2			3			4			5 & above			1			2			3			4			5 & above		
	Age	N	Mean	S.D.	N	Mean	S.D.	N	Mean	S.D.	N	Mean	S.D.	N	Mean	S.D.	N	Mean	S.D.	N	Mean	S.D.	N	Mean	S.D.	N	Mean	S.D.	N	Mean	S.D.
Weight	6	9	17.72	1.51	16	17.53	2.93	8	16.43	1.64	0	0.00	0.00	2	17.00	1.00	12	16.16	1.44	11	15.09	1.72	10	15.40	1.85	3	17.66	0.47	0	0.00	0.00
	7	15	20.16	3.33	12	19.33	1.31	4	18.75	2.58	3	19.16	2.24	1	16.00	0.00	14	20.42	5.71	9	17.83	2.18	8	17.31	1.91	2	17.50	0.50	2	18.00	1.00
	8	16	20.06	2.10	15	21.26	1.98	3	20.83	1.92	1	24.00	0.00	0	0.00	0.00	14	21.07	2.62	12	20.45	2.53	5	21.19	2.20	4	21.00	1.00	0	0.00	0.00
	9	13	23.77	3.28	14	22.60	2.60	4	22.50	3.77	3	26.33	2.86	0	0.00	0.00	16	23.31	3.56	12	21.33	2.46	3	21.50	1.22	4	24.87	2.07	1	25.00	0.00
	10	17	23.58	3.49	8	24.00	3.35	9	25.77	4.54	1	25.00	0.00	1	30.00	0.00	15	24.86	3.61	15	26.70	4.38	4	24.66	5.24	1	33.00	0.00	0	0.00	0.00
Stature	6	9	114.07	3.14	16	110.93	6.58	8	108.86	3.75	0	0.00	0.00	2	115.30	0.25	12	107.97	3.84	11	105.96	6.08	10	105.08	6.09	3	111.66	1.24	0	0.00	0.00
	7	15	118.84	6.90	12	118.49	4.44	4	114.45	6.91	3	117.26	3.59	1	108.00	0.00	14	119.47	7.85	9	115.81	4.36	8	113.52	3.08	2	114.05	4.65	2	118.50	3.50
	8	16	119.88	5.28	15	122.76	4.24	3	122.96	4.21	1	131.80	0.00	0	0.00	0.00	14	121.88	6.12	12	120.05	4.53	5	122.24	6.43	4	122.50	2.53	0	0.00	0.00
	9	13	129.40	8.02	14	124.56	5.51	4	124.25	11.69	3	130.23	2.68	0	0.00	0.00	16	126.52	5.94	12	126.00	6.04	3	124.23	1.92	4	129.95	3.96	1	135.70	0.00
	10	17	128.37	5.34	8	129.68	6.91	9	137.83	12.95	1	118.50	0.00	1	142.50	0.00	15	132.34	8.06	15	136.00	6.69	4	135.72	8.33	1	142.50	0.00	0	0.00	0.00
Sitting height	6	9	62.22	2.20	16	62.08	2.96	8	60.68	1.60	0	0.00	0.00	2	63.00	1.00	12	60.33	1.45	11	59.10	2.22	10	59.38	2.65	3	62.03	0.28	0	0.00	0.00
	7	15	64.36	3.87	12	64.76	1.44	4	63.22	3.12	3	63.40	2.35	1	61.00	0.00	14	64.90	3.71	9	62.00	2.02	8	62.92	1.97	2	62.40	1.20	2	63.40	1.90
	8	16	65.12	2.47	15	65.99	2.26	3	65.43	0.33	1	68.50	0.00	0	0.00	0.00	14	65.97	3.20	12	64.52	2.21	5	65.60	2.17	4	65.50	1.69	0	0.00	0.00
	9	13	68.39	3.90	14	66.62	2.97	4	67.50	4.73	3	69.96	2.23	0	0.00	0.00	16	67.68	3.09	12	66.79	2.50	3	65.60	1.57	4	71.62	3.83	1	69.80	0.00
	10	17	68.71	2.41	8	68.92	3.68	9	70.96	4.37	1	64.50	0.00	1	73.50	0.00	15	68.93	3.14	15	71.11	3.34	4	70.87	3.39	1	74.80	0.00	0	0.00	0.00
Biacromial diameter	6	9	24.54	0.67	16	24.03	1.33	8	23.31	0.70	0	0.00	0.00	2	23.50	0.50	12	23.70	1.18	11	22.89	1.45	10	23.18	1.62	3	24.33	1.54	0	0.00	0.00
	7	15	25.58	15.06	12	25.15	1.04	4	23.67	1.28	3	24.50	1.08	1	23.00	0.00	14	25.53	1.52	9	25.12	0.55	8	24.16	0.90	2	24.60	0.60	2	25.00	1.00
	8	16	25.43	1.55	15	26.08	0.87	3	25.33	1.13	1	27.50	0.00	0	0.00	0.00	14	26.28	1.15	12	25.36	1.25	5	25.40	1.46	4	26.25	0.83	0	0.00	0.00
	9	13	27.55	1.50	14	26.73	1.51	4	26.25	2.51	3	27.86	0.65	0	0.00	0.00	16	26.81	1.53	12	26.73	1.21	3	25.50	1.08	4	26.95	1.01	1	28.00	0.00
	10	17	27.10	1.11	8	27.12	1.47	9	28.14	1.57	1	26.00	0.00	1	31.50	0.00	15	27.96	1.56	15	28.98	2.11	4	28.65	1.93	1	31.00	0.00	0	0.00	0.00
Bi-illiac	6	9	18.05	0.63	16	17.65	0.93	8	17.28	0.45	0	0.00	0.00	2	17.25	0.25	12	17.33	0.74	11	16.61	0.92	10	16.77	0.77	3	18.16	0.62	0	0.00	0.00
	7	15	18.08	1.16	12	18.14	0.99	4	17.62	1.07	3	18.30	1.28	1	16.50	0.00	14	18.68	1.25	9	17.97	1.01	8	17.45	1.23	2	16.95	0.25	2	18.25	0.75
	8	16	18.18	1.23	15	18.75	1.10	3	18.75	0.53	1	19.00	0.00	0	0.00	0.00	14	19.00	1.14	12	18.42	0.81	5	18.44	1.04	4	19.07	0.84	0	0.00	0.00
	9	13	19.35	1.14	14	19.20	1.39	4	19.37	1.38	3	19.66	0.94	0	0.00	0.00	16	19.61	0.88	12	19.60	0.76	3	19.06	0.67	4	20.07	0.95	1	20.00	0.00
	10	17	19.25	1.00	8	19.00	1.03	9	19.76	0.80	1	19.00	0.00	1	22.50	0.00	15	21.10	1.73	15	20.87	1.11	4	21.17	1.42	1	22.50	0.00	0	0.00	0.00

Table 17
Distribution of Mean and Standard Deviation of Anthropometric Measurements Per Capita Income

Measure-ments	Age	Boys < Rs.5000 N	Mean	S.D.	Boys Rs. 5000-10000 N	Mean	S.D.	Boys Rs. 10000> N	Mean	S.D.	Girls < Rs. 5000 N	Mean	S.D.	Girls Rs. 5000-10000 N	Mean	S.D.	Girls Rs. 10000> N	Mean	S.D.
Weight	6	7	15.42	2.43	16	17.81	2.08	12	17.71	2.32	5	15.00	2.00	15	16.37	1.88	16	15.41	1.56
	7	12	18.20	2.03	13	19.88	1.38	10	20.60	4.06	4	17.00	0.82	23	18.35	4.65	8	20.75	3.28
	8	3	21.16	2.02	21	20.33	2.33	11	21.45	1.92	6	19.25	2.60	15	21.77	2.09	14	20.86	2.58
	9	3	23.00	3.60	14	23.46	3.51	17	3.51	23.35	6	21.17	2.79	17	24.06	2.83	18	21.69	3.28
	10	8	23.50	3.25	14	25.00	3.70	14	24.43	4.65	6	27.92	6.53	12	26.04	4.84	17	25.53	3.61
Height	6	7	107.10	7.66	16	111.83	3.99	12	114.43	5.54	5	104.95	8.27	15	108.57	4.46	16	105.86	5.52
	7	12	113.73	5.06	13	119.90	3.85	10	119.87	8.07	4	113.18	3.78	23	115.24	4.91	8	123.11	7.51
	8	3	123.13	5.95	21	121.42	5.96	11	121.91	3.94	6	118.92	6.68	15	123.84	5.56	14	120.50	3.64
	9	3	125.16	10.54	14	126.11	8.58	17	12781.00	7.24	6	123.90	5.83	17	128.98	5.42	18	125.28	5.95
	10	8	1258.00	8.67	14	131.14	8.05	14	129.90	5.66	6	137.03	8.33	12	135.45	9.70	17	133.12	6.31
Sitting Height	6	7	60.01	3.44	16	62.16	2.04	12	62.50	2.31	5	59.30	3.13	15	60.67	2.25	16	59.22	1.79
	7	12	62.19	2.20	13	64.80	2.07	10	65.83	3.91	4	62.98	2.82	23	62.95	2.39	8	66.13	3.72
	8	3	64.60	1.03	21	65.65	2.58	11	65.83	2.23	6	62.97	2.53	15	66.55	2.37	14	64.14	2.55
	9	3	67.86	4.76	14	67.62	325.00	17	67.72	4.19	6	66.20	2.70	17	68.82	3.75	18	66.96	2.60
	10	8	68.65	4.06	14	70.06	4.04	14	69.01	2.94	6	72.15	4.71	12	70.15	3.75	17	69.66	2.83
Biacromial diameter	6	7	23.34	1.04	16	24.13	0.82	12	24.19	1.43	5	22.70	1.65	15	23.70	1.46	16	23.34	1.63
	7	12	24.12	1.19	13	25.39	0.44	10	25.73	2.11	4	24.68	1.33	23	24.86	1.28	8	25.70	1.10
	8	3	26.50	0.50	21	25.65	1.36	11	25.77	1.46	6	25.33	1.36	15	25.89	1.59	14	26.00	0.94
	9	3	26.56	2.65	14	27.02	2.03	17	27.24	1.33	6	26.32	1.47	17	27.09	1.44	18	26.42	1.50
	10	8	27.45	1.32	14	27.83	1.81	14	27.09	1.46	6	29.27	2.44	12	29.14	1.82	17	27.91	1.80
Bi-illiocristal diameter	6	7	16.98	0.87	16	17.60	0.74	12	18.06	0.59	5	16.78	0.82	15	17.27	0.96	16	16.88	0.96
	7	12	17.48	1.14	13	18.58	0.90	10	17.95	1.19	4	18.00	1.08	23	17.85	1.27	8	18.85	1.24
	8	3	19.00	0.86	21	18.34	1.38	11	18.71	0.71	6	18.35	0.74	15	19.14	1.03	14	18.46	1.10
	9	3	19.16	1.25	14	19.47	1.23	17	19.22	1.41	6	19.32	0.42	17	19.88	1.03	18	19.43	0.75
	10	8	19.47	1.32	14	19.75	1.06	14	19.03	1.01	6	21.60	1.37	12	20.92	1.36	17	20.96	1.64

The girls of first parity were slightly heavier, taller with slightly more sitting height, broader bi-acromial breadth and bi-iliocristal breadth at 7 years, slightly taller with slightly more bi-iliocristal breadth at 6 years of age. The girls of second parity were slightly heavier, slightly taller with slightly more sitting height at 10 years of age only, the girls of fourth parity were slightly heavier and with more sitting height with more bi-acromial breadth at 6 and 9 years only and slightly taller at 8 years of age only.

From the above discussion it was observed that, though the children of first parity showed comparatively more growth almost in all the anthropometric parameters at 6 and 7 years, conclusion could not be made that parity has an impact on growth of children as the result was not equal through all the age group expectedly.

To see impact of economic or per capita income on growth and development of children the children were classified into three categories according to their per capita income as below rupees 5000/-, 5000 to 10,000/- and above 10,000/- rupees to compare their body measurements accordingly (Table 17).

The Table 17 apparently showed increased values in all the parameters considered for the growth and development of children with the increase of income group of parents at the age of 6 and 7 years at 8 years in sitting height only and at 9 years in height and bi-acromial breadth at 10 years of boys. All the parameters showed higher value in higher income group of 5000/- to 10,000/- rupees compared to lower income group of below 5000/- rupees.

In case of girls too at 7 years of age, all the parameters showed gradually increased values with increase of income group from lower to higher. The girls at 6, 8 and 9 years of age showed higher value in all the parameters in higher income group of 5000/- rupees to 10,000/- rupees than the lower income of below 5000/- rupees.

The aforesaid facts imply the affirmative impact of economic condition on the growth and development of children.

Summary and Conclusion

The gradual increment of mean values with age of weight and all linear measurement through their growth period of 6 to 10 yrs indicated the regular and gradual growth among the Kaibarta children.

Das (1996) studied growth among the Assamese and Rajasthani boys and found the weight of Assamese boys as 19.9.kg at 7 yrs; 23.1 kg at 8 yrs; 25.4 kg at 9 yrs and 25.7 kg at 10 yrs, and among Rajasthani boys 18.1 kg at 7 yrs; 19.9 kg at 8 yrs; 23.3 kg at 9 yrs and 25.4 kg at 10 yrs. The stature among Assamese boys 120.1 cm. at 7 yrs; 125.4 cm at 8 yrs; 133.9 at 9 yrs and 134.9 at 10 yrs. The stature among Rajasthani boys was 116.0 cm at 7 yrs; 119.6 at 8 yrs; 128.8 cm at 9 yrs and 137.4 cm at 10 yrs. The weight among Kaibarta boys was found to be lower as compared to the findings of Das among Assamese boys and higher than the Rajasthani boys in 7 and 8 yrs of age. The stature among the Kaibarta boys was found to be lower as compared to the findings of Das among Assamese boys and higher than the Rajasthani boys in 7 and 8 yrs of age.

The variation in body dimension through growing phase would occur at different age according to the rate of growth. In the present study variability of different body dimension was observed from co-efficient of variation. Higher value was observed during greater transition period and lower value during the period of slower rate of growth of different body dimensions.

It was observed from the absolute growth rate of all body dimensions that stature grows at a faster rate of all the body dimensions, sitting height and weight grow at a slower rate than stature, the rate of growth of biacromial was more slower than the sitting height and weight, and bi-iliocristal diameter grows at slowest rate of all the body dimensions.

The analysis of the nature of distance and velocity curves for all the traits regularly showed the different rate of growth by different body dimensions at different age level through their growth period; due to this change of velocity according to growth rate, marked differences were also observed in either sexes.

Distance curve for girls showed higher value than boys at the age of 10 yrs for body dimension like weight, height, sitting height, bi-acromial diameter and for bi-iliac diameter from 7 yrs onwards. In case of thickness of all the skinfold higher curve showed by the girls through all the age groups except triceps at 7 yrs than their male counter part.

Velocity curves showed growth spurt or acceleration of growth by both the boys and girls for the traits viz. weight, stature and sitting height at the age of 7 years. For bi-acromial and bi-iliac at the age of 9 years by boys. Growth spurt for bi-acromial diameter at the age of 7 years and bi-iliac diameter at the age of 10 years by girls. Negative rate of growth among both the sexes for same age groups clearly indicates that there was no growth of skin fold dimensions at that age.

It is evident from the present study that though the growth in all linear dimensions appeared more at the earlier age in case of boys; at the later age the growth was more in case of girls; it may be due to the pre adolescent spurt, as girls reach at the stage of maturity earlier than the boys. This is supported by the view of Tanner's (1962) who opine that sex differences were mainly due to the differences in timing and intensity of their adolescent spurt. He further added that the male adolescent spurt occur later than female, consequently in male the whole body has a longer period of growth, causing generally a greater size and also those differential growth rates which have been operating equally in both sexes to change the proportions from those of the body to those of the adult continue to act for a longer time.

In intergroup differences significant growth was observed through their growth period in all the aspects except in skin fold thickness. And no significant result was found among the boys at the age of 9 and 10 years. Highly significant growth of bi-iliocristal diameter through all the age groups of girls agrees with Tanner (1962) who pointed out the width of hip in female was largely developed due to specific stimulation of cartilage cells by estrogen.

Significant sexual dimorphism was noticed at the age of 6 years in case of weight, height, sitting height and biceps skin fold; and at the age of 10 years in case of height, biacromial and bi-iliocristal diameter and skin fold at sub scapular and biceps.

More than fifty per cent of the children suffered from malnutrition which is evident from mid upper arm circumference indicating poor nutritional status of Kaibarta children.

In the present study weight for age indicates that around seventy per cent of the children suffered from various groups of malnutrition due to lack of sufficient nutritional rich diet which might have severely affected in gaining their normal weight.

It is evident from the present study of height for age that majority (approximately 30%) of the Kaibarta children suffered from mild retardation may be due to poor diet which might have caused to stunt the normal growth of growing children.

In the eruption of permanent teeth, girls were slightly ahead than the boys in the present study.

Most of the Kaibarta children suffered from riboflavin and vitamin A deficiency as is evident from dry scaly skin and stomatitis.

Socio-cultural factors like economy, education of parents, occupation, nature of family, family size etc. control the growth and development of children. In the present study mostly low paid occupation, with uncertain income, low level of education of majority parents, medium size of family influenced the growth and development of Kaibarta children to a great extent.

Acknowledgement

I express deep sense of gratitude to Dr. R.K. Bhattacharya, former Director, Anthropological Survey of India, Govt. of India, for allowing me to work under this project.

The author gratefully acknowledges Dr. B.R. Rizvi, the then Deputy Director and Dr. Ramesh Chandra, Deputy Director, Anthropological Survey of India, North Eastern Regional Centre, Shillong for providing necessary facilities to complete the project work.

I am indebted to both the co-ordinators (Dr.) (Mrs.) M B Sharma, Superintending Anthropologist (Physical) and Dr. D. B. Mondal, Superintending Anthropologist (Cultural) for their valuable contribution in designing and providing necessary guidelines for the project.

I am thankful to Shri B P Urade, Anthropologist (Physical) and late A C Nath for their valuable guidance and continuous inspiration for bringing this report in the present form.

Last but not the least, I am grateful to Dr. M. N. Panda, Head, Department of Commerce, North Eastern Hill University, Shillong, Miss Juliet Paswett, Smt. Rekha Devi Lohar, the Kaibarta people and school authorities of Guwahati and North Guwahati for their kind co-operation without which this study would not have been possible.

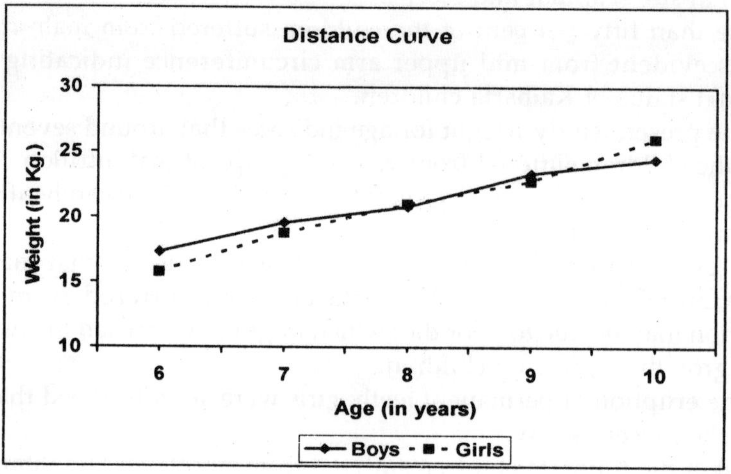

Fig. 1

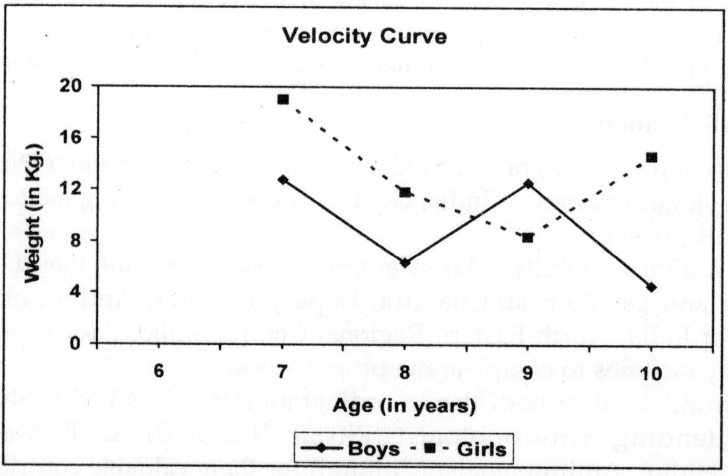

Fig. 2

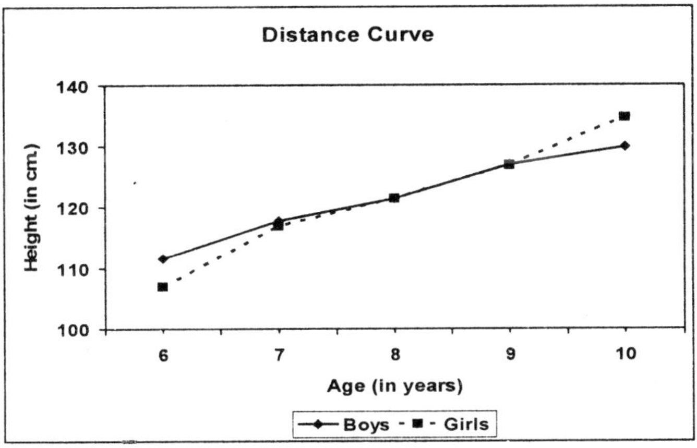

Fig. 3

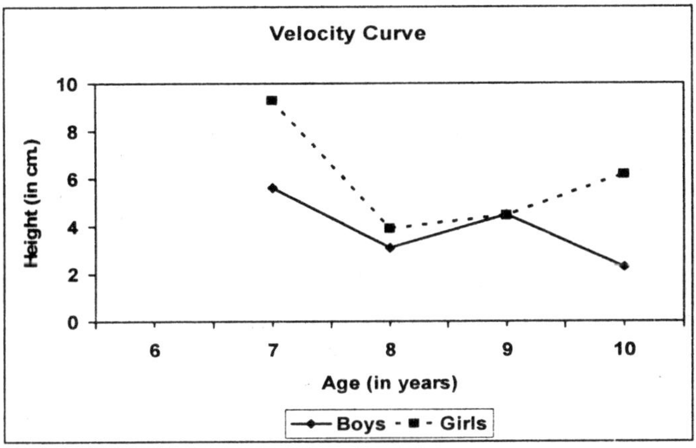

Fig. 4

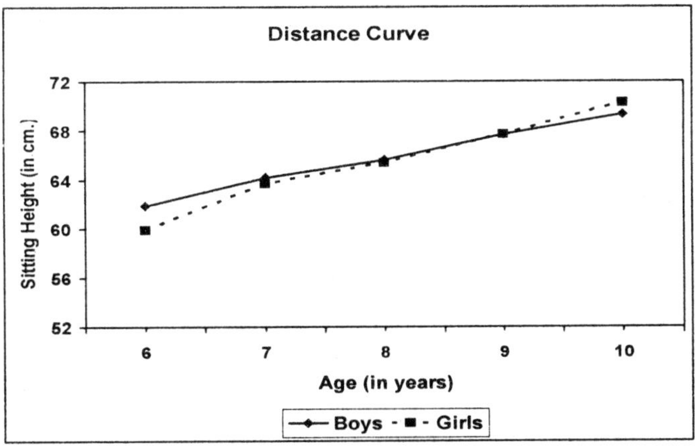

Fig. 5

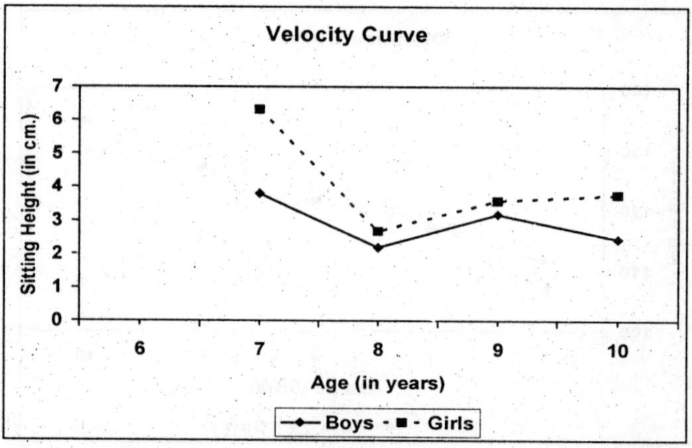

Fig. 6

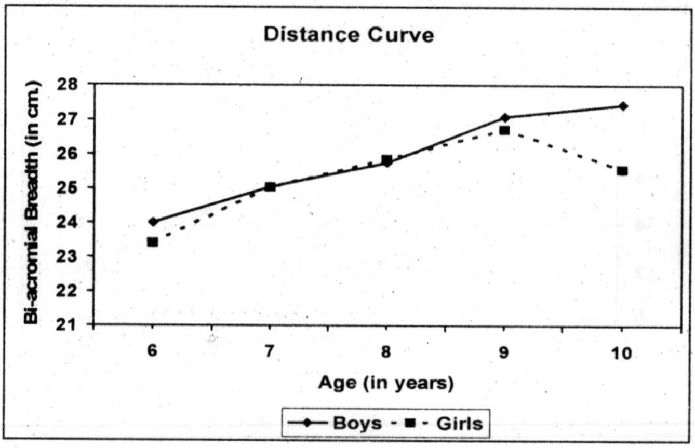

Fig. 7

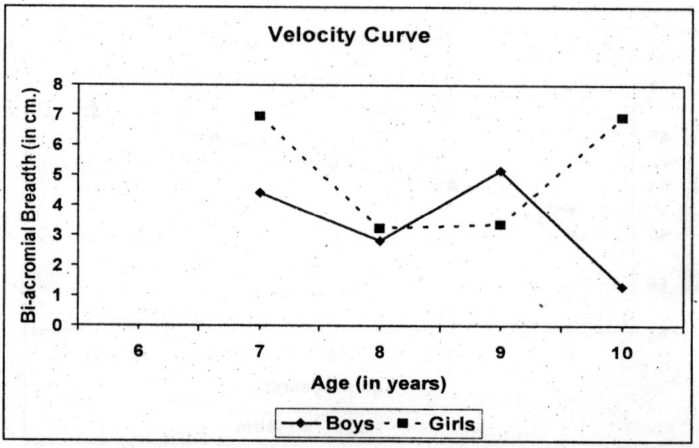

Fig. 8

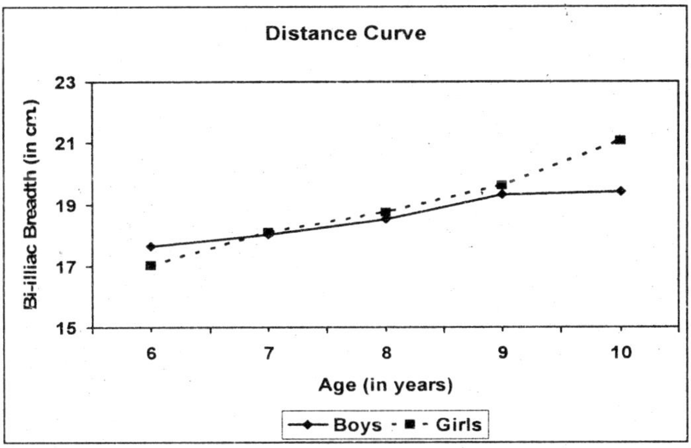

Fig. 9

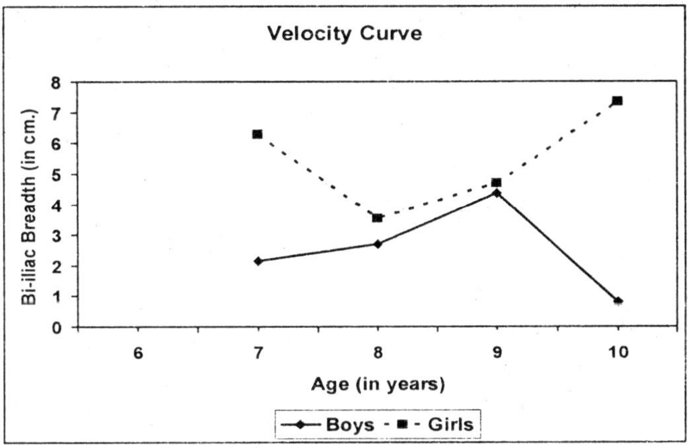

Fig. 10

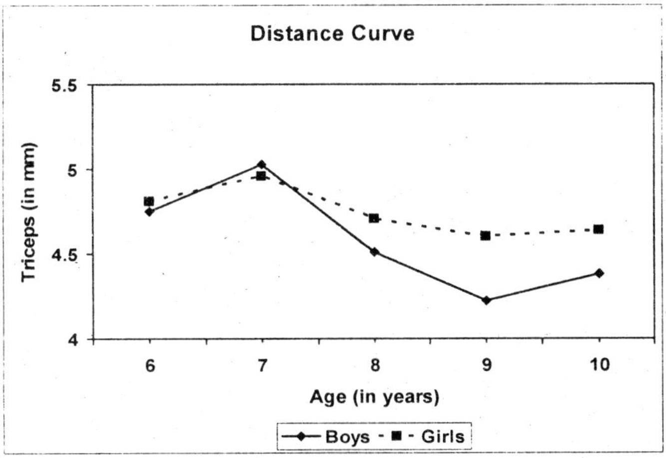

Fig. 11

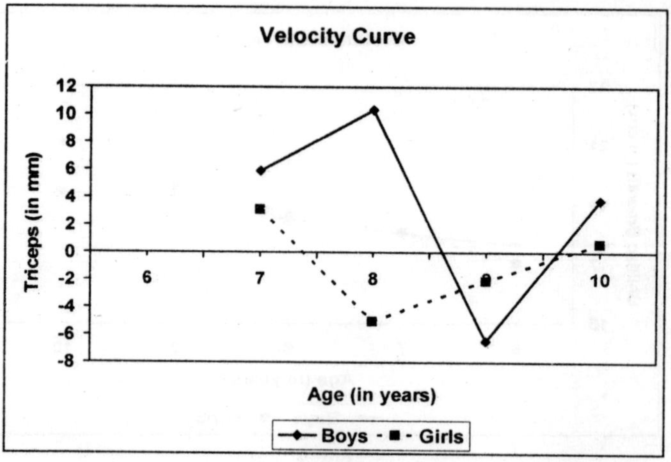

Fig. 12

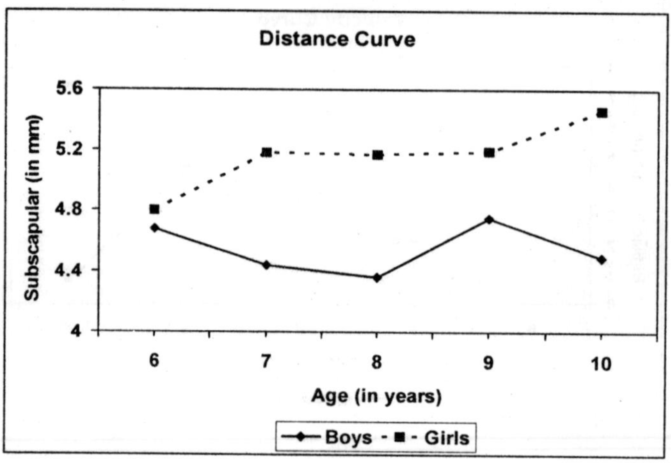

Fig. 13

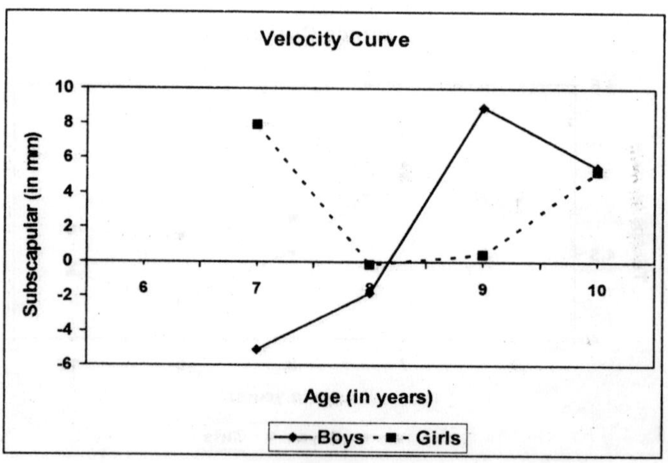

Fig. 14

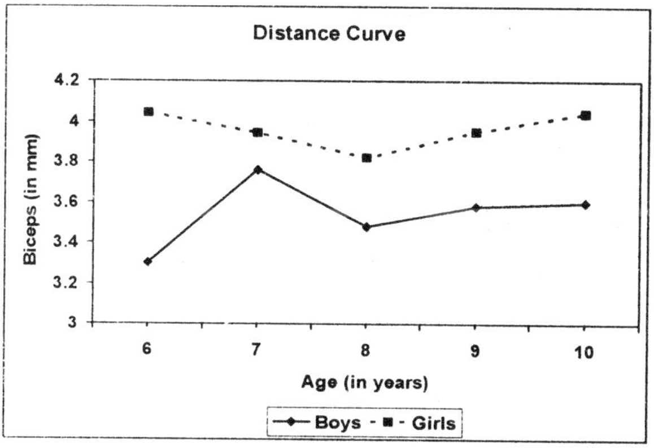

Fig. 15

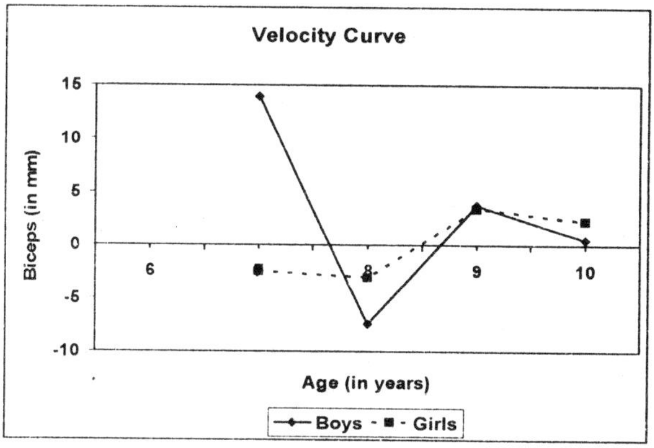

Fig. 16

DISTRIBUTION OF REGRESSION EQUATION OF SOME MEASUREMENTS ON AGE FOR MALE AND FEMALE MEASUREMENTS

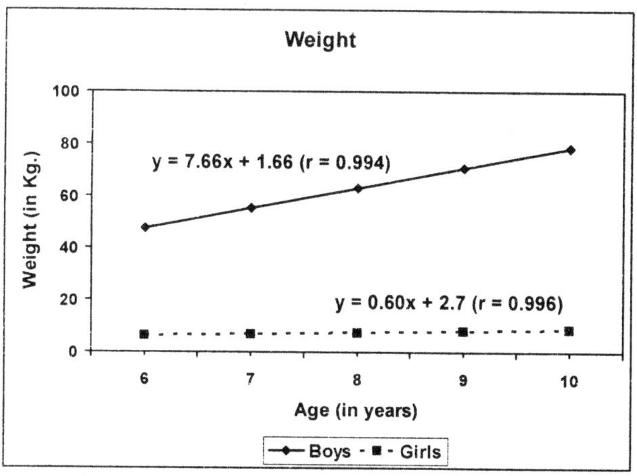

Fig. 17

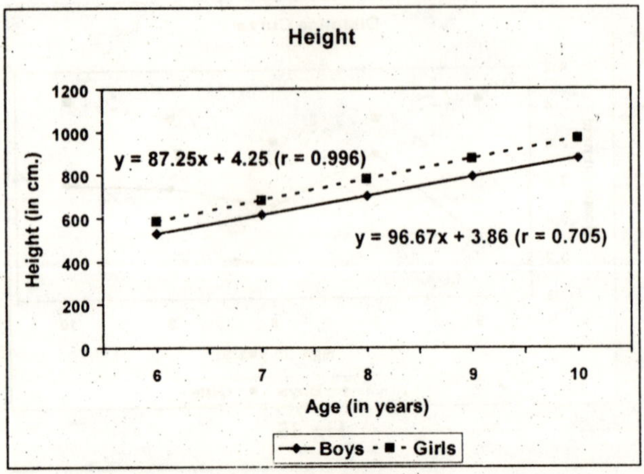

Fig. 18

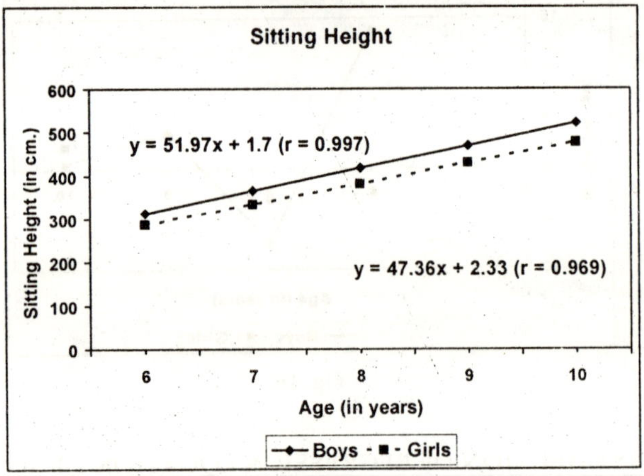

Fig. 19

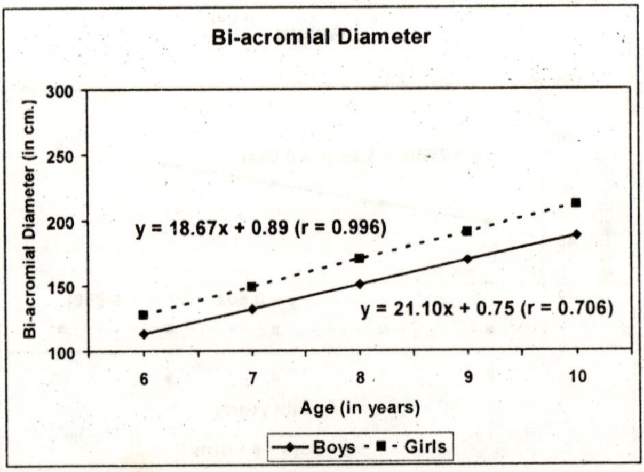

Fig. 20

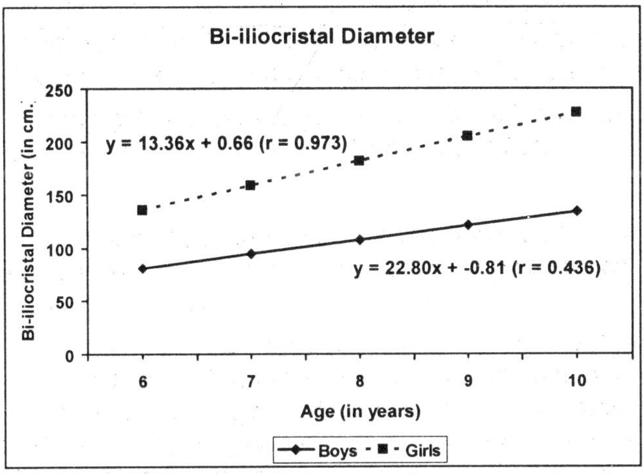

Fig. 21

References

Ahmed Hazarika A.N.Z. (1974), A Comparative Study of Growth of Stature, Growth of Thorax and Weight of Ahom and Kalita Boys of Assam. Contemporary Anthropological Research in North East India, by B.M.Das Dibrugarh University, 73-77.

Beaton, G.H. and J.M.Bengao, (Eds) (1976), Nutrition in Preventive Medicine. Monograph Series No. 62 World Health Organisation, Geneva.

Bordoloi, B.N. (1994), Socio-Economic Condition of the Kaibarta of Assam. A Case Study. A.I. of Research for Tribal & Scheduled Caste.

Das, A.K. (1996), A Study on Growth among the Assamese and Rajasthani boys in 'People of North East India' edt. S. Sengupta, Gyan Publishing House, New Delhi-11002.

Eveleth, P.B. and J.M. Tanner (1990), Worldwide Variation in Human Growth-II Edition, Cambridge Uni. Press, Cambridge.

I.C.M.R. Statistic Division (1972), Growth and Physical Development of Indian Infants and Children. In Technical Report No 18. New Delhi.

Jellife, D.B. (1966), The Assessment of the Nutritional Status of Community. WHO Monograph series No. 53, Geneva: WHO.

NCHS (National Centre for Health Statistics) (1977), NCHS Growth Curves for Children, Birth to 18 Years, United States, Vital and Health Statistics, Series 11, No. 165.

Risley, H.H. (1991), *The Tribes and Castes of Bengal*, Vol. I, 1981-375.382.

Tanner, J.M. (1962), Growth at Adolescence 2nd ed. Oxford & Edinburg, Blackwell Scientific Publications.

6

GROWTH AND DEVELOPMENT OF LUSHAI CHILDREN OF MIZORAM: BIO-CULTURAL PERSPECTIVES

B. P. Urade & S. K. Mukherjee

Introduction

Growth studies in developing countries like India have been inviting attention to go into deeper aspect of impact of both physical and cultural factors on different section of the society and its people. Growth studies of children are utmost important from time to time to assess the potentiality of health or physique and/or a secular trend to possible extent of any community.

The North-Eastern states of our country constitute 1.35% of the total tribal population (Census of India, 1991) invites special attention to study those endogamous tribal groups from various angle. Growth studies in North East India are very few and limited. No study has been carried out on the Lushai children from Mizoram on the age group 6-10 year. Therefore, it was felt necessary to carry out growth study on the Lushai children of Mizoram with a view to make out the relationship between growth and various bio-cultural factors. Such study would be important to understand the nutritional status by means of anthropometry and its impact on growth pattern on the Lushai Children. This study is a part of National project "Growth and Development of Children: Bio-cultural perspective" undertaken by the Anthropological Survey of India, during Ninth five year plan.

Land and People

Mizoram is situated in the North-Eastern part of India. It is surrounded by Bangladesh and Tripura in the west and Myanmar in the east and south, in the north with Manipur and Cachar district of Assam. It has an international boundary of about 650 miles with Myanmar and Bangladesh.

Mizoram lies between $21^0.58'$ to $24^0.35'$ north latitude and $92^0.15'$ to $93^0.29'$ east longitude. It covers an area of 21087 Sq. Km. with a population of 6,89756 (1991 census). Its literacy rate is 82.87% (as per Mizoram statistical Hand Book 1998). The temperature ranges between 11^0c to 21^0c in winter and 20^0c to 30^0c in summer. The monsoon starts from May to September. (Bandopadhyay, 1985).

Mizoroam is the new name given to the region which was formerly known as the Lushai Hills. Mizoram was divided into two districts namely the North Lushai Hills and South Lushai Hills. Presently, these are called Mizo Hills district.

Mizoram is a land of deep valleys and hills. It is inhabited by multi-ethnic groups having a Mongoloid strain. The Lusei was referred to by British Ethnographer as Lushai. The word *'Lu'* means head, and *'shai'* means to cut means–Head Hunters. Another meaning of the word is long headed as to some people 'Shai' means long. In the Duhlian language the equivalent meaning of word 'sei' means long. But many people are of opinion that the word Lushai does not exist in Duhlian language. (Singh, 1995; Shakespear, 1912).

Material and Method

In the present study a sample of 407 children (215 boys and 192 girls) from the age group 6-10 years of the Lushai tribal (endogamous) group of Aizwal district in Mizoram have been drawn. In order to make the study more qualitative and comprehensive the research was confined to rural area of Mizoram state. To maintain uniformity of the study the subjects were selected from more or less similar socio-economic status and dietary habits of the same ecozone.

Eight anthropometric measurements viz., weight, stature, sitting height, biacromial diameter, bi-iliocristal diameter, triceps, biceps and subscapular skinfold thickness were taken on either sexes. Following the technique given by Singh and Bhasin (1989) the data have been collected. The entire data have been reduced into various statistical constants. The mean, standard deviation,coefficient variation, standard errors (Tables 4 and 5), t-test for sexual diamorphism (Table 7), absolute growth with increment, weight deficit, height deficit, classification for mid upper arm circumference have been computed age and sex-wise. The distance and velocity curves were plotted for all variables (Figs. 1 and 2). The regression equation Y=a+bX have been fitted for all linear measurements (Table 6). Correlation coefficient were calculated between some selected related variables (Table 9). (Arora and Mathur, 1996).

Results and Discussion

Agriculture is the principal occupation of the Lushai people. Majority of the Lushai (50.64%) are engaged in Jhum cultivation. Some of them are

Table 1
Occupation of Parents of Lushai Children

	Age in Years															
	6		*7*		*8*		*9*		*10*							
Occupation	*Father*	*Mother*	*Father*	*Mother*	*Father*	*Mother*	*Father*	*Mother*	*Father*	*Mother*	*Total Father N*	*%*	*Total Mother N*	*%*	*Total F+M*	*%*
Jhum Cultivation	11	5	18	12	15	17	14	25	20	21	78	46.99	80	54.79	158	50.64
Govt.Service																
Active	11	8	10	2	1	9	9	5	9	13	42	25.30	39	26.71	81	25.96
Pensioner					1	1	1			1						
Teacher	1	1	2	5	4	1	5	4	5	1	17	10.20	12	8.22	29	9.29
Artisan	2			1	3		3	1	3		11	6.63	2	1.37	13	4.17
Business			1	2		2	4	2	4	2	9	5.42	8	5.48	17	5.45
Others	3		2	3	3			1	1	1	9	5.42	5	3.42	14	4.49
Total	28	14	33	25	27	30	36	38	42	39	166	99.96	146	99.99	312	100

engaged as govt. servant (24.7%) and teachers (9.3%) (Table 1). Besides they also do other works like carpentary, blacksmithy, tailoring, knitting, basketary, weaving and some of them run small hotels, tea stalls etc. as a subsidiary source for their livelihood. As parents are busy in their respective works, so they can not devote sufficient time to take proper care of their children. Most of the people are below poverty line and may not be able to spend much on food items due to which the child lacks nutrients viz., minerals, vitamins, protein, fats and carbohydrates that are essential for normal growth.

Majority of the Lushai people have nuclear family (83.98%) and only 16.02% of them were found under joint family (Table 2). Majority of children (74.04%) have medium sized family i.e. 4 to 6 members Table 3 . Only 19.55 % children are having large and very large families. It is evident from the present study that, though the nuclear family exhibits higher frequency than that of joint family, its role among Lushai has not been obvious in bringing up their children as expected. However, its impact might have affected growth and development to the possible extent and it cannot be denied even at the lesser degree as the growing children fails to get psychological treatment, love and affection, protection, security etc. from elder member of the family.

Table 2
Family Type in which the Lushai Children Live

	Age in Years											
	6		7		8		9		10		*Total*	
Type of family	N	%	N	%	N	%	N	%	N	%	N	%
Nuclear	36	85.71	50	86.21	48	84.21	63	84	65	81.25	262	83.98
Joint	6	14.29	8	13.79	9	15.79	12	16	15	18.75	50	16.02
Total	42		58		57		75		80		312	

Literacy Level

Literacy level among the Lushai population is shown in Table 3 and observed that majority of the parents are literate i.e. father (98.64%) and mother (96.72%). The literacy was found to be higher in males than the female ones. Non-literate mothers (3.28%) are more than fathers (1.36%). Majority of the parents have achieved middle and high school education. More number of fathers (8.84%) are graduate than mothers (1.64%).

Weight

The distance curve (Fig. 1) of weight for boys shows higher than that of girls at 6 and 7 years; whereas, the curve for girls crosses that for boys after 8 years and then continues to accelerate compared to boys at 10 years. Thus the boys are heavier than girls upto 7 years. After that period, the

Table 3
Distribution of Literacy Level of Parents And Family Size of Lushai Children

	Literacy Level						*Family Size*				
	Boys		*Girls*		*Total*						
	Educated Father	*Mother*	*Father*	*Mother*	*Father*	*Mother*	*Family Size*		*Boys*	*Girls*	*Total*
Illiterate	3	6	1	4	4	10	1	Small	9	11	20
	1.89	3.70	0.74	2.8	1.36	3.28	(1-3)		5.49	7.43	6.41
Primary	29	38	24	31	53	69	2	Medium	126	105	231
(1-4)	18.24	23.45	17.78	21.68	18.03	22.62	(4-6)	76.83	70.95	74.04	Middle
School	39	57	37	54	76	111	3	Large	21	26	47
(5-7)	24.53	35.18	27.41	37.76	25.85	36.39	(7-9)	12.80	17.57	15.06	High
School	55	53	52	47	107	100	4	Very Large	8	6	14
(8-10)	34.60	32.72	38.52	32.87	36.39	32.79		(10 and above)	4.88	4.06	4.49
Jr .College	16	5	12	5	28	10					
(11-12)	10.06	3.09	8.89	3.50	9.52	3.28					
Graduate	17	3	9	2	26	5					
	10.70	1.85	6.67	1.40	8.84	1.64					
Total	159	162	135	143	294	305	Total		164	148	312

*Figures in parenthesis are percentage.

Table 4

Distribution of Mean, Standard Error, Standard Deviation (S.D.), Coefficient of Variation Absolute Growth and Increments of Linear Measurement Among the Lushai Children

		Boys						Girls					
		No.	*Weight (kg.)*	*Height (cm)*	*S1. Ht. (cm)*	*Biacro (in cm)*	*Bi-illiac (in cm)*	No.	*Weight (kg.)*	*Height (cm)*	*St. Ht. (cm)*	*Biacro (in cm)*	*Bi-illiac (in cm)*
6 YR.		40											
	M		18.05	110.84	60.82	24.93	16.00		16.17	108.10	60.00	24.10	15.74
	SE		0.47	1.06	0.54	0.25	0.16		0.20	0.76	0.40	0.21	0.17
	SO		2.95	6.70	3.40	1.56	1.02		1.21	4.44	2.30	1.25	1.00
	CV		16.34	6.05	5.60	6.27	6.36		7.48	4.10	3.90	5.18	6.35
7 YR.		50						38					
	M		19.27	114.72	63.15	25.39	16.30		17.84	111.80	61.00	24.83	16.22
	SE		0.35	0.80	0.36	0.19	0.17		0.37	0.92	0.60	0.22	0.16
	SO		2.45	5.70	2.59	1.36	1.19		2.28	5.47	3.50	1.37	1.01
	CV		13.74	4.96	4.10	5.35	6.85		12.78	4.88	5.70	5.17	6.21
	AB.G		1.22	3.88	2.33	0.46	0.30		1.67	3.75	1.50	0.73	0.52
	%		6.75	3.50	3.83	4.01	1.87		10.32	3.71	2.70	3.02	3.30
8 YR.		41						38					
	M		20.23	118.06	64.39	26.13	16.62		20.84	118.20	65.00	26.16	17.35
	SE		0.38	0.71	0.46	0.22	0.13		0.53	0.96	0.50	0.21	0.19
	SO		2.40	4.56	2.93	1.44	0.86		3.29	5.90	3.30	1.28	1.15
	CV		11.86	3.57	4.55	5.51	5.17		15.78	4.99	5.00	4.89	6.62
	AB.G		0.96	3.34	1.24	0.74	0.32		3.00	6.39	3.70	1.33	1.09
	%		4.98	2.91	1.96	2.91	1.96		16.81	5.71	6.00	5.35	6.70

Contd...

			Boys								Girls			
		No.	Weight (kg.)	Height (cm)	S1. Ht. (cm)	Biacro (in cm)	Bi-illiac (in cm)	No.	Weight (kg.)	Height (cm)	St. Ht. (cm)	Biacro (in cm)	Bi-illiac (in cm)
9 YR.		42						43					
	M		23.05	122.64	66.14	27.23	17.04		23.01	123.60	66.00	27.37	17.61
	SE		0.41	0.98	0.53	0.24	0.18		0.51	0.91	0.50	0.22	0.17
	SO		2.65	6.36	3.43	1.55	1.16		0.04	5.99	3.60	1.48	1.16
	CV		11.49	5.18	5.16	5.69	6.80		14.73	4.84	5.40	5.39	6.58
	AB.G		2.82	4.58	1.75	1.10	0.42		2.17	5.38	4.10	1.21	0.26
	%		13.93	3.72	2.71	4.20	2.52		10.41	4.55	1.20	4.74	1.49
10 YR.		42						39					
	M		25.63	128.10	68.95	28.72	18.58		25.92	129.00	70.00	28.72	18.58
	SE		0.46	0.69	0.50	0.43..	0.24		0.81	1.32	0.70	0.43	0.24
	SO		3.01	4.45	3.28	2.72	1.55		5.07	8.29	4.30	2.72	1.55
	CV		11.74	3.47	4.75	9.47	8.34		19.56	6.42	6.10	9.47	8.34
	AB.G		2.58	5.46	2.81	1.35	0.97		2.91	5.44	3.90	1.35	0.97
	%		11.19	4.45	4.25	4.93	5.50		12.64	4.40	5.80	4.93	5.50

*Note AB.G. (Absolute growth)

Table 5
Distribution of Mean, S.E., S.D., C.V. of Skinfold Thickness at Different Site in Lushai Children

		Boys				Girls		
		Triceps (in mm)	*Subscapular (in mm)*	*Biceps (in mm)*		*Triceps (in mm)*	*Subscapular (in mm)*	*Biceps (in mm)*
6 Yr.	40				40			
	M	5.79	3.94	3.24		6.25	4.38	3.66
	SE	0.22	0.09	0.09		0.31	0.13	0.14
	SD	1.40	0.57	0.56		1.84	0.76	0.81
	CV	24.04	14.39	17.31		28.09	17.35	23.49
7 Yr.	50				38			
	M	5.68	4.00	3.30		6.49	4.37	3.61
	SE	0.15	0.00	0.08		0.23	0.12	0.14
	SD	1.04	0.47	0.53		1.41	0.72	0.86
	CV	18.30	11.75	16.06		21.72	16.47	23.61
Absolute Growth	-0.11	0.04	0.06			-0.01	-0.05	
	%	-1.89	1.52	1.85		3.84	-0.22	-1.36
8 Yr.	41			0.24	38			
	M	5.42	4.09	3.18		6.90	4.45	3.76
	SE	0.16	0.08	0.09		0.31	0.13	0.18
	SD	1.02	0.48	0.57		1.93	0.82	1.09
	CV	18.81	11.73	17.81		27.97	18.42	29.06
Absolute Growth	-0.26	0.09	-0.12		0.41	0.08	0.14	
	%	-4.57	2.25	-3.63		6.31	1.83	3.87

Contd...

		Boys				Girls		
		Triceps (in mm)	*Subscapular (in mm)*	*Biceps (in mm)*	40	*Triceps (in mm)*	*Subscapular (in mm)*	*Biceps (in mm)*
9 Yr.	42				43			
	M	5.70	4.26	3.17		6.60	4.65	3.70
	SE	0.19	0.08	0.09		0.33	0.18	0.13
	SD	1.24	0.52	0.56		2.16	1.17	0.86
	CV	21.75	12.83	17.66		32.72	25.16	23.24
Absolute Growth	0.28	0.17	-0.01		-0.30	0.20	-0.05	
	%	4.15	0.97	-0.31		-4.34	4.49	-1.33
10 Yr.	42				39			
	M	5.59	4.3	3.15		7.56	5.34	4.25
	SE	0.19	0.16	0.09		0.54	0.32	0.27
	SD	1.24	1.03	0.54		3.36	2.03	1.68
	CV	22.18	19.73	17.14		43.97	38.01	39.52
Absolute Growth	-0.11	0.04	-0.02		0.96	0.69	0.55	
	%	-1.92	0.94	-0.63		14.54	14.83	14.86

Table 6
Distribution of Regression Equation Between Some Measurements and All Age Groups Among the Lushai Children

	Measurements				
Sex	*Weight*	*Height*	*Sitting height*	*Bi-acromial diameter*	*Bi-illiocristal diameter*
Male	y=1.89 + 6.087x r = 0.988	y = 4.246 + 84.907x r = 0.997	y = 1..929 + 49.255x r = 0.995	y =0.818 + 19.816 x r = 0.995	y = 0.443+13.215x r = 0.986
Female	y =2.466 + 1.029x r = 0.998	y = 5.370 + 75.191x r = 0.998	y =2.478 + 44.645x r = 0.993	y = 1.214 + 16.562x r = 0.999	y = 0.702+11.493x r = 0.993-

Table 7
Distribution of T-test In Sexual Di-morphism among the Lushai Children

Age/ Sex	No. of child	Weight	Stature	Sitting height	Bi-acromial diameter	Bi-illiocristal diameter	Fore arm length	Total arm length	Head circum.	Chest Circum.	Mid. Upp. arm Circum.	Calf Circum.	Triceps Skinfold	Sub-scapular Skin fold	Bi-ceps Skin fold
		Name of the Measurements													
		1	2	3	4	5	6	7	8	9	10	11	12	13	14
6 MF	74	3.68*	2.11	1.45	8.54*	1.11	4.36*	4.70*	2.86*	1.62	1.21	2.17	1.31	2.78*	2.52
7 MF	88	2.80*	2.37	2.65	1.92	0.17	2.37	3.33*	4.96*	4.55*	1.85	2.10	2.94*	2.75*	1.92
8 MF	79	0.93	0.13	1.34	0.00	3.17*	1.00	0.16	3.87*	1.30	0.72	1.05	4.24*	2.36	2.73*
9 MF	85	0.06	0.71	0.30	0.43	1.25	0.51	0.16	3.98*	1.83	0.97	0.10	2.36	3.04*	3.35*
10 MF	81	0.31	0.54	1.23	1.35	2.53	0.79	0.18	2.66	1.13	0.7	0.20	3.44*	2.90*	3.86*

* shows significant results at 1% level

curve for girls rises and exceeds that of boys and continues to prolong upto 10 years. The curve for girls remain at a higher level than for boys which indicated that girls are heavier than boys probably, to attain pre-adolescent growth more faster and earlier than boys.

The velocity curves (Fig. 2) for either sexes shows that growth spurt occurs at 9 years for boys and at 8 years for girls, the peak for girls remaining at a higher level than for boys showing apparent sex difference at that age. The rate of change of increment is more rapid in girls than boys upto 10 years. Thereafter the curve for girls accelerated whereas, in boys the curve is comparatively decelerated at 10 years resulting into a gradual declines of gain in body weight.

The regression equation for weight on age for boys and girls, Y=1.89+6.09X (r=0.988) and y=2.466+1.029 X (r=0.998) respectively have been recorded.

The 't' values for sexual diamorphism, however shows a significant difference for 6 and 7 years at 1% level while no significant difference was recorded for 8,9 & 10 years. The intergroup of boys shows a significant difference for 8 & 9 and 9 & 10 years while the intergroup of girls showed a significant difference in all age groups at 1% level.

Stature

Stature is the actual distribution of such a quantitative character that truly represents the character for the population. A comparison of the distance curves of stature between boys and girls exhibits that the curve for boys shows higher than the girls from the age group 6-7 years; indicating slightly taller stature of boys during the early period of age. After 7 years, the growth of girls slightly accelerates and it surpasses that of boys from 8-10 years indicating taller stature of girls than boys. The growth spurt of girls was found to be faster than boys at 10 years, probably, girls attain pre-adolescent growth spurt and skeletal maturity earlier than boys. The present finding is in conformity with the earlier study by Harrison *et. al.,* (1997) and Tanner (1962).

The velocity curve(Fig. 4) for boys fall at 8 years and thereafter rises sharply upto 10 years whereas the rate of growth for girls falls at 10 years. Thus, boys attained maximum stature at 10 years whereas among girls it was recorded at 8 years.

The regression equation of stature on age for boys and girl i.e., Y=4.24+84.9X(r=0.997) and Y=5.37+75.19X(r=0.998) have been recorded.

The degree of correlation between weight and height was found to be very high among both the sexes and was found to be highly significant at 1% level for all ages.

The 't' for sexual diamorphism shows significant difference for 6 and 7 years at 5 % level while all intergroup shows a significant differences at 1% level.

Sitting Height

The study of sitting height of growing children plays an important role in growth and development of the trunk which helps in assessing body proportion.

A comparison of the distance curves (Fig.-5) of sitting height for both sexes reveals that the curve for boys rises more rapidly from 6-7 years than that of girls, whereas in case of girls it remains higher at the age of 8 and 10 years. Both the curves were crossed at 9 years and after that, the growth of girls rapidly accelerates and surpasses that of boys and continues to grow intermittently upto 10 years. The growth of boys was slow between the age 7-10 years whereas, girls shows faster growth for the same age groups, probably, the endrogenic hormones which stimulated the vertebral column growth, are more active among girls than that of boys as suggested by Eveleth and Tanner (1990).

From the velocity curve (Fig. 6) it was seen that the curve for boys declined at 8 years whereas for girls it declined at 9 years, the rate of decline being higher in girls than that of boys indicating a sharp retardation in growth. Thereafter both the curves accelerates upto 10 years. However, the peak for girls at 8 years remains at higher level than that of boys. Both the sexes show prolong rate of growth of increment at and beyond 10 years.

The regression equation of sitting height on age for boys and girls Y=1.93+49.25 X (r=0.995) and Y=2.48+64 X (r=0.993) respectively have been recorded.

The degree of correlation between height and sitting height was found to be very high among girls at 8 and 10 years and was found to be highly significant for all age groups at 1% level.

The 't' values however shows non-significant difference in sexual diamorphism except 7 years. The 't' for intergroup of boys shows significant difference between 6 and 7 and 9 and 10 years, whereas, among girls it was seen between 7 and 8 and 9 and 10 years at 1% level.

Biacromial Diameter

The distance curves(Fig. 7) for bi-acromial diameter of both the sexes show that they increase almost at the same rate. The curve for boys remains at a higher level than that of girls from 6-7 years, after which the curve for girls accelerates more rapidly than boys upto 10 years. Both the curves crosses each other at 8 years and curve for girls surpasses boys from 8-10 years showing changes more rapidly during this period. From this it was apparent that the boys attained higher growth spurt from 6-8 years than girls whereas the girls attained higher growth spurt from 8-10 years. However both curves show prolong growth at and beyond 10 years too.

The velocity curve(Fig. 8) of girls shows higher absolute growth than for boys from 8-10 years which indicates that the growth was more rapid among girls compared to boys. The maximum rate of growth among girls was noticed at 8 years whereas the boys shows peak at 9 years. Thus, the growth spurt for girls shows prolong beyond 10 years whereas for boys it was diminishing for the same age, this situation may be because of more activeness of hormone endrogen among girls than boys for those age groups.

The regression equation of biacromial diameter on age for boys and girls, Y=0.818+19.816 X (r=0.995) and Y=1.214+16.562 X (r=0.99) respectively, have been recorded.

The 't' values for sexual diamorphism shows highly significant difference for 6 years at 1 % level while no significant difference was seen for other age groups. The 't' for intergroup of girls however shows a significant difference between 7 and 8 and 8 and 9 years; whereas among boys it was seen between 8 and 9 and 9 and 10 years at 1 % level.

Bi-iliocristal Diameter

The distance curve (Fig. 9) of bi-iliocristal diameter of both sexes shows that in girls the acceleration was gradual throughout the age period and the range of variation in growth rate was much larger than that in boys. On the other hand, the increase in boys was uniform and the range of variation in growth rates was smaller than in girls. The curve for boys remains comparatively at a higher level than that of girls for 6 and 7 years; whereas, the distance between the curves accelerates among girls compared to boys as age increases. This means that the increase was more rapid in girls from the age 8-10 years than that of boys.

Though the rate of growth remains almost same in either sex but a sharp rise in the velocity curve(Fig. 10) of girls at 8 years was noticed. The rate of growth in boys slightly accelerates from 6 to 10 years; whereas, in girls it was rapidly decelerates at 9 years and thereafter abruptly rises up to 10 years; may be pre-adolescent growth spurt starts from 9 years in case of girls. Because of this dimension and due to specific stimulation of cartilage cells by the hormone oestrogen, the width of hips and buttock of female is relatively greater than males. Thus, from this it may be stated that-the pelvic girdle is broader among girls than boys for 9 and 10 years. of age groups and the girls reach at puberty as evident from pre-adolescent growth spurt, earlier than that of boys.

The regression equation of bi-iliocristal diameter on age for boys and girls Y=0.44+13.21 X (r=0.986) and Y=0.70+11.49 X (r=0.993) respectively have been recorded.

The correlation coefficient between biacromial and bi-iliocristal diameters for boys was found to be highly significant at 1% level for 6,7,8 and 9 years whereas in case of girls it was highly significant for all age groups at 1% level except for 6 years.

The 't' value shows significant difference for sexual diamorphism for 8 years at 1% level. The 't' for intergroup of 7 and 8 and 9 and 10 years boys and 9 & 10 years girls shows a significant difference between them at 1% level.

Triceps Skinfold

When the two sexes were compared it was seen that the distance curves (Fig. 11) run almost parallel to each other from 6-8 years. The curve for girls remains at a higher level than for boys throughout the age period. After the age of 9 years the acceleration of growth in girls was more rapid than in boys. The decrease of growth spurt in boys was slow and gradual from 6-8 years and from 9-10 years, on the other hand it increases among girls from 6-8 years and decreases at 9 years and again accelerates at 10 years.

A comparison of the rate of growth for both sexes shows distinct variation. The velocity curve (Fig. 12) for boys shows negative increment from 6-8 years which means there was no gain of growth for that period. After that there was an abrupt increment at 9 years and again rate of growth was declined at 10 years. Thus, the peak velocity for boys was observed at 9 years. A quite reverse trend was noticed among girls wherein a continuous gain of increment was recorded with the change of age, except 9 years where the growth was diminished. The peak velocity in girls occurs at 10 years indicating prolong growth beyond that age. Thus, it can be said that the deposition of fat and muscles among girls was higher due to which the thickness of skin at triceps was greater than boys during this period because of attainment of puberty earlier than their male counterparts.

The 't' for sexual diamorphism shows a significant difference for 7,8 and 10 years at 1% level whereas no significant difference was seen for any intergroup of either sexes.

Subscapular Skinfold

The distance curves (Fig. 13) of subscapular skinfold of either sexes runs almost parallel to each other from 6-10 years and accelerates with the change of age. The curve for girls remains at a higher level in comparison to boys for all age groups. Both the curves were intermittently accelerates uniformly throughout the age period with small range of variation in growth rate. The range of variation in growth rates in girls was much larger than that of boys at 10 years.

The rate of growth remains almost the same in boys from 6-10 years but in girls a steep velocity curve was noticed from 8-10 years. This means that the gain of increment was more rapid in girls than in boys from 7-10 years. But in case of boys the gain of increment was decelerates from 8-10 years. In girls the growth rate declined at 7 resulting into stunting of growth for that age.

The velocity curve (Fig. 14) for girls shows peak at 10 years indicating prolong growth beyond that age whereas for boys it shows at 8 years.

The correlation coefficient between triceps and subscapular skinfold among girls was found to be significant for all age groups where the 't' shows a significant difference between them at 1% level for all age groups, except for boys from 8-10 years age group.

The 't' values for sexual diamorphism shows a significant difference at 1% level for all age groups except 8 years where no significant difference was noticed for any intergroup of any sex.

Biceps Skinfold

The distance curves (Fig. 15) of biceps skinfold of either sexes show that in boys it was slightly accelerates from 6-7 years and again decelerates from 7-10 years with very small range of variation growth rate. This means there was no gain of growth among boys from 8-10 years. On the other hand in girls the growth rate was intermittently accelerates from lower age to higher age groups. However, the distance curve for girls remains at a higher level than that for boys for all age groups. The growth in girls was seen to be prolonged beyond 10 years whereas in boys it was seen to be diminished for the same age.

The velocity curve (Fig. 16) for girls shows two peaks at 8 and another at 10 years, may be pre-adolescent growth, whereas in boys, the relative rate of growth was declined for the same age groups. The distinctive feature of the two velocity curves among girls was similar to that found in case of the distance curve at the age of 8 and 10 years.

The 't' for sexual diamorphism shows a significant difference from 8-10 years. at 1 per cent level while no significant difference was recorded for 6-7 years. The 't' for intergoup shows non-significant difference for all age groups.

Dental Pattern

From the Table 8 it appears that the frequency of deciduous teeth was decreasing with the advancing age while the frequency of permanent teeth was found to be increasing. The occurrence of 2nd premolar and 2nd molar teeth among boys started from the age of 10 years whereas in case of girls it started from the age of 8 years. Thus it seems in girls the dental maturity sets in earlier than that of the boys.

Assessment of Nutritional Status

Weight for Age Deficit Classification

The weight deficit classification Visweswara Rao (1980) (Table 10) exhibits that majority of boys suffered from different categories of malnutrition compared to their female counterparts due to which the wasting seems to be more common among them. However, the higher frequency of wasting among boys was found at 9 years followed by 7 and 8 years while in case

Table 8
Distribution of Mean of Dental Pattern Among Lushai Children

	Boys									Girls								
	Deciduous			*Permanent*						*Deciduous*			*Permanent*					
Age in Years	*i*	*c*	*m*	*I*	C	*P1st*		*M1st*		*i*	*c*	*m*	*I*	C	*P1st*		*M1st*	
6	26.75	36.25	36.50	8.62	2.00	0.12		19.00		22.12	34.00	31.37	7.50	-	6.00		17.25	
7	24.87	43.25	44.62	19.75	4.50	0.50		38.25		15.50	35.00	33.37	16.12	2.00	0.25		28.50	
8	9.12	32.50	35.75	28.25	5.00	0.75		38.50		5.50	26.25	31.50	29.62	9.50	1.00	0.25**	37.75	
9	3.37	24.00	33.37	36.25	13.00	2.50		41.50		2.00	23.50	35.75	39.50	15.00	2.00	1.00**	42.00	
10	0.62	12.25	32.50	41.00	24.75	2.75	0.25**	41.00	1.00**	0.75	15.75	32.00	38.25	18.00	5.75	22.50**	38.25	2.25**

of girls it was found at 10 years followed by 9 and 7 years. On the whole, 38.82% of boys were found to be weight deficit against 35.38% of girls.

Height for Age Deficit Classification

The height for age deficit classification (Table 11) reveals that boys shows higher frequency of mild retardation at 8 years whereas among girls it was recorded at 7 years. About 24.57% of boys were found to be retarded from normal growth compared to their female counterparts for which frequency of 23.17% was recorded.

Table 9
Distribution of Co-relation Co-efficient between Selected Measurements Among the Lushai Childen

		Name of the Measurements			
Age in Years	*Sample Size*	*Weight and Height*	*Height and Sitting Ht*	*Bi-acromial breadth and Bi-iliocristal bdh.*	*Triceps and Subscap. Skinfold*
6M	40	0.8097**	0.7649**	0.6412**	0.5308**
6F	34	0.7042**	0.8062**	0.3791**	0.619**
7M	50	0.7984**	0.8363**	0.5652**	0.3912**
7F	38	0.7617**	0.7701**	0.666**	0.614**
8M	41	0.6593**	0.6023**	0.4092**	0.3464
8F	28	0.8365**	0.8756**	0.665*	0.7225*
9M	42	0.7886**	0.7718**	0.7286**	0.3131**
9F	43	0.7174**	0.7188**	0.7137**	0.7574**
10M	42	0.7314**	0.7483**	0.3194**	0.2904
10F	39	0.7916**	0.9431***	0.7297**	0.8941**

* Significant at 1% level.
**Highly significant at 0.1% level.

Mid Upper Arm Circumference for Age Classification

The classification of mid upper arm circumference (Table 12) reveals that the highest frequency of 7.86 % of boys of all age groups was found to be under malnutrition category whereas girls show highest frequency of 9.58% for the same category. Both the sexes show very less frequencies for moderate and severe malnutrition categories. The highest frequency of boys was recorded at 9 years under malnutrition while girls show at 8 and 9 for the same category. When boys and girls were compared, it was noticed that girls were seems to be higher (13.51%) in all categories of malnutrition than boys (10.32%).

The effect of malnutrition based on classification of mid upper arm circumference has not borne out much here on growth and development as majority of children were found to be under normal category. However, this lesser degree of malnutrition might have checked the normal growth pattern of the children.

Table 10
Weight for Age or Weight Deficit Classification of Lushai Children

	Boys						Girls						
Categories	*6*	*7*	*8*	*9*	*10*	*Total Boys*	*6*	*7*	*8*	*9*	*10*	*Total Girls*	*Total Boys+Girls*
Grd. IV M.N.	0	0	0	0	0	0	0	0	1	0	1	2	2
									2.6		2.56	1.04	0.49
Grd. III M.N.	1	1	1	1	1	5	0	1	2	7	6	16	21
	2.5	2	2.44	2.38	2.38	2.33		2.63	5.3	16.28	15.39	8.33	5.16
Grd. II M.N.	3	12	16	18	10	59	8	18	10	14	13	63	122
	7.5	24	39.02	42.86	23.8	27.44	23.53	47.37	26	32.56	33.33	32.81	29.97
Grd. I M.N.	19	22	16	17	20	94	21	12	13	11	6	63	157
	47.5	44	39.02	40.47	47.62	43.72	61.77	31.58	34	25.58	15.39	32.81	38.57
Normal	17	15	8	6	11	57	5	7	12	11	13	48	105
	42.5	30	19.52	14.29	26.2	26.51	14.7	18.42	32	25.58	33.33	25	25.8
Total	40	50	41	42	42	215	34	38	38	43	39	192	407

M.N. = Malnutrition; Grd. = Grade

Table 11
Height for Age or Height Deficit Classification of Lushai Children

Categories	Boys						Girls						
	6	7	8	9	10	Total Boys	6	7	8	9	10	Total Girls	Total Boys+Girls
Poor	0	1	0	1	0	2	0	0	1	0	1	2	4
		2		2.38		0.93			2.6		2.56	1.04	0.98
Mild Retarded	17	17	23	21	20	98	12	21	20	22	17	92	190
	42.5	34	56.1	50	47.62	45.58	35.3	55.26	53	51.16	43.59	47.92	46.68
Normal	23	32	18	20	22	115	22	17	17	21	21	98	213
	57.5	64	43.9	47.62	57.38	53.49	64.2	44.74	45	48.84	53.85	51.04	52.33
Total	40	50	41	42	42	215	34	38	38	43	39	192	407

Table 12
Nutritional Status Classification Based on Mid-upper Arm Circumference of Lushai Children

	Boys						*Girls*						
Categories	*6*	*7*	*8*	*9*	*10*	*Total Boys*	*6*	*7*	*8*	*9*	*10*	*Total Girls*	*Total Boys+Girls*
Severely M.N.	1	0	0	0	0	1	0	0	0	2	2	4	5
	2.5					0.47				0.49	5.12	2.08	1.2
Moderate M	2	1	2	3	1	9	2	2	2	1	5	12	21
	5	2	4.87	7.14	2.38	4.19	5.88	5.27	5.26	0.24	12.82	6.25	5.16
Mild M.N.	25	4	8	9	9	32	5	7	10	11	6	39	71
	5	8	19.51	21.43	21.42	14.88	14.7	18.42	26.31	27	15.38	20.31	17.44
Normal	35	45	31	30	32	173	27	29	26	29	26	137	310
	87.5	90	75.61	71.42	76.19	80.46	79.41	76.2	68.42	7.12	66.67	71.35	76.17
Total	40	50	40	42	42	215	34	38	38	43	39	192	

Nutritional Deficiency

It is evident from the present findings that the girls were found to be healthier than boys. About 25.11% of boys were found to be sufferer from various clinical signs; whereas, in case of girls its frequency 16.07% was recorded (Table 13). The occurrence of clinical symptoms is due to various vitamin deficiency. Those vitamins are essential for metabolic activities, growth and development of body organs and combating diseases. Probably the Lushai children may not be getting those vitamins through their diet which has a direct impact on health and body build and as such those factors might have caused their normal growth pattern and body development as the frequency of nutritional deficiencies found to be higher.

Table 13
Distribution of Clinical Signs and Morbidity Among the Lushai Children

Clinical Signs	*Boys*	*Girls*	*Age (Year)*	*Morbidity Boys*	*Morbidity Girls*
Pigmentation of Skin	81 (15.85)	29 (8.87)	6	14 (3.44)	17 (4.17)
Angular Stomatitis	29 (5.67)	8 (1.96)			
Dry Scale Skin	26 (5.09)	14 (3.4)	7	32 (7.86)	20 (4.91)
Discoloured Hair	3 (0.59)	17 (4.18)			
Flag/Coarse Hair	1 (0.20)	2 (0.49)	8	40 (9.83)	33 (8.11)
Spongy Bleeding Gums	95 (18.59)	64 (15.72)			
Yellowish Teeth	180 (35.26)	152 (37.35)	9	40 (9.83)	32 (7.86)
Pale Conjunctive	63 (12.33)	30 (7.37)			
Yellow Colour in the base of nail	33 (6.46)	11 (2.70)	10	32 (7.86)	33 (8.11)
	511 (100.04)	327	Total	158 (38.82)	135 (33.17)
Mean	102.2 (25.11)	65.4 (16.07)			

*Figures in parentheses are percentage.

Morbidity

Most of the Lushai children were suffered from various kinds of diseases like pneumonia, typhoid, diarrhoea, malaria (PF), jaundice, T.B., Chicken pox and others. The highest frequency of 38.82 % among boys was recorded for various kinds of diseases; whereas, in girls it was recorded to 33.17% for different diseases. This means that about 72% of the children were suffered from morbid condition which is a great concern for health and growth and development of growing children. This impact of magnitude of morbidity prevalent among them, probably, might have affected normal growth and development of the Lushai children, as evident from the present study.

Impact of Various Socio-economic Factors on Growth

Mean and standard deviation were calculated for weight, stature, sitting height, bi-acromial diameter and bi-illiac diameter based on per capita income of family size, family type and birth order (parity) of the child measured.

From the Table 14 it appears that the weight of 7 and 8 years among the boys under Rs. 5000 to 10,000 income group was found to be higher whereas it shows higher for 6 and 9 years boys whose income was more than Rs. 10,000. The height and sitting height among the boys of 6, 9 and 10 years shows higher against the income group of more than Rs.10,000. The bi-acromial diameter among the boys of 6, 7, 9 and 10 years was found to be greater for the same income group. The bi-iliac diameter of 9 and 10 years boys was also found to be greater.

Table 14
Incomewise Distribution of Mean and Standard Deviation of Measurements Among Lushai Children

	Boys			Girls		
Measurements	*5000*	*5000-10000*	*Above 10000*	*5000*	*5000-10000*	*Above 10000*
6 Years						
Weight	17.33	18.07	18.72	16.66	16.16	16.38
	-3.04	-4.04	-1.95	-1.6	-1.04	-1.21
Height	109.18	109.38	111.9	111.06	109.5	107.12
	-5.08	-5.03	-5.77	-4.51	-2.46	-5.83
Sitting Height	60.31	58.51	62.82	60.36	60.83	59.97
	-2.39	-2.71	-1.56	-1.81	-0.55	-2.9
Biacromial Diameter	24.84	24.15	25.22	25.76	24.5	23.87
	-1.55	-1.62	-1.2	-1.65	-1.11	-1.55
Bi-iliac Diameter	16.15	15.84	16.14	14.86	15.8	16.08
	-1.46	-1.07	-0.77	-0.6	-1.08	-1.24
7 Years						
Weight	19.25	19.43	19.23	17.66	17.61	17.85
	-2.94	-2.04	-1.65	-1.36	-1.61	-2.4
Height	113.99	115.88	115.77	112.01	111.85	112.71
	-7.72	-4.04	-4	-5.41	-3.7	-7.01
Sitting Height	62.36	62.53	63.88	62.01	61.41	61.92
	-3.66	-2.1	-1.71	-2.96	-1.99	-3.98
Biacromial Diameter	24.98	25.2	25.8	24.86	24.97	25.01
	-1.22	-1.11	-1.6	-1.28	-0.57	-1.11
Bi-iliac Diameter	16.1	16.25	16.24	16.4	16.52	16.21
	-1.38	-1.4	-1.02	-0.95	-1.06	-0.78
8 Years						
Weight	20.2	20.8	20.42	21.7	19.5	23.5
	-1.61	-2.84	-2.87	-3.06	-2.85	-3.78
Height	118.72	118.1	117.57	118.74	115.77	123.08
	-3.99	-4.81	-6.72	-4.69	-3.91	-7.21
Sitting Height	65.55	64.05	63.17	65.25	63.68	67.84
	-2.56	-3.92	-3.71	-2.52	-2.74	-4.11
Biacromial Diameter	26.15	26.62	25.88	26.52	25.88	26.55
	-1.52	-1.82	-1.1	-0.86	-1.44	-1.11
Bi-iliac Diameter	16.85	16.83	16.77	17.38	16.92	18.06
	-0.86	-0.87	-0.83	-0.52	-1.1	-1.46
9 Years						
Weight	22.94	22.86	23.53	24.2	24.81	20.62
	-1.87	-2.49	-2.72	-3.48	-3.13	-2.21

Contd...

		Boys			*Girls*	
Measurements	*5000*	*5000-10000*	*Above 10000*	*5000*	*5000-10000*	*Above 10000*
Height	122.15	118.97	126.25	124.61	122.81	121.16
	-4.44	-4.63	-5.08	-5.3	-7.95	-4.34
Sitting Height	66.01	64.77	67.56	66.3	66.43	64.76
	-2.11	-2.26	-4.12	-3.83	-3.31	-2.51
Biacromial Diameter	26.97	26.49	27.85	27.78	26.59	26.98
	-1.36	-1.71	-1.13	-1.26	-1.24	-0.71
Bi-iliac Diameter	16.68	16.94	17.38	17.78	17.28	16.95
	-1.12	-1.35	-1.64	-0.93	-1.05	-1.34
10 Years						
Weight	26.125	25.78	24.79	25.54	25.64	26.72
	-2.09	-4.06	-2.83	-4.65	-5.6	-5
Height	127.92	127.07	129.59	130.59	128.22	128.75
	-3.11	-5.65	-4.44	-8.44	-6.31	-6.84
Sitting Height	68.73	68.69	69.53	70.51	69.47	69.87
	-2.56	-3.94	-3.42	-3.68	-5.09	-3.67
Biacromial Diameter	27.96	27.87	28.45	28.9	28.76	28.47
	-1.04	-1.46	-0.98	-2.57	-2.21	-2.13
Bi-iliac Diameter	17.66	17.95	18.05	18.56	18.65	18.47
	-1.1	-1.17	-0.94	-1.73	-1.7	-1.24

Figures in parentheses are the values of standard deviation.

The mean value of stature and sitting height of 8 years boys was found to be higher against the income group of less than Rs.5000, the weight of 10 years boys was found to be higher for the same income group. The bi-iliac diameter among boys of 6 and 8 years was also found to be greater against the income group of Rs.5000. The height and bi-acromial diameter among the girls of 6, 9 and 10 years show higher for the same income group. The weight of 6 years girls, the bi-iliac diameter of 9 years girls and the sitting height of 10 years girls also shows higher values against the same income group.

Under Rs. 5000 to 10,000 income group, the bi-iliac diameter among the girls of 7 and 10 years was found to be greater. The mean value of weight and sitting height of 9 years among the girls was found to be higher for the same income category. Under more than Rs. 10,000 income category, the mean value of weight among the girls of 7 and 10 years and all dimensions of 8 years was found to be higher. The height and bi-acromial diameter of 7 years old girls were found to be greater for the same income group.

From the above it can be said that the income has not played a significant role in general as no specific trend of a particular income group was observed. However, the high income i.e. above Rs.10,000 has necessarily brought about the little change over the growth of boys as majority of the measurements shows higher frequency except weight followed by the income category of Rs. 5000 to 10,000. A quite reverse

Table 15
Mean and S.D. of Selected Measurements of Lushai Children Aged 6 and 10 Years by Family Size

		Boys								Girls							
		1 to 3		4 to 6		7 to 9		10+		1 to 3		4 to 6		7 to 9		10+	
	Age	Mean	S.D.	Mean	S.D.	Mean	S.D.	Mean	S.D.	Mean	S.D.	Mean	S.D.	Mean	S.D.	Mean	S.D.
Weight	6	17	0.5	18.1	3.3	19	2.4	0	0	0	0	16.4	1.1	16.5	1.8	0	0
	7	19.5	3.53	19.2	2.1	0	0	0	0	0	0	17.7	1.9	0	0	0	0
	8	0	0	20.4	2.4	20.8	2.6	0	0	21.7	1.4	21.1	4.8	19.9	3.3	0	0
	9	24.5	2.12	23.1	2.1	24.3	5.9	23	2.1	24.2	2.6	22.4	3.5	23	3.9	24.7	2.3
	10	29.75	3.18	25.5	3.1	25.6	2.1	24.5	3.5	29.5	3.5	26.4	5.2	24.4	4.4	0	0
Stature	6	108.6	4.73	110.8	5	110.7	7.7	0	0	0	0	107.9	5.1	110.2	5.7	0	0
	7	118.5	1.48	114.9	5.4	0	0	0	0	0	0	112.2	5.7	0	0	0	0
	8	0	0	117.6	4.5	120.8	5.3	0	0	119.1	3.9	118.5	6.8	117.3	5	0	0
	9	127	0.49	122.3	4.8	128.2	11.1	119.2	5.2	128.8	8.7	122.9	6.1	121.3	4.2	127.1	4
	10	132.7	3.11	127.8	4.6	129	4.2	124.8	2.1	133.9	1.8	129	8.4	129.6	8.2	0	0
Sitting Height	6	61.6	0.5	60.7	3	61.6	2.6	0	0	0	0	60.2	2.5	60.2	2	0	0
	7	61.2	2	63.1	2.6	0	0	0	0	0	0	61.7	3.2	0	0	0	0
	8	0	0	68.1	3.5	65.4	3.1	0	0	66.2	1.7	65.4	3.7	63.8	3.5	0	0
	9	69.5	1.4	66.3	2.9	65.8	8.2	65.3	2.5	68.9	4.9	65.8	2.7	64.5	4.7	68.1	3.5
	10	72.2	2.1	68.6	3.4	69.6	3.4	68.7	1.8	71.5	0.1	70.1	4.4	69.9	3.5	0	0
Biacromial diameter	6	24.3	0.6	24.7	1.4	26.2	1	0	0	0	0	24.1	1.4	25.7	1.8	0	0
	7	23.2	0.7	25.5	1.9	0	0	0	0	0	0	25	1	0	0	0	0
	8	0	0	26.2	1.6	26.6	1.1	0	0	26.8	0.9	26.3	1.2	25.5	1.4	0	0
	9	27.8	0.6	27.2	1.5	28	2.1	26.8	1.4	28	1.5	27.2	1.3	27.3	1.4	27.2	0.2
	10	29.6	0.2	28.1	1.1	28	1.4	28.1	1.7	31.4	0.2	28.6	2.2	28.7	2.4	0	0
Bi-illiac diameter	6	15.8	0.9	16.3	1.1	15.7	1.1	0	0	0	0	15.9	1.1	15.3	1.3	0	0
	7	16.1	1.8	16.1	1.1	0	0	0	0	0	0	16.4	0.9	0	0	0	0
	8	0	0	16.8	0.9	16.9	1	0	0	17.5	0.7	17.6	1.3	16.8	1.2	0	0
	9	18	0.6	16.9	1.2	17.1	1.3	17.5	1.5	17.8	1.4	17.5	1.2	17.4	1	17.4	0.3
	10	18.6	1.3	17.8	1.1	17.9	1.1	18.2	0.5	19.9	1	18.7	1.6	18.4	1.3	0	0

trend was noticed in case of girls that majority of the measurements were shown high frequency under lower income group i.e. below Rs.5000 category followed by middle income group i.e. Rs. 5000 to 10,000 category.

From Table 15 it shows that the mean value of weight of medium family of both sexes was found to be higher at lower age group whereas it was observed to be higher at higher age group in small family size. The height among the boys of large family was found to be higher at 8 and 9 years which it shows higher at 7 and 10 years of boys of small family. On the other hand the height among the girls of small family was found to be greater from 8 to 10 years. The sitting height of boys of small family shows higher mean value at 6, 9 and 10 years whereas the girls shows higher frequency from 8 to 10 years for the same family size.

The bi-acromial diameter among the boys of large family shows higher frequency at the age group of 6, 8 and9 years whereas the girls of small family shows higher frequency from 8 and 10 years. The bi-iliac diameter among the boys of medium family was noticed to be higher at the lower age group of 6 and 7 years while that of small family it was observed to be higher at the higher age group of 9 and 10 years. The same trend was noticed among the girls too, that is, the lower age group of 6 to 8 years of girls of medium family shows higher mean value and the higher age group of 9 to 10 years of small family shows higher mean value of bi-illiac diameter.

Thus from the above it can be said that the higher age group of both sexes of small family shows higher frequency which might have played a significant role in the growth and development of the Lushai children. On the other hand the lower age group of both children of medium and large family size shows higher frequency compared to small family size.

As the parents of small family size could look after their children in a better and effective way as a whole this may be reason, why the children of higher age group i.e. 9 and 10 years shows relatively higher frequency for almost all measurements. On the other hand, the parents of medium and large family size could provide better family entertainment, less psychological stress, more sharing hands, dependency etc. which is very much needed during the early childhood days for their growth and development.

The Table 16 portrays the higher mean value of stature and sitting height among the boys of 6 and 7 years under joint family type. The frequency of bi-acromial diameter among the boys of 6 and 8 years of joint family was found to be higher compared to nuclear family type. The higher frequency of bi-iliac diameter among boys of 9 and 10 years was also noticed under joint family. Only the weight of both children of all age groups was found to be higher in nuclear family except 9 year where the joint family of both sexes shows higher frequency for it.

The stature among the boys of lower age group of joint family shows higher frequency while that of girls it was observed to be higher in higher age group. A quite reverse trend was apparent in case of nuclear family where the height among boys shows lower frequency for higher age group while that of girls it was observed to be higher in lower age group. The girls of 9 years of joint family shows higher frequency for all dimensions. As a whole it may be mentioned that the nuclear family has played a crucial role in the growth and development of children for all age groups except 9 years of girls.

Table 16
Distribution of Mean and Standard Deviation of Selected Measurements of Lushai Children Aged from 6 Through 10 Years by Family Type

		Nuclear		*Joint*		*Nuclear*		*Joint*	
	Age in Years	*Mean*	*S.D.*	*Mean*	*S.D.*	*Mean*	*S.D.*	*Mean*	*S.D.*
	6	18.1	3.01	18	1.41	16.54	1.12	16	1.41
	7	19.33	2.27	19	1.22	17.72	1.92	17.66	1.52
Weight	8	20.52	2.44	19.67	1.52	21.18	3.61	20.58	3.54
	9	22.98	2.44	24	2.3	22.57	3.43	24.75	3.4
	10	25.79	3.1	24.4	1.94	26.31	5.16	24.8	4.89
	6	110.05	5.39	114	2.26	108.9	3.55	106.95	8.71
	7	115	5.62	116.5	3.37	112.38	5.73	111.16	2.2
Stature	8	118.18	4.88	117.37	5.55	118.7	5.99	118.5	6.57
	9	123.26	5.74	121.91	5.47	122.66	5.73	129.8	4.81
	10	127.98	4.41	127.02	4.19	128.95	8.21	129.95	9.29
	6	60.72	2.8	62.7	1.55	60.06	1.59	60.67	4.07
	7	62.94	2.73	63.94	1.02	61.7	3.19	62.16	1.62
Sitting Height	8	64.42	3.49	63.73	2.47	65.32	3.36	65.21	4.2
	9	66.5	3.53	65.57	2.54	65.39	3.31	70	2.71
	10	69.06	3.4	68.12	2.36	69.8	4.32	70.1	4.35
	6	24.77	1.41	25.4	2.4	24.21	1.48	24.8	2.01
	7	25.43	1.42	25.24	1.36	24.97	1.01	24.87	0.41
Biacromial diameter	8	26.13	1.55	26.87	1.07	26.39	1.25	25.61	1.06
	9	27.26	1.51	27.01	1.42	27.16	1.2	28.3	1.41
	10	28.16	1.15	27.98	1.43	28.77	2.19	28.56	2.49
	6	16.06	1.04	15.9	0.98	15.64	0.93	16.17	1.75
	7	16.22	1.21	16.02	1.16	16.48	0.9	15.53	0.2
Bi-illac diameter	8	16.9	0.81	15.83	0.65	17.6	1.15	16.46	0.98
	9	17.01	1.13	17.32	1.54	17.36	1.03	18.37	1.32
	10	17.8	1.13	18.06	0.85	18.81	1.56	17.9	1.39

As 60 per cent of the children were influenced by the nuclear family compared to joint family whose the frequency was restricted to 40 per cent. This may be due to effectiveness of greater share of nutrition, extra care of children, relatively large space in house, strong intimacy between parents and child, better emotional attachment etc. which are very much essential for growing children at the early stage.

Table 17
Mean And S.D. of a Selected Measurments of Lushai Children Aged and 10 Years by Parity

		Boys										Girls									
		1		2		3		4		5 & above		1		2		3		4		5 & above	
	Age/ Parity	Mean	S.D.	Mean	S.D.	Mean	S.D.	Mean	S.D.	Mean	S.D.	Mean	S.D.	Mean	S.D.	Mean	S.D.	Mean	S.D.	Mean	S.D.
Weight	6	18.08	3.15	17.42	2.04	19.2	4.65	17.5	0.86	21	2.82	16.44	1.05	16.31	1.03	16	1.96	16	1.67	0	0
	7	19.03	2.07	20.17	2.63	16.44	2.83	18	1.76	19.37	3.01	17.83	2.25	18.16	1.96	17.55	2.38	17	2.09	0	0
	8	21.15	2.16	20.53	2.83	18.72	1.29	19.75	2.06	22	3	21.29	3.67	19.75	3.37	21.56	2.62	19.75	3.5	0	0
	9	23.4	2.33	23.05	2.67	22.89	3.88	0	0	22.75	1.5	22.6	3.23	23.04	4.14	22.56	2.41	23.41	3.41	23.71	3.94
	10	25.91	2.12	24.9	4.18	24.6	3.97	26.28	1.97	0	0	28.81	4.93	26.83	5.86	24.9	4.06	27	8.48	22	4.58
Stature	6	112.41	8.58	109.36	5.14	112.78	6.17	100.1	2.4	111.45	13.78	106.77	4.87	109.05	3.93	108.81	3.45	106.61	6.45	0	0
	7	115.48	4.58	116.6	4.09	111.04	4.76	111.95	4.36	114.25	9.24	114.88	4.76	115.55	4.97	108.74	5.56	108.36	4.86	0	0
	8	120.24	3.04	117.8	15.14	115.34	3.94	119.35	2.07	120.16	7.57	118.6	5.35	117.52	6.54	119.36	6.59	115.1	7.41	0	0
	9	123.83	3.41	123.57	5.81	119.87	10.18	0	0	122.7	4.34	123.85	6.88	121.43	6.41	124.55	5.13	125.26	7.09	124.48	4.28
	10	128.3	3.84	126.83	5.89	128.68	5.74	129.12	3.13	0	0	129.6	6.98	130.98	8.38	127.41	6.86	133.95	16.33	122.16	13.15
Sitting Height	6	62.11	3.23	59.31	3.92	61.86	2.43	59.75	2.28	62.9	1.98	59.33	1.53	60.48	2.57	60.12	1.71	59.28	3.9	0	0
	7	62.84	2.07	64.35	1.39	61.18	3.99	63.16	2.27	63.27	4.63	63.15	2.68	62.44	3.68	60.13	3	58.73	2.77	0	0
	8	64.99	3.1	64.25	3.34	63.37	2.24	64.42	2.69	60.6	3.37	65.27	3.22	62.25	3.34	65.9	3.85	62.02	1.33	0	0
	9	65.93	2.96	66.74	4.01	65.41	3.85	0	0	66.02	1.5	65.41	5.03	66.07	2.89	67.42	2.99	66.78	4.22	65.25	2.39
	10	69.4	2.46	67.57	3.26	70.16	5.21	69.72	3.32	0	0	70.4	4.22	70.84	3.85	69.17	3.34	71.75	6.55	65.43	6.35
Biocrosial diameter	6	24.87	1.9	24.54	1.55	25.42	1.08	24.96	0.92	26.5	127	23.92	1.26	23.1	1.12	24.27	1.24	24.03	1.83	0	0
	7	25.27	1.59	25.71	1.17	25.58	1.25	24.9	0.96	24.92	193	25.04	1.56	26.57	1.5	24.28	1.06	24.45	0.97	0	0
	8	26.81	1.74	26.31	1.31	25.2	1.23	26.24	0.99	26.36	109	26.34	1.4	25.96	1.35	26	10	25.75	1.37	0	0
	9	26.93	1.17	27.57	1.78	27	10	0	0	27.07	1.12	27.68	1.04	27.35	1.79	27.86	1.08	27.23	14	26.87	0.95
	10	28.26	0.86	27.87	1.62	26.1	5.57	27.47	132	0	0	28.73	2.21	29.29	2.26	28.3	1.81	30.3	4.1	26.86	2.67
Bi-iliac	6	16.1	1.05	15.86	1.02	48	1.14	15.7	0.84	16.15	1.34	15.4	0.97	16.32	0.99	15.66	0.74	15.63	1.45	0	0
	7	15.9	1.16	16.95	0.78	15.4	116	16.25	10.9	56	1.83	16.65	1.05	16.1	0.82	15.94	1.33	16.16	0.88	0	0
	8	16.81	1.01	16.6	0.81	16.29	0.77	16.52	0.92	17	0.4	17.57	1.09	17.26	1.27	17.06	133	16.87	0.84	0	0
	9	16.95	1.46	17.1	1.21	16.91	0.73	0	0	17.17	1.37	17.41	0.94	17.88	1.44	17.63	1.48	17.63	1.25	17.4	0.39
	10	20.98	1.28	18.03	0.97	17.36	0.97	17.65	1	0	0	18.54	16	18.87	1.76	18.23	1.29	19.7	0.84	18.03	2.12

From the mean values of weight, height, sitting height, bi-acromial diameter and bi-iliac diameter (Table 17) it was found that the parity has not played a much significant role among the Lushai children as it does not show any clear tendency in any of the above mentioned measurements. However, when the data was pooled, it was noticed that the first parity among the boys shows higher frequency for all measurements followed by second one. Whereas. Among the girls the first parity shows higher frequency for weight and sitting height while second parity shows higher frequency for height, bi-acromial diameter and bi-illiac diameter. Thus, from the above it may be mentioned that the child who are of the first and second parity respectively has a little relatively higher growth rate than the third and fourth.

Conclusion

The different body dimensions were interpreted on the basis of magnitude of increment between the age groups. The different traits of different age groups of the Lushai children show remarkable variations in body dimensions by differential growth rates as observed from the value of coefficient of variation, rate of absolute growth and increment in each measurement.

From the velocity curves of linear measurements it was seen that between the age of 6 and 10 years, bi-iliocristal diameter grow the least of all the body dimensions. Biacromial dimensions grow more than bi-iliocristal dimensions. Sitting height and weight grows more than biacromial and bi-iliocristal diameters. Stature grow more than all the above mentioned dimensions to attain the preadolescent growth stage. The subscapular skinfold grow relatively more than triceps and biceps skinfold.

When the distance curve of either sexes compared, it was seen that all the curves for linear measurements boys remain at higher level than those of girls from 6 to 8 years, whereas the girls were at higher level than that of boys from 8 years onwards indicating broader biacromial and bi-iliocristal dimensions, taller in stature and sitting height (greater in trunk) and heavier in weight than boys towards the periods of pre-adolescent growth. From the skinfold thickness it is observed that all the values in girls surpasses that of boys at all ages indicating girls accumulate more fat and muscles than that of boys.

It is also evident from the present study that in almost all linear measurements, the sex differences were more marked during 6 and 8 years of age in comparison with the later age except bi-iliocristal diameter where the sex difference was greater from 9 to 10 years of age. Thus, the difference between curves decreases with the increase of age. The present findings are also in conformity with that of Kalita children of Assam (Das,1971; Harrison *et. al.* 1977 and Tanner, 1962). Overall, the girls are larger in all body dimensions than boys at 10 years of age. This is also supported by the fact that peak velocities for girls are higher than those of boys at 8 years for most of the characters. As the pre-adolescent growth spurt appear at an early stage among girls than among boys, their size also increases and grow faster than boys and there by girls become taller, heavier and healthier than boys.

The nutritional status of Lushai children assessed through the use of different anthropometric measurements such as weight, height and upper arm circumference reveals that majority of children are marginally malnourished. The girls enjoys better nutritional status as compared to boys.

Nutritional deficiency due to lack of vitamin, has a direct impact on growing children as has been seen from the present findings. Morbid condition prevalent among the Lushai children affected growth and development as majority of the children suffered from various kinds of diseases.

Acknowledgement

We are indebted to Dr. Ramesh Chandra, Deputy Director, Anthropological Survey of India, North East Regional Centre, Shillong for his constant and untiring supervision throughout the study and preparation of this report. We express our sincere gratitude to both the co-ordinators Dr. (Mrs.) M.B. Sharma, Superintending Anthropologist (P) and Dr. D.B. Mondal, Superintending Anthropologist (C) for their valuable contribution in designing the project and providing necessary guidelines.

We are also thankful to Dr. N.M. Panda, Head, Deptt. of Commerce, NEHU, Shillong Dr. (Mrs.) Roshina Gowloog, Shri Sumit Mukherjee and Smt. Rekha Devi Lohar of this Survey for their sparing invaluable time in bringing this report in the present form. At last but not least, we are thankful to the Lushai people for their help and co-operation without which this study would have not been possible.

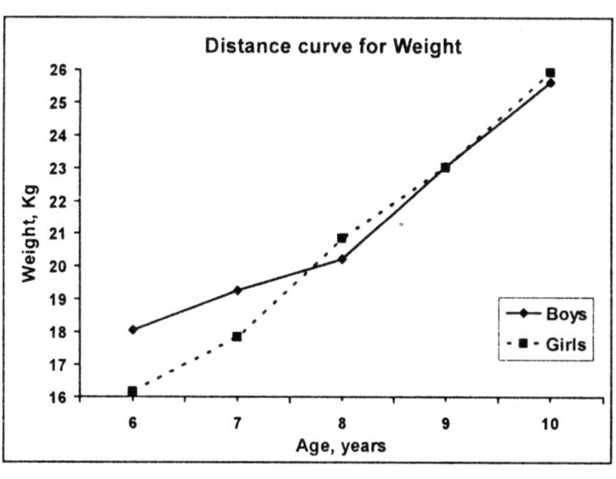

Fig. 1

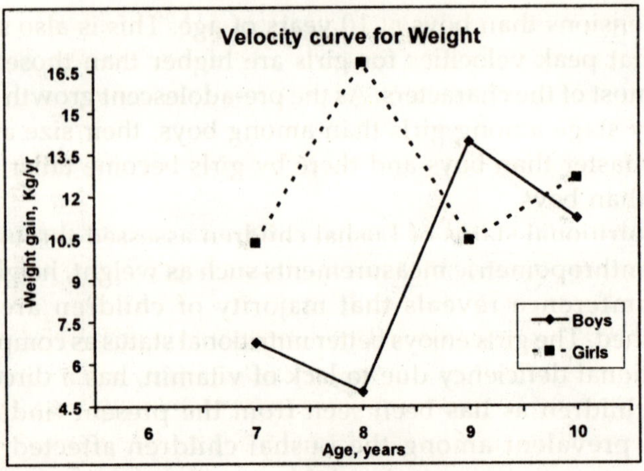

Fig. 2

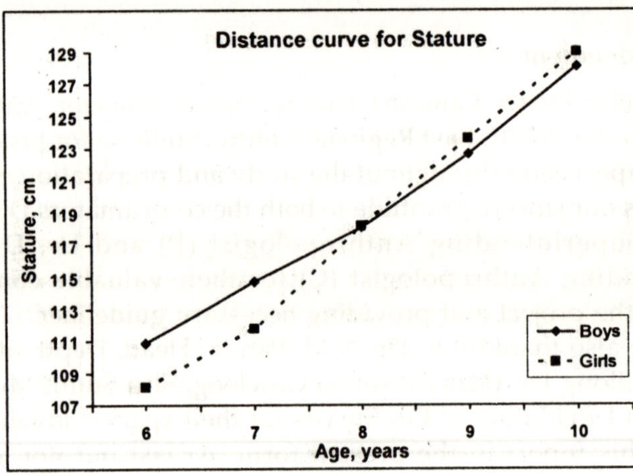

Fig. 3

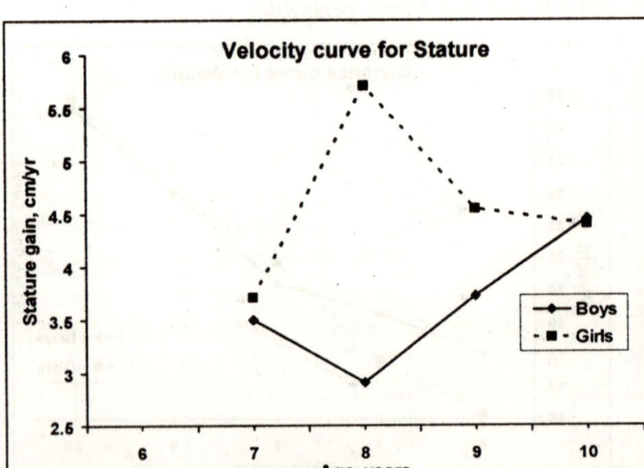

Fig. 4

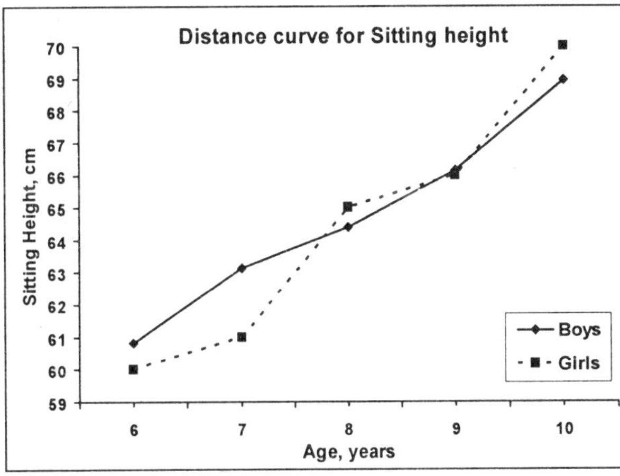

Fig. 5

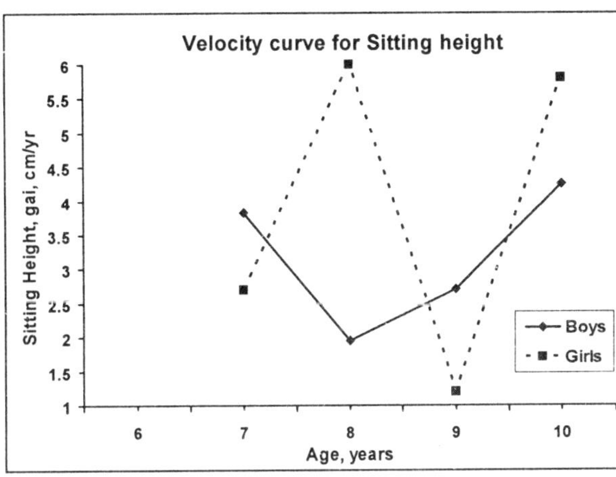

Fig. 6

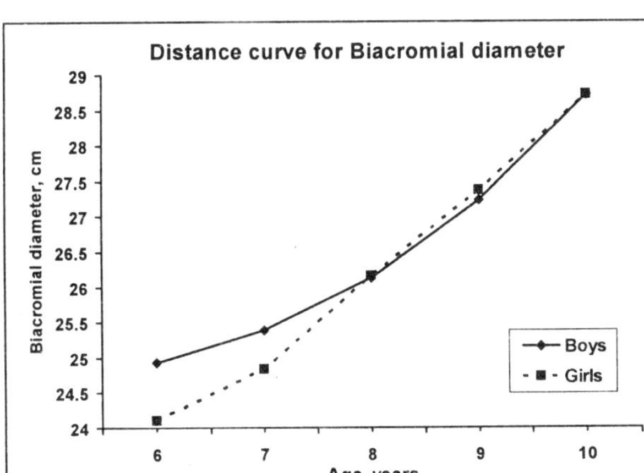

Fig. 7

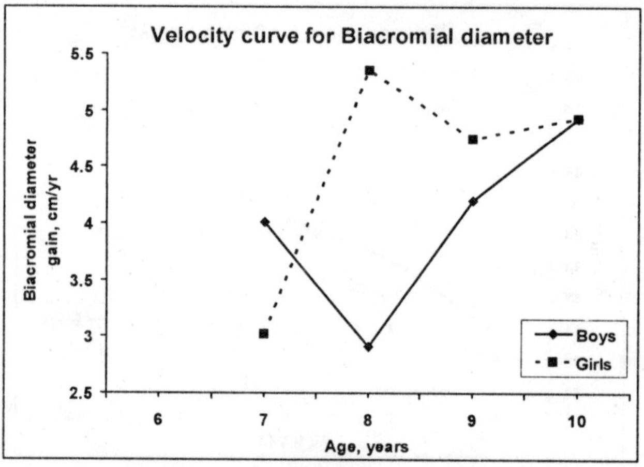

Fig. 8

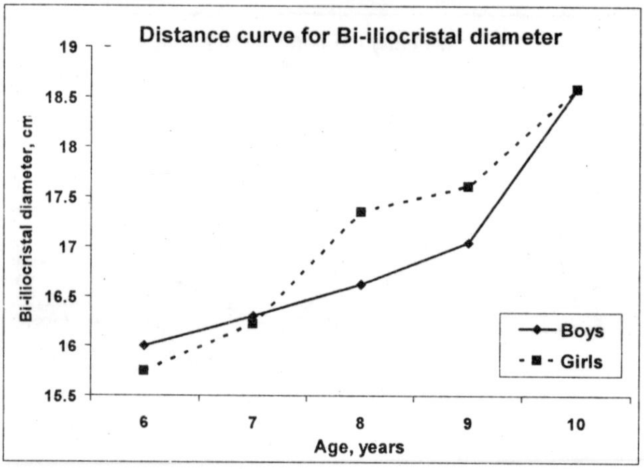

Fig. 9

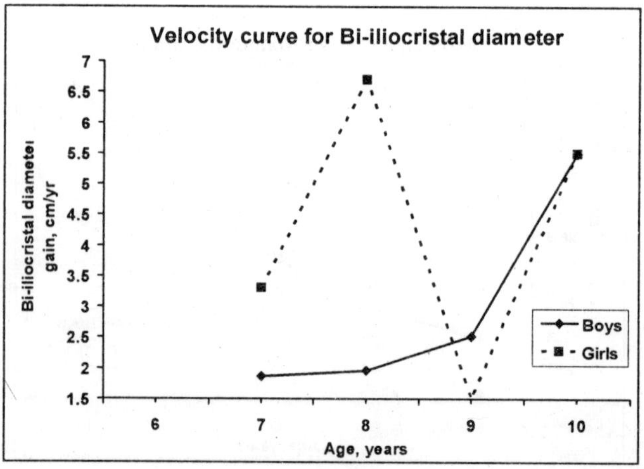

Fig. 10

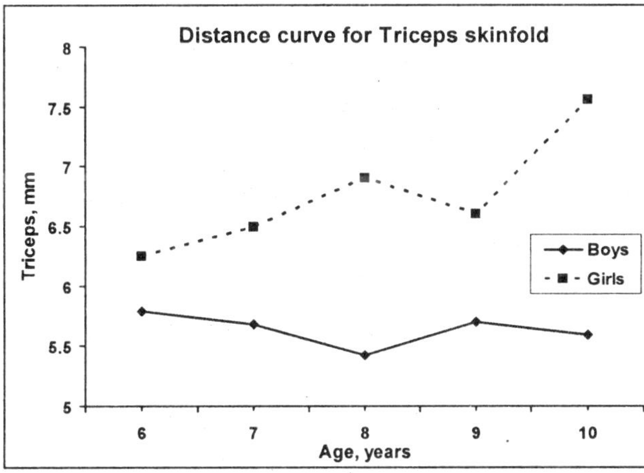

Fig. 11

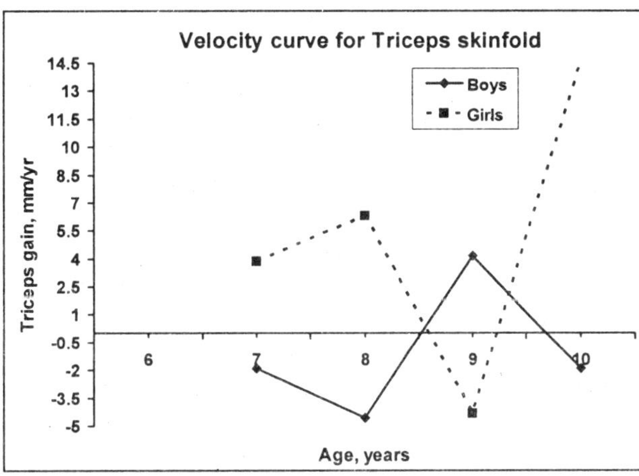

Fig. 12

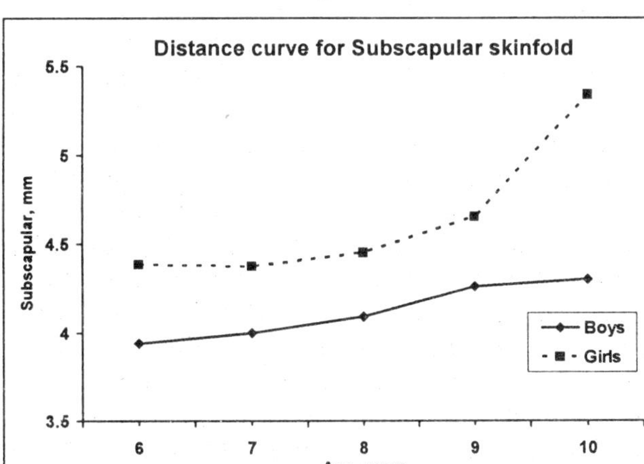

Fig. 13

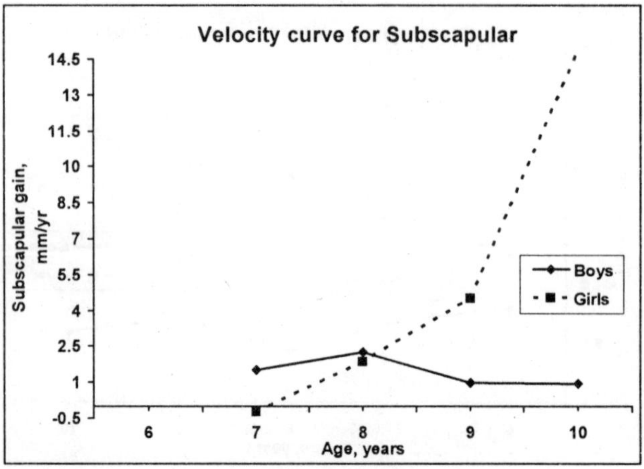

Fig. 14

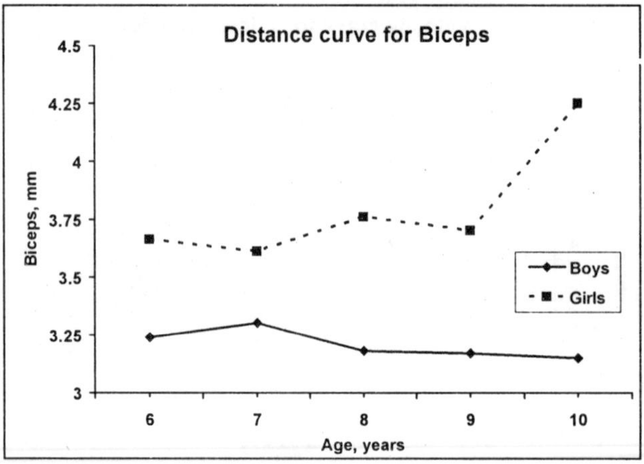

Fig. 15

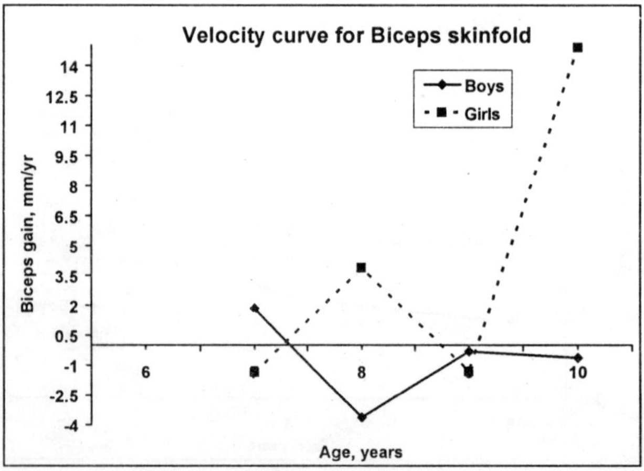

Fig. 16

References

Arora, P.N. and P.K. Mathur (1996), Bio-statistics, Mumbai, Himalaya Publishing House.

Bandopadhyay, P.K. (1985), Leadership Among The Mizos, Delhi. B.R. Publishing Corporation.

Census of India (1991), Final Population Totals, Brief Analysis of Primary Census Abstract. Registrar General and Census Commissioner, India, Series.

Eveleth P.B. and J.M. Tanner (1990), World wide Variation in Human Growth II edition, Cambridge. Cambridge University Press.

Harrison, G.A., J.S. Weiner, J.M. Tanner, and N.A. Barnicot (1977), Human Biology-An Introduction to Human Evolution Variation Growth and Velocity II edition, Oxford University Press.

Mizoram Statistical Handbook (1998), Directorate of Economics & Statistics, Govt. of Mizoram.

Shakespear, J. (1912), The Lushai-Kuki-clans, London; Macmillan & Co. Reprint 1975, Aizwal Tribal Research Institute.

Singh, I.P. and M.K. Basin (1989), Anthropometry-A Laboratory Manual on Biological Anthropology, New Delhi, Kamlaraj Enterprises.

Singh, K.S. (1995), People of India: Mizoram Vol. XXXIII, Seagull Books, Calcutta.

Tanner, J.M. (1962), Growth at Adolescents: with a General Consideration of the Effects of Heredity and Environmental Factors upon Growth and Maturation from Birth to Maturity (2nd Ed.). Oxford: Blackwell Scientific Publications.

Visweswara Rao, K. (1980), Efficiency of Anthropometric Indices for the Diagnosis of Malnutrition Courrier, 30,113.

7

GROWTH AND DEVELOPMENT OF NICOBARESE CHILDREN: A BIO-CULTURAL STUDIES

R. SAHANI & A. DINDA

The children's growth is often used as a marker of health and nutritional status. Growth and Development though genetically determined, is influenced by several factors (Shapiro, 1938; Lasker, 1952; Malhotra, 1984; Frisancho and Baker, 1970; Frisancho *et al.* 1975; Singh *et al.*1986; Chatterjee, *et al.* 1966; Chaudhuri, *et. al.* 1966; Meredith, 1979; Chatterjee and Mandal, 1991; Singh, 1975; and Tanner, 1962) such as heat, cold, relative humidity and socio-economic factors. Roberts (1953) found a significant negative correlation between body weight and mean annual temperature for a worldwide sample of population. It is established that there is direct relationship between the amount of sunlight and the rate of growth. At high altitudes, pre-natal growth retardation as evidenced by low birth weight (Litchy *et al,* 1957; Hass, 1973; Beal *et. al* 1977; Muller, *et. al* 1978, 1980; Frisancho and Baker 1970) and slow rate of post-natal growth stretched is also a well-established fact.

The most important of all the environmental factors is nutrition (Jelliffe, 1966; Garn and Rohman, 1966; Srikantia, 1979; Rao, 1978; Singh and Harrison, 1996; Visweswara Rao and Rao, 1975; Chowdhury et al, 1977; Gopalan, 1957). In the growing human being, the multiplication of cells or their enlargement in size depends upon an adequate supply of energy, amino acids, water, lipids, vitamins and minerals. People require approximately 48 essential nutrients for growth (Gutherie, 1986). Adequacy of the total quantity of food consumed is a major determinant of growth. In population where food shortages are present, growth delay occurs. The famines of the world wars of 1914-18 and 1939-45 retarded the growth of children (Wolff, 1935), Kimura and Katano (1959), Kimura (1948) and it has been observed that when diet to the children were supplemented with nutritious food, the rate of growth improves (Tanner, 1962).

Growth data from Andaman and Nicobar Islands is not available. Therefore, an attempt has been made to evaluate the growth and development of Nicobarese children aged between 6 years to 10 years of Car Nicobar in the background of their socio-cultural and physical environment.

Area and People

The Nicobar Islands, which became the focus of the Media World wide due to Millennium Sunrise at Katchal (one of the Island of this group) are situated in the southernmost portion of the Bay of Bengal. Its location ranges from 6^0 & 10^0 N latitude & the meridians of 89^0 to 94^0 E longitude. The northernmost Island of the Nicobar group of Islands is Car Nicobar which is about 75 miles south of Little Andaman Island, and stretches between the 92^0 422 153 to 92^0 502 523 E longitude and 9^0 172 483 N latitude. The name "Pu" was given for it by the natives. In comparison to other Islands of group, Car Nicobar has almost flat land, except some small cliffs in its north and some small hilly areas in the interiors. The Car Nicobarese are Mongoloid People speaking an Austro-Asiatic sub family language (Das, 1977, Ganguly, 1976, Shyam Choudhury, 1977, Justin, 1990).

Climate

Car Nicobar have a tropical climate it is hot and humid throughout the year. The coolest month are December, January and February and the hottest months are March, April and May. These are also comparatively dry period. The range of average annual variation of minimum and maximum temperature is very low about 10 degree of Fahrenheit scale, between 78.60°F and 86.60°F. Most of the rain falls are due to South-West Monsoon, but the North-East Monsoon also contribute. Car Nicobar has an annual average of about 247 cm rain fall. The peak raining months are May to October. Humidity is high throughout the year with an annual average of 85% with the variation from 77% to 92%. The climate may be broadly classified in two seasons: Rainy and Summer.

The island having 127square kilometer area is roughly an oval shape area, with a tapering projection on the northeast. All around, it is skirted by a sandy beach gradually reaching up the sea. The coast line is not very high above the level of the sea, the average elevation being 2.75 meters. The ecology has largely determine the settlement pattern of the village. On either side of dwelling area, the limits of the village lands converge towards the center of the Islands. The lineage (tuhet) is very important social unit of Car Nicobarese. The significance of the tuhet indicates the socio-economic integrity of its member. According to tuhets norm, the members have no individual ownership. Whatever is available within their resources is a possession of the tuhet as a whole. There is a well-knit society having no discrimination on the basis of caste, class and sex. The tuhet or large joint family system is most prevalent in Car Nicobar. There is no set rule concerning inheritance of property. All members of a tuhet or family (both male and female) have unstatutory rights over the tuhet's property. However, the property remains under the control of the tuhet and family head. They generally respect each other. Children and youngsters are obedient to their parents and elderly members of the tuhet. They do not disobey the advice of their parents, the elders and the tuhet head. Parents treat their children affectionately.

Monogamy is the social norm among the Nicobarese. According to different religious groups among the Nicobarese, the prescribed age of marriage for boys and girls are 22 and 18 years respectively; nevertheless marriage often takes place before the prescribed age.

Food Habits

The food habits of the Nicobarese, especially at Car Nicobar has undergone tremendous change, but still the traditional food are the major part of their daily diets. Among the traditional food yam, pandanus, banana, tapioca, coconut and other wild fruits, roots and tubers are taken. They eat fish mostly marine, beef, pork and chicken. Among the marine resources, the crabs, lobster, prawn, turtle are mostly used, whereas, the octopus and sea cucumber is used mostly when other marine fishes are not available. Many varieties of birds like, kaloh, Maku-ko, Kavov are consumed. Among the reptiles, Pythons and Iguana are also delicacy. The chicken is also taken frequently. Country liquor brewed from rice (Handia) and toddy (coconut) is commonly consumed by them. They also consume tea liquor with milk, the water of tender unripe coconut and lemon juice with sugar as non-alcoholic drink (Justin, 1990).

They smoke yong pop (loose tobacco rolled or wrapped in pandanus leaf) cigarette and bidis also. Chewing tobacco with lime is common. The betel leaves (pan) along with tobacco (zarda), lime and betel nut is frequently consumed by them.

Due to frequent interactions with people from main land now all kind of food are available. They consume rice, pulses, leafy and non-leafy vegetables. Biscuits, Powder milk, Mustard oil, tea, coffee, liquor, wheat flour, Idli, Dosa etc are consumed frequently. It is observed that children relish biscuits more than regular meal. Most of the people prefer coconut oil as a cooking medium.

The study suggests that their diet is nutritious and rich in animal protein (103 gm per consumption unit daily) and fat contents, as reflected by three body build indices like Pignet (16.9), Palidisi (98.8) and Kroperfulla (1.35)(Roy and Roy, 1967).

Economy

Land, forest and sea form the major economic resources of the Nicobarese. Each tuhet and family have land of their own where coconut and arecanut are cultivated. Apart from horticultural activities, the Nicobarese engage in making baskets, mats, wooden and iron spears and repairing canoes, rearing pigs and foul. Now, a sizeable number of Nicobarese are engaged in government jobs. Some have opened petty shops, while others follow traditional economic pursuits like herding and raising coconut groves.

Infra Structure And Other Facilities

Car Nicobar is the District Headquarter of Nicobar District and some of the establishment were made for administrative and other purposes besides Air Force Station. In every village of Car Nicobar, School, ICDS center, Health Centre/Sub-Centre, Road, Bus stand facilities are present. All village have community hall, play ground, and other means of recreations besides electricity, safe drinking water and shops containing goods of daily necessities. Goods are easily available throughout the year. Allopathic, Ayurvedic and Homeopathic systems of medicine facilities are also availed by the community. Goods are also procured from Air Force stations. Literacy rate is high (above 90%) in Andaman & Nicobar Islands. Due to the presence of well organized Tribal Council, Immunization programme besides other Programme launched by Government Agencies for the upliftment of the community is very successful. Personal Hygiene and cleanliness is good. Though some Diseases are prevalent, due to Medical intervention the effect is minimized.

Material and Methods

The study was conducted during the months of September-October 1999 among unrelated 436 Nicobarese children (224 boys and 212 girls) aged between 6 years to 10 years of Car Nicobar. The Anthropometric measurements were taken according to the method suggested by Martin and Saller (1957) and Singh and Bhasin (1968). All the measurements including circumferential is taken nearest to 0.1 cm and the body weight is nearest to 0.5 Kg., while the skin fold measurements were taken nearest to 0.1 mm. The ages were recorded from the school register, birth certificate and also from church record. The data was analysed as per the guideline of the project.

Results and Discussion

Body Weight

The body weight is the most important indicator of growth, health and nutrition of an individual or a population. The graphs 1 and 2 and the

Table 1 gives the details. Up to the age of 7 years, the girls body weight remain lower than the boys, but from 8 years of age and onwards the mean body weight of the girls are more than the boys. The maximum growth or increment took place at the age of 10 years among both the boys and girls i.e. 3.55 Kgs. in girls and 2.08 Kgs. in boys. In terms of percentage of growth per annum, the girls shows maximum value at the age of 8 years and 10 years while in boys it only took place at the age of 10 years. The maximum increment both in terms of absolute and percentage is more among the girls than the boys. The high value of coefficient of variation indicates more variable characteristic of the body weight in the present population.

Stature

The stature is one of the most important linear measurements. The Table 1 and the graphs 3 & 4 show the details of this measurements. It also shows the trend very much close to the trend of body weight. At the age of 6 and 7 years, the boys mean value is more than the girls, but at 8 years of age, the mean value of girls is more than the boys and again at the age of 9 years the mean value of boys is more than the girls, but at the age of 10 years the girls value surpasses the boys mean value. It is necessary to mention here that, at the age of 9 years the low mean value among the girls may be due to small sample size in comparison to boys. The maximum absolute growth among the girls are 7.07 cms and 9.36 cms among the boys at the age of 8 years. The percentage increments also correspond the absolute growth. From 6 years to 7 years of age both boys and girls stature show positive skewness and then the negative in both the sexes though not always.

Sitting Height

The sitting height which gives the value of upper extremity length is also a valuable measurement. Its value also plays a vital role in body weight and varies from individual to individual and population to population. Comparatively, the people of Mongoloid origin gave high value of sitting height. The Table 1 and the graph-3 and 4 gives the details of this measurement. At 6 and 7 years of age, the boys mean value are more than the girls and at 8 years both the mean values are the same, and again at the age of 9 years the mean value of boys is more than the girls, but at the age of 10 years the girls mean value surpasses the boys. Like stature, here also up to 7 years of age the skewness is positive but from 8 years and onward both positive and negative value is noticed. The maximum velocity takes place at the age of 8 years in both the sexes both in terms of absolute as well as percentage. Here also, the maximum value of increment is noticed among the girls.

Table 1
Details of the Anthropometric Measurements of Nicobarese Children as Per Age Group (6-10 yrs)

	Boys									Girls								
	w	*h*	*s/h*	*bd*	*icd*	*t*	*s*	*b*	*BMI*	*w*	*h*	*s/h*	*bd*	*icd*	*t*	*s*	*b*	*BMI*
Age group 6 Year																		
MEAN	18.27	111.24	60.43	24.22	17.62	6.44	4.73	4.06	14.75	17.74	109.39	58.89	24.06	17.53	7.43	5.61	4.5	14.79
SE.OF.M.	0.26	0.64	0.28	0.19	0.11	0.19	0.16	0.16	0.13	0.31	0.8	0.37	0.19	0.16	0.25	0.18	0.14	0.13
S.D.	1.72	4.31	1.9	1.29	0.76	1.3	1.05	1.04	0.89	1.99	5.18	2.37	1.22	1.02	1.63	1.19	0.9	0.86
C.V.	9.42	3.87	3.14	5.33	4.3	20.12	22.3	25.63	6.03	11.23	4.74	4.02	5.06	5.82	21.98	21.25	19.99	5.78
t-testValue	0.19	0.08	0	0.54	0.62	0	0	0.04	0.81									
Age Group- 7 Year																		
MEAN	19.73	114.52	61.62	24.93	18.21	6.59	4.87	4.1	15.01	19.13	112.76	60.61	24.79	17.82	7.17	5.79	4.58	14.98
SE.OF.M.	0.3	0.72	0.41	0.17	0.12	0.18	0.12	0.13	0.11	0.36	0.86	0.98	0.43	0.18	0.19	0.2	0.16	0.12
S.D.	1.89	4.54	2.6	1.08	0.79	1.16	0.74	0.8	0.7	2.6	6.13	6.97	3.1	1.25	1.39	1.46	1.12	0.88
C.V,.	9.6	3.97	4.22	4.35	4.32	17.66	15.25	19.54	4.68	13.59	5.44	5.11	5.24	7.04	19.33	25.19	24.52	5.85
t-testValue	0.18	0.11	0.08	0.6	0.07	0.04	0	0.02	0.79									
Age group 8 Year																		
MEAN	21.31	118.88	64	25.88	18.76	6.67	5.21	3.98	15.03	22.03	119.82	64	25.87	18.94	7.86	6.63	4.73	15.33
SE.OF.M.	0.38	0.87	0.48	0.21	0.16	0.16	0.13	0.09	0.12	0.37	0.84	0.39	0.17	0.19	0.23	0.23	0.18	0.17
S.D.	2.66	6	3.31	1.471	1.136	1.13	0.9	0.64	0.84	2.41	5.53	2.57	1.14	1.27	1.53	1.5	1.17	1.11
C.V.	12.48	5.05	5.18	5.68	6.05	16.89	17.37	16.02	5.58	10.94	4.62	4.02	4.39	6.7	19.48	22.62	24.72	7.25
t-test Value	0.18	0.44	0.99	0.97	0.49	0	0	0	0.14									
Age Group-9 Year																		
MEAN	23	123	65	26.64	19.33	6.48	5.44	4	15.16	23.29	122.84	64.6	26.59	19.06	7.81	6.75	4.65	15.4
SE.OF.M.	0.35	0.81	0.35	0.2	0.13	0.23	0.15	0.11	0.14	0.38	0.99	0.49	0.21	0.22	0.24	0.26	0.18	0.17
S.D.	2.45	5.5	2.34	1.37	0.86	1.56	1.03	0.72	0.95	2.22	5.77	2.84	1.2	1.28	1.4	1.51	1.07	1
C.V.	10.66	4.47	3.57	5.14	4.45	24.07	18.99	18.04	6.3	9.51	4.69	4.4	4.53	6.72	17.88	22.35	23.03	6.51
t-testValue	0.96	0.65	0.93	0.95	0.79	0.78	0.82	0.95	0.47									

Contd...

	Boys									Girls								
	w	*h*	*s/h*	*bd*	*icd*	*t*	*s*	*b*	*BMI*	*w*	*h*	*s/h*	*bd*	*icd*	*t*	*s*	*b*	*BMI*
Age Group - 10 Year																		
MEAN	24.86	126.8	66.52	27.63	19.59	6.5	5.58	3.92	15.44	26.85	128.84	67.93	27.56	20.56	8.39	7.65	5.28	16.11
SE.OF.M.	0.34	0.64	0.39	0.14	0.16	0.19	0.16	0.11	0.15	0.57	0.88	0.44	0.22	0.21	0.39	0.32	0.26	0.21
S.D.	2.25	4.32	2.63	0.96	1.09	1.26	1.05	0.76	0.99	3.67	5.72	2.84	1.43	1.38	2.51	2.07	1.69	1.36
C.V.	9.06	3.41	3.96	3.48	5.58	19.37	18.82	19.26	9.13	13.68	4.44	4.19	5.18	6.71	29.92	27.1	32	8.43
t-testValue	0.01′	0.07	0	0	0	0	0	0	0.08									

Abbreviation : W =weight; h= Stature; s/h= Sitting Height; bd= Biacromial Diameter; icd = Iliocristal Diameter; t= Fat Fold AT Triceps s = Fat Fold AT Sub Scapular region; b = Fat Fold AT Biceps, BMI = Body Mass Index S.D. = Standard Deviation; S.E. = Standard Error; C.V = Coefficient of Variation; t-test = Test of Significance

Biacromial Diameter

The graphs 5 and 6 and Table 1 show the details of Biacromial Diameter. The mean value gradually increases with the increase of age and at all ages, the mean value of boys are more than the girls. The maximum increment took place at the age of 8 years in both the sexes.

Iliocristal Diameter

The mean value of Iliocristal Diameter in adult show that the values of female's are more than the males and the difference is also statistically significant (Ganguly, 1976). But for the children here, the value of this measurement does not show clear-cut trend. At the age of 8 years, the girls mean value show higher value than the boys and at the age of 9 years the boys mean value is more than the girls. But like weight and height, at the age of 10 years the girls values is higher (Fig. 1). The maximum increment in girls took place at the age of 10 years while in boys it happens at the age of 7 years. At the age of 10 years, the girls show maximum velocity both absolute as well as percentage, while boys show the maximum value at the age of 7 years (Fig. 2).

Triceps Skin Fold

The triceps skin fold show different trend in comparison to other measurements. The Table 1 and the graphs 7 and 8 show the details of this measurement. The mean value of this measurement is always more in girls than the boys. The lowest mean value is seen at the age of 6 years among the boys; while in case of girls this value is found at the age of 7 years. In girls, at the age of 7 years and 9 years the reverse velocity is noticed, while in boys this happens only at the age of 9 years but at this age the reverse trend is found in both the sexes. The minimum and maximum both the values are more in girls than the boys. The mean value of triceps of both boys and girls does not differ significantly. The value of coefficient of variation is very high here; indicating the variable nature of this measurement in both the sexes. It is highest at 10 years of age, among girls 29.92%, while in boys the highest value is 24.10% at the age of 9 years. Comparatively the range of this value is more wide even sometimes the maximum value is more than 2 times of the minimum value and even from the mean value.

Sub Scapular Skin Fold

The Sub scapular skin fold does not show the trend like the triceps. Though, here also the mean value of boys is always lower than the girls, but the negative increment is not seen at any age groups and sexes. The increment is highest at the age of 8 years among the boys (0.34 mm) 6.98%, while in girls this is maximum at the age of 10 years (0.9 mm) and 13.33%. The coefficient of variation is also high in both boys and girls indicating again the more variable nature of this value. The Tables 1 and graphs 7 and 8 give the details. The difference between the mean values of boys and girls are not significant.

Biceps Skin Fold

The Table 1 and the graphs 9 and 10 show the details of Biceps skin fold measurement. The maximum mean value in boys is noticed at the age of 7 years and in girls it is at the age of 10 years; whereas, the minimum value is noticed at 6 years among the girls and at 10 years in boys. Like triceps skin fold, the distance and velocity curve both show negative trend. In boys the negative growth is found at the age of 8 years and 10 years; while in girls, it is only seen at the age of 9 year. The coefficient of variation here also high, showing the variable nature.

Correlation

There is high correlation between Stature and Weight, Sitting Height and Stature, Biacromial and Iliocristal diameter and Fat Fold at Triceps and Fat Fold at Sub Scapular region in all age groups among the boys and girls; whereas, correlation between Head and Chest Circumference varies from low to moderate among boys and girls. The correlation coefficient value is more in total sample than at the age group level for all the considered characters. (Table 2).

Regression

Regression analysis is used to examine the bivariate relationship between two continuous variables when there is dependency or when the researcher wants to plot the best fitting line. For computing the regression of some of the measurement on age, it is better to express the chronological age in decimal age. The coefficient of determination or R^2 which express in a scale of 0 to 1, the proportion of the total variation of Y explained by X. The Table 3 show the details of Regression computing by using total sample and age converted in decimal age the value of R^2 is more in boys than girls for all the variables except Body weight–Stature, where the value is same. The value R^2 is always more than 0.50 except the Age-Iliocristal Diameter in both the sexes and only 0.50 in the case of Age-Biacromial Diameter in girls only. Table 4 also gives the detail of R^2 value computed considering decimal age and age group wise. The R^2 value is very low in comparison to total sample for all the value on age and when regression is done in accordance to age group-wise. But for the related variables though the value is less but not to such an extent. So it can be said that, here age is not the best predictor of the considered variables than the related variable.

The growth patterns of Nicobarese childrens show all the value above the mean value of ICMR pooled value; whereas, it remains below from

Table 2
Correlation Between Selected Measurements

	Age Group											
	6		*7*		*8*		*9*		*10*		*Total*	
Correlation Coefficient Between	*Boys*	*Girls*	*Boys*	*Girls*	*Boys*	*Girls*	*Boys*	*Girls*	*Boys*	*Girls*	*Boys*	*Girls*
Height – Weight	0.78	0.81*	0.88*	0.90*	0.89*	0.74	0.80*	0.81*	0.53	0.79*	0.90*	0.92*
Height – Sitting Height	0.68	0.92*	0.83*	0.90*	0.89*	0.85*	0.68	0.88*	0.90*	0.80*	0.89*	0.94*
Biacromial – Biilliac Breadth	0.49	0.42	0.61	0.6	0.68	0.66	0.55	0.69	0.34	0.31	0.72**	0.73**
Triceps-Sub-ScapularFat fold	0.64	0.63	0.68	0.74	0.59	0.53	0.43	0.62	0.59	0.79*	0.53**	0.70**
Head – Chest Circumference	0.37	0.51	0.41	0.2	0.62	0.37	0.61	0.48	0.31	0.42	0.52**	0.37

* High Co-relation
** Moderate co-relation

socio-economic category 1. When the value is compared with the Rabha, a Mongoloid tribe of north east India the value again is higher in both boys and girls. The impact of parity on growth and development does not show any clear cut trend.

Table 3
Regression of Some Measurements and Regression Equation

	Coefficient of determination (R2)		*Regression Equation*	
Regression of	*Boys*	*Girls*	*Boys*	*Girls*
Age-Body Weight	0.62	0.53	Y=2.40x+1.78	Y=1.7x+7.11
Age-Stature	0.65	0.59	Y=5.21x+75.16	Y=4.09x+84.72
Age-Sitting Height	0.59	0.46	Y=2.35x+43.54	Y=1.66+49.75
Age-Biacromial Diameter	0.53	0.5	Y=0.94x+17.92	Y=0.87x+18.61
Age-iliocristal Diameter	0.42	0.37	Y=0.77x+12.35	Y=0.51x+14.45
Body weight-Stature	0.8	0.8	Y=0.4x-29.3	Y=0.40x-25.54
Body Weight-Sitting Height	0.82	0.7	Y=0.90x-34.87	Y=0.80x-29.56
Stature -Sitting Height	0.88	0.79	Y=0.49x+10.55	Y=0.41x+14.77
Biacromial IliocristalDiameter	0.52	0.52	Y=0.49x+5.95	Y=1.06x+6.05

Dentition

The children have both the milk and permanent type of teeth: Deciduous incisors–1 (i) are retained up to the age of 8 years in both boys and girls and the Deciduous incisors–2 (i2) up to 9 years of age, while Deciduous canine (c), first molar (m1) and second molar (m2) are until 10 years of age. Among the permanent teeth, Incisors and first Molar (M1) are found from the age of 6 years, while Pre-molars are reported from the age of 9 years and onward and second Molar (M2) at the age of 10 years (Table 5). Dental health are not so good, a significant prevalence of caries and tartar are reported.

Assessment of Nutritional Status of Children

Height-for-Age or Height Deficit Classification

It reflects gained linear growth and its deficit indicate long term cumulative inadequacies of health and nutrition. Table 5 gives the distribution of H-A in detail. Only boys fall under poor category at the age of 8 and 9 years which is 2.08% and 2.17% respectively and 0.89% of total boys and 0.46% of total children respectively. In total 65.14% children classified under normal category whereas 34.40% comes under mild malnourished category.

Weight for Age or Weight Deficit Classification

Weight for Age (W-A) reflects body mass relative to chronological age. Table 7 shows the distribution of W-A in both the sexes. Boys at age 7 and

Table 4
Regression of Some Measurements (Age Groupwise)

	Age Group									
	6		*7*		*8*		*9*		*10*	
Regression of	*Boys*	*Girls*	*Boys*	*Girls*	*Boys*	*Girls*	*Boys*	*Girls*	*Boys*	*Girls*
Age-Body Weight	0.04	0.28	0.30	0.29	0.11	0.08	0.01	0.05	0.03	0.09
Age-Stature	0.02	0.16	0.26	0.27	0.18	0.04	0.05	0.17	0.00	0.11
Age-Sitting height	0.01	0.13	0.38	0.22	0.11	0.06	0.00	0.09	0.00	0.10
Age-Biacromial Diameter	0.07	0.14	0.10	0.13	0.10	0.16	0.00	0.04	0.02	0.14
Age-Iliocristal Diameter	0.00	0.23	0.18	0.06	0.04	0.00	0.01	0.01	0.13	0.00
Body weight stature	0.60	0.73	0.77	0.81	0.80	0.54	0.64	0.66	0.28	0.62
Body weight-Sitting height	0.52	0.55	0.71	0.74	0.73	0.85	0.34	0.75	0.30	0.55
Stature-Sitting height	0.46	0.65	0.68	0.81	0.79	0.73	0.46	0.78	0.80	0.64
Biacromial IliocristalDiameter	0.24	0.17	0.37	0.35	0.46	0.44	0.30	0.47	0.12	0.10

Table 5
Details of Dental Pattern of Nicobarese Children (Value in Percentage)

Age			6				7				8				9				10			
Dentition			Boys		Girls		Boys		Girls		Boys		Girls		Boys		Girls		Boys		Girls	
Side	Jaw		L	U	L	U	L	U	L	U	L	U	L	U	L	U	L	U	L	U	L	U
	i - 1	P	44.4	80.00	42.90	61.90	25.00	47.50	25.50	33.30	6.30	8.30	0.00	2.30	0.00	0.00	0.00	0.00	0.00	0.00	0.00	0.00
		F	8.90	8.90	9.50	2.40	0.00	5.00	5.90	13.70	6.30	6.30	0.00	0.00	0.00	0.00	0.00	0.00	0.00	0.00	0.00	0.00
	i - 2	P	86.70	93.30	64.30	83.30	55.00	82.50	49.00	78.40	14.60	43.80	2.30	23.30	0.00	2.20	0.00	2.90	0.00	0.00	0.00	0.00
		F	4.40	4.40	9.50	11.90	0.00	10.00	9.80	5.90	4.20	12.50	0.00	7.00	0.00	4.30	2.30	2.90	0.00	0.00	0.00	0.00
Left	i - 1	P	48.50	80.00	71.40	88.90	25.00	42.50	27.50	33.30	0.00	8.30	0.00	0.00	0.00	0.00	0.00	0.00	0.00	0.00	0.00	0.00
		F	2.20	6.70	7.14	9.50	0.00	5.00	0.00	19.60	6.30	4.20	0.00	2.30	0.00	0.00	0.00	0.00	0.00	0.00	0.00	0.00
	i - 2	P	88.90	93.30	71.40	88.90	52.50	87.50	47.10	72.50	10.40	43.80	2.30	16.30	0.00	2.30	0.00	0.00	0.00	0.00	0.00	0.00
		F	2.20	4.40	7.10	9.50	5.00	2.50	2.00	7.80	6.30	8.30	0.00	14.00	0.00	4.30	0.00	0.00	0.00	0.00	0.00	0.00
Right	I-1	P	40.00	6.66	52.38	30.95	70.00	45.00	64.70	49.01	91.66	81.25	100.00	97.67	100.00	97.82	100.00	100.00	100.00	100.00	100.00	100.00
		J	6.70	4.40	0.00	4.80	5.00	2.50	3.90	3.90	2.10	4.20	0.00	0.00	0.00	0.00	0.00	0.00	0.00	0.00	0.00	0.00
	I-2	P	6.70	2.20	16.70	4.80	35.00	5.00	39.20	9.80	79.20	35.40	93.00	60.50	100.00	87.00	97.10	88.20	100.00	95.60	95.20	90.50
		J	2.22	0.00	9.52	0.00	10.00	2.50	1.96	5.88	2.08	8.33	2.32	9.30	0.00	6.52	0.00	5.88	0.00	0.00	2.38	7.14
Left	I-1	P	40.00	6.66	52.38	30.95	70.00	45.00	64.70	49.01	91.66	81.25	100.00	97.67	100.00	97.82	100.00	100.00	100.00	100.00	100.00	100.00
		J	6.66	4.44	0.00	4.76	5.00	2.50	3.92	39.20	2.08	4.16	0.00	0.00	0.00	2.17	0.00	0.00	0.00	0.00	0.00	0.00
	I-2	P	6.66	2.22	16.66	4.76	35.00	5.00	39.21	9.80	79.16	35.41	93.02	60.46	100.00	86.95	97.05	88.23	100.00	95.55	95.23	90.47
		J	2.22	0.00	9.52	0.00	10.00	2.50	1.96	5.88	2.08	8.33	2.32	9.30	0.00	6.52	0.00	5.88	0.00	0.00	2.38	7.14
Right	c	P	100.00	100.00	100.00	100.00	100.00	100.00	98.03	98.03	95.83	100.00	90.69	93.02	58.70	6.30	35.29	55.88	6.66	20.00	7.14	30.95
		F	0.00	0.00	0.00	0.00	0.00	0.00	1.96	1.96	4.16	0.00	4.65	2.32	2.17	0.00	2.94	2.94	2.22	6.66	2.38	0.00
Left	c	P	100.00	100.00	97.61	100.00	100.00	100.00	100.00	100.00	97.91	100.00	95.34	97.67	52.17	63.04	35.29	55.88	6.66	24.44	4.76	33.33
		F	0.00	0.00	2.38	0.00	0.00	0.00	0.00	0.00	2.08	0.00	4.65	0.00	4.35	2.32	2.94	8.82	2.22	0.00	7.14	0.00
Right	C	P	0.00	0.00	0.00	0.00	0.00	0.00	0.00	0.00	0.00	0.00	0.00	0.00	36.96	36.96	52.94	29.41	84.44	62.22	83.33	66.66
		J	0.00	0.00	0.00	0.00	0.00	0.00	0.00	0.00	0.00	0.00	4.65	4.65	2.17	0.00	8.82	11.76	6.60	11.11	7.14	2.38
Left	C	P	0.00	0.00	0.00	0.00	0.00	0.00	0.00	0.00	0.00	0.00	0.00	0.00	43.48	32.65	61.76	29.41	88.88	68.88	76.19	64.28
		J	0.00	0.00	0.00	0.00	0.00	0.00	0.00	0.00	0.00	0.00	4.65	2.32	0.00	2.32	0.00	5.88	2.22	6.66	11.90	2.38
Right	m-I	P	100.00	100.00	100.00	100.00	100.00	100.00	100.00	98.03	95.83	100.00	97.67	100.00	63.04	60.86	58.82	67.64	55.55	64.44	59.52	64.28
		F	0.00	0.00	0.00	0.00	0.00	0.00	0.00	1.96	0.00	0.00	2.32	0.00	0.00	0.00	0.00	2.32	2.22	0.00	0.00	0.00
	m-2	P	100.00	100.00	100.00	100.00	100.00	100.00	100.00	98.03	100.00	100.00	97.67	100.00	88.88	93.33	88.23	94.11	55.55	64.44	59.52	64.28
		F	0.00	0.00	0.00	0.00	0.00	0.00	0.00	1.96	0.00	0.00	2.32	0.00	0.00	0.00	0.00	0.00	2.22	0.00	0.00	0.00

Contd...

Age			6				7				8				9				10			
	Dentition		Boys		Girls		Boys		Girls		Boys		Girls		Boys		Girls		Boys		Girls	
Side	Jaw		L	U	L	U	L	U	L	U	L	U	L	U	L	U	L	U	L	U	L	U
Left	m-1	P	100.00	100.00	100.00	100.00	100.00	100.00	98.03	100.00	97.91	100.00	100.00	97.67	56.52	63.04	61.76	67.64	24.44	26.66	28.57	33.33
		F	0.00	0.00	0.00	0.00	0.00	0.00	1.96	0.00	0.00	0.00	0.00	2.32	0.00	0.00	0.00	0.00	0.00	0.00	0.00	0.00
	m-2	P	100.00	100.00	100.00	100.00	100.00	100.00	98.03	100.00	97.91	100.00	100.00	100.00	88.88	91.30	91.77	91.77	55.55	59.55	59.52	64.28
		F	0.00	0.00	0.00	0.00	0.00	0.00	1.96	0.00	2.08	0.00	0.00	0.00	2.17	0.00	0.00	0.00	0.00	0.00	0.00	0.00
Right	Pm-1	P	0.00	0.00	0.00	0.00	0.00	0.00	0.00	0.00	0.00	0.00	0.00	0.00	36.96	39.13	41.18	26.47	73.33	60.00	71.42	54.76
		J	0.00	0.00	0.00	0.00	0.00	0.00	0.00	0.00	0.00	0.00	0.00	0.00	0.00	0.00	0.00	0.00	0.00	0.00	0.00	4.76
	Pm-2	P	0.00	0.00	0.00	0.00	0.00	0.00	0.00	0.00	0.00	0.00	0.00	0.00	13.04	8.70	11.76	5.88	35.55	35.55	40.76	35.71
		J	0.00	0.00	0.00	0.00	0.00	0.00	0.00	0.00	0.00	0.00	0.00	0.00	0.00	0.00	0.00	0.00	6.66	0.00	0.00	0.00
Left	Pm-1	P	0.00	0.00	0.00	0.00	0.00	0.00	0.00	0.00	0.00	0.00	0.00	0.00	36.96	36.96	8.82	5.88	100.00	66.66	71.42	59.52
		J	0.00	0.00	0.00	0.00	0.00	0.00	0.00	0.00	0.00	0.00	0.00	0.00	0.00	0.00	0.00	2.32	0.00	4.44	0.00	7.14
	Pm-2	P	0.00	0.00	0.00	0.00	0.00	0.00	0.00	0.00	0.00	0.00	0.00	0.00	10.86	8.69	8.82	5.88	44.44	44.44	40.47	35.71
		J	0.00	0.00	0.00	0.00	0.00	0.00	0.00	0.00	0.00	0.00	0.00	0.00	0.00	0.00	0.00	0.00	0.00	0.00	0.00	0.00
Right	M-1	P	57.77	53.33	100.00	76.19	100.00	100.00	100.00	98.03	100.00	100.00	100.00	100.00	100.00	100.00	100.00	100.00	100.00	100.00	100.00	100.00
		J	4.44	0.00	0.00	0.00	0.00	0.00	0.00	1.96	0.00	0.00	0.00	0.00	0.00	0.00	0.00	0.00	0.00	0.00	0.00	0.00
	M-2	P	0.00	0.00	0.00	0.00	0.00	0.00	0.00	0.00	0.00	0.00	0.00	0.00	0.00	0.00	0.00	0.00	8.88	4.44	14.28	2.38
		J	0.00	0.00	0.00	0.00	0.00	0.00	0.00	0.00	0.00	0.00	0.00	0.00	0.00	0.00	0.00	0.00	4.44	2.22	0.00	2.38
Left	M-1	P	25.55	48.88	100.00	68.88	100.00	100.00	100.00	100.00	100.00	100.00	100.00	100.00	100.00	100.00	100.00	100.00	100.00	100.00	100.00	100.00
		J	0.00	0.00	0.00	0.00	0.00	0.00	0.00	0.00	0.00	0.00	0.00	0.00	0.00	0.00	0.00	0.00	0.00	0.00	0.00	0.00
	M-2	P	0.00	0.00	0.00	0.00	0.00	0.00	0.00	0.00	0.00	2.32	0.00	0.00	0.00	0.00	0.00	0.00	6.66	6.66	16.66	4.76
		J	0.00	0.00	0.00	0.00	0.00	0.00	0.00	0.00	0.00	0.00	0.00	0.00	0.00	0.00	2.32	0.00	6.66	0.00	2.38	2.38

**Abbreviation used in Table 5
L=Lower, U=Upper, R=Right, L=Left, P= Present, F=Fallen, J=Just erupted, i = incisor deciduous, I = Incisor permanent
c=Canine deciduous, C=Canine permanent, m=Molar deciduous M= Molar permanent, Pm = Pre Molar

Table 6
Height-for-Age or Height Deficit Classification (Based on Modified Gomez's Classification)

Category		6		7		8		9		10		
		Boys	*Girls*	*Boys*	*Girls*	*Boys*	*Girls*	*Boys*	*Girls*	*Boys*	*Girls*	*Total B+G*
Poor (80% of the Standard)	No	0	0	0	0	1	0	1	0	0		2
	%	0	0	0	0	2.08	0	2.17	0	0	0	0.46
Mild (81-90% of the Standard	No	7	13	15	20	16	12	17	15	21	14	150
	%	15.6	31	37.5	39.21	33.33	27.9	36.95	44.11	46.66	33.33	34.4
Normal (91-100% of the standard	No	38	29	25	31	31	31	28	19	24	28	284
	%	84.4	69	62.5	60.78	64.58	72.09	60.86	55.88	53.33	66.67	65.14

Age Group spans columns 6–10.

Table 7
Weight-for Age or Weight Deficit Classification (Based on Modified Gomez's Classification)

		Age Group									
		6		7		8		9		10	
Category		*Boys*	*Girls*	*Boys*	*Girls*	*Boys*	*Girls*	*Boys*	*Girls*	*Boys*	*Girls*
Grade-IV Malnutrition	No	0	0	0	0	0	0	0	0	0	0
	%	0	0	0	0	0	0	0	0	0	0
Grade-III Malnutrition	No	0	0	0	2	1	0	1	0	0	2
	%	0	0	0	3.92	2.08	0	2.17	0	0	4.76
Grade-II Malnutrition	No	3	4	5	5	12	5	13	11	15	10
	%	6.66	9.52	12.5	9.8	25	11.62	28.26	32.35	33.33	23.8
Grade-IMalnutrition	No	10	19	14	23	20	22	19	15	20	21
	%	22.22	45.23	35	45.09	41.66	51.16	41.3	44.11	44.44	50
Normal	No	32	19	21	21	15	16	13	8	10	9
	%	71.11	45.23	52.5	41.17	31.25	37.2	28.26	23.52	22.22	21.42

9 years (0.89%) and girls at the age of 7 and 10 years (1.88%) comes under Grade-III malnutrition category. In total 37.61% (40.62% boys and 34.43% girls) children are only normal and the remaining comes under Grade I and II malnutrition category. The frequency of normal category is decreasing with increasing age in both the sexes.

Weight for Height for Age

It reflects body weight in relation to height. The mean value as well as the distribution of W-H-A show better status than H-A and W-A. The Harvard value is even not in the position to give the proper weight-for-height-for-age in accordance with the age group. In girls and boys the W-H-A is incorporated from the lower age value, since the W-H-A do not fall in the same age range; but it can be negligible due to small number, only 5 individual at the age range of 6 and 7 as well as 8 and 9 years of age. The minimum mean value is above 97% in both the sexes; and maximum value is above 130%. So, it can be said that the value are more or less constant for increasing age in contradiction to W-A and H-A.

The distribution of W-H-A (Table 8) is maximum between 91-100% in both the sexes, 55.35% in boys and 44.33% in girls. The percentage value which falls between 81-90 is also less in boys (11.11%) and in girls (12.26%).

Mid Upper Arm Circumference

The NCHS/WHO reference of MUAC is only get for comparison at present for the age of 6, 8 and 10 years. The girls mean MUAC value are above 90% of the reference value with the range of 91% to 94%. The boys MUAC mean value show some what lower percentage value, it ranges from 87% to 90% of the reference, 3.67% boys and 4.76% girls at the age of 10 years only comes under moderate malnutrition category which is only 1.89% of total children and 21.58% boys and 7.93% girls (15.09% of total children) comes under malnutrition category and the remaining 83.01% children are Normal. On the basis of standard for Indian children only 8 children (1.83%) comes under malnutrition category and the remaining are normal. Table 9 gives distribution in detail.

BMI-z-score

As mentioned earlier, that for the assessment of Growth and Nutritional Status, in place of W-A and H-A, BMI may be useful. Body Mass Index reference curves are now available for most of the developed countries including Hong Kong; Cole, *et.al.* (1995) suggested to use Dutch Reference in place of NCHS/WHO Reference due to various reasons. The most important one is the low occurrence of Obesity. But at present it will be useful to use Hong Kong reference. On the basis of mean Z-score reporting system, the prevalence level ranges from 3.6% to 6% among the boys and 2.8% to 4% among the girls when we use the Dutch reference of BMI.

Table 8
Weight-for-Height-for-Age (Reference-Baldwin & Wood Table or Harvard Standard)

		Age Group in years											
		6		*7*		*8*		*9*		*10*		*Total*	
Category in per cent		*Boys*	*Girls*	*Boys*	*Girls*	*Boys*	*Girls*	*Boys*	*Girls*	*Boys*	*Girls*	*Boys*	*Girls*
81-90	No	6	4	4	5	7	5	6	7	2	5	25	26
	%	13.33	9.52	10	9.8	14.58	11.62	13.04	20.58	4.44	11.9	11.16	12.26
91-100	No.	20	20	26	21	26	21	26	13	26	19	124	94
	%	44.44	47.61	65	41.17	54.16	48.33	56.52	38.23	57.77	45.23	55.35	44.33
101	No	19	18	10	25	14	14	13	13	14	13	70	83
	%	42.22	42.85	25	49.02	29.16	32.55	28.26	38.23	31.11	30.95	31.25	39.15
110+	No	0	0	0	0	1	3	1	1	3	5	5	9
	%	0	0		0	2.08	6.97	2.17	2.94	6.66	11.9	2.23	4.24

Table 9
Mid Upper Arm Circumference Classification (Based on Reference for Indian Children)

		Age Group in Years										
		6		7		8		9		10		
Category		*Boys*	*Girls*	*Boys*	*Girls*	*Boys*	*Girls*	*Boys*	*Girls*	*Boys*	*Girls*	*Total*
Severe malnutrition	No.	0	0	0	0	0	0		0	0	0	0
(75% of the Standard)	%	0	0	0	0	0	0	0	0	0	0	0
Moderate Malnutrition	No.	0	0	0	0	0	0	0	0	0	0	0
(75.1-80% of the Standard)	%	0	0	0	0	0	0	0	0	0	0	0
Malnutrition	No.	0	0	0	2	0	0	2	0	2	2	8
(80.1-85% of the standard)	%				3.92			4.34		4.44	4.76	1.83
Normal (85.1%+ of the Standard)	No.	45	42	40	49	48	43	44	34	43	40	428
	%	100	100	100	96.07	100	100	95.65	100	95.55	95.23	98.17

Only one boy's of 6 years of age Z-score value fall-2-Z-score (6 years of age).

But when, Hong Kong reference is used to calculate the Z-score of BMI, then the prevalence level ranges from 2.3% to 3.6% in boys, and in girls this ranges from 2.3% to 6% only on the basis of mean Z-score based reporting. Here, not an individual's Z-score value comes under the below-2-Z-score.

Percentiles

WHO (1995) recommended a cut-off value below 5th percentile of NCHS/WHO reference for the thinness and below 3rd percentiles for stunting or low H-A of Body Mass Index (BMI). Due to accessibility of only the percentile value of BMI, Triceps and sub scapular skin folds value are only available of NCHS/WHO reference data, presently.

On the basis of percentile 8.69% boys and 13.33% girls (total 4.19% of children) of age 9 and 10 years fall below 5th percentile (Body Mass Index) under the category of thinness but not in low H-A or stunting. The Skin fold measurements i.e. triceps and sub scapular, also give some additional information about the Nutritional status. It is well known that, in Indian scenario low skin fold value is the common feature. The skin fold thickness value of boys which comes below 5th percentiles is 6.59% for triceps and one individual value (1.09%) of sub scapular skin fold. On the other hand girls value of triceps 5.26% fall below the 5th US percentile; whereas, all sub scapular values are above the 5th percentile values.

General Health and Clinical Signs

The observation on general health shows that majority of the boys and girls show good to very good health (4.46% boys and 4.12% girls); whereas, the weak type is represented by one boy only, while 2.23% boys and 3.9% girls show satisfactory health condition. In total only 1.60%(6) show satisfactory health condition and 4.12% (18) very good and only 0.22% (1) weak body constitution.

Table 10 gives the details of the prevalence of clinical signs due to nutritional deficiencies.

Pigmentation of the Skin

6.25% boys and 3.60% girls show this symptom and it is 5.05% of the total children. The boys of 10 years of age and 6 years of girls does not show the symptom.

Angular Stomatitis

Only 1.83% children show this clinical sign. It is absent among the boys of 9 years age while only at the age of 7 years one girl (1.96%) show this symptom. In boys the prevalence is 3.13% and in girls only 0.47%.

Table 10
Clinical Signs Due to Nutritional Deficiency

Age Group		*6*		*7*		*8*		*9*		*10*		*Total*	
Clinical Signs in per cent		*Boys*	*Girls*	*Boys*	*Girls*	*Boys*	*Girls*	*Boys*	*Girls*	*Boys*	*Girls*	*Boys*	*Girls*
Pigmentation of Skin	No	4	0	4	1	5	1	1	1	0	5	14	8
	%	8.9	0	10	1.96	10.4	2.32	2.22	2.94	0	11.11	6.25	3.6
AngularStomatitis	No	1	0	2	1	3	0	0	0	1	0	7	1
	%	2.22	0	5	1.96	6.25	0	0	0	2.22	0	3.13	0.47
Dry Scaly Skin	No	0	0	0	0	2	1	0	0	0	0	2	1
	%					4.16	2.32	0	0	0	0	0.89	0.47
DiscolouredHair	No.	0	0	0	0	0	2	0	0	0	0	0	2
	%	0	0	0	0	0	4.65	0	0	0	0	0	0.94
Flag/Coarse Hair	No.	2	4	1	3	0	0	0	0	0	0	3	7
	%	4.44	9.52	2.5	5.88	0	0	0	0	0	0	1.33	3.3
Spongy Bleeding gum	No	0	0	3	0	4	2	1	1	2	0	10	3
	%	0	0	7.5	0	8.3	4.7	2.2	2.9	4.8	0	4.46	1.42
Yellowish Teeth	No.	0	0	4	4	8	6	7	3	9	3	28	16
	%	0	0	10	7.8	16.66	12.5	15.21	8.8	20	6.7	12.5	7.54
Yellow Colour at the	No	0	0	0	0	0	0	0	0	0	0	0	0
Base of Nail	%	0	0	0	0	0	0	0	0	0	0	0	0
PaleConjunctiva	No.	0	0	1	0	1	0	0	1	0	0	2	1
	%	0	0	2.5	0	2.1	0	0	2.94	0	0	0.89	0.47

Dry Scaly Skin

This sign is only found at the age of 8 years in both boys (4.16%) and girls (2.32%).

Discoloured Hair

Totally absent in boys and at the age of 8 years only two girls (4.65%) show discoloured hair and the percentage value of the total children is only 0.46 while for the girls this is 0.94 only.

Flag/Coarse Hair

Totally absent in girls; while, at 6 and 7 years of age it is found in boys (1.3%) out of 0.69% of the total children.

Spongy Bleeding Gum

It is absent at the age of 6 years only in boys, and at the age of 6, 7 and 10 years among the girls. In terms of percentage 4.46 per cent and 1.42 per cent boys and girls show this symptom whereas, in total children this is only 2.98%.

Yellowish Teeth

Absent at the age of 6 years in both the sexes but the prevalence is comparatively higher than the other earlier mentioned signs. 12.5% boys and 7.54% girls show the yellowish teeth in boys the prevalence is maximum at the age of 10 years 20.00% while in girls this is at the age of 8 years (14.00 %) in total 10.09% children possess this type of teeth.

Pale Conjunctiva

Among the girls it is found only in a single individual (2.94%) at the age group of 9 years, a single individual (2.94%) in boys one individual at the age of 7 years and the other at the age of 8 years (2.5% and 2.1%), and it is observed only in 0.68% of the total children.

Yellow Colour at the Base of the Nail

It is totally absent.

Except the discoloured hair, all the clinical signs are comparatively more prevalent in boys than the girls and only yellowish teeth show the prevalence of above 10% level and the next is pigmentation of skin, otherwise the prevalence is very less.

Inference

The Geographical location, Socio-economic condition and other factors are favourable for Growth and Development in Car Nicobarese children which is reflected by body dimension like Body weight and Stature are more than the ICMR pooled data as well as from Rabha and some other

Table 11
Mean Value of Variable in Relation to Parity Considered

			Age group									
			6		7		8		9		10	
			Boys	*Girls*	*Boys*	*Girls*	*Boys*	*Girls*	*Boys*	*Girls*	*Boys*	*Girls*
Body Weight	P1	Mean	17.8	18.3	19.3	19.1	21.1	21.4	23.2	23.3	25	28.5
	P2	Mean	18.9	17.6*	20.2	20	21.2	22.2	23.2	24	24.3*	27.2*
	P3	Mean	18.2*	18.3	19.3*	19.4*	21.5	22.3	22.4	23.5*	25.4	25.9*
	P4	Mean	18.6	16.8*	19.4	18.5*	20.8	22.2*	23.5	22.2*	26.2	24.4*
Stature	P1	Mean	111.2	111	112	111.7	118.2	118.3	123.7	122.5	126	131.1
	P2	Mean	112.5	108.3	115.3	115.9*	119.2	119.8	123.3*	123.9	126.4	130.1
	P3	Mean	111.1*	112	113.9*	113.9*	119.2	120.1	122.2*	123.5*	128.8	125.7*
	P4	Mean	109.4*	107.1*	115.7	111.6*	117.8*	120.8	123.1	121.8*	130.3	125.9
Sitting Height	P1	Mean	60.5	59.4	60.4	60.2	64.2	62.8	65.8	64.7	63.3	69.1
	P2	Mean	60.9	58.6*	62.2	61.8	64.3	64	65.1*	65.6	66.4	68.1*
	P3	Mean	60.9	59.9	61	61,3*	64.1*	64.1	66.3	64.4*	67.1	64.4*
	P4	Mean	59.7*	57.4*	62	59.6*	63.2*	64.8	66.0*	63.7*	67.6	66.1
B.A.D.	P1	Mean	23.9	25.1	24.5	24.9	25.7	25.4	26.8	26.3	27.4	27.7
	P2	Mean	24.8	23.7*	25	25.1	25.7	25.7	26.7*	27.3	27.6	28
	P3	Mean	23.7	24.1*	24.9	24.9	25.9	26.5	26.4*	26.6*	28.3	27.1*
	P4	Mean	24.1	23.4	25.1	24.5*	26	25.7	27.1	26.0*	27.8	27.1*
I.D.	P1	Mean	17.8	17.4	18.1	17.7	18.5	18.7	19.3	19.1	19.6	20.9
	P2	Mean	17.7*	17.5	18.3	18.3	18.8	18.9	19.5	19.4	19.4*	20.9
	P3	Mean	17.3*	17.6	18.0*	18.1*	18.4*	18.8*	19.0*	19.3*	19.7	20.3*
	P4	Mean	17.8	17.4*	18.5	17.6*	19.1	19.1	20.1	18.3*	20.2	19.5*
Triceps	P1	Mean	5.9	7.6	6.3	7.2	6.2	8.6	7.1	7.6	6.7	8.9
	P2	Mean	6.3	7.9	6.4	6.7*	6.8	7.8*	6.1*	8.5	6	8
	P3	Mean	6.6	7	6.6	7.3	6.9	7.7*	6.3	7.9	6.7	9
	P4	Mean	7.8	7	7.6	7.5	6.7*	7.6*	5.4*	7.2	6.9	7.2

Contd...

			Age group									
			6		*7*		*8*		*9*		*10*	
			Boys	*Girls*	*Boys*	*Girls*	*Boys*	*Girls*	*Boys*	*Girls*	*Boys*	*Girls*
Subscapular	P1	Mean	4.6	5.7	4.9	5.4	4.8	6.3	5.8	6.1	5.9	8.2
	P2	Mean	4.5*	5.9	4.8*	5.6	5.2	6.9	5.3*	7.2	5.2*	7.7*
	P3	Mean	4.6	5.5*	4.7*	5.7	5.3	6.5*	5.1*	7.7	5.6	7.8
	P4	Mean	5.6*	4.9*	5.5	6.7	5.3	6.5	5.2	6.2*	5.7	6.2*
Bicep	P1	Mean	4	4.5	4.4*	4.7*	3.9	4.6	4.3	4.6	4	5.6
	P2	Mean	3.8*	4.7	3.9*	4.2*	4.1	4.9	3.8*	5.2	3.8	5.2*
	P3	Mean	4.3	4.2*	4.1	4.7	4.0*	4.8*	3.7*	4.3*	3.9	5.9
	P4	Mean	4.7	4.1*	4.8	4.5*	4.6	4.5*	3.8	4.4	4	3.9
BMI	P1	Mean	14.4*	14.8	15.4	15.2	15	15.2	15.1	15.5	15.7	16.47
	P2	Mean	14.9	15	15.1*	14.7*	14.9*	15.4	15.2	15.6	15.2*	16.0*
	P3	Mean	14.7*	14.5*	14.8*	14.9	15.1	15.5	15.0*	15.4*	15.3	16.3
	P4	Mean	15.6	14.6	14.5*	14.8*	15.0*	15.1	15.5	15.0*	15.4	15.3*

*The value highlighted show the decreasing value with respect to ear:y value for the specified parity.

rural Indian children. But always below from the Chinese, American and the Children of Socio-economic Category-1 of Indian children (ICMR). Though low H-A & W-A is noticed when modified Gomez Classification is used, but conversion of W-A in Z-score give some different result. Prevalence of low W-A decreases tremendously but low H-A prevalence are more or less same. Since height is more genetically controlled and also with the increase of age, genetics play a fundamental role. This may be the one of the probable reason for very low H-A. This also gets support when ICMR Socio economic Category-1 data is taken as Reference for W-A and H-A, the prevalence of low W-A and H-A is very low. Since the prevalence increases with the increase of age though not always, but more or less tendency is on the influencing way of genetics. Besides, "although W – H is specific to short term fluctuations it is often reflection of infectious disease rather than moderate change in food availability". The high value of W-H-A does not reflect fluctuation of food supply and prevalence of infectious disease, which again contradict the very high prevalence of low H-A and W-A. But comparison of Nicobarese children with Chinese (Beijing) children is also not wiseful, though both are of Mongoloid stock but the adult Chinese population are more taller than the Nicobarese as well as they are much more affluent than the Nicobarese also.

Stature, Body weight, iliocristal diameter's mean value show that at 6 and 7 years of age though the boys mean value is higher but from 8 year and onward the girls mean value is more. At 9 year of age though some discrepancy is noticed in girls, it may be due to small sample in comparison to boys. The mean value of biacromial diameter is always more boys girls. All the mean value of fat fold of girls are more than the boys and both positive and negative growth signify the different pattern of fat fold growth across the sex and age.

In conclusion it can be said that, for deriving W-A and H-A Gomez's classification is not appropriate for this population and for nutritional assessment in place of W-A and H-A, Body Mass Index is more appropriate and presently need to develop accurate reference for indian children for assessing growth and development.

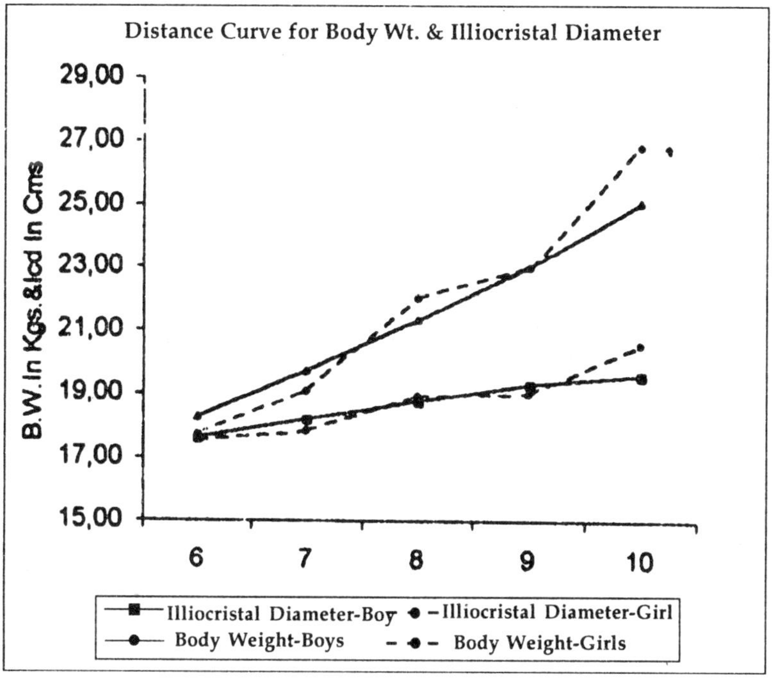
Distance Curve for Body Wt. & Illiocristal Diameter
29,00
27,00
25,00
23,00
21,00
19,00
17,00
15,00
B.W. In Kgs.&Icd In Cms
6
7
8
9
10
Illiocristal Diameter-Boy
Illiocristal Diameter-Girl
Body Weight-Boys
Body Weight-Girls

Fig. 1

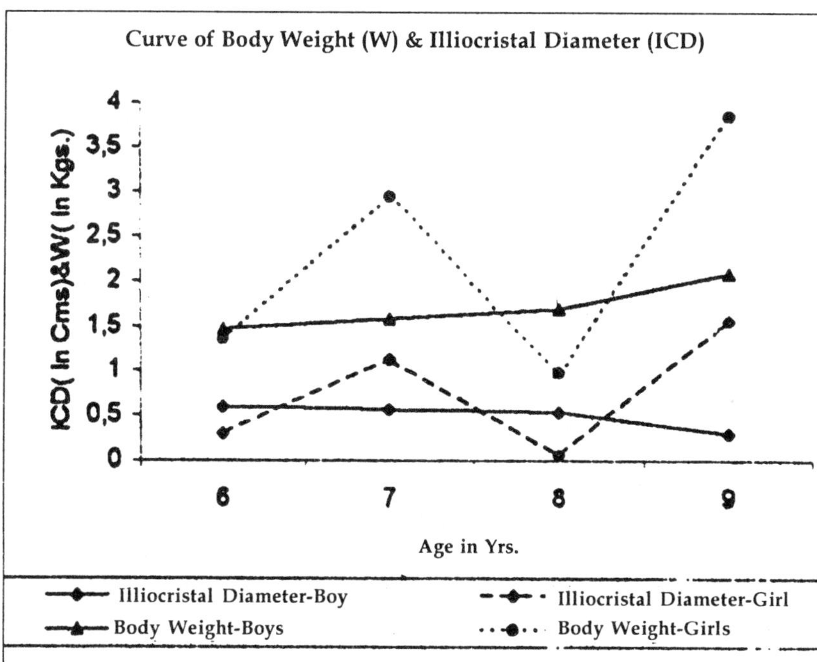
Curve of Body Weight (W) & Illiocristal Diameter (ICD)
4
3,5
3
2,5
2
1,5
1
0,5
0
ICD(In Cms)&W(In Kgs.)
6
7
8
9
Age in Yrs.
Illiocristal Diameter-Boy
Illiocristal Diameter-Girl
Body Weight-Boys
Body Weight-Girls

Fig. 2

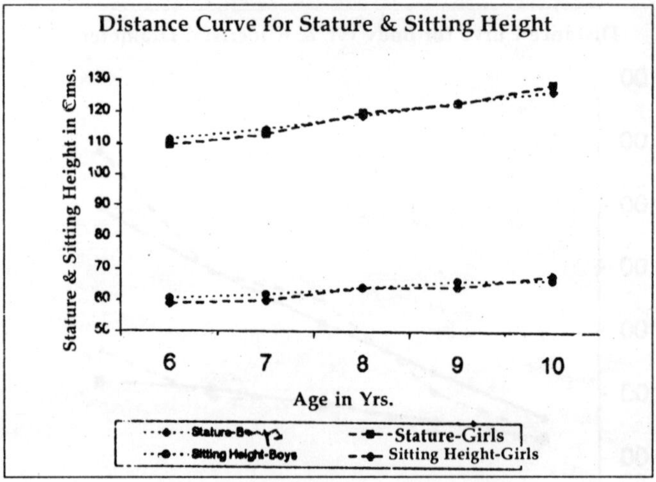

Fig. 3

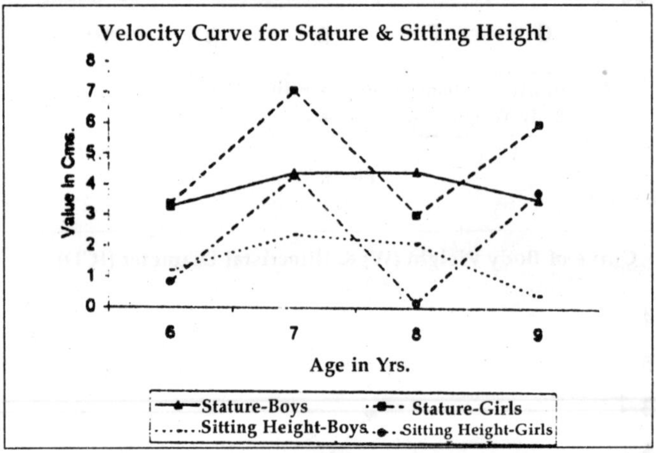

Fig. 4

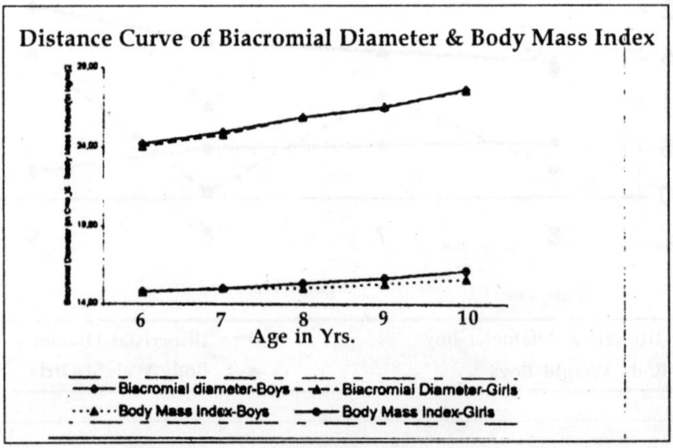

Fig. 5

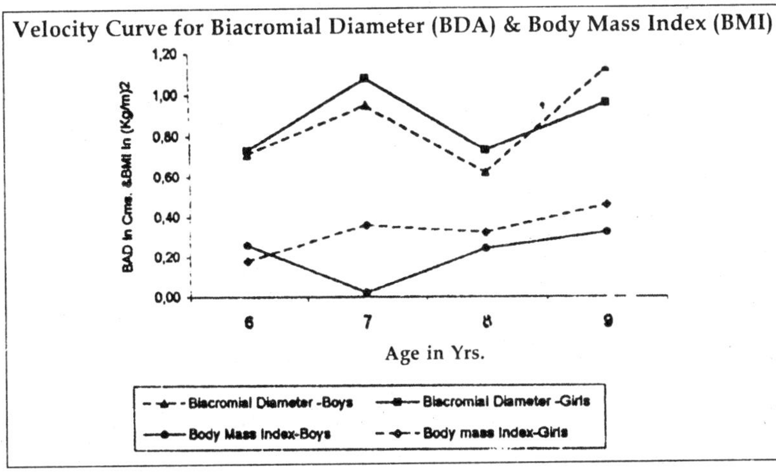

Fig. 6

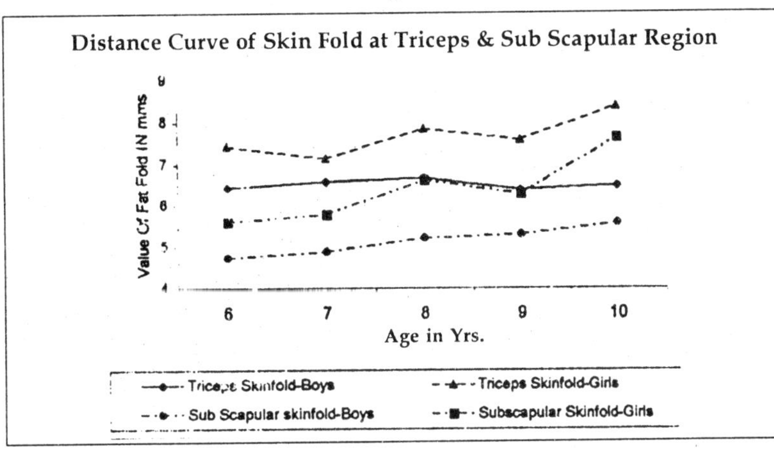

Fig. 7

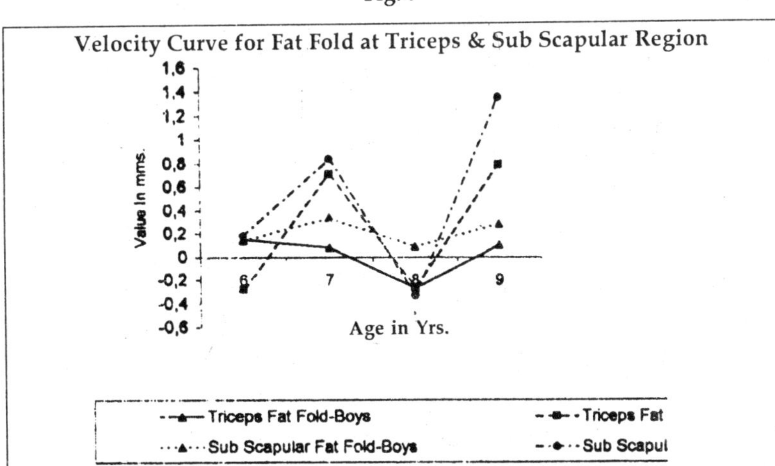

Fig. 8

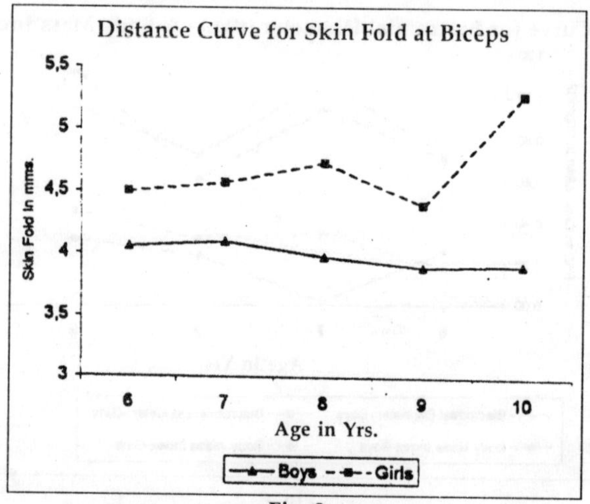

Fig. 9

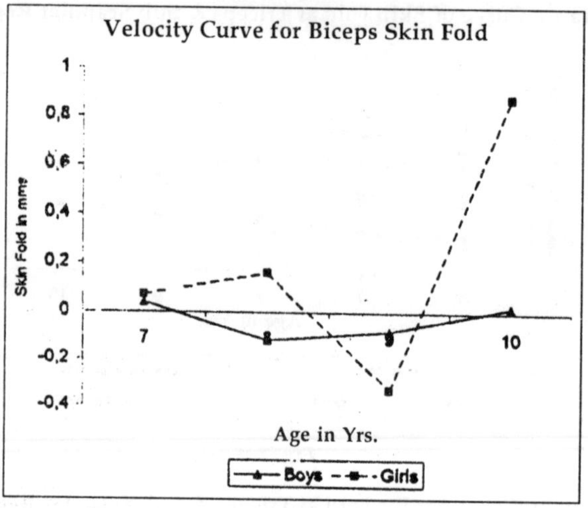

Fig. 10

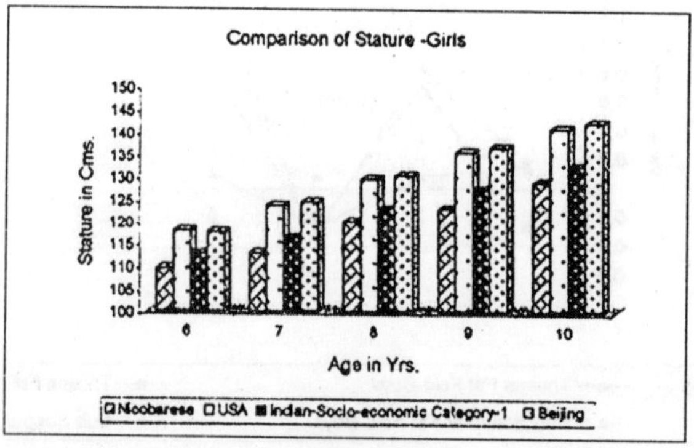

Fig. 11

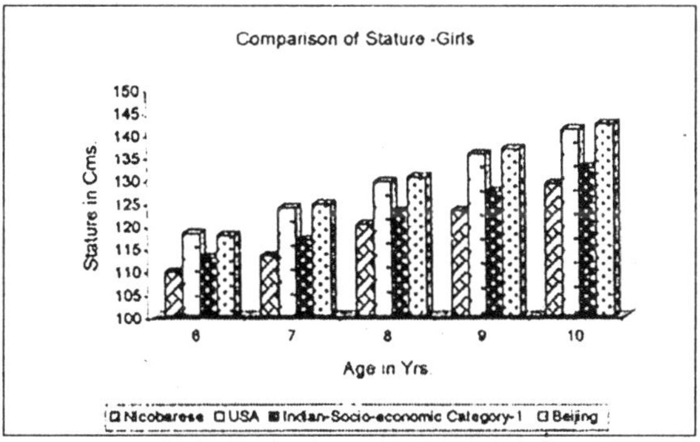

Fig. 12

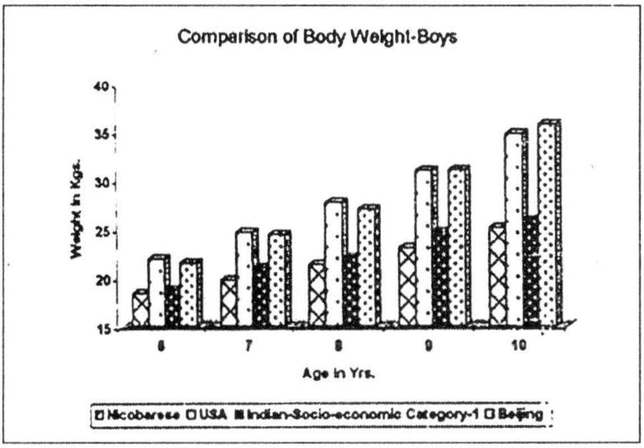

Fig. 13

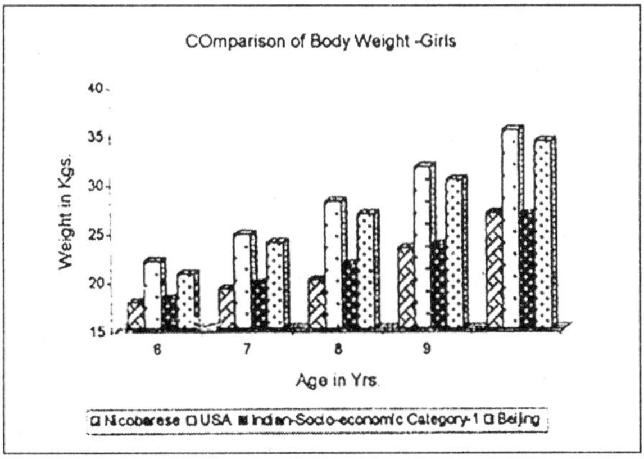

Fig. 14

References

Beal, C.M., P.T. Baker, T.S. Baker & J.J.D. Hass (1977), The Effects of High Altitude on Adolescent Growth in Southern Peruvian Americans. *Human Biology*, 49: 109-24.

Chatterjee, S. and A. Mandal (1991), Physical Growth Pattern of Girls (9-17 yrs.) from Rural West Bengal. *Ind. Jour. of Med. Research*, 94: 346-350.

Chatterjee, G.S., D. Sarkar and G. Paul (1966), "A Preliminary Note on the Relative Variations Between Different Sections of Populations in the Intake of Nutrients in Rural India." In *Human Adaptability to Environments and Physical Fitness.* Edited by M.S. Malhotra. Madras: Defence Institute of Physiology and Allied Sciences.

Chowdhury, A. K., S. L. Huffman, and G.T. Curtin (1977), Malnutrition, Menarche and Marriage in Rural Bangladesh. *Social Biology*, 24:316-325.

Cole,T.J., J.V.Freeman and M.A Preece (1995), Body Mass Index Reference Curve for the U.K. (1990), Archives of Disease in Childhood, 73:25-29.

Das, A.R. (1977), A Study of the Nicobarese Language, Calcutta: Anthropological Survey of India.

Frisancho A.R., P.T. Baker (1970), Altitude & Growth: A Study of the Pattern of Physical Growth of a High Altitude Peruvian Quechua Population, *Am. Jour. of Phy. Anthrop.*, 32, 279-92.

Frisancho A.R., G.A. Borkan and J.F. Klayman (1975), Pattern of Growth of Lowland & Highland Peruvian Quechua of Similar Genetic Composition, *Human Biology*, 47, 233-43.

Ganguly, Pranab (1976), The Physical Anthropology of the Nicobarese. Calcutta: Anthropological Survey of India.

Garn, A.M. and C.G. Rohman (1966), Interaction of Nutrition and Genetics in the Timing of Growth and Development. Pediatric Clinics of North America, 13, 353-79.

Gopalan, C. (1957), Malnutrition Among Infants and Young Children in India, *The Journal of Tropical Paediatrics.*, 3:3-12.

Gutheire, H.A. (1986), Introductory Nutrition. St. Louis:Times Mirror/Mosby.

Hass, J.D. (1973), Altitudinal & Infant Growth & Development in Peru. (unpublished Ph.D Thesis). The Pennsylvania State University, Pennsylvania, USA.

Indian Council of Medical Research (1984), Growth & Physical Development of Indian Infants & Children, *ICMR Technical Report Series*, No. 18.

Jelliffe, D.B. (1966), The Assessment of the Nutritional Status of the Community. WHO Monograph No. 53. Geneva: World Health Organisation.

Justin, Austice (1990), The Nicobarese, Calcutta: Seagull Books on Behalf of Anthropological Survey of India.

Kimura K. (1948), Studies on Growth and Development in Japan. Year Book of Physical Anthropology, 27, 179-214.

Kimura, K. and S. Katano (1959), Growth of Japanese Physique in Four Successive Decades before World War II, Zinruigaku Zassi, 67, 37-46.

Lasker, G.W. (1952), Environmental Growth Factors & Selective Migration, *Human Biology*, 24, 262-89.

Lichty J.A., R.Y. Ting (1957), Studies on Babies Born at High Altitudes, 1. P. Bruna and E. Dyar Relation of Altitude to Birth Weight, *American Journal of Disease in Childhood*, 93,666-69.

Malhotra, R. (1984), Effects of Various Altitudes on Human Growth and Some Adaptive Responses, *Hum. Science*, 33(3): 234-240.

Martin, R. and K. Saller (1957), Cited in Singh, I.P. and M.K Bhasin. 1968.

Meredith, H.V. (1979), Comparative Findings on Body Size of Children and Youth Living at Urban Centres & in Rural Areas. Growth, 43:95-104.

Mueller, W.H. and V.N. Schull, W. J. Schull, P. Soto and F. Rothammer (1978), A Multinational Andean Genetic and Health Programme: Growth & Development in an Hypoxic Environment, *Annals of Human Biology*, 5:329-52.

Mueller, W.H., F. Murillo, H. Palamino, M. Badzioch, R. Chakraborty, P. Furest and W.J. Schull The Aymara of Western Bolivia: V. Growth & Development in an Hypoxic Environment, *Human Biology*. 52:529-46.

Rao, K.V. (1978), Nutritional Status of Pre School Children and the Related Factors, *Indian Journal of Nutrition & Dietetics*, 15 : 112-119.

Roy, J. K. and B.C. Roy (1967), Cited in Pandit T.N. & Sarkar B.N. 1994.

Roberts, D.F. (1953), Body Weight, Race and Climate, *Am. Jour. of Phy.l Anthrop.*,11, 533-58.

Shapiro, H.L. (1938), Migration & Environment, Oxford University Press.

Shyam Chaudhuri, N.K. (1977), The Social Structure of Car Nicobar Islanders. Calcutta, Anthropological Survey of India.

Singh, L.P. and G.A. Harrison (1996), Impact of Migration, Environment and Socio-economic Conditions on Physique of Sikhs, *Journal of Biosocial Science*, 28:101-116.

Singh S.P., L.S. Sidhu and P. Malhotra (1986), Body Morphology of High Altitude Spitians of North West Himalayas, *Zeits. fur Morpho. Und Anthrop*, 76: 189-95.

Singh, I. P. and M.K. Bhasin (1968), Anthropometry, Kamala Raj Enterprises, Delhi.

Singh, R. (1975), Nutritional Anthropometric Measurements of Male Tamil Clerks in Madras (Sea-coast Plains) and Ooty (hills), *Annals of Human Biology*, 2:301-304.

Srikantia, S.G. (1979), Repurcussions of Early Malnutrition in Later Intellectual Development, *Journal of Indian Education*, January, 1-2.

Tanner, J.M. (1962), Growth at Adolescence, 2nd Ed., Blackwell, Scientific Publictions, Oxford.

Visweswara Rao, K. and Rao N.P. (1975), Association of Growth Status & the Incidence of Nutrition Deficiency Signs, *Am. Jour. of Clin. Nutrition*, 23:83.

WHO 1995 Physical Status: The Use and Interpretation of Anthropometry, WHO Technical Report Series 854: Geneva.

Wolff, G. (1935), Increased Bodily Growth of School Children Since, The War. *Lancet*, 1 : 1006-11.

8

GROWTH AND DEVELOPMENT OF GHASE MALI CHILDREN (AGED 6 YRS TO 10 YEARS) OF NAGPUR DISTRICT, MAHARASHTRA: A BIOCULTURAL PERSPECTIVES

P. Aditi Mukherjee & S. Dasgupta

It is well known that every human population vary from each other in respect of growth patterns, body size and composition; depending on their socio-economic condition. In India there are on an average 5000 different caste and tribal populations. The present report deals with the study of growth and development of children aged 6 to 10 years of Ghase Mali community, one of the OBC group of Maharashtra with low socio-economic condition. Under the Mali generic term, there are many sub-groups like; Phool Mali, Ghase Mali, Halda Mali, Kachha Mali, Kadu Mali, Lonare Mali, Bagaloan Mali, Babne Mali, Unde Mali, Adh shethi Mali, Jeere Mali, Lingayetmali, Koshre Mali, Fule Mali, Adhprabhu Mali etc. of which Ghase Mali is the larger sub-group and their main concentration is in the Vidarbha region of Nagpur district, Maharashtra. The Ghase Malis are generally agriculturist by occupation and they are distributed in Nagpur, Amravati, Wardha and Chandrapur districts of Vidarbha region. The 'Mali' word has been derived from the Sanskrit word 'Mala', a garland. According to Risley (1891) the Malis are a caste employed in making garlands. In Central Provinces Malis are generally employed in the temples of Devi because animals offered to the goddess so the worship can not be performed by Brahmans. It is informed by the people that initially Mali was a garland maker and supplied to the household of Raja-Kansa of Mathura. Later on they are divided into number of sub-groups depending on their occupational pattern viz. Phool Mali (grows and sells flowers), Ghase Mali (grows turmeric) and Jeere Mali (who grows only jeera i.e. cumin etc.).

Material and Method

The data for the present study have been collected from the Ghase Mali (OBC) of Nagpur district with special reference to physical and cultural aspects, nutritional deficiency and dental pattern so as to have a synthetic view of the problem in growth and development of the children.

The present study is based on apparently normal and unrelated 427 children including 195 boys and 232 girls aged six to 10 years school children of Nagpur district especially from malmeshwar taluka. The data were collected mainly from primary and middle schools covering two municipal areas Kalmeshwar and Mohpa and also two villages Dehawardi and Maschipathar of Kalmeshwar taluka.

In order to study the socio-economic status of the parents, information relating to the occupation and income of the parents, family size, parents education and parity of the child were also collected by household survey. Actual date of birth of the child has been recorded from the school register and also confirmed from the parents during household survey. Cross sectional data on the following body measurements have been collected-Weight, Stature, Sitting height, Bi-acromial diameter, Bi-iliac diameter, Mid upper arm circumference, Triceps skinfold, Biceps skinfold and Subscapular skinfold following the techniques of Martin & Saller (1957). The anthropometry data was analyzed as per the guideline of the project. Cross-tabulation of the mean values and standard deviation of five selected measurements has been done for parity, family size, family type, per capita income and literacy level of parents in order to see the impact of these socio-cultural factors on growth.

Dentition pattern for both deciduous and permanent teeth were recorded and main attention was given to the eruption of permanent teeth as it is indirectly related to the growth and development at different ages of the child. Dental pattern has been observed with the help of a dental probe in the natural light.

Out of 427 household data on living conditions around the homestead have been collected from 100 households. Clinical estimation is an important method for assessing the nutritional status of a community, especially in the regions where malnutrition are widespread. Clinical deficiency signs such as (1) Irregular pigmentation/patches of skin, (2) Angular Stomatitis, (3) Dry skin/Scaly skin, (4) Discoloured hair, (5) Flag/ Course hair, (6) Spongy bleeding gums, (7) Pale conjectiva, (8) Yellow colour of the nails, (9) Deformities of limbs if any have been recorded according to Jelliffe (1966) and Latham (1979).

Living Condition

Living condition of the Ghase Mali have been surveyed and it has been observed that majority of them live in thatched houses (81%) with good ventilation and proper sunlight, only 11% houses are not having any sunlight. Cleanliness of the houses and personal cleanliness are satisfactory. About 52% houses are having their own latrine and rest of the people goes to field for toilet. In most of the houses utensils are cleaned very poorly. They generally get water supply two times a day. Almost all the houses have electricity but in two Zilla Parisad, the Maschipathar and in Debwardi villages the condition is very poor.

Agriculture is their prime occupation (Table 1). They cultivate mainly chana, tuar dal, wheat, soyabean and cotton and in addition they also cultivate different vegetables and sell it in the village weekly market. Besides, some of the persons owned orange garden and during orange seasons females also does work as labourer in orange garden. Very few families are having their own land and majority of the children's parents are landless and does labour work either on other's land or in nearby factory, or as daily wage labourer on road or in the shops or market (Table 2).

Table 1
Occupational Catagories of the Mali

	Male		*Female*		*Total*	
Occupation	*No.*	*%*	*No.*	*%*	*No.*	*%*
Agriculture	61	5.39	71	5.93	132	5.67
Agricultural Labour	152	13.44	164	13.69	316	13.57
Service	180	15.92	10	0.84	190	8.16
Labour	25	2.21	2	0.17	27	1.16
Agriculture & Agricultural Labour	7	0.62	3	0.25	10	0.43
Agriculture & Labour	0	0.00	1	0.08	1	0.04
Business	41	3.63	1	0.08	42	1.80
Temporary Service	2	0.18	0	0.00	2	0.09
Cattle Grazing	3	0.27	0	0.00	3	0.13
Tailoring	2	0.18	1	0.08	3	0.13
Vegetable Vending	3	0.27	0	0.00	3	0.13
Business & Agriculture	2	0.18	0	0.00	2	0.09
Business & Labour	1	0.09	0	0.00	1	0.04
Retired Employess	9	0.79	0	0.00	9	0.39
Pensioners	2	0.18	1	0.08	3	0.13
Other	0	0.00	a	0.00	0	0.00
Unemployed	22	1.95	12	1.00	34	1.46
Non-workers	619	54.73	932	77.80	1551	66.60
Total	1131		1198		2329	

Table 2
Agricultureal Land-holding Pattern Among the Mali

Range (acres)	*Households*	
	No.	*Per cent*
0 to 2	94	22.01
2.1 to 5.0	50	11.71
5.1 to 10.0	27	6.32
10.1 to 20.0	15	3.51
20.1 & above	5	1.17
Landless	236	55.27
Total	427	

Table 3
Income Catagories of the Mali

Income Catagories (Range in Rs.)	*Households*	
	No.	*Per cent*
<5000	1	0.23
5001 to 10,000	32	7.49
10,001 to 20,000	100	23.42
20,001 to 30,000	111	25.99
30,001 to 40,000	68	15.93
40,001 to 50,000	33	7.73
50,001 to 1,00,00	60	14.05
> 1,00,000	21	4.92
Dependent	1	0.23
Total	427	

Of the surveyed population 89.313% live in nuclear family having four to six members and 3.817% live in nuclear families having with seven to nine members (Table 4). There are higher percentage of medium sized joint families (60.00%).

Table 4
Type and Size of Family in Which Boys and Girls Live Among the Mali

Size of family	*Type of family*			
	Nuclear		*Joint*	
	No.	*Per cent*	*No.*	*Per cent*
Small family (<3)	18	6.87	-	-
Medium family (4-6)	234	89.31	99	60.00
Large family (7-9)	10	3.82	48	29.09
Very large family (10+)	-	-	18	10.91
Total	262	100.00	165	100.00

Literacy level among the studied Mali population has been shown in Table 5 and observed that the percentage of primary level education is more 30.4% (in males) and 25.2% (in females) respectively than the higher education or even the upper primary level of education. Non-literate females (21.5%) are more than the males (14.4%). Percentage of graduation and post-graduation level education is very low. Those who are graduate, most of them are attached with teaching profession.

Data on Growth

The cross-sectional anthropometric data on boys and girls of Mali community, Nagpur district have been statistically analysed and the results are presented in Table 6.

Weight

Weight gives an idea of the total body growth and it changes with the advancement of age. Weight is easily affected by environmental factors,

Table 5
Level of Litercy Among the Mali

	Litercy Level																		
	Non Literate		*Balwadi*		*Primary*		*Upper Primary*		*Secondary Secondary*		*Higher graduate*		*Graduate*		*Post-*		*Total*		
	M	*F*	*M*	*F*	*M*	*F*	*M*	*F*	*M*	*F*	*M*	*F*	*M*	*F*	*M*	*F*	*M*	*F*	*TOTAL*
<1	7	8	-	-	-	-	-	-	-	-	-	-	-	-	-	-	7	8	15
1 to 5	87	68	10	6	-	-	-	-	-	-	-	-	-	-	-	-	97	74	171
6 to 10	17	17	3	5	282	239	29	29	-	-	-	-	-	-	-	-	331	290	621
11 to 15	1	-	-	-	8	7	98	130	8	23	-	-	-	-	-	-	115	160	275
16 to 20	1	1	-	-	1	4	3	6	15	18	8	16	1	-	-	-	29	47	76
21 to 25	-	1	-	-	-	1	1	4	9	8	2	5	4	2	-	-	16	24	40
26 to 30	-	9	-	-	-	10	7	29	8	69	5	31	5	3	3	2	28	156	184
31 to 35	2	10	-	-	3	12	10	41	25	73	21	25	8	4	4	4	73	169	242
36 to 40	7	9	-	-	13	9	26	21	69	35	45	11	15	2	3	-	178	87	265
41 to 45	7	2	-	-	4	4	11	5	58	13	23	-	7	2	5	-	115	25	140
46 to 50	3	3	-	-	6	3	9	1	21	1	11	-	3	1	2	-	55	8	63
51 to 55	2	10	-	-	2	3	2	1	3	1	-	-	-	-	1	-	10	15	25
56 to 60	1	32	-	-	3	4	4	-	1	2	-	1	-	-	-	-	9	39	48
61 to 65	11	49	-	-	8	4	3	-	4	2	1	-	-	-	-	-	27	55	82
66 to 70	4	23	-	-	8	-	4	-	2	-	-	-	-	-	-	-	18	23	41
71 to 75	5	10	-	-	4	2	-	-	2	-	-	-	1	-	-	-	12	12	24
76 to 80	6	4	-	-	2	-	1	-	-	-	-	-	-	-	-	-	9	4	13
81 to 85	2	1	-	-	-	-	-	-	1	-	-	-	-	-	-	-	3	1	4
86+	-	1	-	-	-	-	-	-	-		-	-	-	-	-	-	-	1	1
Total	163	258	13	11	344	302	208	267	226	245	116	89	44	14	18	6	1132	1198	2330
Per cent	14.412	21.53	1.15	0.99	30.39	25.21	18.37	22.29	20	20.45	10.25	7.43	3.89	1.5	1.59	0.5			

Table 6
Anthropometric Variables of Mali Children by Age and Sex

	Boys					Girls				
Age	*6*	*7*	*8*	*9*	*10*	*6*	*7*	*8*	*9*	*10*
Weight (in kg.)										
N	48	41	59	62	22	47	50	33	32	33
Mean	15.60	17.07	19.17	20.77	23.01	15.19	16.43	18.81	19.69	21.88
S.E.of mean	0.32	0.36	0.40	0.36	0.58	0.30	0.34	0.54	0.52	0.53
S.D.	2.22	2.28	3.08	2.83	2.70	2.06	2.37	3.12	2.93	3.03
C.V.	14.21	13.33	16.05	13.63	11.73	13.56	14.41	16.57	14.86	13.84
Absolute growth	-	1.47	2.10	1.61	2.23	-	1.24	2.38	0.88	2.19
% growth	-	9.41	12.28	8.37	10.74	-	8.16	14.46	4.69	11.13
Stature (in cm)										
N	48	41	59	62	22	47	50	33	32	33
Mean	111.63	116.54	121.48	124.96	131.31	109.93	114.43	118.87	123.25	129.26
S.E.of mean	0.72	0.74	0.76	0.65	1.33	0.67	0.80	3.18	0.96	1.17
S.D.	4.97	4.74	5.85	5.08	6.22	4.59	5.65	18.24	5.45	6.71
C.V.	4.46	4.07	4.82	4.07	4.73	4.17	4.94	15.34	4.42	5.19
Absolute growth	-	4.91	4.94	3.48	6.35	-	4.50	4.44	4.38	6.01
% growth	-	4.40	4.24	2.87	5.08	-	4.09	3.88	3.68	4.88
Sitting hight (in cm.)										
N	48	41	59	62	22	47	50	33	32	33
Mean	61.16	62.65	65.06	65.90	68.27	60.04	61.62	65.33	65.29	67.09
S.E.of mean	0.81	0.44	0.44	0.37	0.57	0.63	0.45	0.56	0.46	0.54
S.D.	5.58	2.84	3.38	2.92	2.65	4.31	3.15	3.24	2.59	3.08
C.V.	9.12	4.53	5.20	4.42	3.88	7.18	5.11	4.95	3.97	4.59
Absolute growth	-	1.48	2.41	0.85	2.37	-	1.58	3.71	-0.04	1.81
% growth	-	2.43	3.85	1.30	3.59	-	2.63	6.02	-0.06	2.77

Contd...

	Boys					Girls				
Age	*6*	*7*	*8*	*9*	*10*	*6*	*7*	*8*	*9*	*10*
. ... (in cm)										
N	48	41	59	62	22	47	50	33	32	33
Mean	23.92	25.09	25.99	26.73	27.76	23.50	24.50	25.85	25.91	27.49
S.E.of mean	0.18	0.21	0.22	0.17	0.27	0.23	0.21	0.27	0.24	0.22
S.D.	1.27	1.36	1.66	1.32	1.26	1.56	1.45	1.53	1.35	1.29
C.V.	5.31	5.43	6.39	4.94	4.52	6.62	5.92	5.92	5.23	4.68
Absolute growth	-	1.16	0.90	0.75	1.03	-	0.99	1.35	0.07	1.58
% growth	-	4.87	3.59	2.88	3.85	-	4.22	5.52	0.25	6.10
Biiliocristal breadth (in cm.)										
N	48	41	59	62	22	47	50	33	32	33
Mean	17.92	18.80	19.59	20.17	21.39	17.90	18.84	19.64	19.97	21.19
S.E.of mean	0.14	0.17	0.17	0.17	0.22	0.16	0.15	0.26	0.22	0.24
S.D.	0.98	1.08	1.30	1.34	1.01	1.09	1.06	1.48	1.26	1.37
C.V.	5.45	5.76	6.66	6.62	4.71	6.11	5.62	7.55	6.29	6.46
Absolute growth	-	0.88	0.80	0.58	1.22	-	0.94	0.80	0.33	1.23
% growth	-	4.89	4.23	2.94	6.06	-	5.27	4.24	1.67	6.14
Mid upperarm circumference (in cm.)										
N	48	41	59	62	22	47	50	33	32	33
Mean	14.16	14.21	14.82	15.25	17.71	14.30	14.21	14.97	15.00	15.45
S.E.of mean	0.17	0.16	0.16	0.16	2.11	0.15	0.15	0.25	0.20	0.18
S.D.	1.16	1.02	1.25	1.25	9.89	1.04	1.05	1.44	1.15	1.02
C.V.	8.16	7.20	8.41	8.17	55.88	7.25	7.39	9.58	7.69	6.62
Absolute growth	-	0.05	0.61	0.43	2.46	-	-0.10	0.77	0.03	0.45
% growth	-	0.32	4.32	2.88	16.14	-	-0.69	5.40	0.20	2.97

Contd...

	Boys					Girls				
Age	*6*	*7*	*8*	*9*	*10*	*6*	*7*	*8*	*9*	*10*
Triceps skin fold (in mm)										
N	48	41	59	62	22	47	50	33	32	33
Mean	5.04	4.46	4.38	4.39	4.30	5.81	4.79	4.82	5.16	4.75
S.E.of mean	0.14	0.22	0.15	0.18	0.19	0.20	0.20	0.29	0.26	0.18
S.D.	0.95	1.38	1.12	1.42	0.87	1.34	1.39	1.64	1.49	1.04
C.V.	8.82	30.97	25.48	32.27	20.19	23.05	29.00	34.04	28.82	21.94
Absolute growth	-	-0.59	-0.08	0.01	-0.09	-	-1.02	0.03	0.34	-0.42
% growth	-	-11.62	-1.80	0.21	-2.05	-	-17.53	0.56	7.09	-8.10
Subscapular skin fold (in mm.)										
N	48	41	59	62	22	47	50	33	32	33
Mean	4.22	3.99	3.97	4.26	4.28	4.52	4.08	4.22	4.61	4.49
S.E.of mean	0.10	0.18	0.10	0.09	0.11	0.10	0.11	0.15	0.13	0.15
S.D.	0.67	0.75	0.75	0.74	0.52	0.71	0.80	0.87	0.75	0.85
C.V.	5.90	18.73	18.95	17.27	12.11	15.73	19.70	20.68	16.31	18.83
Absolute growth	-	-0.23	-0.02	0.28	0.02	-	-0.44	0.14	0.39	-0.12
% growth	-	-5.52	-0.38	7.12	0.49	-	-9.71	3.41	9.12	-2.56
Biceps skin fold (in mm.)										
N	48	41	59	62	22	47	50	33	32	33
Mean	3.56	2.87	2.94	2.78	3.04	3.99	3.48	3.22	3.22	3.11
S.E.of mean	0.16	0.13	0.11	0.10	0.13	3.13	0.16	0.16	0.16	0.14
S.D.	1.07	0.81	0.86	0.76	0.62	0.91	1.13	0.90	0.89	0.82
C.V.	30.20	28.28	29.09	27.34	20.42	22.76	32.51	27.87	27.77	26.40
Absolute growth	-	-0.69	0.07	-0.16	0.28	-	-0.51	-0.26	0.00	-0.11
% growth	-	-19.26	2.37	-5.27	9.23	-	-12.77	-7.51	0.03	-3.42

so, it is highly variable parameter. It has been observed from the Table 6 that the boys are heavier in weight than the girls especially in the ages 7 + years to 10 + years but in 6 + years of age the mean weight for girls and boys are almost same. There is a gradual increase in weight among the boys and girls have been observed from 6 + years to 10 + years.

The distance curve for weight (Fig. 1) reveals that there is steady increase of weight from 6 + years to 8 + years but after 8+ years to 9 + years there is a slight decline in the spurt for both boys and girls and after 9 + years weight increases faster. Velocity curve shows that the weight increases upto 7 to 8 years and after that a lower trend is observed between 8 to 9 years and from 9+ years the velocity curve (Fig. 2) again start increasing. The regression equation of weight for boys and girls are, Y = 1.812X + 4.596 and Y = 1.667X + 5.047 respectively. (Fig. 19).

Height

It has been observed from the Table 6 that the mean height of boys are slightly higher than the girls from the 6+ years to 10+ years but the increase of mean height from 6+ years to 10+ years of age are steady. The mean height of boys at 6+ years is 111.63 cm. and of girls 109.95 cm. respectively. The mean height of both boys and girls at 10+ years are 131.31 cm. and 129.26 cm. respectively. In both boys and girls the height increases continuously as the age advances from 6 years to 10 years.

Absolute growth of the boys shows more values than girls in all the age groups except between the ages 8 and 9 years where female shows little higher value (Table 6). This distance curve of stature also showed (Fig. 3) a steady increase from 6+ to 10+ years in both the sexes. The velocity curve (Fig. 4) shows the increment of growth rate among boys and girls came down to minimum after the 8+ years and again it start increasing after 9+ years to 10+ years. The regression equation for stature on age has been shown in fig. 20 and for boys it is recorded Y = 4.653X + b 83.825 and for girls Y = 4.791X + b 81.361 respectively. (Fig. 20).

Sitting Height

Mean sitting height of both boys and girls increases from 6 years to 10 years of age (Table 6). But the mean sitting height is higher among boys than the girls. It was observed that the boys shows higher absolute growth than the girls in all age groups except in 7 and 8 years. The distance curve shows a steady increase from 6+ years to 10+ years (Fig. 5). The velocity curve (Fig. 6) shows that the growth trend among boys and girls came down to minimum in the 8+ years to 9+ years and again increases after 9 + years to 10 + years for both boys and girls. The regression equation of stature on age for Mali boys Y = 1.701X + b50.96 and for girls Y = 1.812X + b49.320 shown in the Fig. 21.

Biacromial Diameter

This measurement gives the transverse growth of the body and measures the straight distance between the two acromian points. Among the boys and girls the gradual increase of the mean values has been observed with the change of age (Fig. 7). The value of absolute growth rate indicate that maximum increment rate in case of boys i.e. 4.87% at 6 and 7 years; whereas, in girls 6.10 % increment rate at 9 and 10 years. From the trend of growth for boys and girls under study, it was apparent that the rate of increment has slow down at 7 and 8 years and 8 and 9 years and it gains after 9+ years of age (Fig. 8). The regression equation have been recorded for boys and girls are Y = 0.931X + b18.438 and Y = 0.945 X + b17.881 respectively (Fig. 22).

Biiliocristal Diameter

This is also transverse measurement shows the transverse body growth. The table reveals that with the change of age from 6+ years to 10+ years the mean values of biiliac diameter also gradually increases both among the girls and boys (Fig. 9).

The velocity curve (Fig. 10) that shows that the rate of increment slow down between age 8 yrs. to 9 years in both boys and girls but rate of increment is more in girls than boys between age 9 and 10 resulting in slightly more bi-iliac breadth in girls than boys at age 10 years. The regression equation (Fig. 23) have been recorded and it is for boys Y = 0.798X + b13.143 and for girls Y = 0.772X + b13.332.

Mid-Upper-Arm Circumference

The mid-upper arm circumference of boys and girls increases with the advancing age, but for girls the mid-upper arm circumference is relatively stable from 6+ years to 8+ years of age. The absolute growth (Table 6) is quite higher (16.13%) among boys than the girls from 9 + years to 10+ years. The distance curve (Fig. 11) for both boys and girls depict that the mean values of mid-upper arm circumference is stable. The velocity curve (Fig. 12) reveals that the rate of growth started increasing from 6 + years among boys and between 7 and 8 years the rate of growth slow down and after 9+ years it again started increasing and same is the case for girls and this may be because of preadolescent growth spurt.

Triceps Skinfold

The mean value of triceps skinfold for both boys and girls reveals that the skinfold thickness decreases with the advancing age up to 8 years in case (Table 6) of girls; whereas, in case of boys up to age 9 years. The rate of growth started after 8 and 9 years then started decreasing after

9 + years through 10 + years. The distance curve (Fig. 13) shows the continuous increase of mean values. The velocity curve shows (Fig. 14) that the pattern of increment of fat deposition. There is cyclical nature of fat gain and loss in alternative years after 8+ years through 10+ years of ages. After a period of negative growth from 6+ years to 7+ years a rapid accumulation can be seen, and after 9 + years the rate of growth again shows negative rate may be because of preadolescent period for both the sexes.

Sub-scapular Skinfold

The sub-scapular Skinfold mean values reveals that among the boys fat deposition decreases from 7+ through 9+ years and started increasing after 10+ years; but among girls the mean values shows that the fact deposition is uniform from 6+years through 10+ years. The growth rate shows negative growth from 6+ years to 7+ years both among boys and girls but among both girls and boys after 8+ years to 9+ years the rate of growth started positive increment and it is higher among the girls but after 10+ years the rate of growth again started decreasing. The velocity curve confirms the above rate of growth in the Fig. 16. The distance curve has been shown in Fig. 15 and shows that the mean increases and decreases in a zig-zag way and after 9 + years among both boys and girls the mean value shows stable.

Biceps Skinfold

Biceps skinfold thickness decreases gradually from age 6 years through 10 years among the boys; whereas, in case of girls it also decreases up to age 8 years and after 9 years onward it start increasing (Table 6, Fig. 17). The biceps skinfold thickness in girls is more than boys at all ages but the bisexual difference is not statistically significant. It has been observed from velocity curve (Fig. 18) among the boys the growth rate started with negative values from 6+ years through 10 + years; whereas, among girls after 9+ years the positive growth is observed.

In Table 7 the t-test values of sexual difference has been shown for each selected measurements and has been observed that there is no sexual difference from 6+ years through 10+ years for all the 14 measurements of the Mali children.

Correlation-Coefficient of selected measurements

The Correlation coefficient between some selected measurements have been calculated and presented in Table 8. The result shows relatively moderate to high positive correlation significant at 0.01 percent level between Stature and Weight, Stature and Sitting Height, Biacromial diameter and Biiliocristal diameter, Chest Circumference and Head Circumference, Skinfold at Triceps and Skinfold at Biceps for both boys and girls.

Table 7
't' Values of Comparisons between Boys and Girls for Different Measurements Among the Mali Children

Age Group	*6*	*7*	*8*	*9*	*10*
Measurement					
Weight	0.94	1.31	0.54	1.74	1.41
Stature	1.74	1.91	0.34	1.51	1.14
Sitting Height	1.10	1.62	0.37	1.01	1.46
Bi-acromial Diameter	1.43	1.98*	0.39	2.83**	0.77
Bi-ilio Cristal Diameter	0.09	0.22	0.18	0.69	0.56
Fore Arm Length	0.77	2.89*	0.89	0.97	1.08
Total Arm Length	2.34*	4.03**	0.51	0.08	1.15
Head Circumference	1.68	2.01*	0.65	1.47	0.47
Chest Circumference	3.45**	2.22*	2.37*	3.24**	2.37*
Mid Upper Arm Circumference	0.64	0.01	0.54	0.92	1.31
Calf Circumference	0.17	0.28	0.33	2.19*	0.96
Triceps	3.24**	1.16	1.54	2.48**	1.68
Sub-scapular Skin Fold	2.12*	0.57	1.43	2.17*	1.04
Biceps	2.10*	2.87**	1.46	2.45**	0.32

** Significant at .01
* Significant at .05

Dental Pattern

The studies suggest that eruption of tooth is genetically controlled and is not affected by environmental non-genetic factors. It is also established that among the females formation and eruption of specific tooth is earlier than among the boys of corresponding age. On the basis of number & type of tooth erupted the chronological age can be estimated by comparing it with the standard. It has been observed from Table 9 that at any given age girls have more number of permanent teeth erupted than boys. The biological age or maturity rate based on eruption of number of permanent teeth indicate that the girls mature earlier than the boys of corresponding age.

Nutritional Status Assessment Based On Height For Age, Weight For Age, Mid-upper Arm Circumference For Age Deficit Classification

In Table 10, 11 and 12 the Weight, Height, and Mid-upper arm deficit classification on age has been classified from 6+ years through 10+ years, and it has been seen that majority of boys and girls shows grade II malnutrition when weight has been classified on age; but when height has been classified on age, it shows normal boys and girls from 6+ years to 10+ years. Mid-upper arm circumference also classified on age and it is observed that most of the boys and girls were in the moderate malnutrition to malnutrition category except the 9+ years boys were in the normal category.

Table 8
Correlation Between Selected Measurements

	Age Group											
	6		*7*		*8*		*9*		*10*		*Total*	
Correlation Coefficient Between	*Boys*	*Girls*	*Boys*	*Girls*	*Boys*	*Girls*	*Boys*	*Girls*	*Boys*	*Girls*	*Boys*	*Girls*
Height – Weight	0.78	0.81*	0.88*	0.90*	0.89*	0.74	0.80*	0.81*	0.53	0.79*	0.90*	0.92*
Height – Sitting Height	0.68	0.92*	0.83*	0.90*	0.89*	0.85*	0.68	0.88*	0.90*	0.80*	0.89*	0.94*
Biacromial – Biilliac Breadth	0.49	0.42	0.61	0.6	0.68	0.66	0.55	0.69	0.34	0.31	0.72**	0.73**
Triceps-Sub-ScapularFat fold	0.64	0.63	0.68	0.74	0.59	0.53	0.43	0.62	0.59	0.79*	0.53**	0.70**
Head – Chest Circumference	0.37	0.51	0.41	0.2	0.62	0.37	0.61	0.48	0.31	0.42	0.52**	0.37

* High Co-relation
** Moderate co-relation

Table 9
Eruption of Permanent Teeth Among the Mali Children

			Incisors		*Canines (1st & 2nd)*		*Pre-molars (1st & 2nd)*		*Molar (IInd)*		*Molar (1st)*	
Age in years	*Sex*	*No.*	*No.*	*%*	*No.*	*%*	*No.*	*%*	*No.*	*%*	*No.*	*%*
6	Boys	48	38	79.16	12	25.00	-	-	-	-	-	
	Girls	47	40	85.11	15	31.25						
7	Boys	41	32	78.04	35	85.36	5	12.19				
	Girls	50	46	92.00	37	74.00	12	24.00				
8	Boys	59	59	100.00	50	100.00	55	93.22	50	84.74	38	64.04
	Girls	33	33	100.00	33	100.00	33	100.00	31	93.93	25	75.75
9	Boys	62	62	100.00	62	100.00	59	96.16	60	96.77	58	93.54
	Girls	32	32	100.00	32	100.00	32	100.00	32	100.00	32	100.00
10	Boys	22	22	100.00	22	100.00	22	100.00	22	100.00	22	100.00
	Girls	33	33	100.00	33	100.00	33	100.00	33	100.00	33	100.00

Table 10
Weight for Age Deficit Classification of the Mali Children

Age (Years)	*Sex*	*Weight For Age* *N*	*%*	*Classification*
6+	Boys	48	70.00	Grade II Malnutrition
	Girls	47	70.32	Grade II Malnutrition
7+	Boys	41	69.10	Grade II Malnutrition
	Girls	50	67.89	Grade II Malnutrition
8+	Boys	59	68.92	Grade II Malnutrition
	Girls	33	68.11	Grade II Malnutrition
9+	Boys	62	66.57	Grade II Malnutrition
	Girls	32	62.67	Grade II Malnutrition
10+	Boys	22	68.24	Grade II Malnutrition
	Girls	33	62.13	Grade II Malnutrition

Table 11
Height for Deficit Classification of the Mali Children

Age (Years)	*Sex*	*Weight For Age* *N*	*%*	*Classification*
6+	Boys	48	94.12	Normal
	Girls	47	93.31	Normal
7+	Boys	41	93.65	Normal
	Girls	50	92.64	Normal
8+	Boys	59	93.43	Normal
	Girls	33	91.86	Normal
9+	Boys	62	92.21	Normal
	Girls	32	90.95	Normal
10+	Boys	22	93.65	Normal
	Girls	33	91.73	Normal

Table 12
Mid-Upper Arm Circumference for Age Deficit Classification of the Mali Children

Age (years)	Sex	Mid-upper Arm Circumference N	%	Classification
6+	Boys	48	84.79	Malnutrition
	Girls	47	84.10	Malnutrition
7+	Boys	41	81.60	Malnutrition
	Girls	50	80.22	Morderate Malnutrition
8+	Boys	59	83.67	Morderate Malnutrition
	Girls	33	83.16	Malnutrition
9+	Boys	62	82.37	Malnutrition
	Girls	32	79.78	Morderate Malnutrition
10+	Boys	22	93.15	Normal
	Girls	33	80.00	Malnutrition

Clinical & Nutritional Deficiency Signs

In the present study mainly nine types of nutritional deficiency signs are observed for both boys and girls and have shown in the Table 13. General health of each child has also been recorded using respective grading technique such as very good, good, satisfactory and weak.

General Health

It has been observed from the Table 13 that majority of the children's health for all the ages is seems to be satisfactory but only in the case of 6+ years boys are weak upto 25%. In the above table girls are also showing satisfactory health condition. Children from 6+ years to 10+ years showing very few number are in good health condition. It has been observed from the Table 13 that at the age of 7 + years maximum number of boys are weak whereas at 6+ years maximum number of girls are weak out of total studied 427 children.

Nutritional Deficiency Signs

Pigmentation of Skin

From the Table 13, it has been observed that 72.73% boys have pigmentation on skin at 10+ years of age and 82.25% girls also having pigmentation at 9+ years of age. Higher number of pigmented boys and girls has been seen in the age group 9+ years and 7+ years of age.

Angular Stomatitis

This is a vitamin B-Complex deficiency signs found on both the angles of the mouth. All the 427 children were examined. Out of studied children this deficiency has been recorded only among the boys of 8+ years (8.47%) and among the girls of 7+ years (2%) and 8+ years (6.06 %).

Dry Skin or Scaly Skin

This condition arises generally due to vitamin A deficiency. It has been observed from the Table 13 that the boys of 6+ years shows higher percentages (14.58%) than 6+ years girls (4.26 %) whereas 7 + years girls shows higher percentage (14 %) than the boys of corresponding age.

Discoloured Hair

Most of the studied children shows discoloured hair. Among the girls at 6+ years the percentage of discoloured hair is more (72.34 %) than the boys (31.25 %).

Flag/Coarse Hair

It has been observed from the Table 13 that most of the children are having the hair with rough texture and split ends. Out of total studied 427 children this type of hair can be seen higher (74.6 %) at the age of 8+ years and 6+ years (64.58%) among the boys but among the girls this type of hair is higher (78.1%) only at the age group of 9+ years.

Spongy Bleeding Gum

The spongy bleeding gum has been observed higher (6.25%) in the 6+ years age group boys but among the girls it has been observed very negligible number from the Table 13.

Yellowish Teeth

Almost in all the age-groups the boys and girls shows this yellowish teeth from 6+ years to 10+ years (Table 13). This may be because of dental flourosis or they are not cleaning their teeth properly.

Pale Conjectiva

Out of 427 children except in one girl of 10+ years age, no other children is having this sign from 6+ years through 10+ years boys and girls.

Yellow colour at the base of the nail - This yellow colour at the base of the nail has been observed in all the age groups from 6+ years to 10+ years boys but among the girls it has been observed higher at the age of 7+ years (78%) Table 13.

Impact of Socio-economic Factors on Growth of Children

Cross tabulation of mean value and standard deviation of some selected measurements such as weight, stature, sitting height, bi-acromial breadth and bi-iliac breadth have been done by parity of the children measured, family type, per capital income and literacy level of both parents in order to see the impact of these socio-economic factors on growth of children.

Measurements of Girls and Boys from 6 to 10 Years by Parity

Parity of the child in the present study was considered as pregnancy number of the mother. It has been observed (Table 14) that the third parity child has higher mean value for all the five measurements in case of 6+ years girls and boys. In 7+ years children the higher mean value of stature and weight are observed in girls of first parity; whereas, in case of boys higher values are observed in second and third parity child. Higher mean value of stature(124.61 cm) and weight (20.44 kg.) have been seen in case of 8+ years children where parity is second. For boys higher mean value of stature (121.76 cm) has been observed in case of third parity. In case of 9+ years boys and girls the mean value of stature has been observed higher (126.00cm) in case of fourth parity for girls and second parity in case of boys (125.83 cm). The measurements of boys and girls age 10+ years, it can be observed from the above number of tables that higher mean value of stature can be seen (132.7 cm) for the fourth parity for girls and third parity for boys (132.97 cm). But the weight of the girls child shows higher mean value (22.31 kg.) in case of second parity and for boys the higher mean value shows (24.4kg.) in case of fourth parity.

Measurement of Girls and Boys from 6+ Years to 10+ Years by Family Size

Measurements of boys and girls aged from 6+ years to 10+ years by family size have been shown in Table 15. Higher mean value of weight (15.25 kg.) for girls have been observed where the family size remain 7 to 9 members and of boys higher mean value of weight (15.7 kg.) have been observed where the family size is medium i.e. 4 to 6 members. From the above-mentioned table it can be observed that the higher mean value of weight (17 kg.) where family size is small i.e. 1 to 3 members and same is the case for stature also. Same type of explanation can be seen in case of boys and girls aged 8+ years, 9+ years and in 10+ years of age. Depending on the family size and family income, the children's weight and stature may vary.

Measurements of Girls and Boys Age 6+ Years to 10+ Years by Family Type

The impact of family type i.e. nuclear or joint on five selected measurements of Mali boys and girls have been studied. Mean values of the selected measurements and family type has been tabulated from 6+ years through 10+ years of the boys and girls in Table 16. It has been observed that mean body weight and stature for boys and girls aged 6 and 7 years exhibits almost the same values living in nuclear and joint family. In case of 8+ years through 10+ years the mean weight value is higher (22.68 kg.) among the nuclear family girls but

Table 13
Nutritional Deficiency and Clinical Signs among the Mali Children

Age		6				7				8				9				10				Total			
Sex		M		F		M		F		M		F		M		F		M		F		M		F	
		No.	%	No.	%	No.	%	No.	%	No.	%	No.	%	No.	%	No.	%	No.	%	No.	%	No.	%	No.	%
General Health	Very Good	-	-	-	-	-	-	-	-	-	-	-	-	-	-	-	-	-	-	-	-	-	-	-	-
	Good	3	6.25	2	4.25	1	2.48	2	4.00	[illegible]	1.69	2	6.06	3	4.84	-	-	-	-	-	-	8	3.45	6	3.08
	Satisfactory	33	68.75	23	48.93	32	78.05	30	60.00	45	76.30	24	72.70	41	66.13	26	81.30	15	68.18	23	69.70	166	71.55	126	64.62
	Week	12	25.00	22	46.81	8	19.57	18	36.00	13	22.00	7	21.20	18	29.03	6	18.80	7	31.82	10	30.30	58	25.00	63	32.31
Nutrional Deficiency Signs																									
Pigmenation of Skin/ Patches on Skin	Present	10	20.83	6	12.79	7	17.07	15	30.00	21	35.60	12	36.40	23	37.10	10	31.30	16	72.73	10	30.30	77	33.19	53	27.18
	Absent	38	79.17	41	87.23	34	82.93	35	70.00	33	64.40	21	63.60	39	62.90	22	68.80	6	27.27	23	69.70	155	66.81	142	72.82
Angular Stomatis	Present	-	-	-	-	-	-	1	2.00	5	8.47	2	6.06	-	-	-	-	-	-	-	-	5	2.16	3	1.54
	Absent	48	100.00	47	100.00	41	100.00	49	98.00	54	91.50	31	93.90	62	100.00	32	100.00	22	100.00	33	10.00	227	97.85	192	98.46
Dry/Scaly Skin	Present	7	14.58	2	4.26	3	7.31	7	14.00	1	1.69	2	6.06	2	3.22	2	6.25	1	4.54	1	3.03	14	6.03	14	7.18
	Absent	41	85.41	45	95.74	38	92.68	43	86.00	53	98.90	31	93.90	60	96.77	30	93.80	21	95.45	32	96.97	218	93.97	181	92.82
Discoloured Hair	Present	15	31.25	34	72.34	15	36.59	28	56.00	25	42.40	13	39.40	30	48.39	13	40.60	12	54.55	12	36.36	97	41.81	100	51.28
	Absent	33	68.75	13	27.66	26	63.41	22	44.00	34	57.60	20	60.60	32	51.61	19	59.40	10	45.45	21	63.64	135	58.19	95	48.72
Flag/Coarse Hair	Present	31	64.58	22	46.81	23	56.10	32	64.00	44	74.60	22	66.70	43	69.35	25	78.10	16	72.73	20	60.61	157	67.67	121	62.05
	Absent	17	35.41	25	53.19	18	43.90	18	36.00	15	25.40	11	33.30	19	30.65	7	21.90	6	27.27	13	39.39	75	32.33	74	37.95
Spongy Bleeding of Gums	Present	3	6.25	2	4.26	1	2.44	2	4.00	2	3.39	1	3.03	-	-	-	-	1	4.55	-	-	7	3.02	5	2.56
	Absent	45	93.75	45	95.74	40	97.56	48	96.00	57	96.60	32	97.00	62	100.00	32	100.00	21	95.45	33	100.00	225	96.98	190	97.44
Yellow Colour of Teeth	Present	43	89.58	41	87.23	39	95.12	48	96.00	59	100.00	32	97.00	62	100.00	32	100.00	20	90.91	32	96.97	223	96.12	185	94.87
	Absent	5	10.42	6	12.77	2	4.88	2	4.00	-	-	1	3.03	-	-	-	-	2	9.09	1	3.03	9	3.88	10	5.13
Pale Coniectiva	Present	-	-	-	-	-	-	-	-	-	-	-	-	-	-	-	-	1	4.55	-	-	1	0.43	-	-
	Absent	48	100.00	47	100.00	41	100.00	50	100.00	59	100.00	33	100.00	62	100.00	32	100.00	21	95.45	33	100.00	231	99.57	195	100.00
Yellow Colour of Nail	Present	36	75.00	30	63.83	27	65.85	39	78.00	32	54.20	22	66.70	36	58.06	20	62.50	15	68.18	23	69.70	146	62.93	134	68.72
	Absent	12	25.00	17	36.17	14	34.15	11	22.00	27	45.80	11	33.30	26	41.94	12	37.50	7	31.82	10	30.30	86	37.07	61	31.28
Any Other Deformities of Limbs	Present	-	-	-	-	-	-	-	-	-	-	-	-	-	-	-	-	-	-	-	-	-	-	-	-
	Absent	48	100.00	47	100.00	41	100.00	50	100.00	59	100.00	33	100.00	62	100.00	32	100.00	22	100.00	33	100.00	232		195	

Table 14
Mean and S.D. of a Few Measurements of Mali Children Aged 6 and 10 Years by Parity

		Boys												*Girls*											
	Age	*1*			*2*			*3*			*4 & above*			*1*			*2*			*3*			*4 & above*		
		N	*Mean*	*S.D.*	*N*	*Mean*	*S.D.*	*N*	*Mean*	*S.D.*	*N*	*Mean*	*S.D.*	*N*	*Mean*	*S.D.*	*N*	*Mean*	*S.D.*	*N*	*Mean*	*S.D.*	*N*	*Mean*	*S.D.*
Weight	6	25	16.220	2.363	16	14.688	1.887	3	15.500	2.179	4	15.500	1.915	22	15.114	1.889	14	14.679	2.163	8	16.188	2.375	3	15.500	2.000
	7	18	17.111	2.410	12	17.792	2.291	9	16.556	1.629	2	14.750	3.182	18	17.306	2.669	14	15.507	1.595	12	15.708	2.463	6	17.167	2.041
	8	14	18.714	2.547	18	18.417	2.686	20	19.850	2.710	7	20.071	5.396	11	18.227	2.514	9	20.444	4.164	10	18.360	2.592	3	17.500	2.598
	9	20	21.175	3.392	17	20.324	2.755	18	20.889	2.852	7	20.429	0.732	12	20.375	3.530	11	19.227	3.044	7	18.786	1.680	2	21.250	0.354
	10	2	20.500	0.000	12	23.167	2.949	4	22.375	3.351	4	24.400	0.638	6	21.833	3.920	16	22.313	3.386	7	21.071	1.813	4	21.625	2.394
Stature	6	25	112.908	5.071	16	109.681	3.968	3	112.800	7.804	4	110.600	5.092	22	110.314	4.982	14	109.480	4.050	8	110.988	3.610	3	106.367	6.646
	7	18	115.672	4.266	12	117.275	5.601	9	117.367	5.010	2	116.300	4.243	18	116.028	4.136	14	112.480	7.352	12	113.592	5.418	6	115.850	5.094
	8	14	121.164	4.694	18	121.733	5.826	20	121.765	5.945	7	120.614	8.580	11	120.455	6.716	9	124.610	4.817	10	120.870	3.827	3	122.500	5.456
	9	20	124.920	5.664	17	125.835	5.594	18	124.850	4.895	7	123.200	1.858	12	124.683	6.547	11	122.960	5.174	7	120.443	3.298	2	126.000	4.384
	10	2	129.400	14.850	12	131.900	6.230	4	132.975	6.047	4	128.800	1.435	6	128.783	6.936	16	129.340	7.025	7	127.500	3.771	4	132.700	10.079
Sitting Height	6	25	61.824	5.477	16	60.963	6.650	3	60.367	4.050	4	58.425	0.988	22	59.850	2.999	14	60.479	6.673	8	59.913	2.472	3	59.700	4.484
	7	18	62.578	2.503	12	62.558	3.649	9	63.144	2.788	2	61.550	1.626	18	62.339	3.942	14	61.207	2.088	12	61.000	2.852	6	61.650	3.416
	8	14	65.543	2.583	18	64.961	3.098	20	64.950	3.755	7	64.643	4.833	11	64.864	2.955	9	67.156	3.608	10	64.340	3.058	3	64.833	2.875
	9	20	66.340	3.274	17	66.118	3.029	18	65.828	2.814	7	64.329	1.366	12	65.817	2.554	11	65.300	2.848	7	64.157	2.630	2	66.000	0.566
	10	2	66.850	3.323	12	68.258	3.303	4	68.550	1.652	4	68.725	1.031	6	66.267	3.322	16	67.619	3.674	7	66.514	1.591	4	67.250	2.553
Bi-illiac diameter	6	25	18.040	0.916	16	17.644	1.077	3	18.267	0.777	4	18.000	1.166	22	17.759	1.186	14	17.936	0.997	8	18.038	1.229	3	18.400	0.529
	7	18	18.628	0.848	12	19.067	1.148	9	18.556	1.236	2	19.750	2.051	18	19.089	0.879	14	18.307	1.058	12	18.825	1.121	6	19.400	1.137
	8	14	19.257	1.612	18	19.628	0.966	20	19.910	1.100	7	19.243	1.890	11	19.082	1.336	9	19.856	1.699	10	20.100	1.423	3	19.533	1.620
	9	20	20.045	1.445	17	20.153	1.213	18	20.078	1.535	7	20.757	0.655	12	20.442	1.268	11	19.400	1.210	7	19.814	1.189	2	20.800	0.566
	10	2	21.000	1.131	12	21.200	0.995	4	21.425	1.179	4	22.100	0.860	6	21.033	1.966	16	21.300	1.383	7	21.257	0.929	4	20.900	1.421
Biacromial diameter	6	25	24.084	1.252	16	23.525	1.019	3	24.600	1.637	4	23.975	2.066	22	23.136	1.510	14	23.943	1.071	8	23.588	2.283	3	23.933	1.686
	7	18	24.889	1.632	12	25.300	1.127	9	25.033	1.216	2	25.800	0.849	18	25.089	1.348	14	23.529	1.354	12	24.275	1.226	6	25.417	1.137
	8	14	25.821	1.486	18	26.233	1.683	20	26.155	1.309	7	25.200	2.710	11	25.400	1.362	9	26.733	2.203	10	25.750	0.753	3	25.167	0.945
	9	20	26.645	1.160	17	26.876	1.581	18	26.600	1.428	7	26.986	0.895	12	26.342	1.133	11	25.264	1.220	7	25.600	1.369	2	28.000	0.566
	10	2	26.850	2.051	12	27.883	1.432	4	27.725	0.685	4	27.900	1.010	6	27.217	1.048	16	27.619	1.489	7	27.514	1.071	4	27.376	1.486

Table 15

Mean and S.D. of A Few Measurements of Mali Children Aged 6 and 10 Years by Family Size

		Boys												Girls											
	Age	1 to 3			4 to 6			7 to 9			10>			1 to 3			4 to 6			7 to 9			10>		
		N	Mean	S.D.	N	Mean	S.D.	N	Mean	S.D.	N	Mean	S.D.	N	Mean	S.D.	N	Mean	S.D.	N	Mean	S.D.	N	Mean	S.D.
		N	Mean	S.D.	N	Mean	S.D.	N	Mean	S.D.	N	Mean	S.D.	N	Mean	S.D.	N	Mean	S.D.	N	Mean	S.D.	N	Mean	S.D.
Weight	6	4	15.250	1.250	40	15.700	2.356	3	15.333	1.528	1	14.000	-	1	13.000	-	32	15.281	1.892	12	15.250	2.527	2	14.500	2.828
	7	3	17.667	3.753	31	17.097	2.027	4	16.375	3.945	3	17.167	1.756	2	17.000	2.828	40	16.513	2.355	6	15.500	0.775	1	12.500	-
	8	0	-	-	48	19.240	3.196	9	18.500	2.761	2	20.500	0.707	3	19.333	4.041	22	18.527	3.167	7	19.571	3.168	2	16.500	2.121
	9	4	22.375	3.816	48	20.260	2.447	6	22.750	4.356	4	22.375	2.056	1	15.000	-	24	19.854	2.917	6	20.250	2.752	1	17.000	-
	10	1	25.000		20	22.880	2.794	1	23.500	-	0	-	-	0	-	-	27	22.130	3.164	4	20.875	2.780	2	20.500	0.707
Stature	6	4	113.525	2.018	40	111.635	5.142	3	111.567	4.798	1	104.200	-	1	109.400	-	32	109.663	4.356	12	110.650	5.702	2	110.100	3.536
	7	3	121.133	5.460	31	116.835	4.108	4	114.975	7.223	3	111.033	2.274	2	105.250	20.435	40	115.343	4.258	6	110.600	3.493	1	110.500	-
	8	0	-	-	48	121.390	5.993	9	120.978	5.437	2	125.800	4.667	3	122.367	4.206	22	122.473	5.611	7	121.286	4.180	2	115.250	6.435
	9	4	125.725	5.726	48	124.285	4.831	6	127.533	6.331	4	128.375	4.724	1	118.300	-	24	123.554	6.024	6	122.517	3.193	1	125.200	-
	10	1	132.500	-	20	131.370	6.502	1	128.800	-	0	-	-	0	-	-	27	128.896	6.301	4	132.800	10.041	2	127.050	6.576
Sitting Height	6	4	60.300	2.237	40	61.355	5.957	3	61.000	4.454	1	57.400	-	1	59.400	-	32	60.000	4.843	12	60.242	3.132	2	59.750	4.313
	7	3	64.933	2.871	31	62.623	2.837	4	62.875	2.748	3	60.300	2.193	2	62.300	4.950	40	61.838	3.025	6	59.483	2.778	1	59.000	-
	8	0	-	-	48	65.019	3.506	9	64.911	2.817	2	66.650	4.031	3	65.100	2.722	22	65.750	3.350	7	64.714	2.633	2	62.050	4.455
	9	4	67.875	3.235	48	65.590	2.740	6	66.317	4.198	4	67.075	2.518	1	63.100	-	24	65.308	2.504	6	65.100	3.191	1	68.100	-
	10	1	69.200	-	20	68.145	2.754	1	69.800	-	0	66.800	-	0	-	-	27	67.019	3.234	4	67.750	2.049	2	-	4.101
Bi-iliac diameter	6	4	17.700	0.406	40	17.970	1.048	3	17.667	0.569	1	17.500	-	1	17.500	-	32	17.753	1.103	12	18.308	1.115	2	18.000	0.849
	7	3	19.733	1.332	31	18.819	1.005	4	18.600	1.479	3	17.867	0.723	2	18.400	1.414	40	18.923	1.049	6	18.717	0.778	1	16.500	-
	8	0	-	-	48	19.552	1.337	9	19.633	1.297	2	20.300	0.000	3	20.333	0.862	22	19.782	1.439	7	18.971	1.650	2	19.300	1.980
	9	4	20.400	1.512	48	20.119	1.277	6	20.117	1.854	4	20.550	1.537	1	19.400	-	24	19.904	1.384	6	20.167	0.821	1	20.900	-
	10	1	20.500	-	20	21.375	1.007	1	22.500	-	0	21.250	-	0	-	-	27	21.307	1.326	4	20.400	1.913	2	-	0.636
Biacromial diameter	6	4	24.175	0.988	40	23.908	1.351	3	23.933	0.379	1	23.400	-	1	22.400	-	32	23.266	1.435	12	24.342	1.783	2	22.850	0.354
	7	3	25.233	1.677	31	25.245	1.305	4	24.500	1.824	3	24.067	1.002	2	25.100	3.536	40	24.545	1.347	6	24.250	1.408	1	22.200	-
	8	0	-	-	48	26.027	1.753	9	25.622	1.283	2	26.650	0.354	3	26.767	1.692	22	26.086	1.520	7	25.214	0.701	2	23.600	1.414
	9	4	27.325	1.307	48	26.825	1.261	6	25.933	1.558	4	26.250	1.597	1	24.900	-	24	25.796	1.447	6	26.400	1.008	1	26.800	-
	10	1	27.500	-	20	27.790	1.318	1	27.500	-	0	27.050	-	0	-	-	27	27.589	1.323	4	27.075	1.387	2	-	0.636

Table 16
Mean and S.D. of a Few Measurements of Mali Children Aged 6 and 10 Years by Family Type

		Boys						*Girls*					
		Nuclear			*Joint*			*Nuclear*			*Joint*		
	Age	*N*	*Mean*	*S.D.*	*N*	*Mean*	*S.D.*	*N*	*Mean*	*S.D.*	*N*	*Mean*	*S.D.*
Weight	6	28	15.375	2.150	20	15.925	2.324	24	15.188	2.004	23	15.196	2.162
	7	23	17.043	1.858	18	17.111	2.779	32	16.547	2.333	18	16.222	2.481
	8	38	19.211	3.308	21	19.095	2.686	18	18.894	3.590	15	18.700	2.555
	9	18	21.444	3.548	44	20.500	2.478	14	19.393	2.536	18	19.917	3.251
	10	4	20.750	3.797	18	23.506	2.232	22	22.682	3.107	11	20.273	2.195
Stature	6	28	111.239	5.121	20	112.185	4.836	24	110.208	4.342	23	109.635	4.906
	7	23	117.104	4.289	18	115.828	5.304	32	114.838	6.195	18	113.700	4.612
	8	38	121.255	5.858	21	121.876	5.964	18	122.294	5.942	15	121.427	4.800
	9	18	125.789	5.631	44	124.616	4.863	14	123.729	5.492	18	122.872	5.539
	10	4	130.150	8.985	18	131.561	5.752	22	129.536	6.083	11	128.700	8.118
Sitting Height	6	28	61.743	6.818	20	60.360	3.117	24	60.446	5.311	23	59.613	2.998
	7	23	62.426	2.840	18	62.928	2.897	32	61.950	3.224	18	61.028	2.999
	8	38	65.137	3.536	21	64.914	3.159	18	65.411	3.466	15	65.227	3.055
	9	18	65.794	3.126	44	65.948	2.861	14	65.529	2.661	18	65.100	2.596
	10	4	66.875	3.876	18	68.578	2.340	22	67.736	2.706	11	65.809	3.499
Bi-illiac diameter	6	28	17.836	0.963	20	18.035	0.980	24	17.796	1.020	23	18.009	1.177
	7	23	19.057	1.066	18	18.461	1.037	32	18.841	1.049	18	18.850	1.107
	8	38	19.550	1.445	21	19.662	1.028	18	19.983	1.585	15	19.233	1.285
	9	18	19.850	1.446	44	20.293	1.282	14	19.900	0.826	18	20.022	1.533
	10	4	21.025	1.223	18	21.467	0.976	22	21.541	1.264	11	20.500	1.360
Biacromial diameter	6	28	23.754	1.264	20	24.155	1.275	24	23.392	1.280	23	23.622	1.821
	7	23	25.213	1.163	18	24.922	1.599	32	24.459	1.527	18	24.561	1.339
	8	38	25.989	1.694	21	25.981	1.638	18	26.083	1.098	15	25.567	1.934
	9	18	26.328	1.399	44	26.900	1.265	14	26.057	1.233	18	25.800	1.465
	10	4	27.375	2.294	18	27.850	0.989	22	27.636	1.346	11	27.209	1.167

the mean weight is higher (23.50 kg.) among the 10+ years boys of joint family and when other measurements compared the same situation was prevailed. The children of joint family type show the higher mean values.

Mean Measurements of Boys and Girls by Per-capita Income

All the five measurements mean values of boys and girls have been exhibited with per capita income of the family and presented in Table 17. It has been observed from the above table that 6+ girls and boys shows higher mean value of weight (16.05 kg.) where per capita range is more than 10 thousands and the stature also shows the higher mean value in this range for both boys and girls. At 7 + years of age both boys and girls shows higher mean of weight (17.75 kg. and 17.85 kg. respectively) where more than ten thousand per capita income range exists. The stature also shows the same sequences as above. It has been observed from the above mentioned tables that the mean values of weight and stature of both boys and girls are higher in the category per capita income is ten thousand and above per annum. The mean value of stature is (132.68 cm) for the 10+ girls in the ten thousand per capita income range but for boys the same mean values shows in the different income range.

Mean Measurement of Boys and Girls by Parent's Literacy Level

The mean measurements of boys and girls by their parent's literacy level has been cross-tabulated in Table 18. this has been observed that weight and stature and other three measurements are higher among the boys and girls of 6+ years where father literate and mother illiterate than both parents literate. But for 7+ years boys and girls the weight and stature is higher where both parents are literate than other three categories, like both parents illiterate, father illiterate and mother literate, father literate and mother illiterate. Among the 8+ years boys and girls (Table 18) it has been observed that girls shows higher mean weight (24 kg.) where both parents are illiterate than other three categories. Girls and boys of both parents where literate were not shows remarkable weight or stature or other three measurements. At the age of 9+ years (Table 18) it has been seen that boys shows higher mean of weight (23 kg.) and higher mean of stature where father illiterate and mother literate than other three categories but in this age group girl sample is having father illiterate and mother literate. In Table-18 the 10+ years boys and girls, mean values of different measurements has been categorized according to parent's educational level. There were no studied girls having both parents illiterate and only one boy was having both parents illiterate. Mean value of weight and stature is higher both among boys and girls where father illiterate and mother literate than other two categories.

Table 17
Mean and S.d. of a Few Measurements of Mali Children Aged 6 and 10 Years by Income Per Annum

		Boys									*Girls*								
		<Rs. 5000			*Rs. 5000-10000*			*Rs. 10000>*			*<Rs. 5000*			*Rs. 5000-10000*			*Rs. 10000>*		
	Age	*N*	*Mean*	*S.D.*	*N*	*Mean*	*S.D.*	*N*	*Mean*	*S.D.*	*N*	*Mean*	*S.D.*	*N*	*Mean*	*S.D.*	*N*	*Mean*	*S.D.*
Biacromial	6	18	23.822	1.368	14	24.236	1.125	16	23.756	1.301	15	23.280	1.747	22	23.655	0.941	10	23.510	2.127
Diameter	7	17	25.235	1.116	17	25.006	1.579	7	24.914	1.504	25	24.276	1.040	21	24.357	1.676	4	26.600	0.688
(in cm.)	8	23	25.839	1.508	28	25.979	1.748	8	25.438	1.897	11	25.500	1.725	18	26.100	1.493	4	25.675	1.261
	9	23	26.235	1.094	25	26.788	1.307	14	27.457	1.409	16	25.894	1.468	11	25.955	1.255	5	25.880	1.475
	10	10	27.720	1.552	8	27.450	0.974	4	28.500	0.787	18	27.522	1.119	9	27.044	1.185	6	28.083	1.821
Bi-lliac	6	18	17.683	1.030	14	18.057	0.853	16	18.063	0.923	15	17.447	1.190	22	18.118	8.276	10	18.100	1.304
Diameter	7	17	18.924	0.871	17	18.500	1.058	7	19.200	1.522	25	18.844	0.810	21	18.767	1.379	4	19.250	0.370
(in cm.)	8	23	19.435	1.192	28	19.646	1.532	8	19.838	0.630	11	19.909	1.662	18	19.544	1.482	4	19.350	1.179
	9	23	19.722	1.173	25	20.340	1.214	14	20.579	1.660	16	19.988	1.597	11	19.991	0.955	5	19.860	0.611
	10	10	21.180	1.098	8	21.563	1.035	4	21.550	0.850	18	21.306	1.397	9	20.911	1.069	6	21.283	1.826
Sitting	6	18	60.233	6.205	14	62.714	5.395	16	60.850	3.071	15	59.387	3.202	22	60.400	1.093	10	60.220	3.169
Height	7	17	61.847	2.759	17	62.947	2.654	7	63.857	3.304	25	60.752	2.550	21	62.171	3.338	4	64.125	4.312
(in cm.)	8	23	64.970	3.683	28	64.975	3.240	8	65.850	3.346	11	65.000	3.085	18	65.411	3.541	4	26.438	2.852
	9	23	65.261	2.309	25	66.304	2.511	14	66.243	4.247	16	66.100	2.539	11	64.164	2.311	5	65.160	2.887
	10	10	68.490	3.356	8	68.638	1.773	4	66.975	2.307	18	67.511	2.702	9	65.244	2.205	6	68.617	4.302
Stature	6	18	109.878	4.513	14	112.307	4.556	16	113.019	4.700	15	109.300	4.459	22	109.795	6.632	10	111.160	5.072
(in cm.)	7	17	116.329	4.024	17	116.318	4.271	7	117.614	7.515	25	113.380	3.922	21	114.952	7.403	4	118.225	1.837
	8	23	121.283	6.388	28	121.243	5.296	8	122.850	6.693	11	120.873	6.865	18	122.689	4.747	4	121.175	4.066
	9	23	123.109	4.765	25	126.140	3.995	14	125.879	6.594	16	124.413	5.666	11	122.209	3.931	5	121.800	7.734
	10	10	131.080	6.699	8	131.563	7.067	4	131.350	4.340	18	129.850	6.898	9	125.789	4.911	6	132.683	7.134
Weight	6	18	14.861	1.805	14	16.000	1.687	16	16.094	2.653	15	15.167	2.241	22	14.818	5.298	10	16.050	2.466
(in kg.)	7	17	16.765	1.863	17	17.059	1.895	7	17.857	3.837	25	15.980	1.534	21	17.071	3.018	4	17.750	1.443
	8	23	18.783	2.615	28	19.518	3.409	8	19.063	3.343	11	18.545	2.454	18	19.172	3.724	4	17.875	1.652
	9	23	20.043	2.359	25	20.820	2.371	14	21.893	3.943	16	20.750	3.114	11	18.545	2.127	5	18.800	3.094
	10	10	23.350	2.698	8	23.013	2.923	4	22.125	2.780	18	22.028	3.151	9	21.167	2.512	6	22.500	3.661

Table 18

Mean and S.D. of a Few Measurements of Mali Children Aged 6 and 10 Years by Literacy of Parents

		Boys												Girls											
		Both parents literate			*Fa.illiterate & Mo. literate*			*Fa. Literate & Mo.illiterate*			*Both perents illiterate*			*Both perents lliterate*			*Fa.illiterate & Mo. literate*			*Fa. Literate & Mo.illiterate*			*Both perents illiterate*		
	Age	*N*	*Mean*	*S.D.*	*N*	*Mean*	*S.D.*	*N*	*Mean*	*S.D.*	*N*	*Mean*	*S.D.*	*N*	*Mean*	*S.D.*	*N*	*Mean*	*S.D.*	*N*	*Mean*	*S.D.*	*N*	*Mean*	*S.D.*
Weight	6	2	16.75	0.36	2	13.25	1.06	2	18.50	2.121	42	15.524	2.178	1	13.50		2	13.00		1	15.00		43	15.34	2.08
	7	-	-	-	1	16		5	16.10	1.432	35	17.243	2.378	4	15.63	1.44	2	14.75	0.35	3	15.67	1.61	41	16.65	2.51
	8	1	19	-	1	19		2	21.50		55	19.291	3.363	1	24.00		1	20.00		1	20.50		30	18.54	3.09
	9	3	20	3.78	3	23	4.36	4	20.50	2.887	52	20.500	2.578	1	21.00		0	0.00		1	18.00		30	19.70	3.00
	10	1	22		3	24.33	2.08	1	23.00		17	22.829	2.93		0.00		3	21.50	3.04	1	17.50		29	22.07	3.01
Stature	6	2	113.8	2.33	2	111	2.4	2	118.10	9.051	42	111.255	4.865	1	180.00		2	108.15	1.77	1	112.40		43	110.00	4.75
	7	-	-		1	114.2		5	113.90	2.575	35	116.989	4.928	4	113.48	1.71	2	99.75	12.7	3	112.83	2.58	41	115.35	4.76
	8	1	120.7		1	124.7		2	125.50	1.7	55	121.673	6.433	1	122.80		1	122.10		1	127.80		30	121.67	5.55
	9	3	121.1	8.65	3	125.8	6.76	4	124.98	6.8	52	124.719	4.417	1	129.10					1	116.60		30	123.27	5.39
	10	1	126.9		3	135.2	8.23	1	133.30		17	130.765	6.137				3	127.33	10.2	1	124.90		29	129.61	6.55
Sitting Height	6	2	59.96	1.91	2	59.5	0.99	2	62.85	4.596	42	61.219	5.89	1	57.40		2	59.65	0.35	1	61.30		43	60.09	4.49
	7	-	-		1	62.9		5	59.94	2.317	35	63.026	2.762	4	60.28	2.7	2	57.90	1.27	3	61.73	1	41	61.92	3.24
	8	1	65.5		1	64.2		2	67.30	3.68	55	65.140	3.607	1	67.70		1	64.00		1	67.90		30	65.21	3.33
	9	3	64.38	4.83	3	67.8	3.62	4	65.38	2.478	52	65.758	2.646	1	65.60		0	0.00		1	61.90		30	65.39	2.60
	10	1	66.9		3	70	4.36	1	69.70		17	67.959	2.439		0.00		3	66.50	2.03	1	61.70		29	67.34	3.07
Bi-illiac diameter	6	2	18.3	1.27	2	17.9	0.71	2	18.36	0.212	42	17.881	1.011	1	18.40		2	17.65	0.21	1	19.20		43	17.87	1.12
	7				1	17.9		5	18.82	1.128	35	18.817	1.097	4	19.48	0.79	2	17.90	0.71	3	18.73	0.23	41	18.84	1.11
	8	1	20.5		1	20.2		2	20.60	1.13	55	19.605	1.438	1	20.80		1	21.10		1	21.40		30	19.50	1.48
	9	3	20.1	2	3	20.93	1.5	4	20.43	0.785	52	20.019	1.257	1	21.20			0.00		1	18.50		30	19.98	1.25
	10	1	20.2		3	20.83	0.58	1	22.50		17	21.488	1.028				3	21.30	1.15	1	21.40		29	21.18	1.43
Biacoromial diamiter	6	2	24.75	2.05	2	24.05	2.33	2	24.55	0.495	42	23.845	1.245	1	23.30		2	22.35	0.07	1	23.40		43	23.57	1.61
	7	-			1	25.1		5	24.96	1.558	35	25.103	1.375	4	24.65	1.03	2	23.90	1.84	3	23.80	0.56	41	24.56	1.53
	8	1	26.4		1	28.1		2	26.00	0.14	55	26.036	1.81	1	25.30		1	27.20		1	25.50		30	25.83	1.58
	9	3	26.9	0.5	3	27.6	1.15	4	25.75	0.289	52	25.648	1.271	1	28.40					1	25.40		30	25.85	1.32
	10	1	27.6		3	28.4	1.31	1	27.90		17	27.653	1.329				3	27.67	1.12	1	26.90		29	27.50	1.34

So, from the above mentioned cross-tables it can be summarized that not only education of the parents are necessary for the healthy children but their socio-economic condition also is equally important for the children's growth and development.

Summary and Conclusion

The children from Nagar Parishad Primary Schools represents the low socio-economic group; and the children from public schools were from the high socio-economic group, and it is observed that the pattern of growth among the children belonging to different socio-economic groups is different. It has been found from the data that the differences in standard of living causes differences in height and weight among the children. It has been observed that the mean values of the selected measurements are gradually increases with the advancement of ages through these, growing children shares the common environment in the district and habituated with the same type of food habits.

It has been further seen that the girls were shorter and lighter than boys and boys had a broad chest and a large head circumference. The boys are taller than girls at all ages. At 9+ years of age weight and height started decreasing up to 10+ years or up to 11 years among the girls. From 6+ year to 10+ years there were sex differences in the mean values 1 cm. to 2 cm. In the age group 8+ years the boys were heavier and taller than the girls.

The growth is gradual with the advancement of ages from 6+ years to 10+ years. The differential growth rate has been evident from the velocity curve among boys and girls through time in various body dimensions and this analysis has been confirmed by the nature of distance curve and velocity curve. It has been also observed that after 9+ years the rate of increment is gradually decreased with the change of age which indicates that the growth is approaching towards maturity and negative values with respect to certain anthropometric traits in some age groups might have been because the data is cross-sectional. The similar trend has also supported by Sharma, 1992.

During the past two decades there is an improvement in socio-economic condition because of increase in family income and parental educational levels. This may have influenced in the improvement in child's nutrition and now the children growth patterns shows a positive trend. The Mali children also shows improvement in their health and growth according to their parent's economic conditions and educational levels.

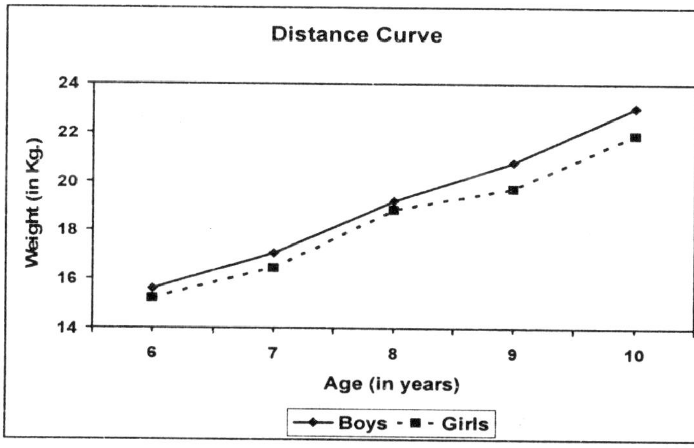

Fig. 1

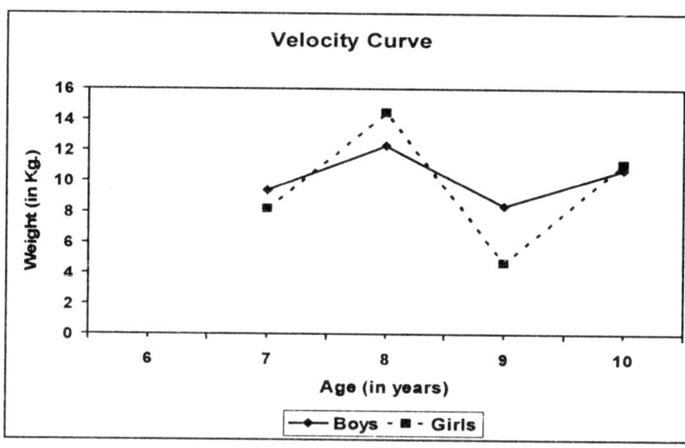

Fig. 2

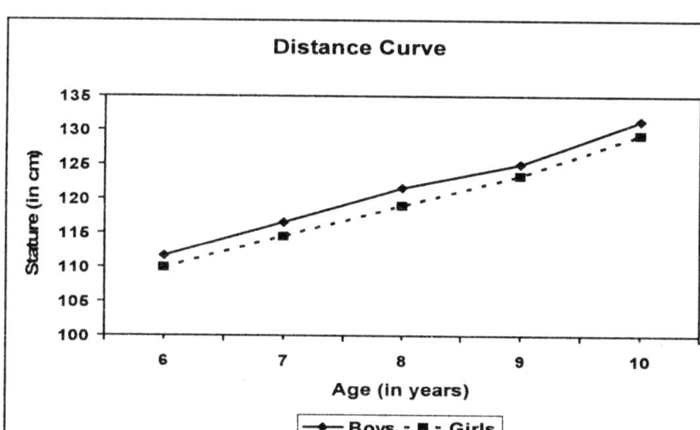

Fig. 3

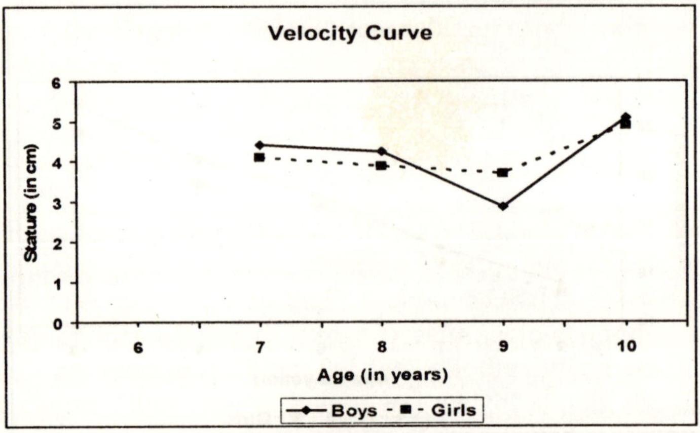

Fig. 4

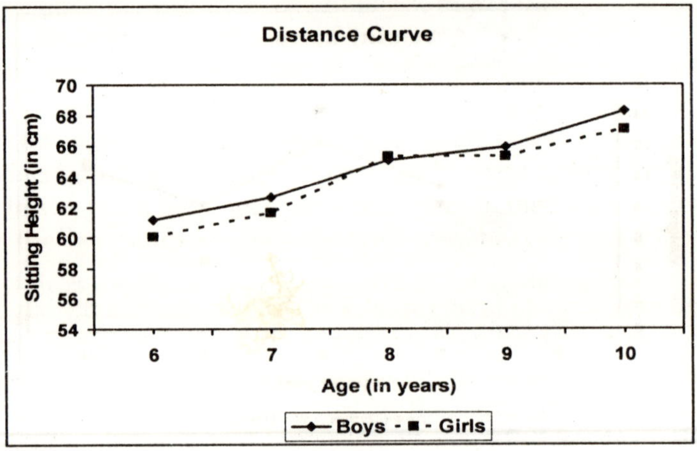

Fig. 5

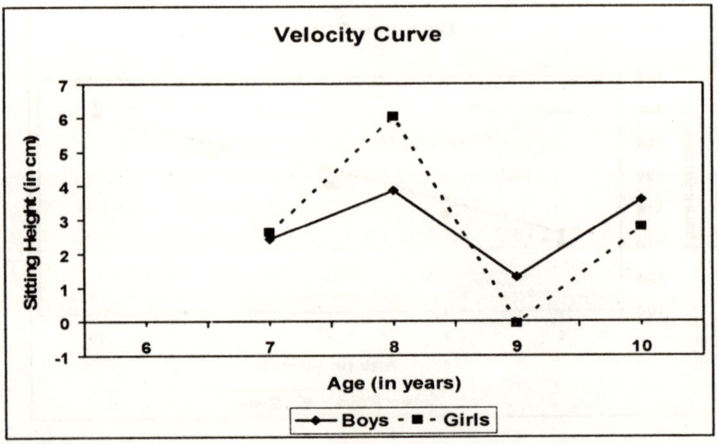

Fig. 6

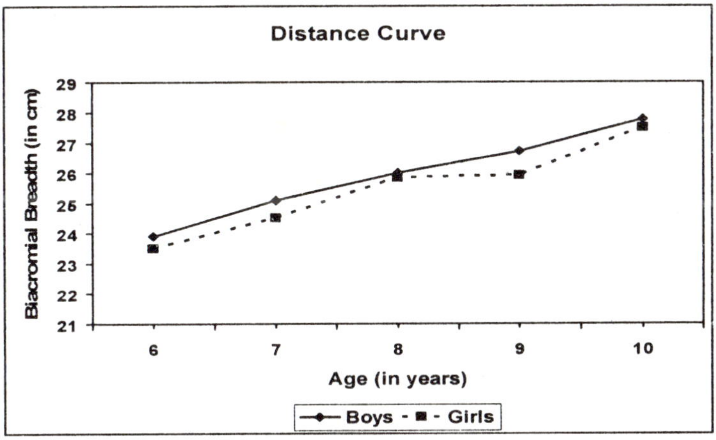

Fig. 7

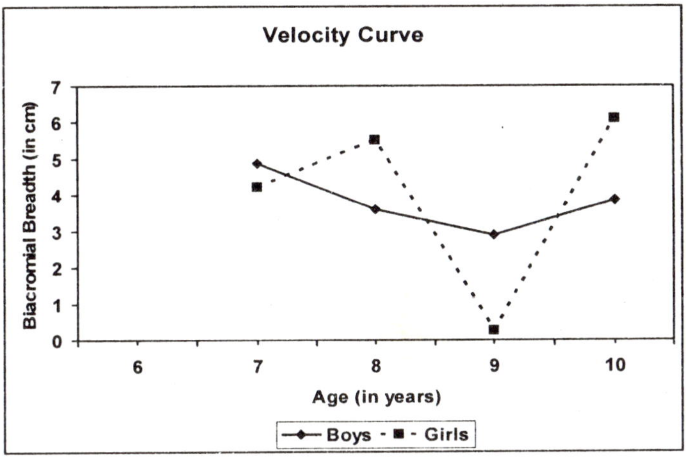

Fig. 8

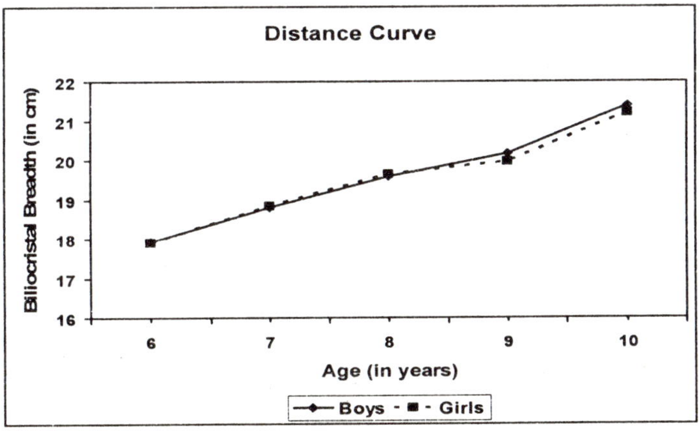

Fig. 9

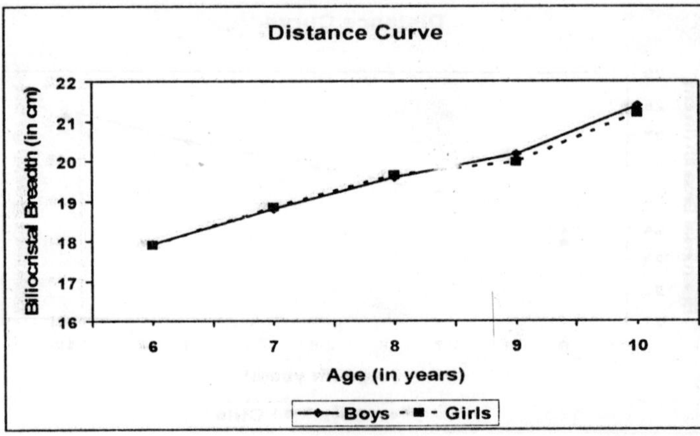

Fig. 10

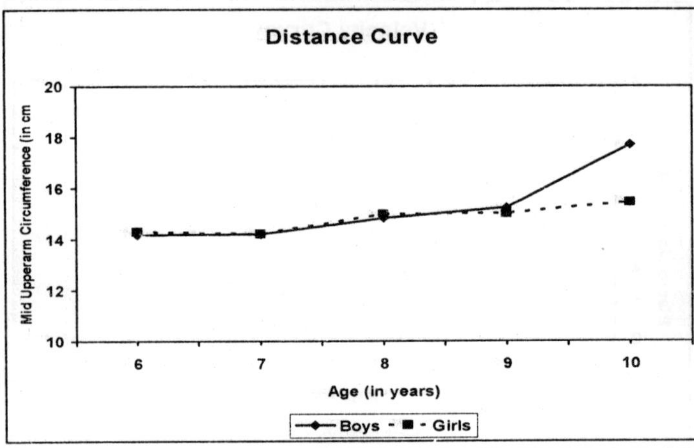

Fig. 11

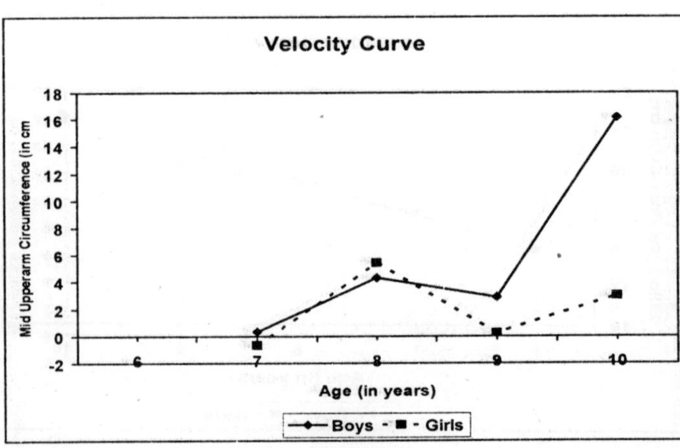

Fig. 12

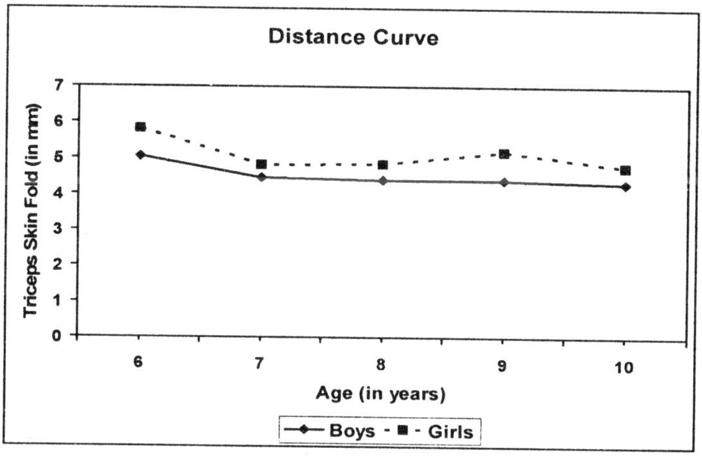

Fig. 13

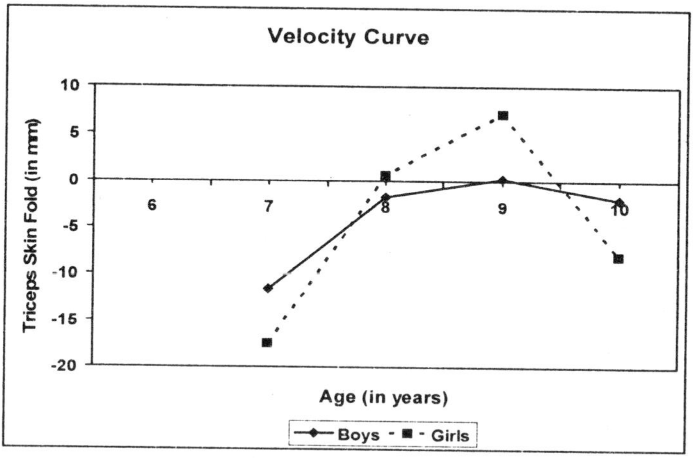

Fig. 14

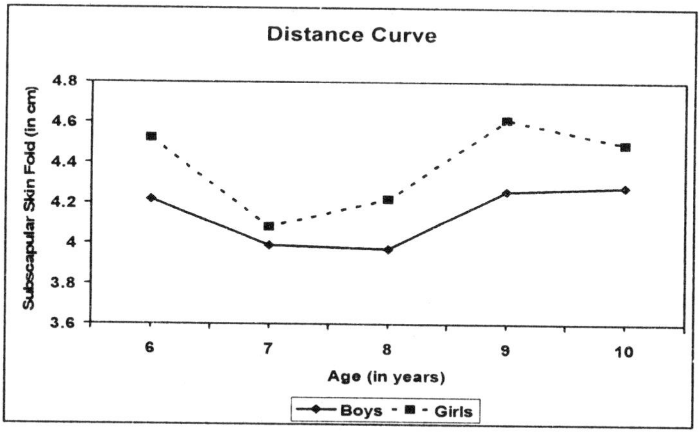

Fig. 15

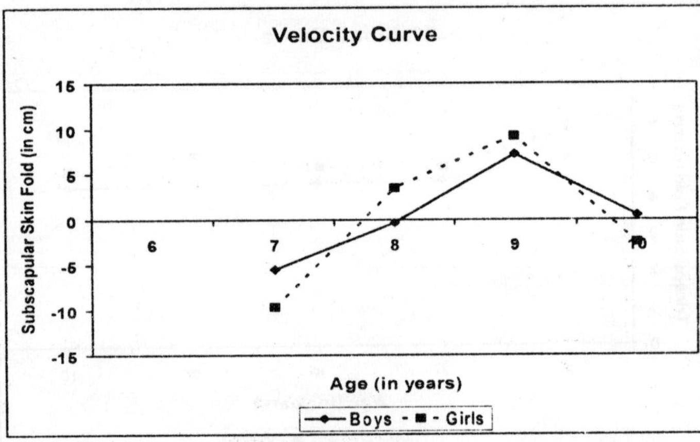

Fig. 16

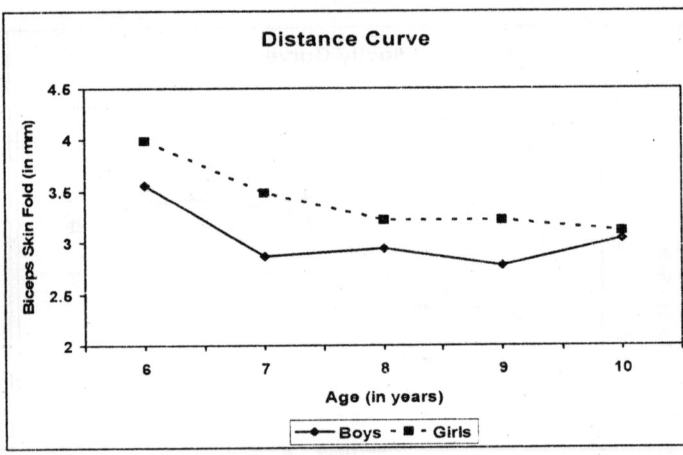

Fig. 17

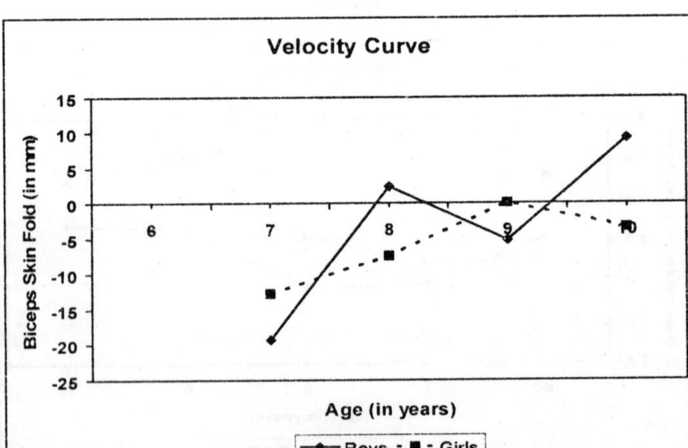

Fig. 18

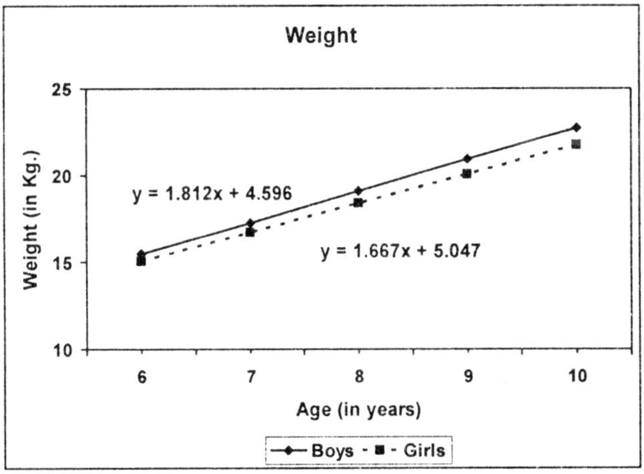

Fig. 19

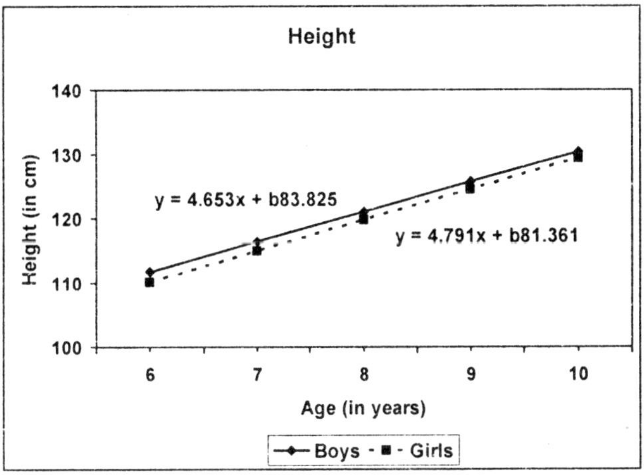

Fig. 20

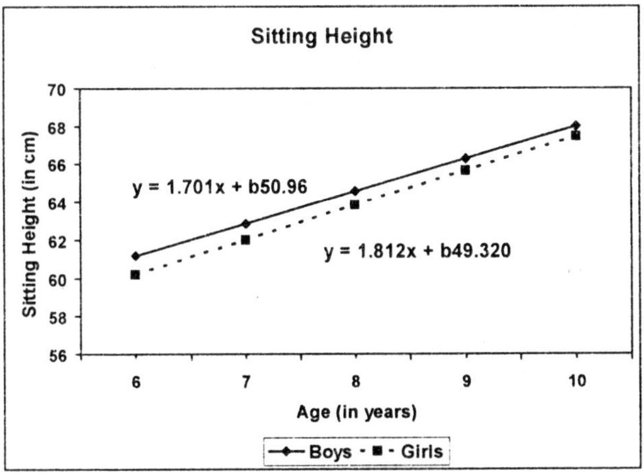

Fig. 21

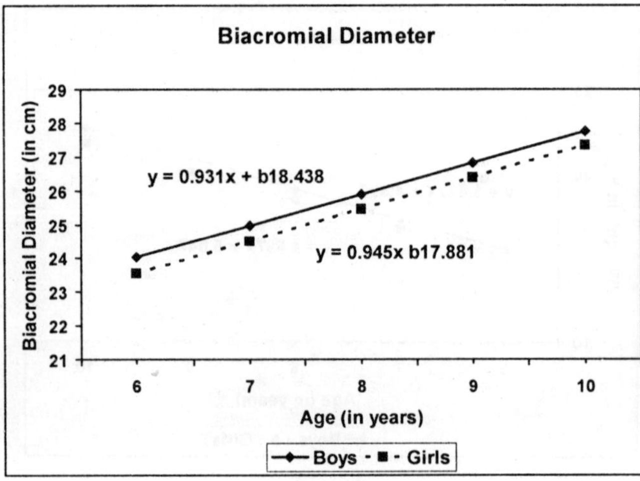

Fig. 22

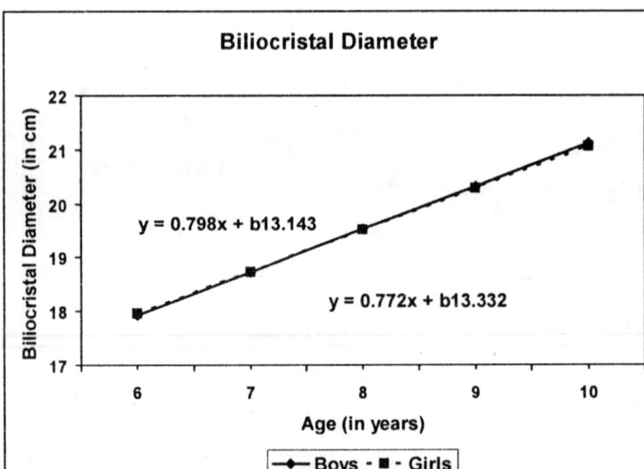

Fig. 23

References

Bhowmik, D.C. (1993), A Cross-sectional Growth Study of the School Children of Midnapur, Published by Director, Anthropological Survey of India, Government of India, Calcutta.

Census of India (1991), District Census Hand Book. Nagpur, Series 14; Part-XII A & B Government of India.

Eveleth, P. B. and J. M. Tanner (1990), Worldwide Variation in Human Growth, 2nd Edition, Cambridge, Cambridge University Press.

Jelliffe, D.B. (1966), The Assessment of the Nutritional Status of the Community, WHO Monograph Series No. 53, Geneva:WHO.

Karve, I. (1948), Anthropometric Measurements of the Marathas. Poona, Deccan College, Post Graduate Research Institute.

Kaul, S.S. (1990), Ecology, Growth and Nutritional Status, New Delhi, Ashish Publishing House.

Latham, M. (1979), Human Nutrition in Tropical Africa, 2nd ed. Rome: FAO.

Majumdar, D.N. and S. Bahadur (1951), Anthropological Study of Growth Among School Children in Lucknow, *Eastern Anthropologist*, Vol. 5, No. 1, pp. 1-26.

Mahalnobis, P.C. and D.N. Majumdar (1949), Anthropometric Survey of Uttar Pradesh, Sankhya, 9, pp. 90-324.

Martin, R. and K. Saller (1957), Lehrbuch der Anthropologie. Gustav Fischer, Jena.

Mukherjee, R. (1963), Socio-economic Factors in Children's Development, *Jl. of Med. Res.*, 1 &2: pp. 21-38.

Phadke, M.V. (1968), Growth Norms in Indian Children, *Indian Jl. Med. Res.*, 56: pp. 850-57.

Risley, H.H. (1891), The Tribes and Castes of Bengal, Calcutta: Firma, K.L. Mukhopadhyay.

Russel & Hiralal (1975), *Tribe and Caste of Central Province*, Vol. IV, New Delhi, Cosmo Publications.

Sharma, J. C. (1992), Human Growth and Assessment of Nutritional Status. In A. Mahajan & S. Nath (Ed.) Application Areas of Anthropology, Pp. 129-152, Delhi, Reliance Publising Co.

9

GROWTH AND DEVELOPMENT OF MALA CHILDREN OF EAST GODAVARI DISTRICT OF ANDHRA PRADESH: BIO-CULTURAL PERSPECTIVES

Yaseen Saheb S. & G.V. Ramana

Many researchers have tried to enumerate the trends of growth under different situations in India (Singh 1980, ICMR 1972, Nath 1982, Sharma 1971 and 1991, Nath *et. al.* 1991, Rao and Busi, 1993, 1994 and Rao, Vani & Busi, 1997, Rao & Vani, 1997, Kapoor and Kapoor 1991, Injeti & Ranganayaki, 1978. However there is a dearth of published material on the growth and development of scheduled castes and the Indian Council of Medical Research (1972) in their nation wide growth survey did not include the Mala/Adi Andhra of East Godavari district in Andhra Pradesh. A cross sectional study on growth and development of Mala children was therefore undertaken during December 1999 to February 2000, with the aim to study the pattern of growth and development of children in terms of 14 anthropometric variables to evaluate the extent of malnutrition among the children, to find out the prevalence of common nutritional deficiency signs, to evaluate the growth pattern of the children in terms of their socio-economic background such as per capita income and its impact on the occurrence of infectious diseases and to study the differential rate of growth in rural setting. This study is a part of the ninth plan national project "Growth and Development of children : Bio-cultural perspective" launched by Anthropological Survey of India.

The present study on the Mala was carried out in the rural areas of East Godavari district, Andhra Pradesh. The Mala is the second largest scheduled caste and they are concentrated in the coastal districts of East Godavari, West Godavari, Nellore, Guntur, Krishna etc. East Godavari district is situated on the coramondal coast and is bounded on the north east by Visakhapatnam and on the south west by West Godavari district. The total Mala population in the state according to 1981 census was 28,96,642 while in East Godavari they number around 1,55,096 and 3,52,445 under Mala and Adi Andhra groups respectively. The major scheduled castes in the district are Adi Andhra, Mala and Madiga. East Godavari district is closely associated with the river Godavari. The climate of this district is characterized by high humidity throughout the year.

Generally the Mala hamlets are segregated from the main village and their hamlets are locally called 'Mala palle'. A number of houses are built with country tiles, while some are thatched houses with palmyra leaves. Their staple food is rice. They are non-vegetarians. They take milk and milk products occasionally. Their mother tongue is Telugu. Earlier ethnographers like Thurston (1909), Hassan (1920) delineated that Mala are divided into a number of subgroups like Sarindla, Charu, Reddi Bhumi, Pakanati, Poknati, Rampala, Mala Desari etc. Some of these groups are territorial, while others are occupational and servicing communities. Erugula, Saladi, Allampalli, Binepu, Pilla, Gaddam etc., are some of their surnames which regulate their marriage alliances. The Mala are patriarchal and they prefer neolocal residence. The inheritance of property is patrilineal. They follow equigeniture principle. Most of the Mala families are nuclear. They are economically poor and most of them are agricultural labourers and a few are in government and private services.

Material and Method

The present study, a cross sectional one, was carried out among the Mala-Adi Andhra School Children, because of easy accessibilityand availability of exact or approximate date of birth of the child from school admission registers or teachers. The Mala Adi Andhra was selected for investigation based on their numerical strength (1981 census) also of their dominant status among the scheduled castes in Andhra Pradesh. The data were collected applying standard techniques and recorded in prescribed schedules. Anthropometric measurements on Mala children were taken during the school hours, adopting standard procedure cited in Weiner and Lourie (1969) and Singh and Bhasin (1968). The subjects were selected by sampling techniques from different schools and villages. Care was taken to exclude the physically handicapped child. The present study was carried out in rural areas of coastal Andhra Pradesh on 453 school children comprising 214 boys and 239 girls aged between 6 years to 10 years on whom 14 anthropometric measurements and clinical observations were recorded. In every age group of above 6 years age, a minimum of 40 subjects of each sex were selected for anthropometric measurements. In order to obtain the above sample, the Mala-Adi Andhra children were selected from different schools spread over in three rural mandals of East Godavari district namely, Kakinada rural Mandal, Samlkota Mandal and Rajahmundry mandal.

Results and Discussion

Socio-Cultural Background

There are always interactions between the genetic material and the environment in determination of the pattern of growth among the children. Types of marriages, size of family, literacy rates of the parents, occupation of the parents are important factors which affect on the growth and development of children. Of the 400 parents who responded to this question, 70 per cent practiced non-consanguineous marriages and 30 per cent consanguineous marriages. Table 1 delineates that most of the children (86 per cent) belong to the medium size family and a few children (10 per cent) belong to the medium to large size family. Medium size families are more in the age group of 10 years male children (92.5 per cent) and small size families are more in the age group of 8 years male children (10 per cent).

98.5 per cent of the families are nuclear type and a few families (1.5 per cent) are joint families. The distribution of boys and girls according to income group is shown in Table 2. Most of the children belong to lower income group. 42.5 per cent of 9 years aged male children and 40 per cent of 10 years aged male children belong to the lower middle income category, 60 per cent of 10 years aged female children and 45 per cent of 9 years aged female children belong to the lower middle income group category.

Table 3 shows that 33.5 per cent of fathers of male children are literate and 66.5 per cent of fathers of male children are non-literate, 39 per cent of fathers of female children are literate and 61 per cent of fathers of female children are non-literate. 35.5 per cent of mothers of female children are literate and 64.5 per cent mother of female children are non-literate. Regarding the picture of population of children and adults, 57.81 per cent of children are male children and 54.73 per cent are female children, 42.19 per cent are male adults and 45.25 per cent are female adults.

Infra structural facilities including living conditions such as sunshine, good housing, lighting and ventilation influence the growth and development of children. It is observed that most of the houses are of very small size. Among the types of houses, 55 per cent are tiled houses, 34 per cent are thatched houses and the rest are Pucca houses (11 per cent). 80 per cent of the Mala families had their own houses provided by the Government and the remaining 20 per cent families live in rental houses. 24 per cent households had good ventilation, 44 per cent houses had satisfactory ventilation and 32 per cent houses had poor ventilation. While assessing the condition of cleanliness of the houses, it was observed that 59 per cent houses are satisfactory and 17 per cent houses are good. Most

Table 1
Frequency Distribution of Size of Family Among Mala Children

	Male					Female				
Age in Years	*Small size family*	*Medium size family*	*Medium large size family*	*Large size family*	*Total no. of family*	*Small size family*	*Medium size family*	*Medium large size family*	*Large size family*	*Total no. of family*
6	-	34	6	-	40	8	27	5	-	40
		(85)	(15)			(20)	(67.5)	(12.5)		
7	1	34	5	-	40	2	29	9	-	40
	(2.5)	(85)	(12.5)			(5)	(72.5)	(22.5)		
8	4	33	3	-	40	2	32	6	-	40
	(10)	(82.5)	(7.5)			(5)	(80)	(15)		
9	-	985	5	1	40	1	37	2	-	40
		(87.5)	(12.5)	(2.5)		(2.5)	(92.5)	(5)		
10	2	37	1	-	40	4	33	3	-	40
	(5)	(92.5)	(2.5)			(10)	(82.5)	(7.5)		
6-10 Years	7	172	20	1	200	17	158	25	-	200
	(3.5)	(86)	(10)	-5		(8.5)	(79)	(12.5)		

Figures in parenthesis indicate percentages.

Table 2
Frequency Distribution of Annual Income Per Capita Among Mala Children

	Male						Female					
Age in Years	Lower Income	Lower Middle Income	Middle Income	Upper Middle Income	Higher Income	Total No. of Children	Lower Income	Lower Middle Income	Middle Income	Upper Middle Income	Higher Income	Total No. of Children
6	36 (90)	3 (7.5)	-	-	1 (2.5)	40	29 (72.5)	8 (20)	1 (2.5)	2 (5)	-	40
7	30 (75)	8 (20)	-	1 (2.5)	1 (2.5)	40	24 (60)	9 (22.5)	4 (10)	3 (7.5)	-	40
8	28 (70)	8 (20)	3 (7.5)	1 (2.5)	-	40	21 (52.5)	11 (27.5)	4 (10)	1 (2.5)	3 (7.5)	40
9	20 (50)	17 (42.5)	3 (7.5)	-	-	40	19 (47.5)	18 (45)	2 (5)	1 (2.5)	-	40
10	18 (45)	16 (40)	4 (10)	2 (5)	-	40	6 (15)	24 (60)	7 (17.5)	1 (2.5)	2 (5)	40

Figures in parenthesis indicate percentages.

Table 3

Frequency Distribution of Literacy Level of the Parents of Mala Children

	(Male Children Parent's Literacy Level)						(Female Children Parent's Literacy Level)					
Age in Years	No. of Father Literates	No. of Fathers Non-Literates	Total No. of Fathers	No. of Mothers Literates	No. of Mothers Non-Literates	Total No. of Mothers	No. of Fathers Literates	No. of Fathers Non-Literates	Total No. of Fathers	No. of Mothers Literates	No. of Mothers Non-Literates	Total No. of Mothers
6	17 (42.5)	23 (57.5)	40	15 (37.5)	25 (62.5)	40	12 (30)	28 (70)	40	11 (27.5)	29 (72.5)	40
7	13 (32.5)	27 (67.5)	40	15 (37.5)	27 (62.5)	40	15 (37.5)	25 (62.5)	40	14 (35)	26 (65)	40
8	15 (37.5)	25 (62.5)	40	9 (22.5)	31 (77.5)	40	15 (37.5)	25 (62.5)	40	13 (32.5)	27 (67.5)	40
9	8 (20)	32 (80)	40	11 (27.5)	29 (72.5)	40	16 (40)	24 (60)	40	14 (35)	26 (65)	40
10	14 (85)	26 (65)	40	11 (27.5)	29 (72.5)	40	20 (50)	20 (50)	40	19	21 (52.5)	40
6-10	67 (33.5)	133 (66.5)	200	61 (30.5)	139 (69.5)	200	78 (39)	122 (61)	200	71 (35.5)	129 (64.5)	200

Figures in parenthesis indicate percentages.

of the houses had no latrines, so the family members (88 per cent) go to open fields for toilet. Only 12 per cent houses have pit type latrines. The habit of defecation on the open space is one of the factor responsible for diseases.

The water supply in the villages under study reveals that water is available from wells, canals and taps. This water is used for washing, bathing and for drinking. 53 per cent households availed both well and tap water, 23 per cent households availed only tap water and 24 per cent household availed only well water.

The cleanliness of the utensils is an important aspect. 71 per cent scored very good and 29 per cent had a poor score. 69 per cent families do not store their utensils properly but the remaining 31 per cent store it properly.

Health and Hygiene

According to W.H.O, health is "a state of complete physical, mental and social well being and not merely the absence of disease or infirmity". Hygiene means the care of body and its individual parts. Health and hygiene affect the normal growth and development during childhood due to diseases like diarrhoea, anemia, etc. Most of the Mala children do not clean their teeth as their parents do not take proper care. The frequency of bathing is low among the Mala children. Generally, Mala children take bath thrice a week. Soap is used for cleaning their bodies. It is observed that a number of skin diseases are reported among the Mala children. 67 per cent of children's health and hygiene is satisfactory and only 33 per cent of children's health and hygiene is good. In the selected villages, all villages have hospital facilities except one village, Koppavaram. 89 per cent of households availed allopathic health care system and only 11 per cent of households availed indigenous medicines. It is observed that all children are immunized.

Food and Food Habits

Rice is their staple food. Among pulses, red gram and urad are commonly used. They take beef, fish, chicken, meat of goat and sheep. Generally children eat three meals a day. The morning meal of the majority of the Mala children consists of previous left over food. Their mid-day meal usually consists of rice and a vegetable. In the night, they take the same food which is prepared in the afternoon. All school going children get 3 Kg. of rice every month under mid-day meals programme which is being implemented by social welfare department. 80 per cent households consume urad dal. 77 per cent of children consume milk and milk products occasionally. 52 per cent of children get insufficient food, 32 per cent of children get moderate food and only 16 per cent of children get insufficient food. Mala children do not take an adequate amount of pulses; and their diet is unbalanced. The severe malnutrition in some Mala children could be arrived due to their economic condition and unawareness of nutritional science. Faulty cooking practice is one of the major contributing factor in malnutrition in the area. The most common ways of wastage of water soluble vitamins are boiling cereals in excess water, over cooking and throwing away the water in which cereal or vegetable was soaked.

Infra Structural Facilities Available at the Village Level

Out of 8 villages, all the places have access through public transport facility like bus transport. Three places (Samalkot, Rajahmundry and Vetlapalem) have Railway station facilities. National High Way No. 5 passes through East Godavari district linking Rajahmundry and Visakhapatnam. High way passes through the villages namely Rajahmundry, Vetlapalem, Hussainpuram and Samalkot linking Rajahmundry and Visakhapatnam. Post Office, Primary Schools, Public Distribution System, Electricity, Tap and Well Water Resources exist in all villages. One village (Koppavaram) has no Tele communication facility within a distance of 3 Kms. Medical facilities exist in seven villages and only one village, Koppavaram do not possess any medical facility within a distance of 5 Kms.

Development Programmes Available at the Household Level

There are a number of development programmes implemented in the area. These development programmes are DRDA, DWCRA, Mid-day meals programme which affect on the growth and development of children. Almost all households availed a mid-day meals programmes. All school-going children get 3 Kg of rice every month under mid-day meals programme which is being implemented by social welfare department. Only 10 per cent households availed DWCRA programmes (Development of women and children in Rural Areas). Some of the families have purchased the milched animals under DWCRA programmes. Most of the families (90 per cent) have not availed DWCRA programmes. I.C.D.S. programme is implemented in the district but this programme is not implemented especially for Mala children. Most of them are not aware of the DRDA, DWCRA, ICDS programmes because of lack of education and other socio-economic factors.

The data was processed from the schedules and arranged into age groups, sexwise with respect to anthropometric measurements. The statistical constants, viz., arithmetic mean, standard error of Mean, Standard deviation, Coefficient of variation for each anthropometric measurement according to sex and age are shown in Table 4. The pattern of growth shows a regular increase in all the measurements with increase in age.

Weight (Wt)

The Mala children shows a steady increase in weight from 6 years to 10 years in their mean values (Table 4). The mean weight for boys and girls at 6 years is 16.13 Kg. and 16.40 Kg respectively indicating that girls are slightly heavier than boys. The mean body weight of boys at 10 years (24.07 Kg) is lower by 0.95 Kg than girls (25.02 Kg) at the same age. The total gain in mean weight for boys is 7.94 Kg between 6 years and 10 years, which is lesser than that of girls (8.62 Kg) by 0.68 Kg for the same period. But girls are heavier than boys at 9 and 10 years, maintaining a higher trajectory than that of boys. The variability of mean weights increased steadily with advanced age for both sexes. The coefficient of variation for boys range between 11.98 to 16.46 while those for girls range between 13.38 to 17.73. The highest coefficient of variation value for boys is observed at 8 years, while for girls the highest C.V. value is seen at 10 years of age. The mean weight of Indian boys at 6 years (16.3 Kg), (ICMR 1989), is relatively higher than the Mala boys of East Godavari district, but they present slightly higher mean value than the Mala boys of Visakhapatnam district (15.73 Kg) by 0.92 Kg (Rao *et al.* 1997). The Mala girls aged 6 years of the present study register slightly higher mean value than the Indian girls (16.0 Kg) at the same age (ICMR) by 0.40 Kg and the Mala girls of Visakhapatnam district (14.21 Kg) reported by Rao *et al* (1997) by 2.19 Kg, which is significant. The mean body weight value of Mala boys aged 10 years showed higher mean value than that of the Indian boys (23.5 Kg) by 0.57 Kg (ICMR, 1989) and the Mala boys of Visakhapatnam district (22.41 Kg) by 1.66 Kg (Rao *et al* 1997). The mean body weight of Mala girls aged 10 years, of East Godavari district possess higher mean value than the results reported by ICMR (1989) for Indian girls (23.6 Kg) by 1.82 Kg and the findings of Rao *et al* (1997) among the Mala girls of Visakhapatnam (22.75 Kg) by 2.27 Kg for the same age group.

The distance growth curves for body weight, (Fig. 1) show the distribution of mean weights plotted against age of both Mala boys and girls. The distance curve for body weight shows between 9 and 10 years for both boys and girls. In 6 and 7 years, the growth curves show a steady rise as age increases, with minor fluctuations. In older years, the growth curve of girls overtakes the boys at the age of 9 years, with increase in mean values, taking an upward momentum than that of boys. On the whole, the distance curves of Mala children for body weight resembles to the growth curves observed in other populations, with little variation.

The weight velocity curves are drawn taking mean differences in weights between successive incremental years of boys and girls (Fig. 2). The velocity curve for weight reaches the highest peak points at the incremental years between 10 and 11 years for both sexes, where the Mala children record the maximum mean weights. Both boys and girls present a downward path in their velocity curves at 8 years, indicating a loss in their body weight, but there after the velocity curves take progressive upward momentum. The course of the upward momentum in the velocity curve of boys is marginally lower to that of girls, reflecting a decline in

Table 4
Statistical Constants of Anthropometric Measurements of Mala Children

		Weight (in Kg)		Stature (in cm)		Siting Height (in cm)		Bi-acromial Diameter (in cm)		Bi-illiocristal Diameter (in cm)	
Ages (Years)		Male	Female	Male	Female	Male	Female	Male	Female	Male	Female
6	N	41	42	41	42	41	42	41	42	42	42
	Mean	16.13	16.40	109.17	109.72	57.55	57.88	24.58	24.66	17.24	17.32
	SEM	0.37	0.34	101	1.05	0.46	0.51	0.24	0.33	0.28	0.18
	SD	2.34	2.20	6.39	6.75	2.93	3.27	1.54	2.13	1.79	1.17
	CV	14.49	13.38	5.85	6.15	5.09	5.65	6.25	8.63	10.37	6.75
	Ab. growth	0	0	0	0	0	0	0	0	0	0
	% growth	0	0	0	0	0	0	0	0	0	0
7	N	44	47	44	47	44	47	44	47	44	47
	Mean	18.81	18.98	116.36	117.59	61.01	61.55	26.53	26.31	18.10	19.78
	SEM	0.47	0.49	0.93	1.21	0.44	0.59	0.34	0.29	0.16	1.52
	SD	3.08	3.31	6.09	8.24	2.89	4.03	2.26	1.97	1.08	10.34
	CV	16.35	17.44	5.23	7.01	4.73	6.55	8.51	7.47	5.94	52.97
	Ab. growth	2.68	2.58	7.19	7.87	3.46	3.67	1.95	1.65	0.86	2.46
	% growth	16.62	15.73	6.59	7.17	6.01	6.34	7.93	6.69	4.99	14.20
8	N	45	41	45	41	45	41	45	41	45	41
	Mea	20.39	19.74	121.64	118.57	63.27	61.40	26.84	26.11	18.44	18.69
	SEM	0.51	0.51	0.99	1.19	0.55	0.56	0.33	0.29	0.19	0.21
	SD	3.36	3.25	6.57	7.53	3.64	3.52	2.16	1.86	1.26	1.34
	CV	16.46	16.47	5.40	6.35	5.75	5.72	8.05	7.12	6.85	7.15
	Ab. growth	1.58	0.76	5.28	0.98	2.26	-0.15	0.31	-0.2	0.34	-1.09
	% growth	8.40	4.00	4.54	0.83	3.70	-0.24	1.17	-0.76	1.88	-5.51

Contd...

	Weight (in Kg)		*Stature (in cm)*		*Siting Height (in cm)*		*Bi-acromial Diameter (in cm)*		*Bi-illiocristal Diameter (in cm)*	
Ages (Years)	*Male*	*Female*	*Male*	*Female*	*Male*	*Female*	*Male*	*Female*	*Male*	*Female*
9 N	43	48	43	48	43	48	43	48	43	48
Mean	21.84	22.35	125.66	125.59	64.57	64.39	28.17	27.89	19.15	19.56
SEM	0.40	0.56	1.10	1.06	0.55	0.47	0.27	0.34	0.33	0.21
SD	2.62	3.87	7.12	7.26	3.59	3.23	1.74	2.36	2.17	1.44
CV	11.98	17.29	5.67	5.78	5.56	5.02	6.19	8.45	11.32	7.34
Ab. growth	1.45	2.61	4.02	7.02	1.3	2.99	1.33	1.78	0.71	0.87
% growth	7.11	13.22	3.30	5.92	2.05	4.87	4.96	6.82	3.85	4.65
10 N	41	61	41	61	41	61	41	61	41	61
Mean	24.07	25.02	130.06	130.88	66.80	67.24	28.61	28.31	19.80	20.39
SEM	0.54	0.57	0.96	0.98	0.43	0.49	0.46	0.29	0.23	0.21
SD	3.40	4.44	6.09	7.60	2.70	3.81	2.89	2.21	1.43	1.61
CV	14.11	17.73	4.68	5.81	4.05	5.66	10.08	7.82	7.21	7.88
Ab. growth	2.23	2.67	4.4	5.29	2.23	2.85	0.44	0.42	0.65	0.83
% growth	10.21	11.95	3.50	4.21	3.45	4.43	1.56	1.51	3.39	4.24

the velocity for boys compared to that of girls. The gulf between the velocity curves of both sexes show a significant sexual dimorphism in mean body weights in between 9 and 10 years, indicating a spurt in growth rate of girls compared to boys in body weight.

Stature/height (St)

The statistical constants of stature presented in Table 4 reveals a general increase in height for both boys and girls. Boys being slightly taller than girls at 8 years and 9 years, while girls maintain a slight lead in mean values at 6 years, 7 years and 10 years.

The mean stature value of boys (109.17 cm) at 6 years is marginally lower by 0.65 cm. than the mean value of girls (109.17 cm) at 6 years age and the same trend is observed even at the age of 10 years, where girls record a slightly higher mean stature value (130.88 cm) than that of boys (130.06 cm). The total gain in stature from 6 years to 10 years is 20.89 cm in boys and 21.16 cm in girls. The mean stature of boys at 8 years (121.64 cm) is higher by 3.07 cm than the mean value of girls (118.57 cm) at the same age. In comparison to body weight, the coefficient of variation values are much lower for stature, implying that the extent of variability is not as high as that at 10 years (4.68) and the highest (5.85) at 6 years of age, while the corresponding C.V. values for girls are (5.78) at 9 years and (7.01) at 7 years respectively. Girls register higher C.V. values than those of boys at all years i.e. 6 years to 10 years. The mean stature value of Indian boys (108.5 cm) and Indian girls (107.4 cm) are comparatively lower by 0.67 cm and 2.32 cms than the Mala boys (107.07 cm) and girls (108.96) cm respectively at 6 years of age. Even the Mala boys and girls of the neighbouring Visakhapatnam district (Rao *et al* 1997) show relatively lower mean stature value by 0.21 cm in boys and 2.65 cm in girls than the Mala boys and girls of the present study. The mean stature value of Mala boys show 5.56 cm higher mean value than the Indian boys (124.4 cm), and Mala girls also register higher stature mean value (2.48 cm) than the Indian girls (128.4 cm) at 10 years of age (ICMR 1989). However, the mean stature values of Mala boys and girls of the present study are closer to the mean values of Mala boys (128.42 cm) and Mala girls (129.32 cm) of Visakhapatnam district reported by Rao, *et al* (1997).

The distance growth curve for stature of Mala children are plotted in Fig. 3. The distribution of growth curves for boys and girls assumes the familiar growth curves observed in human populations, showing steady progressive course with increasing age. Initially the distance curve of boys shows a downward path indicating deaccelerated growth, compared to girls and then the distance curve takes a steady progressive path. While the distance curve of girls shows a downward trend with decelerated growth rate at 8 years and there after maintains a steady growth rate with upward momentum of the curve.

The growth velocity curves of stature was plotted in Fig. 4. The Mala girls present higher growth velocity in stature than that of boys at 6 years age, but the velocity curves take a downward course in both sexes at 7 years, reaching the lowest point at 8 years, with low intensity in girls; whereas, the velocity curve for boys show a steady downward path till 9 years and from there onwards the velocity curve show a progressive upward momentum till it reaches the highest peak point at 10 years. The Velocity curve of girls show a steep rise in intensity between 8 and 9 years, with a moderate intensity at 10 years. The gap between the velocity curves at various incremental years of boys and girls indicate sex differences in growth velocities.

Sitting Height

The statistical constants for sitting height are shown in Table 4. The increase in mean values of sitting height, with advanced age conformed to that of other anthropometric measurements i.e., boys displaying values higher at 8 years (1.87 cm) and 9 years (0.28 cm) than those of girls; while girls exhibit higher mean values at 6 years (0.33 cm), 7 years (0.54 cm) and at 10 years (0.44 cm) of age. A significantly higher mean value of 1.87 cm is observed in boys of 8 years over that of girls at the same age. In all ages the bisexual difference varies between 0.18 cm to 1.87 cm. The mean sitting height values recorded are 57.55 cm. for boys and 57.88 cm for girls at 6 years. The mean value at 10 years of age is 66.80 cm for boys and it is 67.24 cm for girls at the same age. The total mean increase in sitting height is 9.25 cm in boys and 11.36 cm in girls from 6 years to 10 years, indicating that the net increase in mean value of sitting height is relatively high in girls (2.11 cm) than that of boys. The C.V. values are low and are comparable to those of height and chest circumference. The lowest and highest C.V. values for boys are 4.05 at 10 years and 5.75 at 8 years respectively, while the corresponding values for girls are 5.02 at 9 years and 6.55 at 7 years. The mean sitting height values of Mala boys and girls at 7 years are much below to that of Indian boys (59.4 cm) and girls (58.4 cm) by 1.85 cm and 0.52 cm. respectively ((IMCR 1989). The mean sitting height values of Indian boys (67.5 cm) show a relatively (0.70 cm) higher value than the Mala boys, but the Indian girls (67.1 cm) exhibit 0.14 cm lower value than the Mala girls of the present study.

The mean values for sitting height of the Mala children are plotted in Fig. 5 showing the growth distance curves. The growth curve of sitting height shows an initial small rise with upward momentum of the curves for both boys and girls upto 7 years and there after the growth curve takes a downward path indicating a deaccelerated growth in sitting height, while the growth curve of boys shows a steady progress with increasing age, with little deviations. The low intensity variation in magnitudes in mean values of sitting height between the sexes are observed at various incremental years, but the sex difference is greater in proportion at 8 years of age.

The growth velocity curve for sitting height of Mala boys shows an initial sharp rise at 7 years compared to that of the girls, whose velocity curve shows a horizontal course (Fig. 6). The velocity curve takes a sharp downward bend between 7 and 8 years reaching the lowest point with a negative value (-0.15 cm), indicating a negative deaccelerated growth rate of -0.25 cm. per annum. On the other hand, the velocity curve of boys also shows a downward trend but the fall is not as sharp as it was noticed among girls. The lowest point is reached at 9 years in the velocity curve of boys and there after the growth curve steadily progresses in upward direction. The velocity curve of girls rises sharply between 8 and 9 years and there after the velocity curve takes a stabilized course. The sex differences are marked at 8 and 9 years, while the sex differences are at a lesser magnitude at other incremental years among the Mala children.

Biacromial Diameter (Biad)

The statistical constants of biacromial diameter presented in Table 4 shows that the mean values of biacromial diameter among Mala children range from 24.58 cm to 28.61 cm for boys and 24.66 cm to 28.31 cm for girls. The mean values of boys are slightly higher than that of girls at 7 years, 8 years and at 10 years (0.30 cm) of age, while girls show marginally higher mean values at 6 years and 9 years of age. The lowest coefficient of variation value is recorded at 6 years (6.25) for boys and at 8 years (7.12) for girls. While the highest C.V. values are recorded at 6 years for girls (8.63) and at 10 years for boys (10.08). The C.V. values indicate that the variability is greater among Mala boys compared to girls in Biacromial diameter.

The mean of the biacromial diameter of boys and girls are plotted against age show the growth curves typical of the physical growth in Human populations. The distance growth curves show an upward path in initial years upto 7 years in both boys and girls, with almost similar magnitudes and then the growth curves show a slight deacceleration at 8 years, but the decline is marked in girls compared to that of boys. The growth curves show steady progressive upward course upto 10 years of age in both sexes, where the growth curve of boys is marginally ahead of the growth curve of girls. (Fig. 7).

The growth velocity curves for biacromial diameter of Mala boys and girls present a criss-cross path, with lower magnitudes at 7 and 9 years in both sexes and reach the peak points at the age of 10 years (Fig.8). The velocity curve of girls takes a downward path at 7 years, while the velocity curve of boys moves in upward direction, but both curves drop to their lowest levels at 8 years. Girls record the lowest velocity with a negative value of -0.21 cm. recording a decelerated growth rate of -0.79 cm per annum, though the growth velocity of boys read the lowest value

(0.32 cm), the growth rate is higher (1.2 cm) than that of girls at the same age. The growth velocity curves rise sharply at 9 years but the intensity is higher among girls compared to that of boys and again there is considerable fall in velocity curves at 10 years.

Biiliocristal Diameter (Billd)

The statistical constants presented in Table 4, for the biiliocristal diameter indicates that the mean values increased steadily with age and the trend is almost the same for both boys and girls. The mean values range between 17.24 cm to 19.80 cm for boys and between 17.32 cm to 20.39 cm for girls, aged 6 and 10 years respectively. However, the magnitude of increase in mean values are smaller for both boys and girls. The mean values for girls at 6 to 10 years tend to show higher values than those observed for boys; the differential value i.e. the net gain in mean value of the measurement is 2.56 cm for boys and 3.07 cm for girls, where girls register 0.51 cm. higher mean value than the boys in a span of 5 years period. The standard deviation values increased steadily with age, with magnitudes fluctuating. The lowest and the highest coefficient of variation values respectively are at 7 years (5.94) and at 9 years (11.32) for boys, while the corresponding lowest and highest C.V. values are at 6 years (6.75) and at 7 years (52.97) for girls respectively. The exceptionally high C.V. value for girls at 7 years may be due to extremely high value of the measurement in some cases, in all other ages the C.V. value range between 6.75 to 7.88 in 6 years to 10 years. The range in mean values of the present study are comparable with the ICMR (1989) data on Indian children. The Mala boys present a closer mean value of biiliocristal diameter with the Indian boys, where the mean values range between 17.2 cm and 19.8 cm for boys aged 6 years and 10 years respectively. Whereas, the Mala girls tend to show a slightly higher mean values than that of the ICMR (1989) data, where the mean biiliocristal diameter of Indian girls range in between 17.0 cm to 19.9 cm aged 6 years and 10 years.

The distance growth curves were drawn based on the mean values of the biiliocristal diameter of boys and girls against their age in fig.9. The distance curve of boys shows a steady progress with increase in age without any deviations in its path and resembles to a typical growth curve observed in other human population; whereas, the distance curve of girls presents a sharp upward course, recording the highest growth rate (14.18) per annum, reflecting a marked sex difference in the mean values. In between 7 and 8 years, the growth curve takes a downward momentum, with a sudden fall in the growth rate, indicating a decelerated growth, with a negative value of -5.52 per annum and then onwards the growth curve shows a steady progress, with moderate growth rate upto 10 years and again the growth curve rises to peak point at 11 years. The distance growth curve of girls show fluctuating course and traverse marginally ahead of the growth curve of boys, indicating that the growth rate among girls is proportionately greater than that of boys in biiliocristal diameter of the Mala.

The velocity curves of biiliocristal diameter of Mala children were plotted against age in Fig. 10. The velocity curve of biiliocristal diameter of boys show a steady progress with a horizontal course with increasing age, except a slight deviation in its course at 8 years, where the curve takes a downward course, recording the lowest velocity (0.34 cm) and then onwards, the velocity curve moves in a steady direction. Contrastingly the velocity curve of girls shows a zig-zag momentum with fluctuating velocities at various incremental years. The velocity curve takes an upward path in initial years, reaching the highest peak point at 7 years (2.46 cm) in growth intensity. In between 7 and 8 years, the growth velocity curve takes a downward course, with a drop in velocity to a negative value of -1.09 cm, indicating a deaccelerated growth rate of -5.52 cm and then the velocity curve rises sharply at 9 years (0.87 cm) with a minor loss in velocity at 10 years. A perusal at the velocity curves indicate that the intensity in the growth rate of biiliocristal diameter among girls is relatively greater in magnitude compared to that of boys at several incremental years.

Triceps Skinfold (TSF)

The statistical constants for triceps skinfold measurement presented in Table-5, indicate a decelerate mean values from 6 years to 8 years in Mala boys. Boys aged 6 years record the highest mean value (6.45 mm) and there after the mean values decline upto the age of 8 years (5.67 mm), showing a net loss of 0.79 mm in the triceps skinfold. Boys register a moderate but gradual increase in mean values from 9 years (5.78 mm) to 10 years (5.89 mm); the net increase being 0.22 mm from 8 to 10 years. Similarly girls also show a decreasing tendency in the triceps skinfold upto the age of 9 years. The mean triceps skinfold value of girls aged 6 years is 6.89 mm and there after there is slight fall in mean values at 7 years (6.72 mm) and 9 years (6.73 mm); with a minor distortion at 8 years (6.96 mm). The mean value of triceps skinfold of girls aged 10 years (7.36 mm) is higher by 1.47 mm than the mean of boys (5.89 mm) at the same age. The net loss in the triceps skinfold is -0.67 mm in boys, while the net loss in the mean value is -0.47 mm in girls over a span of 5 years. It is evident from the table, that the mean values of the triceps skinfold increases steeply among girls than that of the boys and girls present higher mean values in all the ages over that of boys. The coefficient of variation for boys range between 17.27 at 9 years and 21.16 at 10 years in boys, while the C.V. values range between 17.81 at 8 years and 23.61 at 10 years in girls. The C.V. values show a greater degree of variability for each group, with fluctuating values, Rao, et.al. (1997) reported higher mean values for Mala boys of Visakhapatnam district than the Mala boys of East Godavari district in all the age groups i.e. 6 years to 10 years, where the mean triceps skinfold values varies from 6.91 mm at 7 years to 7.76 mm at 6 years, with intermediate values in other age groups (7.24 mm at 8 years, 7.40 mm at 9 years and 7.25 mm at 10 years). The mean triceps skin fold values of the Mala girls of East Godavari district are significantly lower than the mean values of Mala girls of Visakhapatnam district as reported by Rao et.al (1997), where the mean triceps values range from 8.04 mm at 6 years to 8.72 mm at 10 years of age, with highest value at 7 years (9.21 mm), but the trend is similar in both the studies.

The distance growth curves for triceps skinfold of Mala boys and girls are presented in fig.11. The growth curve of girls show deceleration in mean values at 6 years and then the growth curve shows a steady progress with increasing age, reaching the peak point after 10 years. Contrastingly the growth curve of boys starts at a lower level, relative to that of girls and progress in a downward course, with advancing age, running almost horizontally to the base line and records the lowest value at 11 years. The distance curve of girls deviates apart as age increases with that of boys, indicating marked sex differences in mean values for triceps skinfold.

The growth velocity curves of boys and girls for triceps skinfold are plotted against age (Fig.12). The growth velocity registers progressive negative values in the younger age groups of both sexes with differing velocities. The velocity curve of boys starts at a lower level compared to girls, shows a progressive upward momentum in growth intensity, reaching the maximum levels at 9 and 10 years. The velocity curve of girls takes a progressive upward course in the initial younger ages upto 8 years and then there is a deceleration at 9 years registering a negative growth and there is a spurt in the growth intensity of triceps skinfold, reaching the highest peak at 11 years. Girls present significantly higher values in the growth velocity at 10 years than that of boys in the triceps skinfold.

Sub Scapular Skinfold (sssf)

The mean subscapular skinfold at 6 years of age is 5.10 mm for boys and 6.21 mm for girls, wherein the girls show a proportionately higher mean value (1.12 mm) than that of boys (Table 5). The Mala boys register a slightly higher mean value of 0.22 mm at the age of 7 years over that of 6 years, contrastingly the girls exhibit a loss of 0.08 mm mean value for the same period. A decreasing trend is observed in mean values of boys from 7 years, the loss in the mean measurement being 0.30 mm, while girls tend to show a steady gain in mean value (0.56 mm) for the same period. The mean values for boys (5.25 mm) and for girls (7.80mm) are recorded at 10 years. The total gain in the subscapular skinfold measurement is 0.15 mm for boys and 1.59 mm for girls over a span of 5 years. The difference in the net increase in the measurement is markedly higher in girls compared to boys. The mean subscapular skinfold values of girls are relatively higher to that of boys in all the age groups (Table 5). A greater degree of variability is observed among girls than in boys. The coefficient of variation values range between 15.09 to 22.19 in boys, while it ranges between 17.85 to 28.92 among girls. The mean subscapular values of the Mala boys of the present study are relatively lower to that of the mean values reported by Rao *et. al* (1977) among the Mala boys of the neighbouring Visakhapatnam district, wherein the mean values range between 5.89 mm at 6 years to 6.43 mm at 10 years of age. The Mala girls of Visakhapatnam also record higher mean subscapular skinfold values than the mean values obtained for the Mala girls of the present study. Rao *et.al* (1997) reported that the mean subscapular skinfold of Mala girls range between 6.53 mm at 6 years, but the trend is almost similar with the present study.

The distance growth curves for subscapular skinfold of Mala children are shown Fig.13. The growth curve of girls show a steady rise with increase in age and reach the highest peak point after 10 years and deviates further apart from the growth curve of boys. Contrastingly the distance curve of boys starts at a lower level, relative to that of girls and progress in a parallel course, running almost horizontally to the base line, with advancing age. The distance growth curve, girls shows marked deviation in its path, with that of the boys, indicating sex difference in subscapular skinfold.

The growth velocity curves of boys and girls for subscapular skinfold are plotted against age in Fig.14. The velocity curve of girls shows a decline in velocity from 6 years to 7 years, recording negative growth rate, followed by a steady progress upto 9 years and there after the velocity shows a sharp rise between 9 and 10 years, recording the maximum velocity after 10 years age. Contrastingly, the velocity curve of boys starts with negative velocity, with a slight progressive rise in value at 7 years and then there is deacceleration in velocities, registering the lowest negative value at 7 years and there after the velocity curve for subscapular skinfold of girls shows a steady progressive trend, with higher velocities than that of boys and the differences are significant in the latter years, i.e. 9 and 10 years.

Biceps Skinfold (Bisf)

The statistical constants for biceps skinfold measurement presented in Table 5, indicate that the mean values of biceps skinfold decreased steadily from 4.02 mm at 6 years to 3.37 mm at 9 years among boys, registering a loss of 0.65 mm and then mean value shows a minor gain of 0.06 mm at 10 years. The mean biceps values of girls also show declining trend from a value of 4.42 mm at 6 years to 4.13 mm at 7 years, the net loss in mean value being 0.29 mm and there after the mean values shows a minor gain of 0.31 mm at 8 years, 0.07 mm at 9 years and 0.35 mm at 10 years of age. The net gain in mean values of biceps skinfold among girls (0.07 mm) is comparatively lesser than that of boys (0.58 mm) over a span of 5 years. The fluctuations in the mean values are of minor nature both for boys and

Table 5
Statistical Constants of Anthropometric Measurements of Mala Children

		Triceps Skinfold (in mm)		*Sub Scapular Skinfold (in mm)*		*Biceps Skinfold (in mm)*	
Ages (Years)		*Male*	*Female*	*Male*	*Female*	*Male*	*Female*
6	N	41	42	41	42	41	42
	Mean	6.45	6.89	5.10	6.21	4.02	4.42
	SEM	0.20	0.20	0.15	0.19	0.14	0.13
	SD	1.27	1.27	0.93	1.24	0.86	0.85
	CV	19.64	18.39	18.24	19.95	21.30	19.29
	Ab.growth	0	0	0	0	0	0
	% growth	0	0	0	0	0	0
7	N	44	47	44	47	44	47
	Mean	5.94	6.72	5.32	6.13	3.86	4.13
	SEM	0.17	0.20	0.16	0.20	0.14	0.14
	SD	1.11	1.34	1.06	1.35	0.92	0.93
	CV	18.68	19.87	19.91	22.00	23.91	22.51
	Ab.growth	-0.51	-0.17	0.22	-0.08	-0.16	-0.29
	% growth	-7.91	-2.47	4.31	-1.29	-3.98	-6.56
8	N	45	41	45	41	45	41
	Mean	5.67	6.96	5.28	6.33	3.56	4.44
	SEM	0.17	0.20	0.16	0.18	0.11	0.15
	SD	1.12	1.24	1.06	1.13	0.70	0.97
	CV	19.71	17.81	20.10	17.85	19.75	21.83
	Ab.growth	-0.27	0.24	-0.04	0.2	-0.3	0.31
	% growth	-4.55	3.57	-0.75	3.26	-7.77	7.51
9	N	43	48	43	48	43	48
	Mean	5.78	6.73	5.01	6.69	3.37	4.20
	SEM	0.15	0.21	0.12	0.21	0.09	0.12
	SD	1.00	1.46	0.76	1.47	0.61	0.81
	CV	17.27	21.62	15.09	22.01	18.05	19.24
	Ab.growth	0.11	-0.23	-0.27	0.36	-0.19	-0.24
	% growth	1.94	-3.30	-5.11	5.69	-5.34	-5.41
10	N	41	61	41	61	41	61
	Mean	5.89	7.36	5.25	7.80	3.44	4.49
	SEM	0.20	0.22	0.18	0.29	0.10	0.12
	SD	1.25	1.74	1.16	2.25	0.63	0.93
	CV	21.16	23.61	22.19	28.92	18.25	19.96
	Ab.growth	0.11	0.63	0.24	1.11	0.07	0.29
	% growth	1.90	9.36	4.79	16.59	2.08	6.90

girls. The mean biceps values for girls are slightly higher than that of boys in all the ages. The variability is greater among girls than in boys. The C.V. values among boys range between a minimum value of 18.05 to a maximum value of 23.91 and the corresponding values for girls range between 19.24 to 22.51. The mean biceps value of Mala girls of Visakhapatnam (Rao et.al 1997) are significantly higher than the Mala girls of the present study. Rao *et. al* (1997) reported that the mean biceps value of 6 years Mala girls as 5.70 mm, higher by 1.28 mm than the Mala girls of East Godavari. In all other ages, the Mala girls of Visakhapatnam showed higher mean biceps values compared to the Mala girls of East Godavari, wherein the former recorded 1.85 mm higher value at 7 years, 1.20 mm at 8 years, 2.10 mm at 9 years and 1.60 mm at 10 years of age than the present study. Similarly the Mala boys of Visakhapatnam (Rao *et.al* 1997) recorded higher mean biceps skinfold values than that of the Mala boys of East Godavari district.

The distance growth curves for biceps skin fold of Mala boys and girls are plotted in Fig.15. The distance curve of boys shows steady deceleration in mean values with increase in age and the growth curve takes downward course, reaching the lowest point at 10 years. Both the growth curves take divergent course, where the magnitudes increase with advanced age, widening the gap between the growth curves. The sex difference in biceps skinfold is clearly visible in the distance growth curves.

The velocity curves of skinfold for Mala boys and girls presented in Fig.16. The velocity curve of boys shows a steady progressive upward course, with slight deceleration in between 7 and 8 years and reaches the highest peak at 10 years. Whereas, the velocity curve of girls shows an initial drop in intensity between 6 and 7 years, with a sudden increase and decrease in velocities in between 8 and 9 years and there after the velocity curve rises sharply, reaching the highest point after 10 years. Girls record varying magnitudes in velocity values compared to that of boys. Marked sex differences are noticed at 8 years and 10 years among the Mala children.

Body Mass Index (BMI)

The body mass index for Mala children is calculated by dividing weight in kilograms by the square of height in meters. The average body mass index of 6 years girls (13.60) is slightly higher than that of boys (13.50). Boys of 7 years old record an average BM index of 13.81, while girls register a slightly lower BM index of 13.64, the difference being 0.17. It is evident that both boys and girls have gained in body mass indices from the preceding year. There is a loss in BMI value of boys (13.69) at 8 years, whereas girls register a marginal increase (13.95) in their average body mass index. Both boys (14,18) and girls (14.50) show an increase in their average body mass indices at 10 years where as the BMI values at 9 years are 13.81 for boys and 14.09 for girls.

Correlations Coefficients of Some Related Anthropometric Traits

The correlation coefficient values for some related anthropometric traits are presented in Table 6. The correlation coefficient calculated between height and weight measurements of Mala boys (0.804569) is higher by 0.149585 than that of girls (0.654984) at 5 years age. But a reverse trend is observed at 6 years, where girls record higher correlation coefficient value (0.840991) than that of boys (0.791033) and this trend continues upto the age of 10 years. The increase in correlation (r) values of girls over boys are 0.049958 at 6 years, 0.036506 at 7 years, 0.020011 at 8 years and 0.005914 at 10 years. Boys in 11 years record higher correlation value (0.91722) than that of girls (0.874996) at the same age, the difference being 0.042296. The highest correlation value (r) is observed at 8 years for girls (0.906732) and at 11 years for boys (0.917292).

Table 6
Correlation Co-efficient of Related Measurements of Mala Children

Age	*Traits*	*Male*	*Female*
5 Years	HT vs WT	0.804569	0.654984
	HT vs SH	0.504872	0.539211
	BID vs BIILD	0.559425	0.144804
	TSF vs SSSF	0.530248	0.606133
6 Years	HT vs WT	0.791033	0.840991
	HT vs SH	0.879174	0.85164
	BID vs BIILD	0.696195	0.335909
	TSF vs SSSF	0.729229	0.479026
7 Years	HT vs WT	0.826115	0.062621
	HT vs SH	0.822971	0.804961
	BID vs BIILD	0.461082	0.189257
	TSF vs SSSF	0.714041	0.63974
8 Years	HT vs WT	0.886721	0.906732
	HT vs SH	0.805607	0.882148
	BID vs BIILD	0.481128	0.818874
	TSF vs SSSF	0.571119	0.566569
9 Years	HT vs WT	0.815583	0.821497
	HT vs SH	0.857416	0.817646
	BID vs BIILD	0.515294	0.578869
	TSF vs SSSF	0.427897	0.7427
10 Years	HT vs WT	0.782229	0.847911
	HT vs SH	0.866854	0.887085
	BID vs BIILD	0.346506	0.691171
	TSF vs SSSF	0.616862	0.693237
11 Years	HT vs WT	0.917292	0.874996
	HT vs SH	0.854152	0.920181
	BID vs BIILD	0.256896	0.809783
	TSF vs SSSF	0.113896	0.820944

WT = Weight
HT = Height
BID = Bi-acromial diameter
BILD = Bi-illiac diameter
TSF = Skin fold thickness at tricep
SSSF = Skin fold thickness at subscapular region

The height versus weight correlation indicates that the 'r' value increased in both the sexes from 6 years to 8 years, though the magnitude is fluctuating and then after the 'r' values decreased upto the age of 10 years and gained momentum again at 11 years with a higher magnitude in boys over girls at that age. The increase in 'r' values with advancing age is in conformity with the mean values for these measurements, indicating a close association of these traits with age changes for both sexes, though the magnitude fluctuate in middle age groups.

In height versus sitting height correlation the lowest coefficient 'r' values are reorded at 5 years for both boys (0.504872) and girls (0.539211). The highest 'r' value is noticed at 6 years for boys (0.879174), while it is at 11 years for girls (0.920181). The difference in the lowest 'r' value of boys and girls is 0.034339 and the differential in the highest 'r' value is 0.041007. Boys at 6 years show higher correlation coefficient value (0.879174) than that of girls (0.85174) at the same age, the sex difference being 0.027534 in 'r' values. Girls record higher correlation values at 7 years (0.8795) and at 8 years (0.882143) than that of boys at the respective ages, with sex difference of 0.056529 and 0.076536 respectively. Boys register great 'r' values at 9 years (0.857416) over girls (0.817646), with a sex difference of 0.3977. But girls score higher 'r' values at 10 years (0.887085) and at 11 years (0.920181) than boys at their respective ages. The sex difference in 'r' values are 0.020231 at 10 years and 0.066029 at 11 years. The sex gain in 'r' value for boys (0.34928) is slightly lower compared to net gain in 'r' values for girls (0.38097) over a period of 6 years. The difference in net gain in 'r' value between the sexes is 0.03169.

The correlation coefficient value between biacromial diameter and biiliocristal diameter is higher for boys (0.559425) than the 'r' value of girls (0.144804) at 5 years, with sex difference of 0.414621. Similarly the correlation value for boys of 6 years is also higher than that of girls by 0.360286. The 'r' values show a steady increase from 7 years (0.461082) to 9 years (0.515294) among boys, the net increase being marginal (0.05212) and then there is decrease in 'r' values upto the age of 11 years (0.258398). The total decrease in 'r' value for boys aged 5 years to 11 years is 0.302529. The correlation value 'r' for girls show an increasing trend from 6 years to 11 years age. The increase in 'r' value being 0.473874. Though at the age of 7 years there is considerable fall in the 'r' value for girls. The highest 'r' value is recorded for girls at the age of 8 years (0.818874), which is greater than the 'r' value recorded at 11 years by 0.009091. There is a significant sex difference in 'r' value at 6 years (0.360296) and at 7 years (0.271825), where boys score higher value than that of girls. A reverse trend in 'r' value is observed at 8 years, where girls overtake boys, the difference being 0.337746. The sex difference is marginal at 9 years (0.063575), but the sex difference is significant at 10 years (0.344665) and at 11 years (0.552887), where the 'r' values for girls are higher than that of the boys in all the 4 older age groups. The net gain in 'r' value for girls is 0.664979, while there is a net lose in 'r' value (0.302529) for boys.

Correlation between head circumference and chest circumference measurement show the lowest 'r' value at 11 years (0.103894) and the highest 'r' value at 7 years (0.516818) for boys. The net loss in 'r' value being 0.412924. The lowest 'r' value for girls is recorded at 5 years (0.289644) and the highest value at 9 years (0.520134), the net gain in the 'r' value is 0.23049. Boys register higher values than in girls at 6 years by 0.054865 and at 7 years by 0.010672, whereas girls exhibit higher 'r' values than boys at 8 years by 0.26634 at 9 years by 0.32...., at 10 years by 0.16687 and at 11 years by 0.394291. There is a significant sex difference in 'r' values of boys and girls at 8 years, 9 years and 11 years age. A steady increase in 'r' values is observed in younger age groups of both boys and girls upto the age of 7 years. There is a sudden fall in the 'r' value of boys at 8 years and 9 years, while there is a steep increase in 'r' values of girls, as is evident from the Table 8. There is a differential rate of increase in 'r' values. The 'r' values are comparatively higher in girls than in boys as age advances.

The correlation coefficient value between triceps and subscapular skinfold record the highest value at 6 years (0.729229) followed by at 7 years (0.714041) for boys, while the highest 'r' value for girls is recorded at 11 years (0.820944). The lowest 'r' value for boys is at 11 years age (0.112896), whereas the corresponding value is at 6 years for girls (0.479028). Boys register a steady decline in 'r' value upto the age of 9 years (0.427897) and then after the value increases to 0.616862 at 10 years. There is greater fluctuation in 'r' values of girls. The greatest 'r' value for girls is recorded at 11 years (0.820944) followed by at 9 years (0.7427) and at 10 years (0.693237). Girls show slightly higher value at 5 years than boys, while the trend is reversed at 6 years and at 7 years. The 'r' values between the sexes at 8 years show minor difference (0.00455) while the sex difference is highly significant at 11 years (0.707048). There is greater degree of variability in 'r' values of both boys and girls. The correlation values decreased in boys, while the girls showed remarkable increase in 'r' values.

Assessment of Nutritional Status of Children by Following Methods

Weight Deficit Classification

The data on body weight of Mala children are classified, basing on the modified Gomez *et. al.* (1956) classification as proposed by Vishveswara Rao (1980) using NCHS standards for age and sex. The frequency distribution of boys and girls falling under different grades of weight for each age group is depicted in Table 7. In the total Mala sample, 4.88% of girls aged 8 years and 2.27% of boys aged 7 years ae placed in grade IV malnutrition category, according to weight deficit for that age. Boys having normal weight as per the NCHS standards register highest frequency at 7 years (40.91%) and in other ages they show varying proportions ranging from 17.07% to 20.93%, whereas girls having normal weight exhibit the highest frequency at 7 years (44.68%), followed by at 6 years (35.71%) while in all other ages, they record a frequency around 17 per cent. Interestingly, both boys and girls having normal weight as per the NCHS standards, show higher proportions at 7 years age, while the frequency in 8 to 10 years, fluctuate around 20% in both sexes. Boys, who are grouped under grade-I category of malnutrition show highest proportions at 8 years (53.33%), followed by at 6 years (41.46%) and at 10 years (34.15%). Girls grouped in grade-I malnutrition, show the highest frequency at 8 years (43.90%), followed at 9 years (39.58%) and at 10 years (34.43%), while in other ages, girls show a frequency ranging from 23.81% to 25.53% under grade-I category of malnutrition. Both boys and girls grouped under grade-I malnutrition record highest frequency at the age of 8 years. In grade-II category of malnutrition boys record 36.64% at 7 years, 36.58% at 10 years and 34.15% at 6 years of age. Girls falling in grade-II malnutrition category are found in higher proportions at the age of 6 years (38.10%) followed by at 9 years (29.17%) and at 10 years (27.87%). Around 30 per cent of both boys and girls fall in grade-II category of malnutrition as per the NCHS standard in body weight. Both boys and girls falling under grade-III malnutrition category record below 10 per cent in 6 to 8 years of age, while girls aged 10 years register higher frequency than that of boys in grade-III malnutrition category.

Height Deficient Classification

The data on stature (height) of Mala children is grouped into categories of Nutritional Vishveshwar Rao's, the height deficit classification, using NCHS standards for age and sex. The distribution of various categories of height deficit classification on Mala children show that only one girl aged 8 years (2.44%) is found to be in the poor category of height deficit classification for that age (Table-8). The Mala girls in all ages except 7 years old, exhibit higher proportions in mild retardation category than that of boys. The frequency of mild retardation ranges in between 34.14% of 8 years to 21.28% at 7 years among girls, while the frequency ranges in between 31.71% at 6 years to 24.39% at 10 years among boys. The Mala boys register higher frequency in the normal category of height deficit classification than that of girls. Boys with normal height as per the NCHS standards show higher proportions in younger age groups, i.e. 6 years to 9 years, than that of girls, while the trend is reversed in 10 years age group. The frequency of normal children varied from 68.29% to 60% in boys, while the frequency ranges from 68.85% to 46.81% in girls of all ages.

Table 7
Weight Deficit Classification Among Mala Children

	Males				Females				
Ages	*Standard Wt.*	*Kg.*	*f*	*%*	*Standard Wt.*	*Kg.*	*f*	*%*	*Grades*
6 Yrs	50% of 22	11	0	0	50% of 21.6	10.8	0	0	IV malnutrition
	60%	13.2	3	7.32	60%	12.96	1	2.38	III malnutrition
	70%	15.4	14	34.15	70%	15.12	16	38.1	II malnutrition
	80%	17.6	17	41.46	80%	17.28	10	23.81	I malnutrition
	80+%	17.6+	7	17.07	80+%	17.28+	15	35.71	N Normal
7 Yrs	50% of 24.7		12.35	1	50% of 24.2	12.1	0	0	IV malnutrition
	60%	14.82	0	0	60%	14.52	3	6.38	III malnutrition
	70%	17.29	17	36.64	70%	16.94	11	23.4	II malnutrition
	80%	19.76	8	18.18	80%	19.36	12	25.53	I malnutrition
	80+%	19.76+	8	18.18	80+%	19.36	21	25.53	N Normal
8 Yrs	50% of 27.8	13.9	0	0	50% of 27.6	13.8	2	4.88	IV malnutrition
	60%	16.68	6	13.33	60%	16.56	5	12.2	III malnutrition
	70%	19.46	7	15.56	70%	19.32	9	21.95	II malnutrition
	80%	22.24	24	53.33	80%	22.08	18	43.9	I malnutrition
	80+%	22.24+	8	17.78	80+%	22.08+	7	17.07	N Normal
9 Yrs	50% of 31.2	15.6	0	0	50% of 31.4	15.7	0	0	IV malnutrition
	60%	18.72	7	16.28	60%	18.84	7	14.58	III malnutrition
	70%	21.84	12	27.91	70%	21.98	14	29.17	II malnutrition
	80%	24.96	15	34.88	80%	25.12	19	39.58	I malnutrition
	80+%	24.96+	9	20.93	80+%	25.12+	8	16.67	N Normal
10 Yrs	50% of 33.7	16.85	0	0	50% of 35.2	17.6	0	0	IV malnutrition
	60%	20.22	4	9.76	60%	21.12	13	21.31	III malnutrition
	70%	23.59	15	36.58	70%	24.64	17	27.87	II malnutrition
	80%	26.96	14	34.15	80%	28.16	21	34.43	I malnutrition
	80+%	26.96+	8	19.51	80+%	28.16+	10	16.39	N Normal

Table 8

Height Deficit Classification Among Mala Children

Ages	Males				Females				Categories
	Standard Wt.	*Cms.*	*f*	%	*Standard Wt.*	*Cms.*	*f*	%	
6 Yrs	80% of 118.6	94.88	0	0	80% of 117.8	94.24	0	0	Poor
	90%	106.74	13	31.71	90%	106.02	14	33.33	Mild retardation
	100%	118.6	26	63.41	100%	117.8	23	54.76	Normal
	100+		2	4.88	100+		5	11.91	Above Normal
7 Yrs	80% of 124.5	99.6	0	0	80% of 123.5	98.8	0	0	Poor
	90%	112.05	12	27.27	90%	111.15	10	21.28	Mild retardation
	100%	124.5	29	65.91	100%	123.5	22	46.81	Normal
	100+		3	6.82	100+		15	31.91	Above Normal
8 Yrs	80% of 130.0	104	0	0	80% of 129.4	103.52	1	2.44	Poor
	90%	117	13	28.89	90%	116.46	14	34.14	Mild retardation
	100%	130	28	62.22	100%	129.4	22	53.66	Normal
	100+		4	8.89	100+		4	9.76	Above Normal
9 Yrs	80% of 135.5	108.4	0	0	80% of 135.5	108.4	0	0	Poor
	90%	121.95	12	27.91	90%	121.95	15	31.25	Mild retardation
	100%	135.5	28	65.12	100%	135.5	28	58.33	Normal
	100+		3	6.97	100+		5	10.42	Above Normal
10 Yrs	80% of 140.2	112.16	0	0	80% of 140.9	112.72	0	0	Poor
	90%	126.18	10	24.39	90%	126.81	16	26.23	Mild retardation
	100%	140.2	28	68.29	100%	140.9	42	68.85	Normal
	100+		3	7.32	100+		3	4.92	Above Normal

Clinical Signs

For the incidence of pigmentation or patches on skin among Mala children, observations were made on face, especially cheeks, fore head, fore arm and neck. In the total sample, 7 children are observed to be having irregular patches on their skin, where only two male children one in 6 years and another in 8 years age group show niacin deficiency, while 4 girls in 10 years and one girl in 6 years are afflicted by this condition (Table 9).

The incidence of angular stomatitis among Mala children occurred in a low frequency at 7 years, and reached higher frequencies at 8 and 10 years of age. The incidence of angular stomatitis is more frequently occurring among Mala children of all ages, compared to female children, among whom the frequency is much lower. In the total sample, 35 males are suffering from angular stomatitis, while only 9 females are affected with fissures or cracks, radiating from the angles or corners of the mouth (Table 9).

The occurrence of dry scaly skin is prominent in male children compared to female children. In male children this clinical sign is observed in all age groups, while its occurrence among the female children varies but in lesser proportions (Table 9).

The prevalence of discoloured hair among Mala children reveals that this condition is more frequent among female children than in male children, though the incidence is significantly low. The maximum frequency is recorded among females aged 6 and 7 years, while in latter age groups the frequency shows a declining trend (Table 9).

The prevalence of flag or coarse hair among male children among whom the texture of hair is rough with split ends is recorded in Table-9. Only two male children aged 8 years and 9 years are observed to be having coarse hair in the total sample observed for this trait.

Observations made on Mala children for the occurrence of spongy bleeding gums reveal only 3 males and one female in the 7 years age groups, and one male in 9 years and one female in 10 years, are affected with this sign, indicating the deficiency of Vitamin C.

Incidence of flourosis is characterized by mottled enamel among the Mala children are recorded in Table 9. The incidence of this particular clinical feature shows higher prevalence among male children compared to female children. In younger age groups of both sexes, the prevalence rate is in higher proportions than in older age groups and presents a declining trend as the age of the child increases, replacing the deciduous teeth by permanent teeth.

The incidence of dental caries among the Mala children is characterized by cavities produced by certain micro organisms that live on the teeth and produce acids from ingested sugars and starches. The general trend as depicted for this variable show a decreasing frequency from younger to older children. The incidence is in higher proportions in 7 years and 8

Table 9
Distribution of the Prevalence of Different Nutritional Deficieny Signs Among Mala Children

Age	Sex	Sample	Skin Pigmentation	Angular Stomatitis	Dry Scaly Skin	Discoloured Hair	Coarse Hair	Spongy Bleeding gums	Flourosis Yellowish teeth	Dental caries	Pale conjuctive	Yellow colour at the base of nails
5 Yrs.	M	14		1.68	0.84				3.36	1.26	0.84	
	F	11		0.37					2.21	1.47	0.74	
	M+F	25		0.98	0.39				2.75	1.37	0.78	
6 Yrs.	M	41	0.42	2.52	2.1	0.84			5.46	4.2	0.84	0.42
	F	42	0.37	0.74	0.74	7.35			3.68	3.31	1.1	
	M+F	83	0.39	1.57	1.37	4.31			4.51	3.73	0.98	0.2
7 Yrs.	M	44		1.26	2.52	0.84		1.26	5.88	7.98	1.26	
	F	47		0.37	1.1	7.35		0.37	4.41	5.51	1.47	
	M+F	91		0.78	1.76	4.31		0.78	5.1	6.67	1.37	
8 Yrs.	M	45	0.42	3.78	1.26	0.84	0.42		8.4	7.98	2.94	
	F	41		0.74	0.37	4.78			4.41	6.62	1.47	
	M+F	86	0.2	2.16	0.78	2.94	0.2		6.27	7.25	2.16	
9 Yrs.	M	43		2.52	0.84	1.26	0.42	0.42	6.3	6.3	2.1	0.42
	F	48		0.37	1.84	4.78			5.88	2.94	1.1	
	M+F	91		1.37	1.37	3.14	0.2	0.2	6.08	4.51	1.57	0.2
10 Yrs.	M	41		2.94	1.26	0.84			3.78	3.36	1.68	
	F	61	1.47	0.74		5.88		0.37	2.94	1.84	0.74	0.74
	M+F	102	0.78	1.76	0.59	3.53		0.2	3.33	2.55	1.18	0.39
11 Yrs.	M	10			0.84	0.42		2.1	0.84	0.84		
	F	22			1.1	0.37			0.37	0.37		
	M+F	32			0.98	0.39		0.2	0.59	0.59		
Total	M	238	0.84	14.71	9.66	5.04	0.84	2.1	34.03	31.93	9.66	0.84
	F	272	1.84	3.31	5.15	30.51		0.74	23.9	22.06	6.62	0.74
	M+F	510	1.37	8.63	7.25	18.63	0.39	1.37	28.63	26.67	8.04	0.78

years old children in both sexes and the incidence of dental caries are in moderate proportions in other age groups. It is observed that boys maintain slightly higher prevalence rate than that of girls. However the differential proportion in the incidence of flourosis is small compared to that of the dental caries in both sexes (Table 9).

The incidence of pale conjuctiva in Mala children is slightly in higher proportions compared to females and higher frequencies are recorded in 8 years and 9 years age groups (Table 9).

The occurrence of yellow colour in the base of the nails, among Mala children reveals that only 2 male children, one each in 6 years and 9 years age groups were affected with this clinical sign, whereas 2 females in the age group of 10 years showed this clinical sign.

The general health condition of most of the Male children, is reported to be satisfactory in all the age groups. Only a few children are reported to be weak and anaemic.

Impact of Socio-cultural Factors on Growth

The impact of cultural variables like literacy levels of parents, family size, family type, per capita income on the growth and development of Mala children are assessed through some of the selected anthropometric traits like; weight, height, sitting height, biacromial diameter and biiliocristal diameter of boys and girls. The statistical constants calculated for each of the parameters are presented in Tables 10-14.

The anthropometric data on growth and development of Mala children are analysed as per parents' literacy levels. For weight the boys of non-literate parents show higher mean value in the sixth age group, ninth and tenth age-group, while 7 years age group and 8 years of age group children show higher body weight among the literate parents; and mother non-literate and father literate group respectively. Among girls the gain in weight is not so clear for all ages wherein, in some age group the weight is high in mother-father non-literate group and mother literate – father non-literate group. It is evident from the Table (-)10; that only 8 year girls recorded higher mean body weight for the father-mother literate group. Similarly for stature and sitting height the readings doesn't show a perfect growth trend in either of the groups for all ages. Among boys and girls the mean height is accelerating in the tenth age-group in the parents non-literate group which shows that growth is purely biological, irrespective of socio-cultural factors. Exactly the same pattern is observed even for biacromial diameter and biiliocristal diameter i.e. uneven increase in growth for different ages in different groups, probably, it so happened due to small sample size in different sub-groups.

The growth pattern among the Mala children is observed according to the size of the family. It is seen from the Tables 10-14, that majority of the boys belong to the medium size family (4-6) category. The gain in mean weight for boys is high in medium large family (7-9) than medium size family for all age groups. Girls also show more number in medium family category. 9 year and 10 year girls show more weight in medium family while 7 year and 8 year girls show more weight in medium large family. The mean value for stature among boys is high among medium large family and medium size family. Similarly girls also show higher mean value among medium family and medium large family for different age groups. When height and weight are in one line, obviously sitting height will also follow the similar line. Biacromial diameter and biiliocristal diameter also show more number of children in medium size family than to medium large family size, but the mean value is high in medium large family for some ages and in girls few children are seen in small size family. A definite growth trend is not observed because of less number of sample size among different sub groups.

Growth of the children as per the type of the family reveals that all the boys under study falls in nuclear family type and among girls all the children belong to nuclear family type except in the age group seven and nine years wherein, a sample of two and one children is seen in joint family.

The mean growth of the children according to the birth order is calculated and is shown in Tables 10-14. It is observed that in the 7 year age group and 8 year age group the boys show higher weight in the 2nd birth order. 9 year age group and 10 year age group show higher mean value in the 3rd birth order. Among girls the mean weight is high for the 3rd birth order for the age group . Among the 10 year age group the mean weight is high in the 5th birth order. Similarly 7 years and 8 years age group also show higher weight in the 5th birth order. Among boys the mean height is high in the 3rd birth order for the 6 years age group. 10 years age group show high value in the 2nd birth order. Among girls at the 6 years age group the 1st birth order show higher mean value and in tenth years age group the mean height is high in the 5th birth order child group. The mean values for sitting height, biacromial diameter and biiliocristal diameter according to the birth order were shown in Tables 10-14 respectively. Here also it is seen that from 4th birth order onwards the mean value is high it is because of less sample size which in turn reflects to the mean value of 2nd and 3rd birth order.

The growth data of selected anthropometric traits of Mala children are grouped and analysed for five income group categories, namely lower, lower middle, middle, upper middle and higher income groups, baring on the per capita annual income of parents. It is observed from the table 10–14 a majority of the boys and girls fall in the lower income group. Among boys the mean height is high in the lower income group than the lower middle income group. Similarly, among girls the mean height is high in lower income group for 6, 7 and 8 years of age group while in 9

Table 10
Impact of Socio-cultural Factors on Stature Among Mala Children

Boys

	6 N	6 Mean	6 S.D.	7 N	7 Mean	7 S.D.	8 N	8 Mean	8 S.D.	9 N	9 Mean	9 S.D.	10 N	10 Mean	10 S.D.
Literacy Level															
Father & Mother both literate	10	15.15	1.99	9	20.56	3.13	5	20.6	2.19	5	21.7	2.17	5	23.7	2.64
Mother lit., Father Non-lit.	5	15.7	1.2	6	19.42	2.9	4	19.75	2.63	6	21.5	3.45	6	23.08	3.17
Mother Non-lit., Father lit.	7	16.43	3.52	4	16.67	3.33	10	21.1	4.44	3	20	1.73	9	23.44	2.4
Mother & Father Non-Lit.	17	16.76	2.26	21	16.31	2.84	21	19.5	2.51	25	22	2.6	20	24.82	4.01
Family Size															
Small family (<3)	1	20		4	18.5	3				2	24	1.41	9	17.06	2.27
Medium family (4-5)	33	15.91	2.25	34	16.71	2.96	33	20.15	3.2	33	21.73	2.67	37	23.99	3.44
Medium large family (7-9)	6	17.5	2.89	5	19.5	4.21	3	21.17	1.2	5	21.4	2.51	1	29	
Large family (10>)										1	23.5				
Family Type															
Nuclear	39	16.15	2.39	40	19.84	3.06	40	20.06	3.09	39	21.73	2.6	40	24.11	3.4
Joint															
Birth Order															
Birth order 1	11	16.64	3.15	12	18.42	2.39	14	19.04	2.42	9	21.72	3.09	12	22.5	1.77
Birth order 2	10	15.75	2.29	16	19.26	3.66	10	21.7	4.08	9	20.39	2.39	6	25.25	3.71
Birth order 3	9	15.99	1.09	9	17.87	1.83	11	19.27	2.71	11	22.64	2.3	12	26.67	3.26
Birth order 4	4	14.97	0.63	3	18.67	1.53	4	21.5	2.36	8	21.87	2.5	10	22.3	2.98
Birth order 5	3	16	1	1	25										
Birth order 6	1	16					1	21		1	21	1			
Birth order 7	1	23								1	23.5				
Birth order 11															
Per Capita Income															
Lower 1	37	18.11	2.44	31	18.56	2.54	30	20.02	3.21	22	21.82	2.76	22	23.98	2.8
Lower Middle 2	1	16		7	18.36	4.15	9	20.67	2.6	17	21.62	2.47	17	24.23	4.22
Middle 3				1	24		1	16					1	25	
Upper Middle 4	1		18	1	25										

Girls

	6 N	6 Mean	6 S.D.	7 N	7 Mean	7 S.D.	8 N	8 Mean	8 S.D.	9 N	9 Mean	9 S.D.	10 N	10 Mean	10 S.D.
Literacy Level															
Father & Mother both literate	7	15.86	2.1	10	18.05		9	20.59	3.73	10	21.95	2.47	14	23.18	3.43
Mother lit., Father Non-lit.	4	16.87	1.75	4	19.12	2.39	3	16.67	0.59	4	24.75	3.96	5	22.6	2.3
Mother Non-lit., Father lit.	5	17.6	2.3	5	18.3	3.31	6	18.83	2.71	6	23.83	2.7	6	24.83	4.35
Mother & Father Non-Lit.	24	16.56	2.06	21	18.31	3.26	21	20	3.25	20	22.15	4.87	15	25.2	4.83
Family Size															
Small family (<3)	2	16.5	2.12	2	16.75	3.23	1	22		4	24	4.24			
Medium family (4-5)	27	16.63	2.1	29	18.5	3.07	31	19.96	0.1	37	22.14	4.04	33	24.17	4.12
Medium large family (7-9)	5	15.7	1.49	9	19.94	4.01	6	21.42	3.04	2	19	3.04	3	23.7	4.51
Large family (10>)															
Family Type															
Nuclear	40	16.6	2.06	36	19.54	3.27	39	19.73	3.21	39	22.61	3.9	40	24.11	4.05
Joint				2	17.75	3.18				1	19.5				
Birth Order															
Birth order 1	13	17.36	2.09	14	17.39	2.32	7	18.93	2.96	5	22.6	1.85	14	25.36	4.78
Birth order 2	14	16.18	2.16	10	18.2	2.19	11	18.77	2.77	19	22	2.6	10	24.35	4.45
Birth order 3	5	16.3	1.56	9	19.89	4.23	12	19.37	2.84	11	24.38	8.34	9	22.99	2.42
Birth order 4	5	16.6	2.16	4	18.62	4.64	7	22	4.11	3	21.67	1.53	4	22.25	2.99
Birth order 5	3	15.67	2.06	3	20.33	4.51	2	22	2.83	1	18		2	26	2.83
Birth order 6													1	19	
Birth order 7															
Birth order 11										1	19.5				
Per Capita Income															
Lower 1	32	16.58	2.02	27	18.68	3.3	23	20.15	3.04	21	22.38	4.6	11	126.6	6.26
Lower Middle 2	6	15.56	1.36	12	17.96	3.26	12	19.08	3.94	19	22.74	3.27	27	129.8	7.3
Middle 3	2	20	0	1	20		4	19.25	1.5						
Upper Middle 4													2	136.4	3.89

Table 11
Impact of Socio-cultural Factors on Stature Among Mala Children

	Boys															Girls														
	6			7			8			9			10			6			7			8			9			10		
	N	*Mean*	*S.D.*	*N*	*Mean*	*S.D.*	*N*	*Mean*	*S.D.*	*N*	*Mean*	*S.D.*	*N*	*Mean*	*S.D.*	*N*	*Mean*	*S.D.*	*N*	*Mean*	*S.D.*	*N*	*Mean*	*S.D.*	*N*	*Mean*	*S.D.*	*N*	*Mean*	*S.D.*
Literacy Level																														
Father & Mother both literate	10	107	6.47	9	118.91	6.78	5	121.82	5.664	5	124.28	3.238	5	130.96	5.64	7	106.3	4.09	10	117.1	10.09	9	117.56	8.389	10	124.13	5.74	14	126.9	5.41
Mother lit., Father Non-lit.	5	111	4.28	6	118.45	4.88	4	119.22	5.9	6	122.8	6.183	6	123.73	5.61	4	112.47	3.165	4	117.1	5.47	3	113.03	5.462	4	131	10.1	5	127.9	9.017
Mother Non-lit., Father lit.	7	109.38	9.43	4	108.58	4.44	10	122.79	8.824	3	125.8	5.179	9	128.1	5.16	5	112.3	7.738	5	115.1	10.44	6	116.76	8.141	6	127.3	9.46	6	130.6	7.62
Mother & Father Non-Lit.	17	109.8	5.97	21	115.9	4.9	21	121.07	5.7	25	125.8	7.195	20	131.6	6.1	24	110.6	6.869	21	117	7.893	21	119.18	6.969	20	125.61	6.64	15	131.2	7.84
Family Size																														
Small family (<3)	33	108.55	6.35	1	117.1		4	119.47	7.123				2	130.55	2.76	8	111.46	5.98	2	113.7	1.897	2	110.7	7.212	1	121.7		4	129.2	8.187
Medium family (4-6)	6	112.57	7.1	34	115.93	5.65	33	121.38	6.667	33	125.05	6.839	37	123.99	3.44	27	109.9	6.99	29	117.1	8.465	31	118.06	0	37	126.32	7.37	33	129.1	7.17
Medium large family (7-9)				5	117.18	8.29	3	124.26	2.358	5	126.2	7.33	1	129		5	110.28	4.21	9	116.5	9.172	6	122.85	7.556	2	122.05	6.01	3	129.2	9.06
Large family (10>)										1	123.1																			
Family Type																														
Nuclear	39	109.16	6.54	40	116.11	5.65	40	121.4	6.455	39	125.15	6.731	40	130.3	6.07	40	110.26	6.42	38	117.1	8.3	39	118.42	7.341	39	126.13	7.29	40	129.2	7.18
Joint																			2	111.8	9.097				1	122.3				
Birth Order																														
Birth order 1	11	109.9	8.49	12	115.11	3.53	14	119.55	6.59	9	125.52	6.76	12	127.99	2.51	13	112.49	6.452	14	114.5	6.34	7	116.12	5.436	5	126.56	3.15	14	131.7	8.158
Birth order 2	10	108.09	6.49	16	116.46	7.98	10	123.38	7.97	9	122.42	6.53	6	134.21	8.48	14	108.86	7.375	10	115.1	6.66	11	116.56	6.619	19	125.45	6.65	10	128	7.95
Birth order 3	9	109.05	3.34	8	115.35	4.28	11	120.47	5.08	11	127.14	6.756	12	133.58	4.69	5	110.64	3.76	9	118.4	11.48	12	117.57	7.619	11	126.7	10.4	9	128.2	5.24
Birth order 4	4	106.35	5.59	3	117.85	4.05	4	124.27	4.69	8	124.69	7.878	10	126.79	6.32	5	108.2	6.585	4	120.4	10.24	7	123.24	7.409	3	126.76	2.1	4	125.3	2.64
Birth order 5	3	106.6	1.99	1	123.5											3	109.87	5.35	3	123.5	7.29	2	124.95	11.53	1			2	134.4	1.41
Birth order 6	1	118.1					1	126.5		1	127.9																	1	118.8	
Birth order 7	1	122.7								1	123.1																			
Birth order 11																									1	122.3				
Per Capita Income																														
Lower 1	37	109.07	6.7	31	115.94	5.21	31	121.25	6.8	22	125.47	7.73	22	130.57	5.69		3216.578	2.02	27	117.2	8.9	23	119.36	6.293	21	125.69	7.32	11	126.2	6.26
Lower Middle 2	1	109.7		7	113.91	6.54	9	122.9	4.785	17	124.72	5.371	17	129.83	6.85		615.583	1.357	12	115.9	7.54	12	116.2	9.833	19	126.4	7.3	27	129.8	7.307
Middle 3		111.9		1	129.4		1	112.5					1	132.5		2	20	0	1	118.8		4	119.72	2.973				2	136.4	3.889
Upper Middle 4	1			1																										

Table 12
Impact of Socio-cultural Factors on Sitting Height Among Mala Children

	Boys															Girls														
	6			7			8			9			10			6			7			8			9			10		
	N	Mean	S.D.	N	Mean	S.D.	N	Mean	S.D.	N	Mean	S.D.	N	Mean	S.D.	N	Mean	S.D.	N	Mean	S.D.	N	Mean	S.D.	N	Mean	S.D.	N	Mean	S.D.
Literacy Level																														
Father & Mother both literate	10	56.63	3.041	9	614	3.519	5	64.52	2.655	5	64.74	2.97	5	6774	2.07	7	56.24	2.654	10	61.91	4.988	9	60.91	3.01	10	64.21	2.88	14	85.83	2
Mother Irt. Father Non-lit.	5	57.98	1.497	6	6258	2.913	4	80.02	6.266	6	63.78	4.07	6	65.366	3.066	4	59.02	1.02	4	51.5	2.08	3	59.63	3.84	4	64.925	3.788	5	64.84	4.4
Mother Non-lit. Father Irt.	7	57.61	4.13	4	57675	1.95	10	64.75	3.074	3	61.858	5.11	9	66.188	2.89	5	:59.6	5.07	5	60.54	4.318	6	61.45	3.1	6	64.716	3.85	6	67.716	3.52
Mother & Father Non-Lit.	17	57.87	2.81	21	6086	2.29	21	6227	2.659	25	64.78	3.44	20	67.38	2.576	24	58.17	2.93	21	60.885	3.72	21	61.795	3.86	20	64.415	3.366	15	66.6	4
Family Size																														
Small family (<3)				1	60.5		4	59.95	6.449				2	69.3	0.595	8	59.125	2.86	2	61	1.555	2	58.7	4.38	1	85.2		4	67.12	3
Medium family (4-5)	33	57.38	2.906	34	60.89	2.856	33	63.28	3017	33	64.22	3555	37	66.675	2.72	27	58.018	3.069	29	61	0.396	31	61.36	4	37	64.475	3.26	33	66.166	4
Medium large family (7-9)	6	58.28	3.4	5	61.3	3.5	3	63.23	1.6	5.	5.22	4.148	1	66.6		5	56.9	4.086	9	61.7	4.365	6	62.316	3.725	2	63.8	2.828	3	66.33	3
Large family (10>)											66.4																			
Family Type																														
Nudear	39	57.52	2.958	40	6093	2.86 .	40	62.947	3.438	39	64.4	3.556	40	66.855	2.69	40	58.1	3.14	38	61.205	3.966	39	61.37	3.499	39	64.517	3.19	40	66.277	3.87
Joint																			2	60.3	3.818									
Birth Order																														
Birth Order 1	11	58.118	3.96	12	6054	2.19	14	61.81	3.79	9	65.255	3.5	12	65.9	1.58	13	59.346	2.788	14	60.485	3.058	7	59.97	2.926	5	64.9	2.12	14	67.96	3.1
Birth order 2	10	57.34	2.249	16	60.46	3.58	10	64.08	3.95	9	2.5	3.96	6	68.38	2.02	14	57.85	2.52	10	60.25	2.92	11	60.76	2.9	19	64.32	2.88	10	85.91	4.8
Birth order 3	9	57.355	2.11	8	61.175	1.45	11	62.66	2.796	11	65.45	3.39	12	68.07	2.676	5	57.74	3.569	9	62.755	5.33	12	61.166	3.427	11	64.95	4.43	9	65.05	2.6
Birth order 4	4	56.275	3.18	3	62.53	2.8	4	64.77	1.844	8	63.625	3.32	10	65.62	3.298	5	57.08	4.119	4	59.7	4.62	7	63.51	4.337	3	64.4	2.42	4	54	3.1
Birth order 5	3	56.03	1.234	1	664											3	56.2	5.1	3	64.5	3.798	2	63.35	5.44	1	61.8		2	68.15	0.41
Birth order 6	1	57.1					1	63.3		1	66.7																	1	62.7	
Birth order 7	1	64.1								1	66.1																			
Birth order 11																									1	62.2				
Per Capita Income																														
Lower 1	37	57.5	3.03	31	60.76	2.587	30	63.003	2.903	22	64.768	3.81	22	66.78	2.629	32	57.92	3.17	27	61.1	4.14	23	61.72	3.6	21	54.547	3.17	11	64.66	3.5
Lower Middle 2	1	58.7		7	60.17	3.07	9	64.11	2.666	17	63.92	5.25	17	66.78	2.845	6	57.33	1.9	12	61.13	3.68	12	60.64	3.689	19	64.36	3.25	27	66.64	3.82
Middle 3				1	661		1	50.8					1	69.7		2	62.6	3.39	1	63		4	61.55	2.638						
Upper Middle 4	1	57.1		1	66.4																							2	70.2	3.6

Table 13
Impact of Socio-cultural Factors on Bio-acromial Breadth Among Mala Children

	Boys															Girls														
	6			7			8			9			10			6			7			8			9			10		
	N	Mean	S.D.	N	Mean	S.D.	N	Mean	S.D.	N	Mean	S.D.	N	Mean	S.D.	N	Mean	S.D.	N	Mean	S.D.	N	Mean	S.D.	N	Mean	S.D.	N	Mean	S.D.
Literacy Level																														
Father & Mother both literate	10	24.26	1.708	9	27.4	1.65	5	27.04	1.105	5	27.92	1.72	5	28.62	1.49	7	23.457	1.11	10	26.07	2.145	9	25.82	1.949	10	27.05	1.589	14	27.04	2.906
Mother lit., Father Non-lit.	5	24.58	1.03	6	26.166	1.56	4	27.475	1.819	6	27.98	2.24	6	26.95	4.15	4	27.375	5.15	4	27.1	1.94	3	25.53	1.8	4	28.8	1.888	5	27.62	1.455
Mother Non-lit., Father lit.	7	24.428	2.468	4	25.325	1.29	10	25.92	3.45	3	27.566	1.059	9	27.92	3.847	5	25.38	0.985	5	25	2.6	6	26.316	1.888	6	28.5	1.71	6	28.2	1.89
Mother & Father Non-Lit.	17	24.88	1.228	21	26.52	2.85	21	26.738	1.579	25	28.128	1.786	20	29.615	2.06	24	24.62	1.25	21	26.29	1.856	21	26.285	1.9	20	28.1	3.069	15	28.43	1.92
Family Size																														
Small family (<3)																														
Medium family (4-5)	33	24.518	1.62	1	26.5		4	26.35	2.16				2	28.65	0.212	8	24.437	0.939	2	25.55	0.919	2	25.5	2.828	1	27.2		4	28.4	1.669
Medium large family (7-9)	6	25.066	1.28	34	26.51	2.47	33	26.59	2.25	33	28.145	1.79	37	28.64	3.01	27	25	2.4	29	26.14	1.99	31	26.07	1.887	37	28.07	2.547	33	27.68	2.37
Large family (10>)				5	26.78	1.77	3	27.6	0.916	5	27.12	1.45	1			5	24	1.437	9	26.32	2.407	6	26.61	1.57	2	26.3	0.28	3	28.4	2.42
Family Type																														
Nuclear	39	24.6	1.57	40	26.547	2.35	40	26.65	2.15	39	28.035	1.75	40	28.71	2.929	40	24.787	2.079	38	26.26	1.93	39	26.125	1.846	39	27.99	2.51	40	27.81	2.28
Joint																			2	24.1	3.535				1	27.2				
Birth Order																														
Birth order 1	11	24.85	1.839	12	26.98	3.5	14	26.535	1.695	9	28.6	1.96	12	27.28	2.72	13	24.53	1.245	14	25.37	1.369	7	25.485	1.45	5	26.08	1.826	14	28.59	1.637
Birth order 2	10	24.31	1.876	16	26.506	1.82	10	26.14	3.405	9	26.955	1.706	6	29.866	2.24	14	25.1	3.117	10	25.7	1.655	11	25.9	1.829	19	28.04	3.054	10	27.14	3.746
Birth order 3	9	24.688	1.285	8	25.787	1.29	11	26.57	1.45	11	28.227	1.66	12	29.558	3.787	5	25.16	0.929	9	27.06	2.69	12	25.666	1.86	11	28.1	2.26	9	27.43	1.28
Birth order 4	4	24.1	0.637	3	25.966	0.46	4	28.2	1.18	8	28.175	1.689	10	28.71	1.705	5	24.48	1.525	4	26.88	2.337	7	27.457	1.64	3	27.6	1.5	4	27.15	0.26
Birth order 5	3	24.33	1.12	1	29.8											3	24.33	1.85	3	27.67	2.15	2	27.7	2.4	1	26.5		2	29.7	1.27
Birth order 6	1	24.6					1	27.8		1	28.5																	1	25.8	
Birth order 7	1	26.8								1	29																			
Birth order 11																									1	27.2				
Per Capita Income																														
Lower 1	37	24.559	1.595	31	26.567	2.49	30	26.89	1.76	22	28.13	1.76	22	28.13	3.478	32	24.959	2.235	27	26.19	2.208	23	26.378	1.535	21	28.09	3.007	11	27.47	1.88
Lower Middle 2	1	26.1		7	25.757	1.36	9	25.92	3.23	17	27.91	1.789	17	29.25	2.119	6	23.83	0.985	12	26.03	1.71	12	25.625	2.358	19	27.83	1.805	27	27.79	2.45
Middle 3				1	28.2		1	25.7					1	28.5		2	27.9	1.55	1	26.6		4	26.175	1.297						
Upper Middle 4	1	24.7		1	29.8																							2	29.95	0.919

Table 14
Impact of Socio-cultural Factors on Bi-illiac Breadth Among Mala Children

	Boys															Girls														
	6			7			8			9			10			6			7			8			9			10		
	N	*Mean*	*S.D.*	N	*Mean*	*S.D.*	N	*Mean*	*S.D.*	N	*Mean*	*S.D.*	N	*Mean*	*S.D.*	N	*Mean*	*S.D.*	N	*Mean*	*S.D.*	N	*Mean*	*S.D.*	N	*Mean*	*S.D.*	N	*Mean*	*S.D.*
Literacy Level																														
Father & Mother both literate	10	16.81	0.96	9	18.588	0.88	5	18.36	0.626	5	19.34	1.213	5	19.8	1.369	7	17.657	1.62	10	18.44	1.57	9	15.51	1.24	10	19.28	1.33	14	19.607	1.21
Mother lit., Father Non-lit.	5	16.56	0.53	6	18.7	0.89	4	18.35	0.59	6	19.116	1.74	6	19.75		4	17.15	0.618	4	19.25	1.25	3	17.666	0.776	4	20	1.276	5	19.8	0.868
Mother Non-lit., Father lit.	7	18.1	3.74	4	17.4	0.83	10	18.71	1.71	3	18	0.529	9	19.92	1.008	5	17.78	1.42	5	17.4	1.809	6	18.68	1.49	5	19.7		6	20	2.006
Mother & Father Non-Lit.	17	17.38	1.24	21	17.938	1.16	21	18.1	1.14	25			20	19.81	1.648	24	17.27	1.046	21	18.01	1.47	21	18.95	1.317				15	20.08	1.518
Family Size																														
Small family (<3)	0	0	0	1	18.2	0	4	17.7	1.2	0	0	0	2	20.35	0.35	8	17.61	1.565	2	17.9	0.565	2	17.15	0.63	1	19.3	0	4	19.975	2.087
Medium family (4-5)	33	17.12	1.897	34	18.047	1.04	33	18.36	1.26	33	18.8	1.24	37	19.77	1.46	27	17.325	1.12	29	18.158		31	18.677	1.24	37	19.6	1.24	33	28.16	1.35
Medium large family (7-9)	6	17.98	1.316	5	18.8	1.41	3	18.47	0.64	5	19	0.18	1	20.7		5	17.36	0.67	9	18.255		6	19.05	1.48	2	18.65	1.32	3	18.466	2.28
Large family (10>)										1	19.3																			
Family Type																														
Nuclear	39	17.25	1.83	40	18.145	1.08	40	18.15	1.08	39	18.838	1.72	40	19.83	1.418	40	17.387	1.156	38	18.18		39	18.66	1.29	39	19.55	1.39	40	28.09	1.46
Joint																									1	19	0			
Birth Order																														
Birth order 1	11	17.68	2.885	12	18.2	0.97	14	18.05	1.036	9	18.94	1.168	12	19.23	1.006	13	17.646	1.32	14	17.757	1.06	7	18.04	0.95	5	19.76	0.96	14	20.45	1.7
Birth order 2	10	17.08	1.259	16	18.28	1.41	10	19.04	1.48	9	17.94	0.92	6	20.37	2.006	14	17.185	1.23	10	17.81	0.86	11	18.48	1.25	19	19.67	1.68	10	19.95	1.596
Birth order 3	9	16.83	0.817	8	17.71	0.38	11	17.75	1.076	11	19.29	1.277	12	20.82	1.128	5	17.62	0.545	9	18.84	1.99	12	18.58	1.23	11	20.05	2.07	9	20.14	0.798
Birth order 4	4	16.55	0.6	3	18.1	1.13	4	18.95	0.619	8	19.037	1.07	10	19.03	0.998	5	17.14	1.297	4	18.5	1.909	7	19.42	1.41	3	18.87	0.29	4	19.55	0.988
Birth order 5	3	17.63	0.8	1	18.9		1	18		1	18.9					3	17.23	0.85	3	18.8	2.02	2	19.5	2.26	1	18.6	0	2	20.7	1.13
Birth order 6	1	16.7	0							1	19.3																			
Birth order 7	1	20.3	0																											
Birth order 11																									1	19	0			
Per Capita Income																														
Lower 1	37	17.17	1.838	31	18.13	1.05	30	18.3	1.266	22	19.045	1.21	22	19.76	1.187	32	17.33	1.05	27	18.17	1.607	23	18.869	1.21	21	19.3	1.45	11	19.96	1.557
Lower Middle 2	1	19.4	0	7	17.94	1.34	9	18.38	1.169	17	18.57	1.097	17	19.89	1.34	6	16.85	0.81	12	18.058	1.076	12	18.4	1.475	19	19.81	1.27	27	20.05	1.44
Middle 3				1	19.2	0	1	17.7	0	0	0	0	1	20.1	0	2	19.85	0.636	1	19.4	0	4	18.2	1.191						
Upper Middle 4	1	18.3	0	1	18.9	0	0	0	0	0	0	0	0	0	0	0	0	0	0	0								2	21.35	1.34

and 10 year age group the mean height is high in lower middle income category. Among boys the mean weight is high in 6 years, 7 years, 8 years, 9 years in lower income group than to lower middle income group. Among girls the mean weight is high in 6,7,8 years in lower income group which in 9 and 10 years it is high in lower middle income group. Similarly sitting height also show more number of children in lower income group, similar trend is observed for biacromial and biiliocristal diameter. It is no doubt that higher mean values are seen in middle income and upper middle income group when compared to lower income and lower middle income groups, the reason behind to have higher values in the former than the latter is very less sample size which is highly difficult to come to a conclusion that the higher income group show higher growth.

Summary and Conclusions

The study on the growth and development of Mala children was carried out in East Godavari district, in coastal Andhra Pradesh, during the months of December 1999 to February 2000, to assess the pattern of growth and development of children aged between 6 to 10 years, in terms of several anthropometric traits, and to evaluate the extent of malnutrition prevalent among the scheduled caste children, and also to delineate the impact of several socio-economic parameters on the growth rate of children. The data were collected from several rural schools, spread over three Mandals on the Mala-Adi Andhra subgroup, who's subsistence economy is primarily based on agricultural labour. The findings among the Mala children suggest that they are shorter in stature and lighter in weight compared to the results reported by Singh (1980). Jhingon and Nath (1985), ICMR (1972) and Sharma (1991). The Mala children of present study show close similarity with the results reported by Rao, et al (1997) on the Mala of Vishakapatnam district of Andhra Pradesh. The growth trend among the Mala children is in close agreement with several studies in human populations (Eveleth and Tanner, 1976). The growth of children shows regular increase in all the anthropometric traits with increase in age, with deceleration in between 7 and 8 years, like in other human populations and presents the universal nature of growth among the children (Jhonston, et al. 1975), except the skinfold measurements. The present study on Mala children show comparatively lower growth rate in triceps, subscapular and biceps skinfolds than that of the findings of Rao, et al (1997) and Singh (1980), but show the similar trend. The height and weight deficit classification of Mala children reveal that very few children are observed to be normal, while a majority of them are found to be malnourished and fall below the NCHS standards of height and weight for their respective ages. But the present study can be comparable with that of Indian data (ICMR, 1972). The various clinical signs observed in Mala children indicate that they are suffering from Vitamin A, Vitamin B and Vitamin C deficiencies and are also prone to various diseases due to lack of proper health and medicare facilities in the areas of their habitation.

There is always interaction between the genetic material and the environment in determination of the pattern of growth and development among the children. Most of the parents of children practiced non-consanguineous marriages. Most of their families are of small size. Most of their households come under lower-income group and most of the parents of children are illiterates. It is observed that milk consumption among the Mala children is very irregular. So the malnutrition among some children could be arrived due to their poor economic condition and unawareness of nutritional science.

Acknowledgement

The authors are grateful to Dr. A.Chandrashekar, R.A. (P), for his help and assistance in computerizing the data for statistical analysis of the anthropometric and cultural data presented in this report. The authors wish to express their heart felt thanks, to all the teachers and Mala students, who cooperated in the collection of the data during the field work.

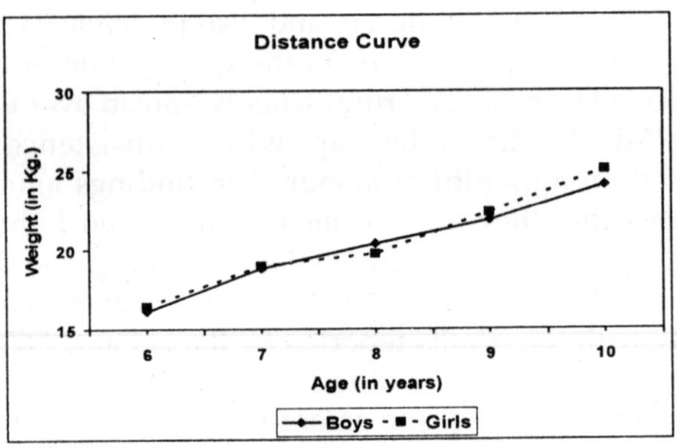

Fig. 1

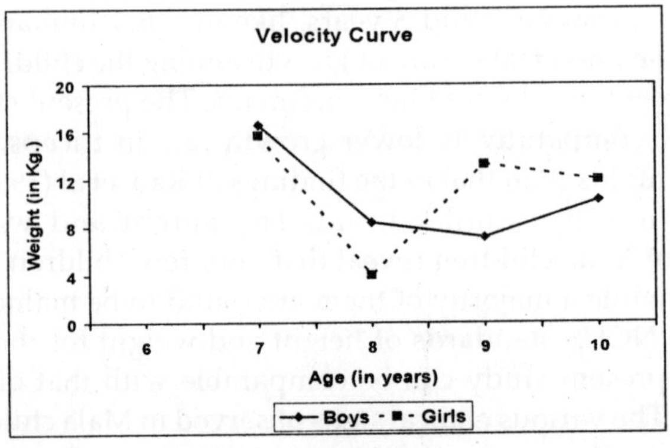

Fig. 2

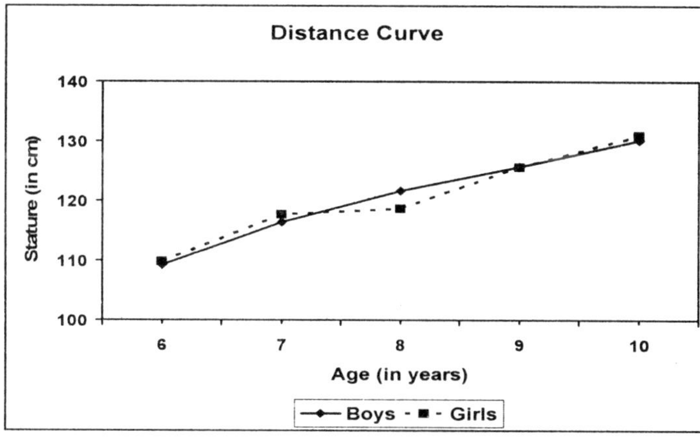

Fig. 3

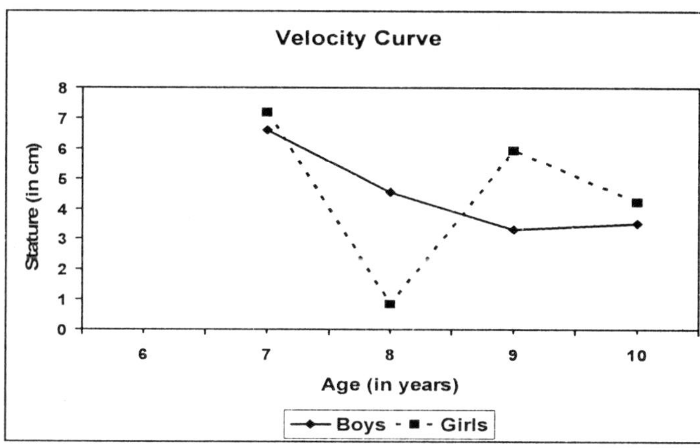

Fig. 4

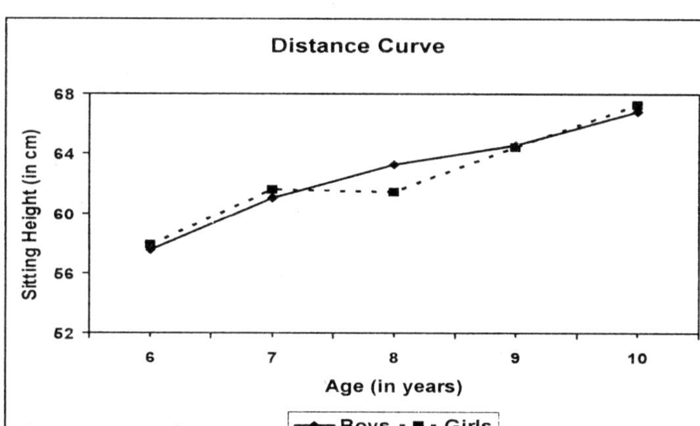

Fig. 5

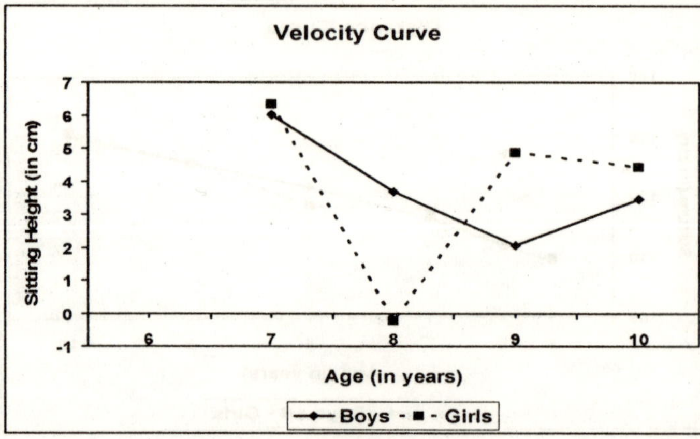

Fig. 6

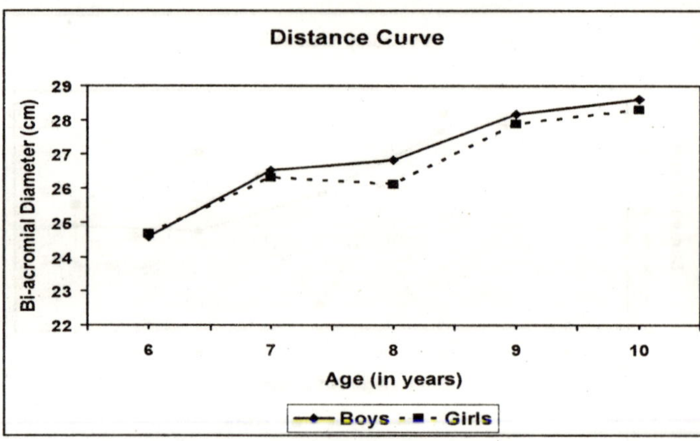

Fig. 7

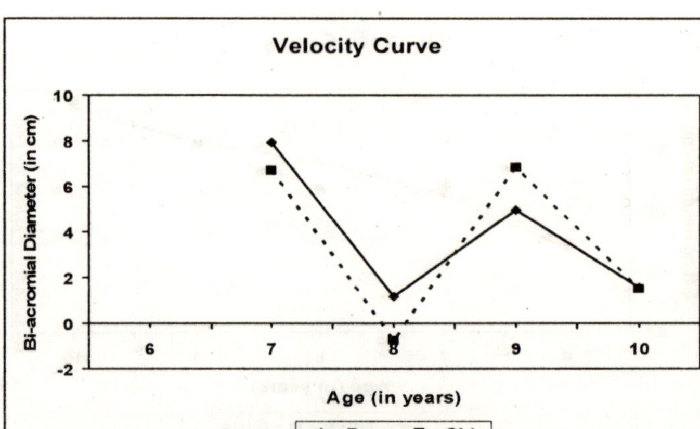

Fig. 8

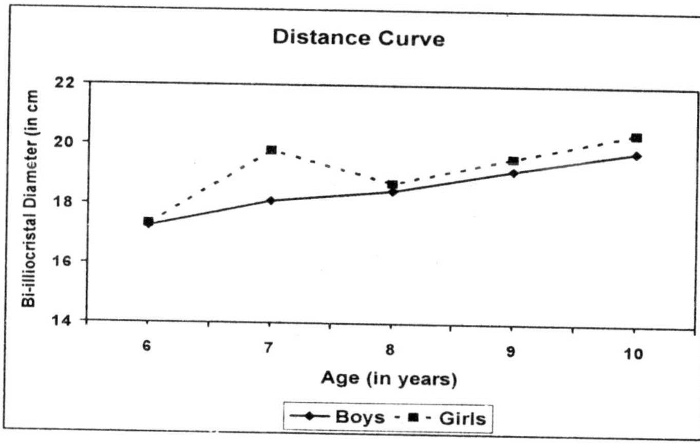

Fig. 9

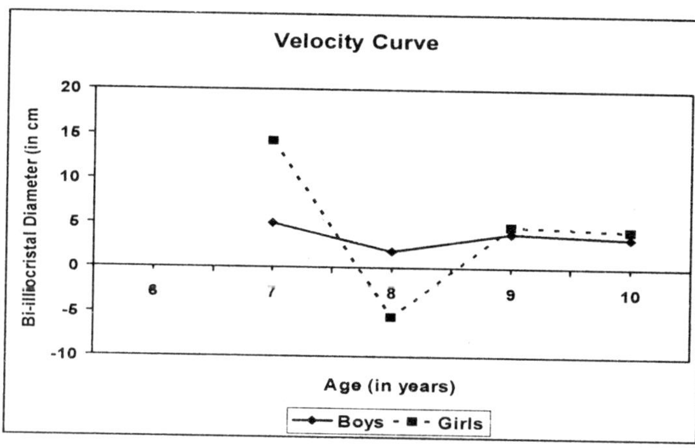

Fig. 10

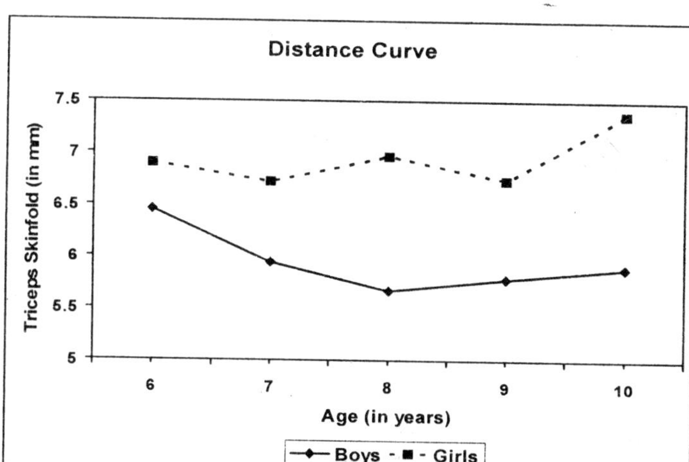

Fig. 11

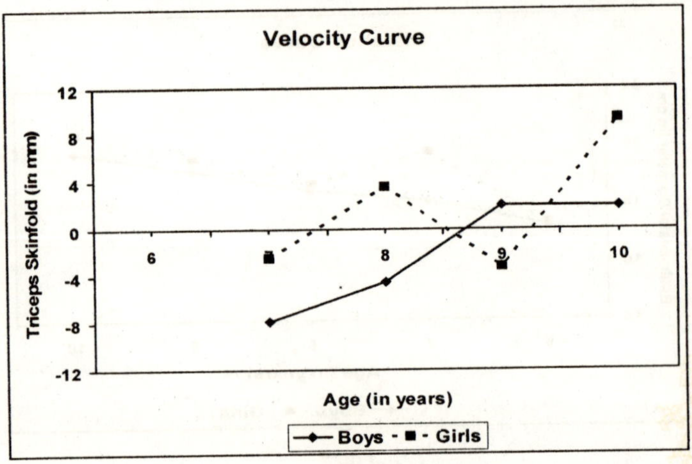

Fig. 12

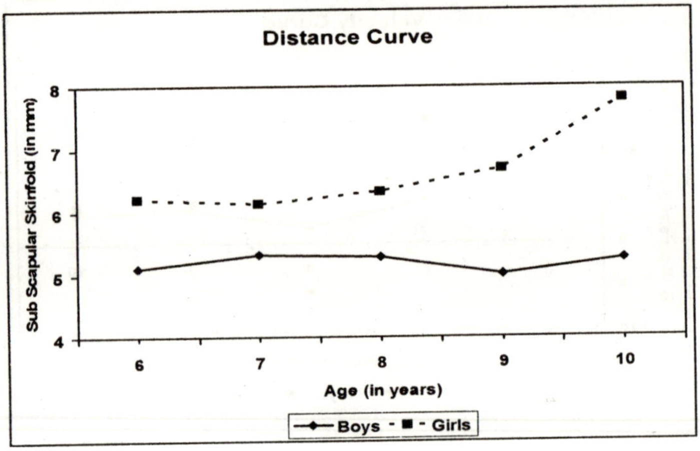

Fig. 13

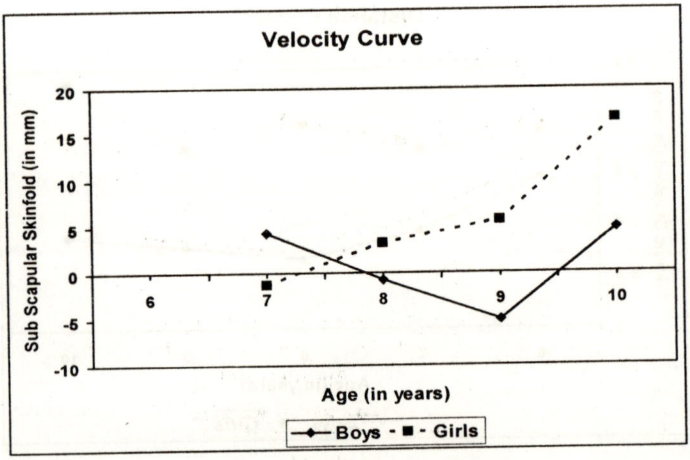

Fig. 14

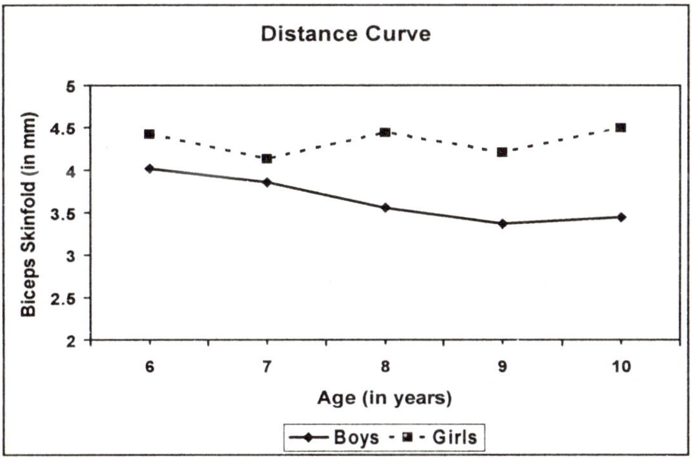

Fig. 15

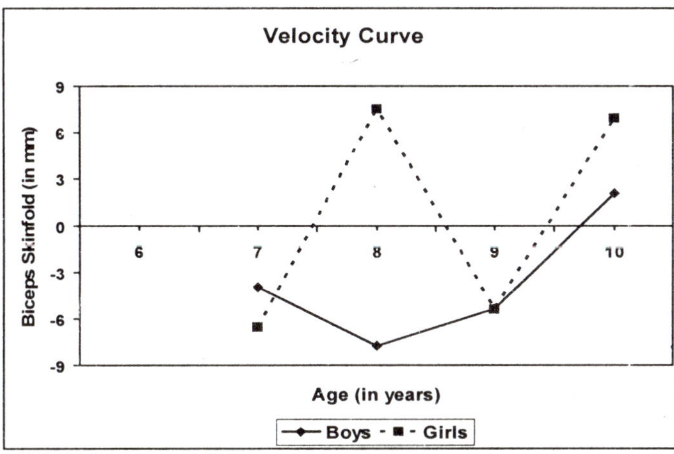

Fig. 16

References

Census of India (1981), Special Tables for Scheduled Castes and Scheduled Tribes, Andhra Pradesh, Series 2, Part 9 (1). Controller of Publications, Delhi.

Chakravarthy (1999), Quality of Life of Scheduled Castes and Tribes in Rural India, '*Yojana*', Publication Divisions, New Delhi.

Eveleth, P.B. and J.M. Tanner (1976), World Wide Variation in Human Growth, Cambridge University Press, Cambridge.

Gomez F., R.R. Galvan, S. Frenk, J.C. Munoz, R. Chavez and J. Vasquez, (1956), Mortality in Second and third degree malnutrition. *J. of Tropical Paediatrics*, 2: 77-83.

Hassan, S. S. (1920), *The Castes and Tribes* of H.E.H. The Nizams Dominions. Hyderabad State (Bombay: Govt. Central Press, 1920).

Indian Council of Medical Research (ICMR), (1972), Growth and Physical Development of Indian Infant and Children, *Technical Report Series No. 18*, New Delhi. Reprint, 1989.

Injeti M.S. and L. Ranganayak (1978), A Cross Sectional Study of Growth Among School Children of Visakhapatnam (A.P.). *Ind. J. Paediatr*, 45(37): 375-380.

Jhingon, Bela and S. Nath (1985), Trends of Growth and Maturation Among Worlis: A Tribal Population of Maharashtra, India, *Ind. J. Phys. Anthrop. & Hum. Genet.*, 11(1&2): 39-46.

Kapoor, Satwanti and A.K. Kapoor (1991), Growth in Physical and Physiological Variabls of Santal Tribals, West Bengal, *Ind. J. Phy. Anthrop. & Hum. Genet.*, 17(2 & 3). 219-222.

Kaul, S. S. and I.K. Nyamongo (1990), Ecology, Growth and Nutritional Status, New Delhi, Ashish Publishing House, pp. 1-210.

Nath, Surinder, Varsha Sachdeva and Neena Chauhan (1991), Progression of Maturation Sequence in Stature and Linear Measures of Extremities and Sex Differences Among Lodhas of West Bengal, *Ind. J. Phy. Anthrop. & Hum. Genet.*, 17(2 & 3): 219-222.

Nath, S. (1982), Maturational Trends of Growth Progression Among Jat Males of North India. Modern Man Anthropos., 22:311-320.

Rao, B., Dharma & B.R. Busi (1993), Growth Pattern and Maturity Gradients of Bicondylar Femur and Wrist Breadth among Yadava and Vadabalija Girls of North Coastal A.P., India, A Comparative study, *J. Hum. Ecol.*, 4(2): 145-147.

Rao, B., Dharma & B.R. Busi (1994), Growth Indices in Certain Selected Measurements Among Yadava and Vadabalija Girls of N. Coastal A.P.–A Comparative Study, *J. Hum. Ecol.*, 4(3): 297-300.

Rao, B. Dharma, V.L. Rao and B.R. Busi (1997), A Study of Growth in Physical and Pysiological Variables Among Koya Doria Tribal Boys of A.P., *J. Hum. Ecol.*, 7:1-3.

Rao, B.D., D.S.S. Girija Vani and B.R. Busi, 1997. A study of growth in physical and physiological variables among Mala boys of Visakhapatnam district, Andhra Pradesh, *J. Hum. Ecol.*, 8 : 361-367.

Rao, B.D., B.R. Busi, and D.S.S. Girija Vani (1997), Growth in Physical and Physiological Variables Among Mala Girls of Visakhapatnam District, Andhra Pradesh, *South Asian Anthropologist*, 18: 105-112.

Singh, I. P. and M. K.Bhasin (1968), Anthropometry, Bharti Bhavan, Delhi.

Singh, S.P. (1980), Physical Growth of Dhaula Dhar Gaddi Rajputs of Dhaula Dhar Range of the Himalayas, *J. Morph. Anthrop.*, 71:15-81.

Sharma, J.C. (1971), Physical Growth and Development of Maharashtrians, Ethnographic and Folk Culture Society, Monograph, Lucknow, India, Pp. 1-56.

Sharma, J.C. (1991), Human Growth and Assessment of Nutritional Status, In: Application Areas of Anthropology. (eds) Anil Mahajan and Surinder Nath, New Delhi, Reliance Publishing House, pp. 129-152.

Tanner, J.M. (1964), Human Growth and Constitution. In: Human Biology (eds) G.A. Harrison, J.S. Weiner, J.M. Tanner, and N.A. Barnicot, Massachusotts, Cambridge, Oxford University Press. pp.1-243.

Thurston, E. 1909, Castes and Tribes of Southern India, Govt. Press, Madras, Vol. IV, pp. 329-387.

Rao Visweswara K. (1980), Efficiency of Anthropometric Indices for the Diagnosis of Malnutrition, Courrier, 30, 113.

Weiner, J. S. and J.A. Lourie (1969), Human Biology: A Guide to Field Methods, I.B.P. Hand Book, No. 9, Oxford, Blackwell Scientific Publications.

10

GROWTH AND DEVELOPMENT OF CHILDREN: BIO-CULTURAL PERSPECTIVES OF THE DANGI OF MEWAR REGION, RAJASTHAN

D. B. Mandal & Mandira Nanda

In India, the children upto the age of 14 years constitute 36.3 per cent of the total population (Census of India 1991). Though they are numerically dominant, yet they are the most vulnerable segment of the population as per socio-cultural parameters and the biological stresses faced by them in formative period and in adulthood. The human resource is by and large, depends upon the upbringing of these children who are the future citizens of this nation. To project their health and to ensure their sound growth a necessary strategy is to be evolved for development of the country's human resource and better quality of life by eradicating poverty.

Physical growth of an individual is a regular and gradual process of increase of body dimension upto certain age. Environmental hazard and malnutrition greatly affect the growth of an individual. Besides hereditary factors, the growth rate of children is directly affected under unfavorable environmental conditions. If all the essential nutrients are available from the surrounding environment then only an individual can be able to derive its inherent capacity.

The term development has much wider connotation. One of its objective is to provide increasing opportunities to all the people for better living conditions. Growth and development of children is not only concerned with the physical growth, but it is also concerned with the socio-cultural and mental development of the child.

Since independence government has launched a number of welfare schemes to develop the rural people of India, As a part of it, some educational, nutritional, health care measures have been implemented by various government as well as non-government organizations. These measures have not only promoted socio-economic upliftment of these people but also developed the quality of life. Hence, genetic factors, environmental conditions, nutritional status along with the induced developmental programmes are responsible for the growth of the children.

This report is a part of the national project "Growth and Development of children: Bio-Cultural Perspective" launched by Anthropological Survey of India during ninth Five Year Plan. In the present treatise an attempt has been made to undertake a study among the Dangi residing in rural areas of Rajasthan, where infrastructural facilities are available.

The Dangi

The Dangi are one of the patrilineal, little known, distinct, numerically less dominant peasant caste of Mewar region of Rajasthan, mostly inhabit on plains and on either banks of Ahar river. They have a distinct cultural affinity with other agricultural castes of this area, like the Patel caste of Gujarat.

The word 'Dangi' has been referred to as upland inhabitants. The Dangi of Udaipur area speak a modified form of 'Bhilli' dialect with little admixture of words borrowed from Gujarati and Mewari languages. According to 'Bhat' (genealogist), the Dangi are the Chandra vanshi/ Yaduvanshi, who have originally migrated from Mathura, from there they moved to Gujarat and finally settled in Mewar region of Rajasthan in search of pastoral land. The largest number of them is found in Udaipur basin with 1916 families inhabited unevenly in 25 villages. The Dangi prefer to live in compact settlement either in centralized villages or in hamlets. Customary food habits during childhood, availability of foodstuffs and intake capacity are the main criteria for maintaining an optimum growth, health and vigour, which in turn regulate the growth scale. Virtually the Dangi regularly consume food items having rich nutrients with high calorific value.

The Dangi were non-vegetarian in the past, but nowadays most of them (82%) have shifted to vegetarianism. The change took place by taking oath (*sankalpa*) at various Hindu pilgrimage centers. Some of them took initiation from Saint Dharam Raj Bahoja. Maize and wheat are the main staple food. Maize is consumed especially during rainy as well as winter seasons. They prepare number of traditional food items i.e., *raita, kadhi, rabri, khamand,* etc., from the flour of maize. *Rabri* is a popular gruel, which is prepared from maize flour and butter milk and consumed regularly. They take considerable amount of milk, butter milk (*chhachh*), chilli and pickle regularly. Their traditional dietary pattern contains high quantity of protein, Vitamin A and C which is energy oriented as well as antibacterial preparation. They observe certain taboos during consumption of food items and perceive the knowledge of 'hot' and 'cold' food stuffs which causes the physiological disorder. During illness, they consume *dalia, rabri, chhachh,* etc. Most of their children consume adequate diet at home, which have direct impact on positive growth of the children.

The Dangi strictly follow caste endogamy. They are divided into several exagamous sub-groups or *gotra*. There are about 110 number of *gotras* namely, *Kai, Dongaria, Betda, Purbia* etc. which regulate their marriage alliance, and indicate their traditional place of origin. Lineage (*Khunt*) is also considered before selection of spouses. There are eight *bhats* who keep genealogical records of the Dangi of a zone (*chakia*).

Ecology and Habitat

Rajasthan has diverse cultural and ecological zones. Aravalli ranges of hills run through the heart of the state dividing the area into two ecological zones, namely the North-Western region which comes under desert eco-system, while the South-Eastern region is basically a semi-arid region.

The field work was conducted in Udaipur district of the Mewar region which is located in southern Rajasthan. Physiographically the studied areas are located in Udaipur basin and enriched by Aravalli ranges. This region comes under semi-arid zone with less than 40% relative humidity. The area is characterized by dry climate, high temperature and hot wind flows during the summer. On an average annual rainfall is about 57.45 cms. Soil structure in this area is moderately sandy loom with partially weathered rock. Here, the rivers are non-perennial. As water resources many big and small tanks and lakes are scatterly located in this area.

Material and Method

The survey among the 400 Dangi school going children between 6 to 10 years of age was conducted in six villages namely Manpura, Hundar, Siyalpura (uni-ethnic village), Thoor, Madar and Dangi-o-Guda (multi-ethnic village) of Badgoan Panchayat area of Girwa tehsil of Udaipur district.

To assess the growth process among the Dangi children of Udaipur (Rajasthan) the data were recorded in four schedules, namely, household census, anthropometric measurements, health and hygiene and area survey schedule. The following anthropometric measurements have been taken into account: ie. weight, stature, sitting height, bi-acromial diameter, bi-iliac diameter, mid upper arm circumference, triceps skinfold, biceps and sub-scapular skinfold. The pattern of dentition both deciduous and permanent teeth was recorded by visual observation. Observation on the nutritional deficiency was taken according to Jelliffe (1966) and Latham (1979) method. Statistical analysis of the present data was done as per the guideline of the project.

Besides data regarding origin and distribution of the communities, occupational pattern and changes, per capita income, child care practices, welfare activities, information on housing pattern, ventilation, health and health care practices, food habit, basic amenities available, availability of infrastructural development programmes launched in villages were collected from head of the households and from key informants by questionnaire method.

Results and Discussion

Total population of the studied 400 households 2182 persons constituting 1110 (50.87%) males and 1072 (49.13%) females. The sex ratio of the Dangi population do not differ much (1000 M: 966 F). Average family size is 5.5. Medium size families (75%) are predominant among them. (Table 1) The percentages of the Dangi children (0-15 years) is higher (54%) than the percentage of the children in the state level which is 42%. This reflects either higher reproduction rate or lower rate of child mortality in the population level. Larger section of population comes under children category. This shows that the population is growing.

Joint family system was in vogue in the past among the Dangi; as land was the main resource of their livelihood. But due to shortage of agricultural land, presently they have inclined towards diverse economic pursuits. Nowadays nuclear type of families (76%) are most prevalent probably due to impact of modernization (Table 2).

Most of the people under study are marginal farmers having only 3.48 *bighas* of land (1 acre = 1.5 *bighas*). The main crops namely maize, wheat, gram, etc., and different varieties of vegetables are produced in their field primarily by their own efforts. Apart from traditional occupation a good number of the Dangi males (50%) are now engaged in other vocations.

Educationally they are not an advanced community. Dropout rate beyond middle school level is high. Among the literate parents, 67% have studied only upto primary standard. Among the mothers, the most neglected segment of the Dangi community, 78% are illiterate. (Table 3).

Living Condition, Health and Hygiene

The Dangi are living within close proximity of Udaipur city. Their houses in rural areas, are by and large spacious and located openly. They mostly live in two roomed (85%) houses. 62% of houses are *pucca* and 38% of houses are *kachcha* which is made up of stone blocks and mud walls with tiled roofs (*kelu*) (Table 4). They perceive that *Kachcha* houses are more comfortable for living during the summer. Only 17% households possess poor ventilation and inadequate sunlight. They keep clean their houses porch and surrounding by regular sweeping. They are habituated of going to the open field for defecation. Use of flash latrine is not yet popular. They mostly take unprocessed potable water from the field wells. However, some (36%) collect purified drinking water either from hand pumps or tap water. Personal cleanliness of the 43% children is quite good and 54%

Table 1
Family Size Among the Dangis in Six Villages

Family Size	Boys					Total		Girls					Total		Grand Total	
	6 yrs.	7 yrs.	8 yrs.	9 yrs.	10 yrs.	N	%	6 yrs.	7 yrs.	8 yrs.	9 yrs.	10 yrs.	N	%	N	%
Small (<3)	4	2	1	2	-	9	4.50	-	3	-	-	2	5	2.50%	14	3.50
Medium (4-6)	30	34	27	34	30	155	77.50	28	31	26	30	30	145	72.50%	300	75.00
Large (7-9)	6	4	12	4	10	36	18.00	11	6	14	10	8	49	24.50%	85	21.25
Very Large (10+)	-	-	-	-	-	-	-	1	-	-	-	-	1	0.50%	1	0.25
Total	40	40	40	40	40	200	-	40	40	40	40	40	200		400	

Table 2
Family Type in Which the Children Live

Family Type	Boys						Girls							
	6 yrs.	*7 yrs.*	*8 yrs.*	*9 yrs.*	*10 yrs.*	*Total*	*6 yrs.*	*7 yrs.*	*8 yrs.*	*9 yrs.*	*10 yrs.*	*Total*	*Total*	*%*
Nuclear	23	32	31	29	32	147	30	30	31	34	31	156	303	76
Extended	2	1	-	3	2	8	1	2	1	1	-	5	13	3
Joint	15	5	8	8	6	42	8	7	8	5	8	36	78	19
Broken/ Incomplete	-	2	1	-	-	3	1	1	-	-	1	3	6	2
Total	40	40	40	40	40	200	40	40	40	40	40	200	400	100%

Table 3
Literacy Standard of the Dangi Parents

	Boys												*Girls*																		
Standard	*6 yrs.*		*7 yrs.*		*8 yrs.*		*9 yrs.*		*10 yrs.*		*Total*		*6 yrs.*		*7 yrs.*		*8 yrs.*		*9 yrs.*		*10 yrs.*		*Total*		*Total*					
	Fa	*Mo*	*Fa*	*Mo*	*Fa*	*Mo*	*Fa*	*Mo*	*Fa*	*Mo*	*Fa*	*Mo*	*Fa*	*Mo*	*Fa*	*Mo*	*Fa*	*Mo*	*Fa*	*Mo*	*Fa*	*Mo*	*Fa*	*Mo*	*Fa*		*Mo*		*G. Total*	
Primary (I-V)	25	09	17	09	24	06	24	12	19	03	109	39	25	08	25	07	17	09	22	06	18	04	107	34	216	69%	73	64%	289	67%
Upper Primary (VI-VIII)	9	-	12	-	04	-	08	-	11	-	44	-	11	-	06	-	10	-	07	-	10	-	44	-	88	28%	-	-	88	21%
Secondary (IX-X)	01	-	01	-	01	-	03	-	-	-	06	-	-	-	-	-	01	-	03	-	-	-	04	-	10	3%	-	-	10	2%
Above Secondary	-	-	-	-	-	-	-	-	-	-	-	-	-	-	-	-	-	-	-	-	-	-	-	-	-	-	-	-	-	-
Semi-literate	-	06	-	03	-	01	-	01	-	06	-	17	01	01	-	08	-	04	-	04	-	07	01	24	01	1%	41	36%	42	10%
Total	35	15	30	12	29	07	35	13	30	09	159	56	37	09	31	15	28	13	32	10	28	11	156	58	315	73%	114	27%	429	54%
Illiterate	04	25	10	28	11	33	03	27	10	31	38	144	03	31	08	25	12	27	08	30	12	29	43	142	81	22%	286	78%	367	46%
Total	39	40	40	40	40	40	38	40	40	40	197	200	40	40	39	40	40	40	40	40	40	40	199	200	396	400	796			

Table 4
Living Conditions Among the Dangi (Based on 100 Households)

Living Conditions	*No. of Households*
No. of thatched houses	38
No. of masonary built house	62
No. of bunglows	-
No. of households having owned house	100
No. of households staying rented house	-
Average no. of rooms	1.80

No. of rooms	*No. of Households*
1	35
2	49
3	11
4	4
5	0
6	1

Living Conditions	*No. of Households*
No. of houses having good ventilation	29
No. of houses having satisfactory ventilation	54
No. of houses having poor ventilation	17
No. of houses having sun light	80
No. of Houses having no sunlight	20
Cleanliness of the houses-good	05
Cleanliness of the houses- satisfactory	91
Cleanliness of the houses-poor	04
No. of houses having flush latrines	02
No. of houss having pit type latrine	00
No. of houses who go field for toilet	98
No. of households avail protected water supply	-
No. of households avail unprocessed water supply	100
No. of households availing pipe water	31
Wells	36
Hand pumps	33
No. of household availing stream water	-
No. of households having washing and bathing facilities- near their dwellings	100
No. of households having washing and bathing facilities-far away from their houses.	-
Personal cleanliness-Good	43
Personal Cleanliness- satisfactory	54
Personal Cleanliness- Poor	03
Utensils cleaned properly	80
Utensils not cleaned properly	20
Utensils stored properly	75
Utensils not stored properly	25

children is satisfactory. Affluent families use detergent, toilet soap, tooth paste, etc., in large scale. Though sanitation and drainage facilities are not yet improved in the villages, but their overall living condition is hygienically good. Community awareness is needed to improve their health and hygienic condition.

It is customary among the Dangi that, in case of illness or ailment, they visit the temple of 'Bheruji' and consult the *Bhopa,* the indigenous medicineman for treatment. They believe that evil spirit causes some of the diseases. But, nowadays due to awareness majority of the Dangi households have tendency to avail modern health care facilities through P.H.C and hospitals and also consult the private physicians for taking allopathic medicines. Almost all the children availed immunization, especially the polio drops and DPT vaccine. Regular breast feeding upto 1 and 1½ years of children is an universal phenomenon. Majority of the households observed some sorts of food taboos during advanced stage of pregnancy, early period of lactation and illness. More than half of the children have availed supplementary food scheme through Anganwari during pre-school age.

Impact of Development Programme

The Dangi people mostly inhabit in the developed areas from where they can avail minimum facilities. Most of the Dangi have access to infrastructural facilities which are available in rural areas of Rajasthan. The aim of the rural community development programme is to promote the welfare activities for the people. Under GDP the Badgoan Block was established in 1959 for extending infrastructural facilities to the people. Major development has taken place in various spheres such as education, agriculture, animal husbandry, credit system etc. Marketing net works have also benefited them in the fields of farm products and allied sectors. Similarly, opening up of non-formal schools, ICDS, primary health care centers and services rendered by the multi-purpose health workers, mass media, etc., have materially affected the life style of the Dangi people as a whole. Way of life of the Dangi's is also gradually changing as a result of the introduction of electricity. Under integrated rural development programmes, the Dangi are benefited by Jawahar Rojgar Yojana, Indira Awas Yojana, Bio-gas, dairy development schemes, etc. Dairy farming can contribute a great deal to the Dangi's economy and rural prosperity.

The statistical constants calculated for different measurements are shown in Table 5 which shows gradual increase in value with the change of age. Absolute gain and rate of increment is different in different age groups in both the sexes.

Weight (Wt)

Mean weight of boys at 6 years is 15.7 Kg. and at 10 years it is 24.2 Kg. In case of girls it is 16.2 Kg. at 6 years and 24 Kg. at 10 years. The boys of 10

Table 5
Anthropometric Variables of Dangi Children by Age and Sex

Measurement			*Boys*					*Girls*		
Age	*6*	*7*	*8*	*9*	*10*	*6*	*7*	*8*	*9*	*10*
N	*40*	*40*	*40*	*40*	*40*	*40*	*40*	*40*	*40*	*40*
Weight (in kg.)										
Mean	15.70	18.10	19.90	21.42	24.20	16.28	18.30	20.25	22.92	24.02
S.E. of Mean	0.24	0.49	0.41	0.51	0.47	0.42	0.50	0.48	0.69	0.77
S.D	1.53	3.09	2.60	3.21	2.99	2.64	3.17	3.03	4.36	4.83
C.V	9.74	17.10	13.10	15.00	12.40	16.22	17.32	14.96	19.02	20.11
Absolute Growth		2.37	1.81	1.54	2.78		2.02	1.99	2.67	1.10
% Growth		15.10	10.00	7.70	12.90		12.40	10.60	13.20	4.80
Stature (in cm)										
Mean	109.60	118.00	121.00	125.00	123.00	110.43	117.16	122.09	128.56	132.21
S.E of Mean	0.87	1.24	0.92	1.13	1.08	1.54	1.15	0.98	1.52	1.33
S.D	5.49	7.82	5.83	7.13	6.78	9.69	7.26	5.89	9.55	8.38
C.V	5.01	6.65	4.83	5.71	5.08	8.77	6.19	4.83	7.43	6.39
Absolute Growth		8.01	3.19	4.17	8.42		6.73	4.93	6.47	3.65
% Growth		7.30	2.70	3.40	6.70		6.10	4.20	5.20	2.80
Sitting height (in cm)										
Mean	58.80	62.10	63.91	65.55	68.10	58.80	61.40	64.19	66.81	67.61
S.E of Mean	0.52	0.60	0.56	0.54	0.53	0.77	0.62	0.45	0.71	0.68
S.D	3.31	3.79	3.52	3.39	3.37	4.46	3.88	2.81	4.45	4.30
C.V	5.62	6.12	5.51	5.17	4.95	7.58	6.31	4.38	6.65	6.35
Absolute Growth		3.29	1.83	1.64	2.49		2.60	2.78	2.62	0.87
% Growth		5.60	2.90	2.60	3.80		4.40	4.50	4.10	1.30
Bi-acromial breadt h(in cm)										
Mean	26.70	27.71	28.10	28.40	29.54	26.19	27.21	28.55	29.61	30.13
S.E of Mean	0.28	0.47	0.29	0.37	0.31	0.35	0.35	0.39	0.34	0.39
S.D	1.79	2.94	1.89	2.32	1.96	2.23	2.20	2.52	2.11	2.47
C.V	6.72	10.61	6.72	8.16	6.62	8.52	8.10	8.82	7.13	8.19
Absolute Growth		1.07	0.34	0.31	1.18		1.01	1.34	1.06	0.53
% Growth		4.00	1.20	1.10	4.10		3.80	4.70	3.70	1.80
Bi-illiac breadth (in cm)										
Mean	24.19	24.52	24.80	25.00	25.10	22.34	23.50	24.31	25.02	25.20
S.E of Mean	0.26	0.43	0.34	0.46	0.39	0.21	0.29	0.35	0.31	0.45
S.D	1.64	2.70	0.28	2.92	2.52	1.52	1.87	2.22	1.94	2.84
C.V	6.79	11.00	8.79	11.70	10.10	6.82	7.96	9.13	7.77	11.28
Absolute Growth		3.30	0.26	0.18	0.09		1.16	0.81	0.71	0.18
% Growth		1.40	1.00	0.70	0.04		5.20	3.40	2.90	0.70
Mid Upper Arm Circumference (in cm)										
Mean	14.00	14.20	14.50	15.20	15.60	14.35	14.59	15.08	15.78	15.95
S.E of Mean	0.09	0.17	0.16	0.17	0.12	0.17	0.19	0.16	0.19	0.23
S.D	0.56	1.04	0.99	1.09	1.20	1.08	1.20	1.03	1.21	1.44
C.V	4.03	7.33	6.83	7.17	7.71	7.51	8.25	6.83	7.65	9.05
Absolute Growth		0.17	0.38	0.63	0.44		.24	0.49	0.69	0.17
% Growth		1.20	2.70	4.40	2.90		1.70	3.40	4.60	1.10
Tricep skinfold (in mm)										
Mean	2.05	2.09	2.15	2.29	2.46	1.81	1.99	2.03	2.28	2.38
S.E of Mean	0.06	0.08	0.08	0.08	0.11	0.05	0.08	0.06	0.11	0.13
S.D	0.35	0.51	0.47	0.48	0.67	0.31	0.53	0.39	0.67	0.83
C.V	17.20	24.27	21.86	20.88	27.25	17.35	26.65	19.11	29.36	34.86
Absolute Growth		0.03	0.06	0.13	0.17		1.70	0.04	0.24	0.10
% Growth		1.70	2.90	6.30	7.40		9.70	2.30	12.10	4.40

Contd...

Measurement			*Boys*					*Girls*		
Age	*6*	*7*	*8*	*9*	*10*	*6*	*7*	*8*	*9*	*10*
N	*40*	*40*	*40*	*40*	*40*	*40*	*40*	*40*	*40*	*40*
Bi-cep skinfold (in mm)										
Mean	1.54	1.68	1.70	1.70	1.74	1.44	1.57	1.58	1.60	1.62
S.E of Mean	0.05	0.06	0.06	0.05	0.70	0.04	0.07	0.05	0.06	0.07
S.D	0.32	0.36	0.38	0.33	0.44	0.24	0.43	0.33	0.42	0.38
C.V	19.67	21.73	22.47	19.47	25.28	16.93	27.45	27.28	24.55	25.10
Absolute Growth		0.14	0.02	0.02	0.03		0.13	0.01	0.02	0.02
% Growth		9.10	1.20	0.90	1.70		9.40	0.63	1.30	1.25
Sub-scapular skinfol (in mm)										
Mean	3.99	4.11	4.28	4.42	4.72	4.44	4.51	4.60	4.69	4.87
S.E of Mean	0.09	0.11	0.09	0.11	0.12	0.09	0.13	0.08	0.11	0.09
S.D	0.51	0.70	0.56	0.67	0.75	0.59	0.81	0.52	0.71	0.62
C.V	12.37	15.16	13.00	15.23	15.87	13.42	17.96	11.26	15.07	12.73
Absolute Growth	0.12	0.17	0.14	0.30		0.07	0.09	0.08	0.18	
% Growth	3.00	4.10	3.40	6.80		1.60	2.10	1.80	3.90	

years show the maximum absolute gain of 2.78 Kg. with rate of increment 12.9 per cent, while the girls obtain the maximum 13.2 per cent at the age of 9 years i.e. one year earlier than the boys. It may be inferred from the distance curve (Fig.1) that during 6 to 9 years girls dominate over the boys. At 9th year the girls become heavier than the boys while the boys start their gain at 10 years of age.

Table 6

Test of Significance 't' Test Value

Character	*6 yrs. male vs 6 yrs. female*	*7 yrs. male vs 7 yrs. female*	*8 yrs. male vs 8 yrs. female*	*9 yrs. male vs 9 yrs. female*	*10 yrs. male vs 10 yrs. female*
Weight	1.21	0.31	0.59	1.76	0.16
Stature	0.45	0.29	0.95	1.88	0.71
Sitting height	0	0.79	0.39	1.41	0.42
Bi-acromial diameter	0.99	0.88	1.00	0.49	1.19
Bi-illiac diameter	5.23	1.96	0.96	0.11	0.24
Mid upper arm circumference	1.89	1.73	2.45	2.37	1.15
Triceps skinfold	0.32	0.86	1.24	0.08	0.48
Biceps skinfold	1.64	1.18	1.23	1.12	0.09
Subscapular skinfold	3.67	2.37	2.71	1.71	0.97

Height (Ht)

The mean height of the boys at 6 years is 109.64 cm. whereas it is 110 cm. for the girls. At 10 years boy's mean height is 123.43 cm. and 132 cm. for the girls. Distance curve (Fig. 3) shows that at the age of 8 years and 9 years the girls surpassed the boys and on reaching 10th year of age boys started dominating over the girl. Velocity curve (Fig. 4) does not show any significant trend of maturity attainment. Coefficient correlation between height and weight in Table 7 shows positive relationship.

Sitting Height (Sh)

The mean sitting height varies from 58.8 cm. to 68.1 cm. among the boys; in case of girls it is 58.8 cm to 67.6 cm. (Table 5) Distance curve (Fig. 5) for sitting height shows that the girls were at par with the boys upto 7th year, after that girls were higher than the boys at 8th and 9th year, and at 10th year boys surpassed the girls.

Velocity curve (Fig. 6) also depicts the same picture. Coefficient of correlation between height and sitting height shows perfect positive relationship. (Table 7).

Bi–acromial Diameter

Bi-acromial diameter with all its statistical reductions are presented in Table 1. The growth trend of boys shows that the rate of increment continues beyond 10 years of age, whereas, among the girls rate of increment gradually reduces and comes down to minimum at 10 years indicating that the major part of juvenile growth for bi-acromial diameter have been completed earlier than the boys.

Both distance curve and velocity curve (Figs. 7 and 8) shows that 'F' line dominates over the 'M' line during pre-adolescent stage.

Bi-iliac Diameter

Growth curve for Bi-iliac diameter shows that until the age of 9th year 'M' line dominates over the 'F' line but with the advancement of pre-adolescent age 'F' line dominates over the 'M' (Fig. 9).

Velocity curve (Fig. 10) depicts the picture of female dominating character over the male in the rate of growth during juvenile to pre-adolescent period. This trend helps to recall Tanner's realization of sexual dimorphism.

Mid Upper Arm Circumference

The distance curve (Fig.11) indicates that the curve lime for girls show at each age level higher value than the boys. Velocity curve (Fig. 12) indicates that at the age of 10 years among the girls the rate of growth came down to 1.7; whereas, for the boys it is again higher than the girls as it relates with the development of body muscles.

Subcutaneous Tissue Fat at Biceps, Triceps and Sub-scapular Region

Subcutaneous fat is associated with energy storage and expenditure during the process of growth and was measured at three sites i.e. biceps, triceps and sub-scapular regions.

Table 7
Correlation Co-efficient (R) Between Some Related Measurments

	Height & Weight		*Height & Sitting Height*		*Bio-acromial diameter & Bi-iliac diameter*		*Chest Circumference & Head Circumference*		*Skinfold thickness at triceps & sub scapular region*	
Age	*Boys*	*Girls*	*Boys*	*Girls*	*Boys*	*Girls*	*Boys*	*Girls*	*Boys*	*Girls*
6	0.8O	0.80	0.60	1.00	0.50	1.00	0.10	0.50	0.10	0.50
7	0.90	0.80	0.80	0.90	0.40	0.70	0.20	0.50	0.40	0.20
8	0.70	0.60	0.80	0.80	0.20	0.40	0.30	0.10	0.10	0.10
9	0.80	0.90	0.80	0.80	0.40	0.80	0.20	0.20	0.10	0.10
10	0.70	0.80	0.70	0.90	0.50	0.50	0.20	0.20	0.10	0.10

The growth line for biceps fat (Figs. 15 and 16) for boys and girls show a steady rise through ages 6-10 yrs. with regard to rate of increase of fat there is a deeline in velocity from 6-7 years for both the sexes and remain steady from 8-10 years in boy, but in female there is a sharp rise between 8-9 years and it slopes down.

The growth as well as rate of increase of subcutaneous fat at triceps region among the boys show gradual rise from 6-10 years whereas among the girls there is decline in velocity from 6-7 years and 9-10 years (Figs. 13 and 14).

The distance curve for subscapular skinfold shows gradual increase in both the sexes and 'F' line dominates over the 'M' line but in the rate of increment 'M' line dominates over the 'F' line (Figs. 17 and 18).

Impact of Socio-cultural Factors on Growth

Weight and Stature According to Parity

Agewise mean weight and stature were calculated in terms of parity of the subjects, keeping in view family's economic condition and attention towards their first child. The researchers hypothesized that growth of child has an inevitable effect of above factors. But it reveals from the analysis (Table 8) that mean weight values in different parities do not support the hypotheses. In both the sexes mean weight values; in increasing parity, do not show any definite trend. Growth of the child diminishes from first to onward parity among the boys of 6, 7 and 9 years except third parity in 7 years age group and for the parity in 9 years age group, but reverse picture is noted among the boys of 8 and 10 years with an exception in third parity at 10 years of age. While among the girls, increase in growth in 2nd parity has been recorded in 6 and 10 years age groups and in 7 years age group shows increase in 3rd parity. 8 and 9 years girls show increase growth in 4th parity.

The disagreement with the hypotheses may be due to the fact that in cross sectional study the subjects were pooled from different socio-economic family environments and parental care with different genetic make up which has also an inevitable effect on growth.

Family Size

The mean values along with SD for both the sexes were taken according to family size and shown in Table 9. It is seen that growth among the boys increases with the increase of family size. But reverse is the case among the girls of 6, 7, 9 and 10 years age group. Where small family size shows increase in growth except in 8 years age group where higher family size is representing an increment in growth. The number of family units have no relation with sex preference. However, this fact supports their customary ideas like more the working hand in agricultural field greater is the income and security which keeps the family healthy and happy.

Table 8
Mean Weight and Stature According to Parity Among the Dangi Girls

Age Group	Measurement	Parity 1			Parity 2			Parity 3			Parity 4		
		No.			No.			No.			No.		
6 Years	Weight (Kg)		X	15.75		X	16.78		X	16.20		X	16.25
			σ	2.49		σ	2.91		σ	2.44		σ	1.78
		12			14			10			4		
	Stature (mm)		X	1072.42		X	1121.93		X	1119.40		X	1100.50
			σ	111.52		σ	102.21		σ	67.34		σ	40.24
7 Years	Weight (Kg.)		X	18.03		X	18.70		X	18.83		X	15.25
			σ	2.99		σ	2.84		σ	3.93		σ	1.25
		15			17			6			2		
	Stature (mm)		X	1168.6		X	1173.53		X	1189.50		X	1123.50
			σ	47.68		σ	69.45		σ	116.89		σ	14.50
8 Years	Weight (Kg.)		X	19.65		X	19.75		X	18.00		X	24.00
			σ	2.76		σ	1.64		σ	2.55		σ	2.26
		17			12			4			7		
	Stature (mm)		X	1205.59		X	1215.83		X	1208.0		X	1274.14
			σ	55.75		σ	36.07		σ	57.79		σ	64.26
9 Years	Weight (Kg.)		X	23.20		X	23.17		X	21.15		X	25.20
			σ	5.53		σ	3.41		σ	1.26		σ	6.11
		10			15			10			5		
	Stature (mm)		X	1274.30		X	1304.06		X	1246.30		X	1332.00
			σ	130.90		σ	71.13		σ	32.17		σ	116.15
10 Years	Weight (Kg.)		X	23.73		X	25.64		X	22.50		X	22.00
			σ	5.68		σ	4.61		σ	2.06		σ	2.83
		15			14			8			3		
	Stature (mm)		X	1313.40		X	1356.14		X	1299.62		X	1265.00
			σ	105.27		σ	64.14		σ	34.91		σ	57.60

Table 9
Selected Measurements of Dangi Children on the Basis bf Family Size

	Family Size: 1-3						Family Size: 4-6						Family Size: 7 +					
		Anthropometric Measurements						Anthropometric Measurements						Anthropometric Measurements				
Age & Sex	*N*	*Wt. (Kg.)*	*Stature (cms)*	*Sitting height (cms)*	*Bi-acro-mial dia-meter (cms)*	*Bi-iliac dia-meter (cms)*	*N*	*Wt. (Kg.)*	*Stature (cms)*	*Sitting height (cms)*	*Bi-acro-mial dia-meter (cms)*	*Bi-iliac dia-meter (cms)*	*N*	*Wt. (Kg.)*	*Stature (cms)*	*Sitting height (cms)*	*Bi-acro-mial dia-meter (cms)*	*Bi-iliac dia-meter (cms)*
6 yr Boys	4	15.50	1097.70	584.00	274.00	255.20	30	15.70	1096.70	592.00	265.50	239.50	6	15.80	1094.20	570.50	266.30	244.00
		1.70	47.20	27.90	8.10	18.50		1.60	59.30	33.90	19.20	15.90		0.70	24.20	20.10	12.50	14.30
6 yrs Girls	0	-	-	-	-	-	28	16.60	1113.40	593.30	268.40	234.90	12	15.50	1083.00	575.60	258.60	237.00
								2.60	105.10	45.30	24.20	15.80		2.40	64.03	38.30	15.20	19.40
7 yrs Boys	2	15.50	1098.00	582.00	255.00	239.50	34	18.00	1175.80	621.70	279.20	243.50	4	19.50	1221.20	632.50	296.00	262.00
		0.50	24.00	14.00	13.00	13.50		3.10	77.60	37.30	24.70	24.80		2.60	55.70	35.50	15.00	38.00
7 yrs Girls	3	16.30	1152.00	611.00	268.00	231.00	31	18.70	1178.40	606.00	276.20	237.80	6	17.20	1146.20	606.80	252.50	222.00
		2.10	41.40	26.90	15.10	5.70		3.12	68.19	63.20	19.11	17.90		2.90	90.80	44.80	26.00	20.00
8 yrs Boys	1	18.00	1192.00	621.00	286.00	232.00	27	19.50	1202.11	635.80	280.92	247.22	12	20.90	1224.00	648.00	279.25	252.90
								2.83	61.66	39.70	20.67	22.90		1.50	46.40	18.90	13.30	18.60
8 yrs Girls	0	-	-	-	-	-	26	19.60	1211.96	636.40	284.50	239.38	14	21.40	1237.50	652.07	287.28	250.00
								2.70	54.73	26.62	20.82	23.30		3.10	60.80	26.90	31.00	15.90
9 yrs Boys	2	21.00	1178.50	626.50	284.00	249.00	34	21.20	1249.70	655.01	281.50	252.47	4	23.50	1289.00	674.00	301.50	225.20
		5.00	104.50	55.50	12.00	34.00		2.90	66.68	31.80	23.30	26.00		2.70	47.80	17.90	15.90	36.50
9 yrs Girls	0	-	-	-	-	-	30	23.20	1287.77	669.80	296.13	248.80	10	22.00	1279.10	662.30	295.80	254.50
								4.70	99.87	15.90	22.50	20.30		2.50	74.90	36.80	14.60	14.60
10 yrs Boys	0	-	-	-	-	-	30	24.30	1339.70	688.20	295.80	249.20	10	24.00	1317.20	672.30	294.10	254.60
								3.10	70.14	36.30	18.78	24.60		2.50	52.50	19.80	20.80	25.20
10 yrs Girls	2	23.50	1338.50	692.00	304.50	254.50	30	24.50	1327.50	679.40	298.67	251.00	8	22.50	1299.75	664.10	310.40	255.00
		1.50	0.50	9.00	0.50	7.50		5.00	90.31	47.40	25.82	31.70		4.00	56.30	15.50	19.00	12.20

Family Type

To find out whether the family type has any effect on growth, mean and SD were calculated for 5 anthropometric characters and are represented in Table 10. It is observed from the table that mean values for boys under joint family type dominate over the girls in respective age groups. Again in nuclear type, the mean values for girls dominate over the boys. As traditions the boys also enjoy privileges in joint family. But in nuclear family both boys and girls are treated as equal and it so happened due to impact of modernization.

Per Capita Income (Annual)

Per capita income of the family shows positive relation with growth of the children (Table 11). To compare the mean values in different age groups of children with different income groups shows that under six years of age, the mean values for boys almost remain unchanged in three economic groups. Perhaps due to tender age, while the mean values for the girls with their expected earlier maturity and development show increased magnitude with better parental care i.e., II + III categories. In subsequent ages, as in the table, the girls and boys also shows the same trend where the mean value increases with the increase of parental income.

Literacy of Parents

Though it is expected that literacy level of the parent has a good deal of effect on growth of their children. But it is revealed from our analysis that mean values for both the boys and girls of all age groups in the illiterate column (11) are dominating over the category I and III (Table 12).

Actually literacy level among the Dangi is very poor particularly among the women. In reality the Dangi fathers (69%) and mothers (64%) are literate only upto primary school level. This literacy level has not shown any effect on growth of their children. However, the differences are not much significant since both the groups of children are exposed to almost identical nutritional and environmental set up.

Nutritional Status

Weight for Age

Weight of an individual represents the nutritional status. Gomes classification has been applied to the present study, frequency along with percentage are shown in Table 13. It has been observed that 94.5% boys and 94.0% girls children are in normal category.

Height deficit classification are shown in Table 14 which reveals that 98.5% boys and 97.0% girls are in normal state of health.

The extent of malnutrition is also observed through the circumference of mid-upper arm, its frequency along with percentages are delineated in Table 15. It is observed that 35.5% of total children surveyed are in

Table 10
Selected Measurments of Dangi Children on the Basis of Family Type

		Nuclear Family						Joint Family					
Age	Sex	No. of family	Weight	Stature	Sitting height	Bi-Acro-mial diameter	Bi-iliac diameter	No. of Family	Weight	Stature	Sitting height	Bi-Acro-mial diameter	Bi-iliac diameter
6 yrs	Boys	23	15.69	1099.22	591.09	267.39	241.00	17	15.76	1092.59	583.96	265.23	243.18
			1.43	48.55	35.12	19.02	17.06		1.63	61.02	28.39	15.62	14.94
	Girls	30	16.77	1127.20	599.10	261.93	232.50	10	14.80	1085.70	554.70	262.00	245.60
			2.47	82.94	40.08	23.84	17.17		2.44	98.58	38.19	15.52	12.36
7 yrs	Boys	32	17.72	1165.84	616.94	276.06	243.87	8	19.50	1219.00	636.37	294.00	250.62
			3.00	77.93	36.62	24.06	21.49		2.87	57.10	37.00	21.49	40.99
	Girls	30	18.27	1169.03	613.03	268.90	232.16	10	18.40	1179.20	616.90	281.40	243.60
			3.45	77.72	41.52	21.34	19.05		1.85	48.25	26.06	20.30	13.37
8 yrs	Boys	30	19.63	1202.27	636.80	279.40	246.40	10	20.60	1226.90	646.10	284.00	252.00
			2.84	59.18	37.16	19.90	22.22		1.20	48.08	24.99	16.62	18.58
	Girls	31	20.68	1229.40	646.29	288.09	243.71	9	18.70	1190.70	626.67	276.44	241.00
			3.14	57.58	28.93	26.62	23.34		1.68	49.68	15.41	14.15	15.89
9 yrs	Boys	30	21.03	1242.73	653.90	283.30	252.63	10	22.60	1272.10	660.50	284.60	240.40
			3.30	75.76	35.47	23.39	23.79		2.37	44.51	25.91	21.20	38.96
	Girls	33	22.91	1284.76	671.94	295.76	248.94	7	23.00	1289.57	650.00	297.43	256.28
			4.49	96.44	44.33	21.98	19.72		3.34	83.55	36.37	14.30	15.08
10 yrs	Boys	32	24.44	1335.22	684.62	296.22	250.53	8	23.25	1330.62	663.75	291.87	250.62
			3.66	66.79	34.17	18.99	26.65		2.22	67.79	22.71	19.98	15.94
	Girls	31	23.93	1317.48	675.00	299.32	251.64	9	24.33	1337.78	679.67	308.11	253.33
			5.07	88.43	48.35	25.43	28.87		8.49	56.72	25.09	18.92	25.09

Table 11
Selected Measurements of Dangi Children on the Basis of Per Capita Income of Family

	Income Group																							
	-11,000			11,001-20,000			21,000-30,000			30,001 +			-11,000			11,001-20,000			21,000-30,000			30,001 +		
	Boys												Girls											
Age in yrs	*No.*	*Wt.*	*St.*	*No.*	*Wt.*	*St.*	*No.*	*Wt.*	*St.*	*No.*	*Wt.*	*St.*	*No.*	*Wt.*	*St.*	*No.*	*Wt.*	*St.*	*No.*	*Wt.*	*St.*	*No.*	*Wt.*	*St.*
6	-	-	-	19	15.89	1109.53	20	15.60	1085.90	1	15.00	10.57	-	-	-	20	15.35	1063.50	18	17.05	1148.94	2	18.50	1155.00
					1.71	60.26		1.32	45.77								2.55	104.77		2.39			0.50	27.50
7	-	-	-	18	17.22	1151.22	15	18.67	1187.40	7	19.00	1218.00	-	-	-	21	17.9	1158.86	17	18.76	1187.41	2	18.50	1170.00
					2.32	57.21		3.82	86.40		2.20	77.71					3.61	80.53		2.55	60.02		0.50	9.50
8	-	-	-	24	19.91	1202.17	12	19.50	1210.08	4	20.50	1241.00	1	21.00	1234.00	19	20.15	1238.50	15	20.60	1197.20	5	19.40	1222.00
					2.59	60.62		2.75	52.07		1.50	41.24					2.72	64.68		3.72	43.38		0.80	51.55
9	-	-	-	18	20.78	1246.83	19	22.00	1254.30	3	21.67	1242.67	1	20.00	1232.00	24	22.96	1281.58	11	23.00	1294.00	4	23.25	1300.00
					2.78	68.58		3.61	77.14		0.47	4.64					5.12	112.47		2.56	50.88		2.77	68.91
10	-	-	-	25	24.64	1335.92	14	23.21	1328.00	1	27.00	1382.00	1	22.00	1339.00	20	23.9	1321.70	15	24.27	1319.33	4	24.25	1329.00
					3.07	64.43		2.48	72.18								5.67	98.07		3.80	63.45		3.27	72.23

Table 12
Selected Measurements of Dangi Children on the Basis of Literacy Level of Both Parents

		Boys									Girls								
		Both Parent Literate			Both Parent illiterate			Father Literate			Both Parent Literate			Both Parent illiterate			Father Literate		
Anthropometric Measurements	*Age*	*No.*	*Mean*	*S.D.*	*No.*	*Mean*	*S.D.*	*No.*	*Mean*	*S.D.*	*No.*	*Mean*	*S.D.*	*No.*	*Mean*	*S.D.*	*No.*	*Mean*	*S.D.*
Weight		15	15.60	1.49	4	15.00	1.87	21	15.90	1.41	9	17.00	1.76	2	18.50	1.50	29	15.80	2.76
Stature			109.20	54.54		1018.25	38.99		1102.38	55.62		1150.55	47.69		1239.50	88.50		1086.62	94.32
Sitting height	6 yrs		575.60	73.11		572.00	18.80		584.14	27.69		615.78	33.37		630.50	41.50		576.45	41.39
Bi-acromial diameter			265.30	18.32		262.75	13.64		258.00	17.76		270.33	18.38		277.00	5.00		258.31	22.66
Bi-iliac diameter			241.47	12.71		231.00	3.67		244.33	18.84		239.67	13.00		232.00	1.00		234.83	18.52
Weight		14	18.36	3.51		20.00	2.09	21	17.43	2.68	7	19.71	3.81	5	19.00	2.61	28	18.18	2.89
Stature			1193.43	94.29		1200.20	65.39		1159.52	61.62		1213.71	70.76		1143.40	59.90		1166.07	69.44
Sitting height	7 yrs		621.28	37.44		633.40	34.76		617.52	37.54		632.71	31.83		605.40	32.45		610.85	39.26
Bi-acromial diameter			280.36	24.27		289.80	29.46		276.76	22.88		279.57	22.58		261.60	16.19		272.03	21.65
Bi-iliac diameter			244.78	24.73		270.80	28.74		239.43	23.61		247.57	25.12		233.20	14.49		232.21	15.64
Weight		7	20.28	2.37		21.18	2.25	22	19.09	2.48	9	19.66	2.58	11	20.36	2.67	20	20.45	3.28
Stature			1220.14	59.92		1216.45	34.29		1200.68	64.56		1238.55	61.81		1215.72	37.20		1215.80	64.14
Sitting height	8 yrs		639.57	24.38		642.82	29.99		637.14	39.33		647.22	27.72		641.27	24.05		639.80	29.28
Bi-acromial diameter			276.43	18.93		289.64	15.77		277.32	18.29		290.55	18.53		283.73	34.41		284.15	20.38
Bi-iliac diameter			257.57	12.59		254.45	13.24		241.36	24.68		250.77	15.36		243.18	22.96		239.60	22.93
Weight		13	21.15	2.63		22.33	2.05	24	21.46	3.51	6	22.33	2.36	7	21.86	3.04	27	23.33	4.83
Stature			1234.15	69.57		1289.66	41.10		1253.75	71.34		1260.00	37.67		1239.28	66.76		1303.29	103.42
Sitting height	9 yrs		653.23	32.57		661.67	28.33		656.04	34.39		645.83	21.54	6	47.57	37.43		678.37	45.41
Bi-acromial diameter			282.23	20.41		286.00	29.07		284.08	23.21		296.83	10.30		281.00	18.65		299.78	21.39
Bi-iliac diameter			256.31	20.63		235.33	22.53		247.71	32.25		255.50	14.97		237.86	8.93		252.26	20.62
Weight		3	23.00	1.41		26.00	3.16	29	23.83	2.80	4	23.25	1.48		23.60	6.74	20	24.31	4.11
Stature			1288.67	16.21		1367.87	55.37		1329.75	69.09		1304.50	22.87		1312.10	114.31		1328.58	72.89
Sitting height	10 yrs		677.67	11.11		693.87	42.68		677.03	30.89		660.25	6.26		682.00	55.73		677.35	38.98
Bi-acromial diameter			304.00	13.69		297.87	13.50		293.79	20.80		306.00	20.26		299.40	24.49		301.31	24.82
Bi-iliac diameter			254.33	15.96		259.00	23.46		247.83	25.43		265.75	11.58		269.10	24.01		241.61	27.70

Table 13
Weight for Age or Weight Deficit Classification Based on Nchs Standards

	Boys						Girls						
Category	*6 yrs*	*7 yrs*	*8 yrs*	*9 yrs*	*10 yrs*	*Total*	*6 yrs*	*7 yrs*	*8 yrs*	*9 yrs*	*10 yrs*	*Total*	*Grand Total*
Grade IV													
Grade III													
Grade III			1			1	1	1				2	3
			(2.50%)			(0.50%)	(2.50%)	(2.50%)				(1.00%)	(0.75%)
Grade I	3	3	1	2	1	10	4	2	1		3	10	20
	(7.50%)	(7.50%)	(2.50%)	(5.00%)	(2.50%)	(5.00%)	(10.00%)	(5.00%)	(2.50%)		(7.50%)	(5.00%)	(5.00%)
Normal	37	37	38	38	39	189	35	37	39	40	37	188	377
	(92.50%)	(92.50%)	(95.00%)	(95.00%)	(97.50%)	(94.50%)	(87.50%)	(92.50%)	(97.50%)	(100.00%)	(92.5%)	(94.00%)	(94.25%)
Total	40	40	40	40	40	200	40	40	40	40	40	200	400

Table 14
Height for Age or Height Deficit Classification Based on NCHS Standards

	Boys						Girls						
Category	*6 yrs*	*7 yrs*	*8 yrs*	*9 yrs*	*10 yrs*	*Total*	*6 yrs*	*7 yrs*	*8 yrs*	*9 yrs*	*10 yrs*	*Total*	*Grand Total*
Poor							1 (2.50%)					1 (0.5%)	1 (0.25%)
Mild retardation	1 (2.50%)		1 (2.50%)	1 (2.50%)		3 (1.50%)	2 (5.00%)	1 (2.50%)			2 (5.00%)	5 (2.50%)	8 (2.00%)
Normal	39 (97.50%)	40 (100.00%)	39 (97.50%)	39 (97.50%)	40 (100.00%)	197 (98.5%)	37 (92.50%)	39 (97.50%)	40 (100.00%)	40 (100.00%)	38 (95.00%)	194 (97.00%)	391 (97.75%)
Total	40	40	40	40	40	200	40	40	40	40	40	200	400

Table 15
Mid Upper Arm Circumference Classification of Dangi Children Based on Reference for Indian Children

	Boys						Girls						
Category	*6 yrs*	*7 yrs*	*8 yrs*	*9 yrs*	*10 yrs*	*Total*	*6 yrs*	*7 yrs*	*8 yrs*	*9 yrs*	*10 yrs*	*Total*	*Grand Total*
Severe	0	6	5	4	4	19	3	6	3	2	6	20	39
Malnutrition		15.00%	12.50%	10.00%	10.00%	9.50%	7.50%	15.00%	7.50%	5.00%	15.00%	10.00%	9.75%
Moderate	6	9	5	11	14	45	7	6	6	8	10	37	82
Malnutrition	15.00%	22.50%	12.50%	27.50%	35.00%	22.50%	17.50%	15.00%	15.00%	20.00%	25.00%	18.50%	20.50%
Mild	15	15	17	12	8	67	13	13	19	15	10	70	137
Malnutrition	37.50%	37.50%	42.50%	30.00%	20.00%	33.50%	32.50%	32.50%	47.50%	37.50%	25.00%	35.00%	34.25%
Normal	19	10	13	13	14	69%	17	15	12	15	14	73	142
	47.50%	25.00%	32.50%	32.50%	35.00%	34.50%	42.50%	37.50%	30.00%	37.50%	35.00%	36.50%	35.50%
Total	40	40	40	40	40	200	40	40	40	40	40	200	400

normal state, 34.25% are in mild malnourished, 20.5% are in moderate malnourished and 9.75% are in severe malnourished state.

In general most of the children (94.5%) are in grade normal and only 5% and 0.75% in grade I and grade II malnourished categories respectively. Only 2.7% children are in mild retarded category and MUAC 35.5% of them are normal only for BMI (97.5%) children falls under calorie energy deficiency III category. This is perhaps the standard set for BMI for the adults does not suit for children for 6-10 years.

Dentition

For the purpose of estimation of age, dentition plays an important role. In the present study the following sequence of dental eruption during the late childhood stage is elaborated in the Tables 16, 17.

Table 16
Loss of Milk Teeth According to Age

		Central incisor		*Lateral incisor*		*Canine*		Pm_1		Pm_2	
Age in yrs.	*Sample Size*	*No.*	*%*	*No.*	*%*	*No.*	*%*	*No.*	*%*	*No.*	*%*
6	80	12	15.00	9	11.20	-	-	-	-	-	-
7	80	17	21.20	11	13.70	-	-	-	-	-	-
8	80	-	-	30	37.50	-	-	-	-	-	-
9	80	2	2.50	4	5.00	12	15.00	14	17.50	3	3.70

In the present study 3% eruption of first permanent molar was observed between 6 years to 8 years of age. This finding is in accordance with Sen's study (1988) on Bengalee girls. Young's study (1964) on whites and Saito's study (1936) on the Japanese girls. All other deciduous teeth were retain at this age with 15% loss of central incisors were noted.

Among 7 years old boys and girls, loss of central deciduous incisors (21%), eruption of permanent central incisors (21.2%) and complete eruption of first permanent molar. In children of 8 years of age loss of deciduous lateral incisors (37%) and eruption of permanent lateral (38%) have been recorded.

Children of 9 years show the combination of permanent 1st molar and 1st incisors, 1.2% deciduous canine and pre-molars. At the age of 10 years eruption of permanent canine (4%), 1st pre-molar (6%), 2nd pre-molar (2%) and one case of second molar has been recorded. South Indian girls of Shouries Series (1946) and Clements *et al* (1953) for British girls showed the age of eruption of canine is 10 years which is at par with the present sample. The present study also shows the similarity with Shouries data on the age of eruption of first pre-molars. Young (1964) gives the approximate age of eruption of second pre-molar as 11 years with a range

Table 17
Emergence of Permanent Teeth According to Age

		Central		Lateral		Canine		Premolar		Premolar		Molar		Molar		Molar	
Age in yrs	Sample Size	No.	%	No.	%	No.	%	No.	%	No.	%	No.	%	No.	%	No	%
6	80	5	5.20	3	3.70	-	-	-	-	-	-	3	3.70	-	-	-	-
7	80	17	21.20	17	21.20	-	-	-	-	-	-	-	100.00	-	-	-	-
8	80	2	2.50	31	38.70	-	-	-	-	-	-	-	100.00	-	-	-	-
9	80	1	1.20	5	6.20	4	5.00	5	6.20	2	2.50	-	100.00	1	1.20	-	-
10	80	-	-	-	-	29	36.20	50	62.50	13	16.20	-	100.00	35	43.70	-	-

Table 18
Incidence of Clinical Signs and Nutritional Deficiency Signs Among Boys

	6 yrs		*7 yrs*		*8 yrs*		*9 yrs*		*10 yrs*		*Total*	
Clinical Signs	*No.*	%	*No.*	%	*No.*	%	*No.*	%	*No.*	%	*No.*	%
General Health												
Very good	0	0.00	2	5.00	0	0.00	1	2.50	0	0.00	3	1.50
Good	12	30.00	9	22.50	13	32.50	10	25.00	25	62.50	69	34.50
Satisfactory	24	60.00	24	60.00	21	52.50	29	72.50	13	32.50	111	55.50
Weak	4	10.00	5	12.50	6	15.00	0	0.00	2	5.00	17	8.50
Nutritional deficiency signs												
Pigmentation of skin												
Present	-	-	-	-	-	-	1	2.50	-	-	1	0.50
Absent	40	100.00	40	100.00	40	100.00	39	97.50	40	100.00	199	99.50
Angular Stomaltis												
Present	-	-	-	-	-	-	-	-	-	-	-	-
Absent	40	100.00	40	100.00	40	100.00	40	100.00	40	100.00	200	100.00
Dry Scaly Skin												
Present	-	-	1	2.50	1	2.50	-	-	2	5.00	4	2.00
Absent	40	100.00	39	97.50	39	97.50	40	100.00	38	95.00	196	98.00
Coloured hair												
Present	1	2.50	-	-	-	-	3	7.50	3	7.50	7	3.50
Absent	39	97.50	40	100.00	40	100.00	37	92.50	37	92.50	193	96.50
Flag/Coarse hair												
Present	-	-	-	-	1	2.50	2	5.00	1	2.50	4	2.00
Absent	40	100.00	40	100.00	39	97.50	38	95.00	39	97.50	196	98.00

Contd...

	6 yrs		7 yrs		8 yrs		9 yrs		10 yrs		Total	
Clinical Signs	*No.*	*%*	*No.*	*%*	*No.*	*%*	*No.*	*%*	*No.*	*%*	*No.*	*%*
Spongy bleeding gum												
Present	-	-	-	-	-	-	-	-	-	-	-	-
Absent	40	100.00	40	100.00	40	100.00	40	100.00	40	100.00	200	100.00
Yellowish teeth												
Present	-	-	-	-	-	-	1	2.50	2	5.00	3	1.50
Absent	40	100.00	40	100.00	40	100.00	39	97.50	38	95.00	197	98.50
Pale Conjactiva												
Present	-	-	-	-	-	-	-	-	-	-	-	-
Absent	40	100.00	40	100.00	40	100.00	40	100.00	40	100.00	200	100.00
Yellow Colour of the base of nail												
Present	-	-	-	-	-	-	-	-	-	-	--	
Absent	40	100.00	40	100.00	40	100.00	40	100.00	40	100.00	200	100.00

Table 19
Incidence of Clinical Signs and Nutritional Deficiency Signs Among Girls

	6 yrs		7 yrs		8 yrs		9 yrs		10 yrs		Total	
Clinical Signs	*No.*	*%*	*No.*	*%*	*No.*	*%*	*No.*	*%*	*No.*	*%*	*No.*	*%*
General Health												
Very good	0	0.00	1	2.50	0	0.00	0	0.00	0	0.00	1	0.50
Good	14	35.00	18	45.00	8	20.00	27	67.50	23	57.50	90	45.00
Satisfactory	23	57.50	19	47.50	30	75.00	13	32.50	14	35.00	99	49.50
Weak	3	7.50	2	5.00	2	5.00	0	0.00	3	7.50	10	5.00
Nutritional deficiency signs												
Pigmentation of skin												
Present	1	2.50	0	-	1	2.50	0	-	0	-	2	1.00
Absent	39	97.50	40	100.00	39	97.50	40	100.00	40	100.00	198	99.00
Angular Stomatitis												
Present	2	5.00	2	5.00	3	7.50	4	10.00	3	7.50	14	7.00
Absent	38	95.00	38	95.00	37	92.50	36	90.00	37	92.50	186	93.00
Dry Scaly Skin												
Present	1	2.50	3	7.50	0	0.00	1	2.50	5	12.50	10	5.00
Absent	39	97.50	37	92.50	40	100.00	39	97.50	35	87.50	190	95.00
Coloured hair												
Present	14	35.00	15	37.50	33	82.50	12	30.00	15	37.50	89	44.50
Absent	26	65.00	25	62.50	7	17.50	28	70.00	25	62.50	111	55.50
Flag/Coarse hair												
Present	4	10.00	3	7.50	1	2.50	-	-	2	5.00	10	5.00
Absent	36	90.00	37	92.50	39	97.50	40	100.00	38	95.00	190	95.00
Spongy bleeding gum												
Present	-	-	-	-	1	2.50	1	2.50	-	-	2	1.00
Absent	40	100.00	40	100.00	39	97.50	39	97.50	40	100.00	198	99.00

Contd...

	6 yrs		7 yrs		8 yrs		9 yrs		10 yrs		Total	
Clinical Signs	*No.*	%	*No.*	%	*No.*	%	*No.*	%	*No.*	%	*No.*	%
Yellowish teeth												
Present	1	2.50	-	-	2	5.00	-	-	-	-	3	1.50
Absent	39	97.50	40	100.00	38	95.00	40	100.00	40	100.00	197	98.50
Pale Conjactiva												
Present	-	-	-	-	-	-	-	-	-	-	-	-
Absent	40	100.00	40	100.00	40	100.00	40	100.00	40	100.00	200	100.00
Yellow Colour of the base of nail												
Present	-	-	-	-	-	-	-	-	-	-	-	-
Absent	40	100.00	40	100.00	40	100.00	40	100.00	40	100.00	200	100.00

from 9-12 years. The similarity in the emergence of this teeth of the present study is also worth noting.

Clinical Signs

In the present study seven types of nutritional deficiency signs are observed for both boys and girls. These signs are due to deficiency of certain vitamins or nutrients.

General health of each child was recorded by using grading technique by simple observation. From the table it is observed that most of the children for all ages seem to be satisfactory. (Tables 18, 19).

Nutrition Deficiency Sign

Pigmentation of Skin: It occurs due to niacin deficiency. It was observed 1% among the girls and 0.5% among the boys.

Angular Stomatitis: This is due to Vitamin B complex deficiency. Frequency of this deficiency among the girls is 7% only. Not a single case among the boys has been recorded.

Dry Scaly Skin: This is due to Vitamin A deficiency. It is observed 2% among the boys and 5% among the girls.

Discoloured Hair: It is found 3.5% among the boys and 44.5% among the girls. Most of the discoloured hair is brown to reddish brown.

Flag Coarse hair: Hair with rough texture with split end was observed 5% among the girls and 2% among the boys.

Spongy bleeding gums: Only 1% has been recorded among the girls and not a single case among the boys. This is due to Vitamin C deficiency.

Yellowish Teeth: Only 1.5% cases has been recorded among the boys and also among the girls.

Summary and Conclusion

The Dangi are one of the distinct, numerically small peasant caste of Mewar region of Rajasthan. They are mainly inhabited in Udaipur basin and found on plain on either banks of Ahar river in rural areas of Girwa tehsil. The Dangi belong to Chandra Vanshi/Yaduvanshi who were descendent of Lord Krishna of Mathura. They migrated from Gujarat and finally settled at South Rajasthan. They speak a modified form of 'Bhilli' dialect. They live in semi-arid area which is experienced by dry climate with extreme summer and winter seasons.

Linguistically they are divided as Mewari Dangi and Gujarati Patel Dangi. Each endogamous section is again divided into a number of exogamous gotra (clan). Child marriage was in vogue among the Dangi. Monogamy is the rule. Medium sized family is predominant among them. Literacy standard of the parents is very gloomy. Besides cultivation and horticulture, the Dangi men are mostly engaged in industrial jobs. By and large Dangi are vegetarian and consume sufficient maize, wheat, milk and milk products regularly. Children get sufficient staple food from their own resource.

They live in good environment and take safe drinking water from the deep tube wells. Overall village hygienic conditions and living conditions of the Dangi are clean and satisfactory. Children live in spacious houses under the natural climate which help them to keep good health. Most of their children are now getting school education as well as covered under various immunization and nutritional programmes. The present cross sectional study delineates the pattern of growth among the Dangi children, living in same eco-cultural background. Clinical signs etc are observed to find out the vitamin deficiency among those children. Fourteen anthropometric measurements have been taken from 400 children from six villages of Badgaon Panchayat Samiti. The respective mean value with all its statistical derivation have been shown in Table 15 and graphical representation have been shown in Fig. 1 to 18.

It is observed that the mean value of the measurements show gradual increase in value with the change of age. Absolute gain and rate of increment is different in different ages in both the sexes. Rate of increment in weight for boys of 10 years is 12.9% while it is 13.2% among the girls at 9 years of age i.e. one year earlier than the boys.

Boys of 10 years show the greater value in stature than the girls.

The distance curve and velocity curve showed a definite trend with the change in age.

From the result obtained, it is evident that as far as weight and stature are concerned, the Dangi children showed higher growth than the values given on Hindus by the ICMR 1984. Five measurements viz., weight, stature, sitting height, Biacromial diameter and bi-illiac diameter were observed for percentile values. All the mean values are closer to 50th percentile value.

Most of the Dangi are in middle income groups. Per capita income is quite higher than other state population. Mean along with standard deviation for height and weight were calculated as per the per capita income of the subject's family. Both the sexes show that more per capita income, better is the growth.

Relation of growth and parity of the subject shows that among the boys growth of the child diminishes from 1st to onward parity, while among the girls increase in growth in 2nd parity.

Growth and family size show that growth among the boys increases with the increase in family size but reverse is the case among the girls. Probably among the Dangi gender discrimination is in practice.

Growth and family type show that 10 years of boys, 6 years and 8 years of girls show increase in growth under nuclear family type and 6, 7, 8 and 9 years of boys, 7, 9 and 10 years of girls show increase in growth under joint family type. In joint family children get more care, security and congenial atmosphere. Though it is expected that proper growth and development have positive relation with the literacy level of parents, but the present study does not show any definite correlation. Very less number of parents are literate, only up to primary standard. In their way of life they do not show any difference.

On the basis of nutritional effect on anthropometry, it is observed from the table that 94.5% boys and 94.0% girls are in normal category. It seems that the growth pattern of Dangi children are quite good.

Height deficit classification reveals that 98.5% boys and 97.0% girls are in normal state of health.

Mid upper arm circumference (MUAC) shows that 35.5% of total children are in normal state, 34.25 are mild malnourished, 20.5% are moderate malnourished and 9.75% are severe malnourished.

In general most of the children (94.5%) are in grade normal and only 5% and 0.75% in grade I and grade II malnourished category respectively. 2% are under mild retarded category and MUAC, 35.5% of them are normal, only for BMI 97.5% children fall under calorie energy deficiency III category. This perhaps is the standard set for BMI. It does not suit to children of 6-10 years age-group.

To conclude we can highlight some of the underlying factors which are responsible for the growth and development of the Dangi children:

1. Apart from genetic factors synergistic environment where the Dangi live, traditional dietary habits, agrarian economical background as well as availability of local infra-structural facilities have concomitant positive affects upon the Dangi children.
2. The present study on growth pattern shows normal increase in all the anthropometric traits with increase in age. Majority of the Dangi children seem to be normal, while a few of them are found to be malnourished because of uncontrolled or personal situation. Anthropometric data on children do not show any significant difference between sexes.
3. Though income has a significant role in growth of the children, but in case of Dangi, it is important to note that irrespective of their economic status food intake pattern is more or less the same among the Dangi households.
4. In rural areas *Anganwari* workers and ANM play an important role in promoting health and hygiene awareness among the mother and the children. Parental awareness through media is also responsible for lowering the morbidity rate particularly in communicable diseases.
5. Among the Dangi, family composition family income and family size, parental education, economic background, etc., do not show significant effect upon growth of the children.

6. Proximity from the urban centers and industrial belts and network of communication are also directly related with parents' economic condition and development of their children's health and growth.
7. The present analysis reveals that growth pattern of Dangi children is better than the average of Indian children (ICMR).
8. Dangi children take adequate amount of maize, milk and milk products as well as seasonal vegetable, which make their diet almost balanced. It is directly responsible for the promotion of growth and development of the children irrespective of age and sex with little exception.

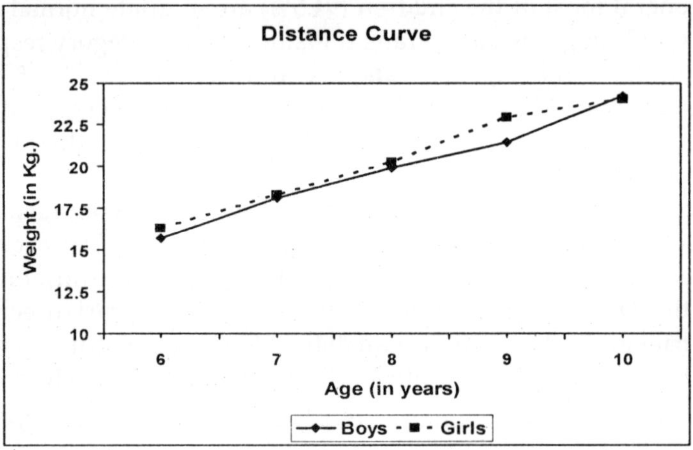

Fig. 1

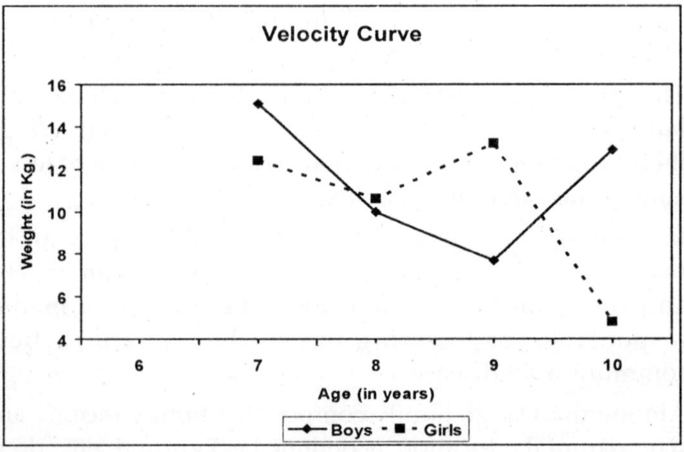

Fig. 2

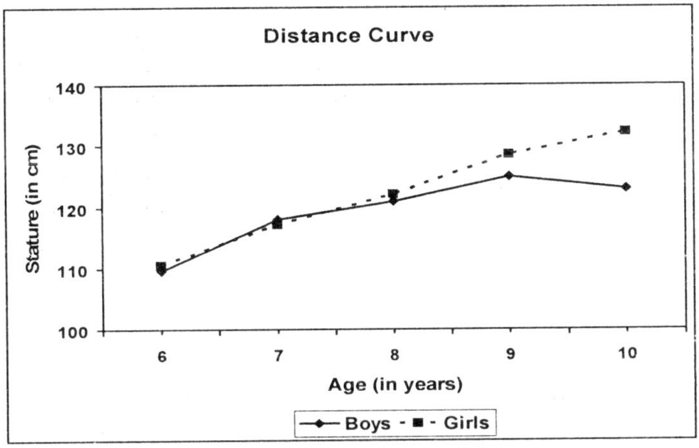

Fig. 3

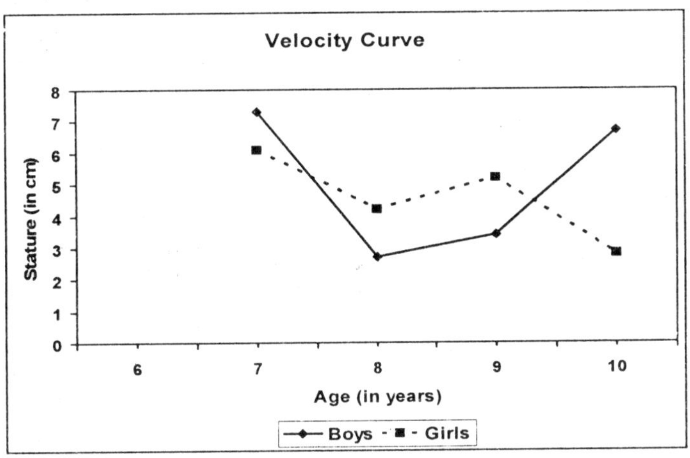

Fig. 4

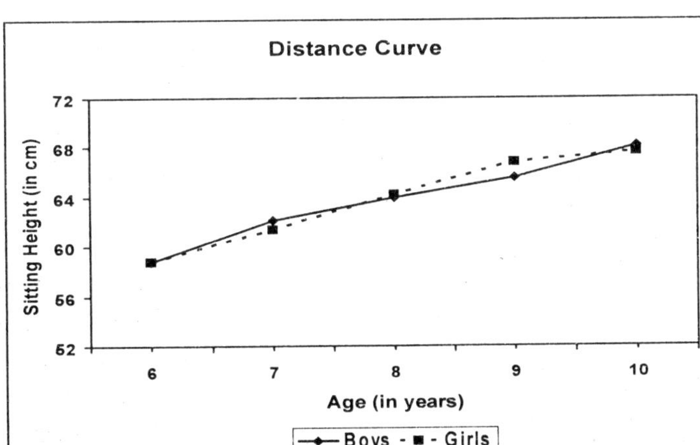

Fig. 5

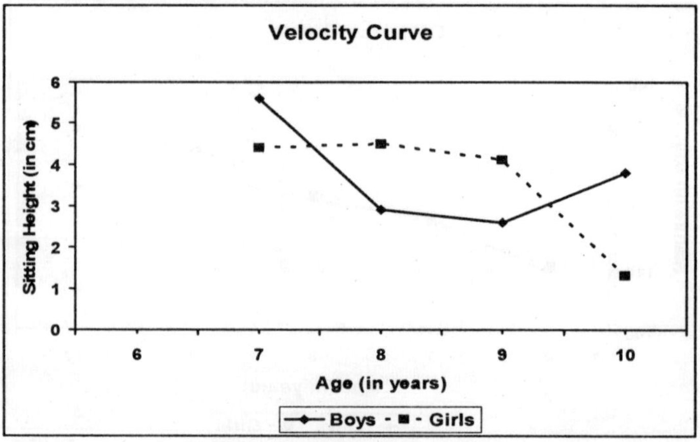

Fig. 6

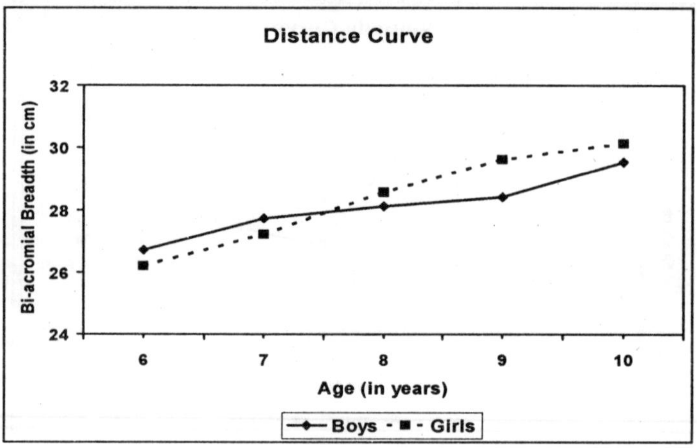

Fig. 7

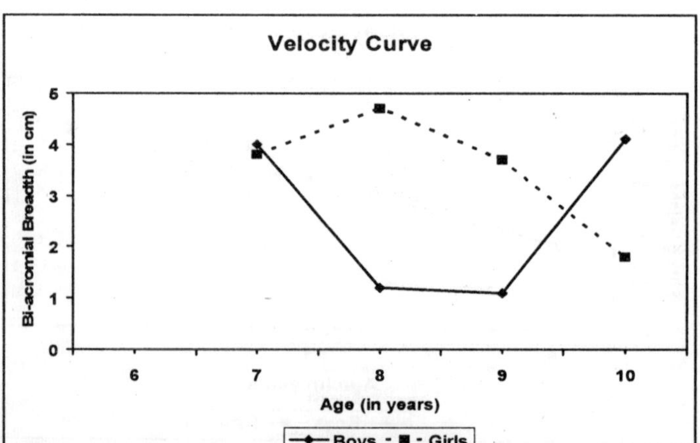

Fig. 8

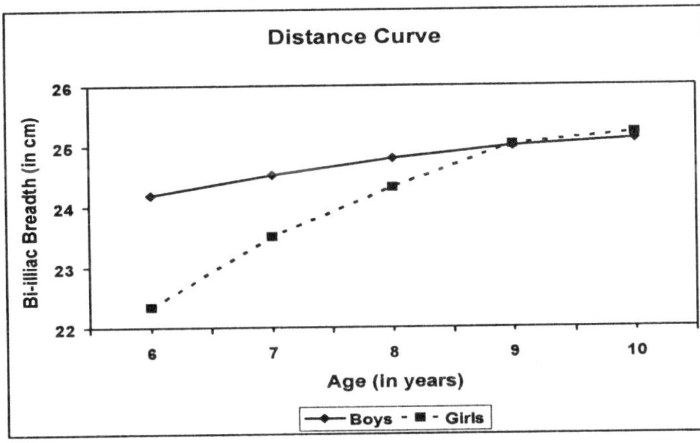

Fig. 9

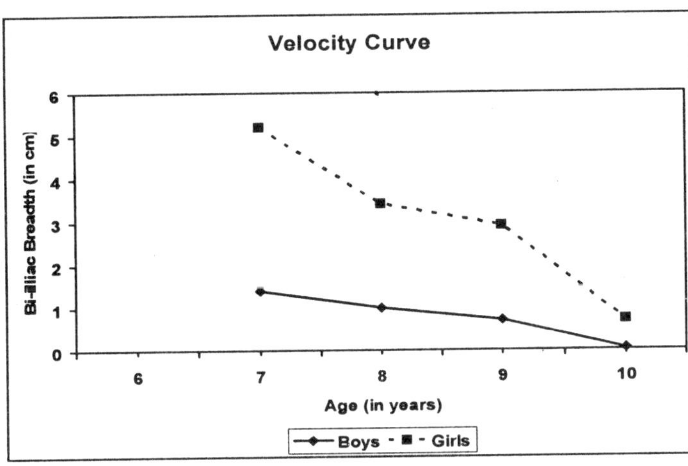

Fig. 10

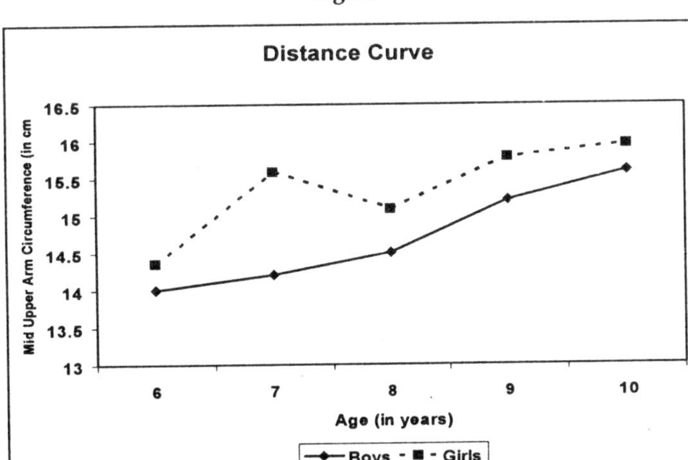

Fig. 11

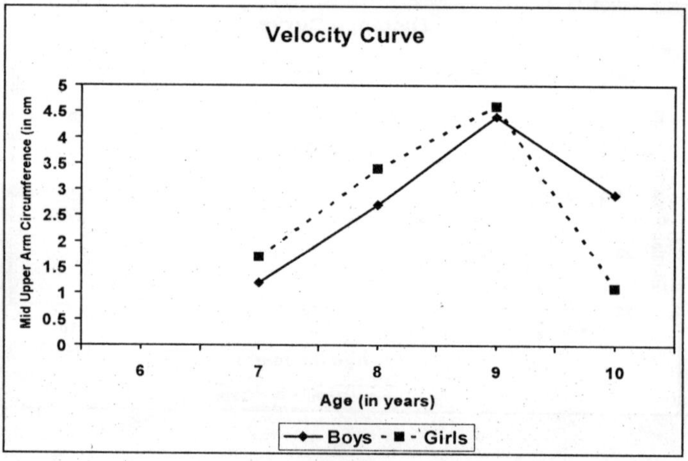

Fig. 12

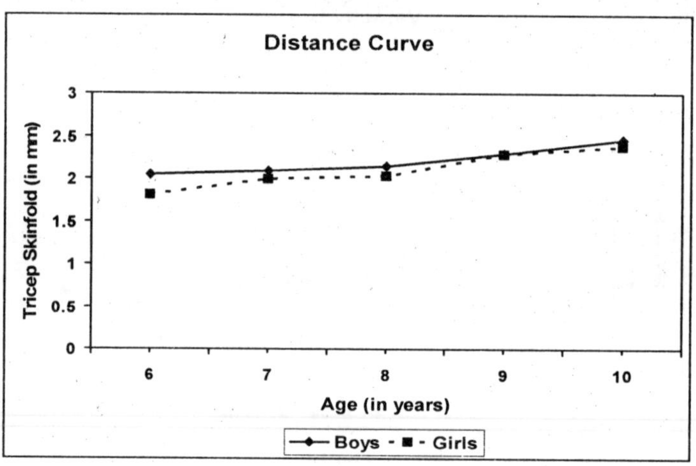

Fig. 13

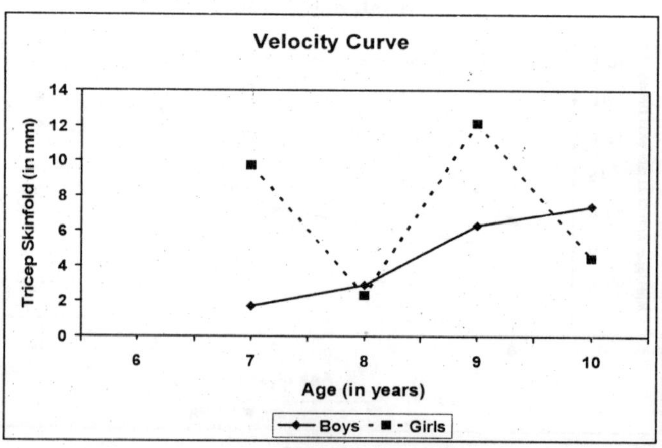

Fig. 14

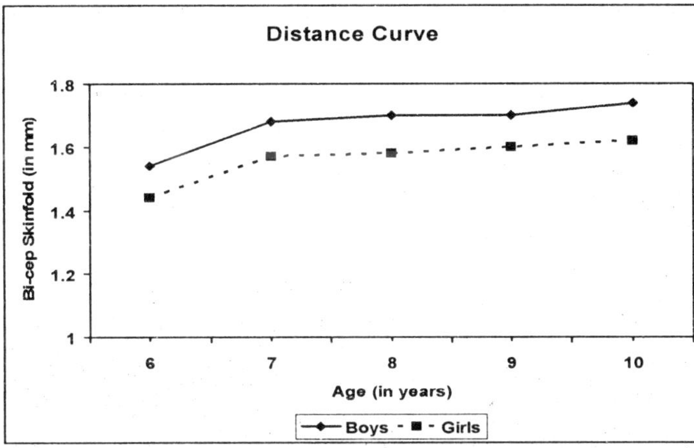

Fig. 15

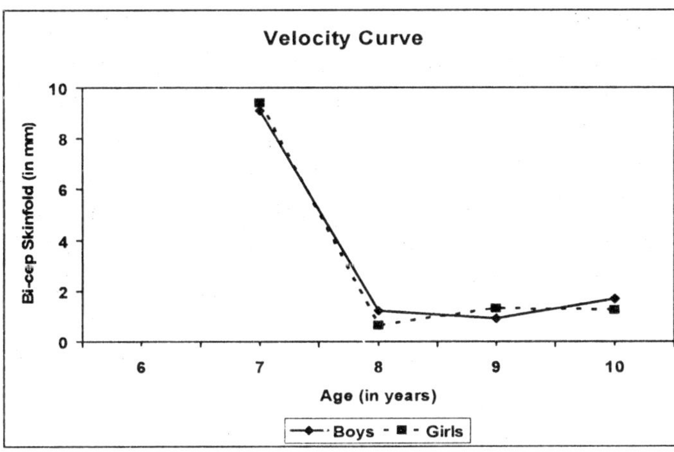

Fig. 16

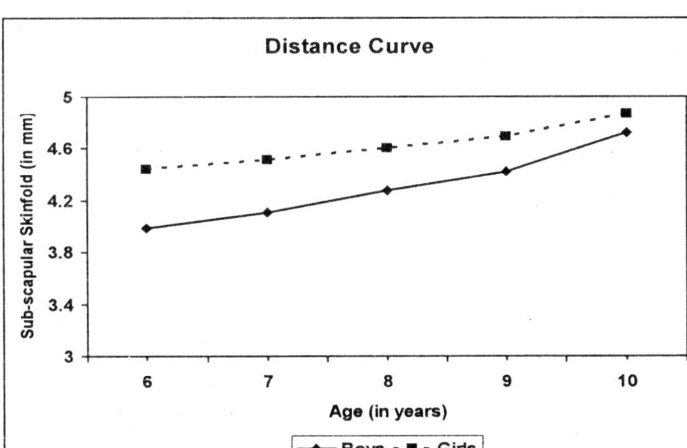

Fig. 17

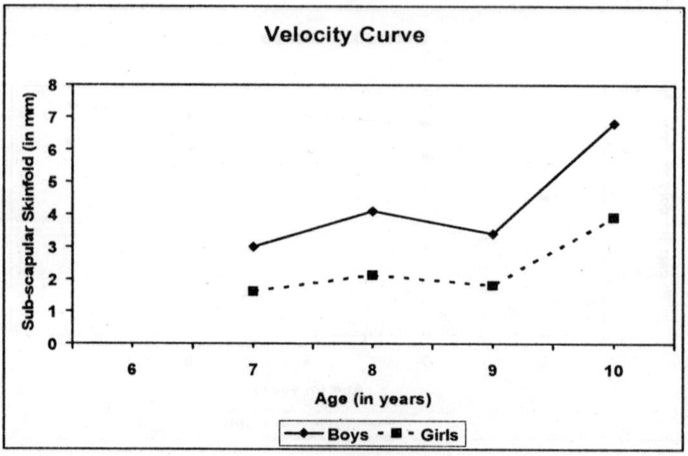

Fig. 18

References

Clements, E.M.B., E. Davies, Thomas and K.G. Pickett (1953), Time of Eruption of Permanent Teeth. In British Children in 1947-48, *British Medical Journal*, 1: 1421-1424.

I.C.M.R. (1984), Growth and Physical Development of Indian Infant and Children. Technical Report No.18, ICMR, New Delhi.

Jelliffe, D. B. (1966), The Assessment of the Nutritional Status of the Communities. Monograph Series 33, Geneva, World Health Organization.

Latham, M. (1979), Human Nutrition in Tropical Africa, 2nd Edition Rome, F.A.O.

National Centre for Health Statistics (1977), NCHS Growth Curves for Children, Birth to 18 Years, United States. Vital and Health Statistics. Series 11, No. 165.

Saito, N. (1936), c.f. Tulika Sen (1988).

Sen, Tulika (1988), Growth and Development of Bengalee girls. Memoir No. 73, An. S.I., Kolkata.

Shourie, K.L. (1946), Eruption Age of Teeth in India, *Indian Journal of Medical Research*, 34(1):105-118.

Young, J. (1964), Outline of Oral and Dental Anatomy. NC Craw Hill Book Co. Ltd. London.

11

EVALUATION OF GROWTH OF CHILDREN BELONGING TO 11 POPULATIONS WITH REFERENCE TO NCHS AND ICMR STANDARDS FOR EUROPEAN AND INDIAN CHILDREN RESPECTIVELY

Madhu Bala Sharma

It has been widely recognized that physical growth of children is one of the sensitive and reliable indicators of health and nutritional status in human populations (Johnston, 1981). Pattern of growth and development of children and youth have been described for most world regions. But there is controversy, for which appropriate data could serve as reference in evaluation of growth. Many investigators refer to such a set of "reference standards", the data are not intended to be a norm i.e. a standard to be attained. Rather, reference data are measures to which growth may be compared. According to Johnston, 1985, it is important to note that not all samples qualify as reference data. Reference values are not simply data of convenience, but are precise estimates of the means, the standard deviations and the percentiles of appropriate age and sex category of a well-defined population. Various problems of planning and execution of growth surveys designed to construct national standards are discussed by Jorden *et al.* (1975) and recommendations for analyzing and presentation of data for international use are presented by Waterlow *et al.* (1977). The controversy arises over whether to use a single international set of reference data, or local data, likely to ethnically and geographically more similar to the studied population than an international standard would be. This issue has been discussed at length by number of authors (e.g. Goldstein and Tanner, 1980; Habicht *et al.* 1974; Jackson and Jackson, 1984; Johnston, 1985; Johnston *et al.* 1984; Kaul, 1983 and Waterlow *et al.* 1977) and concluded that the data set they most widely accepted as an international standard of reference is that of the US National Centre for Health Statistics. The NCHS data based upon a national probability sample of children and youth from the continental United States with numbers in each age/sex cell ranging from 300 to 1600. Furthermore, the percentiles have been developed by smoothening techniques involving a cubic spline function. In the present study the growth of children belonging to 11 communities is evaluated with respect to NCHS reference data and ICMR standards.

The mean body weight, height, sitting height of children belonging to 11 communities are compared with NCHS and ICMR standards, age and sex wise in order to evaluate their growth and are shown in Tables 1-3.

Weight

It is seen from the Table 1 that the US children (NCHS, 1979) are heaviest, whereas, Bauri children are lightest than the other children of all the ages, except at 10 years of age. At 6 years of age the Yadav boys are heavier than the children belonging to socio-economic (S.E.) class I (ICMR, 1972). The weight of the Nicobarese, Lushai, Oroan, Kaibarta and Ahir boys in descending order are lighter than the boys belonging to socio-economic class I (S.E. class I) children but heavier than the Indian (pooled) boys (ICMR, 1972). The Mala, Dangi, Mali and Bauri boys are lighter than the Indian (pooled) boys (ICMR, 1972). At 7 years of age the picture changes due to differential growth rate. At this age group the Oroans boys are heavier than S.E. I (ICMR) ,whereas the Ahir boys are almost of same weight, but the Yadav boys become lighter than boys of S.E. class I (ICMR), the Nicobarese, Kaibarta, Lushai, Mala and Dangi boys occupy the place between boys belonging to the S.E-I (ICMR) and Indian (pooled) boys with respect to weight. Only the Mali and Bauri boys are lighter than Indian (pooled) boys. The Oroan, Ahir and Yadav boys at age 8 years become heavier than boys of S.E- class I due to accelerated growth rate, whereas, the Nicobarese, Kaibarta, Poundrakshtriya, Lushai, Dangi are lighter. The Mali and Bauri remain lighter than Indian (pooled) boys up to 10 years. At nine years of age only the Oroan and Yadav boys are heavier than boys of S.E. class I whereas, the Ahir boys become lighter. The Kaibarta, Lushai and Nicobarese boys are heavier than the Indian (pooled) boys, whereas, the Poundrakshtriya and Dangi boys are almost of the same weight. The Ahir boys become heavier than Yadav boys at age 10 years. The Oroan, Ahir and Yadav boys are heavier than the boys of S.E. class I. The Nicobarese attain weight closer to boys of S.E class I at 10 years, because of accelerated growth between 9 and 10 years. The Poundrakshtriya, Kaibarta, Dangi boys are heavier than the Indian (pooled) boys but lighter than boys belonging to S.E-I (ICMR, 1972). But the Bauri boys are heavier than Mali boys at 10 years because of growth spurt.

The Yadav, Nicobarese, Ahir, Oroan, Dangi girls are lighter than the Indian girls of socio-economic class-I in descending order but heavier than Indian

Table 1
Comperative Data Analysis: Weight (Both Sexes)

	Weight (Mean)										
	Boys					Girls					
Group & Area	6	7	8	9	10	6	7	8	9	10	*Authors*
YADAV, Uttar Pradesh	19.28	19.95	22.72	26.06	26.88	17.80	19.69	21.81	23.07	27.20	Sharma, M. B. & B. Joardar
AHIR (Yaduvanshi), Haryana	17.00	20.95	23.21	24.58	27.10	16.98	19.01	19.60	22.61	24.67	Ravi, K. & J. S. Rao
BAURIS, West Bengal	14.55	16.42	18.53	20.47	23.46	13.73	16.09	17.54	20.70	24.04	Chaudhuri, C. and D. Bhattacharya
ORAON, West Bengal	17.88	21.43	23.58	26.88	30.20	16.56	20.37	23.30	26.77	31.31	Barua, S, Mittali Chatterjee & G. Mallick
POUNDRAKSHATRIYA, W.Bengal	17.19	18.53	19.69	21.60	24.64	15.66	18.90	19.47	21.68	23.44	Devi, Bharati and S. Bhattacharya
KAIBARTA, Assam	17.30	19.51	20.75	23.36	24.44	15.75	18.74	20.96	22.72	26.04	Das, B.
LUSHAI, Mizoram	18.05	19.27	20.23	23.05	25.63	16.17	17.84	20.84	23.01	25.92	Urade, B.P. & S.K. Mukherjee
NICOBARESE, Andaman & Nicobar	18.27	19.73	21.31	23.00	24.86	17.74	19.13	22.03	23.29	26.85	Sahani, R. and A. Dinda
GHASI MALI, Maharashtra	15.60	17.07	19.17	20.77	23.01	15.19	16.43	18.81	19.69	21.88	Mukherjee, P.A. and S. Dasgupta
MALA, Andhra Pradesh	16.23	18.81	20.39	21.84	24.07	16.40	18.98	19.74	22.35	25.02	Saheeb, S.Y. and G.V. Ramana
DANGI, Rajasthan	15.70	18.07	19.88	21.42	24.20	16.28	18.30	20.25	22.92	24.02	Mandal, D.B. and M.Nanda
INDIA(Socio economic class I)	18.70	21.00	22.00	24.70	25.90	18.10	19.70	21.60	23.60	26.70	I.C.M.R., 1972
INDIA (POOLED)	16.30	18.00	19.70	21.50	23.50	16.00	17.60	19.40	21.30	23.60	I.C.M.R., 1972
UTTAR PRADESH	16.30	18.10	19.60	21.80	23.80	16.20	17.70	19.60	21.60	23.80	I.C.M.R., 1972
United States	22.00	24.70	27.80	31.20	33.70	21.60	24.20	27.50	31.40	35.20	NCHS, 1060

(pooled) girls at 6 years of age ,whereas, the Kaibarta, Poundrakshtriya, Mali and Bauri girls are lighter than Indian (pooled) girls. The Mali girls are lighter than Indian (pooled) girls from 6 years to 10 years of age whereas, the Bauri girls are lightest up to 8 years but from 9 years onward become heavier than the Mali girls. It is interesting to note that both Oroan boys and girls experience highest absolute growth between age 6 and 7 years and become heavier than all other groups except that of US boys and girls from 7 years onward. The Yadav girls at 7 years are almost of same weight as that of girls belonging to socio-economic class-I category. The Nicobarese, Ahir, Mala, Poundrakshtriya, Kaibarta, Dangi girls are lighter than the S.E. class-I girls but heavier than the Indian (pooled) girls. The Nicobarese and Yadav girls also become heavier than the girls belonging to S.E class-I category at 8 years of age. The Kaibarta, Lushai, Dangi girls maintain statusquo as at 7 years. But the Ahir, Poundrakshtriya, Mala girls experience negative growth and come closer to the weight of Indian (pooled) girls though slightly heavier. At 9 years of age only the Oroan girls are heavier than the girls belonging to socio-economic class-I and Bauri and Mali girls are lighter than Indian (pooled) girls whereas, the weight of girls of rest of the communities lies between the weight of two ICMR references. The Yadav and Nicobarese girls supercede, with respect to weight at 10 years of age of socio-economic class-I. Kaibarta and Lushai girls are lighter but closer to the weight of girls of S.E class-I category. Mala, Ahir, Dangi, Bauri girls are lighter than girls of S.E class-I category but heavier than Indian (pooled) girls. The Poundrakshtriya and Mali girls are lighter than Indian (pooled) girls.

Based on the values shown in Table 1, distance curves for weight are drawn for boys and girls of all the communities along with the reference data (Fig.1 & 2). The graphs shows that NCHS curve is very far removed from rest of the lines and occupy the highest position on the graphic scale, whereas, the Bauri and Mali distance curves occupy the lowest and second lowest position respectively. The Oroan curves occupy second highest position except at 6 years age. Rest of the lines are closely associated within a restricted area with slight deflections in the points at each age group. It is also clear from the graph, among the girls at 8 years of age the percentage of malnutrition of varied grade is more in comparison to the girls of other age groups. Whereas, among the boys percentages of malnutrition of different grade is comparatively more at 9 years of age.

Stature

It is observed from Table 2 that at 6 years of age height of boys of United States is almost similar to the height of Indian boys belonging to socio-economic class I but as the age advances the differences between the heights of two groups increase. This indicates that the rate of growth was higher among the United States boys than that of Indian boys (Socio-economic

Table 2
Comperative Data Analysis: Stature (Both Sexes)

	Stature (Mean)										
	Boys					*Girls*					
Group & Area	*6*	*7*	*8*	*9*	*10*	*6*	*7*	*8*	*9*	*10*	*Authors*
YADAV, Uttar Pradesh	117.90	119.60	125.90	132.30	134.20	111.60	120.60	123.40	127.40	134.80	Sharma, M.B. & B. Joardar
AHIR (Yaduvanshi), Haryana	111.60	123.20	128.70	132.50	137.90	113.40	120.30	122.40	129.80	134.10	Ravi, K. & J.S. Rao
BAURIS, West Bengal	102.70	109.60	117.10	122.40	128.80	100.40	110.80	116.60	122.70	129.70	Chaudhuri, C. and D. Bhattacharya
ORAON, West Bengal	112.80	122.30	128.30	134.40	140.10	110.10	120.60	128.20	135.00	140.20	Barua, S, Mittali Chatterjee & G. Mallick
POUNDRAKSHATRIYA, W.Bengal	109.20	114.90	117.80	124.70	129.30	107.00	115.20	119.20	123.20	129.00	Devi, Bharati and S. Bhattacharya
KAIBARTA, Assam	111.50	117.80	121.40	126.90	129.80	106.90	116.80	121.40	126.80	134.60	Das, B.
LUSHAI, Mizoram	111.00	115.00	118.00	123.00	128.00	108.10	111.80	118.20	123.60	129.00	Urade, B.P. & S.K. Mukherjee
NICOBARESE, Andaman & Nicobar	110.90	114.50	119.20	123.00	126.80	108.80	112.40	120.30	122.80	128.80	Sahani, R. and A. Dinda
GHASI MALI, Maharashtra	111.60	116.50	121.50	125.00	131.30	109.90	114.40	118.90	123.30	129.60	Mukherjee, P.A. and S. Dasgupta
MALA, Andhra Pradesh	109.20	116.40	121.60	125.70	130.10	109.70	117.60	118.60	125.60	130.90	Saheeb, S.Y. and G.V. Ramana
DANGI, Rajasthan	109.60	117.70	120.80	125.00	123.40	110.40	117.60	122.10	128.60	132.20	Mandal, D.B. and M.Nanda
INDIA(Socio economic class I)	118.80	119.70	123.90	128.40	135.40	112.60	116.30	122.80	127.10	132.50	I.C.M.R., 1972
INDIA (POOLED)	108.50	113.90	119.30	123.70	128.40	107.40	112.80	118.20	122.90	128.40	I.C.M.R., 1972
UTTAR PRADESH	108.10	112.90	118.40	122.80	127.80	106.70	111.10	117.30	122.20	127.90	I.C.M.R., 1972
United States	118.60	124.50	130.00	135.50	140.20	117.80	123.50	129.40	135.50	104.90	NCHS, 1060

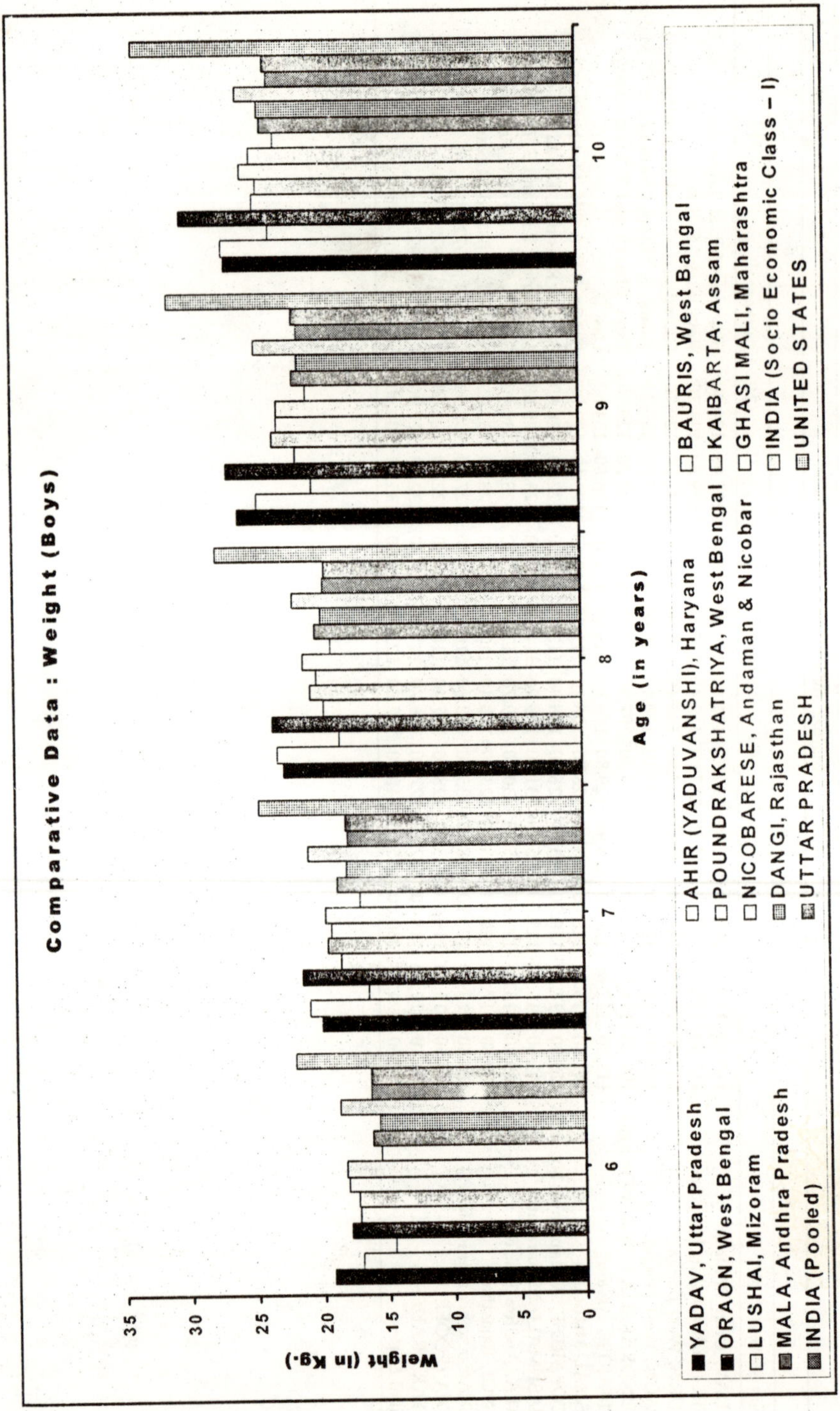
Comparative Data : Weight (Boys)
Weight (in Kg.)
0
5
10
15
20
25
30
35
6
7
8
9
10
Age (in years)
YADAV, Uttar Pradesh
ORAON, West Bengal
LUSHAI, Mizoram
MALA, Andhra Pradesh
INDIA (Pooled)
AHIR (YADUVANSHI), Haryana
POUNDRAKSHATRIYA, West Bengal
NICOBARESE, Andaman & Nicobar
DANGI, Rajasthan
UTTAR PRADESH
BAURIS, West Bangal
KAIBARTA, Assam
GHASI MALI, Maharashtra
INDIA (Socio Economic Class – I)
UNITED STATES

Fig. 1

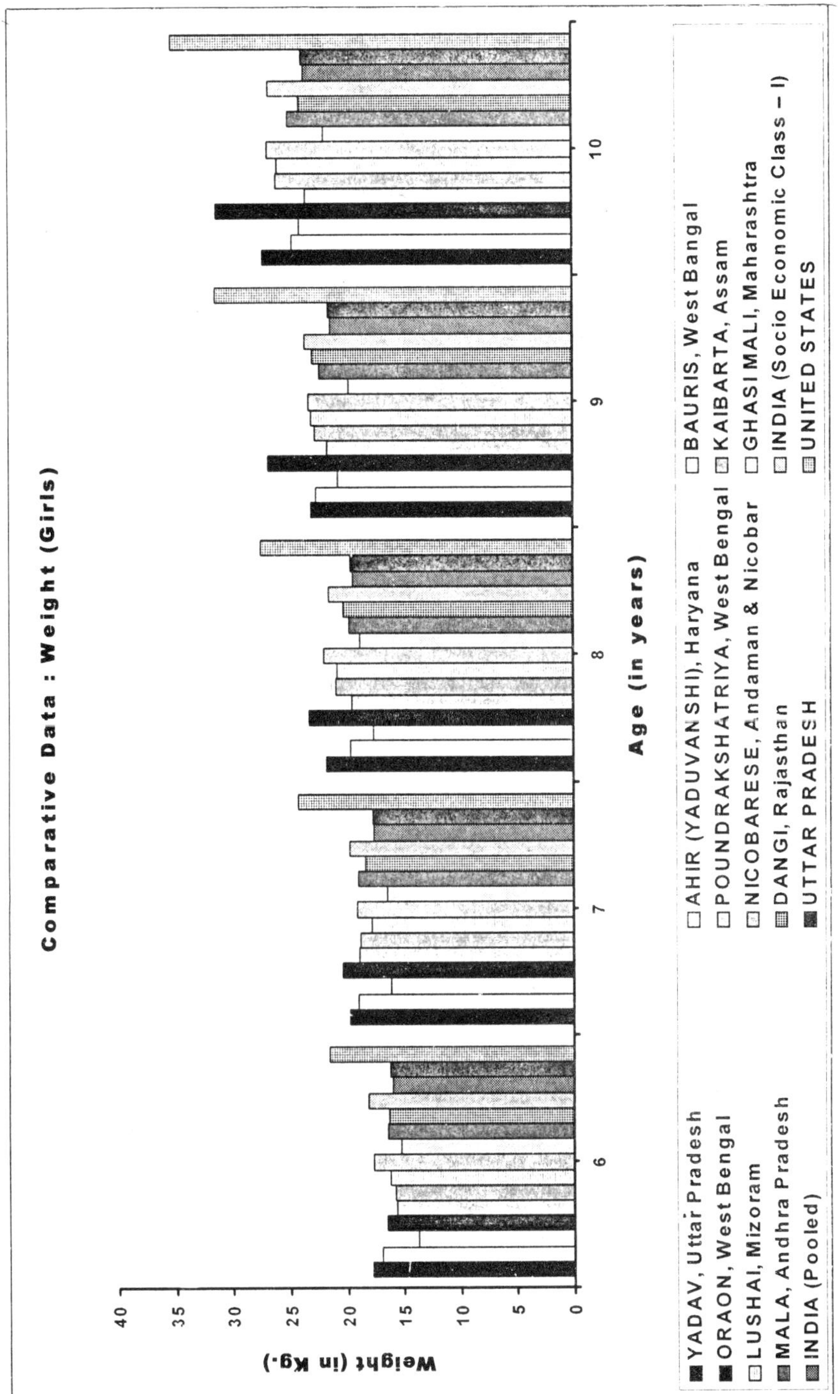
Comparative Data : Weight (Girls)
Weight (in Kg.)
0
5
10
15
20
25
30
35
40
6
7
8
9
10
Age (in years)
YADAV, Uttar Pradesh
ORAON, West Bengal
LUSHAI, Mizoram
MALA, Andhra Pradesh
INDIA (Pooled)
AHIR (YADUVANSHI), Haryana
POUNDRAKSHATRIYA, West Bengal
NICOBARESE, Andaman & Nicobar
DANGI, Rajasthan
UTTAR PRADESH
BAURIS, West Bangal
KAIBARTA, Assam
GHASI MALI, Maharashtra
INDIA (Socio Economic Class – I)
UNITED STATES

Fig. 2

class-I category). This clearly shows that the boys in United States enjoy better living standards and socio-economic status as compared to Indian children. The height of Yadav boys is closer to that of boys of socio-economic class I at 6 to 7 years, but between the age of 7 to 8 years, rate of growth accelerates significantly resulting in taller Yadav boys than the socio-economic class I boys at age 8 years and 9 years. But at age 10 because of stunted growth between 9 to 10 years, the Yadav boys are shorter than that of socio-economic class-I boys. The Ahir and Oroan boys are taller than the boys of S.E class I, except at age 6, as a result of the accelerated growth they experienced between 6 years and 7 years of age. The Kaibarta, Lushai, Nicobarese, Dangi, Mala and Poundrakshtriya boys are shorter than the boys belonging to socio-economic class-I, but taller than Indian (pooled) boys except that Mala and Poundrakshatriya boys ,who are shorter at 8 years of age, because of stunted growth between 7 and 8 years. The Bauri boys are the shortest in comparison to all other boys, under study except at 10 years of age whereby the Bauri boys become taller than Indian (pooled) boys, and also to Lushai, Nicobarese and Dangi boys, because of growth spurt between age 9 and 10 years.

The US girls depict highest mean height as compared to girls of all other groups compared (Table 2). The Oroan girls are almost of same height to U.S girls at age 9 years and 10 years because of growth which they experience between 6 and 7 years and between 9 and 10 years. At 6 years only the Ahir girls are taller than the girls of socio-economic class I category but as the age advances the Oroan, Yadav, Ahir, Dangi, Kaibarta girls also become taller at 7 years age because of growth. But at 8 years age only the Oroan and Yadav girls are taller than the girls of S.E. class I category. At 9 years the Oroan, Ahir, Dangi and Yadav girls are taller than S.E. class I girls. As age advances Oroan, Yadav, Kaibarta, Ahir girls become taller than girls belonging to S.E-class I, whereas, Dangi girls attain almost the same height at 10 years of age. The Poundrakshatriya, Mali, Kaibarta, Dangi, Nicaobarese, Lushai girls are taller than the Indian (pooled) girls but shorter than the girls belonging to socio-economic class-I. The Bauri girls are comparatively much shorter than other girls at 6 years of age and remain the shortest through age 6 to 8 years, but at age 10 years become taller than Lushai and Indian (pooled) girls because of catch up growth they experience between age 6 to 7 years and between 9 and 10 years.

Distance curve for height for boys and girls were drawn for all the comparative groups and are seen in Fig. 3 and 4. It is seen from the graph that the Oroan, Ahir, Dangi, Mala, Poundrakshatriya, Bauri children experience catch up growth between 6 years and 7 years. Whereas, Nicobarese, Lushai, S.E. class I, Indian (pooled) experience growth spurt between 7 and 8 years of age varies among the Oroan and Bauri children, the growth spurt continues up to 8 years. It is observed from the graph that none of the Indian populations observe the steady increase in height from 6 years to ten years like that of U.S children. However, the steady increase to some extent is observed among Oroan, Kaibarta, Bauri Indian (pooled) and S.E-class I children from 7 to ten years, while the rest of the groups showed minor deviations in its increase in height.

Sitting Height

It is observed from Table 3 that US children (NCHS) show the highest trunk height, whereas, the Bauri children are the shortest through 6 years to 10 years of age ,among all the groups compared . The Yadav boys have greater trunk height than the boys belonging to socio-economic class-I from 6 years to 10 years, except at age 7 years. The Kaibarta boys have greater trunk height in comparison to socio-economic class I boys at 6 years to 9 years of age. On the other hand the Mali, Lushai, Nicobarese, Ahir, Oroan boys have shorter trunk height than S.E. class I boys, but greater than the Indian (pooled) boys. The Dangi, Poundrakshtriya, Mala and Bauri boys have shorter trunk height than the Indian (pooled) boys through 6 years to 10 years of age, except for the Dangi boys at 10 years of age where the trunk height exceeds than the Indian boys . The Ahir, Oroan, Dangi and Mala boys show catch-up growth between 6 and 7 years whereas the boys of other groups have the steady growth. Majority of the groups exhibit growth spurt between age 9 years and 10 years, except the Yadav and Nicobarese boys.

The trunk height of the girls belonging to socio-economic class I category (ICMR) have almost the same trunk height as that of Yadav girls at 6 years of age, but as the age advances the Yadav girls exhibit more trunk height from age 7 years to 10 years because of growth spurt between age 6 years to 7 years and 9 years to 10 years. At six years of age the trunk height of Mali, Poundrakshtriya, Kaibarta, Dangi girls is shorter than girls belong the S.E. class-I category but greater than Indian (pooled) girls. The girls belonging to communities such as Oroan, Nicobarese and Mala have shorter trunk height, at age 6 years, than the Indian (pooled) girls. With the advancement of age ,due to differential growth rate, the Kaibarta and Ahir girls exhibit greater trunk height than the girls belonging to S.E- class I category at 7 years age. Whereas, the Oroan, Mali, Poundrakshtriya, Dangi, Mala, Nicobarese girls are of shorter trunk height. Only the Bauri girls have shorter trunk height than Indian (pooled) girls at age seven. The Oroan and Kaibarta girls have greater trunk height than girls of S.E-class 1 category from 8 years onward. At age 8 years, the Mali, Lushai, Dangi, Nicobarese, Ahir girls have shorter trunk height than the girls belonging to socio-economic class-I, but greater than Indian (pooled) girls. The Poundrakshtriya and Mala girls have shorter trunk height than Indian (pooled) girls at 8 years age. At 9 years age same statusquo is maintained with respect to trunk height as at 8 years. The Lushai girls exhibit greater trunk height than the girls belonging to S.E- class I category at age 10

Table 3
Comperative Data Analysis: Sitting Height (Both Sexes)

	Stature (Mean)										
	Boys					Girls					
Group & Area	*6*	*7*	*8*	*9*	*10*	*6*	*7*	*8*	*9*	*10*	*Authors*
YADAV, Uttar Pradesh	63.48	64.23	66.87	69.75	70.39	61.08	64.28	65.93	67.36	70.44	Sharma, M.B. & B. Joardar
AHIR (Yaduvanshi), Haryana	59.40	65.00	66.93	68.00	70.10	60.00	62.90	63.80	66.70	68.60	Ravi, K. & J.S. Rao
BAURIS, West Bengal	55.26	57.57	61.00	62.27	65.51	53.40	57.11	59.76	62.62	65.82	Chaudhuri, C. and D. Bhattacharya
ORAON, West Bengal	59.26	63.25	65.79	68.58	71.65	57.34	61.69	65.59	68.49	71.69	Barua, S, Mittali Chatterjee & G. Mallick
POUNDRAKSHATRIYA, W.Bengal	58.10	61.11	62.59	65.83	67.69	57.32	61.30	62.76	65.02	67.23	Devi, Bharati and S. Bhattacharya
KAIBARTA, Assam	61.85	64.20	65.61	67.69	69.33	59.88	63.67	65.37	67.71	70.25	Das, B.
LUSHAI, Mizoram	60.82	63.15	64.39	66.14	68.95	60.00	61.00	65.00	66.00	70.00	Urade, B.P. & S.K. Mukherjee
NICOBARESE, Andaman & Nicobar	60.43	61.85	63.80	65.60	66.52	58.89	60.61	64.00	64.60	67.93	Sahani, R. and A. Dinda
GHASI MALI, Maharashtra	61.16	62.65	65.06	65.90	68.27	60.04	61.62	65.33	65.29	67.09	Mukherjee, P.A. and S. Dasgupta
MALA, Andhra Pradesh	57.55	61.01	63.27	64.57	66.80	57.88	61.55	61.40	64.39	67.24	Saheeb, S.Y. and G.V. Ramana
DANGI, Rajasthan	58.79	62.08	63.91	65.56	68.05	58.81	61.41	64.19	66.82	67.61	Mandal, D.B. and M.Nanda
INDIA(Socio economic class I)	61.60	64.50	65.20	67.60	69.90	61.00	62.50	65.50	67.00	69.10	I.C.M.R., 1972
INDIA (POOLED)	59.40	61.70	63.80	65.60	67.50	58.40	60.70	62.90	64.80	67.10	I.C.M.R., 1972
UTTAR PRADESH	59.30	61.60	63.60	65.60	67.80	57.80	60.00	62.20	64.20	66.60	I.C.M.R., 1972
United States	64.70	67.00	69.20	71.30	73.00	63.90	66.20	68.50	71.00	73.30	NCHS, 1060

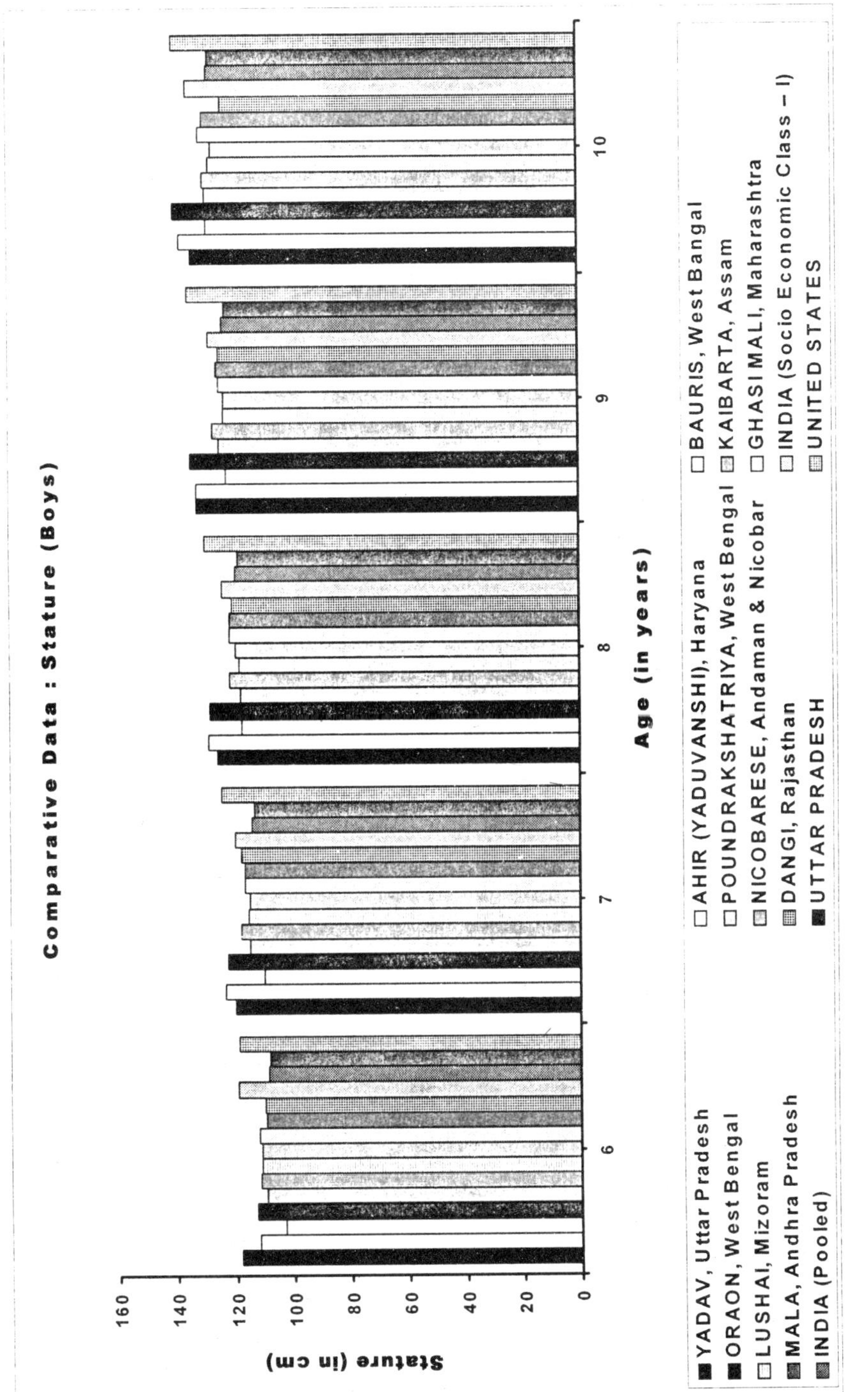
Comparative Data : Stature (Boys)
Stature (in cm)
160
140
120
100
80
60
40
20
0
6
7
8
9
10
Age (in years)
YADAV, Uttar Pradesh
ORAON, West Bengal
LUSHAI, Mizoram
MALA, Andhra Pradesh
INDIA (Pooled)
AHIR (YADUVANSHI), Haryana
POUNDRAKSHATRIYA, West Bengal
NICOBARESE, Andaman & Nicobar
DANGI, Rajasthan
UTTAR PRADESH
BAURIS, West Bangal
KAIBARTA, Assam
GHASI MALI, Maharashtra
INDIA (Socio Economic Class – I)
UNITED STATES

Fig. 3

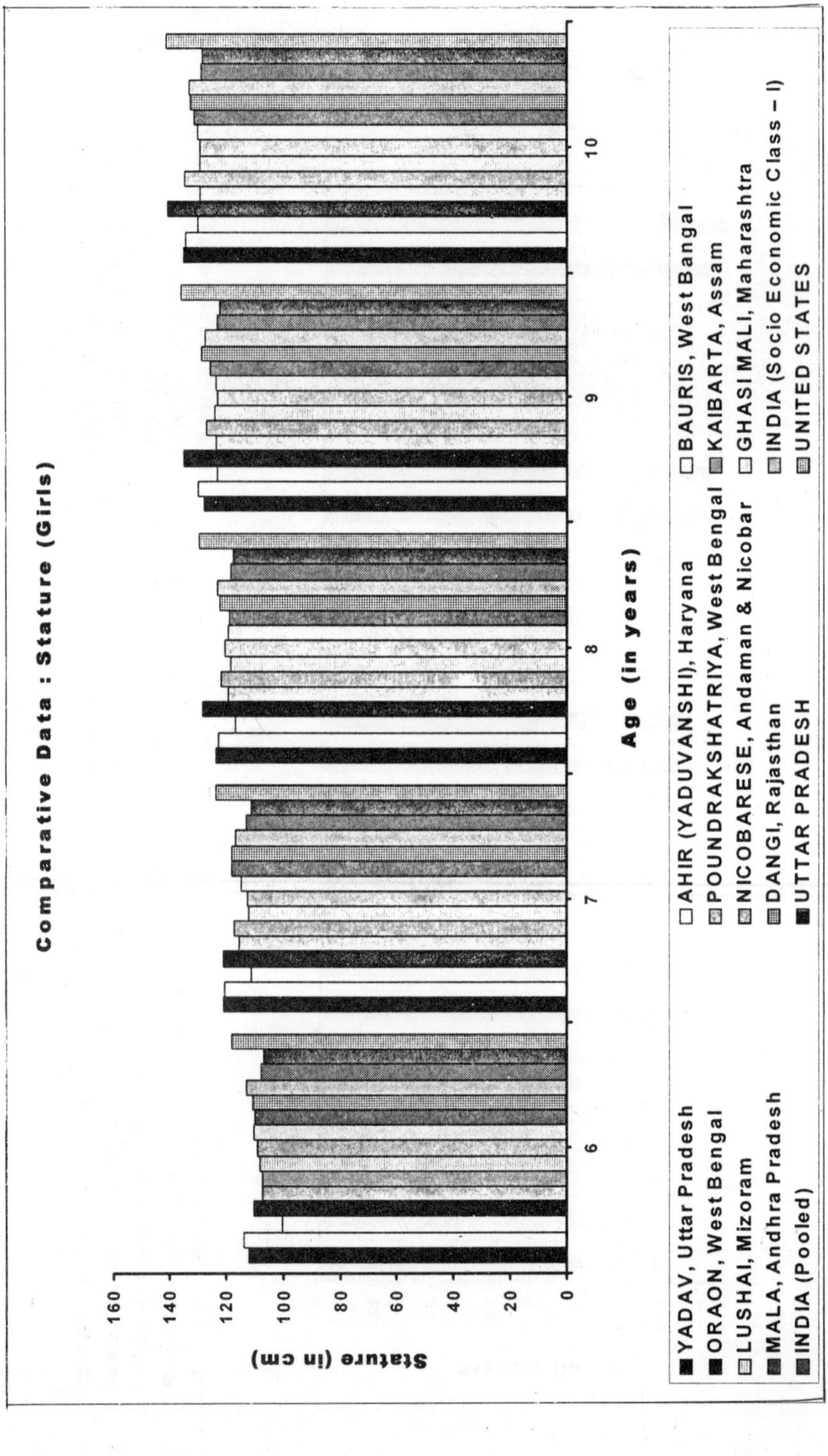
Comparative Data : Stature (Girls)
Stature (in cm)
0
20
40
60
80
100
120
140
160
6
7
8
9
10
Age (in years)
YADAV, Uttar Pradesh
ORAON, West Bengal
LUSHAI, Mizoram
MALA, Andhra Pradesh
INDIA (Pooled)
AHIR (YADUVANSHI), Haryana
POUNDRAKSHATRIYA, West Bengal
NICOBARESE, Andaman & Nicobar
DANGI, Rajasthan
UTTAR PRADESH
BAURIS, West Bangal
KAIBARTA, Assam
GHASI MALI, Maharashtra
INDIA (Socio Economic Class – I)
UNITED STATES

Fig. 4

years, whereas, the Ahir, Nicobarese, Dangi, Poundrakshtriya and Mali girls exhibit lower trunk height.

Based on the values given in Table 3 distance curve for sitting height is drawn for boys and girls of all the groups along with the NCHS and ICMR reference data (Fig. 5 & 6). The graph shows that NCHS curve is very far removed from rest of the lines and occupy the highest position, whereas, the curve for Bauri children occupy the lowest position and are well marked. Rest of lines are closely associated in the limited area between the curve for socio-economic class I and Indian (pooled) children with slight deflection in the points at different age groups depending upon the rate of growth. Some of the groups experience earlier growth spurt; whereas, some experience late growth spurt. This is well documented that variation in the timing of occurrence of catch up growth or growth spurt is the reflection of their environment in term of their living and socio-economic standard which in turn have direct bearing on the nutritional status.

Comparison of growth of Indian children studied under the ambit of project "Growth and Development of children: Bio-cultural perspective" with NCHS reference developed from growth study on US children for selected linear measurement such as Height and Sitting height, and the composite trait i.e. weight reveals that the children belonging to socio-economic class-I category (ICMR), Yadav, Ahir, Oroan show statures matching to those of US children to some extent but in Yadav and S.E-1 groups the difference increases due to slower growth rate with the advancement of age, whereas the Oroan and Ahir children come closer to the stature of US children due to accelerated growth rate with advancing age. This indicates that the Oroan, Ahir and Yadav children have the genetic potential for growth similar to that of US children but due to low standard of living and nutrition, they fail to achieve the maximum genetic potential. The Kaibarta, Dangi, Mali, Lushai, Poundrakshtriya and Mala show stature shorter than the children belonging to socio-economic class I category but taller than Indian (Pooled) children. Among the Indian children the trunk height as compared to stature is much shorter than in US children. This indicates that the rate of growth of trunk in Indian children is slower, whereas, the growth rate of lower extremity is greater than that of US children. Weight at successive ages is much less than that of US children, while the stature is comparatively closer to US children-indicative of leanness. The leanness in Indian children indicates that they are comparatively more undernourished and it is confirmed by weight for age, height for age and upper arm circumference for age classification. The Indian children are suffering with malnutrition of varied degrees i.e. mild to severe. As per the information gathered, the malnutrition among the children ,of the present study is due to ignorance about the consumption of nutritious diet and nature of food consumption , which is

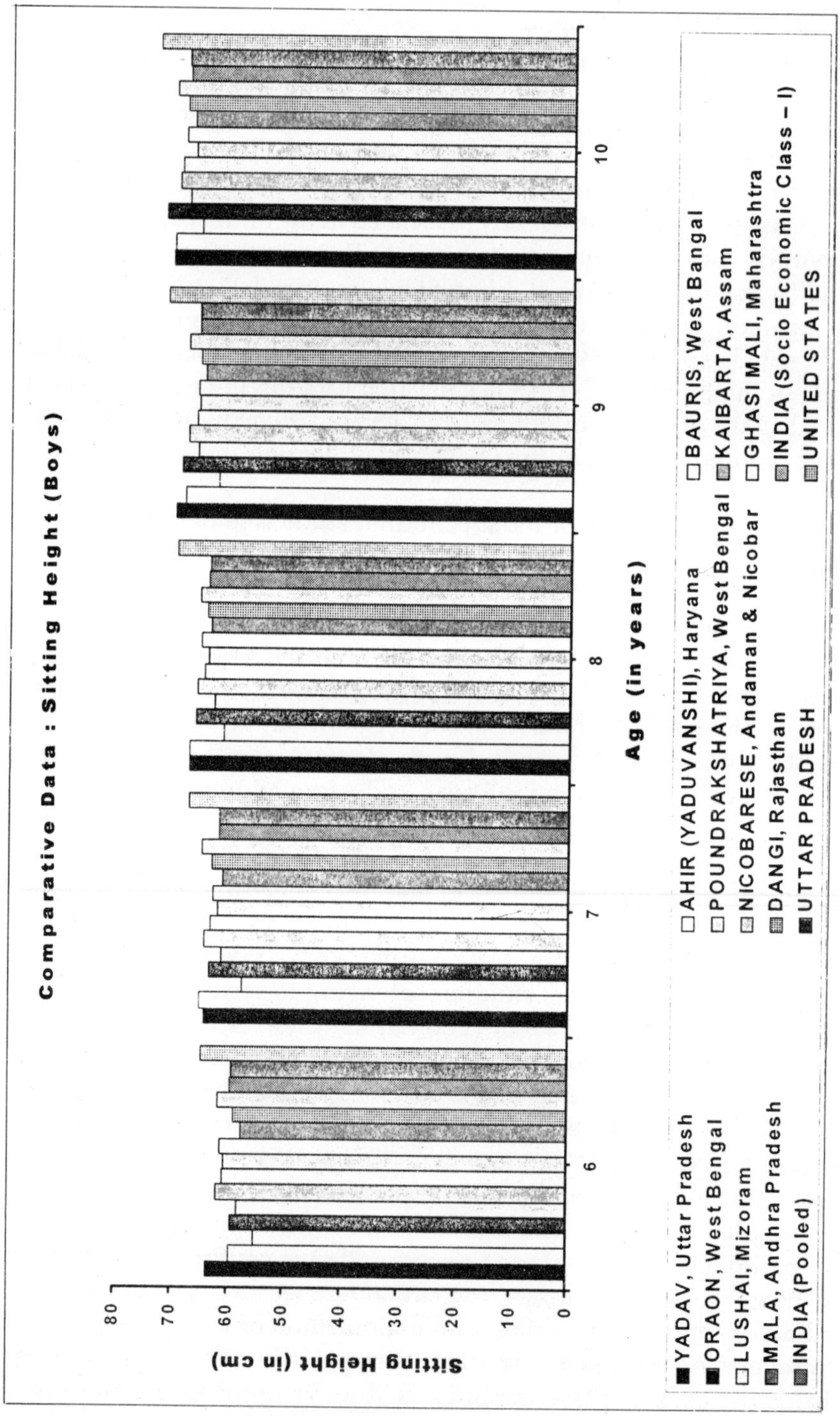
Comparative Data : Sitting Height (Boys)
Sitting Height (in cm)
0
10
20
30
40
50
60
70
80
6
7
8
9
10
Age (in years)
YADAV, Uttar Pradesh
ORAON, West Bengal
LUSHAI, Mizoram
MALA, Andhra Pradesh
INDIA (Pooled)
AHIR (YADUVANSHI), Haryana
POUNDRAKSHATRIYA, West Bengal
NICOBARESE, Andaman & Nicobar
DANGI, Rajasthan
UTTAR PRADESH
BAURIS, West Bangal
KAIBARTA, Assam
GHASI MALI, Maharashtra
INDIA (Socio Economic Class – I)
UNITED STATES

Fig. 5

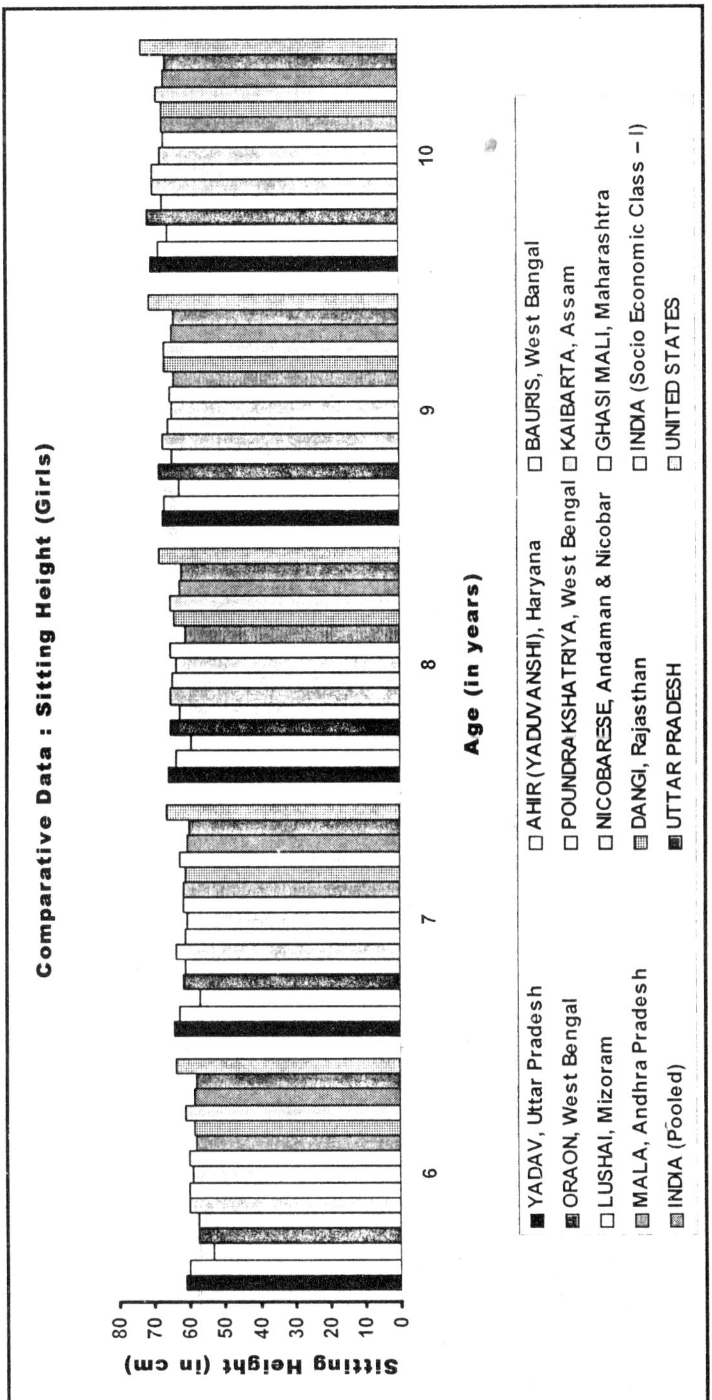
Comparative Data : Sitting Height (Girls)
Sitting Height (in cm)
80
70
60
50
40
30
20
10
0
6
7
8
9
10
Age (in years)
YADAV, Uttar Pradesh
AHIR (YADUVANSHI), Haryana
BAURIS, West Bangal
ORAON, West Bengal
POUNDRAKSHATRIYA, West Bengal
KAIBARTA, Assam
LUSHAI, Mizoram
NICOBARESE, Andaman & Nicobar
GHASI MALI, Maharashtra
MALA, Andhra Pradesh
DANGI, Rajasthan
INDIA (Socio Economic Class – I)
INDIA (Pooled)
UTTAR PRADESH
UNITED STATES

Fig. 6

guided by their religious and caste considerations; rather than non-availability of adequate quality food. The children belonging to lower socio-economic strata such as Mali, Bauri, Poundrakshtriya, Mala and Kaibarta ,reported to be living in poor hygienic conditions, are undernourished and suffering with poor to moderate degree of malnutrition. The under nourished children become more susceptible to infectious diseases like diphtheria, tuberculosis, measles, and cholera including various parasitic and diarrheal diseases. Due to malnutrition the nutritional disorders such as goiter, cretinism, blindness, anaemia and so on are also quite common. A number of World Bank surveys conducted in India in 1984 and later in 1988 showed high disease prevalence and its widespread pattern among the poor. It is also well established that health of a child is the reflection of cumulative effect of number of factors, such as hygienic living conditions, improved purchasing factors and above all education and immunity against communicable diseases. The relationship between literacy, awareness, accessibility of health services, inadequate utilization of health facilities is also noticed. In the present study the majority of children studied for their growth and development belong to lower to middle socio-economic strata and more likely were victims of malnutrition and infectious disease alliance. The children who were the victims of such alliance exhibit retarded growth and development and poor health in comparison with the expected growth and development at their age as per NCHS standard.

References

Eveleth, P. B. and Tanner, J.M. (1976), Worldwide Variation in Human Growth, Cambridge: Cambridge University Press.

Garn, S. M. (1952), Physical Growth and Development, *Am. J. Phy. Anth.*, 10, 169

Garn, S. M. and C. G. Rohamann (1966), Interaction of Nutrition and Genetics in the Timing Growth and Development. In the Peadiatric Clinics of North America, 13: 353-361.

Heirnaux, J. (1968), Bodily Shape Differentiation of Ethnic Groups and of the Sexes Through Growth, *In Human Biology*, 40:44-62.

ICMR (Indian Council of Medical Research) (1972), Growth and Physical Development of Indian Infants and Children. In Technical Report No. 18, New Delhi.

Johnston, F.E., M Borden and R. B. Mac Vean (1975), The Effects of Genetic and Environmental Factors upon the Growth of Children in Guatemala city. In: Watts *et. al.* (eds.), pp. 377-388.

Mead, M. (1964), Food Habits Research: Problem of the 1960's. Mat. Acad. Sci. Mat. Res. Coun. Washington.

NCHS (National Centre for Health Statistics) (1977), NCHS Growth Curves for Children, Birth to 18 Years United States. Vital and Health Statistics. Series 11, No. 165.

Parsons, P.A. (1965), Growth in a Sample of Australian Aborigins from one to Twenty Three Months of Age. In Growth, 29:207-211.

Prader, A, J.M. Tanner and G.A. Van Harnack (1963), Catch up Growth Following Illness or Starvation. An Example of Developmental Canalization in Man. In *Journal of Pediatrics,* 62. 646-659.

Roberts, D. F. (1960), Effects of Race and Climate on Growth of African Children. In Human Growth Ed. J. M. Tanner, pp. 59-72. London, Pergamon.

Tanner, J. M. (1966), Galtonian Engenics and the Study of Growth. The Relation of Body Size, Intelleigence Test Score and Social Circumstances in Children and Adult. *In Eugenics Review*, 58:122-135.

Tanner, J.M. R.H. Whitehouse and M. Takaishi (1965), Standards from Birth to Maturity for Height, Weight, Height Velocity and Weight Velocity: British Children. Archives of Disease in Childhood, 41: 454-464.

SCHEDULE – I

ANTHROPOLOGICAL SURVEY OF INDIA, GOVERNMENT OF INDIA, CALCUTTA

GROWTH AND DEVELOPMENT OF CHILDREN: BIO-CULTURAL PERSPECTIVE

GENERAL INFORMATION OF HOUSEHOLD OF THE SUBJECT

Household Sl. No.: ....

Place: .... City/Town/Village: ....

District :.. State: ....

Name of the Subject :..

Father's Name :..

Address:..

School : ....

Residence : ....

Age (Date of Birth) given by parents : ....

In School Register : ....

Religion:..

Caste/Tribe : ....

Mother Tongue : ....

Level of Education : Primary/Upper Primary/Secondary/Higher Secondary

Consanguineous: Yes/No

If yes, specify the relation :..

Total Family income per annum : Rs. ....

Sl. No.	*Name of members*	*Relation to Head*	*Sex*	*Age*	*Marital Status*	*Literacy level*	*Occupation*	*Income*

Family type: Nuclear/Joint

Family members: Adults: M F Children : M F

Agriculturist: Land owned/Shared/Labourer

Whether the crops grown are sufficient for their subsistence :

Yes/No

Name of the Investigator/s : ....

Signature of the Investigator/s : ....

SCHEDULE – II(i)

ANTHROPOLOGICAL SURVEY OF INDIA, GOVERNMENT OF INDIA, CALCUTTA

GROWTH AND DEVELOPMENT OF CHILDREN: BIO-CULTURAL PERSPECTIVE

ANTHROPOMETRIC MEASUREMENTS

Sl. No.................... Date of Investigation.......................................

Name of the Subject.. Sex ....

Tribe/Caste/Sub-Caste...

Date of Birth.................... Age ....Years..................Month..................

Address..

School..

Residence..

Class in which the subject studying..

Parity of Child ....

ANTHROPOMETRIC MEASUREMENTS

(1) Weight (Kg.) .... (2) Stature/Height vertex (cm) ....

(3) Sitting Height (cm) .... (4) Bi-acromial diameter (cm) ....

(5) Bi-illiocristal diameter (cm) .... (6) Head length (cm) ....

(7) Forearm length (cm) .... (8) Total arm length (cm) ....

(9) Head Circumference (cm) .... (10) Chest Circumference (cm) ....

(11) Mid Upper Arm Circumference(cm) ....

(12) Calf Circumference(cm) ....

(13) Triceps Skinfold (mm)...

(14) Subscapular Skinfold (mm)..

(15) Bi-ceps Skinfold (mm)...

Signs of Puberty : Female

Experienced menstruation : Yes/No

Age at menarche : .... Yrs : .... Months : ....

Dental Pattern* : ....

m m c i i   i i c m m

M M M P P C I I   I I C P P M M M

M M M P P C I I   I I C P P M M M

m m c i i   i i c m m

* **O Tooth present**

/ Tooth fallen

◡ Tooth just erupted

SCHEDULE – II(ii)

DISEASE SUFFERED: IN PAST/RECENTLY

If so, name of the disease/infection suffered.

CLINICAL SIGNS :

(1) General Health	Very good/Good/Satisfactory/Weak
(2) Nutrition deficiency signs :	
(a) Pigmentation of skin	Present/Absent
(b) Angular Stomatitis	Present/Absent
(c) Dry Scaly skin	Present/Absent
(d) Discoloured Hair	Present/Absent
(e) Flag/Coarse Hair	Present/Absent
(f) Spongy Bleeding gums	Present/Absent
(g) Yellowish teeth	Present/Absent
(h) Pale Conjuctiva	Present/Absent
(i) Yellow colour in the base of the nails	Present/Absent
(j) Any other observation	

SCHEDULE–III

ANTHROPOLOGICAL SURVEY OF INDIA, GOVERNMENT OF INDIA, CALCUTTA

GROWTH AND DEVELOPMENT OF CHILDREN: BIO-CULTURAL PERSPECTIVE

GENERAL INFORMATION OF HEALTH AND HYGIENE OF THE HOUSEHOLDS

Sl. No. ....

Subject's Name..

Hygiene and Health ....

House:

(1) Type of House: Thatched hut/masonry Building/Block of flats/Bungalow/any other; owned or rented

If rented, rent paid per month : ....

(2) Number of living rooms : ....

(3) Ventilation : .... Good/Satisfactory/Poor : ....

(4) Sun light : Available/Not available

(5) Cleanliness of the house and its surroundings : Good/Satisfactory/poor

(6) Separate Kitchen : Yes/No

(7) Type of latrine : Flush/pit/scavenger cleaned enclosure/field/any other

Whether they are using these facilities or not : Extent of utility

(8) (i) Drinking water supply : Well/pond/river/sea/tap/any other treated/untreated

(ii) Water supply for washing and bathing : Source and distance from residence :

(9) Personal cleanliness of the children : Very good/good/satisfactory/poor

(10) State of utensils used for cooking : Properly cleaned : Yes/No

Properly stored : Yes/No

(11) Health facilities through Health Centre/Hospital/Private Doctor/any other, Specify:

Available/Not available

If available, facility availed/not availed

If not availed, reason thereof.

(12) Health care system followed : Allopathic/Ayurvedic/Unani/Indigenous/ any other, specify :

Whether child availed immunization : Yes/No

If Yes, detailed information is to be given :

If No, reason thereof :

Breast feeding practiced / not practiced

If practiced duration : Regular/Irregular

Age at which weaning starts : Male Months

Female Months

Taboos regarding consumption of certain food item : If Yes, specify:

(13) Supplementary food facilities : Available / Not available

If available, mention the development programme :

Government/Non-Government

(14) Fuel used for cooking : wood/cow dung cake/coal/kerosene/gas/electricity/ saw dust / any other, specify :

(15) Food Habits :

(i) Staple food (season wise) : Rice/wheat/maize/millets/others Pulses : Urad/arhar/ moong/chana/kulthi/any other

(ii) Vegetarian/non-vegetarian/eggatarian :

(iii) Items of non-vegetarian consumed :

(iv) Consumption of non-vegetarian : Regular/Occasional

(v) Whether milk and milk products consumed.

If Yes : Occasionally/regularly

(vi) Whether child gets sufficient/moderate/insufficient food : Yes/No

(vii) What foods are given to the child if staple food is not sufficiently available :

(16) Basic amenities available in the household :

Radio, Sewing machine, Bicycle, Motorcycle/Scooter/Pump set, Watch, Television, Cart, any other (specify)

(17) Development Programmes facilities availed/not availed at the household level : If yes, specify : I.C.D.S./IRDP/Jawahar Rojgar Yojna/Employment Assurance Scheme/ Rural Sanitation Programme/ Income Assurance Scheme/ Gandhi Kutir Yojna/Indira Avas Yojna/Million Well Scheme/Vikas Mein Jan Sahyog/ TRYSEM/ DWCRA/ ITDA/ SFDA/ MFDA/ NREP.

Impact of these programmes may also be elucidated.

I.C.D.S.	:	Integrated Child Development Scheme
I.R.D.P.	:	Integrated Rural Development Programme
TRYSEM	:	Training of Rural Youth for self Employment
DWCRA	:	Development of Women and Children in Rural Areas
ITDA	:	Integrated Tribal Development Agency
SFDA	:	Small Farmers Development Agency
MFDA	:	Marginal Farmers Development Agency
NREP	:	National Rural Employment Programme

Name of the Investigator/s : ....

Signature of the Investigator/s : ....

SCHEDULE–IV

ANTHROPOLOGICAL SURVEY OF INDIA, GOVERNMENT OF INDIA, CALCUTTA

GROWTH AND DEVELOPMENT OF CHILDREN: BIO-CULTURAL PERSPECTIVE

AREA SURVEY SCHEDULE

Name of the area/village/locality...

Block Development Office: Gram Panchayat/Municipality

J.L.No. .... Ward No. ....

Sub-Division/Tehsil........................ District.......................... State........................

ECOLOGY

Physical features and ecology of the area to be collected briefly :

INFRASTRUCTURAL FACILITIES, THEIR LOCATION AND DISTANCE FROM THE PLACE OF STUDY :

(1) Highway (Kms)
(2) Bus Stand (Kms)
(3) Public Transport System and communication
(4) Post Office
(5) Railway Station
(6) Main Road
(7) Nearest Town
(8) Market (daily/weekly)
(9) Primary School
(10) Secondary School
(11) Junior College
(12) College
(13) Public Distribution System (Fair Price Shop)
(14) Mass Media Centre
(15) Any other extension service
(16) Panchayat Office
(17) Mahila Samiti
(18) Block Development Office
(19) Community Centre
(20) Primary Health Centre
(21) Bank
(22) nearest Industrial Centre
(23) Telecommunication Centre
(24) Facility for Electricity
(25) Facility for Lift Irrigation
(26) ICDS/Anganbari Centre
(27) Library/Club
(28) Sources of Potable Water and Its distance
(29) Sources of water for washing/bath for human and cattles
(30) Play ground or park for the children

DEVELOPMENTAL PROGRAMMES AND ITS IMPORTANCE :

Type of development agencies working in the studied area for welfare of the children as well as parents and public-Government/Non-Government voluntary organizations.

(i) Perception of the people regarding the availability of the infra-structural facilities.

(ii) Name the Developmental Programme launched in the area (see the check list)

(iii) Constraints and compatibilities faced by the beneficiaries.

(iv) Constraints and compatibilities faced by the agencies.

CHECK LIST

HEALTH POINT OF VIEW:

(1) Malaria Eradication Programme

(2) Immunization Schemes : B.C.G., D.P.T., Measles, Pulse Polio, Prenatal care, Antenatal care and any other welfare scheme.

DEVELOPMENT POINT OF VIEW

(1) Integrated Rural Development Programme (IRDP)

(2) Jawahar Rojgar Yojna

(3) Employment Assurance Scheme

(4) Rural Sanitation Programme

(5) Income Assurance Scheme

(6) Gandhi Kutir Yojna

(7) Indira Avas yojana

(8) Operation Black Board

(9) Million Well Scheme

(10) Vikas mein Jan Sahyog

(11) Training of Rural Youth for Self Employment (TRYSEM)

(12) Development of Women and Children in Rural Areas (DWCRA)

(13) Integrated Tribal Development Agency (ITDA)

(14) Small Farmers Development Agency (SFDA)

(15) Marginal Farmers Development Agency (MFDA)

(16) National Rural Employment Programme (NREP)

(This information may be obtained from the local Patwari/Patel/Village Development Officer, Village Panchayat).

Name of the Investigator/s : ....

Signature of the Investigator/s : ....